THE SOLDIER AND THE STATE

Chapel Hill '71

Samuel P. Huntington

THE
SOLDIER
AND
THE STATE

The Theory and Politics of
Civil-Military Relations

A Caravelle Edition

VINTAGE BOOKS
A DIVISION OF RANDOM HOUSE
New York

VINTAGE BOOKS
are published by ALFRED A. KNOPF, INC.
and RANDOM HOUSE, INC.

FOR MOTHER

Preface

This book presents a theory of civil-military relations. The reader will find much historical material, on the United States primarily, but also on Europe and Asia. Yet this book does not attempt an historical description of civil-military relations in general nor of any specific aspect of civil-military relations in particular. It is, rather, an effort to develop a way of looking at and thinking about civil-military relations, in short, a theoretical framework. Understanding requires theory; theory requires abstraction; and abstraction requires the simplification and ordering of reality. No theory can explain all the facts, and, at times, the reader of this book may feel that its concepts and distinctions are drawn too sharply and precisely and are too far removed from reality. Obviously, the real world is one of blends, irrationalities, and incongruities: actual personalities, institutions, and beliefs do not fit into neat logical categories. Yet neat logical categories are necessary if man is to think profitably about the real world in which he lives and to derive from it lessons for broader application and use. He is forced to generalize about phenomena which never quite operate according to the laws of human reason. One measure of a theory is the degree to which it encompasses and explains all the relevant facts. Another measure, and the more important one, is the degree to which it encompasses and explains those facts better than any other theory. The study of civil-military relations has suffered from too little theorizing. The only theory of civil-military relations which has had any widespread acceptance in the United States is a confused and unsystematic set of assumptions and beliefs derived from the underlying premises of American liberalism. This collection of ideas is inadequate in that it fails to comprehend many important facts, and it is obsolete in that it is rooted in a hierarchy of values which is of dubious validity in the contemporary world. The present volume is an effort to suggest a more useful and relevant framework and to raise and define the principal theoretical issues involved in the

vii

study of civil-military relations. Its most important purpose will be served if it stimulates further thinking about civil-military relations and national security.

Two methodological assumptions underlie this book. First, it is assumed that the civil-military relations in any society should be studied as a system composed of interdependent elements. The principal components of such a system are the formal, structural position of military institutions in the government, the informal role and influence of military groups in politics and society at large, and the nature of the ideologies of military and nonmilitary groups. As parts of a total system no one of these elements can change without producing further changes in the other elements. The different ideologies of the Japanese and German officer corps, for instance, were directly related to the difference in the authority and influence which they exercised in their respective societies and to the different ideological complexions of those societies. Similarly, the changes in the power of the American officer corps from 1935 to 1945 had a tremendous impact on the thinking of that officer corps. Any system of civil-military relations thus involves a complex equilibrium between the authority, influence, and ideology of the military, on the one hand, and the authority, influence, and ideology of nonmilitary groups, on the other. Equilibrium may be achieved in an infinite variety of ways. The second methodological assumption of this book, however, is that, starting from certain premises concerning the nature and purpose of military institutions, it is possible to define in the abstract that particular type of equilibria — "objective civilian control" — which maximizes military security. Utilizing this standard, it is possible to analyze the extent to which the system of civil-military relations in any society tends to enhance or detract from the military security of that society. It is also possible to suggest the changes in the component elements of the system which would be necessary if the system were to approximate closer an equilibrium of "objective civilian control."

Portions of this book have been published previously as "Civilian Control and the Constitution," *American Political Science Review,* L (September 1956), 676–699, and "Civilian Control of the Military: A Theoretical Statement," in Heinz Eulau, Samuel J. Eldersveld, and Morris Janowitz (eds.), *Political Behavior: A Reader in*

Preface

Theory and Research (Glencoe, Ill.: The Free Press, 1956), pp. 380–385.

This book was made possible by a Faculty Research Fellowship from the Social Science Research Council. I am profoundly grateful to the Council for this assistance, to Pendleton Herring, President of the Council, for his continuing encouragement and interest, and to Professor V. O. Key, Jr., for his sponsorship of me for this fellowship. Although they may not recognize their influence on the pages that follow, my thinking on politics in general owes much to the wisdom and insight of my senior colleagues: Professors Arthur N. Holcombe, William Yandell Elliott, and Louis Hartz. The manuscript was read in its entirety by Professor Morris Janowitz of the University of Michigan, Dr. Paul Y. Hammond of Columbia University, Professor Ernest R. May of Harvard, and Colonel Trevor N. Dupuy, USA, each of whom contributed a variety of helpful criticisms and suggestions, the range of which far transcended their respective fields of sociology, government, history, and military science. Alexander J. Cella also read the manuscript at an early stage. His labors on it, exceeding the demands of friendship, contributed greatly to the ruthless elimination of surplus wordage and the general improvement of the style of that which remained.

I am grateful to Paul H. Nitze and Henry Rosovsky for their comments on portions of the manuscript, to Lewis Hertzman for his assistance in certain aspects of the research, and to Ann Louise Coffin of the Harvard Press for her patient and helpful editorial criticism. I owe special debts to my mother for her careful reading of the proofs and to Nancy A. Arkelyan, Carolyn N. Carpenter, and Martha Ann Kelleran for assisting in this arduous task. Finally, I wish to express my deep appreciation to my comrades at Kirkland House, Howard L. Erdman, Warren B. Harshman, Stephen I. Hochhauser, Howard H. Muson, Roger C. Ravel, and Stanley E. Tobin, for their yeoman work in checking references and quotations. All these friends, critics, and associates facilitated the creative process, but in the end, of course, it remains my book and my responsibility.

Cambridge, Massachusetts   S. P. H.
November 1956

CONTENTS

Contents

PART II

MILITARY POWER IN AMERICA: THE HISTORICAL EXPERIENCE, 1789–1940

Contents

THE SOLDIER AND THE STATE

Introduction: National Security and Civil-Military Relations

Civil-military relations is one aspect of national security policy. The aim of national security policy is to enhance the safety of the nation's social, economic, and political institutions against threats arising from other independent states. National security policy may be thought of as existing in three forms and on two levels. Military security policy is the program of activities designed to minimize or neutralize efforts to weaken or destroy the nation by armed forces operating from outside its institutional and territorial confines. Internal security policy deals with the threat of subversion — the effort to weaken or destroy the state by forces operating within its territorial and institutional confines. Situational security policy is concerned with the threat of erosion resulting from long-term changes in social, economic, demographic, and political conditions tending to reduce the relative power of the state. Each of these three forms of policy has an operating level and an institutional level. Operating policy consists of the immediate means taken to meet the security threat. Institutional policy deals with the manner in which operational policy is formulated and executed. Civil-military relations is the principal institutional component of military security policy.

The immediate operating issues of military policy normally involve:

(1) the quantitative issues of the size, recruitment, and supply of the military forces, including the fundamental question of the proportion of state resources devoted to military needs;

(2) the qualitative issues of the organization, composition, equipment, and deployment of the military forces, including the types of armaments and weapons, the locations of bases, arrangements with allies, and similar questions; and

(3) the dynamic issues of the utilization of military forces: when and under what circumstances force is brought into action.

1

Public debate usually focuses upon these questions. Yet in the long run the nature of the decisions on these issues is determined by the institutional pattern through which the decisions are made. The fundamental issues of institutional policy are always present; they are continuously redefined but never resolved. The ordering of its civil-military relations, consequently, is basic to a nation's military security policy. The objective of this policy on the institutional level is to develop a system of civil-military relations which will maximize military security at the least sacrifice of other social values. The achievement of this objective involves a complex balancing of power and attitudes among civilian and military groups. Nations which develop a properly balanced pattern of civil-military relations have a great advantage in the search for security. They increase their likelihood of reaching right answers to the operating issues of military policy. Nations which fail to develop a balanced pattern of civil-military relations squander their resources and run uncalculated risks.

THE IMPERATIVES OF CIVIL-MILITARY RELATIONS

The military institutions of any society are shaped by two forces: a functional imperative stemming from the threats to the society's security and a societal imperative arising from the social forces, ideologies, and institutions dominant within the society. Military institutions which reflect only social values may be incapable of performing effectively their military function. On the other hand, it may be impossible to contain within society military institutions shaped purely by functional imperatives. The interaction of these two forces is the nub of the problem of civil-military relations. The degree to which they conflict depends upon the intensity of the security needs and the nature and strength of the value pattern of society. Adjustment and balance between the two forces are not inevitable: some societies may be inherently incapable of providing effectively for their own military security. Such societies lack survival value in an era of continuing threats.

For Americans the problem of balancing the functional and societal imperatives has only recently acquired a new significance. From the second decade of the nineteenth century to the fourth decade of the twentieth century, Americans had little cause to

2

worry about their security. Security was a given fact of nature and circumstance, an inheritance rather than a creation. When Americans did consider military policy, they dealt with immediate practical issues such as the size of the Army's budget or the number of battleships in the Navy. On the other hand, their consideration of civil-military relations was limited to the impact of military institutions upon domestic economic and political values and institutions. One of the more basic and obvious facts of our time is that changes in technology and international politics have combined to make security now the final goal of policy rather than its starting assumption. The functional imperative can no longer be ignored. Previously the primary question was: what pattern of civil-military relations is most compatible with American liberal democratic values? Now this has been supplanted by the more important issue: what pattern of civil-military relations will best maintain the security of the American nation?

The principal focus of civil-military relations is the relation of the officer corps to the state. Here the conflict between functional and societal pressures comes to a head. The officer corps is the active directing element of the military structure and is responsible for the military security of society. The state is the active directing element of society and is responsible for the allocation of resources among important values including military security. The social and economic relations between the military and the rest of society normally reflect the political relations between the officer corps and the state. Consequently, in analyzing civil-military relations, the first necessity is to define the nature of the officer corps. What sort of body is the officer corps? What sort of man is the military officer?

PART I

MILITARY INSTITUTIONS AND THE STATE: THEORETICAL AND HISTORICAL PERSPECTIVES

1

Officership as a Profession

PROFESSIONALISM AND THE MILITARY

The modern officer corps is a professional body and the modern military officer a professional man. This is, perhaps, the most fundamental thesis of this book. A profession is a peculiar type of functional group with highly specialized characteristics. Sculptors, stenographers, entrepreneurs, and advertising copywriters all have distinct functions but no one of these functions is professional in nature. Professionalism, however, is characteristic of the modern officer in the same sense in which it is characteristic of the physician or lawyer. Professionalism distinguishes the military officer of today from the warriors of previous ages. The existence of the officer corps as a professional body gives a unique cast to the modern problem of civil-military relations.

The nature and history of other professions as professions have been thoroughly discussed. Yet the professional character of the modern officer corps has been neglected. In our society, the businessman may command more income; the politician may command more power; but the professional man commands more respect. Yet the public, as well as the scholar, hardly conceives of the officer in the same way that it does the lawyer or doctor, and it certainly does not accord to the officer the deference which it gives to the civilian professionals. Even the military themselves are influenced by their image in the public mind and at times have refused to accept the implications of their own professional status. When the term "professional" has been used in connection with the military, it normally has been in the sense of "professional" as

7

contrasted with "amateur" rather than in the sense of "profession" as contrasted with "trade" or "craft." The phrases "professional army" and "professional soldier" have obscured the difference between the career enlisted man who is professional in the sense of one who works for monetary gain and the career officer who is professional in the very different sense of one who pursues a "higher calling" in the service of society.

THE CONCEPT OF PROFESSION

The first step in analyzing the professional character of the modern officer corps is to define professionalism. The distinguishing characteristics of a profession as a special type of vocation are its expertise, responsibility, and corporateness.[1]

EXPERTISE. The professional man is an expert with specialized knowledge and skill in a significant field of human endeavor. His expertise is acquired only by prolonged education and experience. It is the basis of objective standards of professional competence for separating the profession from laymen and measuring the relative competence of members of the profession. Such standards are universal. They inhere in the knowledge and skill and are capable of general application irrespective of time and place. The ordinary skill or craft exists only in the present and is mastered by learning an existing technique without reference to what has gone before. Professional knowledge, however, is intellectual in nature and capable of preservation in writing. Professional knowledge has a history, and some knowledge of that history is essential to professional competence. Institutions of research and education are required for the extension and transmission of professional knowledge and skill. Contact is maintained between the academic and practical sides of a profession through journals, conferences, and the circulation of personnel between practice and teaching.

Professional expertise also has a dimension in breadth which is lacking in the normal trade. It is a segment of the total cultural tradition of society. The professional man can successfully apply his skill only when he is aware of this broader tradition of which he is a part. Learned professions are "learned" simply because they are an integral part of the total body of learning of society. Con-

8

sequently professional education consists of two phases: the first imparting a broad, liberal, cultural background, and the second imparting the specialized skills and knowledge of the profession. The liberal education of the professional man is normally handled by the general educational institutions of society devoted to this purpose. The second or technical phase of professional education, on the other hand, is given in special institutions operated by or affiliated with the profession itself.

RESPONSIBILITY. The professional man is a practicing expert, working in a social context, and performing a service, such as the promotion of health, education, or justice, which is essential to the functioning of society. The client of every profession is society, individually or collectively. A research chemist, for instance, is not a professional man because the service he renders, while beneficial to society, is not essential to its immediate existence and functioning: only Du Pont and the Bureau of Standards have a direct and immediate interest in what he has to offer. The essential and general character of his service and his monopoly of his skill impose upon the professional man the responsibility to perform the service when required by society. This social responsibility distinguishes the professional man from other experts with only intellectual skills. The research chemist, for instance, is still a research chemist if he uses his skills in a manner harmful to society. But the professional man can no longer practice if he refuses to accept his social responsibility: a physician ceases to be a physician if he uses his skills for antisocial purposes. The responsibility to serve and devotion to his skill furnish the professional motive. Financial remuneration cannot be the primary aim of the professional man *qua* professional man. Consequently, professional compensation normally is only partly determined by bargaining on the open market and is regulated by professional custom and law.

The performance of an essential service not regulated by the normal expectation of financial rewards requires some statement governing the relations of the profession to the rest of society. Conflicts between the professional man and his clients, or among members of the profession, normally furnish the immediate impetus to the formulation of such a statement. The profession thus becomes a moral unit positing certain values and ideals which guide its members in their dealings with laymen. This guide may be a set of unwritten norms transmitted through the professional educational system or it may be codified into written canons of professional ethics.

CORPORATENESS. The members of a profession share a sense of organic unity and consciousness of themselves as a group apart from laymen. This collective sense has its origins in the lengthy discipline and training necessary for professional competence, the common bond of work, and the sharing of a unique social responsibility. The sense of unity manifests itself in a professional organization which formalizes and applies the standards of professional competence and establishes and enforces the standards of professional responsibility. Membership in the professional organization, along with the possession of special expertise and the acceptance of special responsibility, thus becomes a criterion of professional status, publicly distinguishing the professional man from the layman. The interest of the profession requires it to bar its members from capitalizing upon professional competence in areas where that competence has no relevance and likewise to protect itself against outsiders who would claim professional competence because of achievements or attributes in other fields. Professional organizations are generally either associations or bureaucracies. In the associational professions such as medicine and law, the practitioner typically functions independently and has a direct personal relationship with his client. The bureaucratic professions, such as the diplomatic service, possess a high degree of specialization of labor and responsibilities within the profession, and the profession as a whole renders a collective service to society as a whole. These two categories are not mutually exclusive: bureaucratic elements exist in most associational professions, and associations frequently supplement the formal structure of bureaucratic professions. The associational professions usually possess written codes of ethics since each practitioner is individually confronted with the problem of proper conduct toward clients and colleagues. The bureaucratic professions, on the other hand, tend to develop a more general sense of collective professional responsibility and the proper role of the profession in society.

Officership as a Profession

The vocation of officership meets the principal criteria of professionalism. In practice, no vocation, not even medicine or law, has all the characteristics of the ideal professional type. Officership probably falls somewhat further short of the ideal than either of these. Yet its fundamental character as a profession is undeniable. In practice, officership is strongest and most effective when it most closely approaches the professional ideal; it is weakest and most defective when it falls short of that ideal.

THE EXPERTISE OF OFFICERSHIP. What is the specialized expertise of the military officer? Is there any skill common to all military officers and yet not shared with any civilian groups? At first glance this hardly seems to be the case. The officer corps appears to contain many varieties of specialists, including large numbers which have their counterparts in civilian life. Engineers, doctors, pilots, ordnance experts, personnel experts, intelligence experts, communications experts — all these are found both within and without the modern officer corps. Even ignoring these technical specialists, each absorbed in his own branch of knowledge, just the broad division of the corps into land, sea, and air officers appears to create vast differences in the functions performed and the skills required. The captain of a cruiser and the commander of an infantry division appear to be faced with highly different problems requiring highly different abilities.

Yet a distinct sphere of military competence does exist which is common to all, or almost all, officers and which distinguishes them from all, or almost all, civilians. This central skill is perhaps best summed up in Harold Lasswell's phrase "the management of violence." The function of a military force is successful armed combat. The duties of the military officer include: (1) the organizing, equipping, and training of this force; (2) the planning of its activities; and (3) the direction of its operation in and out of combat. The direction, operation, and control of a human organization whose primary function is the application of violence is the peculiar skill of the officer. It is common to the activities of the air, land, and sea officers. It distinguishes the military officer *qua* military officer from the other specialists which exist in the

11

modern armed services. The skills of these experts may be necessary to the achievement of the objectives of the military force. But they are basically auxiliary vocations, having the same relation to the expertise of the officer as the skills of the nurse, chemist, laboratory technician, dietician, pharmacist, and X-ray technician have to the expertise of the doctor. None of the auxiliary specialists contained within or serving the military profession is capable of the "management of violence," just as none of the specialists aiding the medical profession is capable of the diagnosis and treatment of illness. The essence of officership is embodied in the traditional admonition to Annapolis men that their duty will be to "fight the fleet." Individuals, such as doctors, who are not competent to manage violence but who are members of the officer corps are normally distinguished by special titles and insignia and are excluded from positions of military command. They belong to the officer corps in its capacity as an administrative organization of the state, but not in its capacity as a professional body.

Within the profession itself there are specialists in the management of violence on sea, on land, and in the air, just as there are heart, stomach, and eye specialists within medicine. A military specialist is an officer who is peculiarly expert at directing the application of violence under certain prescribed conditions. The variety of conditions under which violence may be employed and the different forms in which it may be applied form the basis for subprofessional specialization. They also form the basis for evaluating relative technical competence. The larger and more complex the organizations of violence which an officer is capable of directing, and the greater the number of situations and conditions under which he can be employed, the higher is his professional competence. A man who is capable of directing only the activities of an infantry squad has such a low level of professional ability as to be almost on the border line. A man who can manage the operations of an airborne division or a carrier task force is a highly competent professional. The officer who can direct the complex activities of a combined operation involving large-scale sea, air, and land forces is at the top of his vocation.

It is readily apparent that the military function requires a high order of expertise. No individual, whatever his inherent intellectual ability and qualities of character and leadership, could perform these functions efficiently without considerable training and experience. In emergencies an untrained civilian may be capable of acting as a military officer at a low level for a brief period of time, just as in emergencies the intelligent layman may fill in until the doctor arrives. Before the management of violence became the extremely complex task that it is in modern civilization, it was possible for someone without specialized training to practice officership. Now, however, only the person who completely devotes his working hours to this task can hope to develop a reasonable level of professional competence. The skill of the officer is neither a craft (which is primarily mechanical) nor an art (which requires unique and nontransferable talent). It is instead an extraordinarily complex intellectual skill requiring comprehensive study and training. It must be remembered that the peculiar skill of the officer is the management of violence not the act of violence itself. Firing a rifle, for instance, is basically a mechanical craft; directing the operations of a rifle company requires an entirely different type of ability which may in part be learned from books and in part from practice and experience. The intellectual content of the military profession requires the modern officer to devote about one-third of his professional life to formal schooling, probably a higher ratio of educational time to practice time than in any other profession. In part this reflects the limited opportunities of the officer to acquire practical experience at the most important elements of his vocation. But to a large degree it also reflects the extreme complexity of the military expertise.

The peculiar skill of the military officer is universal in the sense that its essence is not affected by changes in time or location. Just as the qualifications of a good surgeon are the same in Zurich as they are in New York, the same standards of professional military competence apply in Russia as in America and in the nineteenth century as in the twentieth. The possession of a common professional skill is a bond among military officers cutting across other differences. The vocation of the officer also possesses a history. The management of violence is not a skill which can be mastered simply by learning existing techniques. It is in a continuous process of development, and it is necessary for the officer to understand this development and to be aware of its main tendencies and trends. Only if he is aware of the historical development of the techniques of organizing and directing military forces can the officer expect to stay on top of his profession. The importance of the history of war and military affairs receives sustained emphasis throughout military writings and military education.

The military skill requires a broad background of general culture for its mastery. The methods of organizing and applying violence at any one stage in history are intimately related to the entire cultural pattern of society. Just as law at its borders merges into history, politics, economics, sociology, and psychology, so also does the military skill. Even more, military knowledge also has frontiers on the natural sciences of chemistry, physics, and biology. To understand his trade properly, the officer must have some idea of its relation to these other fields and the ways in which these other areas of knowledge may contribute to his own purposes. In addition, he cannot really develop his analytical skill, insight, imagination, and judgment if he is trained simply in vocational duties. The abilities and habits of mind which he requires within his professional field can in large part be acquired only through the broader avenues of learning outside his profession. The fact that, like the lawyer and the physician, he is continuously dealing with human beings requires him to have the deeper understanding of human attitudes, motivations, and behavior which a liberal education stimulates. Just as a general education has become the prerequisite for entry into the professions of law and medicine, it is now also almost universally recognized as a desirable qualification for the professional officer.

THE RESPONSIBILITY OF OFFICERSHIP. The expertise of the officer imposes upon him a special social responsibility. The employment of his expertise promiscuously for his own advantage would wreck the fabric of society. As with the practice of medicine, society insists that the management of violence be utilized only for socially approved purposes. Society has a direct, continuing, and general interest in the employment of this skill for the enhancement of its own military security. While all professions are to some extent regulated by the state, the military profession is monopolized by the state. The skill of the physician is diagnosis and treatment; his responsibility is the health of his clients. The skill of the officer is the management of violence; his responsibility is the military security of his client, society. The discharge of the responsibility requires mastery of the skill; mastery of the skill entails acceptance of the responsibility. Both responsibility and skill distinguish the officer from other social types. All members of society have an interest in its security; the state has a direct concern for the achievement of this along with other social values; but the officer corps alone is responsible for military security to the exclusion of all other ends.

Does the officer have a professional motivation? Clearly he does not act primarily from economic incentives. In western society the vocation of officership is not well rewarded monetarily. Nor is his behavior within his profession governed by economic rewards and punishments. The officer is not a mercenary who transfers his services wherever they are best rewarded, nor is he the temporary citizen-soldier inspired by intense momentary patriotism and duty but with no steadying and permanent desire to perfect himself in the management of violence. The motivations of the officer are a technical love for his craft and the sense of social obligation to utilize this craft for the benefit of society. The combination of these drives constitutes professional motivation. Society, on the other hand, can only assure this motivation if it offers its officers continuing and sufficient pay both while on active duty and when retired.

The officer possesses intellectualized skill, mastery of which requires intense study. But like the lawyer and doctor he is not primarily a man of the closet; he deals continuously with people. The test of his professional ability is the application of technical knowledge in a human context. Since this application is not regulated by economic means, however, the officer requires positive guides spelling out his responsibilities to his fellow officers, his subordinates, his superiors, and the state which he serves. His behavior within the military structure is governed by a complex mass of regulations, customs, and traditions. His behavior in relation to society is guided by an awareness that his skill can only be utilized for purposes approved by society through its political agent, the state. While the primary responsibility of the physician is to his patient, and the lawyer to his client, the principal responsibility of the military officer is to the state. His responsibility to the state is the responsibility of the expert adviser. Like the lawyer and physician, he is concerned with only one segment of the activities of his client. Consequently, he cannot impose decisions upon his client which have implications beyond his field of special competence. He can only explain to his client his needs in this area, advise him as to how to meet these needs, and then, when the client has made his decisions, aid him in implementing them. To some extent the officer's behavior towards the state is guided by an explicit code expressed in law and comparable to the canons of professional ethics of the physician and lawyer. To a larger extent, the officer's code is expressed in custom, tradition, and the continuing spirit of the profession.

THE CORPORATE CHARACTER OF OFFICERSHIP. Officership is a public bureaucratized profession. The legal right to practice the profession is limited to members of a carefully defined body. His commission is to the officer what his license is to a doctor. Organically, however, the officer corps is much more than simply a creature of the state. The functional imperatives of security give rise to complex vocational institutions which mold the officer corps into an autonomous social unit. Entrance into this unit is restricted to those with the requisite education and training and is usually permitted only at the lowest level of professional competence. The corporate structure of the officer corps includes not just the official bureaucracy but also societies, associations, schools, journals, customs, and traditions. The professional world of the officer tends to encompass an unusually high proportion of his activities. He normally lives and works apart from the rest of society; physically and socially he probably has fewer nonprofessional contacts than most other professional men. The line between him and the layman or civilian is publicly symbolized by uniforms and insignia of rank.

The officer corps is both a bureaucratic profession and a bureaucratic organization. Within the profession, levels of competence are distinguished by a hierarchy of ranks; within the organization, duties are distinguished by a hierarchy of office. Rank inheres in the individual and reflects his professional achievement measured in terms of experience, seniority, education, and ability. Appointments to rank are normally made by the officer corps itself applying general principles established by the state. Assignments to office are normally somewhat more subject to outside influence. In all bureaucracies authority derives from office; in a professional bureaucracy eligibility for office derives from rank. An officer is permitted to perform certain types of duties and functions by virtue of his rank; he does not receive rank because he has been assigned to an office. Although in practice there are exceptions to this principle, the professional character of the officer corps rests upon the priority of the hierarchy of rank over the hierarchy of office.

The officer corps normally includes a number of nonprofessional "reservists." This is due to the fluctuating need for officers and the impossibility of the state maintaining continuously an officer corps of the size required in emergencies. The reservists are a temporary supplement to the officer corps and qualify for military rank by education and training. While members of the corps, they normally possess all the prerogatives and responsibilities of the professional in the same rank. The legal distinction between them and the professional is preserved, however, and entrance into the permanent corps of officers is much more restricted than entrance into the reserve corps. The reservists seldom achieve the level of professional skill open to the career officers; consequently, the bulk of the reservists are in the lower ranks of the professional bureaucracy while the higher ranks are monopolized by the career professionals. The latter, as the continuing element in the military structure and because of their superior professional competence as a body, are normally charged with the education and indoctrination of the reservists in the skills and the traditions of the vocation. The reservist only temporarily assumes professional responsibility. His principal functions in society lie elsewhere. As a result, his motivations, values, and behavior frequently differ greatly from those of the career professional.

The enlisted men subordinate to the officer corps are a part of the organizational bureaucracy but not of the professional bureaucracy. The enlisted personnel have neither the intellectual skills nor the professional responsibility of the officer. They are specialists in the application of violence not the management of violence. Their vocation is a trade not a profession. This fundamental difference between the officer corps and the enlisted corps is reflected in the sharp line which is universally drawn between the two in all the military forces of the world. If there were not this cleavage, there could be a single military hierarchy extending from the lowest enlisted man to the highest officer. But the differing character of the two vocations makes the organizational hierarchy discontinuous. The ranks which exist in the enlisted corps do not constitute a professional hierarchy. They reflect varying aptitudes, abilities, and offices within the trade of soldier, and movement up and down them is much more fluid than in the officer corps. The difference between the officer and enlisted vocations precludes any general progression from one to the other. Individual enlisted men do become officers but this is the exception rather than the rule. The education and training necessary for officership are normally incompatible with prolonged service as an enlisted man.

2

The Rise of the Military Profession
in Western Society

A NEW SOCIAL TYPE

The art of fighting is an old accomplishment of mankind. The military profession, however, is a recent creation of modern society. Historically, professionalism has been a distinguishing characteristic of western culture. The great civil professions originated in the late Middle Ages and existed in highly developed form by the beginning of the eighteenth century. The profession of officership, however, was essentially a product of the nineteenth century. It was, indeed, one of the most significant institutional creations of that century. Only in the Napoleonic Wars did officers begin to acquire a specialized technique to distinguish themselves from laymen and begin to develop the standards, values, and organization inherent in that technique. The professional officer as a social type is as uniquely characteristic of modern society as is the industrial entrepreneur. The emergence of the officer corps as an autonomous professional body cannot, of course, be given any precise dates. It was gradual and faltering. Two facts, however, stand out. Prior to 1800 there was no such thing as a professional officer corps. In 1900 such bodies existed in virtually all major countries.

The emergence of a professional officer corps created the modern problem of civil-military relations in Europe and North America. It is possible to speak of the issues of civilian control, militarism, and the military mind as existing prior to 1800, but the fundamental transformation in the first part of the nineteenth century makes it relatively profitless to go back before that time in search of light on modern problems. Knowledge of the manners and outlook of that aristocratic, individualistic amateur, the medieval knight, is of little help in understanding the professional values and attitudes which constitute the contemporary military mind. The activities of the Praetorian Guard offer few useful lessons for civilian control: the problem in the modern state is not armed revolt but the relation of the expert to the politician. The cleavage between the military and civilian spheres and the resulting tension between the two are phenomena of distinctly recent origin.

This chapter deals with the gradual emergence of the officer corps as an autonomous social institution: its antecedents, its causes, and its early history. Prussia, France, and England, the three major powers which pioneered the way, will be used to illustrate the change from eighteenth-century preprofessionalism to nineteenth-century professionalism. The development of professional expertise, responsibility, and corporateness will be measured in terms of the evolution of five key institutions of the military vocation: (1) the requirements for entry into the officer corps; (2) the means of advancement within the officer corps; (3) the character of the military educational system; (4) the nature of the military staff system; and (5) the general *esprit* and competence of the officer corps. The changes in these factors were accompanied by the development of a professional ethic furnishing the intellectual rationale for the new military man and his new institutions.

MERCENARY AND ARISTOCRATIC OFFICERSHIP

Armies and navies led by officers existed before 1800. If these officers were not professionals, what were they? Generally they were either mercenaries or aristocrats. Neither viewed officership as a profession. For the mercenary it was a business; for the amateur aristocrat it was a hobby. In place of the professional goal of expert service, the former pursued profit, the latter honor and adventure.

The mercenary officer was the dominant type from the breakdown of feudalism to the latter part of the seventeenth century.

His origins were in the free companies which flourished during the Hundred Years War (1337–1453). Under the mercenary system the officer was essentially an entrepreneur, raising a company of men whose services he offered for sale. The mercenary officer might possess a higher or lower level of vocational competence. Success, however, was judged not by professional standards but by pecuniary ones. An army was composed of separate units each the property of a different commander. The mercenaries were individualists, to some degree in competition with each other; they possessed neither common standards nor corporate spirit. Discipline and responsibility were absent. War was a predatory business and the ethics of predatory business prevailed. The end of the mercenary system came with the Thirty Years War (1618–1648) and the success of the disciplined armies of Gustavus Adolphus and Oliver Cromwell.* Remnants of the system, however, persisted almost down to the beginnings of professionalism.

The replacement of the mercenary officer by the aristocratic amateur was fundamentally the result of the consolidation of power by national monarchs who felt the need for permanent military forces to protect their dominions and to support their rule. Prior to this time armies and navies had been raised by kings and others as they were required. But the need of the monarchs was a continuing one, and consequently the standing army and the standing navy came into being. The rank and file of these forces normally consisted of long-term volunteers secured for eight- to twelve-year terms from the worst orders of society by a mixture of bribery and coercion. For officers the monarchs turned to the feudal nobility whom they were still reducing to their will. The nobles were either compelled (as in Prussia) or bribed (as in France) to enter the king's service. The recruiting function was taken away from the

* The Protestant forces of the seventeenth century had many seeming similarities to nineteenth-century professional armies. In the New Model Army, for instance, discipline was strict; promotion was in part by seniority and in part by the recommendation of superior officers; purchase was excluded and politics drastically limited. This apparent professionalism, however, was rooted in a temporary intense ideological-religious fervor instead of being based on an expanding technique and functional differentiation. See Felix Pribatsch, *Geschichte des Preussischen Offizierkorps* (Breslau, 1919), pp. 5–6; Theodore A. Dodge, *Gustavus Adolphus* (Boston, 2 vols., 1895), ch. 5; John W. Fortescue, *A History of the British Army* (London, 13 vols., 1899–1930), I, 279–284; C. Cooper King, *The Story of the British Army* (London, 1897), pp. 39ff.

officers and assigned to special agents of the king. The military forces became the property of the Crown rather than the property of its agents. The officers themselves became the permanent servants of the Crown rather than entrepreneurs operating on a contract basis. In brief, the military function was socialized: national control replaced private control. By 1789, except in artillery and engineering, the aristocracy had a virtual monopoly of officers' positions in the European armies.[1] Aristocratic officership was the last form of preprofessional officership to achieve unchallenged dominance in western society.

EIGHTEENTH-CENTURY ARISTOCRATIC INSTITUTIONS

ENTRY: BIRTH AND WEALTH. During the seventeenth century many commoners served as officers in the Prussian and French armies. The following century, however, saw the gradual exclusion of these elements as aristocratic birth became a requirement for entry into all branches of the military service except the technical arms of the artillery and engineers. Eventually in France even the "bourgeois" arms were closed to nonaristocrats. In Prussia, Frederick William I (1713–1740) compelled the nobility to serve in the army, and Frederick the Great (1740–1786), convinced that only aristocrats possessed honor, loyalty, and courage, systematically expelled bourgeois elements from the officer corps.

Admission to the schools of preliminary military education, founded in both France and Prussia in the middle of the eighteenth century, was limited to aristocrats. As a result, the French Army in 1789 had 6,333 nobles, 1,845 commoners, and 1,100 soldiers of fortune in an officer corps of 9,578. In Prussia in 1806 there were only 700 non-nobles in a corps of 7,100, and virtually all of these were in the technical branches. In France the needs of the aristocracy determined the size of the officer corps. A military commission was a way of pensioning off an impoverished noble. As a result, in 1775 there were 60,000 officers in an army whose total strength was only three times that number. The overstaffing prevailed throughout the century, in war as well as in peace, until just prior to the Revolution.

In mercantile and plutocratic post-Restoration England also, aristocracy prevailed over militarism. But it was an aristocracy of wealth rather than of birth or status. In the army, the purchase of office was the means of both entry and advancement in all branches except the technical services. The purchase system established a property qualification for military rank consciously designed to insure an identity of interest between army and government and to make another military dictatorship impossible in the British Isles. The high price of office, the low pay which made it virtually impossible to live on an officer's salary, and the lack of any system for pension or retirement caused commissions in peacetime to be monopolized by the younger sons of country gentry who possessed some private income. In war the officer corps was expanded by raising new regiments in which commissions might be purchased by virtually anyone who had the necessary funds.

During the last half of the seventeenth century the British Navy also began to have a group of permanent officers. Prior to 1794, however, no regularized system of entry existed for the vast bulk of officer candidates. Most officers began their careers working as servants to ships' captains who personally selected them as future officers. In 1729 the government established a "Naval Academy" to train the sons of gentlemen, from thirteen to sixteen years of age, as naval officers. But this school was never very successful. The more ambitious youths preferred to enter the navy through the "captain's servant" path. Entry into the navy was thus attained more by personal influence and patronage than by the aristocratic requirements of birth and wealth.[2]

ADVANCEMENT: PURCHASE, BIRTH, AND POLITICS. Wealth, birth, and political influence controlled advancement within as well as entry into the pre-1800 officer corps. The operation of the purchase system in the British Army has been discussed above. In the French Army, down to the last quarter of the eighteenth century, promotion was also normally by purchase. The highest military offices were monopolized by the court nobility, while the poorer country nobles remained in the lower ranks. The standard of wealth, however, clashed with that of birth, and in 1776 the country nobility prevailed upon the monarchy to begin the elimination of purchase. The shift from wealth to birth as a requisite for advancement did not, however, disturb the monopoly which the great nobles had on the top positions. Frequently, boys of twelve or fifteen would be made commanders of regiments. It was not until 1788 that the phenomenon of colonels "à la bavette" was restricted and semiprofessional methods of advancement introduced. But by then it was too late to alter the system of the old regime. In Prussia the higher nobility also monopolized the higher offices, although the fiction was maintained of promotion by merit. In actuality personal considerations and the whim of the sovereign were decisive factors. The low pay, further reduced by Frederick the Great, and the absence of any regularized pension system also tended to introduce a property requirement.[3]

Political influence generally determined appointments to the highest command positions in all the military forces. In France court intrigue selected the commanding general of the army; during the Seven Years War the fickle influence of Madame de Pompadour resulted in no less than six commanders in as many years. In Britain influence with Crown, Parliament, or both was essential to securing and retaining high command. Frequently large numbers of officers held seats in Parliament and made use of their legislative position to advance themselves in the army. Their dual role, however, also made them vulnerable to royal pressure, which George III at least did not hesitate to apply. High-ranking officers were frequently removed from their commands for opposing the wishes of the Crown. On occasion, the military hierarchy was prostituted to the purpose of soliciting the votes of officers. In the navy, too, as far as appointments at the higher level were concerned: "Sometimes it was by merit, but more commonly by favour and influence of family, relatives, and friends, in one word by 'interest.' "[4]

EDUCATION: NOBLES AND TECHNICIANS. Education for officership was incompatible both with the primitive state of military science and with the aristocratic belief that the only requirements for command were the inborn talents of courage and honor. The former made military education impractical; the latter made it unnecessary. The military schools which did exist were extremely rudimentary. They may be divided into two general types.

The first were the schools for the preliminary training of officers of noble or gentle birth. Into this category fall Louis XV's Ecole Militaire established in 1751, Frederick the Great's Ritter Akademie founded in 1765, and the English naval school set up in 1729. The quality of the students and the level of instruction in these schools were uniformly poor. The Ecole Militaire was specifically designed as a means of subsidizing the country nobility rather than of improving the army. Military subjects played a small role in its curriculum. It was, as Tuetey said, "une fondation d'intérêt philanthropique plus encore que d'intérêt militaire . . ." [5] Frederick's academy was designed to train nobles for the diplomatic service as well as the army and offered a most incomplete and imperfect education. The sons of nobles entered the Prussian Army at the age of twelve or fourteen and received only the scantiest training before assuming their commands. The English naval academy was of similarly poor caliber, and the English Army possessed no general institution of preliminary training at all.

The second type of pre-1800 military school was designed to train technically competent officers for the artillery and engineers. In the absence of any real military science of general concern to all officers, these were the only branches which offered real food for intellectual exercise. Since these arms were largely staffed by bourgeois officers, military schools to impart this technical knowledge did not conflict with the theory that the aristocratic officer commanded by virtue of inherited qualities. An engineering school was established in Prussia in 1706. The Royal Military Academy at Woolwich for artillery and engineering officers dates from 1741. The French began artillery instruction at Douai in 1679 and established an engineering school at Mézières in 1749. The educational level and character of these schools varied considerably. Woolwich, for instance, offered elements of both a military and a general education, but until a qualifying examination was introduced in 1774 many students were admitted without any real preparation and some without even the ability to read and write. The technical schools and the noble academies were as close as the eighteenth century came to military education. Schools for the advanced training of officers for higher command and staff positions were nonexistent.

STAFFS: ARRESTED DEVELOPMENT. The military staff is essentially a professional institution which collects technical knowledge and applies it practically to the management of violence. The forerunner of the modern military staff appeared in the armies of Gustavus Adolphus and Cromwell. From the middle of the seventeenth century until the end of the eighteenth century, however, the absence of progress in staff organization paralleled the static character of military science. The systems existing in 1790 in general more closely resembled those of one hundred and fifty years earlier than those of fifty years later.

Staff organization, rudimentary as it was, had its origin in the supply activities necessary for the permanent national armies. The key figure in the early staffs was the Quartermaster General. Just as the artillery and engineers were the only branches of the service which required technical training, the logistical activities were the only functions which required expert planning and control. Consequently the staffs had little to do with military operations. Strategy and tactics remained the province of the commanding general assisted by a few aides-de-camp. If the general was of poor caliber he saw no need for organized staff work. If he was an able general — such as Frederick or Saxe — he had little need for it. Staff work was unnecessary until war itself became as complex as its supporting activities.

France possessed the most highly developed staff system in the eighteenth century. But only for five years, 1766–1771, and again after 1783, did France have a true general staff in the modern professional sense. This French staff as organized by Bourcet required examinations and probationary work for admission. Such a scientific institution, however, was isolated and out of place in the aristocratically run French Army. In Prussia the embryo of a general staff existed in the Quartermaster General and his assistants. Their functions were limited, however, to supplies and fortifications, and their influence and significance remained slight until the end of the eighteenth century. In Great Britain virtually no permanent improvements in staff functioning were made over the arrangements which existed in Cromwell's army.[6]

COMPETENCE AND ESPRIT. The eighteenth-century officer corps subordinated the military values of expertise, discipline, and responsibility to the aristocratic values of luxury, courage, and individualism. The aristocrat was an amateur at officership; it was not for him a vocation with ends and standards of its own, but an incidental attribute of his station in society. Along with leisure, hunting, and good living, fighting was part of his ideal — a pastime valued for the opportunities it furnished for sport and adventure. Some of these amateurs turned out to be competent soldiers, but they were the exceptions to the system, not its products. In the French Army the only officers skilled in the practical aspects of their vocation were the soldiers of fortune, who, however, were only a minority of the corps and who were restricted to the lowest ranks. The general level of competence of the French officers drew cries of dismay from their commanders. Conditions were little better in the English and Prussian services. The senility, corruption, and ineptness of the Prussian officer corps increased during the eighteenth century as the higher ranks filled up with aging generals and the lower ranks with the least able sons of the nobility. The deterioration of the officer corps, the product of the entire Frederickan system of selection and organization, culminated in the disaster of Jena and the capitulation of the Prussian fortresses to Napoleon.

In France the intrusion of social considerations into the army made the maintenance of discipline based upon rank virtually impossible. Except when actually drilling troops, officers of higher rank but inferior social position yielded precedence to subordinates of more distinguished family. In the field as well as at court an officer was expected to maintain a household befitting his social status. Influence at court enabled officers to abandon their military responsibilities when they felt so inclined. In Prussia the poverty of the country prevented the excesses of luxury which characterized the French forces. Prussian officers, however, had no greater sense of responsibility and integrity than their French counterparts and regularly seized opportunities to enrich themselves at the expense of the royal treasury. The aristocratic code of the officer undermined military discipline: dueling between junior and senior officers was, for instance, a common phenomenon. In Great Britain the persistent interference of Parliament and Crown in military affairs made discipline impossible. Members of Parliament intervened with the authorities on behalf of mutineers and deserters who were relatives and friends, and officers felt free to quit their regiments when they were ordered to undesirable stations.[7]

SUMMARY. The eighteenth-century officer corps was designed for the needs of the aristocracy rather than for the efficient performance of the military function. Wealth, birth, personal and political influence dictated the appointment and advancement of officers. Children and incompetents frequently held high military rank. No body of professional knowledge existed. Consequently, no institutions, except for a few technical schools, were available to impart military knowledge, and there was no system for applying that knowledge in practice. Officers behaved and believed like aristocrats rather than like officers. The backward state of the military vocation may be contrasted with the condition of the legal, medical, and clerical professions at that time. The rudimentary independent existence of each of these made unthinkable the sort of prostitution to which the military vocation was subject. In brief, the military profession was simply nonexistent.

PREPROFESSIONAL IDEALS: THE MILITARY CRAFT
AND THE NATURAL GENIUS

The eighteenth century saw a tremendous outpouring of military literature which marked the culmination of one epoch in military thinking and the faint beginnings of a modern outlook. A few writers produced noteworthy works on specialized topics; and two eighteenth-century authors — Guibert and Lloyd — anticipated nineteenth-century developments and approached a comprehensive scientific view of war.[8] But these were exceptions. The bulk of the writing was rooted in the past and drew its lessons from the military practices of the Greeks and Romans. It lacked any real comprehension of the substance and limits of its subject matter. In place of a scientific conception of war, writers offered practical advice on a wide variety of disconnected subjects. With respect to military institutions, they substituted glorification of the natural genius for a conception of professional officership. Eighteenth-century military thinking was characteristically preprofessional; it had no unity, no focus, no theory, and no system. It accurately reflected the primitive state of military technique and the absence of professional institutions.

The most striking deficiency in military thinking prior to 1800 was the absence of any conception of military science as a distinct branch of knowledge, unified and complete in itself, susceptible of logical analysis into its component elements, and yet possessing a definite relationship to other branches of knowledge. In fact, military writers generally denied the possibility of ever developing such a science or any fixed principles of war. "War," said Marshal Saxe, "is a science replete with shadows in whose obscurity one cannot move with an assured step . . . All sciences have principles and rules. War has none." [9] This lack of a science of war might be deplored by Guibert and Lloyd; but it was accepted as necessary by most military thinkers. They also failed to recognize the possibility of logically analyzing war into its subcomponents. Only rarely were theoretical distinctions drawn among strategy, tactics, and the other branches of military science. As a result, works on war discussed a miscellaneous hodgepodge of topics bearing little or no logical relation to one another. To the extent that they possessed any scheme of organization at all beyond an alphabetical arrangement, it was chronological in nature. This approach was virtually identical with that of Vegetius who wrote in the fourth century and whose work was in many respects as applicable in the seventeenth century as when it was written. This chronological development is, of course, just the reverse of a logical theoretical approach which would begin with the nature of war and battle and then deduce the desirable type of equipment, training, organization, and recruitment from the purposes which the military forces were designed to achieve. The typical eighteenth-century military work, however, was a catalog rather than a treatise.

The writer whose work stands out in marked contrast is Henry Lloyd. Lloyd made an effort to grasp the essence of war — "War is a state of action" — and to deduce from this the nature of an army. The latter he defined as "the instrument with which every species of military action is performed." He then proceeded to analyze the army as a machine, considering the various parts and their interrelations. Unlike Saxe, Lloyd held that the art of war "like all others, is founded on certain and fixed principles, which are by their nature invariable, the application of them only can be varied: but they are in themselves constant." A contemporary of Bentham, he insisted upon a rigorous military utilitarianism. Reversing the chronological approach, he argued that the type of campaign to be fought and the plan of operations must always determine the number and species of troops and the quantity and quality of magazines.[10] Aside from this English historian, however, there were few efforts at a sophisticated understanding and definition of war.

The accepted eighteenth-century theory of generalship centered about the concept of the natural genius. Military command was an art like music or sculpture which required inherent talent. Military competence could not be transmitted or learned: it was a product of purely subjective factors existing within men rather than the result of anything derived from their environment. This idea is fundamentally romantic and antiprofessional. In effect, it was the application upon the individual level of the aristocratic theory that certain men were born to command and others to obey. The nobility held that only men born to their station were capable of being officers. The military writers of the Enlightenment held that only a man born with superior native ability could be a successful commander. Both theories denied the possibility of producing officers or generals through objective social institutions. The theory of the natural genius was shared by even the advanced thinkers of the period. Saxe argued that a basic similarity existed between war and the other arts. Guibert glorified the "born general." Lloyd held that war was divisible into two parts: a lower, mechanical part which might be taught by rule and precept, and a higher part which could be mastered only through the natural, intuitive knowledge of the genius: "No rule, no study, or application, however assiduous, no experience, however long, can teach this part; it is the effect of genius alone." [11]

THE ORIGINS OF PROFESSIONALISM

THE PRIMACY OF PRUSSIA. If it were necessary to give a precise date to the origin of the military profession, August 6, 1808 would have to be chosen. On that day the Prussian government issued its decree on the appointment of officers which set forth the basic standard of professionalism with uncompromising clarity:

The only title to an officer's commission shall be, in time of peace, education and professional knowledge; in time of war, distinguished valor and perception. From the entire nation, therefore, all individuals who possess these qualities are eligible for the highest military posts. All previously existing class preference in the military establishment is abolished, and every man, without regard to his origins, has equal duties and equal rights.[12]

The great reforms of Scharnhorst, Gneisenau, Grolmann, and the Prussian Military Commission mark the true beginning of the military profession in the West. The work of these leaders reflected an undercurrent of thought, discussion, and writing which appeared in the Prussian Army in the last decade of the previous century and which burst forth after Jena. This movement made a sharp break with the eighteenth century. Scharnhorst and Gneisenau, not Frederick the Great and his father, were the true founders of the modern German Army. They established the institutions and ideals which dominated the Prussian forces for the rest of the century and furnished the model upon which virtually all other officer corps were ultimately patterned. Each nation has made its unique contributions to the culture of western society. To Prussia goes the distinction of originating the professional officer.

Military professionalization was concentrated in two periods in the nineteenth century. During and immediately after the Napoleonic Wars most nations established institutions of initial military education and relaxed the entry bars to the officer corps. In the third quarter of the century, the processes of selection and promotion were overhauled, general staffs organized, and advanced military educational institutions established. In both periods Prussia led the way. While all the nations of Europe by 1875 had acquired the basic elements of military professionalism, in Prussia alone were these elements developed into a rounded and complete system. Requirements of general and special education for entry; examinations; institutions for higher military education; advancement by merit and achievement; an elaborate and efficient staff system; a sense of corporate unity and responsibility; a recognition of the limits of professional competence: these Prussia possessed to an extraordinary degree. In addition, it was a Prussian, Clausewitz, who contributed the theoretical rationale for the new profession. Why was it that this particular country took the lead in such a manner? The answer is to be found in the general causes responsible for the emergence of professionalism in Europe and in the peculiar extent to which they were present in Prussia. These factors were technological specialization, competitive nationalism, the conflict between democracy and aristocracy, and the presence of stable legitimate authority.

THE CONDITIONS OF PROFESSIONALISM. The growth of population in the eighteenth and nineteenth centuries, the development of technology, the beginnings of industrialism, and the rise of urbanism — all contributed to increased functional specialization and division of labor. War, like everything else, was no longer a simple, uncomplicated affair. Armies were larger, and, more important, were composed of increasingly diverse elements. Once, all the men in a military force had performed the same function: engaging the enemy with spears or swords as the case might be. Now armies and navies became complex organisms, embodying hundreds of different specialties, creating the need for still another type of specialist: the specialist in coordinating and directing these diverse parts to their assigned goal. No longer was it possible to master this skill while still remaining competent in many other fields. Most particularly, it became impossible to be an expert in the management of violence for external defense and at the same time to be skilled in either politics and statecraft or the use of force for the maintenance of internal order. The functions of the officer became distinct from those of the politician and policeman. Technological specialization was more or less equally present throughout the West. Professionalism had to arise. The explanation of its especial manifestation in Prussia is found in social and political conditions.

A second underlying factor in military professionalism was the growth of the nation state. The autonomous existence of an officer corps apart from other social institutions requires both that it be needed and that there be sufficient resources to support it. Both of these were supplied by the development of the nation-state system. Competition among the states caused each to create a corps of permanent experts devoted to the interests of military security. The loss or threatened loss of that security by war, or, more especially, by military defeat in war, was for each nation the immediate goad to professionalization. Prussia initiated a professional officer corps after its defeat in 1806 and started a second wave of professionalization following its humiliation by Denmark in 1848. Professionalism made its greatest strides in France after 1815 and 1870, and in England after 1856, 1870, and 1902. The size of the nation state also furnished sufficient resources to support a permanent military profession. As a part of the state bureaucracy, moreover, an officer corps could only be maintained by societies with highly developed governmental institutions.

The element of competitive nationalism had a peculiar applicability to Prussia. Lacking natural boundaries and with her territories scattered all over Germany, Prussia was uniquely dependent upon strong military force to maintain her independence and integrity. The rulers of Prussia had been aware of this since the middle of the seventeenth century and had poured tremendous resources and manpower into the maintenance of an efficient standing army throughout the eighteenth century. If Prussia, as Mirabeau claimed, was not a nation with an army but an army with a nation, this was because in a very special sense the existence of the army was essential to the existence of the nation. The defeat and humiliation of Prussia by the mass armies of Napoleon demonstrated to the Prussian rulers that the eighteenth-century type of force could no longer guarantee her security. To oppose the nationalism of the French Revolution, the Prussian population was enlisted in the army. To oppose the genius of Napoleon and the talents of his marshals selected for their ability in a haphazard but effective manner, the Prussians developed a collectively competent body of officers who triumphed through superior training, organization, and devotion to duty. In the long run, it was advantageous to Prussia that no natural leader appeared to rally the nation in her defeat. This deficiency caused the Prussians to resort to the systematic training of average men. As the most militarily insecure major power in Europe, it was hardly surprising that Prussia pioneered in creating a professional officer corps.

The rise of democratic ideals and parties was a third factor influencing the growth of professionalism. The democratic ideology was basically a system for organizing political institutions. Its proponents, however, attempted to shape military institutions in its pattern also. They substituted the representative ideal for the aristocratic ideal: the officer corps should be democratized and officers selected not by birth but by the choice of their fellow citizens. In the American Revolution the election of officers had been the prevailing means of appointment in the state militia. In the early years of the French Revolution the same system was tried again with equally unsuccessful results. The representative ideal was, of course, just as incompatible with military professionalism as the aristocratic ideal. It was, however, a key factor in breaking the monopoly of the nobles on the officer corps. The conflict between the two ideals in the first half of the nineteenth century produced a stalemate favorable to the advance of professionalism. When each party wished to subordinate the military to its own interests and principles, the only basis for compromise was mutual recognition of an independent officer corps free of partisan or class allegiance and organized in accordance with interests and principles of its own.

The balance favorable to professionalism existed particularly in Prussia and to a lesser extent in France. In the former country the aristocracy and aristocratic values remained strong in the century following Jena. At the same time, liberal ideas flourished, and the bourgeoisie became increasingly powerful. The conflict of rival classes and ideologies for dominance in the officer corps could best be resolved by a professional body isolated from politics. The Prussian reforms of 1806–1812 concretely reflect this situation. The military conservatives wished to maintain the aristocratic basis of the officer corps. The more extreme reformers, on the other hand, wanted to substitute a system of elective officers. Scharnhorst was able to balance one group off against the other and produce a system based on professional standards which satisfied neither but was acceptable to both. Gouvion St. Cyr used the same strategy a decade later in France. The army under Napoleon had become impregnated with liberalism. The reactionaries of the Restoration wished to wipe it clean and return to the 1789 model. St. Cyr put through his reforms of 1818 against the opposition of the extremists at both ends of the political spectrum but with the support of a solid bloc of moderate opinion.[13] In a country like England, on the other hand, where the conflict of aristocracy and democracy while existent was, nonetheless, neither so sharp nor as all-embracing as elsewhere, the same impetus to seize upon professionalism as a device of social compromise was lacking. Finally, in the United States, where there was no aristocracy, and where the democratic ideal reigned almost unchallenged, this incentive to professionalism was virtually absent.

The differing strengths of aristocracy and democracy on the European and American continents explain in part the peculiar historical failure of observers on either side of the Atlantic to recognize the emergence of military professionalism. In Europe professionalism challenged the dominant aristocrats; consequently, they identified it with democracy. In America professionalism challenged the dominant democracy, and hence it became identified with aristocracy. The consequences of this bizarre situation may be seen in De Tocqueville's acute summary of the key characteristics of a professional officer corps. Viewing the world through European eyes, however, he describes these professional elements as characteristic of "democratic armies." [14] Paradoxically, however, at the same time the Jacksonians in the United States were castigating as aristocratic these identical institutions which De Tocqueville labeled as democratic. The institutions, of course, were neither aristocratic nor democratic; they were military. But neither the aristocratic nor the democratic perspective could differentiate them from the socio-political enemy.

A final factor facilitating the growth of professionalism was the existence of a single recognized source of legitimate authority over the military forces. A professional officer is imbued with the ideal of service to the nation. In practice, he must be loyal to some single institution generally accepted as embodying the authority of the nation. Where there are competing authorities, or competing ideas as to what ought to be the authority, professionalism becomes difficult if not impossible to achieve. The conflict of constitutional ideologies and governmental loyalties divides the officer corps and superimposes political considerations and values upon military considerations and values. The nature of an officer's political loyalties becomes more important to the government than the level of his professional competence.

The need of a single locus of authority over the military limits the extent to which class conflict may stimulate professionalism. Professionalism is hindered rather than helped if the opposing classes become identified with competing governmental institutions each asserting some authority over the officer corps or if the two classes have fundamentally differing views on the constitutional structure of the state. Class conflict redounds to the benefit of professionalism only if both parties accept the authority of a particular governmental institution over the military. Professionalism thus requires the removal of party strife and political conflict one step away from the military forces themselves, and the channeling of political influence upon the military through some accepted formal institution of government. Some minimum degree of constitutional consensus is thus essential to military professionalism.

When viewed in the light of these considerations, the outstanding fact with respect to Prussia, France, and Great Britain is that only in Prussia was there a constitutional situation favorable to the growth of military professionalism. Basic to Prussian professionalism was the recognition of the king as Supreme War Lord and sole authority on military matters. Despite their increasing power, the Prussian bourgeoisie were never able, except briefly in 1848–1850 and 1860–1863, to challenge this authority and assert that of the parliament. Consequently, it was relatively easy to isolate the army from constitutional politics.*

In Great Britain, however, the system of dual control established by the constitutional settlement of 1688 delayed professionalization. Parliament had the power to raise and maintain military forces; command and appointments were within the prerogative of the Crown. The institutional rivalry of executive and legislature involved the British military forces in domestic politics until the supremacy of Parliament was firmly established in the nineteenth century. The achievement of this supremacy in the military sphere began with the creation of the office of the Secretary of State for War in the 1790's and ended with the abolition of the office of Commander in Chief one hundred years later. Meanwhile, however, the eighteenth-century system had been exported to the American colonies and copied by the Framers of the American

* A partial exception was the Minister of War, who, after 1850, was responsible in some matters to parliament and in others to the Crown. The position of the minister at times became untenable, and this dual responsibility contributed to the decline of his office. See Gordon A. Craig, *The Politics of the Prussian Army, 1640–1945* (Oxford, 1955), pp. 124–125, 223–225.

Constitution. As a result, many of the problems of military professionalism and civilian control later faced by the United States closely resembled those of Georgian Britain.

In France the constitutional conflict went deeper, continued longer, and had far more adverse effects on professionalism. In isolated instances, such as in 1818, this conflict might be utilized to advance the professionalization of the armed forces. But normally the struggle was so intense, and involved such antithetical constitutional ideologies, that compromise through the isolation of the officer corps from politics was impossible. The schisms dividing the nation were reflected in its military forces. Republicans, Legitimists, and Bonapartists all made direct efforts to control the army. French statesmen were torn between the ideal of a completely nonpolitical, professional officer corps which would maintain a scrupulous neutrality, and the fear that if they did not exercise their influence to insure the loyalty of high ranking officers to their own constitutional ideology, the officer corps might prove unreliable or even revolutionary in an emergency. Although, in the Restoration, St. Cyr attempted to neutralize the officer corps by professionalizing it, the aristocratic leaders of the government insisted upon classifying officers according to their political opinions, purging those considered untrustworthy, and subjecting the army to the surveillance of the secret police.[15] The names of Macmahon, Boulanger, Dreyfus, Sarrail, De la Rocque, Petain, and De Gaulle testify to the subsequent continued involvement of the French officer corps in constitutional politics.

UNIVERSAL SERVICE AND PROFESSIONALISM. The rise of nationalism and democracy had one important product which was closely linked to the emergence of professionalism. This was the concept of the "nation in arms" and its corollary of a national army, with a rank and file recruited through the universal service of all citizens for a brief period of years. The shift in the officer corps from amateurism to professionalism was virtually always associated with the shift in the rank and file from career soldiers to citizen-soldiers. Prussia, the first country to professionalize her officer corps, was also the first to introduce permanent universal service. The law of September 3, 1814 required all Prussian subjects to serve five years in the standing army (three on active service and two in the reserve) and fourteen years in the militia or *Landwehr*. While the terms of service varied from time to time, the basic system established by this law remained in force until the First World War. In France conscription, which had been employed on a temporary and confused basis during the Revolution and Empire, was prohibited by the Charter of Louis XVIII. Along with his reforms of the officer corps, however, St. Cyr attempted to introduce a form of universal service. Aristocratic opposition forced him to compromise upon a law under which the army was raised both by volunteer enlistment and by lot. Substitutes were permitted, however, and as the professionalization of the officer corps stagnated in the middle of the century, France returned to a pre-Revolutionary rank and file composed of career enlisted volunteers. Only with the second spurt of professionalization after the Franco-Prussian War did France adopt the mass army. England, like the United States, did not introduce peacetime conscription until the twentieth century. The triumph of Prussia in 1870, however, led the British not only to abolish the purchase system in the officer corps but also to take a step in the direction of a mass army — reducing the term of service from ten to six years and making strenuous efforts to increase short-term enlistments.[16]

In part the simultaneous introduction of conscription and professionalism was a parallel reaction to the need of military security. Prussia professionalized her officers and conscripted her rank and file as a result of her defeat by Napoleon. The other European countries adopted these twin aspects of the Prussian system as its merits were borne in upon them by either observation or direct and unfortunate experience. Countries such as Great Britain and the United States, which were geographically more secure, were slow in making either change. In addition, however, a more direct relation existed between conscription and professionalism. Aristocratic amateurs could be relied upon only so long as the rank and file were long-term regulars. When the latter became amateur soldiers, armies became larger and a much more capable and experienced leadership was necessary. It became the function of the officers to supply the continuing hard core of the military establishment, to be responsible for the advancement of military technique, and to train the constant stream of enlisted men through the ranks.

The change in the nature of both officer corps and rank and file changed their relations with the rest of society. In the eighteenth-century army the rank and file formed an outcast group, isolated and distrusted, with no roots in, or connections with, the rest of society. The officers, on the other hand, had definite status in society by virtue of their aristocratic position. In the reversal of roles which took place in the nineteenth century, the enlisted men became a cross section of the national population — citizens at heart — and the officers became a separate professional group living in a world of their own with few ties to outside society. While the enlisted personnel were the most "military" part of the eighteenth-century army, the officers are the most "military" part of the modern army.

Some writers have tended to overemphasize the significance of the introduction of universal service and to neglect the importance of the changes in the officer corps.[17] The victory of Prussia over France in 1870 was due as much to the superior professional ability of the Prussian officer corps and particularly its general staff as to the "mass" character of the Prussian Army. By stressing the shift from the old "professional army" to the new "citizen" or "mass" army, these commentators have obscured the appearance of professionalism in the officer corps. Their neglect of this factor has led them to conclude that mass armies inevitably mean total war and bloody national strife of unlimited ferocity. Conscription may indeed produce tendencies in this direction but these are in part balanced by the moderating, rational, calculating expertise introduced into the leadership of armies by the professionalization of the officer corps.

THE EMERGENCE OF PROFESSIONAL INSTITUTIONS, 1800–1875

ENTRY AND INITIAL EDUCATION. The evolution of professional methods of entry went through three phases: (1) the elimination of aristocratic prerequisites for entry; (2) the requiring of a basic level of professional training and competence; and (3) the requiring of a minimum general education and the provision of this education in institutions not operated by the military.

In Prussia the decree of August 6, 1808 abolished class restrictions on entry. An elaborate progression of educational and examination requirements was established to insure the basic competence of the officer corps.* Despite the formal opening of the corps to all qualified candidates, however, aristocratic considerations still remained significant. The more elite guards regiments were usually exclusively aristocratic, the technical arms largely bourgeois, and the regular line units more or less evenly divided. The requirements of nomination by a regimental colonel or, alternatively, admission to cadet school, made it possible to exclude candidates without the proper family background. Nonaristocrats, however, were always a substantial element of the officer corps; in the reaction after 1815 their proportion declined from about one-half to about one-third of the corps in 1860. Thereafter their numbers increased steadily until they made up about two-thirds of the corps on the eve of World War I. The education and examination requirements, which were raised in 1865, insured a basic competence in all officers, aristocratic or bourgeois, which was far higher than that in any other European army.

The early Prussian reformers emphasized the desirability of both general education and special education for officers. At first, however, the two types of education were intermingled with a confusing variety of schools and examining boards. But in 1844 a major reorganization increased the general education requirements and clearly separated general and technical education. The philosophy behind this change was that recruitment for officership should be on the same basis as recruitment for the other learned professions.†

---

* The normal steps to officership for a Prussian gymnasium student, seventeen and a half to twenty-three years of age, about the middle of the century were: (1) nomination by the colonel of a regiment; (2) passage of the general examination in the liberal arts; (3) six months service in the ranks; (4) appointment as a Swordknot ensign (*Portepeefähnrich*); (5) nine months training at division school; (6) special examination on military subjects; (7) acceptance by officers of the regiment; (8) commissioning as a lieutenant. The bulk of the students attending cadet school took the general examination at the ages of eighteen or nineteen and then followed the same procedure as those entering from the gymnasia. The entry procedure of the German Navy at the end of the century was modeled on this army system. See Archibald Hurd and Henry Castle, *German Sea Power* (London, 1913), pp. 160–164.

† Henry Barnard, *Military Schools and Courses of Instruction in the Science and Art of War* (Philadelphia, 1862), pp. 291–292, summarized the theory of the reforms as follows:

"1. The military profession, like every other, requires a general school educa-

Rise of the Military Profession

In the words of one Prussian general:

> The first and great object of the military examinations has been to secure a liberally educated body of officers (*ein gebildetes Offizier-corps*), not, however, over-educated (*übergebildetes*); the second object has been to secure a professionally educated body of officers (*ein berufgebildetes Offizier-corps*).[18]

Future officers were required either to graduate from the gymnasium and to receive the certificate of fitness for the university or, failing that, to pass a rigorous six-day general examination, designed not so much to test the student's factual knowledge as his intellectual capacity and analytical ability. About two-thirds of the officers came from the gymnasia and other schools which prepared students for all walks of life, while the remainder were drawn primarily from the cadet houses maintained by the state for the sons of former officers. Students entered the cadet schools at the ages of ten or eleven, or fifteen or sixteen. Although the cadets were subject to military discipline, virtually all the instruction was in liberal arts subjects. The operation by the War Ministry of general preparatory schools violated, of course, the principle of specialized professional competence; the general education offered in the cadet schools was inferior to that of the gymnasia; and the Prussian military leaders themselves were divided as to the desirability of main-

---

tion intended generally to cultivate the mind, distinct from the subsequent special and professional education for which the former is the necessary ground work.

"The former is tested in the examination for the Swordknot, the latter in the officers' examination.

"2. The preparatory education required for a candidate for a Swordknot is the function of the ordinary schools of the country . . .

"3. The required previous training not only gives the candidate a more certain basis for his subsequent military education, but, as being the ground work for all professions, leaves him afterwards at liberty to cultivate the special knowledge requisite for any profession that he may prefer.

"4. The division schools are freed from a multifarious course of instruction in the scholastic sciences, a task beyond their power; the result of which was that the majority of scholars were little advanced in formal and general education, and but superficially grounded in the elements of the professional sciences, while they spent years in being drilled for an examination, instead of being educated for life.

"5. If the division schools have an able staff of military teachers, they can give a good professional education . . .

"6. By the amount of liberal education required in the examination for the Swordknot, the friends of those destined for the military profession are admonished to provide them an education equal to that received by the members of other professions . . ."

taining the cadet houses. The technical proficiency of the Prussian officers was insured by requiring all entrants, except a few of the top students in the cadet houses, to serve six months in the enlisted ranks, attend a division school for nine months technical military training, and then pass the officers' examination on technical military subjects.

In France, the Revolution swept away aristocratic limitations on entry. Never again was birth to be a formal prerequisite for a military commission. During the Restoration there was strong pressure to go back to the old ways, but St. Cyr succeeded in firmly establishing the principle that entry should be only by competition from the military schools or from the ranks. Similar standards were set for the navy. Throughout the nineteenth century both services had a high, although varying, proportion of aristocratic officers. This fact, however, reflected more the greater interest in a military career among aristocratic families than any weighting of entrance requirements in their favor.

St. Cyr's law and subsequent legislation provided that one-third to two-thirds of the officers should come from the military schools and the remainder from the ranks of noncommissioned officers with at least four years service. The "privates with stripes" promoted from the ranks were frequently unaware of the difference in responsibility and duties between the commissioned and noncommissioned officer, and they contributed little to the intellectual level of the officer corps. Those officers who entered from the military schools possessed in contrast both a good general and a good technical education. There were three institutions of professional instruction. The Ecole Polytechnique (founded in 1794) supplied the army with its artillery and engineering officers and the navy with its marine artillery officers, naval architects, and other technical specialists. The Special Military School to train officers for the cavalry and infantry was established at Fontainebleau in 1803 and transferred to St. Cyr in 1808. Naval schools were set up at Brest and Toulon in 1810 and in 1816 were united in a single institution which came to be established at Brest in 1827. Entry into all these schools was by competitive examination, candidates normally being between sixteen and twenty years of age for the Polytechnic Institute and St. Cyr and fourteen to sixteen for the naval school. In most cases, however, it was assumed that candidates had completed the usual course at the lycée. For the French even more than the Prussians, officers were expected to have gone through the normal secondary schools of the country. The sole exception was the Prytanée Militaire, France's only real military preparatory school, which each year sent a limited number of officers' sons to the military colleges. The course at St. Cyr and the Ecole Polytechnique was two years in length. The curriculum at St. Cyr included in the first year predominantly scientific subjects and in the second principally military subjects. At the Ecole Polytechnique instruction was almost exclusively scientific and technical with only a single course on military art and topography. Students at the naval school studied general and professional subjects for two years at Brest and then underwent a year of practical instruction on board a training ship.[19]

Aristocratic bars to entry prevailed much longer in the British Army than in the French and Prussian forces. The first break in the purchase system (apart, of course, from the artillery and engineers) occurred with the establishment of the Royal Military College at Sandhurst in 1802. Nomination by the Commander in Chief was necessary to enter this institution but graduates received their commissions without purchase. In the middle of the century efforts were made to broaden the avenues of entry which did not require purchase. But it was not until the abolition of the entire system in 1871 that aristocratic qualifications ceased to have a formal place in British entry requirements.* In the British Navy entry as a "Captain's servant" was abolished in 1794. The "First Class Volunteers" which were instituted, however, were still appointed by ships' captains. Approval by the Admiralty of these appointments was required in 1833 and examinations were instituted in 1838–39. In 1848 the captains' powers were still further restricted, and in 1870 a system of "limited competition" was introduced in which two preliminary nominations were made for every appointment. The elimination of patronage from British naval entry thus proceeded

---

* Of 4,003 first appointments to the army between 1860 and 1867, 3,167 were by purchase and 836 without purchase. The opposition to educational requirements for officership was well expressed in the 1850's by the Duke of Cambridge who attacked the Prussian system and insisted that in contrast the "British officer should be a gentleman first and an officer second." Quoted in Roy Lewis and Angus Maude, *Professional People* (London, 1952), p. 31.

at about the same pace as the elimination of purchase from British army entry.[20]

With the establishment of the Royal Military College in 1802, the reorganization and expansion of Woolwich in 1806, and the change of the naval academy into the Royal Naval College in the same year, Great Britain came to possess adequate institutions of preliminary professional education. Attendance at these schools, however, was not required of all officers. In addition, there were no provisions for an adequate general education. Students entered Woolwich and Sandhurst from public school, but the British public school did not offer an education comparable to the gymnasium or lycée. The Admiralty, moreover, had long adhered to a policy of "catch 'em young," enlisting future naval officers at the ages of twelve to fourteen. Accordingly, if the naval officer was to get a general education, he had to get it from the Admiralty. From 1806 to 1837 an effort was made to supply this at the Royal Naval College at Portsmouth. In 1837, however, the college was closed and general education was sent to sea, naval cadets theoretically being educated by schoolmasters on board ship afloat. In actual practice, the training at sea was almost entirely practical and technical. In 1857 this system was ended, and a training ship was established at Dartmouth where cadets from twelve to fourteen received two years instruction before going to sea. In 1886 a special committee urged the Admiralty to secure a "greater degree of intelligence and a better general education" either by furnishing a general education itself or by delaying the recruitment of officers until they had finished secondary school. In 1903 the naval school at Osborne was reorganized in an effort to provide the first of these alternatives, and ten years later the second course of action was also adopted by permitting special entry from the public schools.[21] Thus, about one hundred years after both a general and specialized education were required for the officers of the Prussian Army, they became mandatory for the officers of the British Navy.

ADVANCEMENT. The establishment of professional standards for entry into the officer corps was followed by the establishment of professional standards for advancement within the corps. In general, the new advancement system took the form of promotion by seniority tempered by selection.

Rise of the Military Profession

In Prussia, Scharnhorst introduced the idea of examinations as a prerequisite to promotion and raised the pay of officers so as to decrease their reliance upon outside income. Able officers were advanced rapidly in the General Staff Corps. Despite a lack of formalized rules, influence and favoritism played only a minor role in the advancement of officers. Promotion up to the rank of captain generally followed seniority although unusually able officers, particularly those who had qualified for the General Staff or Adjutant General's Office, might be advanced more rapidly. Above the grade of captain promotion was within the arm or corps and seniority was followed more rigidly. An officer who was passed over, when his turn for promotion by seniority appeared, was expected to resign. Most officers might expect to be advanced in turn to the rank of major, the great weeding out taking place in the promotions from that post to colonelcies. Examinations were utilized as a guide to eliminating officers in the engineers and foot artillery.

The French law of 1818 was a bold attempt to exclude non-professional factors from advancement. It required that two-thirds of all promotions up to the rank of lieutenant colonel should be by seniority. The remaining one-third of the promotions in the lower ranks and all appointments of colonels and general officers were by selection. The law, however, placed too much reliance on seniority, required too lengthy terms of service in the lower grades, and did not entirely prevent aristocratic favoritism. The entire system was revised by the July Monarchy in 1832. The time required in each grade before promotion was significantly reduced, and the proportion of appointments to major going by seniority was reduced from two-thirds to one-half. More significantly, this law merited its title as the "Charter of the Army" because it guaranteed to the officer his rank except in instances of misbehavior punished by court martial. An elaborate system of recommendations for promotion was developed in which lists of officers eligible for advancement were drawn up annually in each arm, and acted upon by either the inspector general or a committee of higher officers. In 1851 a comprehensive and regularized scheme of retirement pensions was introduced. By the middle of the nineteenth century formal regulations for professional advancement existed in the

French Army. In actual practice, however, the system was still subject to certain deficiencies and abuses.

Conditions were somewhat similar in the French Navy. Advancement from one grade to the next required two to four years' service in the lower grade and in certain cases command experience. From the lowest grade up to *capitaine de frégate* (lieutenant colonel) promotion was by both seniority and selection; above this grade, by selection only. In the last quarter of the nineteenth century the disappearance of promotion opportunities caused by the slow retirement of senior officers led to the widespread use of nepotism and favoritism to gain the few appointments available. Whereas under the Empire merit had generally prevailed, in the first years of the Third Republic influence was essential. The situation eventually became so extreme and newspaper criticism of the apparently extraordinary abilities of the sons of admirals and ministers so strong, that the entire system was revised in 1890. The Admiralty Council which had existed since 1824 and which had become the focus of favoritism was abolished and a system of inspector generals instituted to determine those officers eligible for promotion.[22]

Only slowly during the nineteenth century were politics and purchase eliminated from the British Army. The first step toward the restriction of politics was taken in 1794 when the office of Commander in Chief was established. The new position gave the army a professional military head viewed as outside the area of party politics. Gradually this military chief took over appointments and discipline from the more politically vulnerable civilian ministers. In 1861 the Commander in Chief was given complete responsibility for the command, discipline, and appointments in the army, subject only to the general control of the Crown over the government of the military forces and the responsibility of the Secretary of State for War for the exercise of the royal prerogative. To assist the Commander in making appointments, each general officer was required to submit semiannual reports on his subordinates. At about the same time examinations became mandatory for the promotion of junior officers and successful completion of the Staff College course became a prerequisite to duty at general headquarters.

A true system of professional advancement was impossible

in the British Army so long as purchase existed. By 1856 a captaincy cost approximately £2,400 and a lieutenant colonelcy £7,000. The extremely low pay of the officers had not been increased since the reign of William III, and independent income was obviously essential to a military career. Critics of this situation were not lacking. Lord Grey in 1846 made a vigorous attack upon it and formulated a farsighted program of reform. In 1850 a Royal Commission likewise took the system to task. Opposition to reform, however, remained strong. Purchase, it was argued, secured the loyalty of the army to the state by insuring that the former would be controlled by the same property interests which dominated the latter. Direct socio-political controls were preferred to reliance upon a sense of professional responsibility. Conservatives such as the Duke of Wellington strongly condemned proposals to substitute a "mercenary army" for one lead by "men of fortune and character — men who have some connection with the interests and fortunes of the country, besides the commissions which they hold for His Majesty." The ghost of the New Model Army still haunted the minds of British soldiers and statesmen two hundred years after the Restoration. Only the example of the superior efficiency of the Prussian military machine in the war with France enabled Lord Cardwell to secure the abolition of purchase in 1871. Even then much criticism of the idea of a "professional" army still persisted, and Cardwell had to emphasize that:

> . . . if there is one lesson which we have learned from the history of the late campaign, it is this — that the secret of Prussian success has been more owing to the professional education of the officers than to any other cause to which it can be ascribed. Neither gallantry nor heroism will avail much without professional training . . .[23]

With reluctance Parliament conceded that Moltke might be a greater threat than Cromwell and authorized the government to buy up the commissions of its officers and institute a system of promotion based on seniority and selection according to merit.

Professional advancement made easier headway in the British Navy than in the Army. Politics was largely eliminated at the beginning of the nineteenth century. Moreover, there was no purchase system. By the latter part of the century an effective retirement scheme had been introduced, and after 1860 all appointments were made on the basis of "rank" rather than "post." Midshipmen and sublieutenants were promoted by examinations, lieutenants and commanders by selection, and all others by seniority.

EDUCATION. As the science of war increased in scope and complexity, institutions for its advanced study became increasingly necessary. Prussia recognized this long before any other power, and in 1810 Scharnhorst established the famous Kriegsakademie in Berlin. This school was designed to be a military university for the higher study of the science of war. Officers were admitted after five years service, certification by their commanding officers that they had performed their duties competently, and passage of a ten-day special examination. Ordinarily, forty were selected out of sixty to seventy candidates each year. The required subjects included tactics, military history, science of arms, field and permanent fortifications, military and political administration and economy, mathematics, artillery, special geography and geology, staff duty, and military jurisprudence. About one-half of the academic work was elective, and the officer could choose among universal history, universal geography, logic, physics, chemistry, literature, higher geodesy, higher mathematics, French, and Russian. The staff included both military and civilian instructors, and the school possessed an excellent library.

The War Academy was the focal institution of Prussian professionalism. In due course attendance at the Academy became a prerequisite for attainment of either high rank or one of the much coveted positions upon the General Staff. For a long time the Academy was the only institution of its kind in Europe. One measure of its impact is the estimate that in 1859 about 50 per cent of the military literature of Europe was produced in Germany.[24] In the War Academy, as in the lower schools, the great emphasis was on the development of a general understanding and broad theoretical ability on the part of the students rather than detailed factual knowledge committed to memory. Foreign observers marveled at the stress upon encouraging "self-reliance" and the care bestowed upon the "higher objects of education, upon forming and disciplining the mind and encouraging habits of reflection." [25] Judged by the standards of modern educational theory, the Prussian military educational system must have been among the most advanced in Europe — civil or military — during the nineteenth century.

France like Prussia established a number of advanced specialized schools during the first part of the nineteenth century. The French, however, had nothing comparable to the Kriegsakademie. The only institution remotely approaching it was the staff school (Ecole d'Application d'Etat Major) established by St. Cyr in 1818. Admission was limited to a small number of the best students of St. Cyr and the Ecole Polytechnique and to sublieutenants on active service. All candidates had to pass a rigorous examination on military subjects. The course of study was two years in length and was much more narrowly focused and elementary in nature than the curriculum at the Kriegsakademie. Attendance at the school was, nevertheless, necessary for appointment to the general staff corps. Like the other institutions of French professionalism, the staff school did not make much progress during the course of the century. As the French military attaché in Berlin remarked in the 1860's, all French military educational institutions were "only agricultural schools" when compared with the Kriegsakademie.[26]

After the defeat of 1871, the French officers began organizing themselves informally for their own military self-education just as the Prussian officers had done in 1807. In 1874 the government appointed a commission to study the desirability of a war academy, and in 1876 a special course for higher officers was established at the staff school. Finally, in 1878, a true war academy, the Ecole Militaire Supérieure, was founded. Entrance to this school was by competitive examination, and a two-year course was offered to captains and lieutenants destined for the higher command and staff positions. While the Ecole later had its ups and downs, French military education was thenceforth on a much higher level than it had been prior to 1870.[27]

In Great Britain higher institutions of military education lagged behind those of France. In 1799 the Duke of York had opened a special school to educate officers for the staff. In 1802 this was reorganized as the Royal Military College, the staff course becoming the Senior Department of the College. The Senior Department played a relatively small role in British military life, however, until

1857 when it was detached and set up as a separate Staff College. Even then it was still not on a par with the Prussian Academy, and it was not until many years later that the British Army had a really high-level advanced military school. The beginnings of naval higher education occurred in 1837 when the Royal Naval College at Portsmouth was reorganized as an advanced school. In 1873 this college was moved to Greenwich and became the center for high-level instruction in the British Navy with the purpose of educating officers above midshipman "in all branches of theoretical and scientific study bearing on their profession." [28]

STAFFS. The primacy of Prussia was most obvious in the development of a professional staff. The Prussian general staff properly dates from November 25, 1803 when the king ordered the reorganization of the previously existing Quartermaster General's supply staff into a true general staff. Earlier, in 1800, General von Lecoq had carried through some preliminary reforms, but the basic outline of a general staff in modern, professional terms is first found in the memoranda drafted by Colonel von Massenbach in 1802–1803 which served as the basis for the royal directive of the latter year. Under this order officers were appointed to the staff only after passing a special examination, and they were subsequently rotated between staff positions and regimental duties. The duties of the General Staff were divided into two categories: permanent duties involving the development of the fundamental principles of military operations, and special duties involving current military problems and the preparation of war plans.

The General Staff never had the opportunity to function effectively prior to the defeat of Prussia by Napoleon. In 1808, however, Scharnhorst reorganized the staff, redefined more precisely its duties, inaugurated the division between the Great General Staff in Berlin and the Field Forces General Staff, linked the achievement of staff positions to the Kriegsakademie, and instituted the beginnings of the system of dual command whereby general staff officers shared in the responsibility of commanders. After the downfall of Napoleon the General Staff continued to exercise in peacetime the functions which it had previously exercised in war. Throughout the nineteenth century the General Staff tended to be the organizational stronghold of Prussian professionalism. In the early decades it had to struggle for position and recognition against both the War Ministry and the Military Cabinet which tended to be the center of aristocratic reaction. Under the leadership of von Moltke, however, who became its chief in 1857, the General Staff rapidly acquired preëminence. The scientific and rational expertise of Moltke became the dominant ideal of the German officer corps. From the 1860's on, service in the General Staff was the most coveted duty in the German Army. The wine-red trouser stripe of the General Staff officers became the symbol of a new elite within the officer corps, the cream of the profession, signifying the highest standards of knowledge, competence, and devotion to duty. For the General Staff officer, far more than for any other member of the officer corps, all else was subordinated to the requirements of professional service. "Always be more than you seem," was Moltke's injunction to his staff officers. Half a century later von Seeckt summed up the tradition in crisp phrases:

The form changes, but the spirit remains as of old. It is the spirit of silent, selfless devotion to duty in the service of the Army. General Staff officers remain anonymous.[29]

Probably the most revolutionary aspect of the Prussian system was its assumption that genius was superfluous, and even dangerous, and that reliance must be placed upon average men succeeding by superior education, organization, and experience. This approach, on the one hand, subordinated the individual to the collective will and intelligence of the whole, and yet guaranteed to the individual wide freedom of action so long as he remained upon his proper level and within his sphere of responsibility. It was the antithesis of the eighteenth-century theory of the military genius. English observers of the Prussian system were impressed by the absence of the slavish and mechanical obedience to superiors characteristic of other armies and the extent to which each officer performed his particular function without intervening in the duties of others.[30]

In France, in 1800 General Paul Thiebault published the first staff manual of the modern period. In actual practice Berthier, Napoleon's chief of staff, developed a rudimentary general staff organization, although its entire structure and functioning were colored by Napoleon's ability and genius and by Berthier's small-ness and jealousy. During the Restoration, St. Cyr established both a staff corps and a school to train officers for it, but not a general staff itself. Members of this corps were employed with troop com-mands, at the War Ministry and other administrative headquarters, as military attachés in foreign countries, and as instructors in the higher military schools. There was, however, no such thing as a "Great General Staff" with an autonomous existence in the War Ministry, nor was there a chief of staff. Consequently, the educa-tion and work of staff officers lacked purpose and focus. After 1831 the staff corps increasingly became a narrowly technical service concerned with drawing and topography. French staff de-velopment was also handicapped by the continuation of the eight-eenth-century concept, reinforced by the Napoleonic and African wars, that the superior officer was one who relied upon his in-herent natural gifts rather than expert advice and assistance. In general, the level of competence of the staff corps and its ability to grapple successfully with the problems which should have con-cerned a professional staff declined steadily during the forty years from 1830 to 1870. By the Franco-Prussian War the French staff had reached such a low point that it was hardly surprising that it proved no equal of its German counterpart.[31]

During his continental wars Wellington developed an efficient staff for the British Army. With the conclusion of peace, how-ever, the British staff more or less disintegrated, and throughout the nineteenth century Great Britain did not have a general staff in the modern sense of the word. The inept performance of the army in the Crimean War resulted in some steps toward the re-construction of a staff, but the only lasting result was the creation of the Staff College in 1857. The only staff in the British Army was in the adjutant general and quartermaster departments: there was no real staff concerned with military operations and military intelligence — the domain of strategy and tactics as contrasted with administration and supply. This deficiency was not overcome until the first decade of the twentieth century when the work of enthusiasts such as Spenser Wilkinson combined with the lessons of the Boer War to produce a reorganization of the army. In 1904 an Army Council was created and the position of Chief of the

General Staff came into existence. A few years later this was extended to provide for military cooperation with the dominions through the Imperial General Staff.[32]

COMPETENCE AND ESPRIT. The appearance of professional competence and *esprit* among the officers inevitably reflected the extent to which professional institutions were introduced. England remained the most backward of the three major powers. The expertise of her military leaders was severely affected by the aristocratic and social considerations which continued important in her officer corps until the twentieth century. As one of its generals reported, the English Army in 1890 was still split between those who adhered to the tradition of Wellington and those who wished "to make the army a profession." [33] In France before the Franco-Prussian War professional and intellectually inclined officers were viewed with suspicion. Individualism was rampant: the ideal of the army of the Second Empire was the aristocratic *"beau sabreur, a man of boundless courage and audacity but no reflection."* [34] The rejection of intellectual activity and the narrow, rigid confines of the educational and staff systems were the decisive elements in the defeat at the hands of the Germans. After the reforms of the 1870's the professional spirit became dominant within the French forces although it was still hampered by the ideological controversy over the nature of the French state.

Professional competence and the professional spirit reached their fullest development in Prussia. The smooth functioning efficiency of the Prussian armies of 1866 and 1870 stands out in sharp contrast to the bumbling confusion of the English Army of 1856, the American armies of the Civil War, and the Austrian and French armies which Prussia defeated. The central importance of the military schools and the key role of the General Staff gave the Prussian Army an intellectual overcurrent absent from other forces. As one English observer commented sadly in 1859:

> The fact that education is the be-all and end-all of the Prussian officer, is a potent lever in causing him to perfect himself in his profession; and the certainty of promotion through merit and not from caprice, sets the whole of the Prussian officers far above those whom we find in the English army.[35]

Despite the opposition of conservatives like Wrangel and Manteuffel, the spirit of the Prussian officer corps had been slowly transformed from an aristocratic class spirit into a military caste spirit. After the middle of the century the emphasis was increasingly upon the close unity and comradeship of all officers regardless of their social origins. The line was drawn between military and civilian rather than between bourgeois and noble. The aristocracy of birth had been replaced by the aristocracy of education and achievement. The Prussian officer was poor, expert, disciplined, and devoted, an integral part of a tightly knit professional community. The result was a corporate *esprit* unique in Europe. In the words of the British Military Education Commission:

> The whole of the officers of the Prussian army look upon themselves as forming a single corps — the Offizier-corps — united by common ties and sympathies; admission to this body is regarded at once as conferring distinctive privileges, and as imposing peculiar duties.[36]

EUROPEAN PROFESSIONALISM: GENERAL UPTON'S SUMMARY, 1875

Despite the lingering tenacity of aristocratic elements, by 1875 the basic institutions of professionalism had become securely established in the armed services of the major European powers. One indication of this fact is the summary description of the European armies made by the American general, Emory Upton, in that year. Upton had been despatched by General Sherman and Secretary Belknap to study the organization, tactics, discipline, and education of the armies of Europe and Asia, with particular attention to the German military system. In his report Upton stressed the professional institutions which he found to be prevalent throughout Europe and urged their immediate introduction into the American army:

1. Entry into the officer corps was only by graduation from a military school or by promotion from the ranks after pursuing a course of professional study and passing a qualifying exam.
2. A war academy educated officers in the advanced science of war, preparing them for staff positions and high command posts.

3. The general staff demanded officers with "the highest professional training." Officers rotated between staff and line positions.

4. "To enable the Government to profit by the best talent in the army, rapid promotion, either by entering the staff corps or by selection, is provided for all officers who manifest decided zeal and professional ability."

5. So that the government will know the qualifications of its officers, annual or biennial reports were required from commanding officers, showing "the zeal, aptitude, special qualifications, and personal character" of their subordinates.

6. "Officers are maintained for the sole benefit of the Government. If, therefore, an officer is ignorant or incompetent, the Government, by means of personal reports, and special examinations, can stop his promotion, and thus prevent injury to the service . . ." [37]

FORMULATION OF THE PROFESSIONAL ETHIC: THE AUTONOMY AND SUBORDINATION OF WAR IN CLAUSEWITZ'S VOM KRIEGE

The objective emergence of a complicated science of war and of professional institutions devoted to that science rendered obsolete eighteenth-century conceptions of war as an ill-defined craft and of the general as a natural genius. The new conditions required a new theory which received its first comprehensive and explicit formulation in *Vom Kriege* by Karl von Clausewitz published posthumously in 1831. Significantly, Clausewitz had been an assistant to Scharnhorst and Gneisenau in the work of military reform. He wrote his book while director of the War Academy in the years after 1815. In effect, the book furnished the intellectual rationale for the reforms in which he had previously participated.

The problem in discussing Clausewitz and his work is to explain the reputation of the former and the permanence of the latter. Military commentators have been virtually unanimous in hailing this red-nosed Prussian as the preëminent military thinker of western society — the Shakespeare or Goethe of military writers — and in describing his work as the Bible of military science.[38] Most of these commentators have stressed Clausewitz's contributions to the evolution of strategy and tactics, his understanding and formulation of the essence of the Napoleonic method. Clausewitz's views on tactics, however, have long since been outdated, and his statement of the principles of strategy is no more distinguished than that of many other military thinkers. His significant contribution occurs at a higher level of analysis and concerns the inherent nature of war and the relation of war to other forms of human activity. Clausewitz was not, of course, isolated from the intellectual currents about him. Other military writers were groping in the same direction, and many of them anticipated points found in *On War*. They generally dealt, however, with only incidental aspects of the changes which were taking place in the nature of war. Clausewitz was alone in grasping and expressing the essence of this transformation. For this reason he deservedly occupies in military thought a place roughly comparable to that of Marx in the history of socialist theory: most of the writing which came before him was preliminary, fragmentary, and subsequently embodied in his work; most of that which came after him was exegetic and interpretative of the meaning of the master.

The basic element in Clausewitz's theory is his concept of the dual nature of war. War is at one and the same time an autonomous science with its own method and goals and yet a subordinate science in that its ultimate purposes come from outside itself. This concept of war is a true professional one, embodying as it does the essentials of any profession: the delimitation of a unique subject matter independent of other human thought and activity and the recognition of the limits of this subject matter within the total framework of human activity and purpose. Clausewitz expresses many other elements of the professional military ethic. But these are secondary. His seminal contribution is his concept of the dual nature of war and the role of the soldier. Given this, virtually all the other aspects of professionalism must necessarily follow.

For Clausewitz the essence of war when considered as an independent science, as a thing in itself (*Krieg an sich*), is force. *"War is thus an act of force to compel our adversary to do our will."* War in this sense permits of no limitation. The science of generalship is the science of disarming or overthrowing the enemy

by force. In theory this is always necessary. Consequently battle
and bloodshed cannot be avoided. "Let us not hear of generals
who conquer without bloodshed." Clausewitz's stress on force without limit as the essence of war has led some commentators to assume that this is the only side of his thought, that he is exclusively
a glorifier of bloody violence: Liddell Hart refers to Clausewitz
as "the Mahdi of mass and mutual massacre" and "the source of
the doctrine of 'absolute war,' the fight to the finish theory." [39]
This, however, is a misinterpretation of Clausewitz. Only when
considered abstractly, in theory, independent of all else, is war
violence without limit. In practice, war is never an isolated act.
Force is not an end in itself. It is only justified when it is rationally
employed for public purposes. War is always subordinate to the
external political ends which determine the extent and nature of
the violence to be employed. The results of war are never absolute.
"In this way the whole field of war ceases to be subject to the
strict law of forces pushed to the extreme." The costs of military
action are balanced against the ends to be achieved. The political
object of the war remains the guide throughout the struggle.
Bullets merely take the place of diplomatic notes. In his most
celebrated dictum: "war is nothing but a continuation of political
intercourse with an admixture of other means." In short, war has
"its own grammar, but not its own logic."

This concept of war as an autonomous and yet instrumental
science implies a similar theory with respect to the role of the
specialist in war. The fact that war has its own grammar requires
that the military professionals be permitted to develop their expertise at this grammar without extraneous interference. The
"military virtue of an army" is not found in the nature of the cause
for which it fights any more than the skill of the lawyer is judged
by the persons of his clients. The inherent quality of a military
body can only be evaluated in terms of independent military standards. The ends for which the military body is employed, however,
are outside its competence to judge: "the political object of war
really lies outside of war's province . . ." War does not have its
own logic and purpose. The soldier must always be subordinate to
the statesman. The conduct of war is the responsibility of the lat-

ter because it "requires a keen insight into state policy in its higher relations."

The subordination of the political point of view to the military would be unreasonable, for policy has created the war; policy is the intelligent faculty, war only the instrument, and not the reverse. The subordination of the military point of view to the political is, therefore, the only thing which is possible.

A minister of war need not have a detailed knowledge of military affairs, and soldiers often make poor ministers. The military viewpoint will inevitably, of course, interact with the political objective, and policy must take into account the means at its disposal. Clausewitz voices the military warning to the statesman to note carefully the limits of his military strength in formulating goals and commitments. But in the end, policy must predominate. Policy may indeed "take a wrong direction, and prefer to promote ambitious ends, private interests or the vanity of rulers," but that does not concern the military man. He must assume that policy is "the representative of all the interests of the whole community" and obey it as such. In formulating the first theoretical rationale for the military profession, Clausewitz also contributed the first theoretical justification for civilian control.

3

The Military Mind: Conservative Realism
of the Professional Military Ethic

THE MEANING OF THE MILITARY MIND

The unique or functional aspect of the military has often been discussed in terms of the "military mind." This chapter attempts to define this concept precisely enough so that it may serve as a useful tool of analysis. The military mind may be approached from three viewpoints: (1) its ability or quality; (2) its attributes or characteristics; and (3) its attitudes or substance.[1]

Writers employing the first approach have normally emphasized the low caliber of the "military mind." The intelligence, scope, and imagination of the professional soldier have been compared unfavorably to the intelligence, scope, and imagination of the lawyer, the businessman, the politician. This presumed inferiority has been variously attributed to the inherently inferior talents and abilities of the persons who become officers, the organization of the military profession which discourages intellectual initiative, and the infrequent opportunities which an officer has actively to apply his skill. This general approach deals with one feature of the military mind, but it does not help to define the peculiarly "military" aspects of that mind. The mere fact that the military mind occupies a particular point on the intelligence scale says nothing about its distinctive characteristics. The point might well be the same one occupied by the engineering or dental minds.

The second approach holds that the uniqueness of the military mind lies in certain mental attributes or qualities which constitute a military personality. Military and civilian writers generally seem to agree that the military mind is disciplined, rigid, logical, scientific; it is not flexible, tolerant, intuitive, emotional. The continuous performance of the military function may well give rise to these qualities. Intuitively one feels that these descriptions, also intuitive, come close to the mark. But until more knowledge is accumulated about the personality traits of military men and other politically significant groups and also about the relation between personality, values, and behavior in social situations, this approach will not be very useful in analyzing civil-military relations.

A third and more fruitful approach is to analyze the substance of the military mind — the attitudes, values, views of the military man. This has customarily been done through one of two techniques: to define the military mind in terms of content, or to define it in terms of source. The former method describes certain values and attitudes as military in content, and then asserts that these values and attitudes are widely prevalent among military men. Emphasis has generally focused upon two sets of attitudes assumed to be characteristically military: bellicosity and authoritarianism. The military man is held to believe that peace is stultifying and that conflict and war develop man's highest moral and intellectual qualities; he favors aggressive and bellicose national policies. He is also thought to be opposed to democracy and to desire the organization of society on the basis of the chain of command. Irrespective of whether these conclusions are accurate, the method used in arriving at them is both subjective and arbitrary. The *a priori* assumption that certain values are military and that military men therefore hold those values may or may not be true, but there is nothing in the procedure which requires it to be so.

An alternative approach is to define military values by source. This is to assume that any expression of attitude or value coming from a military source reflects the military mind. But the difficulty here is that everything which comes from a military source does not necessarily derive from its character as a military source. Military men are also Frenchmen and Americans, Methodists and Catholics, liberals and reactionaries, Jews and antisemites. Any given statement by a military man may not reflect his attitudes *qua* military man but may instead stem from social, economic, political, or religious affiliations irrelevant to his military role. This difficulty could be overcome if it were possible to cancel out these accidental characteristics of military men by surveying a broad, representative sample of communications from military men from all walks of life, all countries, and all times. The magnitude of such an undertaking, however, makes it desirable to find an alternative path to the military mind: to arrive at the substance of *l'idée militaire* by defining it as a professional ethic.

People who act the same way over a long period of time tend to develop distinctive and persistent habits of thought. Their unique relation to the world gives them a unique perspective on the world and leads them to rationalize their behavior and role. This is particularly true where the role is a professional one. A profession is more narrowly defined, more intensely and exclusively pursued, and more clearly isolated from other human activity than are most occupations. The continuing objective performance of the professional function gives rise to a continuing professional *weltanschauung* or professional "mind." The military mind, in this sense, consists of the values, attitudes, and perspectives which inhere in the performance of the professional military function and which are deducible from the nature of that function. The military function is performed by a public bureaucratized profession expert in the management of violence and responsible for the military security of the state. A value or attitude is part of the professional military ethic if it is implied by or derived from the peculiar expertise, responsibility, and organization of the military profession. The professional ethic is broader than professional ethics in the narrow sense of the code governing the behavior of the professional man toward nonprofessionals. It includes any preferences and expectations which may be inferred from the continuing performance of the military occupational role.

The military mind is thus defined abstractly as a Weberian ideal type in terms of which the beliefs of actual men and groups can be analyzed. Obviously, no one individual or group will adhere to all the constituent elements of the military ethic, since no individual or group is ever motivated exclusively by military considerations. Any given officer corps will adhere to the ethic only to the extent that it is professional, that is, to the extent that it is shaped by functional rather than societal imperatives. Few expressions of the ethic by an officer corps indicate a low level of professionalism, widespread articulation of the ethic a high degree of professionalism. The professional military ethic, moreover, is "non-dated and non-localized" just like the profession of which it is the intellectual expression. So long as there is no basic alteration in the inherent nature of the military function there will be no change in the content of the professional ethic. Simple changes in military technique, such as developments in weapons technology or the increased importance of economics in military affairs, do not alter the character of the military ethic any more than the discovery of penicillin altered medical ethics. The military ethic consequently is a constant standard by which it is possible to judge the professionalism of any officer corps anywhere anytime. For the sake of clarity, this ideal model may be referred to as the "professional military ethic." The views actually held by a concrete group of officers at some specific point in history may be termed the "nineteenth-century German military ethic" or the "post-World War I American ethic."

In the sections that follow an attempt will be made to elaborate the professional military ethic with respect to (1) basic values and perspectives, (2) national military policy, and (3) the relation of the military to the state. The accuracy of this definition of the ethic depends upon the extent to which the views stated are necessarily implied by the performance of the military function. These deductions as to the nature of the ethic will be illustrated by occasional references to typical expressions drawn from military literature. Since the historical evolution of the military ethic in the United States will be described in some detail in later chapters, the citations from American sources will purposely be limited. These references, moreover, are just examples; they do not prove that the views expressed are part of the professional military ethic any more than a completely contradictory statement from a military man would invalidate their inclusion in the ethic. The sole criterion is relevance to the performance of the military function.

THE PROFESSIONAL MILITARY ETHIC

MAN, SOCIETY, AND HISTORY. The existence of the military profession presupposes conflicting human interests and the use of

violence to further those interests. Consequently, the military ethic
views conflict as a universal pattern throughout nature and sees
violence rooted in the permanent biological and psychological nature of men. As between the good and evil in man, the military
ethic emphasizes the evil. Man is selfish. He is motivated by drives
for power, wealth, and security. "The human mind is by nature
one-sided and limited." [2] As between the strength and weakness
in man, the military ethic emphasizes the weakness. Man's selfish-
ness leads to struggle but man's weakness makes successful conflict dependent upon organization, discipline, and leadership. As
Clausewitz said, "All war presupposes human weakness, and
against that it is directed." No one is more aware than the professional soldier that the normal man is no hero. The military
profession organizes men so as to overcome their inherent fears
and failings.[3] The uncertainty and chance involved in the conduct
of war and the difficulty of anticipating the actions of an opponent
make the military man skeptical of the range of human foresight
and control. As between reason and irrationality in man, the military ethic emphasizes the limits of reason. The best schemes of
men are frustrated by the "friction" existing in reality. "War is
the province of uncertainty," Clausewitz said; "three-fourths of the
things on which action in war is based lie hidden in the fog of
greater or less uncertainty." Human nature, moreover, is universal
and unchanging. Men in all places and at all times are basically
the same.[4] The military view of man is thus decidedly pessimistic.
Man has elements of goodness, strength, and reason, but he is
also evil, weak, and irrational. The man of the military ethic is
essentially the man of Hobbes.

The existence of the military profession depends upon the existence of competing nation states. The responsibility of the profession is to enhance the military security of the state. The discharge of this responsibility requires cooperation, organization,
discipline. Both because it is his duty to serve society as a whole
and because of the nature of the means which he employs to carry
out this duty, the military man emphasizes the importance of the
group as against the individual. Success in any activity requires
the subordination of the will of the individual to the will of the
group. Tradition, *esprit,* unity, community — these rate high in
the military value system. The officer submerges his personal in-

terests and desires to what is necessary for the good of the service. As a nineteenth-century German officer put it, the military man must "forego personal advantage, lucre, and prosperity . . . Egotism is beyond all doubt the most bitter enemy of the qualities essential to the officer-corps." [5] Man is preëminently a social animal. He exists only in groups. He defends himself only in groups. Most importantly, he realizes himself only in groups. The "weak, mediocre, transient individual" can only achieve emotional satisfaction and moral fulfillment by participating in "the power, the greatness, the permanence and the splendour" of a continuing organic body.[6] The military ethic is basically corporative in spirit. It is fundamentally anti-individualistic.

The military vocation is a profession because it has accumulated experiences which make up a body of professional knowledge. In the military view, man learns only from experience. If he has little opportunity to learn from his own experience, he must learn from the experience of others. Hence, the military officer studies history. For history is, in Liddell Hart's phrase, "universal experience," and military history, as Moltke said, is the "most effective means of teaching war during peace." The military ethic thus places unusual value upon the ordered, purposive study of history.[7] History is valuable to the military man only when it is used to develop principles which may be capable of future application. The military student of history constantly tries to draw generalizations from his study. Yet the military ethic is not bound to any specific theory of history. While it rejects monistic interpretations, it also emphasizes the importance of force as contrasted with ideological and economic factors. The permanence of human nature makes impossible any theory of progress. "Change is inevitable. Progress is not inevitable." [8] Insofar as there is a pattern in history, it is cyclical in nature. Civilizations rise and fall. War and peace alternate, and so also does the supremacy of offensive and defensive warfare.[9]

NATIONAL MILITARY POLICY. The military view toward national policy reflects the professional responsibility for the military security of the state. This responsibility leads the military: (1) to view the state as the basic unit of political organization; (2) to stress the continuing nature of the threats to the military security of the state and the continuing likelihood of war; (3) to emphasize the magnitude and immediacy of the security threats; (4) to favor the maintenance of strong, diverse, and ready military forces; (5) to oppose the extension of state commitments and the involvement of the state in war except when victory is certain.

The Primacy of the Nation State. The existence of the military profession depends upon the existence of nation states capable of maintaining a military establishment and desiring to maintain such an establishment because of threats to their security. There is no necessary reason why nation states should be the only socio-political groups maintaining professional forces. But with a few peripheral exceptions, this has been true. The military man consequently tends to assume that the nation state is the ultimate form of political organization. The justification for the maintenance and employment of military force is in the political ends of the state. The causes of war are always political. State policy aimed at continuing political objectives precedes war, determines the resort to war, dictates the nature of the war, concludes the war, and continues on after the war. War must be the instrument of political purpose. The purpose of the state cannot be its own destruction. Consequently "total war" or "absolute war" is to be avoided if it is likely to produce the mutual devastation of the combatants.[10]

The Permanency of Insecurity and the Inevitability of War. In a world of independent nation states, the problem of military security is never finally solved. Competition among the states is continuous, and war is only an intensification of this competition which brings to a crisis the ever présent issue of military security. War is always likely and is ultimately inevitable. Its immediate causes spring from conflicting state policies, but its fundamental causes lie deep in human nature where exist the sources of all human conflict. "To abolish war we must remove its cause, which lies in the imperfection of human nature."[11]

If the causes of war are in human nature, the complete abolition of war is impossible. Consequently, the military mind is skeptical of institutional devices designed to prevent war. Treaties, international law, international arbitration, the Hague Court, the

League of Nations, the United Nations are of little help to peace. The decisive factor is always the power relation existing among the states. "In the last analysis the action of States is regulated by nothing but power and expediency." [12] Diplomacy itself only provides a superficial covering for the existence and uses of power. Treaties and other international agreements have meaning only insofar as they reflect the realities of international power. A state can achieve little by diplomacy unless it has the strength and the will to back up its demands with force. As Nelson once said: "A fleet of British ships of war is the best negotiator in Europe."

The Magnitude and Immediacy of the Security Threats. The military man normally views with alarm the potency and immediacy of the security threats to the state. As Lord Salisbury once remarked: "If you believe the doctors, nothing is wholesome: if you believe the theologians, nothing is innocent: if you believe the soldiers, nothing is safe." The military man recognizes the continuing character of threats to the state, but he also stresses the urgency of the current danger. The goal of professional competence requires the military man to estimate the threat as accurately as possible. But the military man also has a professional interest and a professional duty to stress the dangers to military security. Consequently the objective realities of international politics only partially determine the military estimate of the situation. The military man's views also reflect a subjective professional bias, the strength of which depends upon his general level of professionalism. This professional bias, or sense of professional responsibility, leads him to feel that if he errs in his estimate, it should be on the side of overstating the threat. Consequently, at times he will see threats to the security of the state where actually no threats exist.

In estimating the security threats the military man looks at the capabilities of other states rather than at their intentions. Intentions are political in nature, inherently fickle and changeable, and virtually impossible to evaluate and predict.[13] The military man is professionally capable of estimating the fighting strength of another state. But judging its policies is a matter of politics outside his competence. Human nature being what it is, a stronger state should never be trusted even if it proclaims the friendliest intentions. If a state has the power to injure one's own security, it is necessary to assume that it will do so. Safety requires attributing to other powers the worst intentions and the shrewdest abilities. It is a military responsibility to be prepared for any eventuality. The military "opinion must never be coloured by wishful thinking . . . The military man will be dealing with military fact, hard figures, grim realities of time and space and resources." [14] Military planners of one country may prepare elaborate plans for a war with another country without necessarily indicating that it is the purpose of the first country to attack the second.

The Level and Sources of Military Strength. The concern of military men with the dangers to national security leads them to urge the enlarging and strengthening of the military forces available to protect the security of the state. The most common manifestation of this is the demand for a larger share of the national budget. The same concern also leads the military to desire the conversion of military resources (the economic and human potential of the state) into actual military strength. The military man typically prefers regular troops to reserve forces and stockpiles of weapons to factories capable of building weapons. He wants force in being, not latent force. He also desires forces capable of meeting virtually every possible contingency. The limitations of human foresight make it dangerous to assume that security threats will necessarily take one particular form. Consequently the military man favors maintaining the broadest possible variety of weapons and forces provided that each weapons system is kept sufficiently strong so that it is capable of dealing with the threat it is designed to meet. Since the state normally is incapable of maintaining forces to meet all or most possible threats, the military man is usually required to establish a ladder of military priorities. Theoretically he should do this in terms of the objective requirements of military security. In reality, of course, he tends to stress those military needs and forces with which he is particularly familiar. To the extent that he acts in this manner he becomes a spokesman for a particular service or branch interest rather than for the military viewpoint as a whole. No matter what hierarchy of priorities he establishes, however, his military instincts lead him to urge the state to go as far down the ladder as possible.

The military man also favors protecting the state through guarantees and alliances, provided that these arrangements increase the strength of the state more than they increase its commitments. Weak, unstable, and adventurous allies are a liability rather than an asset. Allies should be selected purely on the basis of mutuality of national security interests regardless of ideological and political concerns. "Alliances between States should be regarded entirely from the point of view of might [power] policy." [15] The author of this dictum was a German monarchist but he had no more compunctions about military cooperation with communist Russia in the 1920's than American military leaders had about cooperating with fascist Spain in the 1950's. National strength may also be increased by the expansion of national territory and the acquisition of foreign bases. Here too, however, it is essential that the expansion of territory result in a real increase in power and not simply an overextension of commitments. The military man has no desire to acquire isolated, overseas territories which are vulnerable to attack and difficult to defend.

The Restriction of Commitments and the Avoidance of War. The military man has no concern with the desirability or undesirability of political goals as such. He is, however, concerned with the relation between political goals and military means since this directly affects the military security of the state. The politician must beware of overcommitting the nation beyond the strength of its military capabilities. Grand political designs and sweeping political goals are to be avoided, not because they are undesirable but because they are impractical.* The military security of the state must come first. Moral aims and ideological ends should not be pursued at the expense of that security. The political object is the goal, but in Clausewitz's words, it "is not on that account a despotic lawgiver; it must adapt itself to the nature of the means at its disposal . . ." The statesman furnishes the dynamic, purposive element to state policy. The military man represents the

---

* "The duty of a professional military man obliges him to be a pessimist. He must be the 'no' man for idealism and wishful thinking. Unpopular as it makes him during periods of peace and prosperity he must assume that such conditions are transient, and that the pendulum of history will eventually swing back to the point where the country must risk its well-being and possibly its survival on the final arbitration of armed force." R. A. Hall (Capt., US), "The Peacetime Duties of the Armed Services," U.S. Naval Institute *Proceedings*, LXXX (June 1946), 781.

passive, instrumental means. It is his function to warn the statesman when his purposes are beyond his means.

The military man normally opposes reckless, aggressive, belligerent action. If war with a particular power is inevitable at a later date with decreased chances of success, the military man may favor "preventive war" in order to safeguard national security. Normally, however, he recognizes the impossibility of predicting the future with certainty. War at any time is an intensification of the threats to the military security of the state, and generally war should not be resorted to except as a final recourse, and only when the outcome is a virtual certainty.[16] This latter condition is seldom met except in the case of a powerful state fighting an isolated minor or backward nation. Thus, the military man rarely favors war. He will always argue that the danger of war requires increased armaments; he will seldom argue that increased armaments make war practical or desirable. He always favors preparedness, but he never feels prepared. Accordingly, the professional military man contributes a cautious, conservative, restraining voice to the formulation of state policy. This has been his typical role in most modern states including fascist Germany, communist Russia, and democratic America. He is afraid of war. He wants to prepare for war. But he is never ready to fight a war.

This pacifist attitude may well have its roots in institutional conservatism as well as concern for state security. The military leader is at the top of one of the great power structures of society. He risks everything if that society becomes engaged in war. Whether victorious or not, war is more unsettling to military institutions than to any others. A Tsarist officer once said that he hated war because "it spoils the armies," and American naval officers complained that the Civil War "ruined the navy." [17] This attitude reflects an orientation about means to the point where means become ends, to where, in Merton's terms, the latent function supersedes the manifest function. The military man in his concern with power may come to consider the accumulation of power as an end in itself irrespective of the uses to which it may be put. He may become most reluctant to dissipate that power in any manner.

The military man tends to see himself as the perennial victim of civilian warmongering. It is the people and the politicians, public opinion and governments, who start wars. It is the military who have to fight them. Civilian philosophers, publicists, academicians, not soldiers, have been the romanticizers and glorifiers of war. Military force as such does not cause wars. The state which desires peace must be well armed to enforce its desire. Weak states invite attack. The tendency of the civilian politician is to court popular favor by curbing the arms budget and simultaneously pursuing an adventurous foreign policy. The military man opposes both tendencies. The military ethic thus draws a sharp distinction between armed strength and bellicosity, the military state and the warlike state.[18] The former embodies the military virtues of ordered power: discipline, hierarchy, restraint, steadfastness. The latter is characterized by wild, irresponsible excitement and enthusiasm, and by the love of violence, glory, and adventure. For the professional military man, familiar with war, this type of mentality has little appeal. Believing in the ultimate inevitability of war, he raises the strongest voice against immediate involvement in war.

THE MILITARY AND THE STATE. The military profession is expert and limited. Its members have specialized competence within their field and lack that competence outside their field. The relation of the profession to the state is based upon this natural division of labor. The essence of this relationship concerns the relative scope of competence of the military expert and political expert or statesman. Before the professionalization of military science in the nineteenth century, the same person could be simultaneously qualified in both fields. Now this is impossible. Napoleon embodied the old unity of military science and politics. He was replaced by Bismarck and Moltke who symbolized the new dichotomy.* The exact character of the relationship which should exist between statesman and military officer cannot be defined precisely. But

---

* "Interchangeability between the statesman and the soldier passed for ever, I fear, in the last century. The Germans professionalized the trade of war; and modern inventions, by increasing its technicalities, have specialized it. It is much the same with politics, professionalized by democracy. No longer can one man hope to exercise both callings, though both are branches of the same craft, the governance of men and the ordering of human affairs." Field Marshal Earl Wavell, *The Good Soldier* (London, 1948), pp. 27–28.

it is possible to state some of the principles which should govern that relationship.

Military science is an area in which specialized competence acquired by professional training and experience is necessary for decision and action. This field, which concerns the implementation of state policy by armed force, is divided into constant and variable components. This division was recognized only after the emergence of the military profession. The constant element reflects the permanency of human nature and physical geography. This may be called strategy, and so distinguished from the variable elements, tactics and logistics, or it may be formulated into a set of "fundamental," "immutable," "eternal," "unchanging and unchangeable" principles of war. Military historians differ as to the number and content of these principles but they do not question their existence as the fundamental core of military science. Their application, however, is constantly changing with changes in technology and social organization. The ideal military man is thus conservative in strategy, but open-minded and progressive with respect to new weapons and new tactical forms. He is equally expert in both the constant and variable aspects of military science. The essence of his art may indeed be defined as the relation between the two: "the unchangeable fundamental conditions of good generalship in their relation to changeable tactical forms . . ." [19] It is this area within which the statesman must accept the judgments of the military professional.

Politics deals with the goals of state policy. Competence in this field consists in having a broad awareness of the elements and interests entering into a decision and in possessing the legitimate authority to make such a decision. Politics is beyond the scope of military competence, and the participation of military officers in politics undermines their professionalism, curtailing their professional competence, dividing the profession against itself, and substituting extraneous values for professional values. The military officer must remain neutral politically. "The military commander must never allow his military judgment to be warped by political expediency." [20] The area of military science is subordinate to, and yet independent of, the area of politics. Just as war serves the ends of politics, the military profession serves the ends of the state. Yet the statesman must recognize the integrity of the profession and its subject matter. The military man has the right to expect political guidance from the statesman. Civilian control exists when there is this proper subordination of an autonomous profession to the ends of policy.

The responsibilities of the military man to the state are three-fold. He has, first, a representative function, to represent the claims of military security within the state machinery. He must keep the authorities of the state informed as to what he considers necessary for the minimum military security of the state in the light of the capabilities of other powers. The extent to which he may carry the presentation of his views is difficult to define but he must recognize and accept the fact that there are limits. In general, he has the right and the duty to present his views to the public bodies, whether executive or legislative, which are charged with the apportionment of resources between the military and other claims. Secondly, the military officer has an advisory function, to analyze and to report on the implications of alternative courses of state action from the military point of view. If the state leaders are weighing three possible policies, the military man, of course, cannot judge which is the most desirable. He may, however, say that the first policy could easily be carried out with the military strength currently available, that the second policy would involve serious risks unless there is a considerable augmentation of military forces, and that the third policy is simply beyond the military capability of the state to implement effectively. Finally, the military officer has an executive function, to implement state decisions with respect to military security even if it is a decision which runs violently counter to his military judgment. The statesmen set the goal and allocate to him the resources to be used in attaining that goal. It is then up to him to do the best he can. This is indeed the meaning of military strategy in relation to policy: "the practical adaptation of the means placed at a general's disposal to the attainment of the object in view." [21]

Obviously a considerable area exists where strategy and policy overlap. In this realm the supreme military commander may make a decision on purely military grounds only to discover that it has political implications unknown to him. When this turns out to be the case, considerations of strategy must then give way to considerations of policy. The military man must recognize that a wide number of conceivably purely military decisions, such as the selection of a theater of war, also involve politics, and he must be guided accordingly. As Clausewitz said, "the art of war in its highest point of view becomes policy, but, of course, a policy which fights battles instead of writing notes." The top military leaders of the state inevitably operate in this intermingled world of strategy and policy. They must always be alert to the political implications of their military attitudes and be willing to accept the final decisions of the statesmen. When required in his executive capacity to make decisions involving both military and political elements, the military man ideally should formulate his military solution first and then alter it as needs be on the advice of his political advisers.

The military profession exists to serve the state. To render the highest possible service the entire profession and the military force which it leads must be constituted as an effective instrument of state policy. Since political direction comes only from the top, this means that the profession has to be organized into a hierarchy of obedience. For the profession to perform its function, each level within it must be able to command the instantaneous and loyal obedience of subordinate levels. Without these relationships military professionalism is impossible. Consequently, loyalty and obedience are the highest military virtues: "the rule of obedience is simply the expression of that one among the military virtues upon which all the others depend . . ." [22] When the military man receives a legal order from an authorized superior, he does not argue, he does not hesitate, he does not substitute his own views; he obeys instantly. He is judged not by the policies he implements, but rather by the promptness and efficiency with which he carries them out. His goal is to perfect an instrument of obedience; the uses to which that instrument is put are beyond his responsibility. His highest virtue is instrumental not ultimate. Like Shakespeare's soldier in *Henry V*, he believes that the justice of the cause is more than he should "know" or "seek after." For if the king's "cause be wrong, our obedience to the King wipes the crime of it out of us."

The Soldier and the State

An officer corps is professional only to the extent to which its loyalty is to the military ideal. Other loyalties are transient and divisive. What appeals politically one day will be forgotten the next. What appeals politically to one man will inspire the hatred of another. Within the military forces only military loyalty to the ideal of professional competence is constant and unifying: loyalty of the individual to the ideal of the Good Soldier, loyalty of the unit to the traditions and spirit of the Best Regiment. The most effective forces and the most competent officer corps are those which are motivated by these ideals rather than by political or ideological aims. Only if they are motivated by military ideals will the armed forces be the obedient servants of the state and will civilian control be assured. In the modern army the professional motivation of the officers contrasts with that of the temporary citizen-soldiers who are conscripted or who enlist because of economic or political appeals. The professional officer corps is the instrument of the state in insuring the obedience of the enlisted personnel. The latter, of course, can never develop professional motivation and the sense of professional responsibility characteristic of the West Point or St. Cyr graduate. Nonetheless, the difference between the professional officers and the enlisted personnel is minimized to the extent that the enlisted personnel become indifferent to outside motivations and influences. The professional army which fights well because it is its job to fight well is far more reliable than the political army which fights well only while sustained by a higher purpose. The United States Marine Corps and the French Foreign Legion serve their governments with unvarying and impartial competence whatever the campaign. The military quality of the professional is independent of the cause for which he fights.

The supreme military virtue is obedience. But what are the limits of obedience? This question arises in two separate connections. The first concerns the relation between military obedience and professional competence, the moral and intellectual virtues of the officer. The second concerns the conflict between the military value of obedience and nonmilitary values.

Military Obedience versus Professional Competence. The conflict between military obedience and professional competence usually involves the relation of a military subordinate to a military superior. It arises in two broad senses: operational and doctrinal. The former concerns the execution by a subordinate of a military order which in his judgment will result in military disaster. Assuming he has made his views known to his superior and the superior persists in his order, or assuming he does not have the opportunity to present his views, does the subordinate nonetheless obey? The purpose of obedience is to further the objective of the superior. If the subordinate is thoroughly acquainted with this object, and circumstances unknown to the superior make it possible to achieve the object only through a disobedience of orders, the subordinate may then be justified in disobeying. Only rarely, however, will this be the case. Normally the disruption of the military organization caused by disobedience to operational orders will outweigh the benefits gained by such obedience. The greater competence and knowledge of the superior officer must be assumed. In operations, and even more particularly in combat, ready obedience cannot conflict with military competence: it is the essence of military competence.*

The second possible manifestation of the conflict of military obedience with professional competence involves nonoperational doctrinal issues. Rigid and inflexible obedience may well stifle new ideas and become slave to an unprogressive routine. It is not infrequent that a high command has had its thinking frozen in the past and has utilized its control of the military hierarchy to suppress uncomfortable new developments in tactics and technology. In a situation of this sort, to what extent may a junior officer be justified in disobeying his superiors to advance professional knowledge? There are no easy answers to this question. The authority of superior officers is presumed to reflect superior professional ability. When this is not the case, the hierarchy of command is

* The classic instances of the disobedience of operational orders involve Lord Nelson, who justified his behavior in one case on the grounds that: "I find few think as I do but, to obey orders is all perfection. What would my superiors direct, did they know what is passing under my nose? To serve my King and to destroy the French I consider as the great order of all, from which little ones spring, and if one of these little ones militate against it, I go back to obey the great order." See A. T. Mahan, *The Life of Nelson* (Boston, 2 vols., 2d ed. rev., 1900), I, 56–63, 189–191, 445–451, II, 89–92, and *Retrospect and Prospect* (Boston, 1902), pp. 255–283.

being prostituted to nonprofessional purposes. Yet the subordinate officer must tread judiciously in pushing doctrines which seem to him to be manifestly superior to those embodied in the manuals. In particular, the subordinate must consider whether the introduction of the new technique, assuming he is successful in his struggle, will so increase military efficiency as to offset the impairment of that efficiency caused by the disruption of the chain of command. If it does, his disobedience is justified. Ultimately, professional competence must be the final criterion.[23]

Military Obedience versus Nonmilitary Values. The second set of problems concerns the relation of military obedience to nonmilitary values. What is the responsibility of the officer when he is ordered by the statesman to follow a course which he knows will lead to national disaster? Or when he is ordered to do something which manifestly violates the law of the land? Or when he is ordered to do something which is an equally clear transgression of commonly accepted standards of morality? It appears possible to divide these issues into four groups.

First, there is the conflict between military obedience and political wisdom. We have already said that a military subordinate may be justified in forcing upon military leaders new developments which will increase professional efficiency. Should not the same relationship exist between the higher commander and the statesman? If the statesman is pursuing a course which seems to be sheer political folly, is not the military commander justified in resisting it by appeal to the standards of political wisdom? The subordinate officer "bucking" his superiors defends himself by appealing to professional wisdom. There is, however, a vast difference between these two cases. The criteria of military efficiency are limited, concrete, and relatively objective; the criteria of political wisdom are indefinite, ambiguous, and highly subjective. Politics is an art, military science a profession. No commonly accepted political values exist by which the military officer can prove to reasonable men that his political judgment is preferable to that of the statesmen. The superior political wisdom of the statesman must be accepted as a fact. If the statesman decides upon war which the soldier knows can only lead to national catastrophe, then the soldier, after presenting his opinion, must fall to and make the best of a bad situation. The commanding generals of the German army in the late 1930's, for instance, almost unanimously believed that Hitler's foreign policies would lead to national ruin. Military duty, however, required them to carry out his orders: some followed this course, others forsook the professional code to push their political goals. General MacArthur's opposition to the manner in which the government was conducting the Korean War was essentially similar. Both the German officers who joined the resistance to Hitler and General MacArthur forgot that it is not the function of military officers to decide questions of war and peace.

Second, and at the other extreme, there is the conflict between military obedience and military competence when that competence is threatened by a political superior. What does the military officer do when he is ordered by a statesman to take a measure which is militarily absurd when judged by professional standards and which is strictly within the military realm without any political implications? This situation, provided that the last qualification holds and that it is completely removed from politics, represents a clear invasion of the professional realm by extraneous considerations. The presumption of superior professional competence which existed in the case of a military superior giving a questionable order does not exist when the statesman enters military affairs. Here the existence of professional standards justifies military disobedience. The statesman has no business deciding, as Hitler did in the later phases of World War II, whether battalions in combat should advance or retreat.

Third, and between these two extreme cases, there is the conflict between military obedience and legality. What does the military officer do when he receives an order which his civilian superior does not have the legal authority to issue? Presumably, the military officer as the servant of the state is the servant only of the legitimately constituted authorities of the state. If the statesman in ordering his action recognizes himself that he is acting illegally, then the military officer is justified in disobeying. If the statesman claims to be acting legally, but the action seems illegal to the officer, then the issue is one of the relative competence of the officer and the statesman to judge what is legal and illegal. Most modern states which have military professions also have a group of specialized experts, the judiciary, whose function it is to decide such issues. If their judgment can be obtained, the military officer is bound to accept it. If this is not possible, either because of the urgency of the situation or because the legality of the judiciary itself is in doubt, the military officer can only study the law applicable to the situation and arrive at his own decision. The standards of law are generally far more precise than those of politics but less definite than those of military science. In any event, the officer is bound to give a considerable presumption of validity to the opinion of the statesman. If there are two governments in the state, each claiming to be duly constituted and to be deserving of military obedience, the military officer cannot escape the political choice between them.

Finally, there is the conflict between military obedience and basic morality. What does the military officer do if he is ordered by the statesman to commit genocide, to exterminate the people of an occupied territory? So far as ability to judge and apply ethical standards are concerned, the statesman and the soldier are equal. Both are free individuals morally responsible for their actions. The soldier cannot surrender to the civilian his right to make ultimate moral judgments. He cannot deny himself as a moral individual. Yet the problem is not as simple as this. For politics as well as basic morality may be involved here. The statesman may well feel compelled to violate commonly accepted morality in order to further the political interests of the state. That this is frequently the case, there is no denying. If the statesman rejects the private claims of conscience in favor of the *raison d'état,* is he also justified in implicating the military man too, in subordinating, in effect, the military man's conscience as well as his own? For the officer this comes down to a choice between his own conscience on the one hand, and the good of the state, plus the professional virtue of obedience, upon the other. As a soldier, he owes obedience; as a man, he owes disobedience. Except in the most extreme instances it is reasonable to expect that he will adhere to the professional ethic and obey. Only rarely will the military man be justified in following the dictates of private conscience against the dual demand of military obedience and state welfare.

The Military Mind

SUMMARY: CONSERVATIVE REALISM. The military ethic emphasizes the permanence, irrationality, weakness, and evil in human nature. It stresses the supremacy of society over the individual and the importance of order, hierarchy, and division of function. It stresses the continuity and value of history. It accepts the nation state as the highest form of political organization and recognizes the continuing likelihood of wars among nation states. It emphasizes the importance of power in international relations and warns of the dangers to state security. It holds that the security of the state depends upon the creation and maintenance of strong military forces. It urges the limitation of state action to the direct interests of the state, the restriction of extensive commitments, and the undesirability of bellicose or adventurous policies. It holds that war is the instrument of politics, that the military are the servants of the statesman, and that civilian control is essential to military professionalism. It exalts obedience as the highest virtue of military men. The military ethic is thus pessimistic, collectivist, historically inclined, power-oriented, nationalistic, militaristic, pacifist, and instrumentalist in its view of the military profession. It is, in brief, realistic and conservative.

4

Power, Professionalism, and Ideology: Civil-Military Relations in Theory

THE VARIETIES OF CIVILIAN CONTROL

The role of the military in society has been frequently discussed in terms of "civilian control." [1] Yet this concept has never been satisfactorily defined. Presumably, civilian control has something to do with the relative power of civilian and military groups. Presumably, also, civilian control is achieved to the extent to which the power of military groups is reduced. Consequently, the basic problem in defining civilian control is: How can military power be minimized? In general, two broad answers exist.

SUBJECTIVE CIVILIAN CONTROL: MAXIMIZING CIVILIAN POWER. The simplest way of minimizing military power would appear to be the maximizing of the power of civilian groups in relation to the military. The large number, varied character, and conflicting interests of civilian groups, however, make it impossible to maximize their power as a whole with respect to the military. Consequently, the maximizing of civilian power always means the maximizing of the power of some particular civilian group or groups. This is subjective civilian control. The general concept of civilian control is identified with the specific interests of one or more civilian groups. Consequently, subjective civilian control involves the power relations among civilian groups. It is advanced by one civilian group as a means to enhance its power at the expense of other civilian groups. It thus becomes an instrumental slogan like "states' rights" rather than an end in itself. Just as the banner of states' rights is normally raised by economic groups which have more power at the state than at the national level in struggles with other groups which have more power in the national government, so the slogan of civilian control is utilized by groups which lack power over the military forces in struggles with other civilian groups which have such power. Like states' rights, civilian control may cover a variety of sins. It is always necessary to ask which civilians are to do the controlling. Except very recently in western society, civilian control has existed only in this subjective sense. Subjective civilian control is, indeed, the only form of civilian control possible in the absence of a professional officer corps. In its various historical manifestations, subjective civilian control has been identified with the maximization of the power of particular governmental institutions, particular social classes, and particular constitutional forms.

Civilian Control by Governmental Institution. In the seventeenth and eighteenth centuries in England and America the military forces were generally under the control of the Crown, and the slogan "civilian control" was adopted by the parliamentary groups as a means of increasing their power vis-à-vis the Crown. Since the king, however, was just as civilian as they were, what they actually wanted was to maximize parliamentary control over the armed forces rather than civilian control in general. And parliamentary control was sought, not as a means of reducing the power of the military but as a way of curtailing the power of the king. At the present time, in the United States, Congress and the President engage in a comparable struggle. The Chief Executive identifies civilian control with presidential control — Congress is too large and poorly organized to control the military forces effectively. Congress, on the other hand, identifies civilian control with congressional control — Congress is closer to the people than the President who is likely to become the prisoner of his military advisers. But both Congress and President are fundamentally concerned with the distribution of power between executive and legislative rather than between civilian and military.

Civilian Control by Social Class. In the eighteenth and nineteenth centuries the European aristocracy and bourgeoisie struggled for control of the military forces. Each class attempted to identify civilian control with its own interests. Since the aristocracy generally dominated the military forces, however, the liberal bourgeois groups made the greatest use of the slogan and identified aristocratic control with military control. Military institutions merely furnished one battleground for the struggle between the two classes which permeated all areas of society; the issue was simply whether aristocratic or liberal interests were to prevail in the armed forces.

Civilian Control by Constitutional Form. A broader application of this same identification of civilian control with a particular civilian interest occurs when the claim is made that only a specific constitutional form — usually democracy — can insure civilian control. Civilian control is identified with democratic government, military control with absolute or totalitarian government. In democratic countries, it is argued, policy is determined by persuasion and compromise; in absolutist countries it is determined by force and coercion (or at least the implied threat of force or coercion). Hence, the military, who control the most powerful instrument of violence, will be more powerful in totalitarian countries than in democratic ones. Actually, however, this argument is not necessarily true. In a democratic country, the military may undermine civilian control and acquire great political power through the legitimate processes and institutions of democratic government and politics (for example, the United States in World War II). In a totalitarian regime, on the other hand, the power of the military may be reduced by breaking the officer corps up into competing units, establishing party armies and special military forces (Waffen-SS and MVD), infiltrating the military hierarchy with independent chains of command (political commissars), and similar techniques. Terror, conspiracy, surveillance, and force are the methods of government in a totalitarian state; terror, conspiracy, surveillance, and force are the means by which the civilians in such a state control their armed forces. If employed sufficiently ruthlessly, these means may virtually eliminate military political power (for example, Germany in World War II). Subjective civilian control thus is not the monopoly of any particular constitutional system.

The rise of the military profession transformed the problem of civil-military relations, complicating the efforts of civilian groups to maximize their power over the military. Such groups were now confronted not only with other civilian groups with similar goals but also with new, independent, functional military imperatives. The continued assertion of the particular forms of subjective civilian control required that these imperatives be either denied or transformed. If this could not be done, civilian control in the subjective sense became impossible. Some new principle was needed to govern the relations between the functional military imperatives and the rest of society. So long as civilian control was simply an instrumental value of particular civilian groups, it was, of course, impossible to secure general agreement as to its meaning. Each group defined it as a distribution of power favorable to its own interests. This explains the peculiar historical fact that, although civilian control was regularly invoked in politics and frequently written about in the eighteenth and nineteenth centuries, it was, nonetheless, never satisfactorily defined. The rise of the military profession, however, while making the particular forms of subjective civilian control obsolete, also made possible a new and more meaningful definition of civilian control.

OBJECTIVE CIVILIAN CONTROL: MAXIMIZING MILITARY PROFESSIONALISM. Civilian control in the objective sense is the maximizing of military professionalism. More precisely, it is that distribution of political power between military and civilian groups which is most conducive to the emergence of professional attitudes and behavior among the members of the officer corps. Objective civilian control is thus directly opposed to subjective civilian control. Subjective civilian control achieves its end by civilianizing the military, making them the mirror of the state. Objective civilian control achieves its end by militarizing the military, making them the tool of the state. Subjective civilian control exists in a variety of forms, objective civilian control in only one. The antithesis of objective civilian control is military participation in politics: civilian control decreases as the military become progressively involved in institutional, class, and constitutional politics. Subjective civilian control, on the other hand, presupposes this involvement. The essence of objective civilian control is the recognition of autonomous military professionalism; the essence of subjective civilian control is the denial of an independent military sphere. Historically, the demand for objective control has come from the military profession, the demand for subjective control from the multifarious civilian groups anxious to maximize their power in military affairs.

The one prime essential for any system of civilian control is the minimizing of military power. Objective civilian control achieves this reduction by professionalizing the military, by rendering them politically sterile and neutral. This produces the lowest possible level of military political power with respect to all civilian groups. At the same time it preserves that essential element of power which is necessary for the existence of a military profession. A highly professional officer corps stands ready to carry out the wishes of any civilian group which secures legitimate authority within the state. In effect, this sets definite limits to military political power without reference to the distribution of political power among the various civilian groups. Any further reduction of military power beyond the point where professionalism is maximized only redounds to the benefit of some particular civilian group and only serves to enhance the power of that group in its struggles with other civilian groups. The distribution of political power which most facilitates military professionalism is thus also the lowest point to which military power can be reduced without playing favorites among civilian groups. Because of this, the objective definition of civilian control furnishes a single concrete standard of civilian control which is politically neutral and which all social groups can recognize. It elevates civilian control from a political slogan masking group interests to an analytical concept independent of group perspectives.

The subjective definition of civilian control presupposes a conflict between civilian control and the needs of military security. This was generally recognized by adherents of particular civilian groups who commonly asserted that continued military insecurity made civilian control impossible. By this they simply meant that intensified security threats result in increased military imperatives against which it becomes more difficult to assert civilian power. The steps necessary to achieve military security are thus viewed as undermining civilian control. On the other hand, the effort to enhance civilian control in the subjective sense frequently undermined military security. Because they did not, for instance, recognize the existence of a separate military profession with its own outlook on national policy, civilian groups frequently assumed that the reduction of military power was necessary to preserve peace. This decrease in the power of the military, however, often resulted in increased power for much more bellicose civilian groups. Consequently those civilian groups which tried to minimize the risks of war by reducing the power of the military frequently encouraged exactly what they were attempting to avoid. It is hardly coincidental that the years immediately prior to World War II saw the systematic reduction of the political power of the military in all the future belligerents except Japan, or that the temperature of the Cold War seems to vary inversely with the political power of the generals in the Soviet Union. If civilian control is defined in the objective sense, however, no conflict exists between it and the goal of military security. Indeed, just the reverse is true. Objective civilian control not only reduces the power of the military to the lowest possible level vis-à-vis all civilian groups, it also maximizes the likelihood of achieving military security.

The achievement of objective civilian control has only been possible, of course, since the emergence of the military profession. Subjective civilian control is fundamentally out of place in any society in which the division of labor has been carried to the point where there emerges a distinct class of specialists in the management of violence. The achievement of objective civilian control, however, has been hampered by the tendency of many civilian groups still to conceive of civilian control in subjective terms. Like nineteenth-century aristocrats and bourgeoisie, or twentieth-century French constitutional factions, they are unwilling simply to accept a politically neutral officer corps. They continue to insist upon the subordination of the officer corps to their own interests and principles. Consequently a high level of objective civilian control has been a rare phenomenon even among modern western societies.

THE TWO LEVELS OF CIVIL-MILITARY RELATIONS

What conditions are likely to maximize military professionalism and objective civilian control? The answer depends upon the relation between the two levels of civil-military relations. On the power level, the key issue is the power of the officer corps relative to civilian groups within society. On the ideological level, the key issue is the compatibility of the professional military ethic with the political ideologies prevailing in society. On the one hand, criteria are needed by which to measure military and civilian power. On the other hand, some notion is required as to where the professional military ethic fits into the spectrum of political opinion.

THE OFFICER CORPS AND POLITICAL POWER. Power is the capacity to control the behavior of other people.[2] A power relationship has at least two dimensions: the degree or amount of power, that is, the extent to which a particular type of behavior of one person is controlled by another; and, secondly, the scope or locus of power, that is, the types of behavior which are influenced by the other individual or group. The relations between any two people or groups normally involve the exercise of power in both directions although in all probability in somewhat different if overlapping loci. Power exists in two forms, formal authority and informal influence, both of which may be measured in terms of their degree and scope. Formal authority involves the control of one person over the behavior of another on the basis of their respective positions in a defined social structure. Authority does not inhere in the individual but is an attribute of status and position. Authority, consequently, is ordered, structured, or legitimate power. It is a continuing pattern of relationships which remains relatively constant through successive changes in the individuals involved in the relationships. Its exercise has the sanction of constitution, statute, bylaws, decree, or long accepted custom. It is a truism of politics that formal authority tells only part of the story of power. Informal relationships also exist where one person, or group of persons, controls the behavior of other persons not because they occupy particular positions in a formal structure, but because they control other sanctions or rewards. This influence may stem from personality, wealth, knowledge, prestige, friendship, kinship, or a variety of other sources. Its distinguishing characteristic, however, is always that it inheres in specific individuals or groups, not in the roles or statuses which those individuals or groups occupy.

Authority. In analyzing the pattern of authority in civil-military relations the key criteria are the relative level, the relative **unity**, and the relative scope of the authority of the military and civilian groups. The higher the level of authority of a group, the greater the unity of its structure, and the broader the scope of its authority, the more powerful it will be.

The level of authority refers to the position which the group occupies in the hierarchy of governmental authority. Vertical control is exercised over the military to the extent that they are reduced to subordinate levels of authority. The level of authority of the officer corps is maximized if it is placed at the peak of the hierarchy and the other institutions of government are subordinate to it: if, in other words, it or its leaders exercise military sovereignty. A level of somewhat less authority exists if the military do not possess authority over other institutions, and no other institutions possess authority over them. In this case, two parallel structures of authority exist; one military and one civil. This situation is military independence. Thirdly, the officer corps may be subordinate to only one other institution possessing effective final authority. In other words, the officer corps has direct access to the sovereign. After this, the officer corps might gradually be further subordinated in the governmental structure. Such subordination, however, is generally not carried very far and usually only one level of authority is interspersed between the officer corps and the sovereign. Since this one level is normally in the form of a civilian departmental minister, this level of military authority may be called ministerial control.

The unity of authority refers to the extent to which a given group is structurally unified with relation to another group. A monopolist possesses advantages in dealing with a large number of firms on the other side of the market place. So also, a group which is structurally united possesses great advantages in dealing with a group which is structurally disunited. If the officer corps is originally divided into land, sea, and air elements, and then is unified under the leadership of a single, overall staff and military commander in chief, this change will tend to increase its authority with regard to other institutions of government. It will speak with one voice instead of three. Other groups will not be able to play off one portion of the officer corps against another.

Thirdly, the scope of authority refers to the variety and type of values with respect to which the group is formally authorized to exercise power. The authority of military groups, for instance, is normally limited to military matters. If the chiefs of staff were also authorized to advise the government with respect to agricultural subsidies, the scope of their authority would be significantly expanded. Horizontal civilian control is exercised against the military to the extent that they are confined within a limited scope by the parallel activities of civilian agencies or groups roughly at the same level of authority in the government.

Influence. The political influence of a group and its leaders is even more difficult to judge than their formal authority. Four rough indices exist, however, by which the influence of the officer corps may be evaluated.

(1) The group affiliations of the officer corps and its leaders. One test of the influence of a group is the extent and nature of its affiliations with other powerful groups and individuals. For the officer corps these affiliations are generally of three types. First, preservice affiliations arise from the activities of officers before they enter the officer corps. If the bulk of the officers are drawn from a particular social class or geographical section, this may be assumed to enhance the influence of the corps with that class or section. Secondly, officers may develop inservice affiliations in the course of their military duties, as for example, special ties with congressional committees, or with those industries whose products are consumed by the armed services. Finally, postservice affiliations may reflect a general pattern of officer activities after leaving the corps. If, for instance, officers upon retirement normally entered into a particular type of work, or settled in a particular part of the country, this would also presumably increase the influence of the officer corps in those segments of society.

(2) The economic and human resources subject to the authority of the officer corps and its leaders. The larger the proportion of the national product devoted to military purposes, and the larger the number of individuals serving with the armed services in either a civilian or military capacity, the greater will be the influence of the officer corps and its leaders. An increase or decrease in the resources subject to military authority, however, need not involve any change in that authority itself. The level, unity, and scope of

military authority may well remain constant throughout changes in the resources subject to military control.

(3) The hierarchical interpenetration of the officer corps and other groups. Military influence is increased if members of the officer corps assume positions of authority in nonmilitary power structures. Military influence is decreased to the extent that nonmilitary individuals penetrate into positions within the formally defined officer corps.

(4) Prestige and popularity of the officer corps and its leaders. The standing of the officer corps and its leaders with public opinion and the attitudes of broad sections or categoric groups in society toward the military obviously are key elements in determining military influence.

These four factors will help give some index of the political influence of the military. The more or less quantitative extent of these relationships indicates the degree of military political influence. The specific content and nature of the relationships furnish some idea of the locus of military influence. For instance, an increase in the total number of military men occupying positions of authority in the normally civilian branches of government warrants a conclusion as to an increase in the degree of military influence. The specific type of agency in which the military men are working would lead to conclusions as to the locus of this increased influence: they might all be in the foreign affairs department or they might be scattered generally throughout the government.

THE PROFESSIONAL ETHIC AND POLITICAL IDEOLOGIES. Just as there is a variety of civilian groups engaged in the struggle for power, so also is there a variety of civilian ethics or ideologies. Consequently, it is impossible to assume a continuum stretching from military values at one end to civilian values at the other. The military ethic is concrete, permanent, and universal. The term "civilian" on the other hand, merely refers to what is nonmilitary. No dichotomy exists between the "military mind" and the "civilian mind" because there is no single "civilian mind." There are many "civilian minds," and the difference between any two civilian ethics may be greater than the difference between any one of them and the military ethic. Consequently, the military ethic can only be compared with particular civilian ethics. In this analysis, it will be compared with four manifestations of one species of civilian ethic — the political ideology. A political ideology is a set of values and attitudes oriented about the problems of the state. The ideologies which will be compared with the military ethic are four which have been among the most significant in western culture: liberalism, fascism, Marxism, and conservatism.[3] Each ideology will be considered generally and abstractly, independent of its specific historical manifestations. The point at issue in each case is the extent to which the ideology, viewed as a system of ideas, is compatible with or hostile to the military ethic.

Liberalism. The heart of liberalism is individualism. It emphasizes the reason and moral dignity of the individual and opposes political, economic, and social restraints upon individual liberty. In contrast, the military ethic holds that man is evil, weak, and irrational and that he must be subordinated to the group. The military man claims that the natural relation among men is conflict; the liberal believes that the natural relation is peace. Liberalism holds that the application of reason may produce a harmony of interests. For the liberal, success in any enterprise depends upon the maximum release of individual energies; for the military man it depends upon subordination and specialization. The liberal glorifies self-expression; the military man obedience. Liberalism rejects the organic theory of society. In contrast to the military view, liberalism holds that human nature is pliable and may be improved through education and proper social institutions. The liberal normally believes in progress and minimizes the significance of history. Man is more likely to find solutions to his political problems by consulting his reason than by examining his experience.

The military man emphasizes the importance of power in human relations; liberalism normally either denies the existence of power, minimizes its importance, or castigates it as inherently evil. Liberalism tends to assume the existence of that very national security which the military man considers to be continually threatened. Liberal thinking has been largely concerned with economics and economic welfare and has opposed large military forces, balance of power diplomacy, and military alliances. Liberalism believes that the way to peace is through institutional devices such as international law, international courts, and international organization. Liberalism has many pacifist tendencies, but the liberal will normally support a war waged to further liberal ideals. War as an instrument of national policy is immoral; war on behalf of universally true principles of justice and freedom is not. The liberal thus opposes war in general but frequently supports it in particular, while the military man accepts war in the abstract but opposes its specific manifestations.

Liberalism is generally hostile to armaments and standing armies. They are a threat both to peace and to constitutional government. If military organization is necessary, it must be military organization reflecting liberal principles. Civilian control in liberalism means the embodiment of liberal ideas in military institutions. The military professionals are held to be backward, incompetent, and neglectful of the importance of economics, morale, and ideology. National defense is the responsibility of all, not just a few. If war becomes necessary, the state must fight as a "nation in arms" relying on popular militias and citizen armies.

Fascism. The military ethic and fascism are similar in some respects but they have one fundamental difference. What the military man accepts as the facts of existence to be wrestled with as effectively as possible, the fascist glorifies as the supreme values of existence. The military man sees struggle inherent in human relations; the fascist glorifies struggle as the highest activity of man. The military ethic accepts the nation state as an independent unit; fascism hails the state or the party as the embodiment of moral virtue, the ultimate source of morality. While military thinking accepts war, fascist thinking romanticizes war and violence. The military man recognizes the necessity and uses of power; the fascist worships power as an end in itself. The military ethic recognizes the necessity of leadership and discipline in human society; fascism emphasizes the supreme power and ability of the leader, and the absolute duty of subordination to his will.

The fascist and the military views on human nature and history differ widely. In opposition to military emphasis upon the universality of human traits, the fascist believes in the natural superiority of a chosen people or race and in the inherent genius and supreme virtue of the leader. Military thinking, on the other hand, is skeptical of everybody. While the military man learns from history and the liberal relies on reason, the fascist stresses intuition. He has little use or need for ordered knowledge and practical, empirical realism. He celebrates the triumph of the Will over external obstacles. In this respect, fascism is more individualistic than liberalism and more removed from the military ethic with its emphasis upon the limitations of human nature.

Unlike liberalism, fascism willingly supports the maintenance of strong military forces. While the liberal will fight for ideals and the military man for the security of the state, the fascist fights in order to fight. War is the end not the instrument of politics. In contrast to the cautious, unbelligerent foreign policy of the military man, the fascist advocates a dynamic, aggressive, revolutionary policy with the avowed aims of conflict and the expansion of the power of the state to its ultimate limit. The fascist believes in the internal subordination of all other social institutions to state or party. The military profession itself must have the proper ideological coloring. While fascism does not go as far as liberalism in imposing extraneous forms on military institutions, it is even more hostile to the existence of any potential sources of power apart from the state. Like liberalism, fascism believes in total war, mass armies, and that it is the duty of every citizen to be a soldier.

Marxism. The Marxist view of man is fundamentally opposed to the military view of man. For the Marxist, man is basically good and rational; he is corrupted by evil institutions. He is naturally at peace with his fellow men. This was his condition before the beginning of history. This will be his condition when the dialectical processes grind to a halt. While Marxist thought denies the existence of fundamental distinctions among men, at the present stage in history it views the proletarian as more progressive than other classes. Like the military man, the Marxist is a careful student of history. While there is a cyclical element in the constant repetition of thesis, antithesis, and synthesis, the basic course of history is linear and progressive. Like the military man, the Marxist sees struggle throughout, but unlike him he sees only class struggle. While the military man recognizes the role of chance and human freedom in history, the Marxist holds that all significant events are determined by economic forces. The Marxist view of history is monistic, while the military view is pluralistic. The Marxist also

differs from the military man in his faith that history will come
to an end with the realization of a more or less utopian society.

Both Marxism and the military ethic recognize the importance
of power and groups in human affairs. The Marxist, however,
stresses the importance of economic power, whereas the military
man holds with Machiavelli to the superiority of the sword. For
the Marxist the basic group is the class — mankind is cut horizon-
tally; for the military man, the basic group is the nation state —
mankind is cut vertically. Indeed, Marxism denies the reality of the
state as a reflection of group unity, holding that it is merely an
instrument of class warfare. While the military ethic recognizes
that states will go to war for many reasons, it stresses the concerns
of power and security. To the Marxist economic imperialism is the
basis of interstate wars. The only wars which he can sanction are
class wars, and the only military forces which he can approve are
class instruments. He does not recognize universal military values
and forms; the character of every military force is determined by
the class interests for which it is fighting. He is favorably disposed
towards a military force organized upon "proletarian" lines and
opposing capitalist interests. Like liberalism, therefore, Marxism
insists upon the patterning of military institutions upon nonmilitary
ideas.

Conservatism. Unlike liberalism, Marxism, and fascism, conservatism is basically similar to the military ethic.* Indeed, it was
found appropriate to designate the military ethic as one of conservative realism. In its theories of man, society, and history, its
recognition of the role of power in human relations, its acceptance
of existing institutions, its limited goals, and its distrust of grand
designs, conservatism is at one with the military ethic. Most importantly, conservatism, unlike the other three ideologies, is not
monistic and universalistic. It does not attempt to apply the same
ideas to all problems and all human institutions. It permits a variety
of goals and values. Consequently, conservatism alone of the four
ideologies is not driven by its own logic to an inevitable conflict

* Conservatism, as used here and hereafter in this volume, refers to the philosophy of Burke, and not to the meaning given this term in popular political
parlance in the United States to refer to the laissez-faire, property-rights form of
liberalism as exemplified, for instance, by Herbert Hoover.

with the military values which stem from the demands of the military function. It alone has no political-ideological pattern to impose on military institutions. While inherent contrast and conflict exist between the military ethic and liberalism, fascism, and Marxism, inherent similarity and compatibility exist between the military ethic and conservatism.

THE EQUILIBRIUM OF OBJECTIVE CIVILIAN CONTROL

The distribution of power between civilian and military groups which maximizes military professionalism and objective civilian control varies with the compatibility between the ideology prevailing in society and the professional military ethic. If the ideology is inherently antimilitary (such as liberalism, fascism, or Marxism), the military acquire substantial political power only by sacrificing their professionalism and adhering to the values and attitudes dominant within the community. In such an antimilitary society, military professionalism and civilian control are maximized by the military's renouncing authority and influence and leading a weak, isolated existence, divorced from the general life of society. In a society dominated by an ideology favorable to the military viewpoint, on the other hand, military power may be increased to a much greater extent without becoming incompatible with a high level of professionalism. The realization of objective civilian control thus depends upon the achievement of an appropriate equilibrium between the power of the military and the ideology of society.

The concessions which the military make in order to acquire power in an unsympathetic society are just one example of the general phenomenon of the ameliorating and diluting effects of power. It is a truism that power melts principle and that those who hold to definite, dogmatic, and rigid value systems are excluded from power in a pluralistic society. Only he who is flexible, willing to adjust, and ready to compromise can win widespread support: power is always to be purchased for a price. The price which the military have to pay for power depends upon the extent of the gap between the military ethic and the prevailing ideologies of the society. The effect which the acquisition of power in a nonconservative society has upon military men is similar to the sobering effects that the acquisition of power has upon radicals. Michels remarks at one point in his *Political Parties* that "Socialists may triumph but never socialism." The same is true with the military in an unsympathetic society. The generals and admirals may triumph but not the professional military ethic. The taming effect of political power makes them good liberals, good fascists, or good communists, but poor professionals. The satisfactions of professional performance and adherence to the professional code are replaced by the satisfactions of power, office, wealth, popularity, and the approbation of nonmilitary groups.

In most societies the relation among power, professionalism, and ideology is a dynamic one, reflecting shifts in the relative power of groups, changing currents of opinion and thought, and varying threats to national security. The maintenance of that equilibrium between power and ideology which constitutes objective civilian control is obviously difficult at best. Any profession experiences a tension between its inherent professional aspirations and the extraneous politics in which it may become involved. The military profession, because of its crucial significance to society as well as the vast power which it must wield when the state is threatened, manifests this tension to a higher degree than most other professional bodies. An element of tragic necessity exists in this relationship. Professional success breeds its own downfall by stimulating political involvement. Nonetheless, the professional man who pursues the values of professional competence and obedience and the political man who pursues power as an end in itself are two distinct types. Yet elements of both exist in most human beings and in every group. The tension between the two, consequently, can never be removed; it can only be ordered so as to make it more or less endurable.

Antimilitary ideologies have flourished in western societies, and the demands of military security, or simply the desire for power, have forced many military individuals and groups to play dominant roles in their governments. They have only been able to do this, however, by surrendering their professional outlook. Yet because these military individuals and groups have been the most prominent and politically involved military men, their attitudes have frequently been assumed by nonmilitary groups to be typical of military thinking. Thus, deviant, nonmilitary military men such as De Gaulle, Ludendorff, and MacArthur are often considered to be representative examples of the "military mind." Actually, such men in their political roles express values stemming from nonmilitary sources.

THE PATTERNS OF CIVIL-MILITARY RELATIONS

The general relations among power, professionalism, and ideology make possible five different ideal types of civil-military relations.* These are, of course, ideals and extremes; in actual practice the civil-military relations of any society combines elements of two or more. Three of the five types permit a high degree of professionalism and objective civilian control; two presuppose low professionalism and subjective civilian control.

(1) Antimilitary ideology, high military political power, and low military professionalism. This type of civil-military relations generally is found in more primitive countries where military professionalism has been retarded or in more advanced countries when security threats are suddenly intensified and the military rapidly increase their political power. The export of the institutions and ethics of military professionalism from western Europe to other countries has been as difficult as the export of the institutions of constitutional democracy. Consequently in the Near East, Asia, and Latin America this type of civil-military relations has tended to prevail. Only with great difficulty have nations such as Turkey removed their officers from politics and cultivated professional behavior and outlook. Japan is the only major power to maintain this pattern of civil-military relations over a long period of time. It was, however, also characteristic of Germany during World War I and of the United States in World War II.

(2) Antimilitary ideology, low military political power, and low military professionalism. This combination of elements only appears where the ideology of society is so intensely pursued that

* There are eight conceivable combinations of these three factors, but one (antimilitary ideology, high military power, high military professionalism) is impossible given the theoretical premises stated above, and two others (promilitary ideology, low military power, low military professionalism; promilitary ideology, high military power, low professionalism) are unlikely to occur except in the most unusual circumstances.

it is impossible for the military to escape its influence no matter how far they reduce their political power. Civil-military relations in modern totalitarian states may tend toward this type, a close approximation to it being achieved in Germany during World War II.

(3) Antimilitary ideology, low military political power, and high military professionalism. A society which suffers few threats to its security is likely to have this type of civil-military relations. Historically, this pattern prevailed in the United States from the rise of military professionalism after the Civil War until the beginning of World War II.

(4) Promilitary ideology, high military political power, and high military professionalism. A society with continuing security threats and an ideology sympathetic to military values may permit a high level of military political power and yet still maintain military professionalism and objective civilian control. Probably the outstanding achievement of this variety of civil-military relations was by Prussia and Germany during the Bismarckian-Moltkean epoch (1860–1890).

(5) Promilitary ideology, low military political power, and high military professionalism. This type might be expected in a society relatively safe from security threats and dominated by a conservative or other ideology sympathetic to the military viewpoint. Civil-military relations in twentieth-century Britain have, to some extent, tended to be of this type.

5

Germany and Japan: Civil-Military Relations in Practice

Modern Japan dates from 1868 and modern Germany from 1870. The history of German and Japanese civil-military relations during the following seventy-five years, down to their defeat in World War II, offers excellent material for the application of the theory developed in the previous chapter. Americans have tended to classify both Germany and Japan as fundamentally "militaristic" nations. Yet their patterns of civil-military relations could hardly be more dissimilar. Probably no country has had a wider variety of experiences in civil-military relations than modern Germany. No other officer corps achieved such high standards of professionalism, and the officer corps of no other major power was in the end so completely prostituted. Each chapter of the German story has its lesson and its warning. The imperial experience shows the benefits of civilian control. The republican period demonstrates the difficulty of achieving that control amidst political chaos. World War I illustrates the disastrous results when military men assume political roles. Nazi rule illustrates the equally catastrophic results when military warnings are unheeded and political leaders ride roughshod over the soldiers. The variety of German civil-military relations makes its history a terrifying but highly instructive study. In contrast, Japanese civil-military relations remained in a single relatively stable pattern from 1868 to 1945. From the start, the Japanese military played a persistently active role in the politics of their country. While the high level of German professionalism produced acute tension between the military and popular ethics, the popular thinking of the Japanese officer corps reflected general harmony between military and people. The key to German civil-military relations was sporadic disintegration; the key to Japanese civil-military relations was sustained disorder. Yet the ultimate causes and effects of the breakup of the German equilibrium and the failure of Japan ever to develop an equilibrium were the same. In both countries the disruption of the civil-military balance reflected more basic constitutional disorders. In both countries, too, that disruption helped undermine the nation's security: distorting the perspective and judgment of soldiers and statesmen, confusing their responsibilities and duties, fostering fanaticism and arrogance, and leading to a bellicosity in peace and a weakness in war which contributed to their ultimate downfall.

GERMANY: THE TRAGEDY OF PROFESSIONAL MILITARISM

THE IMPERIAL BALANCE, 1871–1914. Imperial civil-military relations between 1871 and 1914 reflected an extraordinary degree of objective civilian control and military professionalism founded upon a high level and restricted scope of military authority, a broad and gradually changing base of military political influence, and a sympathetically conservative national ideology. In the last decades of this era, however, changes in the national environment began to undermine this balance, and eventually it was completely destroyed in World War I.

Military Professionalism. Modern Germany inherited from Prussia the most professional officer corps in Europe. Its central elements were the General Staff, with its scientific and rational approach to military operations, and the Kriegsakademie where officers were trained in the science of war for the staff corps and high command. Supporting these were the systems of entry and initial training requiring both specialized and general education. Nowhere was war taken more seriously and studied more carefully than in the German military schools and staff offices. Superb technical competence, high intellectual achievement, unwavering devotion to duty — these were the characteristics of the General Staff Corps in particular and, to a greater or lesser degree, of the officer corps as a whole. The preëminence of German professionalism was conceded by the soldiers and statesmen of other powers, large and small, advanced and primitive, who eagerly attempted to model their own military institutions upon the German original.

German institutional professionalism had its counterpart in the dominance of the professional ethic in the German military mind. *On War* was the bible of the officer corps. The two outstanding military leaders of the Empire — von Moltke who was Chief of Staff from 1857 to 1888 and von Schlieffen who occupied the same post from 1891 to 1905 — were both disciples of Clausewitz. Their thinking, writing, and behavior set the intellectual and moral tone of the officer corps. Under their influence the values and attitudes of the German military probably came closer to approximating the ideal-type military ethic than those of any other officer corps in history. The strength of these professional values was reflected in the views of the officers on the two cardinal points of civilian control and the role of war in national policy.

It was accepted gospel in the officer corps that war was an instrument of politics and that therefore the soldier was the junior partner of the statesman. Even von Bernhardi, more politically oriented than most officers, adhered to this basic dogma. Both Moltke and Schlieffen recognized the separate identity and close relationship of politics and war. Moltke was more politically aware than Schlieffen but he had no political ambitions and restricted himself to vigorous presentation of the military viewpoint. His guiding ideal was that of an unpolitical army.

> The commander in his operations [Moltke declared] has to keep military victory as the goal before his eyes. But what statesmanship does with his victories or defeats is not his province. It is that of the statesman.[1]

Even more than Moltke, Schlieffen avoided politics and devoted himself and the General Staff to strictly military matters. He was the military technician par excellence. The rationalism of German military thought also did not permit the glorification of war as an end in itself. War was inevitable — no one would dispute that — but it was also undesirable. Man simply had to endure it: "want and misery," said Moltke, "disease and suffering and war are all permanent elements in man's destiny and nature."[2] Along with most of his military associates, Moltke believed that war for Germany would be a "national misfortune." Yet, in 1875 and 1887 he supported war with France and Russia respectively as necessary to protect German military security. He always viewed the issue from this vantage point; his approach was that of the rational pessimist rather than the utopian romantic. Elements in the naval officer corps, which had been born of imperialistic yearnings and which, as a younger service, had not yet been completely differentiated from the society which created it, were at times inclined toward bellicosity and imperialism. The army leaders, however, almost unanimously opposed both tendencies. The army was, as Vagts says, "non-aggressive before 1914 except in its strategy." That strategy was designed to cope with what the military viewed as the nightmare situation of a two-front war which would require a quick and decisive victory on one front. As the General Staff declared in a confidential statement of 1902:

> We want to conquer nothing, we merely want to defend what we own. We shall probably never be attackers but rather always be the attacked. The necessary quick success can be brought us with certainty only by the offensive.[3]

The German military indeed manifested an almost pathological concern for national security. Far from advocating war, the military leaders generally viewed it as the last resort of policy and looked forward to it with gloomy forebodings and feverish preparations.

Governmental Authority. The structure of governmental authority which helped maintain German professionalism was a unique combination of three elements. First, the scope of military authority was strictly limited to military affairs. The military played no role in determining domestic economic policies. Foreign policy was the concern of the Chancellor and Foreign Minister. The General Staff stuck to strictly military matters. As was natural and proper, the Chief of Staff and War Minister presented the military view on foreign policy. As was also natural and proper, their opinions usually differed from those of the civilian authorities. In the end, however, the civilians, not the generals, made the decisions. Bismarck, for instance, rejected Moltke's advice on the peace treaties with Austria and France and on Russian policy in the

1880's. The only officer who continually exceeded a professional role in foreign policy was Admiral von Tirpitz, and he was generally viewed by the other admirals as an essentially political figure. On the whole, however, the military were confined to their own sphere by the horizontal control of other vigorous offices and officials occupying the areas into which they might be tempted to expand their power.

A second factor restricting military power was the relative unity of civilian and military authority. Civilian power was concentrated in the hands of the Kaiser and his Chancellor while military authority was divided among a multiplicity of offices. The Reichstag never played more than a mildly harassing role in military affairs, and its efforts to increase parliamentary control over military policy were never strong enough to undermine civilian control. The officer corps, moreover, was unconditionally pledged to the Emperor, and, by so binding itself, foreswore the possibilities of enhancing its power by playing executive off against legislature. Military authority, on the other hand, was divided first between the army and navy and then further subdivided within each service. Each had a tripartite headquarters organization consisting of: (1) a ministry, normally headed by a professional officer, and concerned with the administrative, political, and logistical aspects of the service; (2) a cabinet, also headed by an officer, and occupied with personnel matters; and (3) a staff, devoted to the planning of military operations. None of these headquarters had command authority over the fleets and army corps. Consequently, the six chiefs of the headquarters offices, plus the commanding generals and commanding admirals, all reported directly to the Kaiser, who was thus able to pick and choose from the military advice offered him. In addition, there was considerable rivalry in the army among the War Ministry, the Military Cabinet, and the General Staff. The Ministry had initially been the dominant institution, but in the course of the nineteenth century, first the Military Cabinet and then the General Staff acquired preëminence. Eventually, of course, the General Staff was to dominate completely. But, until World War I, an uneasy balance of authority existed among these three military offices.

The effects of the limited scope and multiplicity of military authority were counterbalanced by the high level of that authority.

All the top military leaders had the right of direct access (*Immediatstellung*) to the Kaiser as Supreme War Lord which weakened vertical controls over the military. Since the Kaiser was dependent upon their advice, the military chiefs, except to the extent that they disagreed among themselves, possessed almost complete autonomy and could run their institutions without external interference. While the limited scope of military authority and the unity of civilian power kept the military out of politics, the direct access of the military to the Kaiser kept the politicians out of the military. All in all, given the ideological climate of the times, the entire pattern of authority was uniquely suited to maximize civilian control and military professionalism.

Political Influence. The political influence of the imperial officer corps had three significant aspects: (1) the gradual weakening of the affiliations of the corps with the Junker aristocracy; (2) the temporary incursion of military leaders into politics in the years from 1888 to 1897; and (3) the widespread popularity of the military leaders and the prestige of the military career among the German people.

In the decade of the wars of unification, over two-thirds of the officer corps had been drawn from the aristocracy. The Empire witnessed a steady decline in this proportion as the middle classes successfully asserted their claim to the military career. In 1905, of 102 officers serving with the General Staff, 44, including such future lights as Ludendorff and Gröner, were bourgeois in origin. By 1913 these elements furnished 70 per cent of the entire officer corps.[4] The tremendous naval expansion undertaken after 1890 also increased the size and influence of the naval officer corps, which was much more closely linked with bourgeois than aristocratic groups. The weakening of the ties between the officer corps and the aristocracy aided professionalism, on the one hand, in that it reduced the likelihood that the military interests would be subordinated to class interests. On the other hand, the Junker outlook was highly conservative and sympathetic to the military viewpoint, and the decrease of military affiliations with that group made the military more dependent on general public opinion which was less definitely conservative and more susceptible to change.

During the Empire few individuals crossed the line between

the military profession and politics in either direction. The significant exceptions to this occurred in the years from 1888 to 1897 when a vacuum of civilian political leadership developed which various military figures moved in to fill. This situation was caused by the coincidence of the death of the Kaiser in 1888, the retirement of Moltke in the same year, and the retirement of Bismarck in 1890. The new young monarch had a predilection for personal rule, little respect for the responsibilities and functions of his constitutional advisers, and an intense personal fondness for soldiers and military folderol. Moltke's place was taken by Waldersee, one soldier with political skills and political ambitions, and who, as a favorite of the new monarch, was only too anxious to exert his influence in a variety of fields. He was instrumental in bringing about Bismarck's fall in 1890 and his replacement by another general, Leo von Caprivi. Significantly, it was Waldersee, soldier turned politician, who rejected the two fundamental elements of the military ethic. He was the leading advocate of preventive war and he also entertained the idea of a military *coup d'état*. However, it was not long before he lost favor with the Kaiser; he was fired at the beginning of 1891, and retired to nurture dreams of returning to power as a military strong man. His thirty months as Chief of Staff contrast with the thirty-two years Moltke held the job and the fourteen years of his successor Schlieffen. He was fundamentally out of place in the imperial officer corps, but he was the forerunner of military politicians such as Schleicher, Reichenau, and Blomberg in the 1920's and 1930's. Caprivi, who actively opposed much of Waldersee's wildness, was replaced as Chancellor in 1894, and by 1897 civilian statesmen had resumed political leadership. With Schlieffen's exclusive concern with technical matters the influence of the military retired within professional boundaries.

Decreasing affiliation with the aristocracy was more than compensated for in the years after 1871 by the great popularity of the military with the people as a whole. This stemmed from the great victories of 1866 and 1870 which made Moltke a national hero and permitted a steady increase in military budgets down to World War I. In no other modern western society for such an extended peacetime period have the military career and the military officer had the popular prestige which they had in Wilhelmine Germany. The soldier was "without any challenge, the first man in the State," and the General Staff was held in awe as the oracle of military wisdom and guarantor of state security. "The military man now seemed to be a consecrated spirit — the lieutenant moved through the world as a young god and the civilian reserve lieutenant as a demigod." [5]

Popular Attitudes. The widespread popularity of the military furnished a firm basis for military professionalism so long as the popular mind remained sympathetic to the military ethic. The military were as popular in 1914 as they had been in 1880. The intellectual climate of 1914, however, differed significantly from that of 1880. Subtle forces had drastically altered the value structure of the German nation. As a result, military popularity became a threat rather than an aid to professionalism. A limited and conservative ideology had given way to one which was nationalistic and aggressive. Materialism, bellicosity, the glorification of violence and war, worship of naked *Macht* superseded the more reasonable, idealistic, and humane elements in the German spirit. Mommsen, Droysen, Sybel, Treitschke, Nietzsche supplanted Goethe, Schiller, Kant — and Clausewitz. War and power became ends in themselves and the man of power consequently was viewed not as the servant of the state but rather as the embodiment of the state. The state was power, and power alone; war was, in Treitschke's phrase "political science par excellence," the mainspring of progress and national realization. "Germany," as Paulsen observed, "has been called the nation of poets and thinkers, but to-day it may be called the nation of masterful combatants, as it originally appeared in history." [6]

The ideology of bellicosity was spawned by the universities and embraced by the German people. Its influence was felt in all segments of society. Only the intense adherence of the officers to the military ethic rendered the corps relatively immune down to World War I. Nonetheless the new ideas did make themselves felt about the fringes of the military profession. The navy was a product of the age and susceptible to philosophies of nationalism and expansion. Military officers turned popular writers such as von der Goltz and Bernhardi catered to the bellicose sentiments of the people. They found support with the latter which they did not find with the General Staff, which rejected them and their views. The bulk of the army officer corps, however, was true to the military ethic and rejected the power ethic. In the face of the intellectual and moral deterioration of Germany, it adhered to the old ideas and, in Rosinski's phrase, remained like a "monolithic block in a changing landscape." [7] It was in many respects the last social institution to abandon the conservative morality. Yet the new popular ideology was undermining that balance of power and professionalism which had been the essence of its existence.

WORLD WAR I: MILITARY DICTATORSHIP, 1914–1918. The First World War saw the complete destruction of the imperial balance in civil-military relations. By the end of the war the General Staff was running the German government. Coincidentally, the military leaders abandoned their adherence to military ideals. This German experience well illustrated the difficulties which arise from the conduct of a major war by a nonconservative state. Battle transforms generals into heroes; the heroes transform themselves into politicians; and the result is a loss of professional military restraint and caution.

The involvement of the General Staff in politics began during von Falkenhayn's tenure as its chief from the fall of 1914 to August 1916. During this period a slow but continuous expansion of military authority and influence took place. This was, however, merely a prelude to the virtually absolute power which Hindenburg and Ludendorff exercised in the last two years of the war when the former replaced Falkenhayn and the latter became First Quartermaster General. The fundamental element in this tremendous expansion of military control was the unprecedented popularity of the victor of Tannenberg with the German people. He was a national idol whom the Germans trusted implicitly to bring them success. The Hindenburg adulation far surpassed that accorded any other military or political figure in German history, including Moltke and Bismarck. Consequently, he was the ideal fulcrum for Ludendorff and the General Staff to use in increasing their power throughout the government. The threat of resignation was sufficient to control the Kaiser. By brandishing this weapon, Ludendorff was able to force the Emperor to acquiesce to the military views in most of the conflicts between the General Staff and civilian officials. In the summer of 1917 he secured the ouster of Bethmann-Hollweg as Chancellor and his replacement by Michaelis who was acceptable to the military. A few months later Michaelis proved himself incapable of functioning to the satisfaction of his military masters. He was dropped and, upon the recommendation of the High Command, his place was taken by Count von Hertling. Subsequently, in January 1918 Hindenburg and Ludendorff were able to secure the dismissal of the chief of the Emperor's Civil Cabinet. The other military offices were similarly subordinated to the will of the General Staff.

The military commanders expanded their power into foreign and domestic policy. While the Kaiser refused in January 1918 to give them complete authority over foreign affairs and peace negotiations, they were more or less able to manipulate the foreign office through Count von Haeften, their representative there.[8] In July 1918 they secured the dismissal of the Foreign Minister when he opposed their views on the Brest-Litovsk peace treaty. Previously they had utilized their influence in foreign affairs to overrule civilian opinion in a number of important decisions. With the hope of adding Polish divisions to the military forces of the Central Powers they had in the fall of 1916 successfully insisted upon the creation of an independent Polish kingdom. This prevented the immediate conclusion of a peace treaty with Russia. In the winter of 1917, over Bethmann-Hollweg's opposition, they secured the introduction of unrestricted submarine warfare. By these two excursions into policy the High Command achieved the continuation in the war of one enemy and the entrance into the war of another. Throughout 1917 they insisted upon the maintenance of annexationist war goals, thereby frustrating efforts to bring about a negotiated peace. Military power was also asserted over the domestic economy. The nature of the war early required the expansion of the economic sections of the General Staff into the areas of food, materials, labor, and munitions. Subsequently, virtually no field of policy was beyond its interest. Industrial production was controlled and increased through the so-called Hindenburg Program. All the previously effective horizontal restraints upon military activity were removed as the authority of the generals penetrated into the farthest reaches of German life.

It is impossible to say to what extent the power of the High Command affected the thinking of the bulk of the officer corps. The views of the military leaders themselves, however, were drastically changed by the vision from the heights of power. The old doctrines of civilian control were abandoned. It makes little difference who is Chancellor, Ludendorff is reputed to have said, but "one thing is certain: the power must be in my hands." Expansionist goals were adopted which contrasted markedly with the anti-imperialistic attitudes of the prewar General Staff. In 1917 the war aims of the military included acquisition of Poland, Russia's Baltic provinces, eastern France, and all of Belgium. And even this was viewed as only the nucleus of a vast Germanic realm which would eventually draw into its system virtually all of Europe north of the Alps.

More significant than these immediate policy goals was the fundamental change in values which they reflected. These received their most typical expression, not during the war, but in the literature produced by the generals after their defeat. Blind to the extent to which military dominance had contributed to Germany's misfortune, they argued that military power had not been given its proper scope in wartime Germany. In its effort to shift responsibility to the civilian, this theme was closely tied in with the stab-in-the-back legend. The most authoritative statement of the new doctrine was contained in General Ludendorff's own work, *Der Totale Krieg,* published in 1935. Ludendorff flatly rejected the professional military tradition: "All the theories of Clausewitz should be thrown overboard." The changes in the nature of war since the eighteenth century have made politics subservient to war rather than war to politics. The trouble with Germany in both the Franco-Prussian War and World War I was the division of authority among Kaiser, Chancellor, and Chief of Staff. Instead, at the outbreak of war the entire nation should be subordinated to the Commander in Chief. He supersedes all political leaders and his authority is "all-embracing." Such a man can never be produced by training and experience. He is characterized by creative power, strength of character, willingness to accept responsibility, and indomitable will. He is an artist: he "is either born to his position or he is not." [9] Ludendorff thus resurrected the eighteenth-century concept of the natural military genuis. His theory, with its delusions of omnipotence, its glorification of violence, its adulation of power, and its denial of specialized competence, was a rejection of everything that nineteenth-century German military thought stood for. It was indeed the employment of the more sordid elements of Treitschke, Nietzsche, and Spengler to rationalize absolute military power. Ironically this theory, developed out of military dominance in World War I, in the end achieved its fullest realization in the complete subjection of the military by an Austrian corporal in World War II. The accurate verdict upon the earlier conflict was rendered by another soldier, General von Schoenaich, who, in 1924, concluded that "we owe our ruin to the supremacy of our military authorities over civilian authorities; and that is the very essence of militarism. In fact, German militarism simply committed suicide." [10]

WEIMAR: STATE WITHIN A STATE, 1918–1926. The inauguration of the Weimar Republic saw the role of the military change from complete dominance of the state to essential support for the state. The intellectual and political climate of the Republic was most unconducive to the maintenance of professionalism. The Weimar government had a highly tenuous existence, lacking widespread acceptance and the support of many powerful social groups. Consequently, it had to turn to the army as the one stable and disciplined institution which had survived defeat and revolution and remained a concrete center of power amidst political disintegration. The government was thus absolutely dependent upon the support of the army. Yet this very fact, by confronting the army with a constitutional issue, meant that the government could never be absolutely certain of receiving that support. In 1918, Ebert, President of the Republic, in effect negotiated a treaty with the military leaders receiving the support of the army in exchange for the suppression of the extreme left. In 1920, during the Kapp Putsch, the army maintained a wait-and-see neutrality. Three years later when the government was menaced by the threat of uprisings from both the extreme right and extreme left, the army command defended republican authority, and exercised emergency power in its behalf. That the Weimar government existed as long as it did is due to army support. That support, however, was not something which could be commanded by the government; it was something which was granted by the army.

The general political weakness of the Republic was supplemented by new constitutional difficulties in establishing civilian control. First, under the imperial regime, all officers had sworn obedience to the Emperor. They had little opportunity for doubt as to when and whom they should obey. In the Republic, however, they swore allegiance to the constitution, a lengthy document not entirely clear of ambiguities. The officers might frequently be called upon to determine when obedience to particular individuals constituted obedience to the constitution. This problem was aggravated by a second factor: the division of authority over the military among a large number of civilian institutions. The President was the Supreme Commander of the armed forces, appointing and dismissing all the high officers. The Chancellor, however, was the head of the government, and all the actions of the President with respect to the military had to be approved either by him or by the Minister of Defense. Both Chancellor and Minister of Defense were responsible to the Reichstag, which had full authority over military policy in general and the military budget in particular. In contrast, thirdly, to this civilian disunity was the new unity of the military. Not only were the armies of the various states of the German Empire consolidated into a single national force, but all the headquarters organizations were now brought under a single military chief. This furnishing of the military with a single spokesman contributed, fourthly, to the undermining of the efforts to reduce the level of military authority. Theoretically, the embryonic general staff (*Truppenamt*) was under the Chief of the Army Command who was under the Minister of Defense. Thus, presumably, the right of *Immediatstellung* had been lost by the military. In actuality, however, the increased power of the army commander brought about through his complete control over the military machine made him virtually independent of the Minister of Defense. The first two Ministers of Defense — Noske and Gessler — were spokesmen for military interests, and the last two — Gröner and Schleicher — were generals.

The officer corps in the Weimar Republic retreated from the

ideology of military dictatorship in the direction of the old imperial military ethic. The dominant figure in the Reichswehr from 1919 until 1926 was General von Seeckt who typified the professional soldier and who was thoroughly committed to a nonpolitical army. Seeckt picked his officers according to their capabilities and trained them carefully so as to develop the highest level of professional competence. Seeckt claimed to have the professional hatred for war: "The soldier, having experience of war, fears it far more than the doctrinaire who, being ignorant of war, talks only of peace." [11] In his advice on policy to the republican government, he was guided generally by a proper concern for the military security of the state. Within the army he was adamant in emphasizing the military virtues, in excluding adventurers and opportunists, and in insisting upon correct, nonpolitical behavior. "As for the soldier," he said, "it is not for him to seek to know more or to do better than his commanders: his duty consists in obedience . . . A *Reichswehr* into which the cancer of political discord has entered will be shattered in the hour of danger." [12]

The one deficient element in Seeckt's formulation of the military ethic was a certain haziness as to where the ultimate loyalty of the army lay. This reflected the ambiguity of the Weimar constitution and the political weakness of the republican government. Seeckt's description of the place of the army was contained in the formula: "The Army serves the State; it is above parties." Accordingly,

> The Army should become a State within the State, but it should be merged in the State through service, in fact it should itself become the purest image of the State.[13]

This was fine as far as it went. But it left undefined the relationship of the military to the government. It was a state within a state, not a professional guild serving a government. If the government were the representative or the embodiment of the state, then the army should obey the government and all would be well. But if the existence of the government and the nature of its constitution were issues of party controversy, then presumably the army would remain aloof. In reality the government of the Weimar Republic fitted both these categories and so, consequently, the attitude of the military toward it, as defined by Seeckt, was a curiously dual one. What this meant in practice was well illustrated during the 1923 crisis when Ebert asked Seeckt where the Reichswehr stood. "The Reichswehr, Mr. President," replied the latter, "stands behind me." [14] And there were no general principles which defined where Seeckt stood. At times he seriously considered assuming sovereign power himself. By refusing to accept the Weimar Republic as the permanent embodiment of the German state, the leaders of the Reichswehr were required to make political judgments at any moment of acute crisis.

WEIMAR: FACTION AMONG FACTIONS, 1926–1933. After Seeckt's retirement, his successor, Colonel General Heye, and other generals such as Gröner attempted to carry on his policies. This became increasingly difficult, however, and the last years of the Weimar Republic saw quite a different pattern of civil-military relations from that which had existed previously. Under Seeckt the army had been called upon to make political decisions only when there was an acute constitutional crisis. After his departure it became more and more involved in the day to day affairs and maneuverings of party politics. This involvement was brought about not by any change in the structure of authority but simply by the willingness of the military leadership to apply the political power of the army to immediate political ends.

The two key figures in this change were Hindenburg and General Kurt von Schleicher. The former was elected President of the Republic in 1925. The army now defined loyalty to the state as loyalty to the field marshal and national hero. This would not have had serious consequences if the President had been above party politics as Seeckt had been. Such, however, was not the case. Instead, Hindenburg as president furnished a fulcrum for military politicians such as Schleicher, just as during the war as Chief of the General Staff he had furnished a fulcrum for Ludendorff. Schleicher had been appointed head of the political department of the Defense Ministry in 1926. Trading upon his influence with Hindenburg and negotiating and dealing with party politicians of all stripes, he became a key figure in the government, making and unmaking cabinets with wanton abandon. In 1927, Schleicher eased out the Defense Minister, Gessler, who had appointed him, and had Gröner put in this post. Subsequently, in 1930, he brought about the fall of the cabinet of Chancellor Müller and the replacement of the latter by Heinrich Brüning. Two years later he torpedoed Brüning and Gröner and secured the appointment of von Papen as Chancellor. He himself took over the post of Defense Minister. Late in autumn of 1932, Papen was disposed of; and in December, Schleicher became Chancellor. Generals now occupied the two highest posts in the government. His enemies soon combined against Schleicher, however, and, at the end of January 1933, Hitler succeeded him at the head of a cabinet of Nazis and nationalists. Under Schleicher the Reichswehr had ceased to be a state within the state and had become a faction among factions. The generals had entered into the competition of politics and they had lost. A year and a half later Schleicher paid the price of failure in totalitarian politics when he was assassinated in the Nazi purge of June 30, 1934.

THE THIRD REICH: CIVILIANISM TRIUMPHANT, 1933–1945. The consolidation of power by the Nazis depended upon an informal understanding with the military. The latter would withdraw from politics, leave this field to the Nazis, and in return the Nazis would push an expanded rearmament program and guarantee the army a monopoly of the military function and autonomy within its own sphere. This arrangement received explicit sanction in the spring of 1934 when the army agreed to support Hitler for President; the latter acquiesced in the suppression of Röhm and the S.A., who had dreams of replacing the Reichswehr with a mass, ideologically oriented, people's army. Civil-military relations during the first years of the Nazi regime bore certain resemblances to those of the first years of the Weimar Republic. The army was exempted from much of the Nazi legislation, the authority of the civil courts over its members was abolished, the influence of the party hierarchy and the Gestapo was rigorously excluded. As one after another of the major institutions of German society succumbed before the Nazi policy of *Gleichschaltung,* the army remained an isolated center of health, relatively uncontaminated by the virus of National Socialism. Here the German who wished to escape from the onslaught of the totalitarian state might find refuge in professional patterns of discipline, expertise, duty, and integrity.

It is little wonder that there was rush of former officers back to the colors in what came to be described as "the aristocratic way of emigration."

Military Professionalism. The officer corps during these years was dominated by a professional military viewpoint. After the giddy Schleicher episode about which the great bulk of the corps had never been happy, much comfort was to be found in a purely professional role. The officers welcomed the opportunity to eschew politics and to concentrate upon the training and discipline of their steadily growing forces. Military adherence to civilian control was reaffirmed. For instance, in his volume on *The Art of Modern Warfare*, Colonel Foertsch restated the classical doctrine of the subordination of war to politics and the soldier to the statesman, and took Ludendorff to task for challenging Clausewitz. Ludendorff's book itself was rejected by the General Staff "root and branch." [15] Despite the temporary coincidence of Nazi and military views with respect to rearming and civilian control in the early thirties, a fundamental conflict nonetheless existed between the values of the two groups. Eventually this conflict had to manifest itself. The German military ideals of obedience, loyalty, honor, intellectual integrity, realism, reason could hardly be further removed from the complete unscrupulousness, amorality, and irrationalism of the Nazis.* The latter had little use for the "accursed objectivity" of the General Staff which Hitler described as "just a club of intellectuals." [16]

The conflict between the military approach and the Nazi approach was most sharply focused in foreign policy. The attitude of the German generals was virtually a perfect expression of the military ethic. They wanted to rebuild Germany's armed might, but they wanted to do so slowly, and not in order to wage war but to protect German security. It was necessary to expand the armament industry, build up a trained reserve, equip the army with modern weapons, construct defensive fortifications, and accomplish many other things before Germany would be ready to

* A brilliant restatement of the military ethic was made by General Ludwig Beck, Chief of the General Staff, in a speech at the reopening of the War Academy in October 1935. Beck's theme was Moltke's dictum that "Genius is work" and he vigorously attacked "sudden inspirations" and "wishful thinking." The speech did not make him any friends among the Nazis.

fight. This date in their calculations seemed to recede continuously into the future. There were many who thought that a war could never be fought on terms favorable to Germany because of her geographical vulnerability. If Germany started a war, they argued, she would eventually be confronted by a coalition of powers which would utterly destroy her. In contrast to the sober views of the military, the Nazis wished to rush mobilization, ignore or brush aside obstacles, and embark upon an adventuristic and aggressive foreign policy. The fundamental opposition between the two outlooks was well summed up by one general after the war:

> Hitler taught and believed that reason and knowledge are nothing, and that the unbending will to victory and the relentless pursuit of the goal are everything. Mystical speculation replaced considerations of time and space, and the careful calculation of the strength of one's own forces in relation to the enemy's.[17]

Step by step during the thirties the military opposed Hitler's aggressive actions, and step by step they saw their warnings rejected and Hitler successful. They opposed withdrawal from the League of Nations because it would isolate Germany. They warned against the repudiation of the Versailles Treaty and the reintroduction of conscription in 1935; they were sure it would bring about retaliatory action by the Allies. Fearing French intervention, they protested against the remilitarization of the Rhineland in 1936. Later in that year they opposed sending German forces to Spain. In November 1937, when Hitler unveiled to the military leaders his plans of expansion against Austria and Czechoslovakia, the generals again argued that German military strength was not up to such adventurous exploits. The *Anschluss* with Austria, however, was carried out successfully in the following spring by an adroit combination of internal subversion, diplomatic maneuvering, and military bluff. Hitler's designs on Czechoslovakia aroused even greater military consternation as they could easily embroil Germany in a war with France, and possibly with England and Russia also. The military opposition in the summer of 1938 was led by the Chief of the General Staff, General Beck. Hitler, however, forced Beck to resign and replaced him with Halder. As Hitler's campaign against Czechoslovakia mounted, a military

group with Halder's cooperation planned a *coup d'état* to seize
control of the government before Germany became involved in a
disastrous war. The officers, however, were torn with indecision
and hesitancy which was only finally resolved by the Allied concessions at Munich. The *coup d'état* was cancelled. Hitler had
again defeated his generals.[18] This broke the military. Subsequently, during the war the military objected to the more daring
of Hitler's schemes — such as his desire to attack in the west in
the fall of 1939, the invasion of Russia, and proposals pushed by
the S.S. to attack Switzerland in 1943. But Hitler's continued success in the face of their continued objections had undermined their
self-confidence and their influence with the government. The Nazis
were contemptuous of the timid and overcautious generals. Hitler
himself found the military mind to be much different from what
he expected, commenting on one occasion,

> Before I was head of the German Government I thought the German
> General Staff was like a butcher's dog — something to be held tight
> by the collar because it threatened to attack all and sundry. Since then
> I have had to recognize that the General Staff is anything but that.
> It has consistently tried to impede every action that I have thought
> necessary . . . It is I who always had to goad on this "butcher's
> dog." [19]

The clash of Nazi and military values made accommodation
between the two impossible. The situation in a sense was similar
to that of 1900–1918, except that the tension between the military ideology and the popular ideology was incomparably greater.
An "unpolitical army" is an intolerable anomaly in a completely
politicized totalitarian society. Reasoned military caution is equally
alien to the revolutionary mind. In World War I the military had
relinquished their views and embraced the popular enthusiasm. A
few were to follow that course again. Most did not. Consequently,
the balance could only be restored by the destruction of the political power of the army and the forcible conversion of the military to the Nazi viewpoint.

Governmental Authority. The destruction of the military was
carried out by every conceivable technique. The authority of the
military institutions was reduced, divided, and limited. The level

of the General Staff, which tended to be the center of professionalism, was steadily lowered. In 1935, Hitler assumed the position of Supreme Commander and under him von Blomberg, an officer who cooperated with the Nazis, became Minister of War and Commander in Chief of the Wehrmacht. Under Blomberg were the commanders of the three services, and under each commander the service staff. Also created out of the *Ministeramt* (Schleicher's former office) was an expanded staff, the *Wehrmachtamt,* subsequently headed by Keitel, also a Nazi collaborator, and working directly under Blomberg. Thus, all offices at the ministerial level were filled with either party members or generals willing to work with the Nazis. The General Staff which had previously so jealously guarded its right of *Immediatstellung* was now down at the fourth level in the military hierarchy.

In February 1938 after Blomberg and von Fritsch, the army commander, had been forced out, the War Ministry was in effect abolished. Hitler himself assumed Blomberg's position as Commander in Chief of the Wehrmacht, and transformed the *Wehrmachtamt* into the High Command of the Wehrmacht (OKW) under the direction of Keitel. The principal unit in the OKW was the Operations Staff — under another Nazi sympathizer, Jodl — which now took over many of the planning functions previously exercised by the army General Staff. Subsequently, the doctrine of the co-responsibility for decisions of the Chief of Staff together with the commanding officer was abandoned and the General Staff was thus still further reduced in importance. This organization persisted until December 1941 when the army Commander in Chief, von Brauchitsch, was dismissed and Hitler assumed personal command of the army. He thus combined in his own person the political offices of Chief of State, party leader, and War Minister with the military offices of Supreme Commander of the Wehrmacht and Commander in Chief of the Army. In effect, this meant that military functions of the latter positions were no longer performed.

Military authority was divided as well as reduced in level. The liquidation of the S.A. leadership in 1934 was a Pyrrhic victory for the army in its effort to protect its position as sole arms bearer of the Reich. The real winner was Himmler who, immediately after the June 30th purge, began the expansion of the S.S. Eventually the S.S. became in effect a second army numbering by 1944 twenty-five or thirty divisions, virtually all of them armored, mechanized, or airborne. The Luftwaffe under Göring was also independent of the normal chain of command. In 1935 it took over the anti-aircraft units, thereby insuring that in the event of trouble, the army would not be able to shoot down Göring's planes. In 1942, Luftwaffe Field Divisions, eventually numbering about twenty and designed for ground fighting, were created from surplus Air Force personnel. Thus in effect the Third Reich had three armies: the regular army, Himmler's Waffen-SS., and Göring's varied Luftwaffe units. Hitler also maintained a complicated set of duplicate command relationships. The diminution of the army General Staff's role in planning began in 1938 when Hitler assigned to OKW responsibility for drafting plans for the complete occupation of Czechoslovakia. In 1941, after the invasion of Russia, OKW and OKH (the Army High Command) were given completely different spheres of authority. The latter was responsible for the conduct of the war on the Russian front, whereas the former assumed direction of the military effort elsewhere. The only connection between these two commands was Hitler himself and his own personal staff. Even the transfer of a single regiment from one front to the other had to be approved by Hitler. Independent lines of command persisted out into the field. Numerous special organizations and hierarchies were created for special missions. The so-called Organisation Todt affiliated with the party and independent of the army was responsible for military construction work. In 1943, political indoctrination officers (*National Socialistische Führungsoffiziere*-NSFO) were introduced into the armed forces. These officers were modeled upon the Russian political commissars and had a chain of command independent of the military hierarchy. Competition among the intelligence services was encouraged with disastrous results for the accuracy and efficiency of German reporting.[20]

The scope of military authority was also reduced. With respect to the withdrawal from the League of Nations, rearmament, and the reoccupation of the Rhineland, Hitler either did not inform the military high command or told them of his plans at the last moment. Efforts of Fritsch and Beck to assert the military right to be consulted were devoid of effective result. Subsequently, not only were the military excluded from foreign policy decisions, but they were also not allowed to make purely military decisions. Hitler first began to intervene in the preparation of military plans in the fall of 1938. Once the war was on, however, and particularly after it began to go badly for Germany, Hitler extended his range of decision down to the most detailed tactical level. Time and again the recommendations of the generals were overridden and countermanded by Hitler. He insisted upon a rigid rather than a flexible system of defense, and no withdrawals were allowed without his permission. He personally supervised the movement of battalions, and he neglected long-range strategic planning. "All freedom of action was eliminated. Even the highest commanders were subjected to an unbearable tutelage." [21]

Political Influence. The Nazis were not content merely to eliminate the authority of the officer corps. It was even more necessary to alter its fundamental character, to destroy it as an autonomous group positing its own values and goals. This was done through three principal techniques. First, efforts were made to win over the high commanders to the Nazi cause through propaganda, threats, and bribery with wealth and power. Blomberg, Keitel, and Jodl were undoubtedly in part persuaded by the high office and honors which they received to cooperate with the Nazis. Personal indiscretions might be forgiven by the Führer if the officer were loyal to the regime. Substantial gifts were presented to officers who rendered special services to the party or whose loyalty was thought to be wavering. With middle-ranking officers, persuasion and promotion were employed. The Nazis, of course, had little use for military orthodoxy, and they rapidly advanced military iconoclasts and dissenters such as Guderian and Rommel whose personalities and views were not of the traditional General Staff variety.

More significant in the long run was the infiltration of Nazi-oriented younger officers into the lower ranks. The very speed which the Nazis demanded in the expansion of the army made it difficult, as Beck and others saw it would, for the army to digest its new recruits and indoctrinate them in the code of the corps.

The newer officers were frequently graduates of Nazi youth organizations. Although in the early years of the regime, the army tried to curb the influx of subalterns from this source, the need for leaders eventually forced it to give in. Consequently, a marked difference in outlook rose between the junior and the senior ranks, and by World War II the latter could not be sure of the obedience of their ideologically oriented subordinates if they ordered a military move against Hitler.[22] In the Navy and Air Force the corps of officers had to be built up virtually from scratch; consequently, these services were more predominantly Nazi in outlook.

The final technique of the Nazis in altering the complexion of the officer corps was simply the removal of those who adhered to the professional outlook and values. The first major purge was the Blomberg-Fritsch Crisis of February 1938. Both officers had opposed Hitler's aggressive designs revealed at the conference of commanders on November 5, 1937. Blomberg had also abandoned the soldier's role, embarked upon politics, and aroused the enmity and jealousy of Göring and Himmler. In January 1938, with the Führer's permission, he married a woman beneath his own social level. Two weeks later Göring presented to Hitler police documents proving that the new Frau Blomberg had been a prostitute. This insured Blomberg's dismissal as Commander in Chief of the Wehrmacht. The logical candidate to succeed him, however, was Fritsch, the Army Commander in Chief and a professional soldier through and through. To forestall this appointment Göring and Himmler presented evidence that Fritsch was a homosexual. The charges were untrue, but they were enough to have Fritsch removed from his post pending investigation and to give the Führer opportunity to revamp the officer corps. Six other general officers were retired and a major shake-up of regimental commanders occurred.

The acquiescence of the officer corps to the removal of Fritsch on trumped up charges marked its end as an autonomous organization. Against such machinations, the officers were virtually helpless. Instead of fighting back with the conspiratorial and unscrupulous techniques of totalitarian politics, Fritsch submitted to Gestapo interrogation and considered challenging Himmler to a duel. In the end a special court exonerated him. But by then he was out of a job, and the long arm of the secret police had made itself felt in the army. Subsequently, Fritsch was made honorary colonel of his old regiment. He was, however, a broken, disillusioned man. Just before war began he joined his regiment in East Prussia, writing: "For me there is, neither in peace or war, any part in Herr Hitler's Germany. I shall accompany my regiment only as a target, because I cannot stay at home." [23] On September 22, 1939 he walked into Polish machine gun fire on the outskirts of Warsaw and was killed. Fritsch did not know how to act as a politician in the totalitarian state. But he did know how to die as a soldier on the battlefield. With him died the moral integrity and professional spirit of the German officer corps.

Immediately after Munich three more generals were retired. Two, Beck and Adam, had been outspoken in their opposition to Hitler. The third, von Rundstedt, was a Prussian professional of the old school. From this point on through the war, there was a steady stream of dismissals and retirements of officers who displeased Hitler because of their military caution or their doubtful loyalty. In the fall of 1941, after the Germans had been halted in Russia, Brauchitsch, Rundstedt (who had been called back), Bock, and Leeb left active service. Finally, after the July 20th, 1944 attempt to overthrow the regime, in a mass purge of the high command, twenty generals and one admiral were executed, five other generals committed suicide, and approximately seven hundred officers were either executed or dismissed.[24]

Military Götterdämmerung. The reactions of the military to the Nazi penetration split them into three groups. One clique succumbed to Nazi temptations, abandoned the professional outlook, adopted Nazi views, and were suitably rewarded by the government. Another group, including Hammerstein-Equord, Canaris, Beck, Adam, Witzleben, and most of the July 20th conspirators, also assumed political roles actively opposing Hitler and his policies. Since both these groups abandoned professionalism for politics, it is appropriate to judge them, not by professional, but by political standards. The former share in the guilt of National Socialism; the latter were usually motivated by the highest humanitarian and Christian ideals.

The great bulk of the officer corps had no political yearnings one way or the other and simply desired to follow the proper professional course. In the early days of the Nazi regime this behavior was feasible. The generals did the soldier's job, they issued the soldier's warnings, and, when they were overruled, they did the soldier's duty. After the ouster of Fritsch, however, the military role became impossible. The invasion of the authority of the officer corps and the destruction of its autonomy produced an insoluble conflict. The military code did not permit either total obedience or total resistance. Professional duty to obey the leaders of the state clashed irreconcilably with professional responsibility for the security of the state. "I am a soldier; it is my duty to obey," argued Brauchitsch. Others with equally good military logic disagreed: "The highest commanders in time of war," commented Speidel, "have not always been able to differentiate between the obedience due to God and conscience and the obedience due to men." [25] So the generals struggled along: obeying where there were no grounds for complaint; sabotaging, where possible, impossible policies; temporizing in one place and acquiescing in another; resigning when the situation became intolerable and accepting again the call of duty when it was even worse.

There was nothing politically glorious in this performance. But then they were not trying to act as political figures; they were escaping from politics, and it is not appropriate to judge them by political standards. They were trying to behave like professional soldiers, and it is by the standards of soldiers that they should be judged. By these criteria they come off well. The evil was not in them. It was in the environment which would not permit them to live by the soldier's creed. They could not destroy the evil in the environment without violating that creed and destroying the good in themselves. Their glory and their tragedy was that they adhered to their faith until obliterated by the holocaust.

THE FUTURE OF GERMAN CIVIL-MILITARY RELATIONS. The professional officer corps which was created by Scharnhorst and Gneisenau, and carried to its highest peaks by Moltke, Schlieffen, and Seeckt ceased to exist in World War II. It was a victim of Nazism and its destruction was one of the calamities of the war. It had embodied many of the noblest and best elements of western civilization. Born of enlightened reform, it had been motivated by the ideals of integrity, service, competence, duty, and loyalty. Whatever the uses to which it was put, in and of itself it was a force for reason, realism, and peace. Neither Germany nor the world is better off for its passing.

It remains to be seen what pattern of civil-military relations will emerge in the German Federal Republic. Early plans for the West German army called for a return to some elements of the old tradition. The prevailing tendency, however, seemed to be in a different direction. The Bundestag insisted upon sharing in the control of the military forces. It was stressed that the new army would be basically civilian in character. The decisions of courts martial were to be reviewed by independent boards of civilians. Differentiation among the ranks was to be minimized, the powers of officers curtailed, saluting limited. More significantly, the German government's defense adviser indicated that a commission of civilians would supervise the "inner order" of the army and that all soldiers would go through a special "citizenship course." "Democracy can be defended only by democrats," Herr Blank was quoted as saying, "and freedom only by those who experience it themselves." [26]

The effective implementation of these ideas would inaugurate a third phase in German civil-military relations. The aristocratic army of Frederick the Great was destroyed by Napoleon. The professional army created by Scharnhorst and Gneisenau was destroyed by Hitler. Now the proposal was to create a democratic army, an ideologically motivated force embodying subjective rather than objective civilian control. In part, this approach was a reaction against the professionalism of the past and the product of the false identification of that professionalism with Hitler. Ironically, it was also in part an imitation of the American conquerors of Hitler. But the changes of the Bonn government were not for the better. They were a retrogression to a more primitive form of civil-military relations. Inevitably they will foster the permanent embroilment of the German military in politics and reduce the fighting effectiveness of the new army. Despite what Herr Blank had to say, a democratic state is better defended by a professional force than by a democratic force. The Federal German Republic possesses the confidence of its citizens and strong central in-

stitutions such as the Weimar Republic never had. The obstacles
to civilian control which existed in the twenties no longer exist.
It would be tragic if the new German democracy did not
seize the opportunity to reestablish an effective system of civilian
control and a professional officer corps. It could do far worse
than to resurrect the tradition of Scharnhorst, Gneisenau, and
Clausewitz.

JAPAN: THE CONTINUITY OF POLITICAL MILITARISM

NATIONAL IDEOLOGY: SHINTO AND BUSHIDO. The key factor
influencing Japanese civil-military relations was the persistence of
feudalism through seven hundred years down to 1868. Under
feudalism the ruling class in Japanese society had been composed
of the Emperor who was a figurehead, the shogun who was the
real ruler of the country, the local lords or daimyo, and the samurai or warriors who were the followers of the shogun and the
daimyo. The mass of people, including the peasants and the small
mercantile class, were excluded from political affairs. The Restoration of 1867–1868 ended feudalism. The shogunate was abolished, the Emperor brought out of seclusion and given an active
role in the direction of national affairs, and power transferred from
the local lords to the national government. The samurai were the
leaders in this reassertion of imperial control and in the formation of the new institutions of government.

The national ideology of Japan which set the basic framework
of Japanese thinking down to 1945 was essentially a compound
of two interrelated systems of thought reflecting imperial authority
and samurai rule. These were embodied respectively in State Shinto
and Bushido. State Shinto expressed the unity of government and
religion in Japanese life. It had three basic doctrines.[27] The belief in "unbroken divine imperial sovereignty" was reflected in
Articles I and III of the Constitution of 1889, which provided that
"The Empire of Japan shall be reigned over and governed by a
line of Emperors unbroken for ages eternal" and that "The Emperor is sacred and unviolable." The Emperor was a living god,
his will was absolute, and the highest duty of the subject was not
merely obedience to that will but identification with it: the loss
of self in enthusiasm for the Emperor. Shinto's second element

was belief in the divine origin of the Japanese nation itself. The Japanese were a uniquely gifted people with divinely ordained institutions: "the national gods have given to Japan a divine land, a divine racial psychology, and a divinely established structure in the state." Finally, there was the belief in the divine mission of Japan. Each nation of the world must assume its rightful place in the hierarchy of things. Japan's mission was in the words of one admiral to make "the boundless virtues of the Emperor prevail throughout the whole world." The world was to be brought under one roof through benevolent Japanese leadership although it might be necessary at times to use military force in fulfilling this mission.

The other element in the Japanese national ideology was the ancient ethic of the samurai, the moral code of the military class of Japanese feudalism. After the end of feudalism this code was romanticized and given the name of Bushido: the ways of the military knights. The Bushido code had many resemblances to the standards of conduct of European chivalry. The values of Bushido were the values of the warrior, the lover of violence for its own sake. The sword was "the soul of the samurai" and the "symbol of God." After 1867 this bellicose code which had been the property of a relatively limited class became the ideology of the entire people; Japan became "incontestably a warlike nation." [28] The national ethic combining State Shinto and Bushido was thus a synthesis of imperial nationalism and feudal militarism. It was authoritarian, ethnocentric, nationalistic, imperially oriented (in the sense of both Emperor-worship and glorification of the Japanese empire), expansionist, and bellicose with high value assigned to the warrior and the warrior virtues.

THE JAPANESE MILITARY MIND. The Japanese military strongly adhered to the national ideology. The reasons for this are simple. The same forces which brought about the Restoration of 1868 and stimulated the rise of this national ideology also created the modern Japanese armed services. The armed services, moreover, occupied a very peculiar place in the ideology. They were closely identified with the Emperor; they were an essential if not preëminent requirement for the fulfillment of the world mission of the Yamato race; and they were the continuing embodiment of the samurai tradition. The national ideology served the military and the military served the ideology. The Japanese Army thus, in contrast with the German military, achieved Schleicher's ideal of always being in tune with the dominant spirit of the times. There was no tension between military values and political values. Consequently, Japan had "the most political army" in the world.[29] Given the nature of the national ideology and its strong associations with the feudal tradition, it also made the Japanese officer corps the major military body in the world most lacking in professional spirit.

The impotence of the professional ethic in the Japanese military forces was all the more surprising because in the decades after 1868 the new leaders of the government consciously strove to model their military institutions upon those of the West. French and then German military advisers aided in the creation of the Japanese Army. Military colleges were established. A naval academy was set up in 1872, a naval engineering school in 1876, and a naval staff college in 1888. The system of officer recruitment was very similar to that of Germany. The requirements for promotion were such as might be found in any European officer corps. But it was impossible to import the professional outlook which in the West had developed along with these institutional devices. Japan had the form, the external shell, of military professionalism, but not the substance. The Japanese military mind remained dominated by the popular ideology. Only in the twentieth century did something resembling the professional military ethic gain a foothold in the officer corps and even then it was limited to a relatively weak and distinctly minority group. The dominant ideals of the Japanese military remained fundamentally opposed to this ethic.

The most basic manifestation of this opposition concerned the concept of the ideal officer. The professional military ethic draws a distinction between the military virtues and the warrior virtues. For the Japanese, however, the ideal officer was a warrior — a fighter engaging in violence himself rather than a manager directing the employment of violence by others. This was a feudal, not a professional, ideal. As one observer described the Japanese officer, he was perhaps inferior technically to his western counterpart, but this was compensated for by "magnificent 'nerve' and fighting ardor."

> The Japanese officer . . . is a magnificent leader of men. His weakness consists of his failing to remain master of a combat, as European officers do. He goes through with a battle rather than directs it. His courage and conception of honor are far more inspired by a warring passion than by a real and realistic understanding of the necessities of the craft of arms . . . The Japanese is more of a warrior than a military man, and therein lies his weakness. The difference may be a subtle one, but it does exist: the essential quality of the warrior is bravery; that of the military man, discipline.[30]

Officer indoctrination in the Japanese military forces stressed the importance of courage under fire far more than scientific accomplishment. Associated with this was the close bond which existed between officers and men in the Japanese Army. All were warriors together. The officers did not constitute a fundamentally different group with skills and abilities not possessed by the enlisted men.

The professional military man tends to focus upon the balance of material strength between opposing nations. Japanese military thought, however, minimized the role of material factors. Spirit alone was decisive: this was a basic concept of Bushido. Superior armaments were not responsible for Japanese victories:

> No! What won the battles on the Yalu, in Corea and Manchuria, were the ghosts of our fathers, guiding our hands and beating in our hearts. They are not dead, those ghosts, the spirits of our warlike ancestors.[31]

Or as one officer put it: "The Imperial Army of Japan attaches more importance to spiritual training than to the art of war. Moral strength is greater than physical force."[32] General Araki, War Minister during the 1930's, declared that the mission of Japan was to

> . . . spread and glorify the Imperial way to the end of the Four Seas. Inadequacy of strength is not our worry. Why should we worry about that which is material?[33]

War, consequently, was the test of faith. The nation with the stronger faith not the stronger armaments would come out on top.

Because of their divinely ordained role, this must necessarily be the Japanese. For the western military thinker, God is almost inevitably on the side of the bigger battalions; for the Japanese, He was on the side of the Yamato race. The military had few objections to war with the United States because, despite our incomparably greater resources, our spirit was weaker than theirs. The Japanese military mind was thus subjective rather than objective, involved rather than detached. Because it was imbued with the national ideology it was difficult if not impossible for it to analyze a military situation in a coldly realistic, scientific manner.* Japanese military training emphasized "spiritual mobilization" — *Seishin Kyoiku* — as the most important aspect of preparing troops for battle. Essentially, this was indoctrination in the spirit and principles of the Japanese national ideology: the identification of the individual with the nation and his subordination to the will of the Emperor. It was the continuation of a process which had begun much earlier in the schools. One reason for conscription in Japan was the opportunity it presented for the military to train virtually the entire male population in the ideals of Bushido and the Kodo (the Imperial Way).

The minimizing of the intellect and the exaltation of the spirit produced a notable lack of professional military writing in Japan. Although from 1905 to 1945 Japan was a major naval power, no Japanese writer ever formulated a significant theory on the nature and employment of seapower. Virtually their only writing upon this subject before World War II was either sensationalist or highly elementary. Scholarly analyses were absent. The same was true with respect to land operations. Japan "never produced a standard work on the science of war." [34] Similarly, military history, the

---

* "From a military standpoint the Japanese mind may be described as being subjective rather than objective. In peacetime, an American writer can impassionately discuss a war in the Pacific just as a British student can compose a disquisition upon command of the Mediterranean; and either can discuss at length imaginary campaigns wherein France is opposed to Italy or Germany to Russia. The Japanese, on the contrary, lack interest in waters which do not directly concern them. Whereas the western student will proceed along purely academic lines, concentrating upon the naval factors alone, the Japanese find difficulty in eliminating the national-political approach. As a rule they have been unable to discuss Guam without stating or implying that it was a threat to their country which must be removed." Alexander Kiralfy, "Japanese Naval Strategy," in Edward Mead Earle (ed.), *Makers of Modern Strategy* (Princeton, 1952), p. 459.

core of professional study in the West, was not studied anywhere in the Japanese military educational system except at the Staff College. Only after World War I did military periodicals in a significant number and quality begin appearing in Japan, and so far as naval affairs were concerned these too remained on a very elementary level.

The discipline of the Japanese military forces was a holdover from feudalism. Officers and soldiers had to be instantly prepared to sacrifice their lives for the Emperor. For the Japanese military man, there was no higher achievement than to die in battle with the cry of *"Tenno Heika Banzai"* on his lips. All soldiers who died in battle were deified and their names inscribed in a national shrine. The warrior code, moreover, did not permit retreat. Unlike realistic western professional military thought which recognizes that retreat may well be a military necessity and that consequently it is desirable to prepare for it, Japanese doctrine refused to consider it an admissible alternative. Along with this was the tradition of "death rather than surrender," the refusal to recognize that from a realistic military viewpoint the latter may be a legitimate course of action. In the words of General Araki:

> Retreat and surrender are not permissible in our Army . . . To become a captive of the enemy by surrendering after doing their best is regarded by foreign soldiers as acceptable conduct. But according to our traditional Bushido, retreat and surrender constitute the greatest disgrace and are actions unbecoming to a Japanese soldier.[35]

In contrast to the professional military view that war is generally undesirable and that it is the last resort of national policy, the Japanese feudal warrior tended to praise violence and glorify war as an end in itself. The Japanese Ministry of War declared that: "War is the Father of Creation and the Mother of Culture. Rivalry for Supremacy does for the state what struggling against adversity does for the individual. It is such impetus, in the one case, as in the other, that prompts the birth and development of Life and Cultural Creation."[36] With this philosophy of war in general it is not surprising that the Japanese military in specific circumstances favored war as a means of achieving national goals. The army leaders in particular were bellicose; the admirals, who played a lesser role in politics, tended to be more conservative and professionally oriented. The Japanese military were eager for the 1894–1895 conflict with China. They urged the acquisition of the Liaotung Peninsula at the end of that war. They favored a strong policy against China during World War I. They wanted to expand Japanese influence through Siberia during the intervention there after the war. They were responsible for the intervention in China in 1928 and for the attack on Manchuria in 1931. Finally, they initiated the China incident in 1937, and the army leaders at least (the navy was more hesitant) advocated the attacks upon American and British possessions in December 1941. This record of consistent support for aggression by the politically oriented Japanese military leaders stands in marked contrast to the persistent warnings against adventurism offered to their government by the professionally inclined German generals. Whereas in Germany the military opposed withdrawal from the League of Nations and remilitarization in violation of the Versailles Treaty, in Japan they supported withdrawal and the denunciation of the London Naval Treaty. The more extreme groups within the Japanese officer corps were quite explicit in formulating a philosophy to justify Japanese dominance of East Asia.

MILITARY AUTHORITY: DUAL GOVERNMENT. The legal structure of civil-military relations in the Japanese state was essentially one of military independence. The government was divided into two spheres: military and civil. The theory was *niju seifu:* "dual government." But, while civilians could exercise no authority within the military area, the military, on the other hand, by virtue of their political influence, could easily expand their power into the civil area.

Legal authority for this dual government stemmed from the constitution and from custom. The Constitution of 1889 made the Emperor supreme commander of the military forces, gave him authority to determine their organization and peace standing, and authorized him to declare war, make peace, and conclude treaties. These clauses furnished the constitutional justification for the direct relation between all top military leaders and the Emperor. Unlike the civilian members of the cabinet, the Ministers of War and the Navy did not have to go through the Prime Minister to reach the Emperor. Neither did the Chiefs of Staff nor the commanding generals and admirals. The Emperor exercised military command directly. The military were his personal implements. This close identification of the forces with the Throne provided the objective basis for military adherence to State Shinto with its glorification of the Emperor. It also placed the Japanese military forces in a unique legal position. "Armies abroad," as one general said, "exist on a legal basis, but the Imperial army is founded on that which is infinitely more precious than law." [37] The military exercise of their functions free from civilian interference was guaranteed by an imperial Ordinance of 1889 which provided that, "With the exception of questions of *gunki* (strategy) and *gunrei* (military command), which, having been reported directly to the Emperor, may have been submitted to the cabinet for deliberation, the ministers of state for war and the navy shall report to the minister president of the state." [38] The premier and the cabinet — the civil government of the state — were precluded from rendering advice to the throne on military and naval operations, strategy, and the internal organization, education, and discipline of the armed forces.

The freedom of the military from civilian interference was further guaranteed by the prohibition against appointing civilians to the posts of Minister of War and Minister of the Navy. In 1900 the previously existing custom that only top officers could hold these posts was written into law. Only a general or lieutenant general of the army on active service could be Minister of War. Only an admiral or vice admiral on active service could be Minister of the Navy. In 1912 this restriction was limited so as to permit the appointment of reserve officers of comparable rank. This liberalization, however, only lasted until 1936 when the return was made to the 1900 procedure. It was frequently customary for the service ministers not to resign when cabinets changed but to stay on through many governments, a fact which emphasized their distinct position compared to the civilian ministers.

This complete division of authority between civil and military resulted, of course, in continuous friction between them. Since there was no easy way of defining their respective spheres of responsibility, the support of both was necessary to carry on the government. The vagaries and vicissitudes of civilian politics, however, put the military in a superior position. As General Araki once said: "A Minister of War is able to force the adoption of any measure desired by the Camp or to block any measure that meets his disapproval." [39] This result was brought about simply by the threat to resign. Since the cabinet had to have a Minister of War and a Minister of the Navy, and since only military officers could fill these posts, each service could bring about the downfall of the cabinet by having its representative resign or could prevent the formation of a new cabinet until its demands were met. Time and again, this form of military pressure occurred in Japanese history.* Dual government was further strengthened by the manner in which finances were handled. The Throne — that is, the military leaders in practice — had the authority to set the peacetime strength of the armed services. Appropriations had to be made by the Diet, but if the Diet refused to appropriate funds, the previous year's budget was automatically continued. The estimates for the civilian departments were presented to the Diet by the Finance Minister while the Ministers of War and Navy defended their own budgets before the legislature. Usually the ministers discouraged and frustrated any real parliamentary discussions of military policy.

The one possible weak point which existed in the military

---

* In 1912, when the cabinet of Prince Saionji rejected a demand for an increase in army strength, the War Minister resigned and the cabinet fell. In 1914, Viscount Kiyoura attempted to form a cabinet but no admiral would serve as Navy Minister and he had to give up his efforts. In 1936, when Hirota formed a cabinet, the army vetoed his proposed appointments to the foreign office, the colonial office, and the justice ministry, and forced the selection of men more in accord with its views. A year later the army broke with Hirota, the war minister resigned, and the cabinet fell. A liberal officer, General Ugaki, was called upon to become premier. The dominant forces in the army, however, had old scores to settle with Ugaki and defeated him by refusing to permit any generals to join the cabinet. The army was more lenient with General Hayashi, who succeeded where Ugaki failed, but the army dictated his choice of War Minister and his cabinet program. In 1940 the downfall of the Yonai cabinet was precipitated by the resignation of the army representative, and Yonai was replaced by Konoye who adopted the army program almost completely. See Chitoshi Yanaga "The Military and the Government in Japan," *Amer. Pol. Sci. Rev.*, XXXV (June 1941), 535–539; Hillis Lory, *Japan's Military Masters* (New York, 1943), ch. 5; Hugh Borton, *Japan Since 1931* (New York, 1940), pp. 45–55.

structure of authority was the division of responsibility among a large number of military offices. In this respect Japanese organization resembled pre-World War I German organization. The army was headed by the "Big Three": the Minister of War, the Chief of the Army General Staff, and the Inspector General of Military Training. Naval organization culminated in the minister and the Chief of the Naval Staff. In addition, there was the Board of Field Marshals and Fleet Admirals created in 1898 which, however, was primarily an honorific body. More significant was the Supreme Military Council made up of all the leading generals and admirals and responsible for broad military policy. During war an Imperial Headquarters came into existence drawn from the army and navy staffs. The potential rivalry of these various organizations was curbed by the mutual feeling that they could all increase their power by working together. In 1931, for instance, when the political parties were increasing in importance, the Big Three of the army reached an understanding that all significant personnel appointments would only be made with their mutual concurrence. Subsequently, the War Minister became more powerful and, in 1935, asserted his authority over the Inspector General of Military Training. The understanding of 1931 was abrogated, and the minister assumed full authority with respect to appointments. The Minister of War thus tended to become first among equals. Either cooperation among the military authorities, or the subordination of one to another, prevented civilians from benefiting by the profusion of military offices.[40]

While, theoretically, the two Japanese governments functioned in entirely separate spheres, in practice the civilians remained excluded from military affairs while the military played an active role in civilian affairs. Both the authority and the influence of the military extended into foreign and domestic policy. One Minister of War stated that, "While the generally accepted limits of the deliberations of the Supreme Military Council are matters of policy pertaining to national defence, there are in fact no limitations or qualifications to the scope of its deliberations." [41] Dual government inevitably produced dual diplomacy. The actions taken by military commanders to safeguard their forces and meet the requirements of the situation in the field were not subject to control by the cabinet. In the Manchurian crisis of 1931, for example, the military commanders in the field, supported by the military leadership in Tokyo, pursued an independent line which frustrated the Foreign Minister's efforts to limit the effects of the September 18th incident. The military ordered Japanese forces in Korea across the border into Manchuria despite the opposition of the foreign office and the cabinet. A few weeks later the Foreign Minister assured the United States that the Japanese would not attack the border town of Chinchow, but the army went right ahead and occupied it anyway. One general expressed the military view with respect to Manchuria when he wrote that "it would be very dangerous to have trusted our national diplomacy to the Ministry of Foreign Affairs, which is incapable of visualizing our national destinies . . . only the army is able to conduct a national policy." [42]

The military not only tended to pursue their own foreign policy, but also had no hesitations in pushing the adoption of a definite domestic economic program. General Araki once said, "The army should be prepared not only for military action but for solving economic, social and cultural problems, pursuing in foreign policy an independent line founded on firm, sound and just premises." [43] The war ministry during the 1930's evolved an entire economic philosophy of "Imperial Socialism" which more or less amounted to a military welfare state. The principal opposition to the military in domestic politics normally came from the upper bourgeoisie, and the military economic program was anti-capitalist in spirit. It opposed free enterprise, and favored rigid state controls over the economy, expanded social security and unemployment insurance programs, and revision of the tax system to prevent the accumulation of great concentrations of wealth. Many of the economic ideas of the military found their way into the National Mobilization Law passed in 1938.

MILITARY POLITICAL INFLUENCE. The political influence of the military in Japanese society remained constantly high throughout this period. Its only lapse occurred during the years from 1922 to 1931 when there seemed to be little likelihood of war and Japan had its only real experiences with responsible party government. This low point in military influence also reflected a shift in the foundation of military power from clan support to more widely based popular support. The political influence of the military in Japan had five key elements.

First, there was the affiliation of the military with the powerful western clans of Japan, the Choshu and the Satsuma. These clans had provided most of the leadership for the Restoration of 1868. In the years after the Restoration the Choshu dominated the army and the Satsuma the navy. Down to 1922 virtually all the high officers of the services were drawn from one or the other of these two clans. Since the rivalry between the two pervaded the government generally, this tended to draw the military into politics, but it also afforded each service a secure basis of political support and leadership. In 1909, for instance, the Choshu clan included Marshal Yamagata, the most influential elder statesman in the government, the Prime Minister, the Minister of War and the Chief of the Army Staff. Virtually all the leading admirals (except for the Navy Minister) and a number of generals, on the other hand, were members of the Satsuma clan. The affiliations of the services with these samurai groups began to diminish about the time of the First World War. Choshu influence was greatly weakened by the death of Yamagata in 1922. It became physically impossible for the clans to maintain their monopoly in the officer corps. Representatives of lesser clans and of the bourgeoisie began to find their way into the military hierarchy. By the end of the 1920's the officer corps was drawing its recruits predominantly from the lower middle class: the small landowners, shopkeepers, small factory owners, and the like. This broadening of the base of the officer corps was in many respects similar to the gradual weakening of the affiliations of the German military with the Junker aristocracy. It tended to shift the primary reliance of the military for support from a concentrated social-geographic group to society at large.

A second element in the political influence of the Japanese military was almost entirely missing in the case of Germany. This was the phenomenon of military men holding important nonmilitary posts in government. In Germany the political soldier such as Caprivi and Schleicher was the exception; in Japan the soldier-statesman was the rule, the combination of military and nonmilitary functions in the same person being a continuation of the feudal tradition. In the early days of the Restoration military leaders played an important role in codifying laws, establishing an education system, organizing the national bureaucracy, and carrying out many other reforms. In the following years it became the accepted thing for military men to hold top posts in the government. Their influence was felt in the cabinet, the Privy Council, and the Imperial Household.

From the inauguration of cabinet government in December 1885 to the surrender in August 1945, Japan had thirty premiers heading forty-two cabinets. Fifteen of the premiers were generals or admirals and they led nineteen governments. Three Choshu generals, Yamagata, Katsura, and Terauchi, occupied the premiership for more than half of the thirty years from 1889 to 1918. Military participation in civil government declined during the years of party dominance in the 1920's. But even then Admirals Kato and Yamamoto were premiers in 1923 and 1924, and General Tanaka from 1927 to 1929. After the Manchurian incident military influence was again in the ascendant. Admirals Saito and Okado held the premiership from May 1932 to February 1936, and, from that date to the surrender in August 1945, Japan had nine premiers, four of whom were generals and two admirals. The longest occupant of the office was General Tojo who was in from October 1941 to July 1944. Whether or not the cabinets were headed by military men, officers frequently occupied nonmilitary posts. The military held five of the ten positions in the Yamagata cabinet of 1898–1900. When he was premier from 1927 to 1929, General Tanaka also held the position of Foreign Minister. At various times during the 1930's military men held the posts of Minister of Home Affairs, Foreign Minister, and Minister of Education.

Military influence also was felt in other branches of the government. Marshal Yamagata was president of the Privy Council from 1902 to 1922 and one of the most influential members of the Genro, the body of elder statesmen who advised the Throne. He was regarded "both in politics and in military affairs, as the power behind the throne, the maker or breaker of Cabinets, and the man whose word was law." [44] The Council usually had a promilitary orientation; in 1930, for instance, it blocked for five months ratification of the London Naval Treaty. Traditionally the military were also strong among the advisers to the Emperor in the Imperial Household. In the 1930's, however, their influence there was weakened by the appointment of a number of more liberally minded statesmen to the court positions.

A third important element in the political power of the military was the support which they received from patriotic, fascist, and militaristic societies. These included small secret societies such as the Black Ocean and Black Dragon groups as well as large mass organizations such as the Ex-Servicemen's Association, the Patriotic Women's Society, and the Women's Society for National Defense. The activities of these and other groups ranged from terrorism to propaganda. Military officers frequently played an important role in organizing, leading, and financing them, and the groups invariably supported military foreign and domestic policies of external expansion and internal reforms and control.

With the decline of clan influence the most significant political support of the military came from the people as a whole. The Army in particular went to great lengths to identify itself with the common man. In the years immediately after the Restoration, military service was required of all able-bodied males and the ranks of the officer corps were open to all on the basis of merit. The Army traditionally followed a highly paternalistic policy toward those serving in its ranks and promoted many schemes for improving the welfare of the Japanese masses. Both major political parties before World War II were closely tied in with the interests of big business. The Army frequently attacked this "corrupt" alliance of politicians, industrialists, and bankers, and endeavored to identify itself as standing for impartial, efficient, honest administration of national affairs in the interests of the nation as a whole. It became the embodiment of the national interests and national ideals. While the popular support of the Army waned in the 1920's, the military never lost their fundamental appeal to the average man of Japan.

A fifth and final aspect of military political influence was the reversion in 1931 to terroristic methods of government in Japan. In effect, this involved the superimposing of an extralegal system of violence upon the formal system of constitutional government.

Political leaders who opposed military demands ran the risk of assassination. Premier Hamaguchi who put through the London Naval Treaty was attacked in November 1930 and died of his wounds. His successor, Inukai, was murdered in the military uprising of May 15, 1932. The most elaborate plot was that of February 26, 1936 in which the Lord Keeper of the Privy Seal, the Inspector General of Military Education, and the Finance Minister were assassinated and most of the other high governmental officials barely escaped with their lives. The perpetrators of these assassinations were young officers and cadets who felt that the government was not taking strong enough measures to put through the military program at home and abroad. While the relation between these extremist younger officers and the top military leaders was by no means clear, every outbreak of violence clearly redounded to the benefit of the latter. Each of the major assaults was followed by a substantial increase in military influence and concessions to military demands. After the February 26th incident, the military virtually dictated the composition of the new cabinet and secured a repeal of the 1912 ordinance which permitted reserve officers to become service ministers. The undercover threat of violence was a key component of military political influence. The German officers were psychologically incapable of carrying out even one assassination successfully; their Japanese counterparts suffered from no such inhibitions nor lack of skills.

THE FUTURE OF JAPANESE CIVIL-MILITARY RELATIONS. The pattern of sustained military involvement in politics ended with the destruction of the Japanese officer corps in 1945. The slate was wiped clean, and for eight years after her defeat the only civil-military relations in Japan was between the American occupation authorities and the Japanese civilian institutions. Immediately after Japan regained sovereignty, she still had no armed forces to speak of, and, consequently, no real civil-military relations. This situation could not continue indefinitely. Starting with a *tabula rasa,* Japan, in a sense, possesses an unusual freedom in creating new military institutions. An awareness among Japanese leaders of the political character of the old officer corps and its disastrous consequences could lead to an insistence upon the absolute abstention of the new one from politics. On the other hand, the contemporary ideology of Japan is strongly pacifist. Although vastly different from the prewar bellicose nationalism, it is equally hostile to military professionalism. In addition, the absence of a professional military tradition and the influence of American ideas and practices are likely to complicate further the achievement of objective civilian control. The odds would appear to favor the emergence in Japan of a system of civil-military relations differing in appearance but not in essentials from that which prevailed prior to 1945.

PART II

MILITARY POWER IN AMERICA: THE HISTORICAL EXPERIENCE, 1789–1940

6

The Ideological Constant: The Liberal Society versus Military Professionalism

THE HISTORICAL CONSTANTS OF AMERICAN CIVIL-MILITARY RELATIONS

Liberalism has always been the dominant ideology in the United States. The American Constitution, on the other hand, is fundamentally conservative, the product of men who feared concentrated political power and who provided for the widespread dispersion of that power among numerous governmental units. Yet, the outstanding historical fact of American civil-military relations has been the extent to which liberal ideology and conservative Constitution combined to dictate an inverse relation between political power and military professionalism. From the birth of the Republic through the Second World War liberalism and the Constitution were the relatively unchanging environmental constants of American civil-military relations. Together, they delayed the professionalization of officership in America until it had almost been completed in Europe. Together, they made objective civilian control depend upon the virtually total exclusion of the military from political power.

THE PREVALENCE OF LIBERALISM IN THE UNITED STATES

On the first of June 1784 the American Army numbered seven hundred men under the command of Major General Henry Knox. Six months earlier the Revolution had come to an end; Sir Guy Carleton had evacuated New York; Washington had said farewell to his officers at Fraunces' Tavern. The seven hundred men were the only regular military force in the United States, the last remnant of the Continental Army. On June 2, 1784 the Continental Congress, agreeing with Elbridge Gerry that "standing armies in time of peace are inconsistent with the principles of republican Governments, dangerous to the liberties of a free people, and generally converted into destructive engines for establishing despotism," ordered the disbanding of this remnant:

> Resolved, That the commanding officer be and he is hereby directed to discharge the troops now in the service of the United States, except twenty-five privates, to guard the stores at Fort Pitt, and fifty-five to guard the stores at West Point and other magazines, with a proportionate number of officers; no officer to remain in service above the rank of a captain . . .

Having thus reduced the regular army to eighty caretakers, the Congress then requested the states to furnish it with seven hundred militia to garrison the western frontier.

A little over 131 years later, in the autumn of 1915, the Acting Secretary of War, Henry Breckinridge, was summoned to the presence of Woodrow Wilson. He found the President "trembling and white with passion," holding in his hands a copy of the *Baltimore Sun*. The President pointed to a story in the paper reporting that the General Staff was preparing plans for the eventuality of war with Germany. When the President asked him if this were true, Breckinridge replied that he did not know. The President then directed him to investigate, and, if he found that it was true, to relieve every officer on the General Staff and order him out of Washington.[1]

These incidents together illustrate two basic points concerning the American political mind. First, liberalism dominated American thinking from the Revolution through the first half of the twentieth century. Second, liberalism does not understand and is hostile to military institutions and the military function.

The universality of liberalism in the United States and its essentially static quality contrast with the variety and dynamism of ideologies in Europe. The Frenchman has had firsthand experience with aristocratic conservatism, revolutionary democracy, Bonapartism, clericalism, monarchism, liberalism, socialism, com-

munism. The American knows only liberalism. The political outlook of the Englishman today, be he socialist or Tory, is fundamentally different from that of the average Englishman at the end
of the eighteenth century. The political ideology of Woodrow
Wilson was essentially the same as that of Elbridge Gerry. Liberalism in the United States has been unchanging, monotonous,
and all-embracing.

The American colonists inherited their liberal ideas from the
English tradition of Locke. The dominance of liberalism in America, however, was the product not of inheritance but of economic
expansion and international isolation. Steady economic growth
diluted class conflict. There were few struggles over the distribution of the pie because the pie was always growing larger. No
nascent group ever developed a radical ideology challenging the
established order: it was always too quickly assimilated into that
order. Nor did any established group (with two exceptions) ever
develop a conservative ideology defending its interests against
radical onslaught. The oncoming wave always evaporated short
of the gates of the castle. Radicalism and conservatism were equally
superfluous. Incipient and established groups both adhered to liberalism. In the absence of European feudalism, European classes,
and a European proletariat, political struggle in America was restricted to squabbles for limited objectives among interest groups
all of whom shared the same basic values.[2] The great political controversies of American history with a few exceptions have been
between two or more varieties of liberalism. The isolation of the
United States from world politics in the nineteenth century reinforced the dominance of liberalism. National security was a simple
given fact — the starting point of political analysis — not the end
result of conscious policy. What need was there for a philosophy
to explain America's relation with the rest of the world and to suggest the proper course of conduct in international affairs? Not only
did every group in American society normally feel economically
secure but also American society as a whole normally felt politically
secure. American awareness of the role of power in domestic politics was dulled by the absence of class conflict. American awareness
of the role of power in foreign politics was dulled by the absence
of external threats.

The pervasiveness of the liberal doctrine in the United States has been commented upon by foreign observers from De Tocqueville to Myrdal. Liberalism permeated American society and created a uniformity of belief among the American people which would be the envy of a totalitarian dictator. Even those institutions which inherently seem to be most illiberal capitulated before its influence. Organized religion is normally a conservative force. In America, however, Protestantism was refashioned in the liberal image and even Catholicism was significantly influenced by the liberal environment. More than a century separated Jonathan Edwards from Henry Ward Beecher. While the conquest of religion was perhaps liberalism's most significant victory ideologically, its acceptance by business was much more significant politically. The ideology of American business — that peculiar mixture of Enlightenment rationalism, liberalized Protestantism, Social Darwinism, and orthodox economic individualism — was liberal to the core. Along with the other groups in American society, business never felt impelled to develop a conservative ideology. It joined with the churches, the universities, the professions, and the labor movement in adhering to the liberal creed of individualism, rationalism, and progress.

Only two significant groups in American history failed to adhere to the liberal ideology. Both were genuinely conservative and both existed before the Civil War. The Federalists had their roots in the New England and Atlantic coast commercial and manufacturing interests in the period roughly from 1789 to 1812. Their conservatism derived from both internal and external challenges. At home they believed themselves to be the party of the "rich and well born," and the more extreme Federalists feared a social revolution on the French model by the propertyless elements of the cities and the back country farmers of the frontier. The Federalists were also responsible for the conduct of American foreign policy during the first twelve years of the Republic when European interests still threatened the infant nation. The United States was surrounded by French, English, and Spanish territory, and by the British fleet. They thus had a legitimate concern for the national security. The conservative ideology of the Federalists was reflected in the writing of Hamilton and John Adams, the general temper and attitudes of Washington, and the judicial statesmanship of John Marshall. The domestic source of Federalist conservatism disappeared, however, when the Jeffersonian Revolution of 1800 turned out to be a false alarm. The diluting principle was already at work; there were no mobs in the streets, no confiscation of private property, no guillotines. Class distinctions blurred instead of hardening and eventually melted in the Era of Good Feelings. John Quincy Adams, of impeccable Federalist heritage, was elected President by the Jeffersonian party, thus fulfilling its founder's inaugural dictum that "We are all Federalists; we are all Republicans." Externally, the Treaty of Ghent marked the withdrawal of Europe from America and the beginning of eighty years of splendid continental isolation on the part of the United States. As the threats at home and abroad disappeared, conservative Federalism vanished also.

The second exception to liberal dominance was the ante-bellum South. The causes of Southern conservatism were primarily domestic. The Southern social system was an illiberal island in a liberal society. In self-defense the Southerners, like the Federalists before them, demonstrated their conservatism by creative and original political speculation. Paradoxically, America, the land of liberalism, never produced an outstanding liberal political theorist. Unchallenged at home and from abroad, American liberalism suffered from the absence of competition; liberal writers were content to repeat eighteenth-century formulas. Conservatives, forced to justify themselves in a hostile society, however, were driven to political theory, and the Old South produced notable conservative expressions in the work of George Fitzhugh and John C. Calhoun. Unlike the Federalists, moreover, the Southerners had good grounds for their domestic fears. The slaveowners were the only significant social group in the history of the United States ever to be forcibly dispossessed of their property. The Civil War settled the fate of Southern conservatism. After 1865 liberalism reigned unchallenged on the American scene.*

The American liberal approach to military affairs was hostile, static, and dominant; the conservative approach of the Federalists and the South sympathetic, constructive, and thwarted. It is no

---

* The Neo-Hamiltonians of the turn of the century — Theodore Roosevelt, Henry Cabot Lodge, Elihu Root, Herbert Croly — were semi-conservative. See below, Chapter 10.

coincidence that the two statesmen who displayed the most penetrating insight into military policy and the deepest appreciation of
the military function were the two great spokesmen of the conservative groups: Alexander Hamilton and John C. Calhoun. They stand
in sharp contrast to liberal leaders not just in their views on military
policy but in their interest in military affairs. In more than a
hundred and fifty years American liberalism never produced a governmental leader with comparable ability and interest in military
matters. Hamilton and Calhoun, however, were isolated from the
mainstream of American intellectual and political development.
Their military policy, like their political philosophy, was never
popular with the American people. The avalanche of liberalism
brushed them aside into a discredited cranny of history.

THE LIBERAL APPROACH TO MILITARY AFFAIRS

What I come to is a sense of suddenly being left in the lurch, of suddenly finding that a philosophy upon which I relied to carry us through
no longer works . . . The contrast between what liberals ought to
be doing and saying if democratic values are to be conserved, and what
the real forces are imposing upon them, strikes too sternly on my intellectual senses.[3]

These words of Randolph Bourne six months after America's entry
into World War I poignantly expressed the futility experienced by a
sensitive and acute observer as he tried to apply the philosophy of
liberalism to the problem of war. The stubborn fact facing Bourne
was simply that his philosophy did not furnish means to think
about war, peace, and international relations. These problems were,
to use the phrase of E. F. M. Durbin, "the greater, excluded question" of liberalism. Magnificently varied and creative when limited
to domestic issues, liberalism faltered when applied to foreign
policy and defense. This failure was characteristic of liberalism in
Europe as well as in the United States, but in Europe its implications were not so obvious. Each European country had other philosophies competing with liberalism which furnished more competent ways of dealing with national security. The dominance of the
liberal mind in the United States, however, meant, first, that the
absence of a conservative or other more useful philosophy on foreign affairs was much more keenly felt in the conduct of American

foreign and defense policies, and, secondly, that American liberalism, unable to evade responsibility in this area, tried far more extensively than European liberalism to create a liberal approach to interstate relations. On the other hand, American experience also tended to reinforce and magnify the principal elements in liberal thought which contributed to its incapacity in international relations. These elements of American liberalism were (1) its indifference to international affairs, (2) its application of domestic solutions to international affairs, and (3) its search for objectivity in international affairs.

Liberalism originated in the assertion of the rights of the individual against the state. Liberal thought focused upon the relation of the individual to the state and the relations among individuals within a society. Liberalism never questioned the existence of the state. Instead it presupposed the state's self-sufficiency and external security. In his classic work on European liberalism, for instance, Ruggiero assigned three functions to the liberal state: the political function of adjusting and synthesizing the interests within society; the legal function of guaranteeing the rights of the individual; and the economic and social function of broadening the opportunities for individual self-development. He did not give the liberal state a security function. It was presumed to exist *in vacuo*. Concerned with the defense of the individual against the state, liberalism was ill-equipped to justify the defense of one state against another. Liberal parties in both Europe and America typically neglected foreign policy and defense problems. Few liberals attempted to cultivate the diplomatic and military skills. The assumption of a state in a vacuum was particularly relevant to American liberalism because for almost a century American reality approximated the liberal image. The applicability of the liberal assumption to the United States settled it all the more firmly in the American mind and created problems all the more difficult to solve when the vacuum began to break down.

A second aspect of liberalism in relation to security problems was its application of domestic policies to international affairs. The issues of foreign policy involve the distribution of power among nations. Unable to tackle this problem directly, liberalism tried to reduce foreign policy and defense issues to domestic terms where it could deal with them effectively. This again was particularly characteristic of American liberalism because of the tremendous success of liberal solutions within American society. From the liberal viewpoint, the absence of serious social conflict in the United States was the product of a distinctive legal system and a distinctive economic system. In other countries, where the legal system was not above controversy or where the economic system was not so spectacularly successful, the tendency toward this approach was not so strong as in the United States. But Americans successively urged the adoption of a whole series of domestic reforms as the solution to international problems. The universal acceptance of the republican form of government, international free trade, the industrialization of backward areas, the elimination of poverty, arbitration treaties, the World Court, the outlawing of war, open covenants openly arrived at, intensified cultural contacts among nations, were all proposed at one time or another as essential to American foreign policy. In advocating these reforms, American liberalism attempted to transpose its domestic successes to foreign relations.

A third aspect of the difficulties of American liberalism in foreign affairs was its search for objective standards and ideal goals. Liberalism tended to judge nations by an absolute standard: the extent to which they maximized freedom for the individual. The application of this standard to foreign policy tended to produce a curious sense of detachment and objectivity. For the liberal, to be consistent, had to judge his own nation by the same standard that he applied to others. Consequently, he normally felt alienated from the struggle for power among nations. Liberalism was not a philosophy of involvement. It has always had an Aristotelian air about it. It originated as the philosophy of the middle class, and viewed itself as the rational mean between the extremes of aristocracy and proletarianism. In the twentieth century the liberal came to think of himself as the vital center between communism and fascism. Until recently, this aspect of liberalism was enhanced in the United States by the fact that the United States was detached from the operation of the European state system. The liberal philosophy of the middle of the road accurately described the position of the United States in world politics. The immediate reaction of our first President to European war was a proclamation of neutrality. Only when its neutral rights were violated or when its position as the balancer was threatened did the United States enter the wars of Europe in 1812, 1917, and 1941. The position of the liberal, detached from society and judging it in terms of an ideal standard, coincided with the position of the United States in world affairs. Just as the liberals were willing to fight for their ideals but seldom for their institutions, the United States by virtue of its noninvolvement in the balance of power was able to pursue foreign policy objectives defined in terms of universal ideals rather than in terms of national interests.

AMERICAN AMBIVALENCE TOWARD WAR. The American attitude toward war has fluctuated widely and yet preserved an underlying unity. The American tends to be an extremist on the subject of war: he either embraces war wholeheartedly or rejects it completely. This extremism is required by the nature of the liberal ideology. Since liberalism deprecates the moral validity of the interests of the state in security, war must be either condemned as incompatible with liberal goals or justified as an ideological movement in support of those goals. American thought has not viewed war in the conservative-military sense as an instrument of national policy. When Clausewitz's dictum on war as the carrying out of state policy by other means has been quoted by nonmilitary American writers, it has been to condemn it for coldblooded calculation and immorality. Americans have enshrined much of Washington's Farewell Address in the national ideology, but they have never accepted his view, so similar to that of Clausewitz, that the nation should be able to "choose peace or war as its interests guided by justice shall counsel." The relatively detached, realistic, unemotional attitude toward war which this advice embodies has been distinctly alien to the American mind.

The pacifist current in American thought has been strong. The total rejection of war accords with the liberal view that men are rational and that consequently they should be able to arrive at a peaceable solution of differences. All that is needed is either the proper education — the elimination of nationalistic and bellicose propaganda — or the proper institutions — international organization and arbitration treaties — to furnish the machinery for the pacific settlement of disputes. Organized pacifism in western civilization has normally been a middle-class movement and the United States, as the middle-class country par excellence, has had its full share of such thinking.[4]

The crusading approach to war has not been incompatible with pacifism. It is a common observation that American nationalism has been an idealistic nationalism, justified, not by the assertion of the superiority of the American people over other peoples, but by the assertion of the superiority of American ideals over other ideals. " '[T]o be an American,' " as Carl J. Friedrich reminds us, "is an ideal, while to be a Frenchman is a fact." [5] American idealism has tended to make every war a crusade, fought, not for specific objectives of national security, but on behalf of universal principles such as democracy, freedom of the seas, and self-determination. Indeed, for the American a war is not a war unless it is a crusade. The usual listing of American wars omits all mention of the nineteenth-century Indian struggles, although many were longer and bloodier than some of the seven wars which are normally recognized. The Indian struggles did not have the ideological goals and popular enthusiasm of a crusade; they were waged primarily by regular troops not by special forces enlisted for that war alone. The British, in contrast, have no hesitancy in classifying their border struggles as wars when they were serious enough to warrant the appellation, as, for example, the First and Second Afghan Wars. Aside from the Indian conflicts, however, it was not until June 1950 that the American people were called upon to support a war rather than to enlist in a crusade.

The tendency to swing from one extreme to another has a self-perpetuating quality. War aims phrased in sweeping ideological terms are seldom capable of achievement. Consequently, war is normally followed by a period of disillusionment with the techniques of violence as means for securing liberal goals. After the Spanish-American War there was a wave of anti-imperialism. After World War I there was the isolationist and revisionist reaction. Emphasis was put upon eliminating war or finding a substitute for war. The Hague Court and the arbitration treaties followed the Spanish-American War; the Kellogg pact, disarmament conferences, and neutrality acts followed World War I. Eventually, when these techniques fail to safeguard the national interests, disillusion-ment with liberal pacifism sets in, national interests are rationalized in terms of new ideological goals, and enthusiasm mounts for a new crusade.

THE HOSTILE IMAGE OF THE MILITARY PROFESSION. Liberalism is divided in its views on war but it is united in its hostility to the military profession. The function of this profession is the military security of the state, and the legitimacy of this concern is recog-nized by neither crusader nor pacifist. Both see the military pro-fession as an obstacle to the achievement of their own aims. The pacifist views the professional military man as a warmonger, plot-ting to bring about conflicts so as to enhance his own rank and power. The crusader views the professional soldier as a sinister drag upon the conduct of war, uninterested and unaroused by the ideals for which the war is fought. The pacifist sees the military man con-taminating his peace; the crusader sees him contaminating his cru-sade.

The pacifist view that the professional military man desires war is a widespread one in western society. More peculiarly Ameri-can is the opposition to the professional military man in war. In Great Britain, for instance, the military have traditionally suffered in peace but have been relied upon in war: the shifts of British attitude are well reflected in Kipling's "Tommy Atkins." In Amer-ica, however, the regular has been rejected in both peace and war. Crusades must be fought by peoples not by professionals. Those most interested in the ideological objectives of the war have been most vehement in denouncing the conservative, limited policies of the professional military officers. This attitude was well expressed with reference to the Mexican War by Nathaniel Hawthorne in a campaign biography of Franklin Pierce:

> The valor that wins our battles is not the trained hardihood of veterans, but a native and spontaneous fire; and there is surely a chivalrous beauty in the devotion of the citizen soldier to his country's cause, which the man who makes arms his profession and is but doing his duty cannot pretend to rival.[6]

In the Civil War the Radical Republicans, anxious to pursue a vigorous and aggressive policy toward the South, were bitter in their attacks on the cautious behavior of McClellan and other generals. In a similar vein Woodrow Wilson, during World War I, minimized the role of the professional on the grounds that:

> This is an unprecedented war and, therefore, it is a war in one sense for amateurs . . . The experienced soldier, — experienced in previous wars, — is a back number so far as his experience is concerned . . .
> America has always boasted that she could find men to do anything. She is the prize amateur nation of the world. Germany is the prize professional nation of the world. Now, when it comes to doing new things and doing them well, I will back the amateur against the professional every time.[7]

The essential conservatism of the military outlook has caused American liberalism to identify its external and domestic enemies with military professionalism. The Revolutionary War was described as a war of citizen-soldiers against the standing armies and mercenaries of George III. The Civil War was against the West Point directed armies of the South. President Wilson's words quoted above reflect the American view that German militarism was the principal enemy in World War I. In World War II the American identification of the German Army with the Nazi regime frustrated the possibilities of capitalizing on the opposition of the former to the latter. The professionals, in other words, are always on the other side.

In domestic politics each liberal group tends to identify the military with its own particular enemies. Without any recognized function in a liberal society and standing outside the American ideological consensus, the military have been a universal target group. The identification of the military with the political enemy was initially valid because eighteenth-century military institutions were fundamentally aristocratic and opposed to liberalism. This pattern of thinking persisted, however, after the military had become divorced from the aristocracy and had begun to be professionalized. Each successive emergent liberal group identified the military with the vested interests of the old order. The Jeffersonian Democrats saw the military as the ally of monarchy and a threat to liberty. The Jacksonians saw them as the foundation of aristocracy and a threat to democracy. Business saw the military as the obsolete remnant of a past agrarian age, the refuge of parasites from the competitive ardors of civilian life, and threat to productivity. Labor and reform groups, on the other hand, have pictured a sinister alliance of business and the military. Obviously, all these theories could not be true, and in actual fact, with the exception of their affiliations with the South, the military have had no significant ties with any group in American society. Yet it is precisely this isolation which makes them eligible to be everybody's enemy. The identification of the military with the domestic enemy has a double effect. It enables each liberal group to exaggerate the gap between it and its political opponent by identifying itself with civilian control and its opponent, who was normally within the liberal consensus, with the military profession, which was outside that consensus. This use of the military is thus one manifestation of the tendency of all groups in American society to magnify their political differences by linking their opponents with foreign or "un-American" groups. At the same time, however, this practice also serves to reinforce the antimilitary attitudes already present in the American mind.

LIBERAL MILITARY POLICY: CONFORM OR DIE. These hostile images have been the basis of the military policy of American liberalism. The essence of this policy is sustained opposition to military values and military requirements. Liberalism's injunction to the military has in effect been: conform or die. On the one hand, American liberalism has supported the virtual elimination of all institutions of violence and thus has attempted to do away with the problem of civil-military relations entirely. This is a policy of extirpation. On the other hand, when it has been necessary to maintain armed force, American liberalism has insisted upon a rigorous subjective civilian control, the refashioning of the military institutions along liberal lines so that they lose their peculiarly military characteristics. This is a policy of transmutation. Together these two approaches represent the American solution to the problem of civil-military relations. While different in means, both policies have the same goal of the subordination of functional military imperatives and the professional military viewpoint.

The policy of extirpation has tended to prevail in peace when security needs have not required the maintenance of large armed forces. Its most obvious manifestation has been the devotion to the idea of "a small standing army." It is reflected in a number of attitudes which have been fairly constantly characteristic of the American approach to military affairs.

(1) Large military forces are a threat to liberty. This attitude was particularly popular in the first years of the Republic and was directed principally against the Army. It was revived in somewhat different form at the end of the nineteenth century when it was asserted that military forces tended to infringe upon the civil liberties of citizens. The danger then was viewed not so much to liberty in the abstract as it was to specific liberties such as the right to strike, to refuse military service, and to engage in pacifist propaganda.

(2) Large military forces are a threat to democracy. This attitude appeared with Jacksonianism. It viewed the officer corps as an "aristocratic caste" plotting to subvert popular government. It was directed against both the Army and the Navy, although its most typical expression was resentment at the "West Point clique."

(3) Large military forces are a threat to economic prosperity. Since it was impossible to view the Navy as a danger to liberty, the Jeffersonians attacked it as a danger to the economy. After the Civil War, when the professionalization of the officer corps deprived the "danger to liberty" argument of much of its appeal even against the Army, this "burden of armaments" argument was applied to all military forces in general. It was popular both with business groups and with radical groups, each of whom attacked the unproductiveness of military force.

(4) Large military forces are a threat to peace. The view that armaments races lead to war and that the military are the principal supporters of war was one element in Jeffersonian opposition to a Navy and has, of course, been a consistent part of the pacifist attitude. It became most popular, however, about the beginning of the twentieth century and, like the "burden of armaments" argument, has continued down to the present time.

The policy of transmutation has prevailed more in war when large armed forces were recognized as necessary. Elements of it, however, have also appeared in peace. It is perhaps best symbolized in the slogan that "primary reliance should be placed upon a mi-

The Ideological Constant

litia," and in Josephus Daniels' declaration in 1915 with respect to the Navy that: "You cannot have an institution in America that is not Americanized." Three principal arguments have been advanced in support of this policy.

First, military defense is, like suffrage, the responsibility of every citizen. It cannot be delegated to a small exclusive group. This view which originated in the colonies before the rise of military professionalism was perpetuated into the twentieth century in the concepts of the "citizen-soldier" and the "nation in arms."

Second, a democratic country must have a democratic military force. This, too, has come down from colonial times, its most extreme manifestation being the practice of electing officers. In its milder forms it emphasizes the desirability of abolishing distinctions between officers and enlisted men, inculcating the democratic-liberal ideology into the forces, and relying more on individual initiative than upon discipline and coordination.

Third, the armed forces, if they must be maintained, should be utilized to further other socially desirable objectives. This has been a persistent element throughout American history from the beginning of the public works activities of the Corps of Engineers down to the present time. It contrasts with the Calhoun-Root view that the only purpose of military forces is war.

THE MILITARY HERO IN LIBERAL POLITICS

The American temper has been so strongly antimilitary that the question inevitably arises: Why have military heroes been so popular in the United States? How is it that ten of our thirty-three presidents have been generals, and that military exploits have contributed so much to the popularity and success of others such as Theodore Roosevelt? Why is it that careful analysis indicates that the military hero by and large makes a more successful political candidate than the man without military experience? Is not this a peculiar anomaly in a society which has generally had little regard for the military? In contrast, England since 1789 has only had one prime minister, the Duke of Wellington, who was also a successful general.[8]

The answer to these questions is, of course, that the popularity of the military hero in America is the supreme example of liberal

The Soldier and the State

transmutation. The successful military hero has been the man either who was a nonprofessional soldier or who, if he was a professional soldier, abandoned his military trappings and adopted the guise of liberalism. The role of the military hero in America is indeed conclusive proof that political power and military professionalism are incompatible in the American climate. The American public has never hesitated to make heroes out of those figures who forsake their military heritage. The military man *qua* military man, on the other hand, has never been popular. As Dixon Wecter has pointed out, all the great national heroes of American history, with the possible exception of Washington, have been liberals, and the professional soldier, consequently, has had little durable appeal. Instead, it has been the amateur or the defrocked professional, even the military iconoclast, who has gained the sympathy of the American people.

Fifteen major party presidential nominees may be classified as military heroes. Nine were nonprofessional in the sense that the military career was neither their exclusive nor even, in most instances, their primary occupation. These nine included Washington, Jackson, William Henry Harrison, Pierce, Frémont, Hayes, Garfield, Benjamin Harrison, and Theodore Roosevelt. The six professionals were Taylor, Scott, McClellan, Grant, Hancock, and Eisenhower.* The outstanding fact of the political careers of these

* All of the nonprofessionals except Jackson, W. H. Harrison, and Frémont met the primary test of the citizen-soldier: their military service was limited to years of war or the threat of war. Jackson entered the national military service from the Tennessee militia during the War of 1812 and remained in the Army seven years after the end of the war. He had, however, already made a reputation as lawyer, judge, planter, and politician, before becoming a soldier. W. H. Harrison was a Regular Army officer from 1791 to 1798 but his reputation as a military hero was based on his subsequent service as Governor of Indiana Territory and as a major general in the War of 1812. Frémont served for about fourteen years in the Army in peace and war from 1834 to 1848 but his peacetime service was almost exclusively devoted to exploration. Taylor and Scott were not West Pointers, but each spent virtually all his adult life in the Army. Grant was seven years outside the service but never became proficient at any other trade. McClellan was a railroad executive for four years before the Civil War, Eisenhower a college president for an even shorter period. Hancock was never out of uniform. All the professionals, except McClellan, were on active service when advanced for the Presidency. Lewis Cass, Democratic nominee against Taylor in 1848, was a general in the War of 1812, but his military record played little role in his campaign, and consequently he cannot be classed as a "military hero candidate." In a sense, Theodore Roosevelt was only a military hero candidate for the vice-presidency; in 1904 he ran primarily on his record and personality

fifteen men is the extent to which the nonprofessionals had better fortune than the professionals. Only one of the nine nonprofessionals, Frémont, failed to see the inside of the White House; on the other hand, three of the six professionals were unsuccessful. In terms of campaigns, the score is more even: the nonprofessionals won ten out of fifteen campaigns; the professionals, five out of eight. In two of the three elections which regular officers lost, the victor was a nonprofessional military hero: Pierce defeated Scott in 1852 and Garfield defeated Hancock in 1880. In both elections the issue of the citizen amateur versus professional soldier played a significant role. Scott was attacked for his military formality; his war record and his allegedly mercenary motives were contrasted unfavorably with the simple idealism, patriotism, and valor of the citizen-soldier Pierce answering the call to duty. Twenty-eight years later, Scott's namesake, Winfield Scott Hancock, suffered the same sort of attacks. His exclusively military career was claimed to have unsuited him for the Presidency, and his military adherence to civilian control during Reconstruction was interpreted as partiality to the South. Garfield's supporters stressed his variety of experience as lawyer, teacher, scholar, statesman, general, and Senator. While the American people like their political candidates to be military heroes, they want their military experience to be an interlude in, or a sideline to, an otherwise civilian career. With the exception of military heroes straight from the field of victory, they normally prefer a well-rounded candidate who has been a success in law, politics, business, or other civil activity to one whose talents have been exclusively military. The liberal hero is a versatile hero. "Americans," as Dixon Wecter has said. "have a special affection for the man of peace — like Sergeant York in the World War — who leaves his trade only long enough to beat the military at their own game." [9]

The popularity of the military professionals depended on the extent to which they became men of the people rather than men of the military. The three professional officers who became President did so largely through the combination of military victory and

---

as President. Nonetheless, his Spanish-American War exploits played such a significant role in his political rise, that it seems legitimate to classify him with the nonprofessional military heroes.

pleasing personality. Their military service enabled them to be presented as the servants, not of party or faction, but of all the people, and this plus a homey, folksy sort of personality — "Rough and Ready," "Uncle Sam," "Ike" — did the trick. These factors also enabled them to avoid commitment upon most of the issues of the day. They appealed to the public not because they had a definite program, military or otherwise, but because they had so little program. Those professionals who were defeated — Scott, McClellan, Hancock — either were too distinctly the military type, possessed forbidding personalities, or demonstrated too clearly and too early their ineptness in the civilian world. The failure of any naval officer ever to win a presidential nomination or even, with the exception of Dewey, to be seriously considered for such a nomination also reflects the more narrowly professional and isolated character of the naval officer corps. Naval officers, more than their Army colleagues, tended to live in a world apart from civilian society, and consequently have found it difficult to establish a broad political appeal.* That officer has also generally been unsuccessful who has attempted to vindicate himself at the polls for rough treatment accorded him while in the service by a hostile administration. The American people want victorious generals not vengeful ones. Frémont's appeal in 1856 and his abortive candidacy in 1864 reflected his unceremonious exits from the Army in 1848 and 1862. Scott wanted to justify himself against the Democrats for his removal from command at the end of the Mexican War, and McClellan harbored similar grudges against Lincoln. In the twentieth century Leonard Wood was unable to win much support by claiming that he had been unjustly denied a field command in World War I, and General MacArthur's dramatic dismissal did not set up a countering tidal wave of political support in his favor.

Professional officers who have become President have conformed to the civilian pattern not only as candidates but also in office. With one possible exception, their policies as a whole have not significantly differed from the policies of those presidents without military experience. More passively, perhaps, than many civil-

---

* The political disability of naval officers has extended to congressional elections also. In 150 years apparently only six former officers of the Regular Navy were elected to Congress. U.S. Naval Institute *Proceedings*, LXXVII (December 1951), 1339–1340.

ian politicians, they have been the accurate representatives and instruments of the dominant political forces of their day. In particular, they have not tried to impose definite policy views on the government, but have played it largely by ear and have usually paid great deference to the wishes of Congress. "It's easy enough to be President," Admiral Dewey is reported to have declared, "all you have to do . . . is to take orders from Congress." [10] Only with respect to the size of the military forces do the policies of the professional military presidents appear to differ significantly from those of the civilians. The administrations of Taylor, Grant, and Eisenhower all saw substantial reductions in the military establishment. In part, this was due to postwar demobilization. In part, it was also certainly due to an over-adjustment to civilian values and the fact that it is much easier for a general to reduce the size of the Army than for anyone else to do so.

The rise of military professionalism after the Civil War tended to sharpen the line between the military and politics. Prior to that time most politicians held militia commissions, and many moved in and out of the Regular Army. Five of the nine nonprofessional candidates ran for office before the Civil War and three made their military reputations in the Civil War. With the exception of Theodore Roosevelt's fling in the Spanish-American War, the War Between the States was the last opportunity for the citizen-officer to make a name for himself. America has fought its twentieth-century wars under professional leadership. The nonprofessional military hero is probably a phenomenon of the past. Citizen-soldiers in the future will only be able to distinguish themselves by individual exploits of valor — like Sergeant York — not by the command of victorious armies.

What, however, can be said about the professional military hero? Has he tended to become more or less important? Two of the professionals, Taylor and Scott, were candidates in the pre-Civil War years when, even for regulars, the line between military service and politics was not very sharp. Three other professional candidates made their reputations in the Civil War. From 1880 to 1952 no professional military man was nominated for the Presidency. Admiral Dewey and General Wood, the two professionals during these years who most obviously yearned for the Presidency, did not get very far. And Wood, who entered the Army as a physician and made his military reputation as a volunteer officer in the Spanish-American War, was really only a "semi-pro." The seventy-two-year break between Hancock and Eisenhower thus reflected the heightened professionalism of the post-1865 military. Nonprofessional soldiers (except for Theodore Roosevelt) did not become military hero candidates because they did not become military heroes. Professional soldiers did not become military hero candidates because they were professional: they were dubious about venturing into politics and the politicians were dubious about seeking after them. The election of Eisenhower in 1952, on the other hand, signalized the entrance of the military professional into politics in the drastically changed conditions prevailing after 1940.

7

The Structural Constant:
The Conservative Constitution
versus Civilian Control

THE CONSTITUTIONAL ABSENCE OF OBJECTIVE CIVILIAN CONTROL

The United States Constitution, despite the widespread belief to the contrary, does *not* provide for civilian control. That is, it does not permit the objective civilian control compatible with a high level of military professionalism. The essence of civilian control in this sense is a clear distinction between political and military responsibilities and the institutional subordination of the latter to the former. These are unknown to the Constitution, which mixes political and military functions, interjecting politics into military affairs and military affairs into politics. Present in the minds of the Framers when they wrote it and perpetuated in its provisions was an essentially subjective approach to civil-military relations. Civilian control has at times existed in the United States, but it has emerged despite rather than because of constitutional provisions.

The very aspects of the Constitution which are frequently cited as establishing civilian control are those which make it difficult to achieve. Civilian control would be maximized if the military were limited in scope and relegated to a subordinate position in a pyramid of authority culminating in a single civilian head. The military clauses of the Constitution, however, provide for almost exactly the opposite. They divide civilian responsibility for military affairs and foster the direct access of the military authorities to the highest levels of government:

(1) Within the total federal system of government, the militia clauses divide control over the militia between the state and national governments.

(2) Within the national government, the separation of powers divides control of the national military forces between Congress and the President.

(3) Within the executive branch of the national government, the Commander in Chief clause tends to divide control over the military between the President and departmental secretaries.

These latter two provisions reflect the distribution of military powers in the British government in the eighteenth century. The similarity, however, turned into a fundamental difference in the course of a century and a half. The evolution of British government centralized all authority over the military in the Cabinet, and the British constitution today provides for extremely effective civilian control. The American Constitution, however, remains frozen in the eighteenth-century pattern. The centrifugal politics of this country and the written, inflexible character of the Constitution combined to obstruct changes similar to those in Great Britain. American lack of concern with military affairs, furthermore, left the constitutional structure almost unsupplemented by statutory enactments. Prior to the twentieth century the only significant additions were the office of the Secretary of War created in 1789 and the office of the Secretary of the Navy created in 1798. For most of American history, the Constitution and little else determined the legal structure of American civil-military relations.

THE FRAMERS AND CIVILIAN CONTROL

The speeches and writings of the Framers of the Constitution abound with statements that the military should be subordinated to the civil power. If this is the case, how is it that they apparently failed so completely to carry out their intention? The answer is, of course, that military professionalism and civilian control as the subordination of that profession to political institutions were simply unknown to the eighteenth century. In terms of providing for civilian control, the Constitution was drafted at just the wrong time in history. It was a product of the last years of preprofessional officership. If it had been framed twenty-five years later, its clauses with respect to military power might well have been significantly different. But, as it was, for all their political wisdom and insight, the Framers did not, with a few exceptions, foresee the emergence of military professionalism and objective civilian control. It is no criticism of them that they did not provide for something which did not exist when they were drafting the Constitution. Their approach to civilian control was reflected in their ideas on military officership, military forces, and governmental organization.

Military Officership. The Constitution does not envisage a separate class of persons exclusively devoted to military leadership. "I am not acquainted with the military profession," George Mason proclaimed at the Virginia convention and, except for Hamilton, Pinckney, and a few others, he spoke for all the Framers. They knew neither military profession nor separate military skills. Military officership was the attribute of any man of affairs. Many members of the Federal Convention had held military rank during the Revolution; Washington was only the most obvious of the soldier-statesmen. They combined in their own persons military and political talents much as the samurai founders of modern Japan also combined them a hundred years later. Following Blackstone, they believed that in a free state the citizen did not cease to be a citizen when he became a soldier but rather became a soldier because he was a citizen.[1]

Such views were clearly revealed in the ineligibility and incompatibility clauses of Article I, Section 6:

> No Senator or Representative shall, during the Time for which he was elected, be appointed to any civil office under the Authority of the United States, which shall have been created, or the Emoluments whereof shall have been increased during such time; and no person holding any Office under the United States shall be a Member of either House during his Continuance in Office.

The Convention almost unanimously supported the second clause of this paragraph making legislative office incompatible with judicial or executive (including military) office. This was required by the separation of powers. It reflected the necessity of keeping the legislature distinct from the executive rather than the desirability of keeping the political distinct from the military. Attention at the

Convention centered on the first clause of the paragraph. As reported from the Committee of Detail, this clause proposed to make members of the legislature ineligible for appointment to any national office during the time for which they were elected. Opinions on the desirability of permitting legislators to assume civil office varied and were finally resolved by compromise. There was, however, a universal belief that Senators and Representatives should be eligible for appointment to a military office. "Exclude the officers of the army & navy," said Gouveneur Morris, "and you form a band having a different interest from & opposed to the civil power: you stimulate them to despise & reproach those 'talking Lords who dare not face the foe.'" What would occur, he inquired, in the

. . . case of a war, and the Citizen the most capable of conducting it, happening to be a member of the Legislature. What might have been the consequence of such a regulation at the commencement, or even in the Course of the late contest for our liberties?

Others, such as Edmund Randolph, who favored the general ineligibility of legislators for executive office also recognized that military talent might well exist in Congress and supported an exception with respect to military office. Consequently, the final draft applied incompatibility to both civil and military office but the eligibility limitations only to civil office. Subsequently, in the Virginia convention Madison defended the eligibility provisions concerning civil office by citing the absence of any such restrictions upon appointment to military office. His argument plus the lack of any opposition to legislative eligibility to military office in the ratification debates indicates how widespread was the acceptance of this Cincinnatus theory of military leadership.[2]

Military Forces. The Framers' concept of nonprofessional officership could have been embodied in either of the two forms of military organization familiar to eighteenth-century America: the standing army and the citizen militia. These forms, however, were essentially the extension into the military realm of different political beliefs. The standing army with its upper-class officers and lower-class enlisted men was basically an aristocratic institution. It was associated with the British Crown and with European despotism. It was also quite unnecessary in the eyes of many Americans. The distance of the United States from Europe meant that it required no permanent military force with the possible exception of small frontier garrisons to deal with the Indians. Consequently, it was generally agreed that primary reliance must be put upon a citizen militia composed of part-time officers and enlisted men. This was the only form of military force suitable for the new republic. The militia embodied the democratic principle that defense of the nation was the responsibility of every citizen. The distinction between officers and enlisted men was minimized, and the line between them did not correspond to any sharp cleavage in the social structure.

Preference for the militia was almost universal throughout the states. "There was not a member in the federal Convention," Edmund Randolph remarked with only slight exaggeration, "who did not feel indignation" at the prospect of a standing army. The ratifying conventions were even more strongly opposed to regular military forces. Nonetheless, they approved a Constitution which, while barring standing armies to the states, gave the national government unlimited power to maintain a military force, the only restriction being that no appropriations for this purpose could be made for more than two years. The reasons for this apparent anomaly were twofold. First, it was generally recognized that the national government would have to maintain some sort of permanent force along the frontier. Secondly, there was always the possibility that a standing army might be necessary in an emergency. But the hope and expectation were that this emergency would never occur and that the power would never be utilized. Few provisions in the Constitution were agreed to with more reluctance, and some delegates most vehemently opposed to standing forces refused to sign the Constitution. Criticism of this unrestricted congressional power was widespread in the state conventions. A number of states proposed requiring an extraordinary majority in Congress for the maintenance of such a force or suggested amendments declaring the militia to be "the natural defence of a free state" and standing armies in peace "dangerous to liberty." [3]

Preference for the militia had two important results for future civilian control. First, it assigned a major place in the American military scheme to a force which could never be professionally officered or subjected to civilian control. At the time, of course, professional officers were just as rare in standing armies as they were in citizen militias. The former, however, because they were composed of full-time soldiers, could eventually evolve into a disciplined body of professionals. This was impossible in a part-time militia force. Secondly, the expectation that the militia would be the main reliance for defense made the framers relatively unconcerned with devising institutional techniques to control military forces in being. In part, this was the result of the feeling that such devices could never be successful. To a larger extent, it reflected the view that such devices were unnecessary. The republic would be defended by its loyal citizen-soldiers. Civilian supremacy would be maintained by eliminating a distinct military force.

Governmental Organization. The Framers' concept of civilian control was to control the uses to which civilians might put military force rather than to control the military themselves. They were more afraid of military power in the hands of political officials than of political power in the hands of military officers. Unable to visualize a distinct military class, they could not fear such a class. But there was need to fear the concentration of authority over the military in any single governmental institution. As conservatives, they wanted to divide power, including power over the armed forces. The national government if it monopolized military power would be a threat to the states; the President if he had sole control over the armed forces would be a threat to the Congress. Consequently, the Framers identified civilian control with the fragmentation of authority over the military. Concern for the independence of Congress from executive control, rather than an understanding of the distinct nature of the political and military functions, caused them to make legislative and military office incompatible. The issue of the relative desirability of a militia versus a standing army was subordinate to the issues of the relative power of the states and the nation, the executive and the legislature, over the military forces, whatever their character. Those who wished a strong national government had no hesitancy in arguing: (1) that continuation of the Articles of Confederation would mean standing armies in every state; (2) that the proposed national government necessarily had to have the power to raise a standing army; and (3) that to avoid the necessity of exercising this power, the national government should also organize and discipline the militia. Supporters of states rights, on the other hand, argued that it was unnecessary for the national government to have a standing army and that, in any case, the states ought to have exclusive control over the militia in order to protect themselves against the standing army of the national government.[4]

THE MILITIA CLAUSES AND MILITARY FEDERALISM:
THE EMPIRE WITHIN AN EMPIRE

The militia clauses of the Constitution hamper civilian control in two ways. First, they give constitutional sanction to a semimilitary force which can never be completely subordinated to military discipline nor completely removed from political entanglements. Secondly, they give constitutional sanction to a division of control over the militia between state and national governments which necessarily involves the militia in the conflicting interests of the federal system. This unique combination of characteristics — part civilian and part military, part state and part national — tends to make the militia independent of the policy-making institutions of government.

The Framers had good reasons to prefer a militia force to a regular army. But there was little rational justification for splitting up the control of this force. As Madison said, this control "did not seem in its nature to be divisible between two distinct authorities." Politics if not logic, however, forced the Framers, Madison included, to support dual control. Some, such as Hamilton, wanted complete control in the United States. Others wished the national government to be completely excluded from authority over the militia. The clash of these viewpoints produced a variety of compromise suggestions. In the end, the balance of political forces resulted in the following militia clauses:

The Congress shall have Power . . .
    To provide for calling forth the Militia to execute the Laws of the Union, suppress Insurrections and repel Invasions;
    To provide for organizing, arming, and disciplining the Militia, and for governing such Part of them as may be employed in the Service of the United States, reserving to the States respectively, the Appointment of Officers, and the Authority of training the Militia according to the

169

discipline prescribed by Congress . . . The President shall be Commander-in-Chief . . . of the Militia of the several States, when called
into the actual service of the United States . . .

In addition, of course, Congress also has the authority to "raise
and support armies" under the army clause.[5] The exercise of these
authorities can be divided into two periods. From 1792 to 1903,
the militia was under state control in time of peace and dual control
in time of war. After 1903 the militia was under dual control in
time of peace and national control in time of war.*

State control existed in peacetime throughout the nineteenth
century because Congress, in the Militia Act of 1792, which was
the basic legislation in this field until 1903, refused to exercise its
powers under the militia clauses and provided for neither effective
federal supervision nor effective federal support. Consequently, the
militia remained exclusively state forces when not in the active
service of the United States. When they were in such service, however, the dual control under the militia clauses resulted in constant
confusion and bickering over the purposes for which the militia
might be used and the appointment of officers. In 1812, for instance, when the President called out the militia, the governors of
Massachusetts and Connecticut asserted that they and not he had
the right to decide whether the circumstances justified the call.
Later in the war militia on the Niagara frontier refused on constitutional grounds to enter Canada to support regular American
troops fighting there. In the Spanish-American War, militia units
likewise refused to serve outside the United States. The President
was constitutional Commander in Chief of the militia while it was
in federal service. Yet how could he function in this capacity when
his officers in war as well as peace were appointed by state governors? In the War of 1812 state governors challenged the authority
of the President to subordinate militia units to the command of Regular Army general officers. State officials removed their troops from
national service as they saw fit and upset the lines of command by

* The problems raised by the militia clauses have not changed fundamentally
in more recent years, and this discussion of the militia will include events after
1940. In contrast, the discussion of the separation of powers and the Commander
in Chief clause in this chapter will be limited to the period previous to 1940; the
special problems arising after 1940 will be treated separately in Part III.

appointing militia officers to higher rank than the regular officers to whom the militia units were theoretically subordinate. In the Civil War, also, the states appointed the regimental officers of the militia and the national volunteers assigned to the states, while the President appointed the general officers. The Act of April 22, 1898 providing for the Volunteer Army for the Spanish-American War reproduced this division of authority.[6]

Dual control in war did not survive the nineteenth century. The militia has fought twentieth-century wars as an exclusively national force under the army clause. Nor did the system of state control in time of peace extend past 1903. Dual control under the militia clauses became a reality when Congress passed the Dick Act of that year. The effects of these changes were twofold. The military importance of the militia in time of war was enhanced because it now had the wherewithal to become an effective military body. The political power of the militia in time of peace was enhanced because it was placed between two competing authorities. Civilian control of the militia — difficult in time of war in the nineteenth century — became in the twentieth century difficult in time of peace. Thus, the militia clauses are the constitutional base for a potent political organization — the National Guard, and its spokesman, the National Guard Association. It is generally recognized that constitutions are created by political forces. It is also true, however, that constitutions may themselves create or impel the creation of political interests. This is the case with the militia clauses and the National Guard. Were it not for these clauses, the Guard and the National Guard Association would not exist with the influence which they have today.

The National Guard Association was formed in 1878 by a group of militia officers for the primary purpose of getting Congress to exercise its responsibilities under the militia clauses. It was designed to "present a united front" for joint control.[7] Its founders wished the national government to supply money, instruction, standards, and a certain measure of supervision to the state militia. The Regular Army was opposed because it did not think the militia could be an effective national force. The dual control advocates, however, won their first victory in 1903 and subsequently strengthened and maintained their position despite the continuing hostility of the Regular Army. Throughout its existence the Guard has recognized its dependence upon the militia clauses and has stoutly defended its dual status. Guard officers maintain that these clauses embody the true sentiments of the Framers on military policy. Constitutional "dual control" is opposed to central control and to exclusive state control. The latter is impossible because it is not economically feasible for the states to carry the entire cost of the Guard; the former is unconstitutional because, according to the Guard, the army clause gives Congress the power only to maintain a standing army not to keep a federal militia. For the Guard, dual control in peace means that the national government should supply the funds and the know-how while the states supply the command and direction. The Association has consistently sought more federal money for Guard activities but resolutely opposed any extension of federal control. In 1949, for instance, it demanded increased federal aid for armories and construction, a uniform clothing allowance for National Guard officers, and the franking privilege for National Guard mail. At the same time it vigorously condemned further federal control over the Guard, describing the 1948 Gray Board recommendation for a single national reserve force as "unconstitutional, un-American . . . contrary to our concept and philosophy of life . . . ill-advised and illegal." Upon the constitutional base of the militia clauses, the National Guard has created a political force of formidable proportions. As the president of the Association frankly and accurately proclaimed, the Guard is an "empire within an empire." [8] Within its sphere of interest its word is law, or becomes law very quickly. The extent of this power, and the ways in which the militia clauses contribute to it, may be seen in: (1) its legal status; (2) its constitutional symbolism; (3) its official representation in state and national governments; (4) the peculiar position of the National Guard Association; and (5) the influence of the Guard with Congress.

Legal Status. The efforts of the Association to enhance the Guard's dual status have put the latter in a unique legal position. The National Guard is a single organization with a double existence. As the "National Guard of the several states and territories," it is organized under the militia clause and has the mission of preserving law and order within the states under the orders of the

The Structural Constant

state authorities. In this capacity it may be "called forth" by the President under the appropriate authority of Congress for the limited constitutional purposes of executing the laws of the United States, suppressing insurrection, and repelling invasions. If this were its only status, the Guard would be constitutionally incapable of participating, as an organization, in a foreign war. In 1917, without authority permitting overseas service, its members went into the national army as groups of individuals, and Guard organization was disrupted. As a result, the Association in 1933 secured the passage of an act which makes the Guard as the "National Guard of the United States" a reserve component of the Army of the United States under the army clause. In this capacity, its mission is to furnish units for all types of military operations anywhere in the world. As the National Guard of the United States, it may be "ordered" to active service by the President after Congress has declared the existence of a national emergency. The Guard has the best of two worlds. Its status under the militia clause protects it against federal control in peacetime. Its status under the army clause insures it of a prominent role in wartime.

Constitutional Symbolism. As a militia under dual control, the Guard identifies itself with two venerated constitutional symbols: the citizen-soldier and states' rights. Guardsmen are "amateur soldiers," citizens first and soldiers second in the Minute Man tradition. "In the future as in the past," the Association declared in 1944, "and based upon sound tradition, long experience, and this Nation's fundamental law, the citizen-soldier must be the major dependence of the Nation in time of war." The federal reserves, however, can likewise claim to be citizen-soldiers. But only the Guard can also invoke the banner of states' rights. Our "organizations," claimed President Walsh, "belong to the States and are merely loaned to the Federal Government in wartime." The Guard wants the "Federal system adhered to" in the military establishment. The Guard can thus expect the support of the state governments against the national government. In 1943, for instance, the Conference of Governors urged continued dual status for the Guard in the postwar period, and in 1948 the Executive Committee of the Conference joined the Guard in denouncing the Gray Board report. Its state affiliations enhance the political in-

173

The Soldier and the State

fluence of the Guard relative to that of the reserve associations of the national forces. In 1954 the Reserve Officers Association had 60,000 members and the NGA had 34,000. The ROA normally has had more money and a larger staff than the NGA. Nonetheless, without a secure base of operations in the states, the ROA has not equaled the NGA in political influence. In 1946 the president of the ROA described his organization as the "younger brother" of the National Guard Association and admitted that "The National Guard has much of what we the Reserves have not had." [9]

State and National Representation. The position of the Guard is strengthened by its official foothold in both the state and national governments. The heads of the Guard in the states are the adjutants general appointed by the governors. These officials represent the Guard within the state governments and are linked nationally through the Adjutants General Association which is a "corollary" organization of the NGA. The Guard is represented in the Department of the Army by the Chief of the National Guard Bureau, who under the National Defense Act of 1920 must be a Guardsman, and by the National Guard members of the joint General Staff committees which, under the same act, must consider all policies affecting the Guard. These national representatives keep the NGA well informed of what transpires within the Army and the War Department. The Guard has regularly insisted that it be included at an early stage in the preparation of War Department policies which might affect it. Exclusion of the Guard in the development of policy generally means opposition by the NGA when the programs are submitted to Congress.[10]

The National Guard Association. The NGA, like so many other powerful groups, occupies an ambiguous position on the borderline between a private association and a public body. Legally it is simply a voluntary organization of National Guard officers. Nonetheless, it considers itself to be "the authorized Representative of the National Guard of the United States." It is also closely tied in with the official state and national representation of the Guard. In 1948, when only 42 per cent of Guard officers belonged to the NGA, the Association declared it to be the responsibility of the adjutants general "to insist that every National

174

Guard Officer be a member of the National Guard Association."
To this end it urged the states to require each new Guard officer
to fill out an NGA membership application prior to appearing
before the official examining board. Through such techniques,
the NGA by 1953 achieved a 99 per cent membership among
Guard officers. As a private association the NGA carries on public
relations activities, publishes the monthly *National Guardsman,*
and represents the Guard with respect to a wide variety of legislation. At one point in the debate over the Selective Service Act of
1948, for example, when it looked as if the Guard viewpoint would
not prevail, the Association brought members from thirty-four
states to Washington to lobby with their congressmen. In two days
they were eminently successful in getting Congress to adopt the
National Guard position. In President Walsh's words, the great
virtue of the NGA is that it is

. . . the only agency on which the National Guard can rely to protect
its interests, for the Association is free and untrammeled and it does
not have to conform to any particular pattern nor is it bound within
the narrow limits of channels of communication or the chain of command.[11]

Influence with Congress. In the final analysis the influence of
the Guard boils down to its influence with Congress. The fate of
the militia is in the hands of Congress. Conceivably, Congress could
destroy the dual status of the Guard and undermine its political
power by refusing to exercise its functions under the militia clause
and by returning to the pre-1903 situation. Conversely, Congress
could federalize the Guard and make it an exclusively national
instrumentality under the army clause. NGA officers, however,
assert that "We should settle the future of the National Guard."
If the NGA is going to "settle" the fate of the Guard, it must
settle the actions of Congress on National Guard affairs. For half
a century it has been astoundingly successful in doing exactly this.
The local roots of the Guard, its appeals to states' rights and the
citizen-soldier, its support from the state governments, its lobbying and pressure tactics, have made it a power on Capitol Hill.
"Congress," in the words of President Walsh, "has ever been our
refuge and our strength."

The record of National Guard success with Congress begins with the Dick Act of 1903. Representative Dick himself was a former president of the National Guard Association. In 1908 the Association secured the passage of the second Dick Act strengthening federal support of the Guard. In 1916 the Guard "threw every ounce of its energy into an effort to defeat" the Continental Army plan of the General Staff. It was successful, and the National Defense Act of that year was in line with its views. The position of the Guard was greatly strengthened four years later by the National Defense Act of 1920, which the Guard described as "a great achievement and a great victory." In passing the 1933 act making the Guard a reserve component of the Army in peace as well as war "Congress saw eye to eye with the proposals submitted by the National Guard." Throughout the twenties and thirties, the NGA successfully devoted its efforts to increasing the appropriations of the Guard from $13,000,000 in 1920 to $72,000,000 in 1941. In 1940 when the original Selective Training and Service Bill as proposed in Congress did not secure the interests of the Guard, the Association had inserted into it the "National Guard protective clause" which declared it to be "essential that the strength and organization of the National Guard as an integral part of the first line of defense of this nation be at all times maintained and assured." In 1946 the Guard fought efforts by the War Department to set up a large Organized Reserve Corps which the Guard viewed as a "competing" and "parallel" organization. A War Department recommendation for a $40,000,000 appropriation for the ORC was eliminated by Congress at the insistence of the National Guard. The Guard had no difficulty, however, in getting funds for itself. For Fiscal Year 1949 the Budget Bureau recommended $195,000,000 for the Guard. The NGA did not think this enough and got the economy minded Eightieth Congress to appropriate $290,000,000. In 1948 the Association was also successful in getting its views written into the Selective Service Act and in blocking the legislative recommendations of the Gray Board. In 1954 when an Assistant Secretary of Defense suggested that the Guard should be used only for Home Guard and civil defense functions, President Walsh confidently picked up the challenge: "If they want war, let it begin here." [12]

The record shows that Congress has indeed given, in Walsh's words, "generous support" to the Guard. Continuing his reflections on the Eightieth Congress, the president went on to wonder if

. . . any organization has been so successful in the legislative field in so brief a period as the National Guard Association. It is indeed a great accomplishment to have attained all the major legislative objectives of this Association.

Two years later the NGA Legislative Committee reported that the Association had "been phenomenally successful in obtaining the enactment of legislation essential to its well-being and development." [13] So long as the Guard retains its jealously protected dual status, this will continue to be the situation. Ensconced behind the militia clauses as an "empire within an empire," this premier military lobby effectively dominates those congressional proceedings which interest it. It is a Frankenstein monster created by the Constitution of the United States. That document underwrites its slogan that "There will always be a National Guard."

THE SEPARATION OF POWERS: DUAL CONTROL OVER THE NATIONAL FORCES

In many respects the most significant aspect of the separation of powers is not the relative division of power between President and Congress, but the effects which this division has upon the power of other groups. The existence of two coordinate bodies means that the power of each of these bodies vis-à-vis other groups is less than it would be if either possessed full sovereign authority. The principal beneficiaries of this spreading of power have been organized interest groups, bureaucratic agencies, and the military services. The separation of powers is a perpetual invitation, if not an irresistible force, drawing military leaders into political conflicts. Consequently, it has been a major hindrance to the development of military professionalism and civilian control in the United States.

With only minor modifications the Framers reproduced in the Constitution the division of authority over the military which prevailed in England and the colonies in the middle of the eighteenth century. "The purse & the sword," said George Mason, "ought never to get into the same hands [whether legislative or executive]." The President inherited the powers of the English king, Congress the powers of the English Parliament. The executive authority of the President, Hamilton stated in *The Federalist,* "will resemble equally that of the king of Great Britain and of the governor of New York." The Framers did, however, make one major adjustment in favor of the legislature. In giving Congress the war power, they altered British practice and established a significant precedent in the evolution of representative government. The result was that Congress was given the power

To declare War, grant Letters of Marque and Reprisal, and make Rules concerning Captures on Land and Water;

To raise and support Armies, but no Appropriation of Money to that Use shall be for a longer Term than two Years;

To provide and maintain a Navy;

To make Rules for the Government and Regulation of the land and naval Forces . . . And

To make all laws which shall be necessary and proper for carrying into Execution the foregoing Powers, and all other Powers vested by this Constitution in the Government of the United States, or in any Department or Officer thereof.

And the President was made "Commander in Chief of the Army and Navy of the United States." [14]

The general intent of this division of power is clear. Further problems arise, however, from the nature of the grant of presidential power. This clause is unique in the Constitution in that it grants authority in the form of an *office* rather than in the form of a *function*. The President is not given the function "to command the Army and Navy"; he is given the office of "Commander in Chief." This difference in form is of considerable importance. By defining the presidential power as an office, the Framers left undefined its specific powers and functions. This eased the approval of the Constitution in the ratifying conventions, but it gave subsequent generations something to cogitate about and argue about. What, after all, are the powers of the Commander in Chief? They might range from the extremely broad power to conduct war to a narrowly restricted power of military command. They certainly exclude all powers specifically assigned to Congress or the states, and they probably include all purely military powers not so assigned. But does the office possess nonmilitary powers as well? The Framers themselves seemed to hold conflicting opinions on this point. The Supreme Court in 1850, however, declared that the duty and power of the President as Commander in Chief were "purely military," and denied the similarity between the presidential authority and the royal prerogative.[15] So long as the Commander in Chief power is interpreted as purely military, it really adds little authority to the presidential office. Indeed, down to the Civil War it was, in Professor Corwin's phrase, "the forgotten clause" of the Constitution. In the Civil War and in World War II, however, Lincoln and Roosevelt used the clause to justify an extraordinarily broad range of nonmilitary presidential actions largely legislative in nature. The justification of these actions by the Commander in Chief clause was persuasive, however, only because John Rutledge defined that power as an office rather than a function. It may be argued that the office of Commander in Chief possesses authority to seize a strike-bound war plant. It would be impossible to argue that the function of commanding the Army and Navy implied such authority. In other words, the clause has been of relatively little direct use in securing civilian control over the military. Indeed, in one respect it has been directly detrimental to such control. But because it was phrased as an office rather than a function, it has been of great use to the President in expanding his power at the expense of Congress. This, in turn, has broadened the area of conflict between these two institutions and, consequently, has indirectly further impeded civilian control by increasing the likelihood that military leaders will be drawn into this political controversy.[16]

The means through which the President has exercised his powers with respect to military affairs include the appointment of military personnel, the issuance of executive orders and commands, and reliance upon the instrumentality of the civilian secretary. Congressional weapons include statutes, appropriations, and investigations. These weapons have normally been wielded on behalf of Congress by the military and naval affairs committees, the appropriations committees, and special wartime investigating committees. On occasion both sides have found it necessary or expedient to appeal to the military for support of their plans or to seize upon and push military plans for purposes of their own. The involvement of the national officer corps in politics has, consequently, been less consistent and more sporadic in nature than the involvement of the militia officer corps. The division of authority between two separate governments demanded a permanent political spokesman for the interests of the militia. The division of authority between two branches of the same government led to the transitory involvement of individuals and cliques of officers in controversies over military strength, military strategy, military organization, and military appointments. Until 1940 these issues generally were not of great importance in national politics. Consequently, the separation of powers was primarily a passive, latent obstacle to the emergence of military professionalism. Its implications for civilian control were not clearly obvious because military policy was of relatively minor concern to both Congress and President.

Military Strength. The pattern of national politics respecting the strength of military forces tended to obscure the extent of military participation in politics. Prior to 1940 the executive was generally more favorably inclined toward a larger military establishment than was Congress. Congress had less immediate contact with foreign dangers and was under greater popular pressure to cut spending. In addition, the easiest way to assert congressional authority in the budget process was simply to reduce executive requests. Thus, the institutional jealousy of the two branches, even apart from constituent pressure, tended to make Congress less favorable to military appropriations. The result was that military leaders were generally on the side of the President; they appeared before congressional committees to support his program. Military involvement in politics on the side of Congress tends to be conspicuous and dramatic. Military involvement in politics on the side of the President tends to be subtle and less obvious. Undoubtedly, some administrations did use popular officers to rally congressional support for their military proposals. But it is extremely difficult to draw the line between the soldier giving professional advice to Congress as to what the country needs for its defense and the soldier lobbying with Congress for the administration. The two roles are distinct in theory but blended in practice. In the period following World War II on the other hand, a number of significant variations from this pattern have occurred, with Congress taking a more sympathetic view to military requests than the President.

Military Strategy. It is more difficult to identify continuing executive and legislative positions on strategy than on military strength. To the extent that there were persistent patterns, Congress generally favored a more aggressive and offensively minded strategy, while the President supported caution and restraint. When the issue was joined, both have been able to find elements in the officer corps favorable to their positions. Officers who did not find support for their strategic views in the top levels of the executive branch had no trouble in locating congressmen willing to push their strategy. Similarly, congressmen who wanted to attack the administration with respect to its strategy were usually able to find officers willing to lend an air of professional respectability to their criticism.

The most extreme example of the mixing of politics and strategy occurred in the Civil War. The purpose of the congressional Committee on the Conduct of the War was defined by one of its founders as "to keep an anxious, watchful eye over all the executive agents who are carrying on the war at the direction of the people . . . We are not under the command of the military of this country. They are under ours as a Congress." [17] The Committee favored a "radical" policy involving stringent opposition to slavery and an aggressive "On to Richmond" strategy. The President and General McClellan were for going slow on both counts. Consequently, the Committee had little hesitancy in using its power to undermine McClellan and force his withdrawal from command. Its members were certain that their own capabilities with respect to military strategy made them at least the equal of the generals. In opposing McClellan, they were assisted by many Army officers who shared their views and who actively subverted "Little Mac's" authority. On the other hand, generals such as Hooker and Burnside, who were sympathetic to the Committee's position, were hamstrung by the conspiratorial activities of more conservative subordinates.

Military Organization. With respect to military organization

181

a natural coincidence of viewpoints led military officers to side with Congress against President. Congress normally tried to enhance its own power against the executive by detailed legislative prescription of military organization. Military officers generally supported this as tending to strengthen their position against the President and civilian secretaries. Consequently, military organization issues present many more obvious examples of military involvement in politics than do those with respect to strategy.

During the Civil War, Congress undertook to lay out the details of military organization, and forced Lincoln to divide the army into corps so as to reduce the number of troops under McClellan's command. After the war, the Army Appropriation Act in 1867 directed the President to issue all orders and instructions relative to military operations through the General of the Army (Grant). It also provided that the General of the Army should not be removed or assigned to command elsewhere than at Washington, except at his own request or with the approval of the Senate. This effort to transfer some of the President's authority as Commander in Chief to a military subordinate was undoubtedly unconstitutional, but it is not the only instance in American history where it has been attempted.

Congress has generally supported military officers in the War Department opposed to the centralization of authority in the Secretary of War or in the General Staff. The independent position of the Corps of Engineers with respect to its civil functions is only the most extreme example of this tendency to combine military and legislative power against executive power. In 1901, four staff chiefs — the quartermaster general, the surgeon general, the paymaster general, and the chief of engineers — got Congress to strengthen their position despite the opposition of the Secretary of War. Subsequently, in the controversy over the relative powers of the Chief of Staff and the adjutant general, the Secretary of War successfully backed the former, but the latter received vindication at the hands of a congressional committee. In the army organization act of 1920, Congress required the Secretary of War to submit the comments of the General Staff, pro and con, with any proposed legislation unless this was "incompatible with the public interest." The effect of this provision was to invite general staff officers "to try their controversy with their chief before a Congressional committee." In 1914 and 1915 naval officers under the leadership of Admiral Fiske worked with congressional sympathizers to secure the creation of the office of the Chief of Naval Operations despite the opposition of the President and Secretary Daniels.[18]

Military Appointments. No single pattern of military involvement in politics prevails with respect to personnel appointments. The extent to which individuals become involved and the side they choose are functions of their views on policy and their political affiliations. Both Congress and the President, however, usually tried to maximize their own influence by securing the appointment of officers generally sympathetic to their views on military affairs and by blocking the appointment of those who were hostile. In the Mexican War, for instance, the two senior generals in the Army, Major Generals Scott and Taylor, were Whigs. President Polk, a Democrat, feared that he could not trust these officers and did not wish them to become popular military idols. Hence he asked Congress to create the position of lieutenant general whose occupant would outrank Scott and Taylor. To this position he planned to appoint a Democratic senator, Thomas Hart Benton. But Congress refused to go along with the idea, and in 1848 Taylor was elected President. During the Civil War, the Committee on the Conduct of the War actively tried to advance its favorite generals and get rid of those who opposed its policies. A routine, if unusually important, exercise of congressional influence occurred in the appointment of Dewey to the command of the Asiatic Squadron prior to the outbreak of the Spanish-American War. Secretary of the Navy Long was opposed to Dewey; Assistant Secretary Theodore Roosevelt supported him. T. R. called in Dewey and asked him if he knew any Senators. When the naval officer admitted to knowing Senator Proctor of Vermont, that legislator was induced to approach President McKinley, and the appointment went through.[19]

The differing interests of Congress and the President thus determined the side which military officers supported. On issues of military strength they were normally with the President, on organizational issues they were with Congress, on strategy they were divided, and on personnel issues they followed their own best interests. Whenever significant questions of military policy arose, the national officers were drawn into the legislative-executive struggle on one side or the other. The separation of powers made it impossible for American officers ever to be at ease in their professionalism.

THE COMMANDER IN CHIEF CLAUSE: THE
POLITICAL-MILITARY HIERARCHY

One major function of the Commander in Chief clause has been to justify the exercise of broad Presidential powers in times of national emergency. A second principal function has been to complicate the achievement of civilian control in the executive branch. Just as the separation of powers is a standing invitation to military leaders to bypass the President and go directly to Congress, the Commander in Chief clause is a standing invitation to bypass the civilian secretary and go to the President.

The Commander in Chief clause is the outstanding example of the Framers' mixing of political and military functions. The same thinking which permitted them to envision Senators becoming generals in war also permitted them to accept a civilian President as military commander in chief. In most societies, from primitive nomadic tribes down to their own time, it had been customary for the chief of state also to be the chief military commander. This had been true of the Greek city state, the Roman republic, and the European national monarchies; it was to be true of Napoleonic France. Virtually all the state constitutions at the time made the governor commander in chief of the militia. Military command was as much a function of the chief executive as the appointment of administrative officials or the negotiation of alliances. It was only natural for this role to be assigned to the President. He was to be a republican Soldier-President patterned upon the Royal Warrior of the European states.

The extent to which the Framers expected the President to exercise military functions may be seen in their failure to curb his authority personally to lead troops on the field of battle. Such a restriction was contained in the New Jersey plan and had the support of Hamilton. The Convention, however, explicitly rejected these attempts to limit his authority to command in person. Some criticisms of this power were voiced in state conventions but there, too, efforts to curtail it were unsuccessful. The intention and the expectation of the Framers and of the people was that the President could, if he so desired, assume personal command in the field. Early presidents did not hesitate to do this. Washington personally commanded the militia called out to suppress the Whiskey Rebellion. James Madison took a direct hand in organizing the ineffectual defense of Washington in 1814. During the Mexican War, President Polk, although he did not command the army in the field, nonetheless personally formulated the military strategy of the war and participated in a wide range of exclusively military matters. The last instance of a President directly exercising military functions was Lincoln's participation in the direction of the Union armies in the spring of 1862. The President personally determined the plan of operations, and, through his War Orders, directed the movement of troop units. It was not until Grant took over in Virginia that presidential participation in military affairs came to an end. No subsequent President essayed the direction of military operations, although Theodore Roosevelt in World War I argued conversely that his previous experience as Commander in Chief proved his competence to command a division in France.[20]

Until the middle of the nineteenth century, no real distinction existed between political and military competence. Any man of affairs was capable of command, and the exercise by the President of his military functions created no difficulties. There was a single, clear political-military hierarchy running from the President through the Secretaries of War and the Navy to the uniformed commanders. Political and military responsibilities and abilities were mixed all along the line. The President frequently had previous military experience; the Secretary of War almost always had. The top generals, on the other hand, were usually involved in politics. The organization of the service departments, consequently, was little different from that of any other department.

This unified hierarchy began to break up as the military function became professionalized. The President was no longer qualified to exercise military command, and even if he were qualified by previous training, he could not devote time to this function without abandoning his political responsibilities. The political functions of the Presidency became incompatible with the military functions of the Commander in Chief. Nor were the civilian politicians appointed Secretaries of War and the Navy competent to exercise military command. On the other hand, the emergence of the military profession produced officers whose experience had been exclusively military, who were quite different types from the politician secretaries, and who were technically qualified to command. The constitutional presumption that the President exercised command still remained, however, and complicated the relations among President, secretary, and military chief. Under the Constitution the military chief was military, the secretary political, and the President political and military. Normally, one would assume that the secretary, with his duty to represent the interests of his department, would be more military in outlook, if not in capability, than the President with his broader interests and responsibilities. The Constitution, however, reversed this relationship, and obscured the clearness of the hierarchy. Did the chain of command go up through the secretary, a civilian politician, to the President? Or were there two lines of authority emanating from the Presidency: a political-administrative line to the secretary and a military command line directly to the highest professional officer? These issues have befogged American military organization down to the present day.

THE BALANCED, COORDINATE, AND VERTICAL TYPES OF EXECUTIVE CIVIL-MILITARY RELATIONS. It is possible to conceive of three different types of executive civil-military relations among the President, secretary, and military chief.* The *balanced pattern* assigns to the President a purely political function: the decision of the highest policy issues and the general supervision of the military establishment. Beneath him is the secretary, also a purely political figure, reponsible for the entire military organization. Below the

* There are, of course, other possible structures of executive civil-military relations, such as one making a military officer departmental secretary. This analysis, however, will be confined to the three ideal types relevant to American experience. Although professional military men have occasionally been appointed Secretary of War, this is unusual and contrary to accepted practice. The only plan seriously advanced to put military men in the place of the secretary was the unsuccessful 1815 proposal to substitute a board of three naval officers for the Secretary of the Navy.

secretary, the hierarchy divides into military and administrative components. The highest professional officer is the leading military adviser to the secretary and normally has command of the military forces. The military chief is subordinate to the secretary who is subordinate to the President, but neither of the two civilian officials exercise military command. Military command stops at the level of the military chief. Also subordinate to the secretary are administrative officials (civilian or military) who direct the nonmilitary supply, logistical, and financial activities of the department.

This balanced pattern of organization tends to maximize military professionalism and civilian control.[21] Civilian and military responsibilities are clearly distinguished, and the latter are subordinated to the former. The President and the secretary handle political matters; the military chief military matters; and the staff or bureau chiefs administrative matters. The scope of the authority of the professional military chief is limited to the military realm by the administrative bureaus, and the level of his authority, subordinate to the secretary, does not involve him in political decisions. Administrative and military interests are balanced by the secretary under the authority of the President. English civil-military relations have been organized along comparable lines since the last half of the nineteenth century. Between 1794 and 1870 the War Office administered the civilian affairs of the army, and the Commander in Chief, directly under the sovereign, was responsible for military command and discipline. In 1870, however, the Cabinet insisted that the military chief be subordinated to the Secretary of State for War. A fully balanced scheme was achieved with the abolition of the post of Commander in Chief in 1895 and the subsequent creation of the office of Chief of the Imperial General Staff. The same system also existed at the Admiralty. This organization was possible only because the sovereign consented, however reluctantly, to have his role as first general and admiral become, in Bagehot's phrase, a "dignified" part of the constitution. The "efficient" hierarchy of control ran from Parliament to Cabinet to Prime Minister to Secretary of State for War and then to the military chief and the administrative bureaus of the War Office. In the United States, however, no President has permitted his constitutional functions as Commander in Chief to atrophy. These remain efficient and not dignified. Consequently, the balanced pattern of organization has been difficult to achieve and even more difficult to maintain. American civil-military relations almost inevitably gravitate in the direction of other arrangements which tend to weaken military professionalism and civilian control.

The *coordinate scheme* involves the separation of military and administrative functions immediately below the President. The secretary is limited to nonmilitary administrative duties, and the military chief discharges his military functions directly under the President. The chain of administration goes from President to Secretary to bureau chiefs; the chain of command from President to military chief to the military forces. This accords with constitutional theory and keeps civilians, except the President, out of the military hierarchy. It tends, however, to undermine civilian control. The scope of the authority of the military chief is limited to military matters, but the level of his authority with direct access to the President involves him in political issues. The President is normally too busy with other affairs to devote sufficient attention to the interrelation of political and military policies, and the military chief consequently has to make political decisions. His direct access to the President also encourages the latter to try his hand at military affairs and to intervene in professional military planning and command where he has no special competence.

The *vertical pattern* solves the problem of the Commander in Chief clause in a different manner, but one which is equally inconsistent with civilian control. In this scheme the secretary and the military chief have identical responsibilities. The administrative bureau heads are subordinated to the professional military chief, and the professional military chief is subordinated to the secretary who is in turn responsible to the President. Since the President is still Commander in Chief, and some connection must exist between him and the rest of the military hierarchy, the secretary is given a place in the military chain of command and is described as the President's deputy commander in chief or in some similar terms. The military chief, however, is given control over all the activities of the department under the secretary, the specifically military command and planning functions being delegated down the hierarchy to a subordinate of the military chief's on the same level as the administrative chiefs of bureaus. This prevents the military chief from achieving direct access to the President because his responsibilities are identical with those of the secretary. Consequently, he can claim no peculiar relation to the President and must be subordinate to the secretary. On the other hand, he supervises all the activities of the department below the secretary and, consequently, may be able to reduce the secretary to a figurehead. By combining in his own person political and administrative responsibilities, as well as functions of military command, the military chief transgresses his competence. He sacrifices higher level for broader scope, which is equally damaging to his professional status. Also, the extension of the constitutional myth so that not only the President but also the secretary is assumed to exercise military command violates the facts of reality.

The American constitutional system thus does not facilitate the stable existence of a balanced pattern of executive civil-military relations. The President's power as Commander in Chief inevitably tends to push the executive structure in the direction of either the coordinate or the vertical pattern. The interests of the military chief lead him to seek both direct access to the President and over-all supervision of both the military and administrative aspects of his department. The secretary, on the other hand, attempts both to maintain exclusive access to the President and to have a multiplicity of subordinates reporting to him. Neither secretary nor military chief ever completely achieve their two objectives. The level and scope of military authority tend to be inversely related. Inevitably, the secretary tends to get cut off from his department by a military head who oversees both military and administrative aspects, or he tends to surrender the military aspect to the professional chief who maintains a direct command relationship with the President.

CIVILIAN CONTROL AND CONSTITUTIONAL GOVERNMENT

Objective civilian control has existed in the United States but it has been the product of geographical isolation and the international balance of power, which permitted the virtual elimination of standing military forces and the exclusion of the military from political power. Civilian control in this sense has been so effective that Americans have called it a fundamental principle of their system of government. But they have been deluding themselves. They have ascribed to the Constitution a virtue of geography. Objective civilian control has been extraconstitutional, a part of our political tradition but not of our constitutional tradition. Civilian control has, in a sense, been like the party system. The Framers did not foresee the rise of popular democracy; consequently, they did not provide for political parties. They did not foresee the rise of the military profession; consequently, they did not provide for civilian control. Neither is contemplated in the Constitution, yet both have been called into existence by nonconstitutional forces. The Constitution has contributed its share to obstructing the growth of a strong party system such as exists in Great Britain. It has also contributed its share to obstructing effective civilian control such as exists in Great Britain. The restraints of a written constitution have proved effective against some of the most powerful functional imperatives.

The question thus arises: to what extent is it possible, short of amending the Constitution, to provide for civilian control in the existing framework? The difficulties are constant but they are not all of equal strength. The extent to which the Commander in Chief clause operates to damage civilian control depends largely upon the individuals who occupy that office. It adds nothing and detracts much from military professionalism and civilian control. The British Prime Minister who is not commander in chief and has no military functions has more effective control over his military forces than does the American President. The principal positive use of the clause has been to expand presidential power against Congress in nonmilitary areas. If the clause can come to be viewed primarily in this nonmilitary sense, and if the presidents can exercise constitutional self-restraint so as to make their military command of the armed forces as honorific as that of the king of England, this obstacle to civilian control would be removed, and a balanced pattern of executive organization be made workable.

The militia clauses only directly hamper the development of military professionalism in one segment of the armed forces. Conceivably, of course, Congress could abolish dual control over the militia. But in the face of the political strength of the National Guard this hardly seems possible. And, given the existing situation, it probably would not even be desirable. The more appropriate course is to make the best of the situation of military federalism. The existence of the Guard will necessarily prevent the development of a strong and ready national reserve organization. The Constitution has made the Guard into a powerful political force, and it is not inconceivable that this political strength may make the Guard into an effective military organization. At the end of 1954, the Army and Air National Guard had almost 400,000 men on drill pay status — twice the number of the Army and Air Force Reserves. At the beginning of 1956 Guard ground forces consisted of 21 infantry divisions, 6 armored divisions, 9 regimental combat teams, 9 armored cavalry regiments, 123 antiaircraft battalions, 74 field artillery battalions, and miscellaneous other units. The Air National Guard was organized into 27 combat wings. The readiness of the Guard was at a higher level than ever before in its history. Many of the antiaircraft units and interceptor squadrons were participating in the air defense of the nation on a semiactive alert status.[22] By its very nature the National Guard can never be brought fully within objective civilian control. But it may still be possible to create a respectable reserve force within the existing constitutional and political framework.

The real constitutional stumbling block to objective civilian control is the separation of powers. This is the essence of the American system of government, and its impact is felt throughout the armed forces. Short of fundamental constitutional change, the separation of powers cannot be altered. Indeed, it is highly questionable whether, even if such change were possible, it would be worth the price. There are values other than civilian control and military professionalism, and these were the values the Framers had in mind when they wrote the Constitution. Foreign countries may have more effective systems of civilian control but no country has as effective a system of restraints upon arbitrary political power or such a unique balance of executive unity and legislative diversity. Inevitably, both military officers attempting to adhere to professional standards and civilian secretaries attempting to exercise civilian control look with envy to the cabinet system. Such a system, however, is not for the United States. Within the framework of the separation of powers, institutional adjustments can be made which will reduce its deleterious effects upon civilian control. But it will never be possible to eliminate these effects completely. A lesser measure of civilian control and lower standards of military professionalism are the continuing prices the American people will have to pay for the other benefits of their constitutional system.

8

The Roots of the American Military Tradition
before the Civil War

THE THREE STRANDS OF AMERICAN MILITARISM

Technicism, popularism, and professionalism are the three strands of the American military tradition. All originated prior to the Civil War. The technical element emphasized the mechanical crafts and specialized sciences which contributed to the trade of the soldier; the good military officer was expert in a technical skill such as civil engineering, ship design, cartography, or hydrography. The roots of military technicism were widespread in American culture in the first part of the nineteenth century, but primarily they were found in the Jeffersonian contributions to American militarism. The technical influence was heaviest in military education and in staff organization, particularly in the Navy. The popular strand of the American military tradition stressed the general capability of all Americans, irrespective of knowledge or training, to excel in the military art; the military officer was the citizen-soldier inspired by the ideals of democracy and liberty. The popular element was derived principally from Jacksonian Democracy. Its institutional manifestations were most notable in the systems of entry and advancement in the officer corps and in the Army organization which crystallized during the Jacksonian period. Finally, the idea of a science of war and of a military profession expert in that science — the Southern contribution to the military tradition — also existed by the middle of the century. Unlike the technical and popular strands, however, which were outgrowths of the dominant strains of American liberalism, military professionalism was identified with a conservative sectional minority which during the course of the century became increasingly isolated from the mainstream of American development. The Southern support which permitted military professionalism to be expressed as an idea, also condemned it to defeat in practice. Unlike technicism and popularism, it lacked institutional manifestations. Prior to the Civil War no significant professional military institutions existed in the United States.

THE FAILURE OF FEDERALISM: HAMILTON'S ABORTIVE PROFESSIONALISM

The failure of military professionalism to make institutional headway in the United States was also intimately connected with the failure of Federalism. The Federalists were almost classically conservative; their basic values closely resembled those of the military ethic. Responsible for the preservation of American security during the difficult first years, they had the conservative's interest in military affairs. "Hamilton's hobby was the Army," wrote John Adams, and the second president himself averred that national defense "has always been near to my heart." [1] They stressed the need for military force and the primacy of national defense among the functions of government. The Federalists did not condemn nor eschew power politics; they played the game with some enjoyment and considerable finesse. Washington's Farewell Address advice that the nation should be strong enough and sensible enough so that it could "choose peace or war as our interest guided by justice shall counsel" even reflected the professional military concept of war as the rational instrument of state policy.

If Federalist conservatism had maintained its vitality as an intellectual current and political force into the nineteenth century, it would have been a fertile source of military professionalism. Instead, the Federalists disappeared before the science of war and the military profession became functionally feasible in America. As a result, while they stressed the need for military force, they were not clear as to the need for professional direction of that force. Their two leaders, Washington and Hamilton, were indeed the antitheses of the professional type, moving with ease from military to political office and back again. They likewise had little understanding of objective civilian control. Washington obeyed the Continental Congress not as a soldier but as a citizen. Hamilton alone among the Federalists anticipated important elements of military professionalism. He saw that the prolonged and expert instruction of a small group of military leaders in the essentials of the art of war was a necessary result of the division of labor, and he urged the creation of an elaborate military university to school officers in the "principles of war, the exercises it requires, and the sciences upon which they are founded." [2] Hamilton's views were the most advanced application of the Federalist philosophy to military affairs, but they were, however, not even acceptable to most Federalists. And, more significantly, the conservative Federalist philosophy was not acceptable to most Americans. Its political eclipse in 1800 made Jeffersonian technicism rather than Hamilton's incipient professionalism the starting point of the American military tradition.

TECHNICISM

JEFFERSONIAN SOURCES: THE PRINCIPLE OF SPECIALIZATION. The American officer of the pre-Civil War years was frequently highly trained and scientifically educated but his training was not in a military skill shared with all his fellow officers and distinguishing them from the rest of society. Instead, the officer was expert in one of several technical specialities, competence in which separated him from other officers trained in different specialities and at the same time fostered close bonds with civilians practicing his speciality outside the military forces. The officer corps, in other words, was divided into subgroups, some more important than the rest, but each likely to be more closely tied with a segment of civilian society than with other segments of the corps. The Army officer was frequently more engineering-minded than military-minded, and the naval officer more seamanship-minded than naval-minded. There was as yet in America no distinctive military science which, developing out of the various technical specialities, could modify them, subordinate them, and integrate them into a separate subject directed to the exclusively military purpose of war. Technicism remained a strong force in American militarism after it had been generally superseded by professionalism in Europe. It derived its strength from the many pragmatic, empirical, materialistic, practical aspects of American culture, equally hostile to the generalizations of theory and to teleological definitions of purpose. Insofar as it had its roots in any distinctive political-intellectual current, military technicism was primarily the product of the Jeffersonian influence upon American military institutions.

Like other liberals, Jefferson had little interest in or use for regular military forces, and he had no recognition of the emerging character of professional military officership. Jefferson had no use for objective civilian control, condemning the distinction "between the civil and military, which it is for the happiness of both to obliterate." Unlike most subsequent liberals, however, he did have a definite plan for national defense. Jefferson did not scout the continuing threats to the United States nor the persistent possibility of war. His military policy had its roots in the same unstable state of international relations as did Hamilton's. But in substance it was vastly different, representing an effort to develop a liberal alternative to the Hamiltonian program which would embody the extreme of transmutation based on the "military sovereignty of the people." Far from wishing to disarm the United States, Jefferson desired to turn the nation into an armed camp. "None but an armed nation can dispense with a standing army; to keep ours armed and disciplined is, therefore, at all times important . . ." [3] The militia should be universal in scope — "every citizen a soldier" is a Jeffersonian motto — and well-organized, classified, disciplined, and equipped. In the end, Jefferson's military policy was no more successful than Hamilton's. To universalize the military obligation was in effect to abolish it. Instead of substituting a liberal force for a regular force, Congress preferred to limit the regular force to an inconsequential size. Extirpation triumphed over transmutation. Instead of maintaining a militia in peace to deal with emergencies and creating a regular army in war, as recommended by Jefferson, the United States maintained a regular army in peace to deal with emergencies and enlisted the militia after the outbreak of war. The Hamiltonian program was infeasible in a liberal society because it was contrary to the principles of liberalism; the Jeffersonian program was infeasible because it was contrary to the principles of society.

The Roots of the Military Tradition

The Jeffersonian approach to military science and military leadership mirrored its theory of military force. Just as the Jeffersonians recognized the need for some form of military force, they also recognized the need for some form of military knowledge and education. But just as they identified military force with the civic population, so also they drew no distinction between civil and military skills. Quantitatively, military force was indistinguishable from the whole of society; qualitatively, military science was indistinguishable from the whole of science. "We must train and classify the whole of our male citizens," Jefferson declared. "And make military instruction a regular part of collegiate education." The diffusion of military instruction throughout society was only possible because the skills required for the military vocation were the same as those required for a variety of civilian vocations. Technical subjects figured much more prominently than military ones in the sparse literature produced by American military and naval officers prior to the 1830's. Jeffersonian respect went to the Enlightenment man of science; the good military officer was expert in some special scientific skill.

The tendency toward technicism in the Army officer corps was strengthened by the French influence on American militarism. This, too, was fostered by Jeffersonian sympathies for French institutions and culture. The Americans imitated the French in stressing fortifications, artillery, and engineering. Sylvanus Thayer, the dominating genius of West Point during its early years, studied French education carefully and was convinced that France was the "repository of military science." He consciously strove to pattern his school along French lines, following the great model of the Ecole Polytechnique, and utilizing French instructors and French textbooks. Outstanding Academy graduates in the first half of the nineteenth century, such as Halleck and Mahan, were sent to France not Prussia to continue their education. Jomini was viewed as the final word on the larger aspects of military operations, and American infantry, cavalry, and artillery tactics imitated those of the French Army. The French influence upon the Academy and the Army at large helped to produce a high level of technical and scientific achievement, but it detracted from emphasis upon the Army's military purposes.[4]

EDUCATION: THE ENGINEERING SCHOOL AT WEST POINT. American military education was almost entirely technical in purpose and content until after the Civil War. There was little or no instruction in higher military science and strategy, and there were no American educational institutions comparable to the Prussian preliminary schools or the Berlin Kriegsakademie. The most notable and lasting manifestation of the Jeffersonian impact upon American militarism was in the military academy at West Point. Hamilton's recommendations of 1799 had proposed the creation of five schools: a Fundamental School in which students received instruction for two years in "all the sciences necessary to a perfect knowledge of the different branches of the military art"; and four advanced engineering and artillery, cavalry, infantry, and naval schools, to one of which students would go for specialized study after completing the fundamental courses. This would have been a true professional academy teaching the essence of military science as a whole as well as elements of its more specialized branches.[5] In contrast, the institution which Jefferson established at West Point in 1802 was only one-fifth of the military university urged by Hamilton. It was created almost incidental to the creation of the Corps of Engineers. Its principal object was to produce engineers for military and civil employment. It was the equivalent of the Ecole Polytechnique, not of St. Cyr: a technical institute designed to serve the entire nation as a practical scientific school, not a professional academy for the military vocation. As its first superintendent, Jefferson appointed Jonathan Williams, who had no military experience prior to his appointment but had worked on the construction of fortifications and made a reputation as a practicing scientist. Jefferson's interest was always in the scientific rather than the military activities of the Academy.

The Jeffersonian origins of West Point had tremendous impact upon American military education, initiating a technological emphasis, remnants of which long persisted. The principal contributions of the Academy in the pre-Civil War years were, as intended by Jefferson, in the fields of engineering and science. Until after the Civil War, the school remained a part of the Corps of Engineers, and its superintendent had to be appointed from that branch. Engineering dominated the curriculum. A Department of Engineering was established in 1812, but it was not until 1858 that Congress created a Department of Tactics. Military subjects were taught as a sideline to military engineering, and the military engineering course itself was subordinated to civil engineering. As one observer commented, at the time of the Civil War there was "no instruction in strategy or grand tactics, in military history, or in what is called the Art of War." [6] Graduates of the Academy were much in demand by private employers and were utilized by the government in topographical surveys, railroad building, and the construction of other internal improvements. Throughout the years preceding the Civil War its alumni distinguished themselves to a greater extent in civil occupations than in the military service. West Point produced more railroad presidents than generals. Many students entered the Academy for the explicit purpose of becoming scientists or engineers rather than Army officers, and the Academy was justified to the country in terms of its contributions to science, exploration, and internal development. Prior to 1835, West Point exercised a formative influence over the development of technical education in America. A majority of the nineteen engineering schools established before 1870, including those at Harvard and Yale, had direct pedagogical affiliations with the Military Academy. Thus, before the Civil War West Point was deficient in the two components of a preliminary professional military education. It did not give its students a broad grounding in the liberal arts; neither did it furnish them with the first essentials of military science.

Before the 1860's, technicism was even more pervading in many respects in naval education than in the Army. Its causes, however, were less immediately traceable to Jeffersonian sources. In the early days the emphasis was upon seamanship, and naval officers were frequently commissioned directly from the merchant marine. Subsequently, coincidental with the introduction of steam, a shift in concern occurred to marine engineering. Prior to 1845 the education of officers was practical and haphazard. The only examinations required of midshipmen were in navigation and seamanship, and a strong tradition existed in the Navy that the only place for the education of an officer was the deck of a ship. Eventually the desirability of securing legislative establishment of a shore school comparable to West Point was generally recognized. The nature of this school, however, was still conceived of in technical terms. In 1814, for instance, Secretary Jones advocated instruction in purely technical subjects, which alone he considered "necessary to the accomplishment of the naval officer." In 1841, Secretary Upshur argued that the introduction of steam vessels required a high order of scientific knowledge among officers.[7] When the Naval Academy was eventually established in 1845, its curriculum closely resembled that of West Point except for the substitution of marine technology for civil engineering. For decades afterward, opposition to theoretical instruction still remained strong in the Navy.

STAFF ORGANIZATION: JEFFERSONIAN NAVAL TECHNICISM, 1815–1885. The prevalence of technicism was also reflected in the key role assigned the administrative staff services in Army and Navy organization. Neither the War Department nor the Navy Department during this period possessed a true general staff devoted to the application of professional knowledge to military operations and war. An Army "General Staff" created in 1813 consisted of the adjutant general, quartermaster general, commissary general of ordnance, paymaster, assistant topographical engineer, and their assistants. Their influence in the Army structure was balanced somewhat by the position of the Commanding General, who theoretically represented the military interests of the Army but who actually became deeply involved in political controversy. The technical arms enjoyed a favored status. Engineering was defined by the Articles of War as "the most elevated branch of military science." [8] Throughout the years leading to the Civil War much of the energy of the Army and the Navy was devoted to the essentially civilian pursuits of exploration, scientific research, and internal development.

The most notable instance of the influence of Jeffersonian technicism in military organization was in the Navy Department, the organization of which was given a lasting character during Madison's administration immediately after the War of 1812. In the pattern of organization which was then established and which prevailed until the twentieth century, military expertise was explicitly identified with technical expertise, and the necessity of professional knowledge for the broad conduct of naval operations in war was equally explicitly denied. Naval organization thus made no provision whatsoever for the representation of the professional military interests in the Navy, and consequently it did not resemble any of the three ideal types of executive civil-military relations. It was instead a strictly preprofessional form of organization.

From 1798 to 1815 the Navy Department consisted only of a Secretary and a few clerks who transacted all departmental business, civil and military. After the War of 1812, the demand for a larger staff arose and Congress established a Board of Navy Commissioners composed of three captains. The Board was placed under the Secretary, and its responsibilities were made coextensive with his. Civil duties — procurement and construction — and military duties — the employment of vessels — were assigned equally to both Board and Secretary. Clearly the intention of Congress was to establish a vertical system of organization. This, however, was not the view of the Secretary of the Navy, Benjamin Crowninshield. In one of its first actions, the Board demanded that the Secretary inform it as to the destination of a squadron. Crowninshield refused this request, claiming that the Board should deal only with civil-industrial matters. The President sustained this interpretation of the law, and thereafter down to 1842 the three naval officers constituting the Navy Commissioners directed the civil activities of the Department, while the civilian secretary directed the military activities.

This system seems absurdly paradoxical on the surface. Actually, logic was behind it. The civil activities of the Navy were much more highly specialized and technical than its military activities. The design, construction, and equipment of naval vessels and the operation of the Navy yards were jobs for experts. Compared to these, discipline, the assignment of personnel, and the employment of vessels were relatively simple matters. The man of affairs might still direct the latter; it was impossible for him to manage the former. The idea that the Secretary was competent to handle the military affairs of the Navy was enhanced by the custom, which prevailed down to the 1820's, of appointing to that post men with maritime experience. The rationale behind naval organization was explicitly stated by Secretary Paulding in

1839. The duties of the Department, he said, divide naturally into two classes. The first class "comprises those connected with the more general and comprehensive interests of the state" — the size and distribution of naval forces, and the direction, employment, and discipline of naval personnel. The second class includes "everything connected with the construction, equipment and maintenance of the naval force." The first class of duties, according to the Secretary, "requires no special technical or professional knowledge or experience . . ." Consequently, these duties may be directly discharged by the Secretary. The performance of the second class of duties, however, "calls for long professional experience, and it is believed can be more completely attained under the ministration of competent naval officers." [9] The replacement of the Navy Commissioners by the bureau system in 1842 did not alter this Jeffersonian pattern. The duties which had been previously collectively exercised by the Board of Navy Commissioners simply devolved on to the heads of the five bureaus for Yards and Docks; Construction, Equipment and Repairs; Provisions and Clothing; Ordnance and Hydrography; and Medicine and Surgery. No provision was made for the representation of the professional military viewpoint in the Navy structure, and the Secretary still attempted to discharge this function.

Inevitably, as the military activities of the Navy became increasingly complicated, the Secretaries became less competent to administer them. This was painfully obvious in war. In the Civil War it was necessary to appoint a former naval captain as assistant secretary to act as professional military head of the Navy and to direct its strategy and operations. This official also dealt directly with Lincoln, and during the war years naval organization thus briefly approximated the coordinate pattern. In 1869, however, the post of assistant secretary was abolished, and the Navy reverted to its prewar preprofessional organization. At various times in the next thirty years, whenever a war threatened, the Navy was forced hastily to establish an *ad hoc* professional board for military planning. During the Spanish-American War, a Naval Strategy Board was created to direct military operations. In peace, however, these remained the immediate responsibility of the civilian secretary, and the highest military leadership of the Navy was in the technical chiefs of bureaus. Just as the technical emphasis at West Point hampered the emergence of military professionalism in the Army, the technical interests entrenched in naval organization were a major obstacle to the Navy professional reformers at the end of the nineteenth century.

POPULARISM

JACKSONIAN SOURCES: THE PRINCIPLE OF AMALGAMATION. While the absence of a distinctive military science drew the officer, on the one hand, into technical specialization, it could, on the other hand, lead to the conclusion that no specialized competence of any sort was necessary for officership. The lack of professional standards of judgment invited the use of popular standards. Inevitably, the military service, like the civil service, was utilized to serve the ulterior ends, honorable or not, of the political leaders of the government. The division of the officer corps into technical specialities built individual bridges between the segments of the corps and their counterparts in civil activity; the intrusion of popular politics into the corps created a broad connection with the mainstream of American life. This connection reflected what was popular, amateur, democratic, and idealistic in American culture. It was primarily the product of Jacksonian Democracy.

Jacksonian Democracy began the period of liberal indifference to military affairs. After 1815 there were, aside from the Indians, no significant threats to American security. A liberal plan for military defense was no longer necessary. The disappearance of foreign dangers, plus the emerging imperatives of military professionalism, caused a shift from a positive emphasis upon the citizen militia and technical expertise to negative opposition to all military institutions. The Jacksonians repeated the clichés of Jeffersonian policy but made no effort to realize them in practice. Warning of the dangers of a standing army and hailing the militia as the bulwark of liberty, they neither abolished the Regular Army nor made an effective military force out of the militia. During the thirty years before the Civil War, the militia companies degenerated into almost purely social organizations lacking military discipline and military skill.[10] Jefferson wished to educate all citizens to be soldiers; the Jacksonians assumed that all citizens could be soldiers without training. Technical competence was required of the good Jeffersonian officer; militant enthusiasm of his Jacksonian counterpart. In contrast to Jeffersonian technicism, the Jacksonian approach to military officership was distinctly anti-intellectual.

The distinguishing aspect of the Jacksonian attitude on military affairs was its opposition to the officer corps as an aristocratic institution. This hostility was rooted both in the security of the nation and in the spirit of the times. The Jacksonian concept of the people — united and homogeneous — was incompatible with social differentiations of any sort. The drive for equality became, as De Tocqueville saw, the drive for uniformity. Yet uniformity was also linked with versatility. All citizens were alike because they all could do everything. While Jefferson looked to an armed people expressed in the slogan "every citizen a soldier," the Jacksonians looked to a united people expressed in "the principle of amalgamation." The American nation, as one congressional committee put it, was founded "upon the great principle of amalgamating all orders of society." All professionalism was viewed with suspicion. The military profession which was just beginning was virtually strangled at birth. "In a free State, it was most impolitic and unsafe for the army to be separated in habits, interests, and feelings from the other orders of society." [11]

PERSONNEL: CONGRESSIONAL APPOINTMENT AND LATERAL ENTRANCE. The Jacksonian impact upon the American military tradition was most pronounced with respect to the systems of entry and advancement. West Point was the principal target of Jacksonian hostility, the criticism centering not upon the curriculum and methods of the Academy but rather upon the manner in which cadets were appointed and the extent to which Academy graduates preëmpted junior officer positions in the Army. In Jacksonian eyes, not only was specialized skill unnecessary for a military officer, but also every man had a natural right to pursue the vocation of his choice. Even Jackson's Secretary of War denounced the "exclusive privilege of entering the army" and cited the example of revolutionary France as justification for extensive promotions from the ranks. Jackson himself had an undisguised antipathy for the Academy which symbolized such a different conception of officership from that which he himself embodied. During his administration discipline faltered at West Point, and eventually Sylvanus Thayer, the superintendent and molder of the West Point educational methods, resigned in disgust at the intrusion of the spoils system. The Jacksonian attack reached its peak in 1837 when a select congressional committee appointed to investigate West Point recommended its abolition. In the opinion of the committee, the Academy contravened the principles of the founding fathers and monopolized commissions in the Regular Army, which ought to be kept open to "all citizens, like every other department of government." The basic trouble was the assumption that "education and discipline" were "everything." The military caste produced by West Point was incapable of leading freeborn American citizens. Success in war came to those "qualified to do so by nature." Blasting away at the "tinsels of scholarship" the committee restated in eloquent terms the eighteenth-century concept of military genius. The rich were preferred to the poor in the selection of cadets, the committee declared, although it admitted it had no specific evidence on this point. While Congress did not follow up its committee's suggestions and do away with West Point, the hostility which the committee reflected remained prevalent, state legislatures condemning the "aristocratical institution" in New York as "wholly inconsistent with the spirit and genuis of our liberal institutions." [12]

The most permanent legacy of Jacksonian opposition was the congressional system of appointment to the Academy. In the first decades of the century, cadets were appointed by the military authorities. In the 1820's and 1830's, however, as the number of candidates began to exceed the number of appointments, and, as the attacks upon the supposedly aristocratic and plutocratic nature of the Academy mounted, the custom developed of distributing appointments among the congressional districts. By the early 1840's appointments were made on the recommendation of the Representatives, and congressmen had come to look upon them as a normal part of their patronage. The system was formalized in 1843 when Congress required that cadets be distributed equally among the congressional districts with each cadet actually being a resident of the district from which he received his appointment. Just prior to the establishment of the Naval Academy in 1845, Congress also required that the appointment of midshipmen in the Navy should be distributed among the states and territories in proportion to the number of Representatives and Delegates. As each appointee had to be a resident of the state from which he was appointed, the Navy Department came to rely upon the recommendations of the congressman from the candidate's district. In 1852, Congress formalized this system requiring congressional nomination as a prerequisite to selection as a midshipman.[13] The congressional system of appointment to the military academies was a crude effort at popular subjective civilian control but it was to have a lasting effect on American military institutions.

Lateral entry directly from civilian life into the higher ranks of the officer corps was also a common phenomenon prior to the Civil War. It was in some respects an ancient practice, but it became much more widespread under the Jacksonians. In 1836, for instance, when four additional regiments of dragoons were formed, thirty officers were appointed directly from civil life and four from West Point graduates. Of the Army's thirty-seven generals from 1802 to 1861, not one was a West Pointer; twenty-three were virtually without military experience and eleven others entered the service at the grade of captain or higher. Army regulations at the time of the Mexican War encouraged the appointment of officers from civil life. Regular officers frequently quit the service, entered civilian occupations, then, in time of war, reëntered the Army as militia or volunteer officers at higher grades than those of the officers who had stayed with the service. Officers were frequently elected in the militia and also in the lower ranks of the Civil War volunteers. Until the last years of the Civil War, politics not merit dictated appointments to the highest Army posts. Influence was equally important in the Navy and Marine Corps, although in these services it was more personal in nature, with nepotism not uncommon. "The most important factor in the selection of midshipmen," writes Paullin of the years from 1815 to 1842, "was political and personal influence; and many statesmen of the olden times left memorials of their families in the navy list by making midshipmen of sundry sons, grandsons, nephews, and cousins." [14]

Many opposed political appointment, but the most generally accepted substitute, the seniority system, was, if anything, a cure worse than the disease. During the first half of the nineteenth century, Congress insisted upon maintaining seniority as the formal system of advancement. The result was that able officers spent decades in the lower ranks, and all officers who had normal or supernormal longevity were assured of reaching the higher ranks. Seniority, like politics, was also attacked by those who wanted rank to reflect merit. Even the British system of purchase, some felt, was superior to the American reliance upon seniority, especially since the latter failed in its ostensible purpose of minimizing politics. "Our army," one officer complained, "is much more open to this kind of favoritism and political partiality, than that of almost any of the governments of Europe, which we have been accustomed to regard as aristocratic and wholly unfriendly to real merit." [15] Efforts to substitute a more professional system of advancement failed of success in both the Army and the Navy. Lacking generally accepted criteria for judging professional competence, it was impossible to develop standards for promotion by merit. The absence of a retirement system in the Army and the Navy caused officers to hang on to their posts until they died in their boots, holding up the advancement of juniors. The Navy received a limited retirement system in 1855, but the Army had to wait until after the Civil War. In addition, the Navy had hardly a hierarchy of professional grades, there being only the three officer ranks of lieutenant, commander, and captain. With only two promotions in a lifetime, there was little incentive to distinguished effort and professional improvement.

The influence of popularism in the officer corps encouraged the officers to be active in politics. The pattern was set by the Commanding Generals of the Army. Generals Jacob Brown and Scott were active political figures, and the latter campaigned for the Presidency while commanding the Army. The majority of the officers favored military participation in politics. In a discussion of the issue in the *Army and Navy Chronicle* in 1836, the prevailing opinion was that the Founding Fathers had set the proper example. Every officer in the Revolutionary Army, it was argued, was also a politician. "The feeling and the opinion that an officer should take no part in politics are conceived in the most servile spirit, and inculcated by heartless military aristocrats, whose interest it is to hold the minds of their subordinates in entire subjection to their domineering propensities." [16] The rights of an officer to speak and act politically were no different, it was agreed, than those of any other American citizen.

ARMY ORGANIZATION: THE COORDINATE PATTERN, 1836–1903. The nineteenth-century pattern of naval organization had been fixed along Jeffersonian lines during Madison's administration. The system of Army organization which was to prevail until the first years of the twentieth century was formalized in 1836 and reflected distinctly Jacksonian influences. Prior to 1821 the Army, like the Navy, had no single professional head. The Secretary of War administered the Army through generals commanding geographical districts and supervised the operation of the staff agencies in Washington. He could, if he wished and as Secretary Armstrong did in 1813, exercise direct command of the troops in the field. He thus had complete control over his department; the political and military functions were as yet undifferentiated. In 1821, however, Secretary of War John C. Calhoun ordered the sole remaining major general to Washington so as to bring "the military administration of the army, as well as its pecuniary, through the several subordinate branches, under the immediate inspection and control of the Government." [17] Calhoun's intention was to establish a balanced system of organization. On the one hand, the Secretary would supervise the "General Staff" officers in charge of the technical departments of medicine, subsistence, quartermaster, pay, the adjutant general, and the Corps of Engineers. On the other hand, through the Commanding General, the Secretary would direct the military operations of the Army. Calhoun, however, soon left office, and the system began to function in a manner quite different from that which he had intended. Particularly after Jackson became President, his previous military experience, the constitutional role of the President as Commander in Chief, the personalities of the President, the Commanding General, and the Secretaries, and the pulls of politics and interest, combined to warp Calhoun's organization into a coordinate pattern. The Commanding General became independent of the Secretary and directly responsible to the President on military matters. The authority of the Secretary was limited to fiscal and administrative affairs including the supervision of the technical bureaus. Lewis Cass, Jackson's Secretary of War, endorsed this development, declaring that it was the function of the Commanding

General "to superintend and direct those parts of the administration of the army which are strictly military in their character, and which, to be properly conducted, require not only the advantage of military experience, but of a military connexion with the army." [18] The coordinate system of dual control by the Secretary and Commanding General was formally written into Army Regulations at the close of Jackson's administration in 1836:

> The military establishment is placed under the orders of the Major-General Commanding-in-Chief, in all that regards its discipline and military control. Its fiscal arrangements properly belong to the administrative departments of the staff, and to the Treasury Department under the direction of the Secretary of War.[19]

With the exception of a few years before and after the Civil War, this provision remained in the Regulations until Root's reorganization of the War Department in 1903.

The coordinate Army organization was justified on the grounds that the Commanding General represented the permanent military interests of the Army and that the Secretary of War as an untutored civilian could not interpose himself on military matters between the Commanding General and the constitutional Commander in Chief. Within the military establishment the function of the Commanding General was command, that of the Secretary administration. As a civilian it was impossible for the latter to exercise military command. "In all matters strictly military," declared James A: Garfield, "the General of the Army is second in command under the President." [20] Nor could the President delegate his command authority over the Army to the Secretary because the latter was not part of the Army and, hence, could not be authorized to direct it. The Army and War Department were distinct agencies.[21] The corollary to the responsibility of the Commanding General to the President was the responsibility of the bureau chiefs to the Secretary. After the 1820's the bureau heads reported directly to the Secretary, and all Secretaries insisted upon issuing direct orders to the bureaus without the intervention of the Commanding General. Legislation establishing bureaus virtually always placed them under the "direction" or "supervision" of the Secretary. War Department organization under the coordinate plan was in part a conscious imitation of the similar British system prevailing between 1795 and 1870. The division of responsibilities between the English Secretary of State for War and the Commander in Chief was hailed in American military writing as the wisest form of military organization.

While in theory the Commanding General embodied the professional military interests of the Army and was divorced from politics, in actual practice, quite the reverse was generally true. The direct access of the General to the President and the ill-defined allocation of responsibilities between him and the Secretary kept the Army's top military officer continually involved in political controversy. The biggest eruption was in 1855 when General Scott and Secretary Davis engaged in one of the most vitriolic exchanges ever to enliven American public administration. This struggle became a continuing characteristic of military affairs. McClellan fought Secretary Stanton during the Civil War; Sherman fought Secretary Belknap during the Grant administration; Sheridan quarreled with Secretary Endicott in the 1880's; and General Miles and Secretary Alger were openly at swords' points during the Spanish-American War. Scott moved his headquarters from Washington to New York because he could not get along with the Taylor administration. Sherman shifted his command to St. Louis as a result of his disagreements with the civilian authorities. In addition, just as the Secretary strove to extend his authority over the Commanding General, the latter also attempted to exert control over the bureaus. In 1829 the adjutant general protested to the Secretary that the Commanding General was meddling in affairs which did not properly concern him, and two years later the General in turn complained that the "staff departments hardly seemed to belong to the same service." Throughout the remainder of the century the political struggle of the bureaus versus the General and the General versus the Secretary successfully prevented the General from functioning as a true professional military leader. "Constant discord" was the inevitable result of the coordinate system.[22]

The coordinate organization established by the Jacksonians was the first attempt to reconcile the constitutional provisions making the President Commander in Chief with the existence of a specialized profession devoted to military command and planning. Its history demonstrates the virtual impossibility of achieving objective civilian control through this form of organization. The prolonged War Department experience with the coordinate pattern is probably unique in the history of American public administration. Other major departments and agencies have virtually always been headed by a single individual or a board or commission acting as a single individual. The War Department, however, for sixty-five years operated under a system of dual control, the peculiar result of constitutional forms and of initial Jacksonian unwillingness to permit a balanced pattern of executive civil-military relations.

PROFESSIONALISM

SOUTHERN SOURCES: THE TRADITION OF MILITARY INTEREST. The South gave military professionalism its only significant support in the pre-Civil War years. A "Southern military tradition" existed in a way in which there was never a New England, Middle Western, or Rocky Mountain military tradition. The sources of Southern interest in military affairs were varied. First, the South had peculiar sectional needs for military force. On the western frontier the Indian threat was ever moving westward with the advancing line of settlements. No locality felt the need of military protection for more than a few decades, and there was no basis for a continuing promilitary group. In the South, however, the frontier was more static. Three generations of Southerners were troubled by the depredations of the Seminoles and Creeks, and the threat was not finally removed until the end of the exhausting six-year Florida War in 1842. The active Indian threat was also supplemented by the potential danger of a slave revolt, the two not being entirely unrelated since escaped slaves often teamed up with the Indian tribes. As a result of these two threats, strong military forces and the widespread dissemination of military knowledge and skill were held necessary to the security of the plantation system. A second source of Southern militarism was the romantic cult which infused antebellum Southern culture. This stemmed in large part from the agricultural nature of the South, the admiration of Southerners for the English ideal of the "gentleman," and the desire, fanned by the novels of Scott, to ape the manners and customs of medieval knighthood. All these contributed to the glorification of violence, chivalry, and the martial ideal.[23] Thirdly, the agrarian character of the section and the relative absence of commercial and industrial opportunities present in other parts of the country naturally stimulated Southern interest in the military career.

Sectional self-interest, an atavic allegiance to feudal romanticism, and an agrarian economy — all nurtured Southern militarism. These sources, however, were not in themselves sufficient to lead to an appreciation of military professionalism. In fact, in many respects they reflected motivations incompatible with professional ideals. Transcending these sources, however, was the conservative cast of Southern society and Southern thinking, the product of the South's defensive position as an illiberal island in a liberal society. This conservatism furnished a sympathetic environment for the growth of the professional ideal and channeled the military concern aroused by the other aspects of Southern life into an active recognition of the nature of the military profession and a preference for that profession as a career. The attraction of this conservative environment was manifest at the outbreak of the Civil War. The Southern professional officer in 1861 was confronted with a cruel choice symbolized in Lee's anguished pacing at Arlington. On the one hand, the Southern officer's political allegiances drew him to the Confederacy; on the other, his professional responsibility was to the Union. The decision, however, was not simply a clear cut one between political and professional values. For the South itself was more sympathetic to the military profession than the North. As one Northern officer declared during the war, "For many years previous to secession, the profession of arms had, at the North fallen from disrepute to contempt . . . To be an officer of the Regular Army was, popularly, to be an idle gentleman, well paid for doing nothing, scarcely worthy of respect, and assuredly not of esteem." A Southern Marine captain exclaimed to Alfred Mahan that of course Mahan's father, a Virginian and a professor at West Point, would come South: "All your father's antecedents are military; there is no military spirit in the North; he must come to us." [24] Thus, setting aside political considerations, the Southern officer faced a strange paradox: his professional duty demanded that he support the society which rejected his profession and fight the society which had given it birth. Fortunately for the Southern officers, the policies of the Union government in 1860 and 1861 permitted them to resign their commissions without violating their professional trust. Even so, 40 to 50 per cent of the Southern West Point graduates on active duty in 1860 held to their posts and remained loyal to the Union. The course of the conflict, however, revealed even more strongly the different attitudes of the two sections. Professional officers were pushed aside and passed over in the Union, the higher commissions going, in the first stages of the war at least, to officers called back into service or directly appointed from civil life, many of them "political" appointees. In contrast, the South welcomed its professionals and capitalized upon their talents. Sixty-four per cent of the Regular Army officers who went South became generals; less than 30 per cent of those who stayed with the Union achieved that rank.[25]

Throughout the half century before the Civil War Southerners preëmpted the principal positions of leadership in military affairs. While the leadership of the entire government was predominantly Southern in the first three decades of the nineteenth century, the military departments had an even more pronounced Southern complexion. The gradual displacement of Southern personnel in the civil side of government which occurred toward the middle of the century also had no counterpart on the military side. Instead, Southern influence tended to become more concentrated in the military departments. Despite the congressional system of appointments, the South furnished a heavily disproportionate share of the cadets at West Point. The ideals and atmosphere of the Military Academy became more markedly Southern toward the middle of the century, and the Naval Academy also was characterized by the "prevalence of a Southern flavor." On the Army list of 1837, three of the four active generals were from Virginia, and nine of the thirteen colonels of the line were Southern, six of them Virginians. Ten of the twenty-two highest ranking officers of the Army were from the Old Dominion. Many of the officers who held the top posts over long periods of time came from the South. Winfield Scott, Commanding General from 1841 to 1861, Colonel Roger Jones, adjutant general from 1825 to 1852, and Brigadier General T. S. Jessup, quartermaster general from 1818 to 1850, were all Virginians. The geographical center of the naval officer corps also moved South. In the early years of the Republic, New England had predominated in the Navy. Subsequently, in the first quarter of the nineteenth century, the "naval clans" of the Middle Atlantic seaports were the principal source of naval officers. By 1842, however, 44 per cent of the midshipmen appointments were going to the Maryland-Virginia area. Northern concern about this concentration was one of the factors leading Congress to distribute the midshipmen appointments among the congressional districts. The civilian Secretaries of War — including the two most vigorous, Calhoun and Jefferson Davis — and Secretaries of the Navy, as well as the congressional leaders in military affairs — were frequently Southerners.[26]

Southern support both aided and obstructed military professionalization. The identification of military institutions and ideals with that portion of American society which was distinctly "different" from the dominant elements in American culture strengthened the tendency in the north and west to view military professionalism as something inherently alien and aristocratic. Southern support was insufficient to enable military professionalism to prevail against the predominant Jeffersonian and Jacksonian attitudes. It was not until the South was defeated in the Civil War that American liberalism, instead of fighting professional development, simply ignored it. But if Southern support was a short-term political liability, it was also a long-term intellectual asset. While the institutions of military organization, education, entry, and advancement were shaped along Jeffersonian and Jacksonian lines, the ideas deriving from Southern sources were capturing the mind of the American military man. Southern interest sparked the emergence of military professionalism as a concept and paved the way for the institutional reforms of the post-Civil War era. The roots of American military professionalism go back to mid-nineteenth-century Southern conservatism.

JOHN C. CALHOUN: THE FRUSTRATIONS OF THE SOUTHERN MILITARY STATESMAN. The problems inherent in the relationship between Southern military professionalism and the rest of American society were well illustrated by John C. Calhoun's career as Secretary of War under James Monroe from 1817 to 1825. Calhoun was in many respects the model Secretary of War, energetically concerned with both the administrative and military aspects of his responsibilities. He initiated numerous lasting institutional reforms in the administration and management of the War Department. He rationalized the Army supply system and placed procurement upon a responsible and efficient basis. He vitalized the office of the Inspector General as the Secretary's instrument for checking upon the activities of the military establishment. He created a Medical Department and persuaded Congress to reorganize and strengthen the General Staff departments, laying down the essentials of their organization which were to persist for most of the nineteenth century. He overhauled the Army accounting system and instituted a new centralized method of fiscal responsibility and control. He had the Army Regulations rewritten and codified. He improved the subsistence of the Army and reduced its cost. He appointed able and respected men to head the various staff bureaus and divisions.[27] When he left office the Army's smoothly functioning administrative organization bore little resemblance to the chaos which had prevailed at the close of the War of 1812. Under his direction the War Department became the most efficient agency in the government. For decades afterward, its clerks aspired to handle Army business as "Mr. Calhoun would have done it."

In the realm of administration and management — the housekeeping functions of the Army — Calhoun was thus a great success. But he was also concerned with the Army as a military organization and with the issues of military policy. His views on these matters reflected an essentially conservative outlook. They were based on a Hamiltonian pessimism with respect to human nature and the inevitability of war. Military preparations were essential, and most important among these was the maintenance of a professional officer corps. More clearly than any other American of his time, Calhoun appreciated the changing character of the military vocation. The "rapid progress of military science," he argued, had professionalized officership while leaving unchanged the duties of the enlisted man. In words worthy of von Moltke, Calhoun rejected the eighteenth-century and Jacksonian idea that natural military genius would suffice and emphasized the necessity of trained collective competence. The survival of the nation depended upon the extent to which citizens of "talents and character . . . make arms their profession," and upon the extent to which the armed forces perpetuate "military skill and experience" in peacetime. West Point, Calhoun believed, should be separated from the Corps of Engineers, because the diverse duties of the Corps had "little reference to the existing military establishment." The Academy should be transformed from a technical institute into a professional school and thus given a "character and importance" which had not "been contemplated in its original institution." With West Point and possibly an additional academy devoted to the elementary study of the "art of war," advanced schools of application should then be established for the topographical corps, the artillery, and the engineers. Basically, Calhoun wanted to reorganize American military education from the Jeffersonian to the Hamiltonian pattern. Calhoun's military policy proposed to organize the Army on a skeleton basis, sufficient to perform its peacetime duties of garrisoning the Atlantic forts and Indian posts, yet by expansion and multiplication capable of rapidly increasing to the size necessary for war. Inherent in this plan for an "expansible standing army" was the premise that those professional officers who commanded the small Regular Army in peace would also command the expanded Army in war: recruits would be siphoned into Regular Army regiments; the militia would play a secondary role.

While Congress supported and approved Calhoun's improvements in War Department administration and efficiency, it frustrated his conservative proposals for military education and military policy. The dominant Jeffersonian-Jacksonian liberals in Congress and the public denounced the Army as a drain on the economy and a threat to republican government. Calhoun fought back. No "arrangement can be called economical," he warned, "which, in order that our military establishment in peace should be rather less expensive, would . . . render it unfit to meet the dangers incident to a state of war." The spirit of the Regular Army was indeed, he conceded, different from the spirit of liberalism. But in the United States the danger was not that the military spirit would overwhelm the civil, but rather the reverse: "that both officers and soldiers will lose their military habits and feelings, by sliding gradually into those purely civil." In this insight, Calhoun described both the fundamental problem of American civil-military relations for a century and a half and the reason for the failure of his own policies. Despite his efforts, the Army was reduced in size. The expansible army plan was rejected. It ran counter to the basic tenet of American liberalism that professional military officers are permissible only when they command small military forces and that large military forces are permissible only when they are commanded by nonprofessional officers. Calhoun's proposals to develop the Army educational system were ignored, and the technical emphasis at West Point was continued. The one new school which he was able to establish, the Artillery School at Fort Monroe, Virginia, was closed down by the Jacksonians in 1835. His efforts to create a balanced pattern of civil-military relations in the War Department were warped into quite a different system. Even his recommendations to Congress on coastal defense were brushed aside. Thus, while his administrative reforms determined the pattern of War Department operation for half a century, his military policies found life only in a series of masterly state papers. More than any other nineteenth-century Secretary of War, Calhoun understood the requirements of military professionalism. Yet, paradoxically, the unsympathetic atmosphere in which he worked determined that his lasting contributions to the War Department were in the civil-administrative area. The hostile American environment overwhelmed and dissipated the drive and the genius which he brought to the cause of professional military reform.

THE MILITARY ENLIGHTENMENT AND THE SOUTH, 1832–1846. The fifteen years from the end of Jackson's first administration to the beginning of the Mexican War saw an outpouring of military thought and writing which was, in many respects, unique in American history. Military societies sprang into being; military journals led brief but active lives; military officers published significant — and original — books; the idea of a military profession was expounded and defended. This eruption may be appropriately termed the American Military Enlightenment. Many factors contributed to its appearance, but the intellectual wells from which it was fed were predominantly Southern. Peculiarly enough, the Enlightenment ceased almost as abruptly as it had begun. The 1850's were as barren of significant military thought as the 1820's. Moreover, this military flowering was exclusively one of awareness and articulation. It was singularly void of lasting institutional reforms. The ideas of the Enlightenment, however, molded the form which professionalism in practice was to take after the Civil War.

The causes of the Enlightenment were complicated. The natural course of military development induced officers increasingly to recognize a "military science" distinct from technical specialities and civil pursuits. The initial, embryonic institutions of military professionalism, particularly West Point, also contributed. The Military Academy had only begun to function effectively in 1817; consequently, it did not become capable of reproducing its kind until a couple of decades later. Dennis Hart Mahan, the leading figure of the Enlightenment, for instance, was graduated in 1824 and, returning to teach in 1830, expounded the gospel of professionalism to successive generations of cadets for forty years. The thinking of the Enlightenment was also stimulated by the developing interest in science which spread through Europe and America in the 1830's and 1840's. In this respect, the Enlightenment was not entirely divorced from technicism and, unlike the professional movement after the Civil War, was rather closely linked to the intellectual currents of the day. Significantly, both Mahan and Matthew Fontaine Maury, the leading naval figure, made their initial reputations as technical specialists, the former as an engineer and the latter as an oceanographer. The military journals generally had more technical articles than professional ones on the art of war. A military society, such as the United States Naval Lyceum founded by officers at the Brooklyn Navy Yard in 1833, sponsored scientific and technical researches and, at times, seemed more preoccupied with meteorology, zoology, botany, and mineralogy, than with more strictly naval subjects.[28] The political conditions of the time also tended to stimulate professional activity. The Jacksonian attack on military institutions forced the officer to produce an *apologia pro vita sua*. The advanced outpouring of military thought was thus not unrelated to the backward state of military institutions. The same blanket hostility of a liberal society which stimulated Federalists and Southerners to political theory drove the advocates of military professionalism to sophisticated thought and pungent expression.

The principal positive impetus to the Military Enlightenment came from Southern conservatism. Southerners dominated the serious thought and discussion of military affairs. Military periodicals flourished during the 1830's and 1840's as they had never done before and as they were not to do again until the 1890's. The *Military and Naval Magazine* was published from 1833 to 1836, the *Army and Navy Chronicle* from 1835 to 1844, and the *Military Magazine* from 1839 to 1842. Preëminent among the journals interested in military affairs, however, was the great magazine of the South, the *Southern Literary Messenger*. The *Messenger* consistently devoted extensive attention to military and naval matters. By 1844 it had "become a sort of organ of the United States Army and Navy" — the closest thing the country had to an army and navy journal.[29] The two outstanding military writers and thinkers of the Enlightenment, Mahan and Maury, were both Virginians; Maury went South in the Civil War and Mahan was sorely tempted to do so. Southern interest in the study of the military art was also manifest in the creation of local military schools. Virginia Military Institute was established in 1839, the Citadel and the Arsenal set up in South Carolina in 1842, Kentucky Military Institute in 1845. By 1860, every Southern state, except Florida and Texas, had its own state-supported military academy patterned on the models of West Point and VMI. With the notable exceptions of VMI and the Citadel, most of the Southern schools, like the military journals, did not survive the Civil War. Nonetheless while they existed, they gave the South a unique sectional system of military education which was absent in the north and west.

The most notable critic of the preprofessional institutions of the American Navy during the Enlightenment period was Matthew Fontaine Maury. His views on naval organization and education, expressed in the pages of the *Southern Literary Messenger* and the *Richmond Whig and Public Advertiser,* reflected a truly professional concept of the officer's function. Like Calhoun, he recognized a sharp distinction between the training required for officers and men. The latter could be recruited in a day from the merchant marine. Officers, on the other hand, "must undergo a peculiar system of previous training, that involves no inconsiderable expense, and requires a period of several years to complete the course." Naval officership should be accorded dignity and training comparable to those of the legal and medical professions. The emergence of professional standards required the differentiation of a greater number of professional ranks in the naval hierarchy. A regularized system of appointment and promotion by merit was needed. Naval officers should receive the "benefit of a professional education" which would be "broad, solid, and comprehensive," and which would combine literary and technical instruction. Maury also deplored the lack of professional writing in the Navy.[30]

The most outstanding military thinker of these years was Dennis Hart Mahan. Appointed Professor of Civil and Military Engineering at West Point in 1832, Mahan insisted that the words "and of the Art of War" be added to his title. Teaching at the Academy until his death in 1871, Mahan was the author of technical works on engineering and professional works on strategy, teacher and inspirer of the military leaders of the Civil War and of the postwar generation that was to make military professionalism a reality in the United States, and father of the Navy's most distinguished writer and publicist. In his *Notes on the Composition of Armies and Strategy* and his *Advanced Guard, Out Post, and Detachment Service of Troops* which were used as texts at the Academy from 1841 until the Civil War, Dennis Hart expressed a thoroughly professional military outlook. As his son correctly observed: "The spirit of the profession was strong in him." He was a Virginian at heart with "strict and lofty military ideals." [31]

Mahan's greatest contribution to American military professionalism was, in all probability, his stress upon the lessons to be learned from history. Without "historical knowledge of the rise and progress" of the military art, he argued, it is impossible to get even "tolerably clear elementary notions" beyond "those furnished by the mere technical language. . . . It is in military history that we are to look for the source of all military science." His emphasis on military history led Mahan to abandon the prevailing distinction between strategy and tactics in terms of the scale of operations. He came to see that strategy, involving fundamental, invariable principles, embodied what was permanent in military science, while tactics concerned what was temporary. History was essential to a mastery of strategy, but it had no relevance to tactics. The line which distinguishes the one from the other is "that which separates the science from the art." This scientific component, Mahan declared, distinguished the warfare of his day from the military art of previous eras. Only after the breakdown of the feudal order was it possible to "raise the profession of arms to its proper level, in which mind and its achievements have the first rank, and brute force combined with mere mechanical skill a very subordinate one." Only study and experience alone produce the successful general, he argued, protesting the prevailing Jacksonian view: "Let no man be so rash as to suppose that, in donning a general's uniform, he is forthwith competent to perform a general's function; as reasonably might he assume that in putting on the robes of a judge he was ready to decide any point of law." Mahan also defined the relation of the military profession to war and the distinction between the military spirit and the bellicose spirit. The trouble with the United States as a country was that "we are perhaps the least military, though not behind the foremost as a warlike one." The object of war was always to "gain an advantageous peace," which can only be achieved by applying superior forces at the decisive point.

The influence of Mahan's teachings may be seen in the work of his most intellectually distinguished pupil, H. Wager Halleck, "Old Brains," graduated from the Academy in 1839. Although not a Southerner, Halleck absorbed completely the conservative military outlook. His *Elements of Military Art and Science*, published in 1846, was the most sophisticated volume written by an American military man prior to the Civil War. In it and in his 1845 report to Congress on national defense, Halleck presented a virtually complete expression of the professional military ethic in all its particulars. Halleck was the most outspoken defender of military institutions against their Jacksonian critics, pleading eloquently for "a body of men who shall devote themselves to the cultivation of military science" and the substitution of Prussian methods of education and advancement for the twin evils of politics and seniority. "If we deem professional instruction requisite for the care of our individual property and health," he inquired, "shall we require less for guarding the honor and safety of our country, the reputation of our arms, and the lives of our citizens?" [32] It was a question which the officers of the Enlightenment might raise but which their countrymen did not choose to answer.

9

The Creation of the American Military Profession

THE DOMINANCE OF BUSINESS PACIFISM:
INDUSTRIALISM VERSUS MILITARISM

The Southern defeat in 1865 permitted the United States to achieve an exceptional degree of ideological homogeneity in the following decades. For the first time in the history of western society the interests of the capitalist were merged with the interests of the populace. The ideals and philosophy of business liberalism, individualism, the Horatio Alger creed, became the ideals and philosophy of the nation, accepted and adhered to by all significant groups in American society. Even those such as the Populists who challenged the rule of big business did so in the name of the business ethic of free enterprise. The approach of this ethic to military affairs was surprisingly coherent and articulate. It was, indeed, in some respects the only explicit theory of civil-military relations produced by American liberalism. The fundamental outlines of this theory, which may be called "business pacifism," were accepted by the leading thinkers of the period and permeated deeply into the popular mind.

Among the expounders of business pacifism, Herbert Spencer stood in unchallenged preëminence. Not only did he state the theory in its most systematic form, but he also wielded tremendous influence over both popular and critical thought. Although an Englishman, his doctrines had greater vogue in the United States than in his home country. He became an intellectual fad which persisted for two generations and which penetrated into the most unintellec-

222

tual strata of society. Also widely popular in the 1870's and 1880's was an American, John Fiske, whose *Outlines of Cosmic Philosophy* presented the Spencerian theory of civil-military relations in more elementary form. Later, about the turn of the century, William Graham Sumner of Yale became the leading exponent of the business ideology. Second only to Spencer in his influence on the intellectual currents of the age, Sumner's thought represented a readjustment of business pacifist theory in the light of the new conditions of the twentieth century. Finally, while Spencer, Fiske, and Sumner might be the competing intellectual high priests of business pacifism, there was no challenging Andrew Carnegie's role as its leading lay prophet. The most spectacular millionaire of the age, the embodiment of the Horatio Alger rags to riches legend, the Scottish-born industrialist was also one of the most tireless, conscientious, and generous supporters of the organized peace movement. Describing himself as a "disciple" of Spencer, Carnegie was in a sense the culmination of a long tradition of American business interest in pacifism which stretched back to Benjamin Franklin.[1]

Business pacifism had three important sources. First, and most important, was the religious moralism associated with the Puritan version of the Protestant ethic. War, of course, was evil, because it involved killing. But the worship of work and the stress on the moral value of economic productivity led this ethic to condemn militarism even more particularly because it was wasteful. War itself was actively destructive of economic wealth. Military forces in peace were passively destructive, pure consumers, parasites living off the fruit of other men's labors. Second, classical economic liberalism and utilitarianism contributed to business pacifism an optimistic belief in human nature, reason, and progress. International free trade by multiplying contacts among nations and creating mutual interests would eventually render war unthinkable. The spirit of Cobden and Bright had a firm hold on the mind of the American businessman, however much he might demand a specific exception for his products. "Trade does not follow the flag in our day," said Carnegie, "it scents the lowest price current. There is no patriotism in exchanges." The third source of business pacifism was the most surprising and most immediate: the Social Darwinism which dominated the intellectual world of the last third of the nineteenth century. On the surface, the application of the survival of the fittest thesis to human society should result in the acceptance and glorification of conflict and war as essential to human progress. In an entirely different intellectual climate such as prevailed in Germany, Social Darwinism was indeed developed along these lines by Bernhardi and others. In England and America, however, the bellicose version of Social Darwinism found less support, although it did contribute to the end-of-the-century rationale of imperialism. Its prevailing form was highly pacifist. The "struggle" of Darwinian theory was redefined to mean economic competition, and the "fittest" who were to survive were identified with the most productively efficient. In previous eras, the struggle for survival had meant the struggle for the most power. Now it meant the struggle for the best price.

The convergence of Protestant morality, classical economics, and Social Darwinism produced a distinctive outlook on military affairs which posited two basic forms of human society: the militant or militaristic type, organized for the primary purpose of war; and the industrial or pacific type, organized for the primary purpose of productive economic activity. Jeffersonian hostility to the military had been largely confined to the limited institution of the standing army as a threat to republican government. Jacksonian hostility had broadened this to opposition to a military caste as the enemy of popular democracy. Business pacifism now expanded it still further so that the conflict was no longer one of institutions or of social groups, but the fundamental struggle of two entirely different ways of life. In its most expanded form, the dichotomy between industrialism and militarism became one aspect of the still broader opposition between economics and politics — the scientific and rational determination of ends and means so as to maximize welfare, versus the arbitrary and irrational actions of governments concerned with their own power and wealth.

The dichotomy between militarism and industrialism was unchallenged dogma in the intellectual world at the close of the nineteenth century, accepted by all the business pacifist thinkers as well as by others such as Brooks Adams. It was given its most careful delineation by Spencer who found the essential difference between the two societies in the role of the individual. In the militant society,

Spencer argued, the individual was "owned by the State" and subordinated to the goal of the preservation of society. The "absence of hostile societies" characteristic of industrialism, however, meant that individual goals took precedence over social goals: "the individuality of each man shall have the fullest play compatible with the like play of other men's individualities . . ." The militant society was one of compulsory cooperation and status; the industrial society one of voluntary cooperation and contract. The industrial society was characterized by decentralization, representative government, and the limitation of the functions of government by a wide variety of private combinations outside its scope. Industrial societies had a high degree of plasticity and developed close bonds of trade and friendship with adjacent societies. An industrial society fostered in its citizens a spirit of independence, little faith in governments, hostility to arbitrary power, reliance on individual initiative, and a respect for the individuality of others. The militant society contrasted sharply with this loose, productive, peaceful utopia. The purposes of war took precedence over all else; the warriors ruled the state. Authority, subordination, and violence were the watchwords. The state was despotic; power was centralized; and state control extended throughout the activities of society. The militant society was autarchic, minimizing its peaceful contacts with other states and striving for the goal of economic self-sufficiency. The dominant character type in this society was physically vigorous, forceful, courageous, vengeful, violent, relentless, patriotic, obedient. He had implicit faith in his leaders and little ability or aptitude for initiative and enterprise.

Except for Sumner, who was too much of a realist to think that war could ever be completely abolished, the business pacifists assumed a natural progress from the militant to the industrial society coupled with the gradual elimination of war. For the Jeffersonian, war had been a thing of the present which required a strong military force in being. For the Jacksonians, war was a thing of the future which could be met by the populace springing to arms in an emergency. For the business pacifist, however, war was a thing of the past, rendered obsolete by the march of industrialism. Spencer and Sumner both argued that while war had served useful social purposes in previous eras, its utility was now over. War was ethically wrong, economically ruinous, and incompatible with modern civilization. The "ever-increasing interdependence of human interests," declared Fiske, "itself both the cause and effect of industrial progress, is ever making warfare less and less endurable." To Carnegie, international law — "proof of the supreme force of gentleness" — was limiting the ferocity of war, and the international arbitration of disputes was the means of displacing it altogether. Eventually, international courts would replace wars just as municipal courts replaced duels. The business pacifists saw the United States as more advanced on the road to peace than the European nations which continued to maintain large armaments. They contrasted the "American temper" of industrialism with the "war ideals" dominant on the European continent.

Since war was fundamentally a thing of the past, the business pacifists wanted to eliminate all forms of military institutions and preparations. Armaments were the cause of wars and the military profession a useless and vestigial remnant of a previous irrational age. The standing army and the regular officer were the natural instruments of aggression. As societies evolved from the militant to the industrial phase, Spencer reasoned, the military profession lost its function, its attractiveness, and its popularity. In the spreading reign of peace, the military arts would wither and die through the lack of interest and support in society. To Carnegie, the military professional was virtually criminal in his denial of conscience, the "Judge within," in refusing to evaluate the rightness or wrongness of the cause for which he fought. When he admitted the possibility of war, the business pacifist usually thought it could be met through Jacksonian means, Carnegie in particular holding forth the vision of the pacific Anglo-Saxon nations springing to arms en masse if set upon by an aggressor. His fundamental premises, however, required the business pacifist to take a dim view of all forms of military force, including the militia. More the Whig and less the democrat than his liberal predecessors, he was for that reason also less intoxicated with the prospect of the armed people.

YEARS OF ISOLATION: THE DARK AND THE BRIGHT

The prevalence of business pacifism made the dominant feature of post-1865 civil-military relations the complete, unrelenting hostility of virtually all the American community toward virtually all things military. The military's source of sympathetic conservatism had gone with the South. The blanket hostility of American society isolated the armed forces politically, intellectually, socially, and even physically from the community which they served. Electionwise the military vote was negligible. Military personnel suffered from many disabilities and restrictions which made it difficult for them to vote when they wanted to, and a number of states denied the franchise to those serving in the Regular Army and Navy.[2] Few economic groups had a direct interest in supporting the military. The Army had relatively little need for the products of industry; neither did the Navy before 1881. Even after the construction of an armored, steam navy began in the 1880's, only a small group of business concerns became regular military suppliers. The isolation of the officer corps was enhanced by the manner in which it was recruited. The mounting effects of the congressional system of appointment to West Point and Annapolis hastened the divorce of the military from the South. Both those entering the officer corps and those reaching its highest ranks in the years after the Civil War were a cross-section of middle-class America.* As the officer corps became the mirror of the nation, it also became isolated from it. Representative of everyone, it was affiliated with no one.

Socially and physically the services tended to be separated from society. Until 1890 the small Army was strung out along the frontier fighting Indians. After its brief but inglorious role in the Spanish-American War, substantial segments were required overseas in Cuba, Hawaii, the Canal Zone, and the Philippines. Both these missions divorced it from a nation which was rapidly becoming urbanized. Before World War I, in the words of one officer,

---

* The occupations of parents of candidates for admission to West Point from 1842 to 1891 and of the parents of cadets admitted to the Academy from 1892 to 1899 inclusive were: farmers and planters, 1,149; merchants, 722; lawyers and judges, 625; physicians, 367; army officers, 632; mechanics, 341; no occupation, 191; manufacturers, 151; clergymen, 128. No other occupation contributed more than a hundred candidates. Charles W. Larned, "The Genius of West Point," *The Centennial of the United States Military Academy at West Point, New York, 1802–1902* (Washington, 1904), pp. 482–483. Richard C. Brown, "Social Attitudes of American Generals, 1898–1940" (Ph.D. Thesis, Univ. of Wisconsin, 1951), pp. 1–34 found the social profiles of the generals essentially the same as those of business and political leaders.

soldiers "lived apart in their tiny secluded garrisons much after the manner of military monks and they rarely came into contact with the mass of our citizens . . ." Naval officers likewise had their life apart, spending a large portion of their careers at foreign stations. "The fact that naval officers are separated so much and so long from each other and from other men," one of them commented in 1905, "must tend to lack of unity of purpose, and therefore to lack of influence with the public." Other officers were conscious of their social isolation, highlighted by the absence of military leaders from important social functions, something unheard of in the early days of the country. The United States Army, one officer complained, was virtually "an alien army" existing in "practically complete separation from the lives of the people from which it is drawn." The military were also divorced from the prevailing tides of intellectual opinion. West Point, for example, gradually lost contact with the rest of American education to which it had made such significant contributions, and went its own way.[3]

Congressional military policy accurately reflected the philosophy of business pacifism. Army expenditures were steadily lowered from their Civil War peak of over a billion dollars to thirty-five million in 1871. They hovered about that figure for the next quarter century, varying from a high of forty-six million in 1873 to a low of twenty-nine million in 1880. The strength of the Army averaged about twenty-five thousand officers and men. Naval expenditures were normally about twenty million dollars a year until after 1890, and the strength of the Navy and Marine Corps was about eleven thousand officers and men. The shortage of funds made it impossible for the military to experiment and develop new techniques and weapons of warfare. Both services, for example, continued to use smoothbore cannon long after foreign powers had replaced them with rifled cannon. The Army seldom was able to bring together more than a battalion of troops at a time; the Navy lagged behind other powers in ship design and marine ordnance. Despite the advantages of steam propulsion, the Navy after the Civil War went back under canvas, and the desire for economy made it almost a crime for a naval officer to utilize the engines on his ship. By 1880 the United States Navy was an ill-sorted collection of obsolete vessels incapable of functioning together as a fleet. The United States

Army was a far-flung Indian chasing frontier police, skilled at that function but quite unsuited and unprepared for any more serious operations. Business pacifism had reduced the military services to rusty decay.

The isolation, rejection, and reduction of the armed services after the Civil War have led historians to mark this as the low point of American military history. They speak of "The Army's Dark Ages" and the "Period of Naval Stagnation." These phrases are accurate, however, only with respect to the social influence and political power of the military. They describe only one side of the civil-military equation. The very isolation and rejection which reduced the size of the services and hampered technological advance made these same years the most fertile, creative, and formative in the history of the American armed forces. Sacrificing power and influence, withdrawing into its own hard shell, the officer corps was able and permitted to develop a distinctive military character. The American military profession, its institutions and its ideals, is fundamentally a product of these years. No other period has had such a decisive influence in shaping the course of American military professionalism and the nature of the American military mind. The practical work of professional reform, frustrated while the military were associated with the South in the prewar years, became possible once all ties with civilian society had been broken. Universal hostility permitted what limited support prevented. The foundation of this advance was the absence of any significant threat to national security. The isolation of the military was a prerequisite to professionalization, and peace was a prerequisite to isolation. Paradoxically, the United States could only create a professional military force when it was lacking any immediate use for such a force. The dark ages of military political influence were the golden ages of military professionalism.

The withdrawal of the military from civilian society at the end of the nineteenth century produced the high standards of professional excellence essential to national success in the struggles of the twentieth century. If the officer corps had not been rejected, if the Army and Navy had not been reduced to the bone in the 1870's and 1880's, the United States would have had a far more difficult time of it in 1917 and 1942. The military officer who, at the end of the period of isolation, rejoined civilian society in World War I and World War II, was a fundamentally different creature from his ancestor who had withdrawn in the 1860's. When he left, he was a citizen-soldier, an accepted member of the liberal family. When he returned, he was a stranger in his own household. His membership in the national family was no longer free, easy, and relaxed. The years of isolation had remade him into a professional with values and outlook basically at odds with those of the mass of his countrymen. They had interjected steel into his soul which was missing from that of the community. His return marked the beginning of the real problem of American civil-military relations: the tension between the conservative professional officer and the liberal society. While his professionalism thus created intense problems of psychological and political adjustment, it was nonetheless the salvation of his country externally. The ability of the professional officers and their impressive record in leading the forces and conducting the operations of the two world wars were acquired because of, not despite, their rejection at the end of the nineteenth century.

THE CREATIVE CORE: SHERMAN, UPTON, LUCE

The professionalization of the American military was preëminently the work of a small group of officers in the two generations following the Civil War. The process was begun by Generals William T. Sherman and Emory Upton and by Rear Admiral Stephen B. Luce. The immediate form which American professionalism took was largely of their making. Sherman is the best known of the three, but his popular fame rests almost exclusively upon his Civil War exploits. For almost fifteen years from 1869 to 1883, however, he was the Commanding General of the Army, heading that service for a longer period of time than any other officer except Winfield Scott. He was the leading military personality for an entire generation of soldiers and civilians from the Civil War until his death in 1891. Unlike Grant, whose record became besmirched and disputed by his entrance into politics, as Sherman predicted it would, Sherman retained his military popularity because he would have nothing to do with politics. As Commanding General, he sparked the professional reform movement. Particularly aware of the importance of military education, he vigorously defended the Artillery School at Fort Monroe which had been reëstablished in 1868. The father of the infantry and cavalry school at Fort Leavenworth, Sherman espoused a complete system of military education in which West Point would furnish both the preliminary liberal education required of any professional man and the indoctrination in military values and discipline required of the military man. Advanced schools would then give the officers the specialized knowledge of their profession and prepare them for the higher posts.

More important than the institutional developments in which Sherman had a hand was the tone which he set for the Army. His outlook and thought were thoroughly military, and the professional spirit which he manifested permeated throughout the ranks of the officer corps. Earthy, direct, limited, he was the epitome of all the virtues and vices of the professional officer. A man of simple truths rather than of brilliant concepts, he glorified in the unadorned title of "soldier" and wished to be nothing more or nothing less. Disclaiming other interests, causes, motives, his constantly reiterated motto was: "It is enough for the world to know that I am a soldier." Loyal to the Union, but opposed to abolition and an admirer of the South, he did his duty during the Civil War in the manner of the professional. His single-minded devotion to military ideals led him in the postwar period to object to the use of the Army as a police force — "That should be beneath a soldier's vocation" — and to assert that the Army must always be "organized and governed on true military principles" so as to preserve in peacetime the "habits and usages of war." Civilian control was essential to securing this objective. Democratic procedures were out of place in the Army which should be "an animated machine, an instrument in the hands of the Executive for enforcing the law, and maintaining the honor and dignity of the nation." Sherman was particularly adamant in stressing the divorce of the military from politics. Three of the six Commanding Generals before him had become presidential candidates. With him begins the tradition of political neutrality which, with the sole exception of Leonard Wood, was to be maintained by subsequent Commanding Generals and Chiefs of Staff until after World War II. "Let those who are trained to it keep the office," he wrote of the Presidency in 1874, "and keep the Army and Navy as free from politics as possible, for emergencies that may arise at any time." On party politics, "no Army officer should form or express an opinion." The essential components of the military ethic — hatred of war and avoidance of politics — were succinctly expressed in Sherman's two most quoted phrases: "War is hell" and "I will not accept if nominated and will not serve if elected." [4]

The most influential younger officer in the work of Army reform was Emory Upton. Graduating from West Point in 1861, Upton distinguished himself in the Civil War, rising to become a major general of Volunteers. After the war, he prepared a new system of infantry tactics for the Army, served as Commandant of Cadets at West Point from 1870 to 1875, toured the world in 1876 and 1877 inspecting foreign military institutions, and became superintendent of theoretical instruction at Fort Monroe. His two great works, *The Armies of Europe and Asia* and *The Military Policy of the United States,* were studies of foreign and American military institutions, clearly expressing the fundamental postulates of the professional military ethic and presenting the case for a wide variety of reforms. Although unfinished at the time of his suicide in 1881 and not published until 1904, *The Military Policy of the United States* was a powerful plea for a strong regular military force. It was endorsed by Sherman and subsequently became the Bible of the Regular Army in its disputes with the militia advocates. Throughout the 1870's Upton was in the forefront of the movement for reform. His contemporary, Admiral Luce, was Commandant of Midshipmen at Annapolis between 1865 and 1869, a founder and president of the Naval Institute, and the driving force in the creation of the Naval War College. A tireless proselytizer for naval professionalism, Luce crusaded against politics and technicism, urging naval officers to focus upon their "real business — war." His views were an almost exact expression of the professional ethic, and he exerted a lasting influence throughout the naval officer corps. As Admiral Fiske once truthfully remarked of Luce, "the United States Navy owes more to him than to any other man who was ever connected with it, directly or indirectly." Matthew Maury, Benjamin Isherwood,

John G. Walker, A. T. Mahan, Theodore Roosevelt, all made contributions. But none rivaled that of Luce. His achievement was as simple as it was great: "Luce taught the navy to think." [5]

The work of Sherman, Upton, and Luce in the 1870's and 1880's was carried on at the turn of the century by a second generation of reformers: Bliss, Wagner, Young, Carter, and others in the Army; Mahan, Taylor, Fiske, Sims, and their associates in the Navy. Just as Scharnhorst, Gneisenau, Clausewitz, and Moltke set the tone and direction of the German military tradition, these two generations of reformers determined the nature of the professional strand of American militarism. This creative core was a distinctly military group in three ways. (1) They were largely cut off from contemporary American civilian influence. (2) They derived their ideas and inspiration from the American Military Enlightenment and from foreign military institutions. (3) They transcended service boundaries, transmitting ideas and encouragement back and forth between the two services and developing professional institutions applicable to both Army and Navy.

The American military profession differed from those of most other countries in that it was almost entirely the product of the officers themselves. In Europe professionalism was normally the outcome of social-political currents at work in society at large: the Prussian reformers, for instance, were only doing in the army what Stein and his associates were trying to do for the state as a whole. In the United States, however, military professionalism was strictly self-induced. The civilian contribution was virtually nil. Professionalism was the reaction of an inherently conservative group against a liberal society, rather than the product of a general conservative reform movement within society. The military profession was probably unique among significant social institutions in the United States in the extent to which it was created independent of American society. In these origins lie much of the reason for American hostility to the profession as an essentially alien body. Even within the liberal society, some intellectual and political movements existed upon which the officers might have drawn, such as the beginnings of the science of public administration and the civil service reform movement. But little contact existed between these developments and the military. The officers

233

went their solitary way, accomplishing their work without the support and largely without the knowledge of civilian society. Within the narrow limits permitted them by the civilians, they could do more or less as they wished. The creation of a professional spirit, and even of professional institutions, did not require much in the way of money. So long as the Army was kept down to twenty-five thousand men, Congress let the West Pointers run it in accordance with their own ideas. So long as the number of officers was kept low, Congress approved changes in promotion and retirement plans. Sherman, for instance, carefully avoided Congress in setting up the School of Application at Leavenworth; he did not wish it to be "the subject of legislation." Subsequently, he repeatedly pointed out that the schools at both Leavenworth and Monroe required no additional funds beyond "ordinary garrison expenses." [6] And Congress, content with this, shrugged its shoulders and let them be.*

The principal American source of the ideas of the professional reformers was the Military Enlightenment of the 1830's and 1840's. The intellectual grandfather of their work was Dennis Hart Mahan and its father H. Wager Halleck. Sherman, Halleck, and Upton had been students of Mahan; Sherman and Halleck had overlapped at the Academy. All the active figures in the war of reform were graduates of the military or naval academies. From this source flowed the native contributions to the professional reforms. Equally important, however, were what the reformers learned from foreign military institutions. Drawing little help and inspiration from nonmilitary American sources, they turned to non-American military sources. The War of 1870–71 freed the American officers from their reverence for French institutions, and aroused their interest in those of Germany and other countries. Sherman was instrumental in sending Upton on his tour of the world in 1876 and 1877 to inspect foreign military establishments with particular reference to Germany. Upton's report revealed to American officers for the first time in any comprehensive manner the extent to which the United States lagged behind foreign developments.

---

* Five of the six other major advanced schools established by the Army between 1865 and 1914 were first set up by departmental order without prior congressional authorization.

Upton urged the establishment of advanced military schools, the creation of a general staff corps, a comprehensive system of personnel reports by superiors on their subordinates, the compulsory retirement of officers, and the use of examinations as a prerequisite to promotion and to appointment to the staff corps. He was particularly impressed by the military institutions of India which in their clear-cut system of objective civilian control offered many lessons for the United States. "In no free country," he declared, "is the subordination of the military to the civil authority more clearly defined than in the politico-military despotism of India." [7] A decade later Tasker Bliss also traveled through England, France, and Germany studying their military schools.

While the American reformers analyzed the experiences of many countries, Germany was their primary focus of attention. Upton himself expressed great admiration for German military institutions: every Prussian general in 1866, he pointed out, was a graduate of the Kriegsakademie, contrasting this with the backward state of military education in the American forces. Sherman thought the German system of military organization "simply perfect." Wagner echoed these sentiments, extolling the "excellence of the military system of Prussia." Clausewitz was translated into English in 1873, and American professional military journals devoted great coverage to Prussian affairs.* American officers became fully conscious, indeed overly conscious, of their backwardness in comparison to Germany, and tended to accept German methods as models to be followed without question. By the end of the century American military thinking on organization, stimulated by Spenser Wilkinson's volume on *The Brain of an Army* and by the report of the American officer Theodore Schwan, fully accepted the German general staff theory. The German lessons were frequently misinterpreted and misapplied, but the desire to imitate German institutions was an important force in furthering American military professionalism. Naval interest in German militarism lagged somewhat behind that of the Army officers; attention still focused upon Britain as the classic seapower. Undoubtedly influ-

---

* The March 1884 issue of the *Journal of the Military Service Institution*, for example, contained an article by von der Goltz, correspondence with the Militarische Gesellschaft, and a discussion of von Moltke. This was not atypical.

enced by his father's Gallomania, Alfred Mahan was a warm admirer of Jomini. Nonetheless, by the twentieth century the younger generation of naval officers attempted to espouse German thought on military organization; German methods were introduced at the War College; and Mahan himself eventually was much impressed by Clausewitz.[8]

While separated from civilian influence, the professionalizing core cut across service boundaries. The fundamental institutions and ideas of military professionalism were the same for Navy and Army; consequently, there was much room for mutual interaction and stimulation by the officers of the two services. Having imbibed the basic ideas of professionalism from Dennis Hart Mahan, Sherman, in turn, inspired Admiral Luce to devote his life to the reform of the Navy by demonstrating in practice the meaning of the professional approach to war. In January 1865, Luce, then a lieutenant commander, reported to Sherman at Savannah to plan the cooperation between Navy and Army for the drive northward into South Carolina. Listening to Sherman describe his plan of campaign, Luce had what Mahan was later to call an "illumination," and what was, in truth, a sudden insight into the meaning of military professionalism. In Luce's own words:

After hearing General Sherman's clear exposition of the military situation the scales seem to have fallen from my eyes. "Here," I said to myself, "is a soldier who knows his business!" It dawned upon me that there were certain fundamental principles underlying military operations which it were well to look into; principles of general application whether the operations were conducted on land or at sea.[9]

This vision enabled Luce to see the need for reorganizing the Navy Department, creating a professional military head for the Navy, and instituting a naval war college. Subsequently Upton became a close friend of Luce and encouraged him in these projects. While Upton was superintendent of theoretical instruction at the Artillery School of Fort Monroe, Virginia, he and Luce exchanged ideas on the means of improving American military education. It was at this time that Luce, citing the Artillery School as a model, first urged the Navy to offer a postgraduate course of instruction "in the Art of War." After securing the establishment of the Naval War College in 1884, Luce brought to it as instructors the son of Dennis Hart Mahan and also an Army lieutenant, Tasker H. Bliss, who at the turn of the century took the lead in organizing the Army War College. Thus, the line of influence ran from D. H. Mahan to Sherman, Halleck, and Upton; from Sherman to Upton and Luce; between Luce and Upton; from Luce to A. T. Mahan and Bliss; from A. T. Mahan to the younger naval officers; and from Bliss back to the Army.[10]

THE INSTITUTIONS OF PROFESSIONALISM

Virtually all the institutions of American military professionalism, except the service academies, originated between the Civil War and the First World War. The common theme in their emergence was the replacement of technicism and politics by military professionalism. They reflected the slowly growing awareness of the science of war distinct from those other sciences existing outside it and from those subordinate sciences contributing to it. The evolution of this recognition may be seen in the areas of education, personnel, and organization.

EDUCATION: COMPLETION OF THE BASIC STRUCTURE. The only national institutions of military education existing in 1865 were the military and naval academies at West Point and Annapolis. Their courses combined elements of liberal, military, and technical education, with the technical component predominating. The three great steps forward in the following half century were: (1) the reduction in importance of technical instruction at West Point and Annapolis; (2) the institution of postgraduate technical schools in the Army and Navy; and (3) the creation of war colleges for advanced military study. In 1865 the United States hardly possessed any professional military education. By 1915, it had a comprehensive system complete in almost all its elements.

Immediately after the Civil War both Annapolis and West Point began to shift away from technicism, in a more military and professional direction. In 1866 the Military Academy was removed from the control of the Chief of Engineers, and its superintendentship was opened to officers of all branches of the Army. In the following years, the proportion of graduates pursuing engineering decreased markedly. "The military schools," as one report put it,

237

"do not serve the profession of civil and mechanical engineering any longer." [11] Military critics of the Academy were still unsatisfied, however, with the heavy emphasis on mathematics, and argued that a broad, liberal, cultural education was as necessary for American officers as for German officers. They consistently urged that technical courses be transferred to postgraduate schools and that more time be allotted to English, history, and foreign languages, on the one hand, and to tactics and military history on the other. By 1902 about 31 per cent of the cadet's time was devoted to strictly technical subjects, about 30 per cent to military instruction, and about 39 per cent to the liberal arts or basic science. The reduction of technicism at the Naval Academy was hampered by stress upon the new technology of steam which replaced the earlier emphasis on sailoring and seamanship. From 1871 until the 1890's, there were two types of cadets at Annapolis: the regular cadet-midshipmen, who were trained for the line of the Navy, and cadet-engineers, who received a special engineering education. Emulating West Point graduates of a previous era, many of the cadet-engineers went out into the civilian world to teach and practice their speciality. This division among the midshipmen, eliminated in part in 1890, was done away with entirely with the amalgamation of the line and engineering corps in 1899. In the first decade of the twentieth century, liberal arts subjects were receiving increased emphasis in the Academy curriculum.

By 1900 professional purposes were foremost at both West Point and Annapolis. The military emphasis distinguished both schools from civilian institutions of higher learning and isolated them from the main currents of American education. In teaching methods, curriculum, organization, stress upon character development, as well as in the substantive content of the courses, the service academies trod their lonely path, impervious both to Eliot's ideas on electives and to Dewey's pragmatic progressivism. While the rest of American education explored the limits to which freedom might be granted college students to go their own ways, the military academies continued to stress obedience, discipline, and regularity through a prescribed course and daily recitations. Just as the military profession as a whole developed in opposition to business liberalism, the military schools remained relatively untouched by the new ideas in education. While reducing their technical content, the service academies, nonetheless, still tried to combine both a general liberal education and a basic military education into a single course. The effort to achieve both goals caused continuous tension, a crowding of the curriculum, dissatisfaction on both sides, and persistent suggestions for reform.[12] Thus, the period after the Civil War made the great step forward of substituting a professional for a technical orientation at the service academies. It left unresolved, however, the relationship of the liberal to the professional elements in the preliminary educational system.

The reduction in technicism at the service academies was intimately associated with the appearance of special postgraduate technical schools. The increasing complexity and depth of the sciences contributing to the military art which made it impossible to find room for them in the service academy curriculum required the creation of distinct advanced technical institutions. Coincidental with the separation of West Point from the Corps of Engineers in 1866, the Army established an Engineer School at Willets Point, New York. In 1868 Calhoun's Artillery School at Fort Monroe was revived. In 1881 Sherman established the School of Application for Infantry and Cavalry at Fort Leavenworth. Congress in 1887 authorized the creation of a practical school for cavalry and light artillery at Fort Riley, Kansas. In 1893 the Army Medical School came into being at Washington to train physicians for military careers. The Signal School was set up at Fort Leavenworth in 1904, the infantry School of Musketry at the Presidio, California in 1907, and the field artillery School of Fire at Fort Sill, Oklahoma in 1911.

Technical instruction in the Navy was also linked to the shift in emphasis at Annapolis. In the 1880's the only postgraduate school for naval officers was the Torpedo School at Newport. During that decade, however, the Navy began to send officers to civilian universities here and abroad for specialized instruction. In 1893 Admiral Luce secured the establishment of a School of Naval Architecture at the Massachusetts Institute of Technology for the training of naval constructors. After the abolition of the cadet-engineer course at Annapolis in 1899, the Navy instituted in Washington its own advanced school in marine engineering, electrical engineering, and ordnance. In 1909 this school was moved to Annapolis and eventually became the Postgraduate Department of the Naval Academy. The Navy continued, however, to rely on civilian institutions to supplement this training.

The third major development in military education was the appearance of schools exclusively devoted to the higher study of the art of war. The first significant step in this direction was Sherman's action in 1881 establishing the Infantry and Cavalry School at Leavenworth. In a sense, this was just a branch school, but it was conceived in terms of a larger purpose and ultimately evolved into something more significant. Prior to its establishment, certain elements of the higher science of war — military history, strategy, logistics — under Sherman's fostering care, and with Upton's participation, had been offered in the theoretical course at the Fort Monroe Artillery School. The initial two-year course at Leavenworth included general education subjects in its first year, but in time the emphasis was shifted to purely military topics. The Spanish-American War caused the temporary suspension of the school's activities, but in 1902 it was reopened under Elihu Root with an expanded and more explicit charter. The Army School of the Line instructed officers of the grade of captain or above in the "higher branches of military art and science." The Army Staff College, also at Leavenworth, trained graduates of the School of the Line for positions upon the higher staffs in war. The dominating figure at the school in these early years was Arthur L. Wagner who, teaching there from 1886 to 1897, insisted upon high standards of instruction and performance. Wagner's books on the *Campaign of Könniggratz* and *Organization and Tactics,* written during those years, were the best military analysis the Army produced between Upton and the First World War. After the Spanish-American War, Wagner became commandant of the Staff College, and by 1904 it was not inappropriate to refer to Leavenworth as a "military university" embodying the basic German premise that war could be taught in school.[13]

The instruction in military science at Monroe and subsequently at Leavenworth was a goad to the Navy to produce something similar. Admiral Luce and his associates pointed repeatedly to the inferiority of advanced naval education compared with that of the Army. Luce's campaign eventually led to the creation of the Naval War College at Newport in 1884. This was a true war academy dedicated like its European counterparts exclusively to the higher study of war. Its early existence, however, was shaky. Many naval officers remained ignorant of its purpose and unconvinced of its desirability. Efforts were regularly made to combine it with the Torpedo School, also at Newport, or to make it a postgraduate course at Annapolis. As Luce and Mahan pointed out, these moves reflected a confusion of technical with military expertise and a failure to recognize the independent existence of the latter.* The support of Admiral David D. Porter, the propagandizing of Luce, and the popularity of Mahan eventually triumphed over the opposition. After the Spanish-American War, the existence of the College was unchallenged. The College pioneered in the development of curriculum and teaching techniques and became a model for similar institutions in the navies of Europe.[14]

The final step in providing for advanced military education prior to World War I was the establishment of the Army War College in 1901. This was a logical outgrowth of Leavenworth and the success of the Naval War College. The demand in the Army for an educational institution more advanced than Leavenworth had been strong for a decade. Its creation, however, was complicated by Elihu Root's confusion of the duties of a war college with those of a general staff. Just as the development of the Naval War College was hampered by a failure to distinguish it from a technical institute, the development of the Army college reflected Root's inability to distinguish the functions of planning and administration from those of education and research. Root wanted the college to be composed of the heads of the staff departments of the Army who would supervise the work of other Army schools, direct the activities of military intelligence, and prepare plans for, and advise the President with respect to, mobiliza-

* Luce subsequently wrote of his opponents: "While urging advanced courses in the higher mathematics, in the science of ordnance, nautical astronomy and the rest of it, they overlooked their own science — the science of war. In advocating the cultivation of the arts of gunnery and navigation, mechanical engineering, and the mechanic arts generally, they took no account of their own special art — the art of war." U.S. Naval Institute *Proceedings*, XXXVI (1910), 560.

tion and military preparation. A more heterogeneous collection of duties could hardly be imagined. When the college itself was established in 1901, under the direction of a board of officers headed by Major General S. B. M. Young, its academic duties were distinctly secondary to its staff and planning activities. When Young in 1903 became the first Chief of Staff, he was succeeded at the War College by Brigadier General Tasker H. Bliss, who had been the first Army instructor at the Naval War College, and who, consequently, was thoroughly imbued with the purposes of such an institution. Under Bliss and his successor, Wagner, who moved up from Leavenworth, the College began to be more concerned with the advanced study of war. But under Root's influence, its principal duty remained assisting the General Staff in the preparation of plans for national defense. Despite the efforts of the military to put the College on the proper course, its ambiguous start meant that even in 1914 its primary purpose was still "to make practical application of knowledge already acquired and not to impart academic instruction." [15]

If Root was hazy as to the functions of a war college, he did have a clear perception of the essential components of a comprehensive system of professional military education. Earlier, military officers had defined the three stages of such a system, in imitation of German institutions, to consist of West Point, the postgraduate schools, and the general service schools and War College. In a brilliant memorandum dated November 27, 1901, Root accepted the essentials of this scheme and redefined the missions of the existing schools of the Army as parts of a unified whole. Similar imperatives were leading the Navy to recognize the same basic stages in officer education. In 1919, the Knox-Pye-King board, surveying naval education, declared that four steps were involved: first, the Naval Academy; secondly, the postgraduate course at Annapolis; thirdly, the Junior War College Course; and finally, the Senior War College Course.[16] Root's memorandum and the naval board's report signalize the completion of the fundamental structure of professional military education in the United States.

The American Military Profession

Associations and Journals. The new military educational system was supplemented by creation of professional associations and professional journals on a scale unprecedented in the United States.* First in the field was the United States Naval Institute founded by a group of officers at Annapolis in 1873 in conscious imitation of the British Royal United Service Institution and with the declared purpose to advance "professional and scientific knowledge in the Navy." In 1874 the Institute began publishing its *Proceedings* which, over the years, was probably the most intelligent and influential military journal in the United States, offering to naval officers a continuing forum for professional discussion. Army officers essayed to follow the lead of the Navy in 1879 by organizing the Military Service Institution, again on the British RUSI model. Both the Institution and the journal it published perished from lack of support during World War I. By this time, however, the Army had many associations and magazines reflecting a variety of professional and technical military interests. Most of these originated at the military schools. The Cavalry Association was formed in 1885 and three years later began publishing the *Cavalry Journal.* The *Journal of the United States Artillery* was founded in 1892 at the Fort Monroe Artillery School. It became the *Coast Artillery Journal* in 1922, the *Antiaircraft Journal* in 1948, and merged into the *Combat Forces Journal* in 1954. In 1893 a group of officers at Fort Leavenworth founded the Infantry Society, renamed the following year the United States Infantry Association. In 1904 the Association was reorganized and began publication of the *Infantry Journal,* which, after the demise of the Military Service Institution *Journal,* became the leading Army professional organ. In 1950 it was expanded into the *Combat Forces Journal* by merger with the *Field Artillery Journal,* which had been established in 1911 after the founding of the Field Artillery Association at Fort Riley. In 1909 the Corps of Engineers began publishing its *Professional*

---

* Prior to the Civil War the most significant military associations had been the West Point Military Philosophical Society, 1802–1812, and the United States Naval Lyceum in the 1830's. Both groups, however, had scientific and technical as well as military interests. Except for the *Naval Magazine,* published by the Lyceum, the journals of the Military Enlightenment had been published by commercial houses rather than by the officers themselves, and all of them had brief existences.

Memoirs as a bimonthly journal.* In both services the new magazines fed a continuing demand for the greater general availability
of professional literature.[17]

PERSONNEL: THE SEPARATION OF THE LAY AND THE EXPERT.
The years between the Civil War and World War I saw the emergence of the essentials of a professional personnel system. Entry
into the officer corps was primarily at the lowest ranks and through
the service academies. The higher ranks were almost monopolized
by academy graduates. The traditional system of promotion by
seniority, which had withstood earlier attacks, was qualified and
restricted although the fear of politics kept it as the basic criterion.
A retirement system, previously virtually nonexistent, was introduced. The prohibitions upon officers participating in nonmilitary activities were sharpened and clarified. All these developments
tended to enhance the separate, corporate existence of the officer
corps, to tighten the bonds among its members, and to widen the
gap between it and other segments of society.

The indifference of business pacifism toward military affairs and
its contrast with the Jacksonian approach were reflected in the willingness with which Congress narrowed the channels of entry into
the officer corps to the military academies. Junior line officer appointments in the Navy were monopolized by Annapolis graduates
in the post-Civil War years. The needs of the Navy were small, and
the Academy was more than able to meet them. At the turn of the
century, when the expansion of the Navy increased the demand for
officers, the number of appointments to the Academy was doubled.
In the event that there were insufficient Annapolis graduates to fill
the quotas, Congress also authorized the promotion of warrant
officers to ensigns, but these opportunities were hedged about by
strict limitations. From 1890 on, all the higher positions in the
Navy, except in the specialized staff departments, were filled by
Annapolis men. The more extensive officer requirements of the
Army did not permit West Point to achieve the same degree of
monopoly which Annapolis did. Nonetheless, Congress in 1878

* Official professional literature also grew in volume and quality, with the
Office of Naval Intelligence, established in 1882, the Military Information Division of the War Department, the Naval War Records Office, and the war colleges, all playing significant roles.

244

firmly established the priority of Military Academy graduates in receiving appointments and required rigorous professional tests for those entering the officer corps by other routes. In 1898 West Pointers made up 80 per cent of the officer corps, but were still in a minority at the highest ranks. Twenty years later World War I was fought under almost exclusively professional leadership, politics and influence being rigidly excluded from appointments and assignments. Almost three-quarters of the 441 Regular Army generals (other than medical officers) commissioned between 1898 and 1940, virtually all of whom entered the service between 1861 and 1917, were West Point graduates.[18]

Continued adherence to the seniority system coupled with the contraction of the Navy after the Civil War caused promotions to stagnate. Officers remained in the lower ranks for interminable lengths of time, reaching the higher grades about when due for retirement. The reforms suggested were either promotion by selection or an efficient system for weeding out the less competent officers. The advocates of promotion by selection were hindered, however, by the efforts of congressmen and others to influence the assignment of officers. Officers were dubious of the possibility of an impartial selection system, fearing that if seniority were abolished, politics would intrude upon promotion as well as assignment. The alternative to promotion by selection was elimination by selection, which was eventually provided for by Congress in the Personnel Act of 1899. Controversy and demands for further reform still continued, however, within the officer corps, and the final step in the completion of the Navy promotion system was made in 1916 when Congress replaced the 1899 scheme by a plan for limited selection which gave the Navy a highly advanced professional system of promotion.

The Army lagged behind the Navy in qualifying the workings of seniority. Under prevailing practice, promotion was by seniority up to and including the rank of colonel. Generals were selected, but here, too, the customs of seniority were usually followed. In 1890 a minimum level of professional competence was insured by requiring examinations for the promotion of all officers below the rank of major. Systematic personnel reports on the character and efficiency of officers were instituted in the middle 1890's. Elihu Root and others strongly supported the introduction of promotion by selection. But the officers feared that selection would only bring about the intrusion of "social or political influence" which at all costs must be avoided if the integrity of the officer corps was to be preserved. Root's efforts for reform were unsuccessful.[19] Here, as in the Navy, professional suspicion of politics led the officers to settle for a lower standard of professionalism, rather than risk a higher standard which might be more susceptible to manipulation by outside forces. The fears of the officers were primarily directed toward congressional influence, and their opposition to selection is another example of the way in which the separation of powers hampered the development of military professionalism.

Prior to 1855 no retirement system existed in either the Army or Navy. In that year, however, Congress, persuaded of the necessity for cleaning out the upper ranks of the Navy, created a "reserved list" for officers incapable of duty. In 1861 Congress approved a continuing scheme of compulsory retirement of Army and Navy officers for incapacity and introduced the first provisions for voluntary retirement. Subsequent legislation in the 1860's and 1870's required the compulsory retirement of naval officers at the age of sixty-two and attempted to stimulate voluntary retirements by increasing retirement benefits. Legislation in 1862 and 1870 provided that Army officers could be retired on their own application after thirty years of service or by compulsion at the discretion of the President. Mandatory retirement at the age of sixty-four, a reform long advocated by professionally minded officers, was finally enacted by Congress in 1882.[20] By the end of the century both services had adequate professional systems of superannuation.

Legal restrictions upon the participation of officers in nonprofessional activities also appeared during these years. In 1870 Congress espoused a concept of civil-military relations fundamentally at odds with the constitutional theory of the Framers when it prohibited any officer on active service from holding any civil office either by election or by appointment. Subsequent legislation elaborated this restriction and placed limitations upon the employment of retired officers. The two services also attempted to curtail the legislative activities of their officers, adding regulations to this effect in 1876, 1896, and 1900.[21]

ORGANIZATION: THE STRUGGLE AGAINST TECHNICISM. The fundamental organizational problem for both the Army and the Navy at the end of the nineteenth century was to provide an organ to perform the professional military function and to represent professional military interests. Inevitably solution of this problem required subordination of the technical-administrative units which played a major role in the structure of both services. At the level of personnel organization, the problem demanded the elimination or limitation of the specialized staff corps. In the Army, appointments to the various staff departments had been awarded more or less upon a patronage basis; officers once appointed spent their entire career with the staff speciality, becoming technical experts rather than military experts. This situation was modified in 1894 when Congress required that all subsequent appointments in the staff departments should be made from the line of the Army. At the turn of the century, Elihu Root led the fight on permanent commissions in the staff corps, pointing out that among the officers of the line serving on the frontier or overseas, the feeling existed that the staff departments were closed corporations "with all the luxuries, and the privileges and all the power" coming from constant association with the members of Congress in Washington. Congress responded to Root's demands in 1901 by establishing four-year details from the line for officers in the staff departments. This effectively broke the isolation of the staff corps from the rest of the Army, and was a major step toward the creation of a homogeneous military profession.

The naval officers were also divided between the line and the several staff corps. Within the Navy, as within the Army, there was a feeling that the staff departments had preëmpted first place. The better pay and promotion opportunities of shore duty in the nonmilitary departments attracted the Annapolis graduates. The most troublesome problem was the relation between the line and the Engineering Corps established in 1842. These two bodies were constantly at swords' points over their respective rights and privileges. By the 1890's, however, the basis for the distinction between the two was disappearing. A Personnel Board under the chairmanship of Assistant Secretary Roosevelt reported in 1898 that all engineers should be line officers, and all line officers should be engineers. The Navy needed, the Board argued, "one homogeneous body, all of whose members are trained for the efficient performance of the duties of the modern line officer." The Navy Personnel Act of 1899 embodied the recommendations of this board and provided for the amalgamation of the two corps.[22]

The other, and more important, aspect of the struggle against technicism concerned the administrative organization of the departments: the relations which should exist between the secretaries, the bureaus, and the spokesmen for the professional military interests. Naval organization still reflected Secretary Paulding's theory that only the technical-administrative operations of the Navy required special expertise and that the Secretary himself could handle the direction of military affairs. This theory had proved impractical in the Civil War, and the increasing complexity of naval science now made it impractical in peace. Some institution was required to deal with the military needs of the Navy, the preparation of war plans, and the employment and distribution of the fleet. This need was articulated by Secretary Whitney in 1885. Repudiating the Paulding theory, Whitney pointed out that the separate executive responsibilities of the bureau chiefs made it impossible for them to furnish the Secretary with the "intelligent guidance" which he needed in the "art of war." In contrast to Paulding's self-confidence in military affairs, Whitney's declaration a half century later represented official secretarial recognition that the military side of the Navy was now an expert profession.[23] No immediate changes were made as the result of Whitney's plea, but his statement touched off a debate on naval organization which continued for thirty years until the establishment of the Office of the Chief of Naval Operations in 1915. This debate took the form of an outpouring of articles, reports, discussions, and proposals which may well be unique in the history of American public administration. The focus of the controversy was the role of the professional military chief in relation to the bureau heads and Secretary.

One school of thought, the naval traditionalists, led by Luce and Mahan, advocated a balanced system of organization. They stressed the neglect of the military side of the naval establishment. The Navy existed for war and, unless departmental organization provided a spokesman for the military needs of the Navy, the civil activities of the bureaus, which properly had a supporting role, tended to become ends in themselves. The traditionalists thus wanted to balance the bureaus by creating an organ to represent the military side of the Navy. Since they emphasized the purely military and professional character of this need, they did not insist that the new office be given supervision over the civil side of the Department. Recognizing the inherent conflict between the Navy's military and civil aspects, they assigned to the Secretary the job of reconciling the two. Accustomed to secretarial direction of the military side of the Department, they were not troubled by the problem of the command relationships existing among the military chief, the Secretary, and the President. The Secretary was viewed as the President's agent in all matters concerning the naval establishment, civil and military. The traditionalists took as their model the British system of naval organization with its division of military and civil duties between the First Sea Lord and the other Admiralty officials, all under the supreme authority of the civilian First Lord of the Admiralty.

Sympathy for a vertical remedy for the Navy Department's organizational ills had long existed in the service, and in the 1890's the vertical system received new support from a younger generation of naval insurgents led by Admirals H. C. Taylor and William S. Sims. The naval insurgents stressed a different imperative from that of the traditionalists, emphasizing not the need for a military representative to balance the bureaus, but the desirability of a military administrator to coordinate the bureaus. They pointed to the independent ways of the bureaus, their overlapping responsibilities, the lack of coordination in the entire Department, and the lack of knowledge and experience of the secretaries. The Secretary, they argued, should have a single responsible adviser, either an individual or a board, for all matters concerning the Department. They viewed this adviser as a general staff whose authority would extend over the bureaus. The insurgents cited German military organization in their support. But in this, they made the same mistake that Elihu Root did: they misinterpreted the German system as establishing the power of the general staff over all elements of the military establishment.[24]

During the years of debate the Secretaries of the Navy and the bureau chiefs tended to side with the traditionalists against the insurgents. The chiefs defended their direct access to the Secretary. The secretaries saw the problem as one of furnishing themselves with professional assistance on military affairs without abdicating policy control to the military head. Except for those who succumbed to Roosevelt's influence, they rejected the vertical scheme, fearful that under it, the Secretary would sign the papers, and the military chief would run the Department. They were virtually unanimous in their support of what Secretary Daniels described as a "calculated policy of dispersion." Their opposition to vertical organization also tended to make them skeptical of the desirability of even a balanced plan of departmental control. Here they were caught in a dilemma. They recognized, with Secretary Whitney in his 1885 report, that the Secretary needed professional military assistance. They were, however, afraid that a military chief, even if originally limited in authority to purely military affairs, would tend to extend his power over the bureaus. Secretary Whitney himself pointed out that a Naval Advisory Board, which had been created to assist the Secretary, had tried to take over executive functions and intrude on the responsibility of the bureaus. Subsequently, in 1904 the Secretaries also complained that the General Board established in 1900 to prepare war plans was encroaching on civilian duties: administering navy yards, running naval reservations, and becoming involved in legal problems. The expansionist tendency of military organs, in itself testimony to the difficulty of maintaining a balanced organization in the American scheme, weakened the enthusiasm of the secretaries for any plan of reform.

The ideas and forces entering into the great organizational debate eventually crystallized in the act establishing the Chief of Naval Operations in 1915. The immediate initiator of the Act was Admiral Bradley Fiske who, going behind the back of the Secretary, urged naval reorganization upon sympathetic congressmen. An amendment was made to a Navy appropriation bill establishing a Chief of Naval Operations who was to be "responsible for the readiness of the Navy for war and be charged with its general direction." This proposed legislation thus provided for a vertical scheme. Secretary Daniels objected strenuously and was successful in getting the bill significantly altered. As finally passed, the law provided that the CNO "shall, under the direction of the Secretary of the

Navy, be charged with the operations of the fleet, and with the preparation and readiness of plans for its use in war." [25] Daniels thus achieved the two essentials of a balanced organization: the level of the authority of the CNO was subordinate to the Secretary; the scope of the authority of the CNO was limited to military affairs, not extending to the civil activities of the bureaus. The Luce-Mahan traditionalist viewpoint had prevailed.

The reform of War Department organization took quite a different course from that in the Navy. It was much more the work of civilian outsiders rather than a product of extensive discussion and debate among the officers themselves. Indeed, prior to the Spanish-American War, Army officers displayed little interest in organizational matters. Apparently they were generally content with the existing coordinate system. Even in 1900, when the Military Service Institution sponsored a prize essay contest on the best staff organization for the Army, none of the articles submitted was judged worthy of the award. The initiative for reform came primarily from Elihu Root who became Secretary of War in 1899. At the time of his appointment Root knew virtually nothing about military affairs, but once in office he made vigorous efforts to inform himself. He absorbed the prevailing admiration for the German general staff system and was much impressed by Spenser Wilkinson's analysis of German organization in *The Brain of an Army*. In approving reorganization plans for the War Department, however, Root attempted to remedy two deficiencies by a single reform. The Department required both improved performance of professional military functions and more effective central coordination and control. The first need could have been met by subordinating the Commanding General to the Secretary and furnishing the General with a staff to prepare military plans. The second need could have been met by enhancing the legal authority of the Secretary and strengthening his office, so that he could effectively control both Commanding General and bureau heads. These reforms would have given the Department a balanced system of organization reflecting in essence both the German system and the ideas of Spenser Wilkinson. Root, however, took but a single step, establishing a Chief of Staff as the principal military adviser to the Secretary. Thoroughly imbued with a Neo-Hamiltonian outlook, Root gave the Army a vertical system of organization reflecting a mixture of military and political functions. The General Staff Act of 1903, embodying Root's theories, marked a sharp break with the old coordinate pattern of organization in three respects.

(1) It abolished the direct command relationship of the military chief to the President. Under the new system, "command should . . . be exercised by or in the name of the Secretary of War, through a Chief of Staff." While the law put the Chief of Staff under the direction of the President as well as the Secretary of War, nonetheless, in practice, the new plan required that the Secretary of War alone become "the representative of the Constitutional Commander-in-Chief — the President." The job of the Chief of Staff was to "assist a superior officer [the Secretary of War] who has command, and to represent him, acting in his name and by his authority, in carrying out his policies and securing the execution of his commands."

(2) The corollary to the assumption of military command by the Secretary of War was the extension of the control of the Chief of Staff over the administrative bureaus of the Department. In return for the demotion in his level of authority, the military chief received a widening of his scope of authority. The original proposals, drafted by General Carter, for a General Staff Corps and a Chief of the General Staff assigned to these units purely military functions connected with war planning, thus providing for a balanced organization. Root, however, urged that it was necessary to give the military chief the "immediate direction of the supply departments, which are now independent of the Commanding General of the Army and report directly to the Secretary of War." This view, requiring a vertical organization, was embodied in the General Staff Act which gave the Chief of Staff power to "supervise" but not "command" the staff departments. This choice of words was a conscious one, Root's view being that "supervision" meant overseeing in the interests of a superior, whereas "command" implied independent and inherent authority. Thus, the wording was designed to insure the subordination of the Chief of Staff to the Secretary, as well as establishing the authority of the Chief over the bureaus.

(3) The third key element in the General Staff theory was the

necessity for mutual confidence between Chief of Staff and Secretary. Under the nineteenth-century organization, the independence of the Commanding General had made conflict with the Secretary inevitable. This system could only prevail, however, so long as the responsibilities of the military chief were purely military. The Chief of Staff, with authority coextensive with that of the Secretary, had to reflect the same interests and thinking as the Secretary. The Chief had to "have the entire confidence of his commander." Consequently, the President was authorized to choose the Chief of Staff from the entire corps of general officers for a four-year period only. Furthermore, because of the necessity of absolute confidence between President, Secretary, and Chief of Staff, the latter's term would "in every case cease, unless sooner terminated, on the day following the expiration of the term of office of the President, by whom the detail is made." Moreover, the Chief was under obligation, if he found that he could not loyally serve his civilian superiors, to ask to be relieved from his position.[26] Under this system, the Chief of Staff became a part of the administration in power. He was not simply the spokesman for permanent military interests. He was also political, and if his sentiments did not coincide with those of the administration, he was expected to resign. His position was, in effect, that of an undersecretary in an executive department. Root's reorganization thus was from the viewpoint of military professionalism and civilian control only a minor improvement over the coordinate system. The General Staff, under the Chief of Staff, did undertake the professional work of military planning. But the reduction of the technical bureaus one level in the departmental hierarchy had been achieved only at the expense of broadening beyond their professional scope the responsibilities of the Army's military chief. While naval organization subsequently evolved into a fully professional balanced system, Army organization remained frozen in this semi-professional, Neo-Hamiltonian form.

SUMMARY. By the First World War both services had achieved a broadly professional set of institutions. In only three areas did American militarism deviate significantly from the professional pattern.

(1) A professional system of preliminary education requires liberal and basic military education separately offered by institu-

tions specializing in these tasks. West Point and Annapolis, however, attempted to crowd into a single four-year course both these elements of professional training.

(2) A professional system of promotion requires advancement according to merit. The fear of politics, however, led the Army to cling to the seniority system.

(3) A professional system of organization requires a military organ devoted exclusively to the performance of the highest level professional tasks and the representation of the military viewpoint. The Army's vertical organization, instituted in 1903, fell short of this, however, mixing, as it did, the political and military responsibilities of the Secretary and Chief of Staff.

THE MAKING OF THE AMERICAN MILITARY MIND

The American professional military ethic is peculiarly a product of the years between the Civil War and the First World War. Prior to 1860, its essential elements had been grasped and expressed by the writers of the Military Enlightenment. But these were exceptional individuals, ahead of their times, and it was not until after 1865 that their ideas became the common property of the bulk of the officer corps. During the post-Civil War decades the officers as a whole developed a uniquely military outlook, fundamentally at odds with business pacifism and the rest of civilian liberal thought. By World War I this corporate military viewpoint had hardened into a stable pattern of belief and a fixed way of looking at the world. While the Army and Navy differed, of course, on their strategic concepts, the fundamentals of this professional ethic were the same for both services. The emergence of the ethic was the necessary corollary to the isolation of the military and the rise of military institutions. Sherman, Upton, Luce developed professional ideas; these led them to create professional institutions; and the institutions, particularly the schools, associations, and journals, fostered the further acceptance and articulation of a professional ethic. The evolution of this ethic may be traced in the articles and books by officers during this period.*

* The analysis of the American military ethic which follows is based upon a comprehensive study of:

(1) the *Journal* of the Military Service Institution, 1879–1917;

The American Military Profession

War as Science and Purpose. In viewing the evolution of human knowledge, the military writers emphasized the emergence of war as a distinct field of study. The science of war was the peculiar habitat of the military man. "War has become a specialty," declared an Army captain in 1883. "It has developed into an abstruse science." The importance of developing a doctrine of war was emphasized. "The Conduct of War" became the focus of professional interest. The naval officer corps was reminded that "the study of every officer should be the science of naval warfare, and his watchword 'preparation for battle,' for war is his profession." The substitution of steam for sails should free the sailor from concern with seamanship and permit the development of abstract and general principles of naval strategy such as Jomini and Clausewitz had already formulated for land operations. The science of war was separated into its permanent and variable elements. Strategy had "underlying principles which have always existed, and will continue to exist" but new conditions and new technological developments affect the application of these principles through tactics and logistics.

Closely associated with the idea that war existed as an independent science was the idea that the practice of that science was the only purpose of military forces. The Army and Navy existed to fight, not for any other reason. Their organization, activities, and

(2) the United States Naval Institute *Proceedings,* 1874–1917;
(3) the *Infantry Journal,* 1904–1917;
(4) *United Service,* 1879–1905;
(5) selected memoirs and textbooks by officers and articles in popular journals.

The professional journals are the best source for military thinking for a variety of reasons. Their articles were by officers on active duty and hence immersed in the military milieu. Few officers had the time or inclination to write books while still in the service, and when they wrote them after retirement, they at times looked back through rose-colored glasses. Most of the articles in the professional journals were by junior and middle-ranking officers whose views may be presumed to reflect the thinking of the bulk of the officer corps. Most of the books were written by generals whose views were more likely to reflect nonvocational influences. Articles in the professional journals were designed for military readers, and hence their authors were less likely to hide or modify their true opinions than if they were writing for the general public. The articles in the professional journals not only expressed military opinion but also shaped it. At the end of each section in the following analysis of the American military ethic, references will be given to some representative expressions of the military viewpoint on the topic of the section including those which have been quoted in the text.

training must be directed to the sole end of efficiency in combat. This teleology of militarism was the theoretical foundation for the assertion of the primacy of the line over the bureaus. The bureaus, representing technicism, existed only to serve the purposes of the line, representing professionalism. The armed services had in the past made many contributions to the advancement of science, exploration, commerce, and navigation. But these "pleasures and satisfactions" must be foregone in order to concentrate upon the single end of military efficiency.[27]

Self-Conceptions. For the first time American officers began generally to view themselves as a learned profession in the same sense as law and medicine, being consciously aware of the progress they had made in this direction. Their self-conception was rooted in the new view of war as a science. The problems of war,

. . . demand for their solution the highest talents and the most persistent application. Its students are students for life. The profession of arms has become a learned profession. When it was simply a fighting profession everybody belonged to it, and there were no military quacks. That it has changed its character seems to have escaped general observation.

Army and Navy officers alike stressed the need for a "military conscience," and emphasized the essentiality of the officer centering his devotion, loyalty, and interest upon his profession. While the military profession resembled other professions in its principal characteristics, it also differed from them in one important aspect: it was an organization as well as a profession. Administration and bureaucracy were essential elements. The unique aim of the military profession — efficiency in battle — meant that, in contrast to the situation of the staff bureaus, there was no profession in civil life analogous or comparable to that of the line officer. The Army and Navy officer corps, moreover, were only different branches of the same basic profession.

The emergence of professional institutions led to the conclusion that genius was superfluous, if not dangerous. Napoleon had been the key to French victory at the beginning of the nineteenth century, it was said, but a hundred years later no one would argue that without Oyama Japan would have been defeated by Russia, nor even that Moltke was indispensable to German victory. What was required was a perfected machine, not a brilliant individual. War had become rationalized and routinized. "Nowadays the general staff, 'the brain of an army,' can take the place of genius in the commander." The German system was seriously praised as the "triumph of organized mediocrity," the personification of teamwork, in which "the efficiency of every part is constantly developed, but subordinated always to the efficiency of the whole." Individual stars were dangerous because their talents would overflow the niches allocated them in the organized structure. "In any office in the military service, whether of the line or of the staff," the students at Leavenworth were told in 1907, "search should be made nowadays, not for a brilliant soldier, not for a genius, but for one that knows thoroughly the duties of the office." [28]

Conservative Values. Prior to the Civil War, the fundamental values of Army and Navy officers did not differ significantly from those of the bulk of the American population. Undoubtedly the officers were more inclined to conservatism but, so long as the South retained a position of eminence in national politics and thought, there was also a significant civilian conservative strain. After the Civil War, however, the nation and the military moved in opposite directions. As the former became more liberal, the latter became more conservative. Withdrawn from the mainstream of American life, realizing that their existence depended upon the probability or at least, the possibility of war, and that war was only likely if human nature contained a substantial streak of cussedness, the military found little in common with the doctrines of optimism and progress. By the turn of the century, when other professions, such as law and the ministry, had thoroughly adjusted to the liberal climate, the military were alone in their uncompromising conservatism. Those officers who did express themselves at a more thoughtful and less practical level took a distinctly conservative line, and the nature of the more widely articulated military views on other subjects implied a conservative philosophy.

In classic fashion, the military emphasized the evil in man, man's natural pride, acquisitiveness, and avarice. For the American officer, the duality of good and evil in human nature made war inevitable. The "well-spring of war is in the human heart" as Luce expressed it, and the military writers vented their scorn on the pacifists who based their theory on man as he ought to be, not man as he was. Francis Wayland, David Dudley Field, and E. L. Godkin were popular targets until Norman Angell appeared to be criticized not only for his wishful thinking, but also for his assumption that man was purely an economic animal. To the officers, human nature was unchanging. Man was the same now as he had been at the beginning of civilization, and no institutional devices would alter his basic make-up.

This low view of man led to a high stress on the virtues of organization and society. Military writers of both services were vehement in their attacks on individualism, and went to extremes in their glorification of the military values: subordination, loyalty, duty, hierarchy, discipline, obedience. The group was supreme over the individual. The highest glory of the soldier was "obedience, unthinking, instinctive, prompt and cheerful obedience." "Military discipline," one officer argued, "is invaluable because it never reasons." Unquestioning obedience and respect for superiors were the two essentials: "theirs not to reason why," the motto of the American military man. Individualism in all its forms was severely condemned as a step on the road to anarchy. The military view of the unchanging character of human nature also led to a stress on history, an interest which, except for D. H. Mahan, had been noticeably absent from earlier American military thinking. Only from history was it possible to develop generalizations about human behavior, and only from such generalizations is it possible to lay down guides to the future. History was opposed to progress. Progress could only take place in technique, and at a more basic level, "moral science . . . has made no progress in eighteen hundred years." To the extent that military writers espoused a theory of history at all, it tended to be a cyclical one.[29]

Politics, Democracy, and the Separation of Powers. In sharp contrast to the opinions of the officer corps in the 1830's, after the Civil War officers unanimously believed that politics and officership did not mix. Not one officer in five hundred, it was estimated, ever cast a ballot. In part this was the result of shifting stations and state restrictions. But, to a much larger extent, the abstention of the officer corps, stemmed, in the words of an Army major, "from settled convictions, from an instinctive sense of its peculiar relation as an organization to the Republic." The teachings of the service academies were now having their effect. "If any convictions . . . were acquired by the cadet," declared one officer, "they were generally of contempt for mere politicians and their dishonest principles of action." The concept of an impartial, nonpartisan, objective career service, loyally serving whatever administration or party was in power, became the ideal for the military profession. The military were proud of the extent to which they had realized this ideal, and compared themselves favorably with the more backward and still largely politics-ridden civil service.

The most immediate challenge to the maintenance of a sharp line between politics and the armed forces came from Congress. When Theodore Roosevelt urged Admiral Dewey to use his senatorial acquaintanceship to further his appointment to the Asiatic Squadron, Dewey expressed a "natural disinclination" to do so and only gave in after considerable persuasion by the forceful Assistant Secretary. Dewey's "natural disinclination" was one manifestation of the professional military hostility to the separation of powers which originated in the years following the Civil War and which has been a latent, but continually present, element in military thinking on government ever since. The new American professional officer had an inbred respect for the integrity of the chain of command stretching from the President as Commander in Chief to the lowest enlisted man. No place existed in this picture for Congress. The legislature could be placed neither above nor below the President; yet it obviously had to be placed somewhere. Congress existed off to the side, an ever present threat to the symmetry and order of the military hierarchy. The officers preferred to simplify matters and stress only their allegiance to the President. "The President is the Army's Commander-in-Chief, and its duty is to render him strict obedience. Duty is the Army's highest law, and supersedes all other law." Military officers at times wished for some mechanism to represent the military viewpoint as a whole before Congress, but they were strong in their condemnation of individual officers who succumbed to the temptation to resort to legislative influence and push special bills. They were equally vehement in denouncing Congress itself for intruding into the military realm. In attempting to ignore or to deny the separation of powers, the professionally minded national officer corps was sharply distinguished from the nonprofessional militia officer corps, which during this same period attempted to make effective its dual responsibility to the states and nation. The militia officers saw the bifurcation of authority as an opportunity for aggrandizement; the national officers saw it as a cause of neurosis. In refraining from exploiting the congressional escape hatch, the national officers demonstrated the same professional self-denial which characterized German officers before World War I when they remained adamantly loyal to the emperor and did not utilize opportunities to play Reichstag off against Kaiser.

At a deeper level the American officers feared the effects of democratic government on their developing profession: popular rule seemed incompatible with professional autonomy. There was little consistency or realism in military policy; the armed forces appeared to be mere playthings of powerful interests and public opinion. The military officer was "often sacrificed to the fetish of party." "Penuriousness and over-scrupulousness urged forward by local interests or party spirit," complained Colonel Wheeler, "seem to be the reasons controlling all plans suggested for the improvement of the present organization." The conflict between the political and military imperatives could not be avoided. At times, warned Wheeler's successor at West Point, a democratic government "in order to arouse popular enthusiasm and lead the people to make necessary sacrifices, [must] adopt measures which may or may not have a direct connection with purely military considerations." Some officers concluded that democracy was implacably hostile to true militarism. Monarchies, with an undisturbed chain of command and a single center of authority, were on this score much to be preferred. The fundamental characteristics of American government made "it impossible to organize and discipline an effective army from the point of view of military experts." [30]

Civilian Control: Army Passivity, Naval Responsibility, and the Council of National Defense. The origins of the theory and practice of objective civilian control in the United States stem from the institutional separation of the military forces from society during these years, the ideas of the officers as to the proper distance between the military forces and politics, and their deepening professional *esprit* and sense of professional autonomy. To the extent that objective civilian control became effective in the United States, it was military in its inception and maintenance. Army and Navy officers emphasized their subordination to the political arms of government. The military services were but the muscle of the government "controlled and directed," as one Navy man put it, "by the intellectual parts comprising the legislative, executive and judicial." The Army's "subordination to the civil power," an officer of that service echoed, "segregates it as a power distinctive from all others, executive, legislative or judicial." Within this fundamental allegiance to civilian superiority, however, the differing experiences of the two services led them to phrase their ideals in slightly different form.

The Army participated in a diversity of tasks — Southern reconstruction, Indian fighting, labor disorders, the Spanish War, Cuban occupation, Philippine pacification, construction and operation of the Canal, the Mexican punitive expedition. Accordingly, the Army developed an image of itself as the government's obedient handyman performing without question or hesitation the jobs assigned to it: "the country's general servant, well-disciplined, obedient, performing civil functions." It had no peculiar field of responsibility; instead, it was a vast, organic, human machine, blindly following orders from on high. The analogy of the Army to a machine, both in the sense of its dependence upon an operative to start it and guide it in action and in the sense of a complicated slowly constructed whole which alone gave meaning to its parts, was frequently employed, underlining as it did the Army's passive role. "When called into action, it is merely a machine, and is as irresponsible." Consequently, "military power is but an instrument in the hands of a superior will. It is passive to the exercise of other governmental functions." Army writers admitted that the military were only bound to obey lawful orders, but they held that it was not for them to judge their legality. "Soldiers are soldiers and not lawyers." By following all orders literally the Army attempted to divest itself of political responsibility and political controversy despite the political nature of the tasks it was frequently called upon to perform.

The situation of the Navy was somewhat different. Its role was more limited to enforcing the national will in foreign affairs. It was also, obviously, the nation's first line of defense. Consequently, while stressing the subordination of the Navy to the political direction of the government, naval officers also stressed its responsibility for the country's safety. "Let us remember," warned Fiske, "that the naval defense of our country is our profession, not that of Congress." The naval profession must obey its civilian superiors, but it also has the duty to make its professional opinions known. If an ordered course of action ran counter to "professional convictions" and seemed "fraught with harm," a "proper representation" to the senior officials was "of course obligatory." The naval profession must have room to work out its own "rules of strategy, tactics, and discipline," but in the end, these were, of course, subject to the "general control of the civil authority, to which it must render absolute obedience." The Navy view of civilian control thus assigned a more positive and active role to the military profession than did that of the Army.

Both branches of the profession had roughly the same ideas on the over-all relationship between strategy and national policy. Military policy depended upon statesmanship. It was the function of the civilian policy-maker to determine the ends of national policy and to allocate the resources which the military might use to achieve those ends. It was then the job of the military to apply the resources to the achievement of the goal. Planning this application constituted strategy. If military activities developed ends of their own which conflicted with those laid down by the statesman, the military goals had to give way. "In the highest sense," one officer wrote about naval policy, "it depends on the foreign policy of the government, and is therefore beyond the sphere of our discussion as naval officers." Officers unanimously agreed that strategy was "the servant of statesmanship" and that the determination of national goals had to precede the decisions on strategy. The continuity of policy through peace and war was also stressed. Policy developed with the nation and would have no end so long as the nation existed in a world of sovereign states. It should be obvious, one naval officer argued, that "policies make war; that war is conducted to further policies, and that treaties carry forward these policies when war decides in their favor." By 1914 the theory of the American military man on war and policy was strictly Clausewitzian.

This view, as Fiske pointed out, presupposed that the ends of policy would be defined before strategy had to be prepared. Given the American system of government, however, this was not always a safe assumption. Frequently, the military men found themselves forced to work in a vacuum and to guess as to the nature of national policy. Such a situation tended to undermine either civilian control or national security, forcing the military men to make their own policy or give up any serious strategic planning. Consequently, the military profession was virtually unanimous in its demand for some sort of organ, such as a Council of National Defense, which would lay down definite policies for them to follow. Over and over again, fifty years before the National Security Council was created, they pleaded the need for such a body. Without it, they were directionless. Most of the military proposals suggested the inclusion of congressional as well as executive leaders, and they were, consequently, another manifestation of military hostility to the separation of powers. The military writers recognized that a defense council was needed more in peace than in war, and buttressed their arguments by pointing to the existing councils in foreign countries. Civilian officials such as Secretary Daniels and members of the State Department opposed the military recommendations. In 1916 when Congress did create a Council of National Defense, it was a far cry from what the military had in mind. The Secretary of State was not a member and there was no provision for regularized professional military advice. The work of the Council, consequently, was largely concerned with economic mobilization.[31]

National Policy: Realism or Pessimism? The attitudes of the American military toward national policy followed closely those of the ideal-type military ethic. Continuously, the officers warned of the inevitability of war. The causes of war were in the "unstable equilibrium" of international politics and the rivalry of sovereign states for power, glory, and trade. Wars might be postponed and they might be limited, but they could not be avoided. The United States, the officers counseled, was no different from any other nation in its susceptibility to conflict. War is "an occurrence," Wagner reminded his countrymen, "to which all nations are subject." While preaching the inevitability of war, the officers had to defend themselves against charges that they viewed it as desirable also. A few of them, to be sure, absorbed the militant version of Social Darwinism, and described the benefits of conflict. The great bulk of the officer corps of both services, however, stressed the evils and horrors of war. Sherman's dictum on war was frequently quoted by Army writers, as were Moltke's words to the same effect. The causes of war, the officers insisted, were civil in nature, and the military who have to fight them have little desire to foment them. Instead, the natural conservatism of the military man leads him to support the maintenance of peace. Before the Spanish-American War and before the United States entered World War I, the officers were conspicuously absent from the ranks of war advocates, and instead warned of the dangers involvement would entail for the United States.

The twenty years prior to World War I were the heyday of the belief that war might be prevented by treaties or institutional devices. Again and again the military warned that Peace Palaces would not bring peace, and that treaties could only be relied upon so long as they reflected the underlying realities of power politics. Particularly popular in the United States, with its legal orientation, was Andrew Carnegie's idea of international arbitration. American military men, consequently, directed most of their fire against this conception, warning that arbitration could settle nothing but the most minor disputes and that arbitration treaties were no substitute for armaments. As American delegates to the Hague Conferences, Admiral Mahan and General George B. Davis expressed these strictly military opinions. "They were an excellent tonic," Andrew D. White remarked on Mahan's views. "When he speaks the millennium fades, and this stern, severe actual world appears."

The military's answer to the problems of war and peace was, of course, stronger military forces. This was probably the most frequent theme in military literature after the 1870's. Every argument which was subsequently to be utilized in the popular controversy over preparedness in the Wilson Administration may be found in the military thinking of these earlier years. The military particularly criticized the idea that the United States could rely on its "latent-strength"; when war came, military power in being, not

potential resources, would determine its outcome. Military preparation was also argued for on the grounds of economy. Efficient forces
in being were in the long run less expensive and would bring about
quicker victory than wasteful efforts to put together an army after
the opening of hostilities. The maintenance of strong forces would
also tend to reduce the likelihood of war by deterring potential enemies from aggression. Germany, it was pointed out, had maintained
the strongest and best army in Europe after 1871 and had been
freer from conflict than any other European power. There was
nothing inherent in the maintenance of substantial military forces
which tended to provoke war. Instead, they prevented war. The
standard by which American military strength should be measured
was "the estimated force which the strongest probable enemy"
could bring against us.[32]

The essence of the military thinking on national policy was
power and the natural rivalry of nations. In this respect, their attitudes were more realistic than most American thinking on foreign
policy. But, on the other hand, the military responsibility was to
be pessimistic, and their pessimism was in many ways unrealistic
during the years of isolation and peace. Their forebodings of disaster
and their repeated pleadings for more force were out of place in the
long, quiet years of the 1880's and 1890's. The officers were ahead
of their times. Civilian complacency more accurately reflected the
realities of international politics than military fears of imminent
war and invasion. Although they started out with realistic assumptions about international relations, the military did not follow these
through to the logical conclusion that the United States actually had
little need for military force and that the protection of the oceans
would give her time to transform resources into power once war
began. Instead, the military writers substituted their own views on
the essentiality of power which were, however, derived not from
the needs of foreign policy, but from the needs of the military
profession. After 1898, on the other hand, the military view more
closely approximated national requirements than did the still com-
placent civilian attitudes. As World War I approached, the coincidence between national needs and military attitudes became closer,
and the distance between national needs and the hitherto prevailing civilian view much greater. By this time, however, the military

suffered the results of crying wolf in the previous century. Although the march of events was making realists out of the pessimists, the civilians by and large were slow in recognizing this change.

American Society: Jingoism, Individualism, Commercialism. The military officers were not pleased by what they saw when they looked out from their professional monastery on the bustling America of their age. Those aspects of American society which were most important were those which seemed most unmilitary. The image of America in the military mind was a picture of jingoism, individualism, and, most particularly, commercialism.

Back in the Military Enlightenment, D. H. Mahan had termed the American people warlike but unmilitary. He had hoped that this would change. A. T. Mahan, however, found it necessary to echo the words of his father: Americans were "aggressive, combative, even warlike," but they were the "reverse of military; out of sympathy with military tone and feeling." The naval Mahan's Army contemporaries concurred in this judgment. Not only were Americans bellicose, but they suffered from an overweening and highly dangerous self-confidence. The military officers expressed great alarm at the "national conceit" rampant in the United States, warning of the effects of the persistent Jacksonian strain of thinking which led the American people to reject military skills and the military profession. Again and again the officers spoke of the danger of "blind faith in the manifest destiny of the Republic." To them, there was nothing manifest about it at all. The American people had made a monetary motto — "In God We Trust" — into a military policy, without regard to the fact that faith must be supported by works. Military men criticized the rash and adventurous psychology, typified by the "On to Richmond" slogan of the Civil War radicals, and urged the primacy of prudence over courage and the necessity of accepting a "patient and costly defense." Some military men almost seemed to regret that the United States had "never known a Jena or Sedan" to curb national arrogance and complacency.

While American national egotism was, according to the military view, a threat to national security, the egotism of individual Americans was viewed as a threat to the military services. Military writers never ceased to inveigh against the evils of individualism which they held to be the dominant social current in the American scene. The individualism and self-assertiveness of the civilian were contrasted with the discipline and subordination required of the professional soldier. The universal hostility of the American people to things military was "the result of our institutions inculcating pride and egotism." Army officers despaired of ever inducing the American public to support universal military service, pointing out that the only compulsory civic responsibilities which Americans had accepted, and even these reluctantly, were jury service and education of the young. The pervading spirit of individualism was seen as infiltrating the services and undermining their effectiveness. "It is high time now," pleaded one naval officer, ". . . that this individualism be brought under proper control."

By far the most serious aspect of the unhealthy national psychology, so far as the military were concerned, was the prevailing spirit of commercialism. They reacted vigorously to the rise of industrialism and the dominance of business pacifism. The military attack, rooted in a thoroughly noneconomic conservatism, was much more fundamental than that of labor and radical groups who shared with business a basic utilitarian ethic. Officers deplored the "tremendous spirit of commercialism" which they had to face and the dominance of Congress by businessmen. Fiske warned that "the insistent requirements of business, society, and pleasure," would enervate the nation and leave it wealthy and powerless, open to attack. Homer Lea, America's brilliant if erratic soldier-romantic, was not always in tune with the conservative officer corps, but in his condemnation of the commercial spirit, he was speaking in true military tones. "The trouble with us," one brigadier general agreed, "is that under the modern devil of sordid commercialism, which corrupts legislators and public servants and dulls public conscience, the average man considers that the state and the government exist for his sole personal benefit; he does not realize that the rights, privileges and immunities resulting from citizenship have corresponding responsibilities and duties." The prevalence of technicism and the emphasis on material in the services were laid at the door of the national values. The cultivation of the proper military spirit, Mahan argued, required the military to withdraw from contact with the materialistic society which they served and to isolate themselves from the corrupting "spirit of the age." The *Infantry Journal* deplored the spread of "scientific materialism." Industrial discipline was opposed to military discipline, and it was the former which was held to dominate the Navy. The only things military about the Navy, it was lamented, were the Naval Academy, the training stations, and the Marine Corps. Otherwise, it was simply a "fighting industrial association," reeking with materialism and commercialism.

Rejected by a commercial society, the military services were contemptuous of the values of such a society and sure of the superiority of their own creed. One of the great advantages of West Point, it was held, was that it isolated its students from the "atmosphere of commercialism." Cadets were strictly confined to the post for four years and were not allowed to receive, possess, or use pocket money — a minor indication of the Academy's isolation as a military monastery. The moral superiority of the military life rested on its freedom "from the sordidness and misery of the money-getting trade." The order, discipline, and regularity of the military existence led to "military contentment," whereas the frantic rush and bustle, chaotic self-seeking, and injustice of civilian life made discontent endemic to civilian society. Peace of mind, freedom from the never satiated drives for material gain, were only possible in the self-discipline and restraint of the military life. In their criticism of American commercial democracy, the officers were treading on classical ground, unconsciously echoing Plato's indictment of Athenian commercial democracy twenty-five hundred years previously.

The arrogance, individualism, and commercialism of American society gave the military the outlook of an estranged minority. "In the United States," as the *New York Sun* observed in 1906, "the professional soldier has a feeling of detachment and futility." The sense of alienation was complete and disturbing, and in the first decade of the twentieth century, the military began to wonder what might be done to effect a reconciliation. The frequency with which they discussed their unsatisfactory relations with the public increased noticeably. But, despite their concern, the basic conflict of values remained. Its deep-rooted nature was unconsciously but brilliantly pinpointed in one officer's comments in 1905 on the "Cardinal Vices of the American Soldier." [33] These included his personal independence, rebellious spirit, excessive wants, deficient sense of obligation, criticism of superior authority, self-interest, ambition, and "contempt of humble things and duties." These very characteristics to which the major objected were those which most civilian Americans would list, under different names, as national virtues rather than vices. With such an ideological gap between the military and civilian worlds, the attempts of officers to justify their services were bound to fall on deaf ears.

10

The Failure of the Neo-Hamiltonian
Compromise, 1890–1920

THE NATURE OF NEO-HAMILTONIANISM

From roughly 1890 (the publication of *The Influence of Sea Power upon History, 1660–1783*) to 1920 (the rejection of Leonard Wood by the Republican National Convention), a group of statesmen and publicists and a school of thought existed in America which might be labeled Neo-Hamiltonian. The outstanding individuals in this group were Theodore Roosevelt, Henry Cabot Lodge, Elihu Root, Albert J. Beveridge, A. T. Mahan, Herbert Croly, Leonard Wood, Henry Adams, and Brooks Adams. The common bond among these diverse personalities was an outlook on politics which transcended the usual American categories. The Neo-Hamiltonians did not fall into the liberal tradition of Jefferson, Jackson, Spencer, and Wilson. Yet neither were they completely conservative, in the sense in which Calhoun was conservative. On economic issues, they bridged the gap from the reforming tendencies of Croly and the *New Republic* group to the staunch standpatism of Elihu Root. More significantly, the Neo-Hamiltonians also combined elements of military and civilian thinking. They were in fact the first important American social group whose political philosophy more or less consciously borrowed and incorporated elements of the professional military ethic.

The fundamental cause of Neo-Hamiltonianism in an age otherwise characterized by business pacifism was the shock of American involvement in world politics at the end of the nineteenth century. Neo-Hamiltonianism was essentially a positive reaction to the end of isolation and a favorable response to the opportunity to play power politics. It briefly captured the attention and support of the American people by its emphasis on power and the primacy of the national interest. Woodrow Wilson, however, dealt it a death blow by developing an alternative philosophy of international involvement which transcended national interest and which was more deeply rooted in the American liberal tradition. Neo-Hamiltonianism had a semi-conservative explanation of the role which America should play in world politics. Wilsonianism offered a completely liberal explanation. Given the overwhelming devotion of the American people to the values of liberalism, it was inevitable that the latter should displace the former. And when the Wilson program failed, the American people reacted in the 1920's, not by going back to Neo-Hamiltonian interventionism, but by abandoning intervention altogether and returning to liberal isolationism. Neo-Hamiltonianism never had a secure base in the continuing interests and outlook of any specific social or economic group. The political vehicle of the Neo-Hamiltonians was the Republican Party, and, when they finally lost control of that party to business elements, they were irremediably excluded from further political influence. The main current of American liberalism flowed majestically onward between 1890 and 1920. Neo-Hamiltonianism was a side eddy of a different hue, which at times diverted a substantial portion of the political water, but which was ultimately reabsorbed by the main channel.*

The civilian expressions of the Neo-Hamiltonian ethic — the writings and speeches of Theodore Roosevelt, the philosophizing of the Adamses, the policies of Elihu Root, the editorials of the pre-war *New Republic* — reveal a peculiar amalgam of liberal-conservative values. Neo-Hamiltonianism differed from liberalism and resembled the professional military viewpoint in its appreciation of the role of power in human affairs. Like the military and unlike the liberals, the Neo-Hamiltonians saw international politics as basically a struggle among independent nations with interests which not infrequently brought them into conflict with each other. Con-

---

* Neo-Hamiltonianism reemerged briefly in 1940 and 1941 when Grenville Clark, Stimson, Robert P. Patterson, Elihu Root, Jr., and others in the Roosevelt-Root-Wood tradition played a major role in stimulating American rearmament and in securing the passage of the Selective Service Act of 1940.

trary to the optimistic doctrines of business pacifism, they held to the military view that war was far from obsolete. Also, like the military and unlike the liberals, the Neo-Hamiltonians argued that national policy must primarily reflect not abstract ideals but a realistic understanding of the national interest. This was the first responsibility of the statesmen. So long as nations exist, force is the ultimate arbiter. Consequently, nations must maintain adequate armaments to back up their national policies, the nature of national policy determining the size and nature of the forces required. The Neo-Hamiltonians shared with the military an essentially Clause-witzian view of the relations of policy and force. They supported the military in their efforts to build up the nation's defenses. They were more willing than most Americans to accept the military profession. Herbert Croly's *New Republic* in 1915 could pour a withering scorn at the liberal illusions of Bryan and Carnegie that a citizen army, springing to arms overnight, was sufficient for the nation's defense. Along with the military, the Neo-Hamiltonians rejected plutocracy and were bitter in their contempt for the prevailing commercialism, materialism, and the values inherent in an economically oriented way of life. They shared with the military a stress on loyalty, duty, responsibility, and subordination of the self to the requirements of the nation. Brooks Adams even went so far as to suggest openly that America would do well to substitute the values of West Point for the values of Wall Street.

Despite this wide agreement with the military ethic, there were, nonetheless, significant differences. Neo-Hamiltonianism was not completely divorced from the popular ideologies of the times. Many of its advocates, particularly Theodore Roosevelt, made an effort to rationalize the national interest in terms of universal moral values of justice and righteousness. The Neo-Hamiltonian interest in politics was much broader than the strictly military approach. Croly's international realism, manifested in *The Promise of American Life,* was part of a broad political philosophy which offered answers to the issues of domestic as well as foreign politics. More fundamental, perhaps, was the value which the Neo-Hamiltonians put on violence and force. In many respects the underlying moral values of the Neo-Hamiltonians were closer to those of aristocratic romanticism than they were to those of military professionalism.

Peace was enervating and degrading. Man was born to struggle and triumph. Virility, adventure, the strenuous life, strife and combat — these were good in themselves. The militant version of Social Darwinism had a much greater influence on Neo-Hamiltonian ideas than it did on military thinking. Unlike the military, the Neo-Hamiltonians supported national expansion. The world was divided into vigorous nations asserting themselves, expanding their power and prestige, and weak, timid nations on the decline. The dividing line between these two groups was frequently given a racial basis, the virile Anglo-Saxon nations with the capacity for self-government opposed to the inferior peoples of the world. "The American nation," as Croly put it, "needs the tonic of a serious moral adventure." And he went on to complain that America had been too comfortable and too safe. No military man could ever agree with this analysis. And here was the root of the difference. For the military, the fundamental aim was national security. For the Neo-Hamiltonians, it was national assertion and national adventure.[1]

MAHAN AND WOOD: THE TRAGEDY OF THE MILITARY PUBLICIST

The participation of Alfred Mahan and Leonard Wood in the articulation of Neo-Hamiltonian ideas was the first and only time in American history that professional military leaders contributed so directly to the outlook and activities of a political movement. Other military officers, before and since, have been prominent in political life. But they have usually been popular heroes identifying themselves with a civilian interest or movement. Their role has been passive and instrumental. The contribution of Mahan and Wood, on the other hand, was active, positive, and intellectual. They brought many elements of the military ethic to Neo-Hamiltonianism. Yet the influence was not simply in one direction. In espousing Neo-Hamiltonianism, Mahan and Wood had to make concessions to American opinion and become something less than military. Despite their popularity and influence, this was their tragedy: to be caught between two worlds. With one foot on the bedrock of military professionalism, and the other in the shifting sands of politics and opinion, they were unable to maintain a standing on either.

Both Mahan and Wood attempted to bridge the gap between the military and American society by riding the tide of temporary popular interest in military might and war. Mahan was the military officer become prophet of expansion in the first phase of Neo-Hamiltonianism in the 1890's; Wood was the military officer become prophet of preparedness in a second phase between 1908 and 1917. Mahan attempted to build a link between the Navy and the public, Wood between the Army and the public. Mahan justified expansion on nonmilitary moral, economic, and political grounds; Wood justified preparedness on nonmilitary moral, economic, and political grounds. Mahan's philosophy was a semi-military explanation of the relation of the United States to the rest of the world, Wood's theory a semi-military explanation of the relation of the armed services to the rest of the country. Each contributed to the development of professionalism in his own service, but was never at home there, and went on to become a political figure. The difference between Luce and Mahan and between Pershing and Wood were the measures of their distances from the professional ideal.

ALFRED THAYER MAHAN. Mahan was, of course, born into the main stream of the American military tradition. His father's military ideals, his early childhood at West Point, his contact with such figures as Lee and McClellan, even his name honoring the father of the Military Academy, all indicated a military career. At an early age he decided upon the Navy, graduating from Annapolis in 1859. During the Civil War and for twenty years afterward, he had a normal naval career, steadily moving up the ladder of rank and responsibility. As he himself subsequently stated, he was at this time merely the average officer "drifting on the lines of simple respectability" and very much the prisoner of his professional environment. Politically, he was a staunch anti-imperialist. In 1885, however, the turning point came when he was invited by Luce to join the Naval War College staff. During the following seven years at Newport, he embarked upon a career of thinking and writing which changed him from naval professional to naval philosopher.

This metamorphosis was largely the result of historical study and the impact upon his thinking of the events and currents of opinion of his day. Nonetheless, elements which propelled him in this direction were already present in his character and thought. He had never been completely satisfied with the professional military life. His interests, his thinking, and his morality went too deep to be completely absorbed within narrow professional confines. His father had warned him that he was more suited for a civilian than for a military career, and, subsequently, Mahan was to acknowledge the wisdom of this paternal insight. "I think myself now that he was right; for, though I have no cause to complain of unsuccess, I believe I should have done better elsewhere." [2] During his early cruises, he developed a deep interest in politics and read widely in international relations. This interest continued and grew right down to his going to the Naval War College. He was much discouraged with the inactivity and routine of the naval profession, and with the indifference it suffered from the American public. He was also extremely religious, his entire outlook colored by his orthodox Episcopalianism. Paternal influence, attendance at an Episcopalian school, and the influence of an uncle who was a minister, all contributed in this direction. At the Academy, and on his early cruises, he devoted much thought, reading, and worry to theological questions. Discontent with the naval profession, political interests, and religious concerns thus all forced Mahan to search for a wider frame of reference and endeavor. These he found in history and in public opinion. Just as his father represented the military technician who became a professional, Alfred Mahan represented the professional officer who became a political figure. In terms of the evolution of social types, the elder Mahan is separated from the younger by the professional generation of Luce, Sherman, and Upton.

The views Mahan expressed in his historical and popular writings from the publication of *The Influence of Sea Power upon History, 1660–1783* in 1890 to his death in 1914 were a typical Neo-Hamiltonian combination of military and nonmilitary elements. Mahan had a basically conservative outlook. The fundamental causes of war were to be found in the nature of man as a creature of passion and reason. Each nation pursued its interest, destiny, and ideals, and clashes between nations could not be avoided. Mahan was highly skeptical of the value of arbitration as a means of settling international disputes. He believed that an equilibrium of power was the best means of preserving peace, and that effective armed preparedness was a national necessity. Following the preachings of Luce, he urged naval officers to concentrate upon the true heart of their profession, the science of naval warfare, and to appreciate the importance of naval history to its mastery. He was a consistent advocate of a balanced system of organization for the Navy Department which he believed would effectively delimit civilian and military responsibilities. He also urged the establishment of a national defense council modeled after the British Defense Committee so as to secure adequate coordination of foreign and military policies. In all these respects, Mahan was enunciating standard military ideas common to both Navy and Army officers of the period.

In four important particulars, however, Mahan's thinking went beyond the purely professional outlook. His theory of the significance of sea power in the rise and fall of nations transcended the limits of military analysis. By sea power, he meant all the elements contributing to national strength on the ocean, not just the military ones. His theory rested primarily upon the examples of Athens, Rome, and, above all, England. Mahan's scope was far broader than that of Clausewitz, Jomini, or other military writers. His theory was a philosophy of history not a philosophy of warfare. As such, it had political, ideological, and even racial overtones. Secondly, in his study of international relations, Mahan went beyond a mere realistic analysis of the conflicts of national interests and the situations in which they led to war. Instead, he formulated a philosophy of national power which glorified national expansion as an end in itself, a national duty and responsibility. At times, he became intoxicated with the mystique of power. The political goal of national expansion prevailed over the military goal of national security. He supported the acquisition of the Philippines by the United States, for example, on grounds of morality and duty without really considering what effects this might have on national security. Thirdly, Mahan went beyond warning of the inevitability of war to justifying it on moral and religious grounds. War was the instrument of the progressive improvement of mankind. "Power, force, is a faculty of national life; one of the talents committed to nations by God." Finally, Mahan deviated from the orthodox military view in his attitude toward the blending of strategy and politics. "Aim to be yourselves statesmen as well as seamen," he advised naval officers, stressing the desirability of political knowledge and political action. Writing in 1911, he acknowledged the change in his own viewpoint on this subject from an earlier, more professional outlook:

I cannot too entirely repudiate any casual word of mine reflecting the tone which once was so traditional in the navy that it might be called professional, — that "political questions belong rather to the statesman than to the military man." I find these words in my old lectures, but I very soon learned better, from my best military friend, Jomini; and I believe that no printed book of mine endorses the opinion that external politics are of no professional concern to military men.[3]

In going beyond professionalism, Mahan became an excellent target for those within the officer corps who fell short of professionalism. Both the requirements of writing as a career and the content of what he was writing tended to separate him from the rest of the officer corps. In 1892, when his turn for sea duty came up, he attempted to avoid it by promising to retire after completing forty years of service in 1896 if he were permitted to remain on shore. He, in his own words, "by this time had decided that authorship had for me greater attractions than following up my profession, and promised a fuller and more successful old age." He would have retired immediately if that had been possible. Despite the efforts of Roosevelt and Lodge to keep him on shore, the naval bureaucracy was indifferent to his literary success — "It is not the business of a naval officer to write books," declared the Chief of the Bureau of Navigation — and Mahan was sent to sea. This thoroughly irked him.

I am enduring, not living [he wrote one friend]; and have the painful consciousness that I am expending much labor in doing what I have indifferently, while debarred from doing what I have shown particular capacity for. It is not a pleasant feeling — especially when accompanied with the knowledge that the headstrong folly of my youth started me in a profession which, to say the least, was not the one for which I have the best endowments . . . I have become exceedingly interested in professional literary work, and have now a fair promise of success in it.

Given this attitude, it is not surprising that his superior officer declared in a fitness report that Mahan's "interests are entirely outside the Service for which, I am satisfied, he cares but little and is therefore not a good officer." [4] After this last tour of sea duty, Mahan did retire in 1896 and thereafter only served on active duty during the Spanish-American War and on a few other temporary occasions.

Mahan's theories thus reflected the civilian intellectual currents of his time as well as the developing naval professional outlook. The change in his activities from professional work to popular writing coincided with the change in his thinking from professional realism to the defense of expansion and violence. To support his position, he called in Christian doctrine, Social Darwinism, utilitarianism, and nationalism. He elaborated upon the civilian doctrines of manifest destiny. Mahan was truly "a child of his age, an age of budding imperialism." [5] In his magazine articles, he consciously appealed to the sentiments for expansion stirring in the American populace. As he himself said, his writings traced "not my development, but the progress of national awakening from 1890 to 1897." His function was that of popularizer and articulator of the political sentiments of the day. Mahan's doctrines were in many respects more widely accepted by the American public than by the American Navy. His immediate influence upon his fellow officers did not equal that of the more professionally inclined Luce and Sims.[6] Separated from his profession, Mahan rode the swelling tide of imperialist sentiment in the 1890's. He was acclaimed at home and honored abroad. His books were best sellers, his articles widely read and quoted. He was the premier spokesman of the new doctrines, the confidant and adviser to Lodge, Roosevelt, and the other Neo-Hamiltonian political leaders of the day. In shifting his base from the naval profession to public opinion, however, he had gained temporary strength at the expense of permanent support. Inevitably, after the turn of the century, the reaction against Neo-Hamiltonianism and imperialism set in. Popular opinion swung back toward liberalism, isolation, pacifism, and indifference to preparedness and the responsibilities of national greatness. His books no longer commanded the audience which they once did. Mahan vigorously criticized *The Great Illusion,* but it was Norman Angell rather than he who was now the best seller. In his autobiography published in 1907, the sense of separation from the public was as manifest as the sense of separation from the profession. The American people, Mahan regretted, were unmilitary, and they viewed the military spirit as "the obtrusion of an alien temperament." His warnings as to the dangers from Germany and the needs of naval preparedness fell on deaf ears. The American people, he declared in 1912, "are singularly oblivious of the close relation between peace and preparation." In 1913 he admitted that his "vogue was largely over." [7] The next year he died.

LEONARD WOOD. Leonard Wood had fewer initial connections with military professionalism than did Mahan. Graduating from Harvard Medical School, he became an Army surgeon and for several years saw service in the final Indian campaigns in the southwest. Ordered to Washington in Cleveland's administration as surgeon to the President, he stayed on with McKinley. When the Spanish War broke out, he joined with Theodore Roosevelt in organizing the Rough Riders. Wood came out of the war a major general of Volunteers and served as military governor of Cuba from 1899 to 1902. McKinley also promoted him from captain in the Medical Corps to brigadier general in the Regular Army. Subsequently, Roosevelt made him a major general and sent him out to be military governor in the Philippines. Returning in 1908, he served as commander of the eastern department of the Army and as Chief of Staff from 1910 to 1914.

Wood's views on military and national affairs were expressed in his speeches, writings, and actions after his return to the United States in 1908. Like Mahan's, his outlook was, to a large extent, that of the military professional. He was instrumental in advocating and instituting professional reforms in the Army.[8] Nonetheless, like Mahan, he also ended up the proponent of an unmilitary political *Weltanschauung.* Wood's thought revolved about the twin ideas of the responsibility of the citizen for military service and the benefits to the citizen from military service. Unlike the professional military man, Wood saw the Army as the embodiment of the people rather than as "the career of a chosen class." [9] While recognizing the military need of preparedness, he stressed even more the civic need: the desirability of stimulating throughout the country the military, or at least semi-military, virtues of patriotism, responsibility, devotion to duty, and manliness. In 1913 he organized summer training camps for college youths. In 1915 this idea was expanded into the Plattsburg camp for businessmen. At the end of World War I, before his unit was demobilized, Wood turned his division into a university, pushing educational plans for both officers and enlisted men. He wanted to combine military training with a broader education in citizenship and the ideals of national service. Wood justified universal military training by its political, educational, and moral benefits. It would give meaning to citizenship, and it was the logical corollary of universal manhood suffrage. It would reduce crime and improve economic efficiency. It would unite the country, forming a single national spirit transcending sectional, class, and nationality group differences. In a similar vein, Wood defended the Regular Army for its constructive work in engineering, public health, sanitation in Cuba, the Canal Zone, Puerto Rico, and the Philippines.[10] Wood's outlook is summarized in the titles of two lectures delivered in 1915: "The Military Obligation of Citizenship" and "The Civil Obligation of the Army." In stressing the universality of military service, Wood harked back more to Jefferson than to Hamilton, although the imperatives he invoked to plead his case — manliness, duty, responsibility, patriotic ardor — were not those which received primary emphasis in Jefferson's formulation.

During the decade prior to American entrance into the World War, Wood was a leading figure in the drive for a positive national policy and the increase in America's armed strength. He played a major role in stimulating the outpouring of preparedness literature which flooded the country.* His support for preparedness went far

* These books of 1914–1917 constitute one of the few significant bodies of writings by American civilians and military men on defense issues. The tone of virtually all those favoring preparedness was thoroughly Neo-Hamiltonian. Many were written by close friends of Wood, others were dedicated to him, and to others he contributed introductions. Some of the more notable were Jennings C. Wise, *Empire and Armament* (New York, 1915); Frederic Louis Huidekoper, *The Military Unpreparedness of the United States* (New York, 1915); R. M. Johnston, *Arms and the Race* (New York, 1915); Eric Fisher Wood, *The Writing on the*

beyond the policies of the Wilson Administration. His close personal ties with Roosevelt and the other Neo-Hamiltonians linked him with their violent attacks upon what they described as the pacifism and vacillation of Wilson. Wood himself was on occasion in his public speeches highly critical of his Commander in Chief. He was also thoroughly identified with the Republican Party, and in 1915 and 1916 was openly receptive to the idea that he might become its presidential nominee.

Political participation further alienated Wood from the military profession of which he never had been a full-fledged member. Lacking the West Point background, entering the Army as a surgeon, becoming the confidant of Cleveland and McKinley and the intimate friend of Roosevelt, making his military reputation as leader of the thoroughly unprofessional Rough Riders, Wood was viewed with suspicion and jealousy by many within the officer corps. Rejecting the 1899 advice of the War Department that he get out of the Army, he had instead risen to its highest post. Inevitably, the rapid rise of this medical man over the heads of deserving career officers was attributed to political favoritism. His political activities barnstorming about the country between 1908 and 1917 did not sit well with a generation of officers indoctrinated in the Sherman-Upton philosophy of a silent, impartial professional service. Eventually, the officer corps settled up with him. In the first war which they directed in their own fashion, the professionals could find no place for Leonard Wood. Eager though Wood was for military glory, Pershing viewed him as an insubordinate political general and refused to have him in France. He was shunted aside and spent the war directing a training camp on this side of the Atlantic. Although he blamed Wilson and the Democrats for the treatment he received, his real enemies this time were the military professionals he had so long flouted.*

Wall (New York, 1916). Theodore Roosevelt was the only figure who overshadowed Leonard Wood in the preparedness campaign.

* Hermann Hagedorn in his highly sympathetic biography of Wood summed up the difference between him and Pershing as follows:

"The conflict between Wood and Pershing went deeper than mere personal antagonism. Their views of what the American army should be differed fundamentally. To Pershing — brought up on the Prussian theorists, Clausewitz, Bernhardi, Treitschke, von der Goltz — the army was a machine, to be used as man, the intelligent, uses any other machine for his own purposes. To Wood, the army

The officer corps evened the score with Wood during the war by denying him combat command. The politicians evened the score after the war by thwarting his second great ambition. Rejected by the military, Wood still hoped to redeem himself in politics. He was a leading contender for the Republican presidential nomination in 1920. But the convention and the country were tired of the martial spirit. Too much the politician for the military, he was too much the soldier for the politicians. His fellow Republicans wanted normalcy not preparedness, the easy dollar not the strenuous life. Theodore Roosevelt, had he lived, might have been flexible enough to adjust to the new mood; but not Leonard Wood. He was swept aside by the postwar antimilitarism. What place was there for him in an America of commercialism and flapperism, gin mills and jazz, Jimmy Walker and F. Scott Fitzgerald, Harding and Mencken? The new administration did the best it could for him by sending him out to the Philippines to resume his post as Governor General. He returned briefly to the United States in 1927 to die in a country which hardly remembered him and which had little use for him.

THE ABORTIVE IDENTIFICATION WITH SOCIETY, 1918–1925

After 1918 the military made every effort to continue the wartime identification with American society and to expand the Neo-Hamiltonian link with the American community. Particularly in the Army, the war was viewed as ushering in a new era of civil-

---

was first and foremost, an aggregation of human beings, gallant, lovable, wonderful human beings, who might be made craven or glorious according to the leadership given them. To take them into battle, to make them fight to gain a position, by means of them to win a campaign, was only one of a general's functions. That was essential; but it was equally important to make these men in his charge true and devoted citizens of the Republic, to give them a vision of their country, to show them what they were fighting for."

Leonard Wood (New York, 2 vols., 1931), II, 268. Wilson explained his reasons for keeping Wood in the United States in a letter to the Springfield *Republican*, June 5, 1918:

"In the first place, I am not sending him because Gen. Pershing has said that he does not want him, and in the second place, Gen. Pershing's disinclination to have Gen. Wood sent over is only too well founded. Wherever Gen. Wood goes there is controversy and conflict of judgment."

Gen. Peyton C. March, wartime Chief of Staff, had little in common with Pershing except his strict professionalism — and his dislike of Leonard Wood. See March's *The Nation at War* (Garden City, N.Y., 1932), pp. 57–68.

military relations. "The 'splendid isolation' of the Regular Army," proclaimed the *Infantry Journal,* "is a thing of the past." The Army was to become a participating member of American society. An Army as a special caste apart from the people, said the Secretary of War in 1920, "is relatively useless." Instead, it must be "in fresh and constant contact with the thoughts and feelings of the civil fireside from which it had come." [11] The hopes of the military largely reflected their belief that the separation of the Army from the populace prior to the war was primarily physical in nature, the result of its being strung out in its frontier garrisons remote from the centers of population, civilization, and commerce. With the end of Indian fighting, the reasons for this isolation were now over. The urge to belong, to be accepted, to identify with the community at large, was the primary goal of the military officers as they stressed the necessity of "getting close to the people."

The basis for uniting the Army with the people appeared to be laid in the National Defense Act of 1920. This was universally hailed by military spokesmen as inaugurating the new age of civil-military relations. The primary mission of the Regular Army was now held to be the training of civilian components — the National Guard and Organized Reserves. The new ROTC program, an extended and much broader form of the old land grant college plan, made military instruction available in any qualified college or high school. In little over a decade, more than three hundred ROTC units were set up at schools and colleges with about 125,-000 students participating in the program which absorbed the energies of about 5 per cent of the Regular Army officers corps. A second link with the civilian population came from the summer training camps for youths, developing out of Leonard Wood's prewar Plattsburg movement. The first of the new camps opened in 1922 and offered a combination of military and civic instruction to ten thousand young men for a thirty day period. Thirdly, the 1920 Act authorized the detail of regular officers as instructors with the National Guard and reserves. The Army goal was to build a nation-wide organization, so that every community in the country would have representatives of at least one of the Army components, whose views, the Secretary of War hoped, would "be felt among their neighbors until all our people come to appreciate the wisdom of supporting" a strong national defense. Finally, in these immediate postwar years, the Army also made a determined effort to institute localized recruiting, assigning each Regular Army unit to a specific geographical area and hoping in that way to build up popular support and to capitalize upon local pride.[12] Not only was the Army as a whole to be reunited with the people, but each regiment was to develop close ties with a particular locality.

This new range of activities inevitably altered the attitudes and behavior patterns which were most highly valued within the military services. The forces must adjust to society. "The character of our Army and Navy," a naval officer argued, ". . . must reflect the character of the American people — American ideas, ideals, and thoughts." The new outlook must embody the spirit of Washington's injunction: "When we assumed the soldier, we did not lay aside the citizen." Officers were told to abandon the appearance of exclusiveness and to develop a "fellow-feeling for all citizens." In training the citizen-soldier, the officer must rely upon "cooperative spirit" rather than discipline. The prewar practice of boasting about their failure to vote must be dropped. The soldier, like any other citizen, had a duty to exercise his franchise; the abstention of the officer from the polls would be "looked at rather askance by the progressive business man with whom he speaks." The military must abandon their old dislike of publicity and actively woo public opinion through all the devices and media utilized by any business corporation. All other social groups, even conservative institutions like the churches, had hired publicity men and public relations advisers; it was time for the Army to do likewise. "We must get on our feet at once and adopt business methods to meet business conditions," it was argued in marked contrast to the prewar military distaste for anything suggestive of business or commercialism. This new approach was formally recognized by the recision of President Wilson's order banning public discussion of national policy by officers, and by the issuance in 1927 of a new Army regulation declaring that public defense and advocacy of the national military policies was "naturally and logically one of the important duties of the officers of the Army." [13]

The instruction of the civilian components in particular required a new type of officer with a new outlook. It was essential, in the words of General MacArthur, that the officer have "an intimate understanding of the mechanics of human feeling, a comprehensive grasp of world and national affairs, and a liberalization of conception which amount to a change in his psychology of command." The officer on duty with the reserves must be qualified in "salesmanship" as well as the professional skills of a soldier. He must be a "good mixer" as well as a good fighter. Officers detailed to reserve duty were advised to make friends with the local Chamber of Commerce, to meet influential businessmen, to work closely with the local American Legion post, and to join the Kiwanis or Rotary. In short, they were to blend with middle-class business America. Above all, they were warned "not to be too military." [14]

The pushing of the military program involved adoption of the values as well as the techniques of a business civilization. In order to persuade their opponents of the validity of their conclusions, the military had to adopt the premises of their opponents' thinking. The defense of the regular services in terms of their nonmilitary benefits to society, which Leonard Wood had argued in the prewar years, was continued and elaborated upon. The Navy was extolled in terms of its contributions to industry and science, above and beyond its role as the country's first line of defense. The Navy, its Secretary declared in 1921, is "engaged continuously in useful and humanitarian enterprises." Two years later it was claimed that the Navy's work in humanitarian causes justified its existence even if it never fired another shot. The Army was praised for its contributions to "national development of resources, science, and manhood." By educating officers and men in civilian skills, it "blended defensive readiness with industrial and civic aid." There should be no reticence in pointing out the "economic value of the Army's peacetime accomplishments." The summer training camps were, in true Wood style, defended on the grounds of their contributions to national unity, and the Regular Army was declared to be one of "the greatest agencies in the nation in the teaching of good citizenship." [15]

The most extreme instances of the military denying themselves, and advocating a military program for nonmilitary reasons, were in their postwar campaign for universal military training. As the prospects of congressional approval for such a plan rapidly receded after 1920, the arguments advanced in its favor became more and more removed from military requirements. In the end, the officers were advancing UMT as more or less the universal panacea for all the social ills which beset America. It would strengthen national unity, promote the amalgamation of ethnic groups, and encourage democracy and tolerance. It would be physically beneficial and would virtually eliminate illiteracy in the United States. Far from injuring industry or retarding the development of occupational skills, it would have just the reverse effects. The Army would discharge its recruits with a basic training in law, commerce, transport, engineering, or any one of a number of other technical fields. Most important were the moral benefits to be derived from universal training. At the same time that it was quite rapidly espousing the values of a commercial civilization, the officer corps could still retain some elements of the old sense of the moral superiority of the military to the business way of life. Loyalty, patriotism, honor, discipline, fairness, a respect for law could be inculcated in the youth of the nation through military training. In short, the officers proved conclusively the need of universal service for every reason except military ones.[16]

The Army's new activities also involved it in political controversy with pacifist, religious, and educational organizations. Refusing to take the officers' arguments at their face value, these groups viewed the ROTC program, the summer camps, and the proposed UMT plans as schemes for the militarization of society which could lead only to war. Civilian memories of the horrors of the French trenches and the natural repugnance against instructing teenagers in the gory techniques of bayonet wielding were capitalized upon in the antimilitary propaganda. The services responded by denouncing the motives and activities of the peace groups. The epithet "pacifist" had been coined just prior to World War I to describe the opponents of the Neo-Hamiltonian preparedness program. It was now widely employed by the military officers to describe anyone who criticized military objectives. In contrast to their prewar perspective of themselves as an outcast minority, the officers now sought to portray themselves as representative of all true Americans and as one hundred per cent patriotic. Their opponents, on the other hand, were visualized as a small, conspiratorial, subversive clique, either insidiously plotting to undermine American institutions or unconsciously serving as the tools of those who did have this as their goal. The officers participated fully in the national denunciation of Reds and Bolsheviks which swept the country in the early twenties, and they did not hesitate to go further and to link their pacifist opponents with the Red Menace. While conceding that some of the pacifists might just be sentimentalists with an unreasoned opposition to war or taxpayers with a desire to reduce military expenditures, they tended to view the core of pacifists as political radicals who opposed military training with the ultimate aim of destroying the Army and Navy and overthrowing the government.[17] The services reflected the true will of the American people; their opponents were the political outcasts.

It was only slowly that the officers were disabused of this illusion. By the end of the decade, however, it had become impossible for them to maintain their identification with the community. The opposition to military ideals and the military program which was so strong within the government could no longer be blamed upon misinformation or the failure of Congress to reflect accurately the sentiment of the country. Nor could the mounting opposition to the military intrusion into education be viewed as only the work of a conspiratorial minority. Army expenditures were reduced far below that level which the officers believed necessary to carry out the purposes of the National Defense Act. The postwar reaction against navalism had reduced appropriations and produced the Washington arms conference. The localized recruiting campaign had failed to produce significant results. Military training in the secondary schools was coming under increasing attack and was being discontinued in some areas. Bills in Congress proposed to abolish the compulsory aspects of ROTC. It was manifestly obvious that "a wave of feeling against military training in our schools and colleges seems to be spreading over this country." When the new Chief of Staff, General Summerall, in 1926 sought to arouse public support for larger defense appropriations, he was abruptly silenced by the President, an action which served to point up the fact that the new freedom of officers to participate in public discussion was limited to supporting established military policies. More fundamental was the resurgence of antagonism against West Point, and the criticism of the purposes and methods of the military academy. "There is a stiff prejudice in civil life against the West Pointer," complained the cadet yearbook of 1927. Another officer diagnosed the existence of "a current epidemic, militariphobia." All the varied antimilitary prejudices came to the fore. Those of pioneer stock disliked the Army because it was the antithesis of rugged individualism. Recent immigrants disliked the Army because of its Old World aristocratic associations. Labor disliked the Army because of its strike duty. And business? "The composite American business mind," wrote one naval officer, signalizing the return to the orthodox military view of commerce, "values present advantage above future security and can see no profit in national insurance in times of peace." Underlying all was American distrust of government and the belief that the military along with the civil branches of the public service were inherently inefficient and largely unnecessary. It was time as one officer bluntly put it, to "face the facts." [18] The military effort to bridge the gap to society had been a failure. The triumphs of antimilitarism were not due to Bolshevism, but to the natural apathy of the American people, their inherent dislike for war, their linking of the military with war, and their faith in a future of peaceful progress. The Neo-Hamiltonian compromise was impossible in the postwar world. The opposition was not a few pacifists and radicals. It was America itself. Rejected again, there was nothing for the military to do but to retreat back to their prewar isolation and find interest and satisfaction in the mundane duties of their profession.*

---

* Illustrative of the withdrawal was the changing content of the Army's foremost professional magazine, the *Infantry Journal*. In the early twenties, its pages were filled with articles on political issues, Communism, national defense policy, social and economic problems. Since the Army was involved in political controversy, very few articles were critical of that service; instead, the virtues of the military program were extolled. By the late twenties and early thirties, however, politics had disappeared from the *Journal*. Its content became more strictly professional, and, at the same time, self-criticism of the military, of Army conservatism, organizational defects, technological backwardness, became much more extensive. Sober discussion of technical military problems replaced the earlier exhortations to political action.

11

The Constancy of Interwar Civil-
Military Relations

BUSINESS-REFORM HOSTILITY AND MILITARY PROFESSIONALISM

The evaporation of Neo-Hamiltonianism in the benignity of
the 1920's reunited the American community in its distaste for
military affairs. In part this reflected the renewed dominance of
business pacifism during the twenties. It was also manifest, however, in the other strand of the liberal tradition preëminent during
the second and fourth decades of the century. Reform liberalism
originated in the 1880's and 1890's in the guise of populism and
swept forward into the twentieth with the muckrakers, the progressive movement, the New Freedom, and, eventually, the New
Deal. Many of the ideas of the reformers with respect to military
affairs, and certainly the language in which they expressed their
ideas, differed considerably from those of the spokesmen of business. Yet the basic substance and the ultimate effects of the reform approach and the business approach were the same. The
antimilitarism of reform liberalism complemented the antimilitarism of business liberalism. In this respect there was no fundamental change from Wilson to Harding to Roosevelt. As a result,
the manifestations of military professionalism during the interwar
period were remarkably static. The ideas and institutions which
had been produced during the years of business rejection reflected
intense professionalism on the outskirts of society. With the postwar collapse of the Neo-Hamiltonian bridge, civil-military relations resumed this pattern and maintained it throughout the
twenties and thirties. The constancy of American military pro-

fessionalism during the interwar period reflected the underlying constancy of the business and reform approaches to military affairs.

REFORM LIBERALISM: THE PRAGMATIC USAGES OF MILITARISM

Reform liberalism was composed of many elements frequently at odds with each other. Yet there was an underlying unity in a general opposition to the interests of "big business" and a general willingness to utilize the government to secure a more equitable distribution of wealth. Superficial diversity and deeper unity were also present in the reform approach to military affairs. On the surface, reform had no consistent and prevailing military policy. Reformers supported and denounced preparedness, conscription, large armies and navies, American intervention in World War I, disarmament, neutrality legislation, the renunciation of war, rearmament in the 1930's, and aid to the allies in 1940 and 1941. Virtually every major defense issue found equally well-qualified reformers on both sides. Yet this diversity of approach was in itself a product of an underlying similarity. Reformers consistently viewed military institutions and military policy not in their own terms with reference to the purpose of military security, but rather in the reformers' terms with reference to the purposes of reform. These purposes, whether world-wide in scope or limited to American society, were essentially domestic in nature: they concerned the relations between individuals and states, not the relations among states. Reformers ended up on different sides of defense issues because they had different immediate objectives, or because they analyzed differently the way in which the issues of defense policy were related to the realization of common goals of reform. The military instrumentalism of reform liberalism accounted for both its unity and its diversity.

The antimilitarism of reform differed in tone from the antimilitarism of business. The business approach rejected all aspects of militarism. Convinced that the military were a vestigial holdover from a barbarous past, business made no effort to utilize the military for its own purposes. The reformer was more pragmatic. His opposition to the military lacked the elaborate theoretical rationale of business pacifism. Faced with the beginning of the twentieth-century age of warfare, the reformer could not so readily assume that war and militarism were obsolete. If military institutions were to exist, however, the reformer wanted to bend them to the purposes of reform. Consequently, the reformer consistently opposed only military professionalism which, being designed exclusively for the purposes of military security, necessarily competed with the demands of reform. Whereas business policy was straight extirpation, reform policy was mixed extirpation and transmutation.* In some ways, the reformer's opposition to the institutions of professional militarism was more bitter than that of the business pacifist. In part, this was the result of his inability to accept the optimistic conclusion that military institutions would die a natural death. Instead, the reformer thought positive steps necessary to eliminate militarism. Like most liberals, the reformer identified the professional military groups with his own worst enemies. "Militarism," said Harold Stearns, quoting Viscount Morley, is "the point-blank opposite of Liberalism in its fullest and profoundest sense, whatever the scale and whatever the disguise." [1] In the reform lexicon, militarism was virtually coextensive with all evil; it was incompatible with the democratic premises of American society.

The reform attack on professional militarism took two general forms. The first was similar in many respects to the business pacifist view from which it was, to a large extent, derived. It looked upon the military profession as backward and primitive. No utilitarian justification existed for the maintenance of exclusively military institutions. While the business pacifists were more or less content to state this as a self-evident truth, the reformers went about documenting it in satirical fashion. Military expenditures were sheer waste. The resources devoted to these useless purposes should be used for the reform purposes of improving human wel-

* Similarly, the reformers viewed war in terms of its contribution to domestic or international reform. They initially opposed American entrance into World War I because it would end reform at home and put business in the saddle. They eventually justified participation when they saw the exhilarating prospects for international reform in the Fourteen Points. The postwar return to power politics, colonialism, and armaments races then soured them on war as an instrument of international reform, and they proclaimed their error in ever supporting American entry. At the same time, however, the reformers became nostalgic for the domestic collectivism of the war years which in retrospect seemed to suggest parallels and techniques applicable to their efforts for social reform at home.

fare. "For in my youth," Walter Lippmann has written, "we all assumed that the money spent on battleships would better be spent on schoolhouses, and that war was an affair that 'militarists' talked about and not something that seriously-minded progressive democrats paid any attention to." [2] Stuart Chase in the 1920's bemoaned the wasted energies of the million workers which he figured were required to maintain America's modest peacetime military forces. Lewis Mumford in the following decade defined the army as a "negative producer" of "illth" in Ruskin's expressive phrase.[3] The reformers also emphasized the conflict between military values and the humanitarian values of liberalism. The mores and customs of the military professional were given a devastating analysis with the weapons of Veblenian social unmasking. The futility, inhumanity, and barbarousness of military life were constantly emphasized, and its formal social code jeered at from the vantage point of modern liberal ethics. This aspect of reform criticism set the tone for the sociological analysis of the military which has continued down to the present time. Military standards of honor, obedience, and loyalty were adjudged either hypocritical or positively dangerous. The military officer, a *New Republic* writer declared, is a "man cherishing an attitude toward life that belongs in the dark ages." The problem of the relation of military obedience to individual moral responsibility, which bothered Andrew Carnegie, also reappeared in the reformist critique. "Absolute obedience to orders," wrote Ernest Crosby, the most prolific antimilitarist of the muckraker period, "involves, of course, the abdication of conscience and reason." The minutiae of military discipline and the customs of the service defining the social gap between officers and enlisted men likewise furnished ammunition for attacks on the military caste. Such criticisms were particularly prevalent immediately after World War I, reflecting the irritation between professional officer and citizen-soldier in the wartime forces.[4] In sum, the reformer viewed military professionalism as economically wasteful, socially useless, and ethically backward.

The reformers also had a second and more positive image of the military as the active allies of big business in the struggle against reform. Here the reformer took over the business antimilitary argument and gave it an antibusiness twist. The economic imperative behind large armies and navies was the need of the capitalist economy for an outlet for over-production. Reformers and businessmen were united in their worship of the economically productive and in their description of the military as unproductive. But they disagreed as to the forces behind militarism. The respectable utilitarianism of the businessman just saw the generals and antiquated aristocrats. The radical utilitarianism of the reformer saw these plus the businessman himself. A few isolated arms manufacturers, such as Hudson Maxim, always furnished just enough evidence to give the "blood and profits" theory some support in fact.[5] Actually, it was highly ironic that what may well be, on the whole, the most pacific dominant social group in world history — American business — should be portrayed as plotting war in an unholy alliance with bloodthirsty and rank-hungry generals. In this case, the reformers were wrong on both counts: as groups, neither generals nor capitalists were eager for war. Nonetheless, the image of this alliance serving the ends of war and reaction was highly pervasive. The generals wanted war and the manufacturers would furnish the arms for that purpose; the manufacturers wished to crush labor, and the generals would furnish them troops for that end. In a distillation of Marxism, it was argued that armaments and military institutions were necessarily associated with the upper class, while the lower classes were inherently pacifist and antiwar. "Armament is fashionable," proclaimed Simeon Strunsky, and Harold Stearns looked back on the prewar preparedness movement as strictly "upper class," its impelling force coming from the social upper crust, who felt a racial and class affinity with their brethren in England. By the early 1930's, this theme had become a significant element in the revisionist interpretation of the first war. At the same time that the professional officers were lamenting the baneful effects of business on military institutions, the dedicated reformers were speaking of the "inevitable alliance between militarism and industrialism," and arguing that reform had to deal "not merely with the military mind, but also with the business mind which has taken it into double harness." [6] The entire reform theory of the business-military alliance, however, illustrated more about the relations between reform and the military than it did about the relations between business and the military.

While the reformers identified the professional military with their domestic class enemies, they did admit the possibility of military institutions which would not be so tainted and which would serve the needs of progress. Even Strunsky cited the possibility of a democratic militarism on the 1789 French model, and contrasted it with the caste militarism that was engulfing the United States. Many reformers were impressed with the democracy of universal military service — the great leveler — and contrasted this progressive military policy with that which relied upon "a hired or professional army which, next after monarchy and hereditary rank, is the most undemocratic thing that man has so far invented." This view, and the appeal of the nation-in-arms concept, were Jeffersonianism in twentieth-century guise. They had a particular attractiveness to the more collectivist and egalitarian reformers, while those who put greater emphasis upon libertarian and humanitarian values were more generally hostile to all military institutions. Like the Neo-Hamiltonians, the reformers wanted to utilize the military services directly for educating and "uplifting" the servicemen, employing them for socially productive purposes, and teaching ideals and skills desirable for civilian life. Wilson's Secretary of the Navy, Josephus Daniels, for instance, set about remedying what he thought to be the two greatest deficiencies of his service — lack of education and lack of democracy — by putting schools on every ship and by reducing the social "chasm" between officers and men.[7]

MILITARY INSTITUTIONS

EDUCATION AND PROMOTION. The basic professional institutions established prior to World War I continued afterward. There were, of course, some alterations and additions. New professional societies and journals were founded; new technical schools reflected the changing nature of war; some new professional organizations were created; and modifications were made in existing ones.* In general, however, there was little change and little need

* The most important new professional societies and journals were those founded immediately after the war for the Army Quartermaster, Ordnance, and Engineering Corps, the *Military Review* started by the Leavenworth schools in 1922, and the Infantry School *Quarterly* established in 1925. Between 1925 and 1940 few new military periodicals appeared. The most important new educational

for change. The earlier generations had built well. On the other hand, the areas which they left incomplete remained incomplete, and the issues they left unresolved remained unresolved. Controversy and unrest during the interwar period centered in three fields: preliminary education, where the legacy of Jeffersonian technicism still crowded the service academies' curriculum; promotion, where the fear of Jacksonian popularism and the separation of powers dictated continued reliance on seniority; and executive organization, where constitutional ambiguities obfuscated the lines of responsibility among civilian and military departmental leaders.

In their early years the service academies had a relatively clear mission: to produce technically competent engineers and seamen. The professionalization of officership substituted for this single technical goal the dual purposes of liberal education and basic military education. The four-year course, however, simply was not long enough to permit achievement of both these purposes, particularly when technical subjects still persisted in the curriculum. Even beyond curriculum difficulties, liberal and military education required different types of institutions: the one flourishing in a relaxed, skeptical atmosphere favorable to intellectual curiosity and discussion; the other requiring a disciplined, purposive, concentrated effort to absorb military values and military knowledge in the shortest possible time. In attempting to crowd these two discordant elements into a single curriculum, the service academies did not succeed in doing either job as well as could have been done if each had been performed separately. Theoretically the academies could have become postgraduate military schools requiring a liberal college education for admission. The general hostility of American society toward the military profession, however, made this unlikely of success in practice. If recruitment were postponed until after college, military opinion feared that the manifold opportunities of American society, the diverse interests

---

institution was the Army Industrial College created in 1924 to train officers in procurement and economic mobilization. In 1932 the Chief of Staff could claim with some degree of truth that the United States Army's "school system is unsurpassed in excellence anywhere in the world." Advanced naval education also expanded, and in 1927 the general line course was established at the Annapolis Postgraduate School. *Ann. Rept. of the Secy. of War, 1932*, p. 73; *Ann. Repts. of the Secy. of the Navy, 1925*, pp. 24–25, *1927*, pp. 157ff.

stimulated by civilian college life, and the relative unattractiveness of the military career would make it impossible to get officers of sufficient quality and quantity. In the unsympathetic American environment it was necessary to begin the military indoctrination and training of the future officer before he completely absorbed the prevailing antimilitary values and motivations. The other alternative was to remove the military and technical courses from academy curricula, deferring them to postgraduate military schools, and to concentrate upon offering a liberal education at West Point and Annapolis. The armed services, however, were neither equipped nor inclined to compete with colleges and universities in the liberal arts area. It would indeed have been hard to justify the national government's moving into liberal arts education even if all the graduates of the federal colleges entered government service.

The changes at Annapolis and West Point in the 1920's and 1930's attempted to increase the liberal arts component in the curriculum without altering fundamentally the nature of service academy education. Annapolis improved its English and History courses in 1923; and in 1932 a drastic change in the curriculum increased the proportion of the midshipman's academic time on cultural subjects from 21.6 per cent to 31.6 per cent. Technical subjects were cut from 33.6 per cent to 31.2 per cent, and professional courses from 44.8 per cent to 37.2 per cent. A department of economics and government was created. Officers still continued to complain, however, of their inferior cultural background compared to those of foreign contemporaries. They urged either the opening of junior academies which could furnish this background, or the relegation of technical and engineering subjects to the postgraduate school, or the extension of the course beyond four years. Virtually every other profession, it was pointed out, required five to eight years of initial training. Admiral Sims seized the bull by the horns in 1933, recommending, in a minority report from the Board of Visitors, that the Academy be changed into a two-year school in professional subjects for college graduates only. At West Point, instruction in English was doubled in 1920 and a chair in Economics, Government, and History was established in 1926. Under the leadership of Colonel Lucius Holt and then of Colonel Herman Beukema, the social sciences came to play an increasingly important role in cadet education. The Academy was still criticized, however, for the extent to which it emphasized mathematics and science as essential to the future officer.[8]

The Act of 1916 remained the fundamental legislation on naval officer promotion throughout the interwar period. It generally worked satisfactorily, although at times it produced hardships and dissatisfaction requiring minor changes in its operation. The Army promotion system was revised by the National Defense Act of 1920 which placed all officers except those in the Chaplain and Medical Corps on a single list, advancing them by seniority up to the rank of colonel as vacancies occurred. Officers judged unfit for promotion by boards created for this purpose were placed in a special category and weeded out, this aspect of the plan introducing a selection-out system resembling that of the Navy between 1899 and 1916. Promotions to general officer rank continued to be by selection. The basic issue confronting the Army was still the old controversy of seniority versus selection. In the early 1920's the Secretary of War recommended supplementing seniority with the more rapid advancement of a small number of highly able officers. It was argued that this would not disturb the impartiality of the seniority system, nor discredit those officers not selected, but that it would furnish an incentive to the more energetic and ambitious officer to distinguish himself to his own advantage and that of the service. The plan was unsuccessful, and many thoughtful military men still felt that it was impossible in peacetime to predict which junior officers would make good higher commanders in wartime, that the Army had to rely upon the general competence of the entire officer corps rather than upon "a relatively small number of brilliant individuals," and that selection always ran the risk of political interference. The division of opinion within the Army resulted in its retention of the seniority system down to World War II.[9]

ORGANIZATION. In theory and in practice the War and Navy Departments after 1915 had differing systems of civil-military relations. The vertical organization of the Army reflected the Neo-Hamiltonian ideas of Elihu Root and the dominance of constitutional and administrative imperatives. The balanced organization of the Navy embodied the naval traditionalist views of Luce and Mahan and the dominance of functional considerations. As a result, the Army system produced harmony and efficiency in peace, but was unequal to the tasks of war. The Navy system, on the other hand, elicited continuous discontent and friction among its constituent elements, but provided a viable basis for wartime operation. The heightening of civil-military tensions in war and the need for greater specialized responsibility at the upper levels of the War Department pushed the Army toward a balanced form of organization in war. The political and constitutional pressures favorable to coordinate or vertical organization, on the other hand, made it difficult for the Navy to maintain its balanced system in peace.

Army Civil-Military Relations. The General Staff Act of 1903 fostered an identity of interest between the Secretary of War and the Chief of Staff. The old alignment of the Secretary and the bureau chiefs versus the Commanding General was replaced by a new alignment of the Secretary and Chief of Staff versus the bureaus. While some Secretaries at times tried to take a few steps toward a balanced system, their efforts ran counter to the spirit of the existing organization and came to naught. It was easier to rely on the Chief of Staff as the secretarial instrument. Harmony and mutual confidence replaced nineteenth-century acrimony between the military and political leaders of the Department: Chiefs of Staff lavishly praised their Secretaries; the Secretaries were equally generous in their response.[10] During the two decades following Root's law, the Secretaries consistently supported the Chief of Staff in extending his authority over all the components of the Army. In the "muster roll" controversy of 1912 between Chief of Staff Leonard Wood and Adjutant General Fred Ainsworth over their respective powers and duties, Secretary Stimson backed Wood. Despite congressional support behind Ainsworth, the adjutant general was fired for insubordination. This victory of the Chief of Staff, in Stimson's words, "expanded his power far beyond that of the commanding generals of former days." When Congress in the National Defense Act of 1916 attempted to weaken the General Staff, Secretary Baker interpreted the law so as to uphold the authority of its Chief. As General Harbord described it, the effects of Baker's decision "were very far-reaching — it settled for all time the ancient struggle between the line and supply staff." General March, appointed Chief of Staff in 1918, also vigorously opposed direct dealings between the bureau chiefs and the Secretary, and Secretary Baker upheld the supremacy of his Chief against the efforts of General Pershing to act independently and to deal directly not only with the Secretary but also with the President.[11] In expanding the power of the Chief of Staff over the Army, however, the Secretaries undermined their own effective authority. Theoretically the Secretary exercised military command and the Chief of Staff was merely his adviser; in actual fact, as even the supporters of the system recognized, the Chief of Staff commanded the military forces.[12] Having little contact with his department except through the Chief of Staff, the Secretary tended to become a figurehead and the Chief of Staff to become the mayor of the palace. In franker moments, the Secretaries admitted their dependence on the Chiefs.[13] At the same time, the broad responsibilities of the Chiefs forced them to adopt a catholic outlook transcending a purely professional military viewpoint and approaching the natural predisposition of the Secretaries.

While the vertical system made effective civilian control difficult in peace, it also made effective military operation extremely difficult in war. In a major conflict it was impossible to maintain General Staff control over all the expanded military, administrative, supply, and procurement functions. In World War I, the centralized General Staff system simply broke down, as General Bullard had predicted that it would.[14] Drastic reorganization in the first part of 1918 created a special Division of Purchase, Storage, and Traffic to handle procurement and supply. Theoretically a part of the General Staff, this division actually functioned primarily under the direction of the Assistant Secretary of War who also had the title of Director of Munitions. While the vertical system was adhered to in theory, in practice the operation of the Department much more closely approximated the balanced system which the pressure of events demanded.* After the war, the As-

---

* The deviation of practice from theory was explained by Assistant Secretary Crowell as follows:

"Since the reorganization had to keep within the law, the central business

sistant Secretary, Benedict Crowell, vigorously urged Congress to
establish a balanced organization for the Department, arguing his
case in the language of Luce and Mahan. The National Defense
Act of 1920 followed his recommendations in part, continuing
some of the responsibilities of the General Staff for supply matters,
but at the same time giving the Assistant Secretary supervision
over procurement and industrial mobilization. This scheme was a
compromise between the vertical and balanced systems. In the
years of peace which followed, however, the functional pressures
favorable to the balanced plan weakened, and the institutional interests supporting the vertical system resumed dominance. While
the Assistant Secretary continued to play a significant role in
procurement planning, the Chief of Staff and the General Staff
reasserted their authority over all elements of the military establishment.[15] The much greater demands of World War II, however,
again made it impossible for the Chief of Staff and the General
Staff to carry the entire load. Again, Army organizers such as
General McNarney began to emphasize the twofold nature of War
Department responsibilities: "mobilization and preparation of the
forces for war" and "operations in the field." In March 1942, for
the United States the most critical point in the war, the War Department organization had to be thoroughly overhauled. All procurement and supply functions were given to the Army Service

office of the Department, the Division of Purchase, Storage, and Traffic, had to
be given a military status . . .
   "This necessity gave to the General Staff . . . an appearance of power which
it did not actually possess. In the chart the General Staff itself, through its Division of Purchase, Storage, and Traffic, has apparently become the great procuring
agency of the War Department, in addition to its purely military functions. This,
however, was only an arrangement *pro forma* to give authenticity to the acts of
the Division of Purchase, Storage, and Traffic. Actually, a different arrangement
was in effect . . . The Division of Purchase, Storage, and Traffic was . . . plotted
as the agency through which the Assistant Secretary . . . could gain control of
the industry. Thereafter the Assistant Secretary of War was the industrial head
of the War Department. But since this arrangement was one of agreement rather
than of law, the executive decisions of the Assistant Secretary went down to the
Division of Purchase, Storage, and Traffic as from the Secretary of War, through
the technically legal channel of the General Staff. In spite of appearance, therefore, the General Staff remained a purely military body. The Chief of Staff was
the Secretary of War's military adviser: the Assistant Secretary was the Secretary
of War's industrial adviser." Benedict Crowell and Robert F. Wilson, *The Armies
of Industry* (New Haven, 2 vols., 1921), I, 10ff. I have been greatly aided on this
point by an unpublished paper by Paul Y. Hammond on "The Civilian Role in
the Administration of the Army Supply Program in World War I."

Forces under the command of General Brehon Somervell and the supervision of Under Secretary of War Robert Patterson. Again, as in World War I, Somervell's command was theoretically under the control of the Chief of Staff. In actuality, however, the General Staff played a minor role in supply matters, and the Patterson-Somervell team operated with almost complete autonomy. The Operations Division of the General Staff, on the other hand, was made into a true military general staff for the Chief of Staff, free from all responsibilities "except strategic direction and control of operations, determination of over-all military requirements, and determination of basic policies affecting the zone of interior." Despite this second example of what one War Department board termed the "devitalization of the General Staff during wartime," the Army in 1945 moved back toward the reintroduction of the vertical system.[16]

Navy Civil-Military Relations. In contrast to the Army, the Navy's balanced organization provided for effective civilian control in peace and effective military operation in war. It obtained these values, however, only at the cost of constant bickering and friction among the Secretary, the Chief of Naval Operations, and the bureau chiefs. Once the naval traditionalist view had been written into law in 1915, the balanced system lost almost all support among the line officers of the Navy. The organizational theory of Luce and Mahan was forgotten by postwar generations of naval officers. The weight of naval opinion favored a vertical system to be achieved by extending the powers of the CNO over the bureaus. The history of naval organization between 1915 and 1945 is the history of continuous struggle between the chief military officer of the Navy, on the one hand, and the Secretaries and bureau chiefs on the other. Every CNO, except one, believed that he should have directive power over the bureaus.* In 1921 the CNO

---

* The exception was Admiral W. V. Pratt, CNO, 1930–1933, who wanted a coordinate organization. Satisfied with the existing bureau system, Pratt and his followers argued that the distinction between command and administration required the CNO to have direct access to the President. Toward the end of the 1930's, the personal ineffectiveness of the Secretary of the Navy, the increasing international tension, and the President's interest in naval affairs combined to introduce elements of the coordinate pattern in the form of frequent contacts between the Chief Executive and the CNO. See U.S. Navy Dept., *Naval Administration: Selected Documents on Navy Department Organization, 1915–1940,* pp.

and the line officers argued their case before the Senate committee investigating the naval prosecution of the war. In 1921 they told a departmental board on organization that the CNO theoretically had legal authority over the bureaus; all that he required were the administration mechanisms to implement this power. In 1924 the CNO won a partial success when he was given coordinating authority over certain activities of the bureaus. Eight years later this grant of power was vitiated by the President who declared that it did not include the authority to give orders to the bureaus. The CNO's, however, continued to plead their case before Congress, and, during World War II, Admiral King made several efforts to reorganize the Department along vertical lines which were only stopped by the determined opposition of the President and Under Secretary Forrestal.[17]

Throughout the twenties and thirties, the Secretaries consistently fought the efforts of the CNO's to expand their powers over the bureaus. The most colorful defense of direct dealings between Secretary and bureau chiefs was made by Secretary Daniels in 1920. The most logical defense was made by Secretary Edison in 1940. "Now, there are," he said, "two distinct professions, you might say, in the Navy. There is the military profession and there is the technical or supporting profession." Rivalry between these two is natural and even "splendid," providing that there is an umpire in the form of the Secretary "to settle any controversies, and to make final rulings." Under no circumstances, however, should one profession be subordinated to the other. This would violate the limits of professional competence and the division of labor.[18] The views of the Secretaries, supported by the President, generally prevailed during the 1920's and 1930's. At times the seesaw tipped in the direction of the Chiefs, at other times in the direction of the bureaus. But the essential balance was maintained: the Navy came out of World War II with fundamentally the same organization with which it had gone into World War I.* While there was

---

V–13–V–14, VI–28–VI–31; U.S. Naval Institute *Proceedings,* LVIII (1932), 806, 1502–1503, LIII (1927), 275–277; Adm. William D. Leahy, *I Was There* (New York, 1950), p. 3.

* At the beginning of World War II, naval organization was altered by Admiral King's combining the two posts of Chief of Naval Operations and Commander in Chief United States Fleet and by the creation of the Office of Pro-

constant conflict among the three elements of the Department, civilian control and military professionalism were both maximized. When Secretary Meyer turned his office over to Josephus Daniels in 1913, he had pointed down to his desk and offered one word of advice to his successor: "Power lies here, and it should remain here!" [19] The organization of the Navy Department down through World War II was calculated to fulfill Meyer's dictum. The one deficiency in the system, the administrative weakness of the Secretary's office as an instrument of coordination and control, was corrected by departmental reforms in 1940. The line officers performed their military duties; the bureaus ran the shore activities; and the Secretaries stayed on top. The continuing friction between the military and civilian elements produced in each a distinctive viewpoint. The line officers carried on the characteristically military outlook of the naval profession which had originated with the generation of Luce and Mahan. Compared to the broad approach of the Army Chiefs of Staff, the Navy CNO's appeared to be narrow military men continually at odds with the civilian Secretaries. As Secretary Stimson once remarked, the admirals were wrapped up in a "peculiar psychology" in which "Neptune was God, Mahan his prophet, and the United States Navy the only true Church." [20] The payoff of the system, however, was in war. Realizing Mahan's, and Calhoun's, organizational goal — that peacetime structure should meet wartime needs, "The order of sailing is the order of battle," in Nelson's phrase — the United States Navy went through both world wars without drastic alteration of its system of civil-military relations.

THE AMERICAN MILITARY ETHIC, 1920–1941

LOYALTY. The fundamental values of the American military profession between the wars did not change significantly from those developed during the previous period. The unfavorable view of human nature, the lessons to be learned from history, the persistent likelihood of war and conflict, the necessity for order and

---

curement and Material. The former change redistributed authority and functions *within* the military side of the Navy; the latter did the same on the supply side. Neither change, however, altered the basic pattern of civil-military relations *among* the professional leadership, the supply organizations, and the political direction of the Department.

subordination in human affairs, all continued to be emphasized. The single most significant change in tone from the prewar years was the stress on loyalty as the cardinal military virtue. The prewar outlook held up the value of objective obedience; the postwar, that of subjective loyalty. Routine obedience was not enough. It was necessary, as Brigadier General MacArthur put it, to substitute "subjective for objective discipline." For the Navy, loyalty, said Sims, was "always indispensable"; loyalty plus initiative was to be preferred to unthinking obedience. The four values asserted by Navy Regulations — virtue, honor, patriotism, subordination — all rested on, and were embraced in, the basic value of loyalty. Throughout the 1920's and 1930's, no other virtue rivaled loyalty for the central place in the military hierarchy of values. Its critical role was stressed again and again, in almost monotonous fashion.[21]

The significance of this concern with loyalty is twofold. First, it indicated the development from the prewar years of a more sophisticated understanding of the characteristics of an efficient military organization. Previously, unthinking obedience, the mere response to orders coming down from on high, had been the keynote. Now, however, the desirability of initiative was recognized, and initiative was reconciled with obedience through loyalty. Superior commanders should restrict themselves to general directives; subordinates should have the skill and the loyalty to apply these to varying situations. The exercise of initiative must reflect the loyal identification with, and understanding of, the desires of the superior. Underlying this changed attitude was a feeling that as the officer corps came to think alike, to adhere to the same body of doctrine, subjective cohesion would replace objective restraints. The new emphasis reflected mutual confidence in each other's professional ability. Also present was a more realistic appreciation of the Moltkean system of trained initiative in the German Army.

The other significance of the military devotion to loyalty was in the extent to which it reflected the separation between the military values and popular civilian values. Loyalty had never ranked high in a country where the supreme virtue was individualism, for loyalty implied the subordination of the individual to a goal or standard outside of and superior to himself. It also presupposed an emphasis upon the collective aspect of human affairs, since common loyalty is the basis of group existence. The American tendencies to extol the rights of the individual over the duties of the individual and to see the social benefits stemming from the pursuit of individual self-interest were incompatible with a high value on loyalty. Loyalty never received much attention in American moral philosophy. The one significant discussion of it was in Josiah Royce's *The Philosophy of Loyalty,* and Royce himself recognized that his views were in the minority. He could attack the pragmatism of James and Dewey, but he could never compete with it in appealing to the American mind. And probably seldom in their history did the American people feel less inclined towards the syndrome of values associated with loyalty than during the halcyon days of the twenties and the experimental environment of the thirties. While Royce was forgotten by the people, however, he was remembered by the military. *The Philosophy of Loyalty* was constantly quoted and referred to in military writings on this subject.

POLICY. The military interpretation of the nature of international politics and their prescription for foreign policy remained remarkably static. Every nation, it was held, was motivated not by "any broad abstract principle but by self interest." When their interests conflicted, the clash might be settled in the first instance by diplomacy, but if that failed, arms were the only recourse. War was the "continuation of policy" and to be expected in the normal course of events. Arbitration treaties, the League of Nations, international law, the Kellogg-Briand Pact, disarmament conferences — none of these could guarantee peace. The only possible way of delaying war was through the maintenance of an adequate balance of power. International politics was a continuous struggle; no sharp line divided war and peace. Foreign policy could extend only as far as the willingness and the ability of the state to support it by force. Military strength, rather than unorganized military resources, was desirable insurance. Actions should be guided by enemy capabilities rather than estimates of their intentions. The military man viewed himself as fundamentally conservative on questions of war and peace; he defended himself against claims that the military were fomenters of strife. Glorification of war by the military was, indeed, conspicuously absent during these years. In the crises of the 1930's the military urged the statesmen to tread cautiously, warning them of American military weakness.[22]

This prevailing military outlook on foreign affairs during the twenties and thirties differed hardly at all from the military perspective developed by the American officer corps in the 1870's and 1880's. This similarity again suggests that the decisive influence shaping the military outlook was not the actual state of world politics, but rather the level of professionalism achieved by the military. Internal causes springing from the essential characteristics of the profession — the inner logic of professional justification — determined what the military man saw when he viewed the world. The officer looking at international politics in 1930 saw fundamentally the same thing that his predecessor had in 1880 — not because the world was the same, but because he was the same. The constant nature of the American military perspective reflected the constant character of American military professionalism. If, like Ludendorff, the American officer had retreated from his professionalism, he would have followed the German military leader in developing a widely different appreciation of international relations. In the 1880's the military outlook had little relation to the realities of the American position in international relations. Over the course of the years, however, the military perspective gained relevance and adequacy. The progressive involvement of the United States in international politics by the 1930's caused the world of American foreign relations to approximate the image which the military had always painted of it.

While the gap between the military perspective and international reality narrowed, that between the military outlook and prevailing civilian opinion broadened. Here, again, the dynamic element was the nonmilitary one. In the 1880's the military and civilian viewpoints had been widely separated. At the turn of the century, Neo-Hamiltonianism had built a bridge of sorts between the two. With the collapse of the Neo-Hamiltonian compromise after World War I, the chasm between military and civilian thinking widened again. The Neo-Hamiltonian fascination with power politics was replaced by either liberal isolationism or liberal internationalism. Both were far removed from military thinking on international relations. American civilian interest in international affairs had its origins in the peace movement before World War I and after the War focused upon international organization, international law, and the intricacies of the League. It reflected the triumph of form over substance. It assumed a harmony of interests among nations. The analytical model underlying its approach was "a world commonwealth characterized by permanent peace." [23] There could hardly be a sharper contrast with the military model of independent states engaged in continuous struggle. Toward the end of the thirties, civilian thinking began to move in the direction of greater realism. A new appreciation of national interests and the role of force became manifest in the work of Earle, Spykman, Wolfers, and Schuman. They represented the first beginnings of the civilian adoption of the military approach to international affairs which was to characterize thinking after World War II. This, however, was a minor current in the civilian outlook between the two wars. The prevailing philosophy was thoroughly unmilitary, and the military reacted sharply against it, complaining constantly of the unwarranted idealism, pacifism, and altruism of American thinking on foreign policy.[24]

GOVERNMENT. The perspective of the officer corps on its relations with the government continued and strengthened the professional outlook of the latter years of the nineteenth century. The classic doctrines of Clausewitz became standard gospel in the Navy as well in the Army. The German theorist was hailed by naval officers as "the master writer on war." It was said that he appeared so frequently in student themes at the Naval War College that the stenographers could be relied upon to supply the quotation marks.* American officers of both services typically referred to the armed forces as "instruments" of the government and constantly reiterated the dictum that national policy dictated military policy. Wars might be limited or unlimited depending upon the goals of policy. It was, however, the duty of the statesman to formulate a "clear, concise, and unambiguous declaration of national policy" to guide the military. The latter could not operate in a policy vacuum. To furnish

* The Infantry School recommended reading list in the early twenties suggested four "classical works," all of the German school: *On War;* von Caemmerer's *The Development of Strategical Science During the Nineteenth Century;* and von der Goltz's *Conduct of War* and *Nation in Arms.*

this policy guidance, the officers continued to demand the creation of a national defense council modeled on the British Imperial Defense Committee and comparable institutions in major foreign countries.[25] As previously, this proposal was frequently advanced, not only as a means of securing a clear statement of policy in the executive branch but also as a way of bridging the continually irritating gap between executive and legislature.

In classic military fashion, the corollary to the subordination of the military to the political was held to be the independence of each within its own sphere. The line between politics and military affairs, it was emphasized again and again, was sharp and clear and must be maintained. "Politics and strategy," said a Command and General Staff School publication in 1936, "are radically and fundamentally things apart. Strategy begins where politics ends. All that soldiers ask is that once the policy is settled, strategy and command shall be regarded as being in a sphere apart from politics . . . The line of demarcation must be drawn between politics and strategy, supply, and operations. Having found this line, all sides must abstain from trespassing." [26] The maintenance of this separation between statesmanship and strategy was menaced, in the military viewpoint, by the tendency of politicians to invade the independent realm of the military. Particularly in a popular government, officers were warned, civilian political leaders might be tempted to interfere with the conduct of campaigns with an eye on the next election. The desire to save money and to win quick victories were constant temptations. The conflict between the statesman and the soldier will be a continuing one, and in the end the latter must simply accept this as one of the difficulties of life. On the whole, the military view of civilian control during this period embodied a highly sophisticated analysis generally absent from civilian writing on this subject.

While the role of the military within the government was clear so far as strictly military operations were concerned, the broadening scope of war raised other questions of delimitation which were not so easily answered. As war became total, it involved economic, political, and psychological factors far beyond the normal scope of military cognizance. Traditionally, the military man had defined war as his peculiar specialty. But the conduct of war now obviously involved many other specialties. Did the military man attempt to encompass all of modern war or did he limit his attention to the military aspect of war? Theoretically, the latter was the right answer, and most military men recognized this. The military man necessarily, of course, had to be concerned with the relation of the military component of war to the other components, but he could not accept responsibility for the other components. In pursuit of this theory, the officer might study procurement and economic mobilization at the Army Industrial College, but this was something different from giving him the authority to direct economic mobilization. American military writing, reflecting this attitude, continued to focus almost entirely on technical military problems.[27] Nonetheless, a tendency in the broader direction did exist in the 1920's and 1930's. This was due primarily to the lack of interest in the nonmilitary aspects of war by the civilian branches of the government, and the absence of civilian institutions equipped to perform these functions. As a result, the War Department assumed the job of mobilization planning. The civilians imposed a civilian war function on a military agency. In this sense, the national mobilization planning of the War Department in the thirties was a forerunner of the vast civilian abdication of function which was to take place during and after World War II.

SOCIETY. The content and tenor of military communications after the early 1920's reflected the isolation forced upon the military by the hostility of a liberal society. There was a renewed emphasis upon military values, and a renewed awareness of the gulf between military values and those values prevalent in American society. The military spirit and its core element of discipline have been neglected, complained the Chief of Staff of the Army in 1927. Members of the Army, he declared, must have "pride in being an officer or soldier." Discipline as well as morale was necessary for the existence of a military force. The military purposes of the armed services must always be kept uppermost. "A technical and mercantile philosophy," posited another officer, "cannot be supreme in an army that has any fighting value." The military and civilian ethics were fundamentally incompatible, proclaimed one writer in 1936, in words which would never have been uttered fifteen years previously:

If a man cannot find satisfaction in living a purely military life, he should get out of the army. The super-imposition of any semi-civilian system will reduce the military consciousness and should not be tolerated. The soldier and the civilian belong to separate classes of society. The code of the soldier can never be the same as that of the civilian; why try to mingle them?

Officers were still conscious of the problem of applying military command to citizen-soldiers, but instead of trying to develop a single theory applicable to both citizen-soldier and regular, they now recognized that the former required a different sort of treatment from the latter. The American civilian was a "sovereign, jealous of his royal prerogative," and the Declaration of Independence was his "personal and daily credo." Consequently, while the traditional type of military discipline was applicable in the regular force, a different type, capitalizing upon enthusiasm and patriotism, was necessary for the large armies called to the colors in emergencies.[28]

The prewar feeling of the moral superiority of the military life reappeared in modified form. While previously the values of the military had been contrasted with the values of a commercial civilization, now the values of the military were contrasted with the lack of any values in the America of the late twenties and thirties. The United States was viewed as a country abandoning its moral anchor and venturing out into a chaotic sea of pragmatism and relativism. The age was an "age of youth, defiance, self-expression, skepticism — an era of new and greater freedom." America was being swept by "insidious doctrines," loose living, "sensuous publicity," crime and rackets, all resulting from carrying to an extreme the ideas of equality and democracy. Pacifism was only a natural by-product of "political uplift, loose thinking, and free speech." The gloomy military perspective on the modern scene was well expressed by the officer who moaned in 1939 that modern man was the product of a "brutal age" and a "materialistic culture" which had its roots in "scientific pragmatism which sees man only as a fairly high-type animal and little else." There was too much hedonism, too little idealism and religion. The horrors of modern war were the result of science, which produced its "lethal tools," and of philosophy, which produced the ideologies that set man against man.[29]

The changing military interpretation of their relation to society was well expressed in their altered attitude toward education. In the early 1920's they had warned that a small group of Bolsheviks and other radicals were infiltrating American schools and colleges. Now they saw the danger as much deeper and more pervasive. American education was dominated by the philosophy of "scholastic liberalism" which emphasized only scientific analysis and research and which rejected the old faiths and ideals. The student was engulfed by naturalism and realism. Deprived of moral values, the college freshman "plunges desperately into a godless philosophy, a behavioristic psychology, a history of sensuous Gladstones and drunken Washingtons, and a literature flavored with risqué Helens and rollicking Galahads." The "inadequate" and "worthless" philosophy of John Dewey and his followers, it was warned, was overwhelming the public schools and producing "a different American." The schoolmasters were generally without brains or distinction and were themselves in need of guidance. The difference between civilian colleges and the military academies was the difference between "institutions of opportunity" and "institutions of obligation." The conservatism of Annapolis was favorably contrasted with the "radicalism and fads" at civilian schools. Military students had no use for isms, it was approvingly stated, and only a very few ever read Nietzsche, Mencken, Russell, or Spengler.[30]

The final summing up of the alienation of the military man from both the business liberalism of the 1920's and the reform liberalism of the 1930's was brilliantly and bitterly expressed by the editor of the *Infantry Journal* in a posthumous essay on "The American Professional Soldier," published just as America moved toward involvement in World War II.[31] In one sense this article was simply an eloquent restatement of the professional military view that human nature does not change; that devices do not prevent wars and soldiers do not make wars; that strength is the only source of security. But it went beyond this to reveal sharply the antagonism between the modern soldier and the modern intellectual. The intellectual associated the military with war and hated them because war was a sorry reflection on the strength of the human intellect. The great virtues of the soldier — Honesty, Duty, Faith, — disqualified "him utterly from ever being a modern intellectual." The world of scholars, writers, and liberals had nothing but scorn for the professional military man:

So these workers in words, ideas, and thoughts, the articulate part of the American folk, were mainly alike in their aversion — to use a mild term — to the Army. Strange, wasn't it, how this heterogeneous list of writers, speakers, idealists, scientists, religionists, philosophers, pseudo-philosophers — practically all the vocal parts of our population — had one powerful emotion in common? They disliked the professional soldier.

Major Burns poured out the bitterness of his profession against the "so-called scientific civilization" which had no use for it, against the sociologists which ignored it, against the intelligentsia which ridiculed it, and against the "fine minds" of the *Nation* and *New Republic* which attacked it. Three-quarters of a century of accumulated resentment and frustration spewed forth in this article. It was a fitting epitaph for the old system of civil-military relations which World War II was to end forever.

PART III

THE CRISIS OF AMERICAN CIVIL-MILITARY
RELATIONS, 1940–1955

12

World War II: The Alchemy of Power

CIVIL-MILITARY RELATIONS IN TOTAL WAR

World War II began a new era in American civil-military relations. The space of a few years saw a remarkable revolution in the power and the attitudes of the military. The new pattern was carried to an extreme during the war. But its fundamental elements, distinguishing it from the pattern which had prevailed since the 1870's, persisted after 1945. The problem then became the construction of a new balance of civilian control and military professionalism to replace the old system irreparably shattered by American participation in the fight against the Axis.

The three key aspects of American civil-military relations in World War II may be stated baldly with only minor oversimplification.

First. So far as the major decisions in policy and strategy were concerned, the military ran the war.

Second. In this area of policy and strategy, the military ran the war just the way the American people and American statesmen wanted it run.

Third. On the domestic front, control over economic mobilization was shared between military and civilian agencies.

The power of the professional military leaders reached unprecedented heights in World War II. But they scaled these summits only by sacrificing their military outlook and accepting the national values. The military leaders blended with the liberal environment; they lost their alien and aloof character and emerged as the supreme embodiment of the national purpose. The subtle alchemy of power worked an amazing transformation in their perspectives and

315

policies. This, however, was true only with respect to external policy and grand strategy, where the military easily moved in to fill a governmental vacuum. On the domestic front, on the other hand, the original decision was for civilian control of economic mobilization, and powerful civilian interest groups rivaled the military. Although the military carved out a broad sphere of influence, they were never able to establish the same supremacy that they did on the international side. Accordingly, they did not develop the catholic outlook on economic mobilization which they did on foreign policy. They remained more narrowly the spokesmen for military interests and the military viewpoint. The result was that an astounding harmony of purpose and policy prevailed on the international front, as the military adopted civilian goals. The domestic front, on the other hand, was the scene of continuous conflict, acrimony, and bureaucratic infighting as civilian and military agencies clashed in the forwarding of their opposing interests. In grand strategy the military exercised their new power in a broadly responsible manner. On the domestic scene, however, they demanded and fought for military control of the economy, since they were reasonably secure in the knowledge that they would never get it. The difference between Hull and Nelson explained much of the difference between Marshall and Somervell.

American civil-military relations in World War II paralleled in some respects those of Germany in World War I. Like the German officer corps before 1913, the American officer corps before 1939 was highly professionalized, although it was also much smaller and more removed from the center of national life. Correspondingly, however, the institutional mechanisms of civilian control were much weaker. When war came, the American military did not reach out after power — Marshall was no Ludendorff. Instead, power was unavoidably thrust upon them. They were given no choice but to accept it, and, with it, the implicit conditions upon which it was granted. They became the agents of American liberalism, just as the German General Staff became the agent of German nationalism. Domestically, however, their control never approximated that of Hindenberg, Ludendorff, and Gröner. The breakdown of civilian control and the weakening of military professionalism in Germany contributed to her losing the war. The parallel developments in the United States contributed to her losing the peace. In both countries the immediate postwar period was marked by only partially successful attempts to reëstablish a viable balance of civil-military relations.

MILITARY AUTHORITY AND INFLUENCE IN GRAND STRATEGY

THE BASIS OF MILITARY POWER. The wartime power of the military leaders was rooted in the American liberal attitude toward war and the military. War was sharply differentiated from peace. When the nation went to war, it went wholeheartedly, turning the direction of the conflict over to those who made that their business. The national aim of total victory superseded all else. The military became the executors of the national will, the technicians called in to implement the basic policy decision. In the American view, their function was not to provide for the military security of the country in war and peace, but simply to achieve victory in war. The American people and the American statesmen were unanimous in adhering to the Ludendorff philosophy. "I have washed my hands of it," Hull told Stimson a few days before Pearl Harbor, "and it is now in the hands of you and Knox — the Army and the Navy." His words were symbolic of the civilian abdication. Stimson himself declared that his wartime duty was "to support, protect, and defend his generals." A not unrepresentative Representative expressed congressional acquiescence when he said:

I am taking the word of the General Staff of the War Department, the people who are running this show. If they tell me this is what they need for the successful prosecution of this war and for ultimate victory, I am for it. Whether it staggers me according to its proportions or not, I am still for it.[1]

The center of wartime military leadership was the corporate organization of the senior military chiefs. Prior to February 1942 this was the Joint Board composed of four high-ranking officers from each of the services. The Board had been established in 1903 but during most of its history its duties had been minor. From 1939 on, however, it played an increasingly significant role in the preparation of the joint Army-Navy Rainbow war plans. Its influence and functions quickly expanded. At the first British-American meeting after Pearl Harbor, the Arcadia conference of December 1941–January 1942, it was obvious that military exigencies required the creation of a unified theater command for American, British, Dutch, and Australian forces in southeast Asia. The theater commander had to report to someone. Accordingly, the conference established in Washington the Combined Chiefs of Staff, consisting of the American chiefs and representatives of the British Chiefs of Staff Committee. In order to coordinate the American viewpoint and present some sort of unified front to the frequently single-voiced British representatives, the American chiefs organized themselves as the Joint Chiefs of Staff. This body superseded the old Joint Board. It consisted of the Army Chief of Staff, the Commanding General of the Army Air Forces, the Chief of Naval Operations, and, after June 1942, Admiral Leahy as Chief of Staff to the Commander in Chief. Its members had the dual function of participating as the American component in the Combined Chiefs of Staff and serving as the collective organ of command and planning for the overseas operations of the American armed forces.

Both the expansion of the Joint Board in 1939 and the establishment of the JCS in 1942 reflected purely military necessities: the need for joint and combined planning and command. Theoretically, the Board and the Joint Chiefs should have been the highest organs of professional military advice to the government and professional direction of the armed services. Although created in response to functional military imperatives, however, both organs were drawn by organizational and political pulls into operating as political as well as military bodies. The Joint Chiefs of Staff became, next to the President, the single most important force in the overall conduct of the war, the level and the scope of their activities far transcending those of a purely professional body. As a result, the Joint Chiefs ended the war with no experience in functioning simply as a military organization. Four years of war had given them a political tradition and role.

THE JOINT CHIEFS AND THE PRESIDENT. The close identification of the JCS with the President rested upon both formal legal position and informal personal relationships. Prior to 1939, the military chiefs collectively had no legal right of direct access to the President. The Joint Board was merely an interdepartmental committee established by agreement between the two service secretaries. All its actions had to be approved by the secretaries. On July 5, 1939, however, the President ordered that the Joint Board and the Joint Army-Navy Munitions Board should thereafter function directly under him as Commander in Chief of the Army and Navy. This action removed the collective military organ from departmental control. When the Joint Chiefs superseded the Joint Board, they too, operated immediately under the President as his military advisers. Although the JCS never, until 1947, had any firmer legal basis than an exchange of letters between General Marshall and Admiral King, there was never any doubt as to its position with respect to the President. In addition, both King and Marshall were, in their individual capacities as service chiefs, authorized to deal directly with the President on matters pertaining to the strategy, tactics, and operations of their respective services.[2]

The formal position of the Joint Chiefs was reinforced by their personal relations with the President. Roosevelt viewed himself as a master strategist and relished the title of Commander in Chief. He liked to consort with the military leaders, and he liked to think that he could consort with them on equal terms. Leahy and Roosevelt were old associates from World War I years when the latter was Assistant Secretary of the Navy and from the late thirties when the former was Chief of Naval Operations. After his appointment as Chief of Staff to the Commander in Chief in July 1942, Leahy was probably more closely and continuously connected with the President in the conduct of the war than any other individual except Harry Hopkins. At the minimum, he had a daily conference with the President, and he was, of course, the principal liaison between the President and the other Joint Chiefs. General Marshall was first called to Roosevelt's attention by Hopkins, who recommended his appointment as Chief of Staff in 1939. For three years thereafter, Hopkins was Marshall's principal contact with the White House. After Pearl Harbor, Marshall acquired Roosevelt's complete confidence, and by 1943 there was no need for any intermediary between them.[3]

THE EXCLUSION OF CIVILIAN ADVICE. The mere fact of direct access to the President did not account for the authority of the Joint Chiefs in the conduct of the war. Their power was rather a product of their direct access combined with the exclusion of civilian advice. During war the Chief Executive necessarily deals directly with his military advisers. As military issues become more important, the level of decision-making rises, and the head of the government devotes more time to military matters. If civilian control is to be maintained, however, a balance must exist between the military viewpoint and the relevant political viewpoints at whatever level decisions are made. An equilibrium at the Presidential level could have been achieved through a political-military council or staff including the Secretaries of State, War, and the Navy, the directors of economic mobilization, and the military chiefs. The British Prime Minister in both wars had such an instrument in the War Cabinet and its secretariat. The American attitude toward war and the military, however, coupled with Roosevelt's opposition to any device which might take policy out of his own hands, prevented the creation of such an agency. Each of the committees which conceivably might have evolved into a war council withered on the vine after Pearl Harbor.* The civilians ceased to consider grand strategy. Ironic as it was, Roosevelt, who normally skillfully played subordinates off against each other in order to maximize his own authority, allowed one set of advisers to preempt the field with respect to his most important decisions. This strange departure from his usual pattern reflected self-confidence, confidence in his Chiefs, and the presence in the President's mind of the prevailing American ideas as to the nature of war and the manner in which it should be conducted. As a result, instead of presenting their advice within the framework

* Three such agencies existed in the immediate prewar years: the Standing Liaison Committee composed of the Under Secretary of State, Army Chief of Staff, and Chief of Naval Operations; the "Committee of Three" composed of the Secretaries of State, War, and the Navy; and the War Council composed of the same three secretaries plus the Chief of Staff and Chief of Naval Operations. The Liaison Committee and the War Council ceased to operate during the war, and the "Committee of Three," its members excluded from grand strategy decisions, played only a minor role. It was not until December 1944 that the State-War-Navy Coordinating Committee, composed of assistant secretaries, became the first successful political-military body. Concerned initially with surrender terms and occupation policy, SWNCC was the direct ancestor of the National Security Council.

of a civil-military war council, the Joint Chiefs themselves substituted for such a council.

Throughout Roosevelt's third administration, the Secretaries of War and of the Navy were excluded from matters of grand strategy. Roosevelt's selection of Stimson and Knox in 1940 was undoubtedly in part motivated by the feeling that he would direct the services himself and that two elderly Republicans would tend to be administratively passive and politically neutralized. The secretaries did not meet with the President and the Joint Chiefs. They did not, with one or two exceptions, attend the wartime allied conferences. They were not on the routine distribution list for JCS papers. They tended to be excluded from contacts between the military and civilian agencies, since the latter preferred to deal with the Joint Chiefs as the single unified spokesman for the military viewpoint. While at times the secretaries were consulted on specific points, they still had "no formal responsibilitity in matters of military strategy." [4] Even procurement and logistics were primarily in the hands of Under Secretaries Patterson and Forrestal. The service secretaries performed two functions. Within their departments, they directed the administrative, housekeeping, and more narrowly civilian matters. Externally, they defended the interests of their services before President, Congress, and the public.

The State Department played a minor role in the direction of the war for political, personal, and organizational reasons. Ideologically, the State Department was peculiarly ill-equipped to deal with the problems of either the war or the immediate postwar periods. During the 1930's, the Department had been largely occupied with Latin American affairs — the good neighbor policy — on the one hand, and economic matters — the reciprocal trade agreements program — on the other. During the war, the State Department continued to believe that its function was diplomacy and that diplomacy was distinct from force. As a result, it devoted itself to relations with neutrals and minor allies and to the development of plans for the United Nations organization. The bitter antagonism between Secretary Hull and Under Secretary Welles also weakened the Department. The President tended to play off one against the other until Hull insisted upon the resignation of Welles in 1943. Throughout, however, Roosevelt did not wish Hull to participate in the major decisions of the war.* Unlike his successors, Stettinius and Byrnes, Hull did not attend the principal wartime conferences. State Department organization during the war also suffered from the confusion of purpose and role. Stettinius attempted to reorganize the Department after his appointment as Under Secretary in 1943 but he was not notably successful. Symbolic of the peripheral role of the Department was the fact that General Clay, prior to his departure to become military governor in Germany in 1945, consulted with the President, Stimson, McCloy, Byrnes, Marshall, and Somervell, but never visited the State Department. As he subsequently remarked, it never occurred to him that this might be a wise thing to do.[5]

The preëminence of the Joint Chiefs in advising the President was reflected in the infrequency with which Roosevelt rejected their recommendations. Apparently, this occurred only twice in the course of the conflict: the decision in the summer of 1942 to invade North Africa and the abandonment of an Indian Ocean offensive at the Cairo conference in December 1943.[6] In both cases, the President initially accepted the view of his Chiefs and then reversed his decision, not as a result of conflicting advice from civilian American sources, but rather due to pressure from the British. On one or two other occasions, Roosevelt may have gone ahead without consulting with the Chiefs, but with these exceptions, harmony reigned between the President and his military advisers.

THE SCOPE OF MILITARY AUTHORITY. As the substitute for a war council, the Joint Chiefs extended their activities and interests far beyond the normal military confines and into the areas of di-

---

* Hull's feelings at this exclusion are well reflected in his *Memoirs* (New York, 2 vols., 1948), II, 1109–1110:

"After Pearl Harbor I did not sit in on meetings concerned with military matters. This was because the President did not invite me to such meetings. I raised the question with him several times . . .

"The President did not take me with him to the Casablanca, Cairo, or Teheran conferences, which were predominantly military meetings, nor did I take part in his military discussions with Prime Minister Churchill in Washington, some of which had widespread diplomatic repercussions . . .

"The question of where the armies would land and what routes they would take across the Continent in the grand military movement to conquer Hitler was a subject never discussed with me by the President or any of his top military officials, although I was early informed of the decision reached.

"I was not told about the atomic bomb."

plomacy, politics, and economics. From the initial great decision to defeat Germany first to the last complex series of decisions on the end of the war with Japan, the major strategic and policy issues of the war were resolved by the President, the Chiefs, and Harry Hopkins. The absence of a formal charter for the JCS facilitated the expansion of its functions since it was impossible for any rival agency to argue that it was exceeding its authority. Tied in close to the President, the interests and power of the Chiefs tended to expand and become coextensive with his. The formulation of the American position preparatory to the great interallied war conferences was normally done by the military and the President. The Chiefs themselves attended virtually all these conferences while the civilian secretaries were left at home. The military carried out diplomatic negotiations for the government, as well as being in constant communication with the British service chiefs. In the field, theater commanders such as MacArthur and Eisenhower functioned in political and diplomatic roles. Civil affairs and military government, at least with respect to overseas operations, were largely areas of military responsibility.

In the early years of the war, the formulation of American policy was handicapped by the absence of any coordinating agency at the top. The military floundered about without any clear notion as to the policy of the government. As a result, they were at a considerable disadvantage in dealing with the British. Eventually, however, when the military realized that they had to furnish themselves with political guidance, the JCS took over the "administrative coordination of national policy decisions." This created, however, a system far different from that of the British. The range of activities covered by the JCS was truly impressive. Comparing the British and American systems, one American participant pointed out that the British military joint planners had much less to do with "matters of an economic, sociological or administrative nature" than their American opposite numbers. These nonmilitary problems were handled by other British agencies which furnished guidance to the British military. In some cases the British officers "didn't even know how some of the subjects handled by our [military] planners were dealt with in the U.K." [7]

Not only did the Joint Chiefs extend themselves beyond the

scope of military competence, but, as the war progressed, the involvement of military organs in political decision-making penetrated to lower levels of the military hierarchy. By 1945 the War Department staff was consciously enmeshed in foreign policy. This involvement had existed almost since the beginning of the war, but, prior to 1944, it had been obscured by the high military content of these political decisions. At the end of the war, the level of military participation remained essentially the same, but the significance of military issues lessened; consequently, with the camouflage being stripped away, the military staffs dealt more and more openly with political questions. Although the military continued to think that it would be "helpful" to get the government's political position before military matters were discussed, they also had to recognize that this was not likely and that, consequently, the military agencies would have to make their own political decisions. As one officer put it, "The time has come when, whether we like it or not, the War Department must face the fact that it has a real interest in political matters of varying categories." Originally, the War Department did *not* like this situation, but by the end of the war, the pressure of events had "overcome all scruples on the part of OPD [Operations Division of the General Staff] about getting into matters that traditionally were none of the Army's business." Considerably more than half the papers OPD prepared for the Potsdam conference were devoted to matters other than military operations.[8]

THE MILITARY AND CONGRESS. The two chief means of congressional control of the military are the power of the purse and the power of investigation. The scarcity of resources during World War II rendered the power of the purse inoperative. Dollar controls were supplanted by administrative priorities and direct allocations. Inevitably, this transferred power from the legislative to the executive branch, and Congress more or less willingly acquiesced in the transfer. The larger the military appropriations, the less information Congress received with respect to them and the less time it spent debating them. As Colonel G. A. Lincoln and his associates have pointed out, the War Department estimates in 1945 occupied 16 pages in a total budget document of 872 pages. In 1950, when the estimates were 5 per cent of those of 1945, the War Department had 90 out of 1,400 pages. While the low Army budgets of the

1930's were debated for four or five days in the House of Representatives, the high budgets of the early forties were debated for one or two days. The reason for this was not that Congress considered the wartime budgets less important than the peacetime ones: it was rather that it considered them less the concern of Congress. It simply felt that the military must have all that they needed, and that it was beyond the capacity of Congress to inquire into military estimates in any fundamental way. The result was that the services got what they wanted and ended the war with some fifty billion dollars in unused appropriations. To achieve victory, Congress was willing to "trust in God and General Marshall." As one congressman remarked, "The War Department, or . . . General Marshall . . . virtually dictated the budgets." [9]

The other possible instrument of congressional control, the investigative power, was voluntarily restrained by Congress. The ghost of the Committee on the Conduct of the War still haunted Capitol Hill. The fear of involvement in technical military matters expanded into a general willingness to stay clear of the realm of grand strategy. Congress' principal watchdog of the war effort — the Truman Committee — supported the differing systems of wartime civil-military relations in strategy and policy on the one hand and production and economic mobilization on the other. The "committee never have investigated," it declared, "and they still believe that they should not investigate, military and naval strategy or tactics." The Committee also made clear that it would defend the military against efforts by executive officials to intrude into that realm. At the same time that it supported military control of the direction of the war, however, the Committee also supported civilian control of the homefront and economic mobilization. Its activities, the Committee said, were restricted to "the nonmilitary aspects of the defense program, that is to say, with seeing to it that the defense articles which the Army and Navy have determined that they need are produced in a minimum of time at a minimum of cost and with as little disruption of the civilian economy as possible." [10] In this area, the Committee was not only on occasion highly critical of the military, but it also supported the War Production Board and the Office of War Mobilization in their struggles with the generals.

THE MILITARY ADJUSTMENT TO WARTIME POWER

HARMONY AND ITS ROOTS. A remarkable harmony prevailed in
the high councils of the American government as to the basic
strategy of the war. Men with lesser responsibilities — theater commanders, bureau chiefs, and the like — fought for their particular
needs as was their interest and their duty. But at the top, with minor
exceptions, soldiers and statesmen, diplomats and secretaries, personal advisers and planning staffs, all viewed the war from extraordinarily similar viewpoints. Indicative of the harmony is the fact
that with the possible exception of the dismissal of Sumner Welles
in 1943 (which was the result of a personal antagonism antedating
the war), there were no conflicts, ill-feelings, or clashes of policy
or personality serious enough to cause anyone to be fired or to quit
in disgust. The same men who began the war finished the war. The
area of consensus even included those civilian leaders excluded
from the major policy decisions. Although Stimson and Hull may
not have had much to do with the making of policy, they nonetheless had little reason to argue with the policies that were made. It
was, indeed, only this fact which, as Stimson recognized, made
their positions tolerable.[11] The record of strategic policy making,
enlivened only by interallied differences, was bland and dull in
comparison with the opposite extreme which prevailed on the economic mobilization front with its constant organizational shifts,
fiery personality clashes, dramatic resignations and firings.

What were the sources of the harmony among soldiers and
statesmen? The civilian and military approaches to national policy
had been poles apart in the 1930's. The unified front achieved during the war meant that either the political leaders abandoned their
positions and accepted the military outlook or that the military
leaders dropped their professional conservatism and adhered to
the prevailing American civilian viewpoint. One widely accepted
school of thought argues for the former. Such critics condemn
the American military chiefs for thinking purely in military terms
and blame the chiefs for American acceptance of the doctrine that
military victory had to be pursued to the exclusion of all other
goals. The critics contrast the "military" attitudes of American de-

cision makers with the "political" motivations and character of British wartime policy.[12]

It is impossible to accept the conclusions of this school of thought. The critics are, of course, correct in saying that America's overriding goal in the war was military victory. They go astray, however, when they say that this goal had its roots in military thinking. They err in assuming that, because military men made the decisions, they must have made them from a strictly military viewpoint, and they are wrong in their assumptions as to the content of the military viewpoint. The professional military mind is concerned with military security not military victory. The very points most emphasized by the critics — unconditional surrender and the rejection of the Balkans in favor of western Europe as a scene of operations — were political decisions supported by almost all the political leaders of the government and virtually required by the prevailing complexion of American public opinion. The difference between British and American policy was not the difference between political thinking and military thinking; it was simply the difference in national political objectives as defined by the people and statesmen of the two countries at the time. If the American policies turned out not to be the wisest ones, it was not because they were products of the military mind; it was rather because they reflected poor political thinking: a failure to appreciate what its long range political goals properly were by a nation immature in the ways of international politics. The argument that our policy was too "military" implies that if the State Department had had more of a say, the policy would have been more realistic and farsighted. Actually, the reverse is true. The State Department was a center of just the type of thinking which the critics deplore. In contrast to American civilian thought, the thinking of the military before the war was, in general, coldly professional and free of illusion. They were, indeed, the only significant group to have such an approach to foreign policy. If they had been able to continue to think in military terms after assuming direction of the war, the policy decisions which their critics mistakenly label the result of the "military mind" might well have been avoided. If their views had not been altered, the military leaders might have warned the country of the permanence of the struggle for power, the improbability of postwar harmony, the weaknesses of international organization, the desirability of preserving a balance of power in Europe and Asia, and the truth of history that today's allies are frequently tomorrow's enemies. But, instead, as they achieved power, the military commanders had to abandon their professional conservatism and adopt the prevailing civilian viewpoint. The trouble with American policy making was not too much military thinking but too little. And this was caused directly by American insistence that their professional military servants assume power and responsibility beyond their competence. The fault was not in the military but in America itself. If the military leaders had not adjusted their thinking to civilian lines, they would have been viewed during the war with the same suspicion and castigated for devious intrigue in the same manner in which Churchill was. Five years after the war, of course, they would, like Churchill, have been hailed as prophetic statesmen. But the freedom to choose between current and future glory was not open to them in 1942.

The real difference between the American and British systems of conducting the war was that the greatly expanded scope of the American military chiefs forced them to adopt a broadly political viewpoint, while the restricted range of activity of the British military permitted them to adhere to a professional military outlook. Sherwood remarks that it was "the American opinion that Churchill dominated his own Chiefs to a much greater extent" than did Roosevelt, and Admiral Leahy in a revealing comment observes:

As we worked in closest liaison with the Chiefs of the British armed forces, there was more than one occasion when we felt that our British colleagues were loyally supporting the views of their defense minister [Churchill] only because it was their duty and because they were carrying out orders. On our side, we never labored under any such handicap. There were differences of opinion, of course, but due to the mutual confidence and daily contact between the President and his military chiefs, these differences never became serious.[13]

Viewing the war from a military point of view, the British chiefs differed from their government which looked at it from a political point of view. As good military men, however, they supported the government decisions with which they disagreed. The American Chiefs, on the other hand, supported their government's policies because, as political directors of the war, they played a major role in formulating them. Accustomed to power, on the rare occasions when they were overruled, they did not take their defeat with very good grace.[14] While they did not envy the British military chiefs their circumscribed role, the American military leaders did have to recognize the superior coordination and unity produced by the British system of civilian control. At least the British military always knew what the policies of their government were, even if they did not agree with them. On the American side, however, confusion existed as to who was making policy, and at times the American military yearned for the orderly division of responsibilities of the British system. The disunity in American organization was, however, simply the corollary of the harmony in American thought. Too much harmony is just as much a symptom of bad organization as too much conflict. On the face of it, something is wrong with a system in which, during the course of a four-year major war, the political Chief Executive only twice overrules his professional military advisers. This can only mean that one of them was neglecting his proper function and duplicating the work of the other.

NATIONAL POLICY: BALANCE OF POWER TO TOTAL VICTORY. The views of the military leaders who began to achieve prominence at the end of the 1930's reflected the conservative professional military ethic prevailing in the American officer corps during the interwar decades. Long before 1939, American officers, adhering to the military belief as to the inevitability of war, were convinced that the United States would become involved in another world conflict.[15] Consequently, throughout the lean years of the 1930's, the services strongly advanced a variety of proposals to build up the forces to a minimum consistent with the needs of national security. After the Administration began to take deeper interest in armament in the fall of 1938, the military continued to advocate a balanced yet sizable increase in military strength. At the same time, in these years prior to the wartime military-civilian harmony, a significant cleavage existed in the Administration in 1940 and 1941 between the military viewpoint and the dominant civilian opinion. Wishing to delay the inevitable conflict so as better to prepare for it, the military consistently advocated caution and the avoidance of any action which might give the Axis powers an excuse for war. Hopkins, Stimson, Knox, Ickes, and Morgenthau, on the other hand, all tended to favor more active and belligerent measures. The President and Secretary Hull wavered between the two, with the President generally tending toward the civilian group and Hull usually coming to conclusions closer to the military school of thought. In a manner reminiscent of the fears of the German General Staff in the 1930's, the military stressed the dangers to the United States of involvement in a two-front war. Throughout 1940 and 1941 they consistently opposed an express or implied commitment by the United States to enter the European war and objected to moves which might provoke Japan, such as the embargo on American exports and the visit of American naval units to Singapore. As tension mounted in the Far East in the fall of 1941, the military leaders urged an agreement with Japan and the avoidance of the "precipitance of military action." Their warnings were, however, overruled by the civilian leadership, and the final American decisions the last part of November which precipitated the conflict were made virtually without military participation and decidedly without military approval.[16]

Not only in their advocacy of military strength and diplomatic restraint, but also in their entire approach to the international situation in these prewar years, America's military leaders adhered to the professional military ethic. The two most comprehensive statements of the military viewpoint during this period were probably the formulation of the American position for the staff conversations with the British in January 1941 and the "Joint Board Estimate of United States Over-all Production Requirements" of September 11, 1941. In the earlier document the military planners warned that the United States must not "entrust our national future to British direction," and emphasized that American planning must be based upon an awareness of America's continuing political goals and interests. The British, the planners declared, would always have in mind "their postwar interests, commercial and military." Consequently, it was necessary that we too should "safeguard our own eventual interests." [17] Nine months later, the military approach was further elaborated in the Joint Board Estimate signed by Marshall and Stark. Both in its specific requirements for immediate American strategy, and in its analysis of Axis strategy and capabilities, the Estimate manifested a coldly realistic and professional approach. It was, in the words of Langer and Gleason, "utterly devoid of false hope or self-delusion." It defined the "major national objectives of the United States" as:

. . . preservation of the territorial, economic and ideological integrity of the United States and of the remainder of the Western Hemisphere; prevention of the disruption of the British Empire; prevention of the further extension of Japanese territorial dominion; eventual establishment in Europe and Asia of balances of power which will most nearly ensure political stability in those regions and the future security of the United States; and, so far as practicable, the establishment of regimes favorable to economic freedom and individual liberty.[18]

Even at this late date the military leaders were still thinking in conservative realistic terms with respect to national policy. The long-run goals of the United States were not the defeat of Germany and Japan, but rather the establishment of a balance of power in Europe and Asia. Victory over the Axis was desirable only insofar as it contributed to this end. This confidential military statement of American aims contrasted markedly with the idealistic and ambiguous public declaration of American goals by the President in the Atlantic Charter a month earlier. The mere fact that the Joint Board had to formulate a definition of national goals was, however, a sign that the military could not long adhere to it. The origin of the Estimate was a presidential request for military production requirements. To state these, however, the military had to know what over-all national policy was. But, in the summer of 1941, the only policies which existed were, in the words of General Gerow, "more or less nebulous." Hence, the military staff had to make its own definition of national policy. In these early days, it could still do this in the spirit of the military ethic. In due course, however, this was to become impossible, and the military planners found their thinking shifting from that typified by the Joint Board Estimate to that typified by the Atlantic Charter.

The foreign policy which the United States actually followed during the war contrasted markedly with prewar military thinking.

Its most important elements were derived almost exclusively from civilian sources. Among these key components were: (1) concentration upon the military defeat of the Axis to the exclusion of all other considerations; (2) postponement of political decisions respecting the postwar settlement until after the war; (3) requirement of unconditional surrender of the major Axis powers; (4) priority to the defeat of Germany ahead of Japan.

Early in the war the President laid down the line that all American military planning was to be based upon the assumption that our political aim was military victory in the most efficient manner. In Stimson's words, "The only important goal of the war was victory, and the only proper test of wartime action was whether it would help to win." [19] This emphasis was deep-rooted in the American approach which assumed a natural harmony in international relations. Disruptions of this harmony were caused by a single transitory evil, the elimination of which would end further conflict. As a result, the Americans rejected Churchill's pleas for an attack through the Balkans and insisted in the final weeks of the war that the western armies concentrate primarily upon the destruction of the German armed forces rather than the occupation of territory and capitals. The desire not to consider or discuss postwar objectives with our Allies was naturally a part of this outlook. Hull and the President strongly resisted British and Russian efforts to engage the great powers in commitments as to the postwar settlement. The goal of unconditional surrender was, in its phrasing, a personal creation of Roosevelt's, but in its substance, it was implicit in American policy and thinking. It was determined upon by the President without first consulting his military advisers. Finally, the Germany-first policy had both civilian and military roots. From the military viewpoint, it was, of course, desirable to defeat first the principal threat to American security. More significant than this consideration, however, was the fact that throughout the two years before American entry our policy had been primarily oriented toward the support of Britain while holding off Japan in the Pacific by adopting a defensive attitude.[20]

As the military acquired authority and influence during the war, they slowly abandoned their prewar attitudes and accepted the assumptions and values of civilian thinking. This adjustment may be seen concretely in the manner in which the Joint Chiefs altered their views to accord with those of the President. As early as April 1941, when Marshall began his strategic briefings of FDR, the Chief of Staff reminded his subordinates that "Army planners had to recognize and adjust their thinking to the fact that the President was governed by public opinion as well as by professional military opinion." [21] The high commanders of the Army and Navy had, indeed, been in part chosen because they possessed the "sense of statesmanship that enabled them to consider the political as well as purely military aspects of the global situation." [22] The acquiescence of the military was in part the result of daily contact with the President and his appealing persuasiveness. But it was even more due to the fact that as the Joint Chiefs became the alter egos of the President in the conduct of the war, it was only natural that similar responsibilities and similar perspectives should produce similar policies. As Captain T. B. Kittredge of the Historical Section of the JCS observed:

It may be true that the President formally overruled them on very few occasions but this was only because informal discussions of the President with Leahy, Marshall, King, and Arnold usually led them to know in advance the President's views. They, no doubt, frequently recognized the advantages of accepting the President's suggestions with their own interpretations, rather than of risking an overruling by presenting formally proposals they knew would not be accepted.[23]

Through this subtle process the values and assumptions of the President were gradually written into the thinking of the military chiefs. The easiest civilian aim for the top military leaders to adopt was the substitution of total victory for continued military security through the balance of power. By 1943 and 1944 Marshall, for instance, had abandoned the views he had put forth earlier, and instead was agreeing with Stimson that military victory was the overriding goal and the requirements of military strategy the decisive component in national policy.[24] Although Cordell Hull had little to do with the basic decisions of the war, his rejection of the balance of power concept was eventually endorsed by the Joint Chiefs. By the time of the Quebec conference in August 1943, the Chiefs of Staff were accepting the implication that the crushing of

Germany in Europe would put Russia in a dominant position. The American response to this, they added, should not be to back Britain's feeble efforts to create a balance to Russia in the Mediterranean area, but rather to give "every assistance" to Russia and to "make every effort" to obtain her friendship. This was, indeed, a far cry from the cold realism of two years earlier. Subsequently, in May 1944 the Joint Chiefs restated their new view on harmony among the Big Three as a substitute for the balance of power: "our basic national policy in postwar settlements . . . should seek to maintain the solidarity of the three great powers and in all other respects to establish conditions calculated to assure a long period of peace, during which, it may be hoped, arrangements will be perfected for the prevention of future world conflicts." [25] In part, this emphasis upon agreement with Russia reflected a military concern for Russian assistance in the Far Eastern conflict. Its content and context, however, indicate that it also reflected a change in political attitude from that of the prewar years. The Joint Chiefs similarly supported the policy of deferring consideration of the postwar settlement until the end of the conflict. As Admiral Leahy put it, the United States should stay clear of European politics and should rest its policy on the Atlantic Charter, "one of the most profound political announcements made during the war." [26] The American high command did not, of course, completely abandon the military viewpoint in their thinking. The tendency of some, if not all, of the commanders to take a pessimistic view of the time and the effort which would be necessary to defeat Japan reflected a normal military conservatism. Similarly, their desire that the United States acquire full ownership of the Japanese mandated islands was a typically military approach which brought them into sharp conflict with civilian agencies of the government. In general, however, on the major issues of policy, the views of the Joint Chiefs were those of the civilian statesmen and of the American public.

The pressure upon the military to make this adjustment varied, of course, with their rank and position. While it is difficult, if not impossible, to draw any lines, it is fairly obvious that politicalization was limited generally to the higher echelons and to officers serving in special capacities which brought them into contact with civilian needs and viewpoints. On the lower levels, the professional ethic remained more or less intact. Throughout the war, lower ranking military officers and the professional military journals warned of the difference between the postwar world and a post-warfare world. They urged the desirability of formulating postwar goals before the conflict ended, maintaining strong forces after victory, and directing policy toward the achievement of a world-wide balance of power.[27] In the Balkans versus western Europe dispute, the Operations Division of the General Staff, which served as Marshall's command post, generally accepted the prevailing political orthodoxy. In the lower ranking staffs, however, there were at least some doubts. A staff study produced in the G–2 (Military Intelligence) Division of the War Department warned of the political dangers of Russian dominance in the Balkans. But this occurred just at the time when the Joint Chiefs were acquiescing in the idea of Russian preëminence in Europe. Consequently, in the words of Hanson Baldwin, the authors of the staff paper "had their ears pinned back by a superior, who told them sharply: 'The Russians have no political objectives in the Balkans; they are there for military reasons only.' "[28]

GOVERNMENTAL ROLE: CIVILIAN CONTROL TO MILITARY DOMINANCE. The changing nature of military thinking may also be seen in the attitudes of the military commanders with respect to civilian control. In the thirties the American military adhered thoroughly to this concept. This continued in the immediate prewar and early war years. It was the function of civilian authorities, the Army War Plans Division affirmed in July 1940, to determine the "what" of national policy and the responsibility of the military to decide upon the "how" in the form of the military operations necessary to support that policy.[29] The top military leaders during the first part of the war and their subordinate planning staffs for a longer part of the conflict favored the creation of a civil-military war cabinet along British lines staffed with an effective secretariat. This was, of course, merely a reiteration of the military pleas of the twenties and thirties for a strong national policy organ to furnish civilian guidance.

The military attitude toward civilian control changed completely during the war. The plans for postwar organization of the armed services, developed by the military in 1944 and 1945, reflected a new conception of their role in government. One would hardly recognize the cowed and submissive men of the 1930's in the proud and powerful commanders of the victorious American forces. Civilian control was a relic of the past which had little place in the future. "The Joint Chiefs of Staff at the present time," Admiral Leahy said quite frankly and truthfully in 1945, "are under no civilian control whatever." And the Chiefs made it clear that they wanted to perpetuate this situation. "There was one point upon which all of us agreed," to quote Admiral Leahy again. "We felt the Joint Chiefs of Staff should be a permanent body *responsible only to the President* and that the JCS should advise the President on the national defense budget." [30] Admiral King attempted to formalize and make permanent his wartime direct access to the President.[31] The Army, in its McNarney plan, explicitly proposed to carry over the wartime JCS system into the postwar years. The plan provided for a United States Joint Chiefs of Staff which were to deal directly with the President on military strategy, force levels, war plans, the size of the military budget, the allocation of funds among the services, and virtually all other significant policy matters. There was also to be a civilian Secretary of the Armed Forces, but he was cut strictly along Stimsonian lines. He was to advise the President on "political and administrative matters," but he was not to participate in the formulation of the military budget. His primary responsibility was to effect "economies and improvements." [32]

When the McNarney plan ran into considerable opposition, the military leaders of the Army came up with a revised proposal the following year in the form of the Collins plan. However, it too was based upon the proposition that the Joint Chiefs should continue to function as they had during the war. While the Chiefs of Staff were now placed beneath the Secretary of the Armed Forces on the organizational charts, they still were to deal directly with the President and to have full authority over "military policy, strategy, and budget requirements." Their budget recommendations were to go to the President through the Secretary, but he was to have no power to change them. In still another plan which received the formal approval of the Joint Chiefs, provision was made for a Commander of the Armed Forces, who would also be Chief of Staff to the President and the head of a central Armed Forces General Staff. The Chiefs of Staff were to be under a civilian Secretary, but the military leaders were to deal directly with the President on matters of strategy and operation. The Secretary was to advise the President on the political, economic, and industrial aspects of military problems, to be responsible for administrative matters, and to participate with the Chiefs of Staff in the formulation of the military budget.[33]

Prior to 1941 the one recurring element in military organizational prescriptions had been a council of national defense to establish authoritative policy guides for the military. A striking feature of the 1944 and 1945 ideas of Admiral Leahy, the two Army plans, and the JCS plan, was the absence of any such provision for political-military coordination between the services and the State Department. The State Department's role of bystander during the war and the central importance of the Joint Chiefs of Staff in the formation of national policy had pushed this to the background. As a result of this sharp break with traditional military thinking, the National Security Council, established in 1947, was not derived from the long strand of military recommendations stretching back to the 1890's. Instead, its sources were in the plan which Ferdinand Eberstadt drew up for Secretary of the Navy Forrestal in 1945. The Eberstadt proposal in turn was inspired, not by the prewar naval tradition favoring such a body, but by the experience of the British Committee of Imperial Defense. While Eberstadt's recommendations provided more effectively for civilian control than did the military proposals, they possessed a different weakness in that no provision was made for a Secretary of Defense. Consequently, the Joint Chiefs were left aloof in limbo dealing directly with the President on strategy and the military budget without any central civilian secretarial organization to balance them.[34]

CIVIL-MILITARY RELATIONS IN ECONOMIC MOBILIZATION

The distinguishing aspect of civil-military relations in economic mobilization was that eventually all the interests concerned received organizational expression in one form or another. By the middle of 1943 there was in operation a rough but effective balanced system of civil-military relations in which the demands of the military agencies were coordinated with those of a number of other claimant agencies by an umpire — the Office of War Mobilization — with the full backing and support of the President. As a result, like the civilians, the military were left free to be spokesmen for their own peculiar needs and interests. The diversity of interests engaged in the "Battle of the Potomac" is reflected in the historiography of the struggle. In contrast with the memoirs and accounts dealing with grand strategy, which in general do not disagree in their interpretation of significant events, each of the postwar accounts of economic mobilization tends to embody the distinct and limited perspective of one of the participants in the conflict.[35]

The initial agency in the field of economic mobilization was the Army and Navy Munitions Board composed of the Assistant Secretaries of the Army and Navy. The 1939 version of the Industrial Mobilization Plan drafted by that agency was the final expression of military thinking on economic mobilization during the premobilization period. It proposed an organizational structure similar to that desired by the military in the foreign policy-strategy field at this time in that it, too, prescribed a limited role for the military and an effective system of civilian control. The key agency suggested in the plan was a War Resources Administration staffed by qualified civilians which was to initiate and enforce in the name of the President all economic measures necessary for the prosecution of the war. Various other civilian agencies were to handle special problems — such as war finance, trade, labor, and price control — but these were to be subordinate to the War Resources Administration. The actual procurement of munitions was to be in the hands of the services.[36] There was thus a reasonable division of responsibility between civilians and military, and, indeed, although the Industrial Mobilization Plan was ignored in 1940, the system of organization which emerged in 1943 was not unlike that proposed in the plan.

Under the plan the Munitions Board was to assist the WRA in getting started and then fade out of existence. Actually, the Board's career turned out to be somewhat more complex. This was primarily because economic mobilization was spread over three years and because there was lacking in this period a strong, central, civilian agency such as proposed in the Industrial Mobilization

Plan. Consequently, as the civilian side of mobilization evolved through a series of short-lived agencies — the National Defense Advisory Commission, the Office of Production Management, and the Supply Priorities and Allocations Board — the ANMB began to accumulate more power, particularly with respect to priorities, than was, strictly speaking, within its contemplated purview. The Board was further strengthened at the end of 1941 by the appointment of Ferdinand Eberstadt as chairman. However, in January 1942, the President established the War Production Board under Donald Nelson and ordered the ANMB, which since 1939, like the Joint Board, had been directly under the President, to report to him through the WPB. The month after that, moreover, the Army Services of Supply under General Somervell were established to integrate all Army procurement activities and to act as the principal spokesman for the Army with respect to mobilization matters. The ANMB was thus caught in a squeeze play. Its ambiguous status as a semimilitary agency — a creature of the service departments, but headed by three civilians — caused it to be viewed within the services as an instrument of civilian control and outside of the services as a spokesman for military interests. The net result was that it lost stature and functions to both sides. The Army and Navy procurement offices preferred to present their claims directly to the WPB and, when the priorities system broke down, the War Production Board took over the administration of the succeeding Production Requirements Plan and Controlled Materials Plan. Indeed, Eberstadt went over to the WPB in the fall of 1942 to put the latter into effect. And with this move the ANMB lapsed into the status of a minor agency.[37]

With the fading away of the ANMB, the key element in civil-military relations on the mobilization front became the relations between the War Production Board and the military procurement agencies: the Army Service Forces and the Office of Procurement and Material in the Navy. The role of the military here was fairly clear and unambiguous. They were responsible for getting the war instruments they needed, and they pursued this goal with a single-minded devotion. They were looking out for military needs and military needs alone. It was the responsibility of someone else to represent the interests of the rest of the economy. The real problem concerned the identity of that someone else. The Presidential directive establishing the WPB had given the chairman of the Board broad, if ill-defined powers over the entire industrial mobilization operation. The Office of Production Management and the Supply Priorities and Allocations Board had been abolished and their powers assigned to the War Production Board along with other grants of authority. The WPB chairman was to "exercise general direction over the war procurement and production program" and to "determine the policies, plans, procedures, and methods of the several Federal departments, establishments, and agencies in respect to war procurement and production." [38] The fairly obvious intent of this order was to make the WPB and its chairman the ultimate arbiters of the war mobilization program. Immediately upon taking office, however, Nelson began to delegate key functions to other agencies. Even more damaging to his powers was the fact that the crucial need in 1942 was not so much for an arbiter of conflicting claims but rather for some agency to represent the needs of the civilian economy. This was a new need. Until the spring of 1942, the civilian supply division within WPB and its predecessors had been primarily concerned with accelerating conversion to war production. However, as the situation began to get tight, and as the statements of military requirements mounted, it became obvious that someone had to defend essential civilian needs. In what was probably poor administrative strategy, the WPB did not expand its civilian supply office nor detach it as a separate agency. Consequently, the WPB itself became the principal spokesman for civilian needs. Instead of being the umpire, it came to be viewed as one of the claimant agencies in the struggle for scarce resources. Less attention and authority were given to the orders of its chairman and more and more frequent appeals were made to the President over his head. Nelson's staff became convinced that the military were out to take over the entire economy, and the military became equally certain that the WPB was only vaguely aware that there was a war on.

The issue was further complicated by the move of Eberstadt from the ANMB to the WPB in September 1942. In effect, Eberstadt represented the military within the WPB structure. In this sense, if Nelson had been able to balance off Eberstadt against his other vice chairman, Charles E. Wilson, he might have been able to salvage his position. But the military were now completely opposed to him, and, at the beginning of 1943, the service departments urged the President to fire Nelson and reorganize the board under the leadership of Baruch and Eberstadt. Nelson forestalled this move by firing Eberstadt and thereby saved his personal position at the expense of his agency. For, with Eberstadt gone, the services could only view the WPB as an open rival. If, on the other hand, Nelson had lost the battle, Baruch and Eberstadt might well have reëstablished WPB's authority as the general supervisor of war production. It was now clear, however, that the WPB "was a member of a team of agencies and not . . . the dominant agency that was created on paper by the President's Executive order of January 1942." [39] The creation of a superior agency to coordinate the WPB, the military, and the other civilian agencies was inevitable.

The Office of War Mobilization, established in May 1943 under the leadership of James F. Byrnes, exercised in fact the authority which the WPB had possessed on paper. This office was the outgrowth of the Office of Economic Stabilization established the previous fall under Byrnes' direction. Although the OES theoretically had no responsibilities for production, nonetheless it, too, had gradually encroached upon the authority of the WPB, because no sharp line could be drawn between production and stabilization and because Byrnes had set himself up in the White House which gave him a prestige and influence not possessed by the chairman of the WPB. With the establishment of OWM, this tendency was formalized, WPB was downgraded, and Byrnes emerged as "Assistant President" in charge of economic mobilization. Subsequently, in the fall of 1944, Congress placed OWM, rechristened the Office of War Mobilization and Reconversion, on a statutory basis. Throughout its existence, this agency was to be able to maintain itself as the umpire primarily as the result of two facts. By the time of its creation, all the major interests involved in the mobilization program had achieved agency representation in one form or another. Thus, it was impossible for OWM to be drawn down into the position of spokesmen for one claimant against another. Instead, the great need was to reconcile and coordinate conflicting claims and requirements. Secondly, while keeping his staff small, Byrnes himself, like the JCS, kept close to the source of authority, the President, so that for all intents and purposes an order from Byrnes was an order from the President. While agencies occasionally appealed over the head of the OWM director, they met with little success. The record indicates that in the last two years of the war OWM was able to play the balancer and umpire role among the conflicting civilian and military agencies. The military were kept in their proper sphere, yet their essential demands were met.[40]

THE FRUITS OF HARMONY AND ACRIMONY

The differing patterns of civil-military relations in foreign policy and strategy, on the one hand, and economic mobilization, on the other, offer considerable food for thought. On the one side, there was cooperation and harmony; on the other, conflict and acrimony. Which pattern was the more successful? Certainly, on the domestic front, much of the sanguinary "battle of Washington" might have been avoided if an agency similar to the OWM had been created earlier in the process. Nonetheless, it is impossible not to conclude that, with all the infighting, hostility, name calling, and maneuvering, the domestic system of acrimony was far more successful than the foreign system of harmony. By any standard, relative or absolute, American economic mobilization was an outstanding success. Starting considerably later than any of the major participants in the struggle, it soon overtook and exceeded them. And this was not due simply to superior resources. It also reflected superior planning and organization. By comparison with the economic mobilization of Germany and Japan, the American effort was conducted with realism and foresight.[41]

The contrast between the formulation of American external and internal war policies was heightened by the differing roles of civilians and military in each. With respect to foreign affairs, the role of the military was essentially instrumental. As the WPD said in 1940, the function of the political leaders was to determine the "what" and that of the military to decide on the "how." On the domestic side, this was reversed. It was the function of the military to determine the broad policies — the military requirements, the "what" — and up to the civilian agencies to determine "how" the military end items were to be produced. In each, the instrumental "how" side had the important function of representing capabilities and the continuing prospect of providing those capabilities. The instrumental side could either act as a restraint or a goad with respect to the mobilization of capabilities for the fulfillment of policy objectives, whether those were the defense of a particular piece of territory or the production of a certain number of tanks. In World War II, the civilian agencies on the mobilization side played this role perfectly. Before the entry of the United States into the war, they urged the military to raise their production goals: at some points in 1940 and 1941, the civilian mobilization agencies were advocating production objectives two or three times those submitted by the military whose thinking was still dominated by the short rations of the thirties. But, once the war was under way, the policies of the two were reversed. The military agencies set their production goals sky high, and the civilian agencies, particularly in the famous "feasibility dispute" of 1942–1943, usefully reminded them of the needs of the nation's civilians, the desirability of preserving capital resources, and the limits on the nation's economic capabilities. Similarly, toward the end of the war, it was Nelson in the WPB who began preparation for reconversion at a time when the military were still demanding all-out war production. Thus, the instrumental agencies, civilian in this case, served to remind the military policy agencies of the temporary nature of their immediate goals. They were always looking toward the capabilities required for the future. The interaction between the military concern for the immediate policy goal and the civilian concern for the development and preservation of the economic instrument resulted in a generally wise mobilization policy.

Contrast this with the situation in foreign policy. Here the political agencies, the President and the State Department, should set the immediate goals, and the military should be concerned with the means to be utilized in the achievement of those goals. Before the United States entered the war, the military did play their proper role in warning of the need for greater military force and urging a delay of conflict until that force could be achieved. Once the United States got into the war, however, they ceased to be

concerned about the continuing problem which it was their function to be concerned with — military security — and instead became wrapped up in the achievement of the political goals of the
moment. Rather than looking to the future, they sacrificed themselves to the present. The goal posited by the policy agency became so overwhelming in its claim that all else had to be forgotten.
This was not the case on the domestic front because at each stage
the military requirements goal was challenged. On the strategic
front, on the other hand, the military abdicated their responsibility
to think in terms of the continuing demands of American security
and rushed headlong after the political goal of total victory.

The prime deficiency in the conduct of World War II was,
therefore, the insufficient representation of the military viewpoint
in the formulation of national strategy. This key interest, which
should have played a major role, was downgraded and neglected.
On the economic front, on the other hand, with all the controversy, all the interests had their say. The result was that economic
mobilization was a brilliant success while the strategic conduct of
the war left something to be desired. "The great mistakes of the
war" were in the field of strategy not mobilization. Less harmony
would have produced better policy. If, instead of moving into the
seats of power and embracing civilian goals, the Joint Chiefs had
preserved their military roles and warned the political leaders that
no war is the last war and that the problem of military security
would still be with us after V-day, the United States would have
come out of the war in a far better strategic position than it did.
The derangement of American civil-military relations was simply
the institutional reflection of a deeper malady: the ignorance and
naïve hopes which led the American people to trade military security for military victory.

13

Civil-Military Relations in the Postwar Decade

THE ALTERNATIVES OF CIVIL-MILITARY RELATIONS

The outstanding aspect of civil-military relations in the decade after World War II was the heightened and persistent peacetime tension between military imperatives and American liberal society. This tension was the product of the continued dominance of liberalism in the American mind and the continued acceptance of the liberal approach to civil-military relations, on the one hand, and, on the other, the intensified threats to American military security, which increased the need for military requirements and the relevance of the military ethic to national policy. The Cold War shifted the emphasis in foreign policy from diplomacy and maneuver to construction and operation. Under the old pattern of international politics with a number of major powers, the static element tended to be the relative power of the various states. The dynamic element was the shifts in coalitions and alignments among the states. After World War II, however, the diplomatic element was relatively static — countries were generally on one side or the other in the Cold War — and the dynamic element was the relative military and economic strength of the two coalitions. The changes of China and Yugoslavia from one side to the other in the Cold War altered the balance of power, but their significance paled before the relative progress of the Soviet Union and the United States in developing thermonuclear capabilities. Military requirements thus became a fundamental ingredient of foreign policy, and military men and institutions acquired authority and influence far surpassing that ever previously possessed by military professionals on the American scene.

345

The basic issue raised was: how can a liberal society provide for its military security when this requires the maintenance of professional military forces and institutions fundamentally at odds with liberalism? Theoretically, three answers were possible. The tension could be relieved by returning to the pre-1940 pattern of civil-military relations: cutting military forces to the bone, isolating military institutions from society, and reducing military influence to negligible proportions. American society would remain true to its liberalism, and the American military would return within the shell of professional conservatism. Pursuit of this policy, however, would realize these values at the expense of the nation's military security. A second solution was to accept increased military authority and influence but to insist that military leaders abandon their professional outlook and that military institutions be reformed along liberal lines. While sacrificing traditional military conservatism, this would assure the continuance of liberalism in American society and would provide, at least temporarily, for the military security of the nation. But, as happened in World War II, it might accomplish these ends at the expense of long-range goals and at the ultimate loss of military effectiveness. Finally, the tension between the military and society could be lessened if society adopted a more sympathetic understanding and appreciation of the military viewpoint and military needs. This would involve a drastic change in the basic American liberal ethic. The most difficult, it would also be the most permanent solution of the problem. In actual practice, American civil-military relations in the decade after World War II followed no one of these paths exclusively. The tension between conservative military outlook, liberal social values, and increased military power largely went unresolved. The dominant tendencies in policy and practice, however, tended toward the first and second solutions: the traditional liberal approaches of the extirpation or transmutation of military values and institutions.

POSTWAR PERSPECTIVES ON CIVIL-MILITARY RELATIONS

THE GARRISON-STATE HYPOTHESIS. The postwar decade saw the appearance on the American scene of the first conscious, systematic, and sophisticated theory of civil-military relations since the business pacifism of Spencer, Sumner, and Carnegie. This was the concept of the garrison state. Originally stated by Harold Lasswell in 1937 as an interpretation of the Sino-Japanese War, the garrison-state idea was not fully elaborated and popularized by its creator until World War II and later.[1] It then became a dominant theory of civil-military relations, adhered to by intellectuals and alluded to by mass media. The significance of Lasswell's concept derived from its attempt to apply the traditional assumptions and values of American liberalism to the apparent reality of continuing military crisis. It combined three elements: an analysis of twentieth-century international conflicts; a prediction that the result of permanent warfare would be the general emergence of a particular form of social organization, the garrison state; and a statement of preference for a world commonwealth as the only possible alternative to the garrison state.

Lasswell's analysis began where Herbert Spencer left off. The natural course of history is progressive and upward from bellicose, militaristic caste society to pacific, bourgeois, democratic society. The polar opposite of the war state or garrison state is the business state, which in the nineteenth century was becoming increasingly dominant. The goals of society at that time were economic — "the peaceable pursuit of prosperity" — and the rise of complex commercial relations "seemed to create a world market which would furnish the material basis for a limited world order." Beginning about the time of World War I, however, history went off the track. The trend was reversed *"from* progress toward a world commonwealth of free men, *toward* a world order in which the garrison-prison state reintroduces caste bound social systems." As a result of this interruption or deflection of history, the tendency "of our time is away from the dominance of the business man, and toward the supremacy of the soldier." War hastens this tendency, but even the "continuing threat of war can bring about a reversal in the direction of history." Lasswell was vague as to the causes of war, crisis, and insecurity. Looking out on the mid-twentieth-century world, he accepted the fact of their existence. Starting from the liberal theory of progress, however, he had no real explanation of why they did exist. They were apparently linked to the "world revolutionary pattern of our times" which began with the Communist seizure of power in Russia in 1917. This caused continuing tension between the universal ideas of communism and the particular needs and institutions of the Russian state. The garrison state is either the logical product of the world revolution or a reaction against it. In his earlier writings Lasswell appeared to assume the latter; in his subsequent ones the former. Once one state adopts the garrison state form of social organization, the pattern tends to be universalized. In both the United States and the Soviet Union, the garrison state will be the necessary product of the prolonged continuation of the Cold War.

Inherent in Lasswell's prediction as to the nature of the garrison state were many misconceptions with respect to the content of military values, the possibility of militarization in a liberal society, and the relation between patterns of civil-military relations and forms of the state. Basic to the garrison state, in his view, was the subordination of all other purposes and activities to war and the preparation for war. The preëminence of bellicose intentions and values is reflected in the dominant role which the military play in the state. Lasswell here made the traditional liberal identification of the military with war and violence. Holding to the erroneous view that the military have a greater preference for war than do civilians, he easily arrived at a magnified estimate of their strength in modern society, concluding that the militarization of belief systems would be relatively easy under the threat of war. In his earlier formulations, he stressed the predominant role of the military skill group in the direction of the garrison state. In subsequent essays, he broadened his view of the ruling elite to include the police as well as the military; the specialists in violence, foreign and domestic, were now the top group. Coincidentally, he spoke more of the "garrison-police" state or "garrison-prison" state than just simply the garrison state. Lasswell continued the liberal pattern of linking the military with the enemy, identifying them here with the totalitarian police. He also tended, more specifically, to identify the garrison state with the immediate threat of the moment. In 1937, Japan was its closest approximation; after the beginning of the Cold War, Soviet Russia most fully manifested garrison-state tendencies.

The garrison state requires the centralization of power in the hands of the few. The executive and the military gain power at the expense of the legislature and civilian politicians. Democratic institutions are abolished or become purely ceremonial. "Authority flows downward from commanders at the top; initiative from the bottom can hardly be endured." Lasswell assumed that military control is incompatible with democracy, identifying a form of civil-military relations with a form of government. With the garrison state, the scope of the government eventually expands and becomes practically coextensive with society. Technology, industry, science, and labor are all regimented for the purposes of war. This utilization of the resources of society for military defense is essentially unproductive. The garrison state differs from both capitalism and socialism where production is for use: indeed, at one point Lasswell defined the "dominant crisis of our time" as "socialism *and* capitalism *versus* the garrison-prison state." The garrison state has an egalitarian aspect but it is the egalitarianism of the camp: an equality of short rations and much danger. The garrison state is, in short, Ludendorff's nation at war, Spencer's militant society plus modern technology. In its ultimate form it is indistinguishable from modern totalitarianism.

Lasswell variously rated the emergence of a garrison state as "probable," "likely," or "what might happen." The only admissible alternative to the garrison state, the "triumph of human felicity" in a world commonwealth is, however, "at least not out of the question." Modern science and technology bind the world together. The fundamental aspirations of mankind are the same the world over. Even Russian and American cultures share many points of similarity. The self-interest of the ruling elites in raising the standard of living and the level of scientific knowledge will lead them to reduce the likelihood of war. If war can be deferred, the factors of "common consciousness and enlightenment" will permit the "steady resumption of cooperation." Once this begins, the "meagre trickle of pacific contact between the two polar camps will swell into an enlarging stream, inaugurating a new era of peaceful association in which the world community makes direct progress toward a more perfect community of free men." The end result will be "a homogeneous world culture combining science and democracy," a "global correlation of power," and an "eventual integration of humanity." Lasswell combined a variety of liberal approaches in his stress on the formative influences of science, culture, reason, psychiatry, economics, and technology.

World unity should be the end of American policy. "Our goals are, in fact, positive and world-embracing." Just as the maintenance of liberal institutions and military institutions is impossible within the same society, so also is the continuance of two conflicting social systems in the same world. Either there is peaceful unity or there is the continued development of garrison states eventually coming into mortal conflict. This conflict can only mean the "near-total annihilation of humanity." It will produce not one Rome but two Carthages. By that time, however, destruction will be preferable to continued life in a militarized society. The undermining of free institutions by war preparation is a "more insidious menace" than a third world war even though this would "devastate man and his works on a scale without precedent." The "final fact of war is likely to be less perilous than perpetual preparation for war."

Lasswell held that there must be either total peace in a world commonwealth or total war and destruction. He ruled out the possibility of continuing strife and adjustment. In this he reflected the liberal refusal to tolerate the prospect of continuous friction among social units. History must come to a stop in one way or another. At the root of this outlook is the psychological intolerance of difference and the psychological craving for universality and harmony. The alternatives are world oneness or world war: the unattainable or the unbearable. Lasswell's theory was a measure of the pessimism and, indeed, desperation to which the liberal was driven in contemplating the post-World War II scene. His was the voice of despair and hopelessness, the anguished recognition of the extent to which liberal illusions had been shattered by the stubborn grimness of the human situation.

POLITICAL-MILITARY FUSION. The theory of the garrison state was an effort to adjust to the fact of protracted military crisis. The theory of political-military fusion was an effort to adjust to the fact of enhanced military power. While the garrison-state hypothesis was a passive expression of helplessness in the face of world-wide conditions, the demand for fusion was a positive attempt to solve one aspect of the problem by denying the possibility of functional specialization. This theory started from the undeniable fact that military policy and political policy were much more closely inter-related in the postwar world than they had been previously. It went on, however, to assert that it had become impossible to main-tain the distinction between political and military functions at the highest level of government. Over and over again it was argued that new developments had rendered the old categories of "po-litical" and "military" sterile, obsolete, and meaningless. Fusionist theory dominated civilian thinking on the administrative problems of civil-military relations in the postwar period.[2] In the specific forms in which it was applied to the analysis of governmental in-stitutions, this demand for the merger of political-military func-tions was itself a new element in the American approach to the military. In part it reflected the inherent constitutional difficulties of maintaining a clearcut delimitation of military responsibilities, and in part it derived from the feeling that because war had be-come total, so also had the sphere of military affairs. To a greater extent, however, it simply reflected liberal fear that the increased power of military leadership would mean increased acceptance of the professional military viewpoint. Consequently, it attempted to weaken and subordinate the professional military approach and to reconcile increased military power with liberal values by posit-ing the inevitable transmutation of military leadership. In effect, the fusionist theory attempted to solve the postwar problem of civil-military relations by denying its existence.

Fusionist theory manifested itself in two forms. One demand was that military leaders incorporate political, economic, and so-cial factors into their thinking. This school of thought answered the recurring question "Should military men have military minds?" by replying: "No, they should not and cannot have military minds, at least at the highest levels of military authority." It condemned narrow-minded "military mechanics" and praised broad-minded "military statesmen" whose perspectives transcended the purely military. It argued that the only means whereby administrative co-ordination could be secured among the Joint Chiefs of Staff, the State Department, and other agencies was for them to share a common national outlook. Every decision on national policy, it was held, contained both military and nonmilitary elements which could not be segregated. "There is no such thing as a purely military decision," choroused the fusionists, thereby begging the issue of what were the proper civil-military administrative arrangements. Of course, there is no "purely military decision" at the level of the Joint Chiefs of Staff. This is the exact reason why the Joint Chiefs are legally constituted as an advisory body rather than a decision-making body. There is very definitely, however, a military viewpoint on national policy which stresses the importance of military security considerations. Any decision on national policy involves choices among competing values. The job of the military is to insure that military security is not neglected by the political decision-maker who must balance the desirability of maximizing military security against its costs in other values. The fusionist call for broad-minded military statesmen was a demand that the military leaders deny themselves in order to play a higher role. As such, it was the most subtle and most persuasive form which liberal antimilitarism could assume. Fusionist theory extended the undeniable fact that every military policy recommendation must rest upon certain political and economic assumptions to mean that the military should furnish themselves with those assumptions. Supporters of this position pointed to the extent to which at interdepartmental conferences State Department representatives brought up military arguments while the Joint Chiefs defended the importance of political considerations. They also praised the establishment of institutions such as the National War College, not just because they would enable military officers to appreciate the complexities of national policy, but because they would also enable military officers to arrive at their own conclusions concerning political and economic issues. The one point on which exponents of this theory remained vague was the substantive content of the political thinking they wished to see the officers engage in. To what, or, more significantly, to whose political ideas were the officers to adhere? This question the fusionists never answered specifically. If they had grappled with it, the almost unanimous civilian opinion that the military leaders should integrate nonmilitary elements into their thinking inevitably would have dissolved into the bitter controversy of one civilian against another.

A second manifestation of fusionist theory was the demand that military leaders assume nonmilitary responsibilities. The argument for nonmilitary thinking on the part of military leaders implicitly rejected functional specialization and objective civilian control. This second demand explicitly preferred subjective civilian control. It was impossible, it was argued, to rely upon the political neutrality of military leaders and their simple obedience to state institutions. Instead, as Lasswell put it, minimizing the possibility of military professionalism, "the perpetuation of civilian supremacy would appear to depend not upon maintaining a specific set of governmental forms but upon ensuring the vitality of the value goals of the free society among all members of society, in or out of uniform." [3] Just as "military mechanics" who restricted their thinking to military considerations had been rejected, so also were "military technicians" who narrowly defined the scope of their responsibilities. One most notable manifestation of fusionist theory was the argument that the German generals shared in the moral and political guilt of Hitlerism by not openly and energetically opposing the domestic and foreign programs of the Nazi regime. Some supporters of this critique rather brazenly defied logic by supplementing their denunciation of von Rundstedt in 1945 with an equally vehement attack on MacArthur in 1951. Other critics, such as Telford Taylor, understood the dilemma and attempted to deal with the implications of their criticism for the American scene.[4] American military officers themselves in the postwar decade did not miss the relevance of the Nuremberg "higher loyalty" philosophy to their own behavior. General MacArthur echoed many of the American civilian critics of the German generals when he denounced the "new and heretofore unknown and dangerous concept that the members of our armed forces owe primary allegiance and loyalty to those who temporarily exercise the authority of the executive branch of government rather than to the country and its Constitution which they are sworn to defend." [5] More explicitly, another American officer defended what he agreed was the "insubordination" of Captain Crommelin in the 1949 B-36 controversy on the grounds that:

The decisions of the Nuremberg International Military Tribunal were in large part based on the tenet that the professional military defendants should have followed their consciences and not the orders of Hitler. There are, then, occasions when the refusal of a military man to comply is not insubordinate, but is positively his duty.[6]

In cutting loose from the safe grounds of objective civilian control, the advocates of fusion brought out a weapon which could be turned to a variety of uses.

MILITARY INFLUENCE IN AMERICAN SOCIETY

The influence of military professionals in American society between 1946 and 1955 was significantly less than it had been during World War II. Nonetheless, it was still at an unprecedented level in the absence of total war. The extent to which professional military officers assumed nonmilitary roles in government, industry, and politics, and developed affiliations with nonmilitary groups was a new phenomenon in American history. Military officers wielded far greater power in the United States during this period than they did in any other major country. Three of the most significant manifestations of their influence were: (1) the influx of military officers into governmental positions normally occupied by civilians; (2) the close ties which developed between military leaders and business leadership; and (3) the widespread popularity and prestige of individual military figures.

In analyzing these postwar military roles, two issues are of peculiar importance. First, was the increased influence of the military due fundamentally to factors associated with World War II, and, consequently, a temporary phenomenon? Or did it arise from causes associated with the Cold War and, consequently, something which might continue indefinitely into the future? Unquestionably, the increased military imperatives stemming from America's involvement in world politics contributed to a much higher level of military influence than ever existed prior to 1940. Nonetheless, military influence during the first postwar decade was also in many respects an aftermath of World War II, a carry-over into peacetime both of the prestige and influence which the military acquired between 1940 and 1945 and of the weakness of civilian institutions and leadership during those years.

Second, was increased military influence accompanied by more widespread acceptance of the professional military viewpoint? In general, the inverse relationship between these two factors which had prevailed earlier in American society continued throughout the 1946–1955 period. A significant gap existed between the rapid and extensive rise of military influence and the considerably less success of military demands and military requirements. Those military elements which acquired the greatest political influence went farthest in abandoning the professional ethic, and their diversified roles made it easier for civilians to reject the postulates of professional military thinking. On issues where there was a clear-cut distinction between the professional military viewpoint and the traditional American civilian attitudes, such as universal military service and the size of the military budget, the latter usually triumphed. Indeed, American military policy throughout these years was in many ways a series of continuing efforts to escape from the professional military conclusion that the best means of achieving military security is through the maintenance of substantial forces in being.

PARTICIPATION IN CIVIL GOVERNMENT. The penetration of professional officers into governmental positions not requiring solely military skills took two forms: military occupancy of conjoint positions combining military and political functions, and military occupancy of civilian positions with exclusively nonmilitary functions.

The most notable examples of conjoint positions were: (1) the military governorships of occupied territories such as existed in Germany until 1949 and in Japan until 1952; (2) international military commands such as the North Atlantic Treaty Organization's SHAPE and the United Nations Korean Command; and (3) military advisory and training groups in nations receiving American aid. The conjoint positions reflected the failure of governmental organization to adjust rapidly enough to increased functional specialization. They were one area where fusionist theory was manifested in reality. In the absence of appropriate institutional mechanisms for the separate performance of the military and political responsibilities, the occupants of the conjoint positions discharged both duties. The occupation governorships were a temporary phenomenon developing out of World War II. While hostilities were still in progress and immediately after their termination, the separation of political and military functions was virtually impossible. Military government and civil affairs were naturally handled through the military command organization. After the end of the war, however, the military security function in the occupied territory declined in importance; the immediate problems were economic, social, political, and constitutional. Theoretically, military control should at this point have given way to civilian direction, and in the French, British, and Russian zones of Germany, civilian control did replace military control. The national popularity and political support of General MacArthur, however, made it impossible to reduce him to the status of a military subordinate to a civilian occupation governor. In Germany, the reluctance of the State Department to undertake the responsibility for occupation rule prolonged military control until 1949. In the Far East and in Germany large staffs, devoted purely to political and civil affairs, developed to assist the military governor in the discharge of his political responsibilities. In one form or another, these staffs, largely civilian in composition, were subsumed under or attached to the military command organization.

The international military commands were a reaction to military security threats stemming from the Cold War. Consequently, as a type they were a more permanent manifestation of conjoint office. The Commanders in Chief of SHAPE and of the United Nations Command in the Far East both had to devote substantial portions of their time to the discharge of political and diplomatic duties. The more *ad hoc* nature of the UN Command precluded any effort to develop means of segregating political and military responsibilities. In Europe, on the other hand, the initial creation of the SHAPE military organization and the piloting of it through its first tests required a unique combination of military, political, and diplomatic skills. Once the structure was established, however, a degree of segregation of function became possible. The more thoroughly military approaches of Ridgway and Gruenther to their job and the emergence of the civilian organization under Lord Ismay both reflected an effort to disassociate military and civilian activities in NATO. The complete segregation of the two functions, however, required the development of new forms of international political institutions which were probably impractical. Consequently, under a military guise and through military mechanisms, the commanders and staffs of NATO continued to perform political functions which the exigencies of politics did not permit to be performed more openly.[7]

The military advisory groups to nations receiving American military assistance combined diplomatic and military responsibilities. By virtue of their control over the most significant form of American assistance, the advisory group and its chief at times tended to absorb duties and influence which properly belonged to the ambassador and the State Department. While the problem of the organizing of civil and military representation in foreign countries on such a scale was relatively new to the United States, it had in the past been effectively dealt with by other nations. American military assistance and advisory groups will undoubtedly continue as a relatively permanent fixture in the conduct of American foreign affairs, and the eventual delimitation of responsibilities and duties between military and civil missions abroad should not present unsoluble difficulties.

Prior to World War II professional military officers occasionally held civilian positions in the national government. However, the scope of military penetration into the civilian hierarchy after World War II was completely without precedent in American history. In 1948 it was estimated that one hundred and fifty military men occupied important policy-making posts in civilian government.[8] Many of the most significant appointive positions in the government were at one time or another occupied by military officers. The reasons behind this influx of officers into civil posts were complex: some represented factors which had long been present in the American scene; some were the result of World War II; some derived from the new and continuing demands of the Cold War.

(1) Traditional appointments had been continuingly characteristic of American civil-military relations. In some areas of the federal government a tradition of military appointments antedated World War II. Officers were appointed to these positions either upon detached duty from their services or after retirement. The most significant areas of traditional appointments were closely associ-

The Soldier and the State

ated with the technical specialties of the two services. Naval officers were frequently selected for federal posts connected with maritime affairs. Between 1937 and 1949, for instance, the United States Maritime Commission always had one to three officers among its five members, and throughout much of its life it was headed by an admiral. From an early period, Army engineering officers had been often appointed to civilian public works positions. In the thirties the New Deal utilized the services of a number of officers in the WPA and similar agencies, and their employment in comparable positions was continued by the Truman and Eisenhower administrations.* In another area, the directorship of veterans affairs to which General Bradley was appointed in 1945 had been occupied by another general since 1923. Although Bradley was succeeded by a civilian, it seems legitimate to conclude that a tradition of military occupancy also inheres in this post. The traditional appointments reflected civilian desire to capitalize upon special types of nonmilitary expertise possessed by certain classes of professional officers. They appeared to be a continuing and relatively constant phenomenon in American government.

(2) Honorific and political appointments were peculiarly characteristic of the years immediately following World War II. After World War II many military appointments were designed primarily to honor or reward military commanders who had distinguished themselves in the war. The selection of leading generals and admirals to serve on the American Battle Monuments Commission, the appointment of various military figures to *ad hoc* commissions, and some appointments of military men as ambassadors fell into this category. Honorific appointments were more frequent under Truman's administration than under Eisenhower's. Many of the military appointments between 1945 and 1953 also undoubtedly reflected the desire of the Truman Administration to utilize the political popularity of the top World War II commanders to carry

* Maj. Gen. Philip Fleming, for instance, was executive officer and deputy administrator of the P.W.A., 1933–35, and Federal Works Administrator, 1941–49. Maj. Gen. Edmond H. Leavy was deputy administrator of the W.P.A. in New York City, 1936–40, and assistant commissioner of the W.P.A. in 1940. The Eisenhower Administration appointed Brig. Gen. Herbert D. Vogel chairman of the T.V.A. and Brig. Gen. John S. Bragdon public works coordinator.

358

the burden of its foreign policies. Probably the most notable instance where this motivation was present was the employment of
General Marshall as presidential envoy to China, Secretary of
State, and Secretary of Defense. Honorific and political appointments were both temporary phenomena. No subsequent administration was likely to have quite the peculiar need for such political
support that the Truman Administration did, and nothing short
of total war was likely to produce popular military heroes of sufficient stature to furnish such support or to be eligible for honorary posts.

(3) Administrative appointments reflected the new but continuing demands of the Cold War. The great bulk of the military appointments to civil positions in the postwar decade occurred in the foreign affairs and defense agencies and may be
termed "administrative" in nature. They derived from new imperatives likely to remain in existence for an indefinite length of
time. Before 1933 the personnel requirements of the federal government were fairly small. The expansion of the domestic agencies
during the New Deal period was handled by the movement to
Washington of program-oriented professional workers, academicians, lawyers, and others. To perform its wartime activities the
government attracted business and professional men through the
double appeal of the temporary nature of its employment and the
patriotic duty of government service. The staffing of those significant foreign affairs and defense activities which continued after
1945, however, presented a difficult problem. The temporary war
employees dispersed homeward; the New Dealers were generally
uninterested in foreign affairs; and the businessmen were generally
unwilling to work for the Democratic administration. No ready
source of civilians with administrative and diplomatic skills was
available. Consequently, the military were called upon to fill the
vacuum. The officers were willing to serve, used to public employment, accustomed to low salaries, untainted by leftist affiliations, and divorced from ties with special interest groups. While
military skills were not prerequisite for the positions to which they
were appointed, their military background furnished them with
certain types of experience and training not possessed by any significant groups of available citizens. The State Department, in

particular among civilian agencies, required experienced, competent personnel in the immediate postwar years and utilized the services of professional officers.* The proportion of officers in civilian foreign affairs and defense posts tended to decline after 1946 and 1947, and the Eisenhower Administration to some extent replaced professional officers with recruits from business. The complete elimination of military administrative appointments, however, depended upon the development of a continuing source of high-level civilian administrators with education and experience in this field superior to those of the military.

The influx of military men into civilian posts aroused considerable criticism, particularly in the years from 1946 through 1948. The military appointments were held to be a sign of the militarization of the government, the abandonment of civilian control, and the imminency of the garrison state. Congress refused to approve three of President Truman's military appointments.† The selection of General Marshall as Secretary of Defense in 1950 stimulated renewed debate of the issue. Some of the Eisenhower Administration's military appointees met vigorous congressional

---

* These included: Gen. of the Army George C. Marshall, Special Representative to China, 1946, Secretary of State, 1947–49; Brig. Gen. Henry C. Byroade, Dir., Bur. of German Affairs, 1949–52, Asst. Sec. of State, 1952–55, Amb. to Egypt, 1955—; Maj. Gen. John H. Hilldring, Asst. Sec. of State, 1946–47; Lt. Gen. Walter Bedell Smith, Amb. to U.S.S.R., 1946–49, Under Sec. of State, 1953–55; Rear Adm. John W. Bays, Chief, Div. of Forgn. Service Adm., 1947–49; Capt. Lee W. Park, USN, Chief, Div. of Cartography, 1944—; Maj. Gen. Thomas Holcomb, USMC, Min. to South Africa, 1944–48; Lt. Gen. Albert C. Wedemeyer, Special Representative to China and Korea, 1947; Adm. Alan G. Kirk, Amb. to Belgium, 1946–49, Amb. to U.S.S.R., 1949–52; Maj. Gen. Philip Fleming, Amb. to Costa Rica, 1951–53; Adm. Raymond A. Spruance, Amb. to Philippines, 1952–53; Brig. Gen. Frank T. Hines, Amb. to Panama, 1945–48; Rear. Adm. Arthur A. Ageton, Amb. to Paraguay, 1955—. Other significant military appointments included: Maj. Gen. Kenneth D. Nichols, Genl. Manager, A.E.C., 1953—; Maj. Gen. Edmund B. Gregory, Admistr., War Assets Adm., 1946; Maj. Gen. Robert M. Littlejohn, Admistr., War Assets Adm., 1946–47; Lt. Gen. William E. Riley, USMC, Dep. Dir., F.O.A., 1953—; Vice Adm. Walter S. DeLaney, Dep. Dir., F.O.A., 1953—; Maj. Gen. Glen E. Edgerton, Mngng Dir. & Chrman. Bd. of Dirs., Export-Import Bank, 1953—.

† Maj. Gen. Lawrence S. Kuter to be Chrmn. of the C.A.B., Gen. Mark Clark to be Ambassador to the Vatican, Flt. Adm. Chester W. Nimitz to be Chrmn. of the President's Commission on Internal Security and Individual Rights. All three cases involved controversial issues other than the military background of the nominees. President Truman reportedly offered the CAB chairmanship to six civilians, all of whom declined the job, before selecting Gen. Kuter.

opposition.[9] Virtually all the criticism of the military influx was couched in terms of abstract constitutional and political principles and generalized dangers to civil government. With a few exceptions, it was impossible to demonstrate that the actions of any particular military officer reflected the inherently dangerous qualities of the military mind. It was all very well to cite the general influx of military men as evidence of a trend toward the garrison state. But, when one got down to the specifics of Bradley as Veterans Administrator or Marshall as Secretary of State, the threat of militarization rapidly evaporated. The professional officers blended into their new civilian milieu, serving nonmilitary ends, motivated by nonmilitary considerations, and performing their jobs little differently from their civilian predecessors and successors. Undoubtedly the officers who moved into the State Department in 1946 and 1947 did contribute to the more conservative outlook which developed in that department during those years. Yet even this was largely an adjustment to the civilian environment, for the new approach to foreign policy which became dominant in the Department in 1947 and 1948 had deep roots in the Department's own professional staff. The general ease with which the officers adjusted to their civilian roles and outlook forced their critics to shift to the argument that, although the particular officers appointed were harmless exceptions to the desirable rule, dangerous precedents were being set for the future. This, too, was unconvincing. The "civilianizing" of the officers was not the exception. It was instead the only rule which American liberalism would permit.

THE MILITARY-BUSINESS RAPPROCHEMENT. Few developments more dramatically symbolized the new status of the military in the postwar decade than the close associations which they developed with the business elite of American society. Prior to World War II, the professional officers and the capitalists in spirit and in fact had been poles apart. The American business community had little use for military needs, little appreciation of the military outlook, and little respect for military men. The military reciprocated in kind. After World War II, an abrupt change took place in this relationship. Professional officers and businessmen revealed a new mutual respect. Retired generals and admirals in unprecedented numbers moved into the executive staffs of American corporations; new organizations arose bridging the gap between corporate management and military leadership. For the military officers, business represented the epitome of the American way of life. Association with business was positive proof and assurance that they had abandoned their outcaste status and had become respected members of the American community. Financially and psychologically, the military men who moved from the officers corps to the corporation gained in security, acceptance, and well-being. The business firms, on the other hand, capitalized upon the prestige of well-known commanders, the special skills and expertise of the officers in nonmilitary technical fields, their general administrative and organizing abilities, and their assistance in doing business with the Department of Defense. The ties that bound the two groups together in the postwar decade were apparently many and strong. In actuality, they rested upon two quite different foundations: one broad in scope but temporary in duration; the other more restricted but also more permanent.

The more ephemeral basis of the military-business alliance was the prestige of the military from World War II. Big business was eager to employ famous battle commanders: MacArthur went to Remington Rand, Bedell Smith to American Machine and Foundry, Bradley to Bulova, Halsey to International Standard Electric. This type of appointment was necessarily a temporary phenomenon, the Cold War producing few military figures of sufficient prestige to be of interest to business. The businesses which appointed these officers were usually large manufacturing corporations, holding sizable defense contracts, but so large and diversified as to be in most cases neither exclusively nor even primarily dependent upon government business. The military heroes came in at the top of the corporate structure, assuming posts as president, vice president, board chairman, or director. Although a few had occurred after World War I, prestige appointments on this scale were quite unprecedented in the United States. They were the American equivalent of the British practice of rewarding successful generals with peerages, a commercial society substituting corporation presidencies and board chairmanships for earldoms and viscounties. The military heroes, on the other hand, brought glamour and public attention to the businesses.* The corporations were honored and so were the generals. The large industrial concerns which hired the military men, however, had been the principal locus of opposition to a large military establishment. They were the major institutional base of business liberalism and the dominating element in the National Association of Manufacturers, which consistently demanded the reduction of military expenditures. There is little evidence that their employment of the military officers signalized any fundamental change in what Walter H. McLaughlin, Jr. has described as their "indifferent attitude" toward military affairs. Nor, apparently, were the officers able to work

---

* The pros and cons of adding General Marshall to the General Motors board of directors were debated among corporation officials in 1945, President Sloan suggesting that: "General Marshall might do us some good, when he retires, following his present assignment — assuming he continues to live in Washington; recognizing the position he holds in the community and among the government people and the acquaintance he has — and [if] he became familiar with our thinking and what we are trying to do, it might offset the general negative attitude toward big business, of which we are a symbol and a profitable business, as well." Lammot du Pont, on the other hand, secured the rejection of Marshall on the grounds of, "First, his age; second, his lack of stockholdings, and, third, his lack of experience in industrial business affairs." *New York Times*, Jan. 7, 1953, pp. 33, 35. Owen D. Young, after World War I, defined the qualifications he wanted in the president of the Radio Corporation of America in the following words, and concluded that they could best be filled by a military man, General James G. Harbord, Pershing's Chief of Staff in France:

"1st. He should be well known both nationally and internationally and he should have made such a place for himself as would enable him to speak with authority either to foreign Governments or to our own Government.

"2nd. He should not have been previously identified with politics because that would mean party alignment and partisan reaction.

"3rd. He should not have been identified with Wall Street or the money interests because it is important that the American people should accept the Radio Corporation as an organization for service to American interests both at home and abroad rather than as an organization primarily to make a profit for Wall Street interests.

"4th. He should have had administrative experience and if possible business experience.

"5th. He should be well known in Washington and in a position to appear before Committees of Congress and before the Departments and have his statements of facts accepted without question. It is particularly important in this connection that no one should be able to question his Americanism, such as they have done in several instances in the case of our international bankers.

"6th. He should be a man of public position whom to attack would be bad politics rather than good politics."
Quoted in Gleason L. Archer, *The History of Radio to 1926* (New York, 1938), pp. 246–247.

any change in the business political outlook. The corporations accepted the officers and utilized their talents and reputations, but they did not accept the professional military viewpoint. Insofar as there was a rapprochement in thinking between the military heroes and their business colleagues, it was the military men who made the concessions, adjusting to their new environment by surrendering their professional outlook.

A more restricted but more lasting tie developed between the military leadership and those businesses supplying goods to the Department of Defense. Prior to 1940, the Army and Navy offered little in the way of markets to American industry. In World War I industry had accepted large defense contracts only to suffer dislocation and hardship when they were abruptly canceled at the end of hostilities. As a result, business was most reluctant to take on military orders again in 1939 and 1940. Once the United States entered the war, of course, industry cooperated wholeheartedly in the production of military goods and equipment, and hundreds of businessmen went to Washington to work in the War and Navy Departments. The rapid demobilization in 1945 and 1946 first seemed to indicate a repetition of the post-World War I pattern. In due course, however, and particularly after the outbreak of the Korean War, it became obvious that the Cold War military demand was going to be substantial and relatively stable. The dollar volume of military orders and the complex technological requirements of the modern armed forces brought a significant permanent defense industry into existence for the first time in the United States. The defense suppliers were composed in part of large general manufacturing corporations, such as those in the automobile industry, which furnished military items while at the same time catering to the civilian market.* On the other hand, some industries, such as the aircraft manufacturers and sections of the electronics industry, were almost totally dependent upon military orders.

The economic nexus which joined the defense producers to the military was reflected both in the large numbers of former

* General Motors was the largest producer of defense goods, yet only 19.3 per cent of its 1951 sales were to the military. *New York Times,* Mar. 11, 1952, p. 42.

officers who entered the management of these companies and in the various organizations which developed to cement the military-business tie. The officers hired by the defense producers were not normally well-known public figures, but rather younger men who entered the corporations in operational rather than honorific positions. Most of the officers were technical experts in some specialized scientific field and many had held high positions in the Army's technical services and in the Navy's bureaus. Some of them resigned from the service to pursue their careers in business. The technical specialists employed by defense industries constituted the largest single group of general and flag officers hired by private business in the postwar decade. The aircraft companies and their associated industries alone accounted for a significant portion of them. Unlike the prestige appointments, this type of business-military arrangement appeared to increase rather than decrease during the course of the postwar decade.[10]

The professionalization of the military in the 1880's and 1890's and their withdrawal from society had been reflected in the organization of numerous military associations designed for officers only. The return of the military to society and their close links with the Cold War defense industries were marked by the formation of a different type of organization open both to officers and to civilians and business firms. Probably most significant among these groups was the National Security Industrial Association organized by James Forrestal in 1944 to insure that "American business will remain close to the services." The Association in 1954 was composed of six hundred industrial firms, virtually all of whom had significant defense contracts. Many officers of the Association were former generals or admirals. The Association was principally active in helping its member firms and the Department of Defense resolve problems of production techniques, procurement, and patents. The Armed Forces Chemical Association and the Armed Forces Communications Association came into existence in the immediate postwar years to bridge the gap between the interested segments of the military and of business. The previously existing Quartermaster Association, formed in 1920 as an organization of military officers only, was broadened to admit civilians to active membership and to provide for company membership. The

Army Ordnance Association, founded in 1919, was reorganized as the American Ordnance Association, covering all three services. While its staff was composed largely of retired military officers, the thirty-five thousand members of AOA were mostly representatives of ordnance manufacturers.[11] Both the Aircraft Industries Association and the Air Force Association provided links between the aviation industries and the military.*

In general, the defense businesses supported for economic reasons the same military policies which the officers supported for professional reasons. Exceptions to this existed, of course, in the case of businesses interested in producing or continuing to produce weapons or equipment not believed essential by professional judgment. But on the whole a coincidence of viewpoint existed which permitted the officers an easier association with defense industry than with those businesses which had more diversified customers. Corporation officials and military officials shared a common interest in technological development, and the defense industries for the first time in American history furnished the military program with a significant base of economic support. In other respects, however, association with the defense industries did not aid military professionalism. Inevitably, the businesses thought of themselves first and attracted to their staffs many younger officers who still had many years of useful service to offer their country. In the middle 1950's over two thousand regular officers each year were leaving the services for the more lucrative positions in business. In addition, there was the likelihood that the ability to move from one of the technical branches of the armed forces into a well-paying industry job would enhance the popularity and attractiveness of the technical staffs as against the line. A very small proportion of the business appointments in the postwar decade went to military commanders who were neither famous public figures nor technical specialists, but simply regular line officers with back-

* The new military-business relationship was illustrated by the career lines of Maj. Gen. Harry C. Ingles — Chief Signal Officer in World War II, organizer of the Armed Forces Communications Assoc. in 1946 and 1947, president of R.C.A. Communications in 1948 — and Lt. Gen. Levin H. Campbell — World War II Chief of Ordnance, later exec. vice pres. of International Harvester and president of the Amer. Ordnance Association, author of *The Industry-Ordnance Team* (New York, 1946) which expresses the philosophy of military-business cooperation.

grounds in military command. The businesses who hired these officers seemed to assume that any general or flag officer must necessarily be a good administrator. Their relatively small numbers, however, were indicative of the gap which still remained between even defense business and the more strictly professional military elements of the services. A major general whose principal experience was in commanding regiments and divisions had little to offer the manufacturing corporation.

THE MACS AND THE IKES: RETURN OF THE SAMURAI. In an engaging article, T. Harry Williams argues that the United States has two military traditions.[12] One is represented by the friendly, folksy, easygoing soldier who reflects the ideals of a democratic and industrial civilization and who cooperates easily with his civilian superiors. This "Ike" tradition is exemplified by Zachary Taylor, U. S. Grant, and Dwight D. Eisenhower. Opposing this is the "Mac" tradition, embodied in Winfield Scott, George B. McClellan, and Douglas MacArthur — brilliant, imperious, cold, dramatic officers deriving their values and behavior from an older, aristocratic heritage and finding it difficult to subordinate themselves to civilian authorities. Williams' dichotomy is obviously real and significant; yet, in a sense, it is restricted in scope, failing to encompass important elements of the American military tradition which fall into neither the "Ike" nor the "Mac" category. Essentially, the Ikes and the Macs represent two aspects of the same strand of American militarism: the tradition of political involvement. The true opposition is not between the Taylor-Grant-Eisenhower line and the Scott-McClellan-MacArthur line, but rather between both of these, on the one hand, and the professional strand of American militarism (which might be described as the Sherman-Pershing-Ridgway line), on the other. The basic distinction is not between the Ikes and the Macs, but between the "Ike-Macs" and the "Uncle Billies" or "Black Jacks." The differences between the Ike type and the Mac type are the differences between two kinds of politicians: the charismatic, inspirational, unbending political leader who leads because he is superior to his followers, and the flexible, earthy, unpretentious political leader who leads because he is representative of his followers. That the Ikes generally have been more successful than the Macs in their political pursuits indicates only that the American environment generally is more favorable to the Ike type, irrespective of whether he is civilian or military. The difference between the Ikes and the Macs is simply the difference between Jackson and Calhoun, Theodore Roosevelt and LaFollette, Wendell Willkie and Robert A. Taft.

Significantly, Williams mentioned no representative of either the Ike or the Mac traditions between the Civil War heroes and the post-World War II figures. During the intervening years both elements of the political strand of the American tradition were subordinated to the prevailing professionalism. Only with the return of the military to society after World War II did the political tradition which had wilted in the 1870's and 1880's reëmerge as a major theme of American militarism. For the first time in American history in the postwar decade, professional officers not only became popular public figures but also became deeply involved in the domestic politics of candidates and elections, political movements and political parties. The most obvious figures were, of course, Eisenhower and MacArthur. But other officers, although not numerous, also assumed conspicuous roles in popular politics. The causes of this political involvement essentially had little relation to the continuing issues and policies of the Cold War. While the officers disputed many points of national policy, their entrance into the partisan political arena does not appear to have been motivated primarily by ideological or policy considerations. Instead, their participation was fundamentally the result of the popularity of Eisenhower and MacArthur and the rivalry between these two great military figures. The conflict between the Macs and Ikes in the postwar decade was real, but it was a conflict of personalities not of traditions. Its roots lay in the confused events of World War I and in the inner tensions and feuds, obscured from public view, of the Regular Army of the 1920's and 1930's. At an early date MacArthur and George C. Marshall became identified with opposing groups within the Army. During and after World War I a rivalry, fed by a series of incidents and misunderstandings, developed between them. Eisenhower was an aide to MacArthur while the latter was Chief of Staff from 1930 to 1935 and military advisor to the Philippine government thereafter. Eventually, however, Eisenhower, too, broke with MacArthur, returning to the

United States in 1939. In due course, he came to the attention of Marshall, now himself Chief of Staff, and was rapidly advanced on the career which eventually led to his appointment as Supreme Commander of the European invasion. In this process Eisenhower became completely identified with the Marshall group. His rapid promotion and the priority given to the European theater over the Pacific necessarily drew the ire of the MacArthur supporters. The emergence of Eisenhower and MacArthur as the two popular military heroes of the war projected the essentially intramilitary feud upon the larger framework of national politics. The personal rivalry was enhanced by the identification of the contests with Europe-oriented and Asia-oriented strategies. Virtually all the significant participation of individual military officers in postwar partisan controversy was a function of the rivalry between these two personalities. On the one hand, there was the Marshall-Eisenhower, Europe, SHAEF-SHAPE, Pentagon group; on the other hand stood the MacArthur, Asia, SCAP, "Bataan" group. Retired officers played active roles on behalf of one or the other generals: MacArthur had his Wedemeyer and Bonner Fellers, Eisenhower his Clay and Bedell Smith. Other officers essayed a neutral role or made a difficult choice between the two.[13] The impact of this controversy continued for some while after the war, but the passing of the World War II generation of military leaders and the rise of a new crop of generals removed from its animosities will undoubtedly diminish military political participation.

The political involvement of Eisenhower and MacArthur affected not only the officer corps but the men themselves. Neither was able to adhere to the fundamentals of the professional military ethic. In due course, both emerged as "unmilitary" military men, deviants from the professional standard, heroic and symbolic figures for millions of Americans. MacArthur's involvement in political roles long antedated that of Eisenhower as did also his deviation from the professional military ethic. From the start, MacArthur had been a brilliant soldier but always something more than a soldier: a controversial, ambitious, transcendent figure, too able, too assured, too talented to be confined within the limits of professional function and responsibility. As early as 1929 his name was mentioned in connection with the Presidency, and in 1944,

1948, and 1952 he was on the fringes of the presidential political arena. The MacArthur ideology which evolved in the 1920's and 1930's was essentially religious, mystical, and emotional, contrasted with the normally practical, realistic, and materialistic approach of the professional soldier. To an even greater extent than Mahan, MacArthur's attitudes appeared to reflect a deeply felt and profoundly personalized version of Christianity. In contrast to the professional stress on military force in being, he emphasized the moral and spiritual aspects of war and the importance of the citizen-soldier. In contrast to the bulk of the officer corps, MacArthur viewed the threats to the United States as arising from insidious political philosophies rather than from other nation states of equal or superior material strength. His sense of mission and dedication gave rise to a sustained and unbridled optimism which contrasted with the normal professional pessimism. The professional officer exists in a world of grays. MacArthur's universe was one of blacks and whites and loud and clashing colors. His articulate and varying views reflected a continuing quest for beliefs and policies which would satisfy his own ideological inclinations and at the same time inspire favorable popular response.

In contrast to MacArthur, Eisenhower was still an unknown lieutenant colonel as the nation moved toward involvement in World War II. While MacArthur had specialized in being different, Eisenhower specialized in adjusting to and reflecting his environment, absorbing the attitudes and behavior patterns of those about him. During the 1920's and 1930's, immersed in a professional milieu, he was the typical professional officer. When he catapulted to the heights of rank and fame, Eisenhower rapidly adjusted to his successive new environments, easily emerging as distinctly "civilian minded." Speaking less and smiling more than MacArthur, he appeared the embodiment of consensus rather than controversy. MacArthur was a beacon, Eisenhower a mirror. While the former attempted to build a variety of bridges to the American consciousness, the latter waited and let the bridges be constructed under him. With few pretensions to philosophy and creative originality, Eisenhower had little need to commit himself on public issues or to identify himself with any except the most widely held American values. The Eisenhower ideology was elusive because it was so familiar and acceptable. Substituted for it was a warm, sympathetic, but noncommittal, understanding.

The full measure of the extent to which both MacArthur and Eisenhower by their different paths departed from the professional code was dramatically indicated in the early 1950's. MacArthur became the leading advocate of the abolition of war. Eisenhower emerged as the most effective instrument in the reduction of the armed forces. Both roles reflected the influence of the civilian environments in which the soldiers had become immersed. By 1956 even Henry Wallace was endorsing the views of the two old soldiers on peace and war.

From an early period MacArthur's attitude toward war embodied the dominant ideas of the American liberal tradition. During the 1920's and 1930's he had justified war on moral and religious grounds, and surrounded the warrior's art with a sentimental romanticism. Unlike Dennis Hart Mahan, but similar to Mahan's Jacksonian opponents, MacArthur preferred the warlike spirit to the military spirit.[14] Some observers detected irony many years later in 1951 and 1952, when MacArthur denounced the dangers of the "military mind." But the general was on firm ground. A vast gulf existed between his thinking and that of the professional officer. After World War II he adopted the pacifist ideas which he had castigated in the 1920's and 1930's, urging in Kellogg-Briand terms that war must be "outlawed from the world." Seldom has a professionally trained military man more completely departed from the cardinal tenet of military doctrine that war is ultimately inevitable and beyond the power of humans to prevent. MacArthur had the ban on the maintenance of armed forces written into the constitution of Japan. He urged his own nation to "proclaim our readiness to abolish war in concert with the great powers of the world." MacArthur's demand for the total abolition of war reflected his unwillingness to accept the frustrations, embarrassment, and burdens of continued international friction. In Lasswellian phrases he declared that "in final analysis the mounting cost of preparation for war is in many ways as materially destructive as war itself." Instead he turned to the abolition of war as the panacea of the world's ills, "the one issue, which, if settled, might settle all others." [15] Despite their differences, an underlying consistency existed between Mac-

Arthur's earlier and later views on war. War was always a total, cataclysmic act. In his earlier years he stressed the heroic self-sacrifice and glory involved in this act. In his later years he saw the destruction and calamity it entailed. But his reactions to war were always extreme. "You cannot control war; you can only abolish it," he declared, rejecting vigorously the concept that "when you use force, you can limit that force." Adherence to the total war-total peace dichotomy necessarily led MacArthur to a theory of civil-military relations closer to Ludendorff than to Clausewitz. War represented the utter bankruptcy of politics, not simply the extension of politics. Consequently, in war full control, "politically, economically, militarily," must be in the hands of the military commanders, and the nation must concentrate its complete trust in the military leadership.[16]

While MacArthur emerged as the nation's most eloquent advocate of the abolition of war, Eisenhower became its most effective instrument in the reduction of American military strength. In this again Eisenhower demonstrated his responsiveness to the forces about him, performing a double service for the Republican Party. As a popular military hero candidate, he helped the minority party secure control of the national government for the first time in two decades. Once in office, his military prestige aided the dominant elements in that party toward a realization of their goals of reducing expenditures, lowering taxes, and balancing the budget. The first three military budgets submitted by his administration all cut back the size of the armed forces, all encountered resistance in Congress, and all were approved on the personal assurance of the President that they would provide adequately for the national defense. When in 1953, for instance, congressional supporters of air power threatened to upset Administration plans to reduce Air Force appropriations by $5 billion, the President intervened and saved the budget, assuring Congress that the cuts had his "personal endorsement in all major particulars." As Senator Ferguson accurately predicted: "I believe . . . most of the Senators will go along with the President on this because he is a military expert and his judgment must be trusted." [17] He was the indispensable instrument of the arms cuts. Neither Adlai Stevenson nor Robert A. Taft could have carried out the reductions with so little resistance. The opposition was disarmed from the start. As one Democrat sadly remarked, "How in the devil can a mere Senator argue about military matters with General Ike Eisenhower?" [18] The result was a rift between the President and his erstwhile professional colleagues, and the identification of America's most popular military officer with its most antimilitary philosophy of business liberalism.

14

The Political Roles of the Joint Chiefs

POLITICAL ROLES: SUBSTANTIVE AND ADVOCATORY

The political involvement of a military leadership institution such as the Joint Chiefs may take two different forms. The military leaders may espouse or recommend policies which are derived from nonmilitary sources and which are unrelated to or contrary to the professional military viewpoint. In this event the military leaders assume a substantive political role. Alternatively, the military leaders may play an active part in the public defense or merchandising of policies (irrespective of their content) before Congress and the public. The political involvement in this case stems not from the substantive views of the military leaders but rather from the place, manner, timing, and effects of their expression of those views. This is an advocatory political role. It is essentially exoteric while the substantive political role is esoteric in the sense that the policy views of the military chiefs may not be known beyond a small group of executive officials. These roles are of course not mutually exclusive: military leaders could assume both at once by publicly urging a nonmilitary policy.

Although the Joint Chiefs in the postwar years retreated somewhat from their World War II heights of power and glory, they still continued a high level of political involvement. The most striking aspect of this period, however, was not the degree of their involvement, which it was to be expected would remain at a high level, but rather the differing forms which it took. During the Truman Administration the views of the Joint Chiefs on policy coincided to an astonishing extent with the professional military ethic. In many respects their attitudes would have done credit to the German General Staff in its heyday of professionalism. In view of the extent to which the Chiefs had deviated from the ethic in World War II, this return to the traditional military line stands out as all the more remarkable. On the other hand, the Truman Chiefs quite obviously did become involved in an advocatory political role as the proponents of policy before Congress and the public. In the first two years of the Eisenhower Administration, on the other hand, the reverse tended to be true. In many important instances the views on national policy of the Eisenhower Chiefs, as reported in the press, showed significant departures from the professional military viewpoint. Although thus assuming a substantive political role, the Eisenhower Chiefs were considerably more reticent than their predecessors in the public exposition of their views. It would be erroneous to overemphasize this difference between the Truman and the Eisenhower Chiefs — both to some extent assumed both political roles — but it would be even more unfortunate to ignore it. Each pattern of behavior was in its own way an effort to ease the tension between the professional military leadership institution and the political environment in which it operated.

What caused the differing tendencies in the political roles of the two sets of Joint Chiefs? The reason cannot be found in organization. The Defense Department was reorganized in 1953, but it had also undergone a more significant reorganization in 1949. Neither reorganization fundamentally altered the position of the JCS in the government. While difference in organization may have been a contributing factor to the differences in behavior, it can hardly be rated as a decisive one. Nor can the change be explained by shifts in the fundamental national attitudes toward the military. Throughout the period these remained basically liberal. The answer must be found in the more specific environments created about the Joint Chiefs by the two administrations, their political leadership, their dominant interests, and their policy viewpoints. The Joint Chiefs operate immediately and primarily in a governmental framework. Inevitably they must be affected by the attitudes and behavior of the policy makers and statesmen with whom they are in constant contact. These immediate surrounding circumstances, the "governmental environment," have a greater immediate influence on the Joint Chiefs than the more basic but also more remote national environment. In the long run, of course, the latter is decisive, but in the short run the two may differ. The differences between the Truman and Eisenhower Chiefs of Staff derive from the differences between the governmental environments of the Truman and Eisenhower administrations.

THE JOINT CHIEFS IN THE TRUMAN ADMINISTRATION

DUALITY. The reasons for the behavior of the Truman Joint Chiefs may be found in one of the most striking characteristics of the Truman Administration: its split personality between foreign affairs and defense, on the one hand, and domestic affairs on the other. In many respects it was two administrations in one. In domestic affairs the Administration pursued a policy of liberal reform which was formulated and executed by one set of officials. In foreign affairs the Administration followed a policy of conservative containment which was formulated and executed by a different set of officials. The contact between these two halves was almost minimal. In fact, the only place where they were really linked together was in the President himself.

This duality is perhaps best reflected in the personnel employed by the Administration to formulate and execute policy in the two fields. On the domestic side Truman relied upon the same type of official which had been present during the New Deal. While a mass exodus from Washington of the older generation of New Deal officials occurred in 1945 and 1946, their places were taken by a younger generation which was not essentially different. This younger group included ideologically oriented reformers, vote-oriented politicians, and program-oriented governmental careerists: Hannegan and Clifford, McGrath and McGranery, Wyatt and Lilienthal, Tobin and Steelman, Olds and Clapp. None would have been out of place in the 1930's. Indeed, their function in the Truman Administration was to carry on the Fair Deal version of the New Deal policies. They were committed to the Fair Deal program of reform liberalism: public housing, expanded social security, farm supports, valley authorities, public power, higher minimum wages, federal aid to education, civil rights for Negroes. All of them were linked in one way or another with one or more of the political forces in the Fair Deal-New Deal coalition: the farmers, labor, public power interests, city machines, ethnic minorities. Virtually all were Democratic partisans.

The situation was quite different on the foreign policy-defense side of the Truman Administration. Here another type of creature held sway. There were few New Dealers, fewer machine politicians, and still fewer liberals. While the domestic leaders sprang from a variety of sources reflecting the diversified interests of the Democratic coalition, the foreign affairs leaders were a fairly close knit band of bankers and lawyers, soldiers and diplomats. Forrestal, Lovett, Acheson, Patterson, Harriman, Nitze, Finletter, Draper, McCloy were typical of the former; Marshall, Bradley, Eisenhower, Bruce, Kennan, Peurifoy of the latter. They were reinforced by a few stray businessmen like Hoffman, Symington, and Foster. The inner heart of this foreign affairs government was the foursome of Forrestal, Marshall, Lovett, and Acheson. One of these was Secretary of Defense for all but eighteen months during Truman's two administrations and Secretary of State for all but two years. In addition, during the two years when Byrnes was Secretary of State, Acheson was Under Secretary and had a major role directing the affairs of the Department since Byrnes was frequently away at conferences. Also, Lovett was Under Secretary of State while Marshall was Secretary of State, and Deputy Secretary of Defense while Marshall was Secretary of Defense. These four, together with Hoffman and Harriman in the foreign aid field, formed the nucleus of the Truman foreign policy-defense government.

The foreign policy leaders and their assistants differed from the domestic policy leaders in being almost completely divorced from partisan politics. They had been selected with little regard to party lines. Some of the most prominent were Republicans: Lovett, McCloy, Foster, Hoffman, Patterson, and Draper. These were reinforced by other Republicans at the second level: Assistant Secretaries of Defense McNeil and Coolidge; Assistant Secretary of War Petersen (later national finance chairman of the Eisenhower clubs); Policy Planning Staff head Paul Nitze; CIA Deputy Director Allen Dulles. The professional diplomats and soldiers, of course, tended to be nonpartisan. Even the Democrats differed from their counterparts in the domestic agencies. Acheson was definitely a Democratic partisan, but he was not cut from quite the same cloth as the Fair Deal domestic leaders, and, to some extent, his partisanship was forced upon him. Forrestal's party ties were hazy; he was *persona non grata* to several key groups in the Democratic domestic coalition, and a wide gap existed between him and the "political characters" in "soft gray hats and turned-up overcoat collars" he encountered in the 1944 campaign. A survey by Reston of the *Times* at the close of the Truman Administration indicated that of thirty-nine major appointments of Republicans or nonpartisans to important posts, twenty-two were in the State Department, ten in the Defense Department, five in other national security agencies, and only two in domestic departments. In addition to Eisenhower himself, four of his most active supporters, Hoffman, Lewis Douglas, Dulles, and Clay, held key positions under the Democrats.[1]

It was rare that a domestic politician or liberal reformer appeared in the Truman foreign-defense agencies. One such example was Louis Johnson. He represented forces, interests, and attitudes quite at variance with those dominating the external half of the Administration. He became the symbol of the popular cause of budget cutting and he was a partisan Democrat reputedly with political ambitions. His intrusion into the foreign affairs-defense field was stormy. The Secretary of the Navy quit; the Chief of Naval Operations was fired; the Secretary of the Air Force openly fought him; the other military leaders and service secretaries engaged him in an administrative cold war; communication between the Defense Department and the State Department declined to a minimum. Eventually his relations with Secretary of State Acheson deteriorated to the point where it was obvious that one of them would have to go. So Truman fired Johnson and brought in Marshall and Lovett, whom Acheson had replaced in the State Department, to replace his opponent in the Defense Department. This restored the harmony and unity of the foreign policy team, and relations between State and Defense again developed the mutual confidence and cordiality which had existed earlier when Marshall and Forrestal had been directing affairs.

DEFENSE CONSERVATISM. The significance of this sharp dichotomy in personnel between the foreign and domestic sides of the

Truman Administration lies in the sharp difference in policy which it reflected. While domestically the Administration followed the path of pragmatic liberal reform, in foreign policy it adhered to a distinctly conservative course. The liberalism of the war years was abandoned. Isolation, universalism, legalism, and crusades were backtracked. The principal characteristics of policy were commitment, caution, firmness, patience, and realism. The entire cast of the policy was well summed up in the name given it by its creators and mocked by its critics: containment. There was nothing revolutionary about this policy and very little that was liberal. It was based on the limited national interests of the United States in self-preservation. Its goals were the creation of "situations of strength," armed alliances, and the bolstering up of weak noncommunist governments. In its essence, as Edgar Ansel Mowrer pointed out, containment was a return to the balance of power policy of the Joint Board memorandum of September 1941. Symbolic of this shift was Secretary of State Marshall's declaration on November 7, 1947 that "the objective of our policy from this point on would be restoration of balance of power in both Europe and Asia and that all actions would be viewed in the light of this objective." [2] From his wartime infatuation with total military victory Marshall thus returned to the goals which he had defined for the nation in 1941.

The sources of this conservative foreign policy were fourfold. Of primary importance was the President. Liberal at home, Harry Truman was profoundly conservative in foreign affairs. It was his peculiar political genius and personality to be able to represent and embody these two facets of policy. He could deal equally with conservative banker and Fair Deal reformer, ward boss and professional soldier. Forrestal caught the essence of this characteristic when he observed shortly after the 1948 election that "We are very fortunate in having Mr. Truman, a man who, while he reflects the liberal forces both in this country and throughout the world, is nevertheless a conservative in the real sense of that word — a conserver of the things we hope to keep." [3] Truman's conservatism stemmed not from political philosophy but from his personal conviction that the only way to get along with the Russians was to get tough with them. Never associated with the wartime policy of the Grand Alliance, Truman had an advantage over many other American leaders in being able to strike out on his own without commitment to the past. Undoubtedly, also, his difficulties, first with Byrnes and then subsequently with Wallace over the desirability of a tough line with the Russians, contributed to the hardening of his viewpoint.[4]

The second source of the Truman Administration's foreign policy conservatism was in the top civilian leadership of the government. The background of these bankers and lawyers gave them a perspective on affairs quite different from that of the usual American industrialist. The latter is typically a go-getter, an "operator," aiming at the building of a business empire through the production of the most goods at the least cost in the shortest time. This stimulates an optimistic, individualistic, progressive ethos. Transferred to government, it had a typical manifestation in the desire for "a bigger bang for a buck." The Truman men, on the other hand, tended to be the investment banker type, concerned less with the concrete production of things and more with the subtle intricacies of high finance. They possessed all the inherent and real conservatism of the banking breed. Transferred to government, they were cautious realists, aware of the complexities of human affairs, the limitations of human foresight and control, and the dangers of extending commitments beyond resources. They were also in some measure another manifestation of the curious way in which Theodore Roosevelt was the intellectual godfather of Democratic administrations after 1933. Former Progressives such as Ickes had contributed much to the New Deal. In the wartime and postwar periods the more conservative wing of Neo-Hamiltonianism played its part. A clear line existed from Root to Stimson to Marshall, Lovett, and McCloy. After the war, the influence of the Forrestal men who spread throughout the government contributed a similar perspective to national policy.

The professional ranks of the State Department and the Foreign Service were a third source of the Truman Administration's foreign policy. During the 1930's, economic concerns had dominated the outlook of the State Department. Subsequently, during the war the Department had become immersed in legalistic and organizational problems involved in planning the United Nations. In both phases the Department's approach had been fundamentally liberal. With the end of the war, however, and the opening of the Cold War, its dominant tone and complexion changed. A group of Foreign Service officers came to the fore who had long been suspicious of the motives of the Soviet Union but who had previously been in subordinate positions and unable to exercise a significant influence on policy. In 1947 and 1948, however, the views of this group began to prevail in the Department.[5] They received their classic expression, of course, in George Kennan's analysis of "The Sources of Soviet Conduct" in the spring of 1947, and under Marshall they became institutionally embodied in the Policy Planning Staff of the Department. During the Marshall and Acheson regimes the views of the State Department on policy were frequently even more hard-boiled, power oriented, and realistic than those of the military. Men such as Kennan laid much stress on the importance of military power, and in their analyses almost completely subordinated the ideological factor to the power factor. While the State Department was at times criticized during these years for succumbing to military pressure, its military viewpoint was by and large the uncoerced product of its own thinking on foreign affairs. The general nature of this new outlook in the Department was reflected in the works produced by its supporters after leaving office.[6] The common elements of this *weltanschauung* were the stress on the necessity of power, the recognition of the limitation of American power, and the defense of the morality of using power to further the national security and the national interests.

The final source of the foreign policy conservatism of the Truman Administration was, of course, the military themselves. Along with Marshall, the Joint Chiefs returned to the professional ethic. But the return was only possible because the wartime union of foreign policy and domestic liberalism had been split asunder. The political outlook of Truman and the top civilian leaders plus the new conservative realism of the State Department furnished a sympathetic environment. The civilians led the military back home. With respect to force levels and the military budget, the Truman Chiefs fairly consistently represented the military needs of national security. As a result, their strategic thinking was frequently divorced from political and economic reality. Their budgetary demands were normally drastically cut. At times, to be sure, they did integrate into their analysis an estimate of what the "country could afford," but subsequently, General Bradley, at least, recognized that in so doing they were abandoning their proper role.[7] With respect to the employment of military force the Truman Joint Chiefs similarly pursued a cautious, conservative line. In 1946, when the Yugoslavs shot down some American planes, the State Department wanted to despatch an ultimatum backed up by a show of force; the Joint Chiefs pointed out the limitations of our military resources and urged moderation. With respect to Korea the State Department again urged intervention and the Joint Chiefs played a passive role.[8] In their recommendations regarding the expansion of the Korean War, Israel, the Japanese peace treaty, German rearmament, and the organization and arming of NATO, the Joint Chiefs similarly reflected a paramount concern with military security and a desire to avoid adventurous forays until the United States had strengthened its defenses. General Bradley's entire outlook with its emphasis on the impossibility of quick and easy solutions, the necessity of basing policy on enemy capabilities rather than intensions, the desirability of a pluralistic strategy embodying many and varied types of force, and the transcendence of political goals over military ones, was an almost perfect formulation of the professional military ethic. In their views on civilian control, the Truman Chiefs likewise espoused the traditional military viewpoint.[9]

IMPLEMENTATION. The ability of the Truman Administration to carry out its conservative foreign policy depended upon the extent of popular indifference to foreign affairs, the extent to which foreign policy decisions could be removed from popular control, and the extent to which the people could be won over to the Administration's viewpoint.

A key factor favoring the Administration was the relative indifference of its supporters to foreign policy. The interests of the Democratic Party coalition were numerous, varied, conflicting — and essentially domestic in nature. The Administration was returned to office in 1948 by appealing to those interests in an election fought primarily on domestic economic issues. Consequently, only on those issues was it politically committed. The political stalemate among the interests of the coalition, moreover, insured that there would be no overwhelmingly dominant group to insist that its viewpoint prevail on both domestic and foreign policy. The largest bloc of Administration voters, in any event, was drawn from the poorer economic classes, who typically are indifferent to and fatalistic toward foreign policy.[10] Consequently, the Administration was left relatively free to pursue a foreign policy derived from unpopular and professional sources. At some points, of course, such as Palestine, conflicts arose between domestic interests and the conservative line, in which case the latter normally had to give way. But in general the Democratic interests had little concern with the foreign policy carried out on their behalf by the bankers, diplomats, and soldiers.

The Administration also attempted to isolate as far as possible foreign policy decisions from congressional and public control. Ironically, the tradition of executive leadership and decision-making developed by Roosevelt to implement a popular domestic policy and a liberal wartime foreign policy was invoked by the Truman Administration to carry out an unpopular and conservative foreign policy. The sense of sweeping, dynamic leadership which had been so present under Roosevelt was lacking with Truman because the latter asserted the presidential prerogative not as a Jacksonian "tribune of the people" but rather as a Burkeian virtual representative of the nation. Roosevelt embodied the popular will; Truman escaped from it. For nonlegislative matters the typical pattern was for the decision to be made first and then to be publicly announced, and debated, ratified, or modified in Congress. Virtually all the great congressional debates on foreign policy in the Truman Administration took place after the executive had committed the nation. The decisions on the Berlin airlift, the hydrogen bomb, Formosa policy, the Korean War, the proclamation of national emergency, the troops to Europe, the firing of MacArthur all tended to follow this pattern. In effect, the Administration so far as possible adhered to Locke's federative power theory that control over foreign policy does not belong to the legislature but instead should be in the hands of those who can better use it for the public good. This theory was, indeed, restated by Kennan who, in almost Platonic terms, argued that foreign policy was no place for mass opinion and that the public should be guided by the judgment of professional experts there just as much as in law and medicine.[11]

At times a serious gap existed between the policies demanded by the external affairs side of the Truman Administration and the policies which were politically feasible for it to put into practice. This was perhaps best illustrated by the history of "NSC 68": the plan for the extensive build-up of American armed strength developed in the winter of 1949–1950 as a reaction to the Soviet explosion of an atomic bomb. The conclusions of NSC 68 were in general vigorously supported by the State Department and by the military echelons of the Defense Department. Louis Johnson, Secretary of Defense, was somewhat less sympathetic toward the expansion program, and the Budget Bureau was definitely opposed to it. The President approved the general principles of NSC 68 in April 1950, subject to the development of the detailed implementing programs and further consideration of their cost. Thus, in the spring of 1950 the Administration, in effect, had two defense policies: a public one embodied in the thirteen billion dollar defense budget recommended for the next fiscal year and a private one embodied in NSC 68. This duality was ended only by the outbreak of the Korean War which permitted the Administration in the summer of 1950 to go ahead with the build-up of forces which had been urged the previous fall by the supporters of NSC 68.

As the history of NSC 68 indicates, Congress and the public could not be excluded from many of the most important decisions on foreign policy. The principal area of continuous legislative participation was, of course, appropriations for defense and foreign aid. Here the policies of the foreign affairs side of the Administration ran into the interests of the domestic agencies pushing the claims of their programs and the everpresent demands for economy, a balanced budget, and reduced taxes. Consequently, it was in this area that the conservative foreign policy was left incomplete.[12] In the long run, no foreign policy was feasible which did not have legislative and popular support. The Administration had to supplement its other efforts by salesmanship.

The merchandising of containment to the American people, however, was far beyond the scanty political resources of the Truman Administration. The President himself did not command the prestige and respect necessary for the job. The State Department had always suffered from the lack of a domestic constituency. It was furthermore under increasing partisan attack. Its personnel were labeled as incompetent or disloyal, and it became the symbol of popular frustration with the course of foreign affairs. Mr. Acheson, moreover, had at times a somewhat cool disregard for the sensitivities of public opinion; by 1951 even most Democrats in Congress favored his dismissal. As Republicans or conservative Democrats in what was normally regarded as a liberal Democratic Administration, the civilian leaders of foreign affairs were in effect politically sterile. New Dealers and party-line Republicans both had their suspicions of a Lovett or a Hoffman.

The Administration consequently was forced to turn to the military professionals to explain and justify its policies before Congress and the public. To a considerable extent this was done by appointing men such as Marshall to civilian posts. Reliance was also placed upon the Joint Chiefs themselves. The Joint Chiefs still retained much of their World War II prestige. They commanded attention as a professional, disinterested body, and the complete aloofness of their members from public affairs prior to 1940 made it impossible to associate them with radicalism or any other form of sordid politics. Thus, although it was the existence of a special conservative foreign affairs environment which permitted the Chiefs to return to their professional outlook, it was also the existence of this special environment which forced them to become its public advocates before the country. Within the foreign affairs side of the Administration the tension between military professional and civilian statesman which had characterized American civil-military relations for seventy-five years evaporated in a unity of outlook as real as that of World War II but far different in substance. Given the prevalence of liberalism in the American mind, however, this tension reappeared along the line between the foreign affairs sector, and the rest of the political community. The military became the principal ambassadors of the former to the latter. They pleaded for foreign aid appropriations, urged the ratification of treaties, defended the assignment of American troops to Europe, justified the dismissal of General MacArthur, defended the conduct of the Korean War, and explained the Administration's decisions on force levels and budgets. Generally speaking, they did not relish this role, but they were drawn into it by the needs of the Administration. Before both congressional committees and civic groups they acted as political advocates. Symbolic of their activities was General Bradley's famous talk before the Pasadena Chamber of Commerce on March 20, 1952 in which he castigated the "Gibraltar theory" of defense advocated by Hoover and Taft as "selfish" and "defensive," and urged a policy of balanced military strength without overweighting of air power. As Hanson Baldwin acutely pointed out at the time, Bradley's views were simply "military common sense," yet he had no business adding them to the rising tide of a presidential election.[13]

For a while the Joint Chiefs were a success in their advocatory role, capitalizing upon the combined prestige of military hero and technical expert. Congress listened to Bradley when it ignored Acheson. Eventually, however, the military currency began to lose value. The unpopularity of the policies which they were advocating lowered the personal and institutional prestige of the men who were advocating them. Although they still adhered to their professional views on the substance of policy, the Joint Chiefs inevitably opened themselves to partisan criticism by ardently defending that policy in public on behalf of an administration which had adopted it as a political course. This mounted rapidly after the outbreak of the Korean War and intensified with the firing of MacArthur. "I have come to the point where I do not accept them as experts," Senator Taft declared in the spring of 1951, "particularly when General Bradley makes a foreign policy speech. I suggest that the Joint Chiefs of Staff are absolutely under the control of the Administration . . ." In more restrained terms the Republican foreign policy spokesman, John Foster Dulles, also criticized the role of the military in foreign policy.[14] By 1952 their persuasiveness had largely been dissipated.

The carrying out for half a dozen years of a conservative foreign policy on behalf of a fundamentally liberal nation was, in a sense, a considerable political achievement for the Truman Administration. But, inevitably, it could not last. Just as it had been impossible for the military to remain conservative in World War II, so also was it impossible for the combined military-civilian foreign policy agencies to maintain a conservative policy in the Cold War. The issue came to a head over the conduct of the Korean War and subsequently was a major element in the Democratic defeat of 1952. A critic might say that this simply proved the Lincolnian dictum that you can't fool all the people all the time. But that is unfair. That the conservative policy lasted as long as it did is a tribute to the ability of the Administration to make the best of scant resources. That it came to an end when it did is a tribute to the vitality of American democracy.

THE KOREAN WAR: THE GENERALS, THE TROOPS, AND THE PUBLIC

The Korean War broke the Truman pattern of civil-military relations. It aroused public interest in and indignation over foreign policy; it stimulated opposition, partisan and otherwise, in Congress; it exhausted the political influence of the Joint Chiefs. The Korean War was the first war in American history (except for the Indian struggles) which was not a crusade. It was also the first time that public resentment of the conduct of a war contributed to the ousting of the party in power.

The war was extraordinary in many ways but certainly no more so than in the peculiar relations which existed among the Administration which was conducting the war, the generals who were directing it in the field, the troops who were fighting it in the front lines, and the people who were supporting it at home. The fundamental decision of the Truman Administration was to fight the war for the limited political objective of maintaining the independence of South Korea. To be sure this decision was not reached overnight. Rather, it emerged out of the confusion of events and the complexities of lesser decisions during the long, hard winter of 1950–1951. But, once it had been established, the Administration held to it with a stubborn persistence. All the civilian and military leaders of the Administration — the President, Acheson, Marshall, Lovett, Bradley, the Joint Chiefs — were in agreement on this fundamental concept. This decision, together with its domestic corollaries of limited mobilization and the rebuilding of conventional military forces, was, of course, an essentially conservative one. The United States had no sweeping goals; it simply wished to reestablish the *status quo ante*. This required the careful measurement and calculated employment of the military force to achieve this goal. Fighting a war according to Clausewitz rather than Ludendorff, however, was a new experience to Americans and one which they generally were unwilling to accept. The fundamental problem of the Administration, consequently, was to secure the support or at least the acquiescence of the troops, the generals and the public in this novel undertaking.

The Administration scored a success with the troops. At the beginning of the war the United States Army was in poor shape. The units pulled suddenly out of the soft life of occupied Japan and thrown into a fight against a more numerous foe had a tough time of it. They were undisciplined, poorly trained, and psychologically unprepared for combat. By the spring of 1951, however, the Eighth Army had been rebuilt into a tough, battle-experienced fighting force. The political objectives of the Administration, however, did not permit it either to push on to complete military victory or to withdraw completely from the peninsula. Consequently, the problem became the maintenance of troop morale in an apparently indefinite and indecisive conflict in a far-off corner of the earth. Both material and psychological means were tried. Materially, once the front had become stabilized, every effort was made to make the existence of the soldier as comfortable as possible: a shower once a day, mail twice a day, and hot food three times a day. No means were spared to incorporate as much of the American civilian standard of living as possible into the Main Line of Resistance. By the end of the conflict American troops were fighting on a level of physical luxury and comfort unique in world history.

Equally important, however, in securing the acceptance of the war by the troops was the policy of rotation which shaped the psychology of the front lines. Unlike the provision of material benefits, this represented a sharp break with the American past. In World War II, soldiers were in for the duration: they could only achieve their personal goal of getting home when the government achieved its political goal of military victory. In Korea, however, rotation divorced the personal goals of the troops from the political goals of the government. The aim of the soldier was simply to endure his nine months at the front and then get out. The war was a necessary evil, and he acquiesced and accepted it as such. His attitude was brilliantly summed up in that classic expression of Stoic resignation which emerged out of the front lines: "That's the way the ball bounces." For the first time in American history the common soldier fought a major war solely and simply because he was ordered to fight it and not because he shared any identification with the political goals for which the war was being fought. Instead he developed a supreme indifference to the political goals of the war — the traditional hallmark of the professional. And "professional" was the one term seized upon by newsmen and observers to describe the peculiar psychology of the Korean fighting man as distinguished from his World War II counterpart.[15]

In some ways the spirit of World War II posed as many problems as the Communists in the conduct of the Korean War. Rotation worked a miraculous change in the psychology of the troops, but there was nothing comparable to change the attitudes of the generals who directed the war in the field. There was "no discharge in the war" for them; they continued to think in World War II terms. The only proper end of war was military victory, and they could not understand why this should be denied them. If the Army had been ordered off to fight the Korean War in 1939 there is little doubt but that, from the Chief of Staff down, obediently and without thinking it would have gone and fought the war under the conditions it was told to fight it under. General Marshall, indeed, contrasted General MacArthur's behavior with Pershing's obedient acceptance of the confining political restrictions imposed by Wilson on the Mexican punitive expedition of 1916.[16] The Joint Chiefs in the sympathetic environment in the Truman Administration could return to their prewar professional moorings. But for the commanders in the field, imbued with the World War II psychology and encouraged by the political and popular resentment at home, this was impossible. Substantively divorced from the military ethic, their subordinate position in a conservative Administration in a liberal country tended to force an advocatory role on them also. The civilian exaltation of military victory as the supreme political goal in World War II thus came back to haunt the civilians ten years later. The responsibility which had once been abdicated was

not easily regained. Ironically, General MacArthur's phrase —
"There is no substitute for victory" — might well have been inspired
by the ghost of FDR.

The result was that, if "professional" summed up the attitude
of the troops, "frustrated" described that of the generals. The
troops were willing to accept the way the ball bounced, the generals
were not. They reacted. They protested. They evaded. They
squirmed. As Homer Bigart reported:

> Few of the soldiers seem able to identify themselves with any na-
> tional goal. Caught up in a stern, primitive and often miserable exist-
> ence, the soldier's perception becomes so blunted that foresight is
> limited to the individual goal — rotation. The officer, with more oppor-
> tunity for thought, broods over the apparent futility of the stalemate and
> yearns for rotation. But the generals are driven almost frantic by job
> frustration.[17]

The extent to which the generals as a group of field commanders
were out of sympathy with the policy of the government probably
had few precedents in American history. Even in the Civil War
there was never the unanimity of military dissent manifested in
Korea. Except for General Ridgway, virtually all the field commanders — MacArthur, Van Fleet, Stratemeyer, Almond, Clark,
Joy — irrespective of whether or not they had previous associations
with MacArthur or the Far East shared what the Jenner Committee
succinctly described as "a feeling of unease because victory was
denied, a sense of frustration and a conviction that political considerations had overruled the military . . ." General Clark reported that all the commanders in the Far East with whom he discussed the issue hoped that the government would remove the political restrictions which denied them victory.[18]

The closest recent parallel to the mass dissatisfaction of the
Korean field commanders was the discontent of the atomic scientists
with government policy toward the construction of nuclear and
thermonuclear weapons. In each case, a well defined body of professional employees took a political stand against the policies of
the government which they served. In each case, the discontent of
the expert group had deep roots in American public opinion and
was directed against an essentially conservative policy embodying

fundamental assumptions of the military ethic. The physicists refused to accept the burdens and frustrations of an indefinite nuclear arms race with Russia and demanded an end to them by negotiated disarmament. The generals in Korea refused to accept the burdens and frustrations of an indefinite limited war with Communist China and demanded an end to them by total military victory. In each case the principal exponent of the discontent — MacArthur and Oppenheimer — was a charismatic figure, touched with an almost religious mysticism, who aroused intense emotional loyalties and hatreds, and who eventually was unceremoniously ejected from the government.

In the final analysis, the continued viability of the Truman Administration's policy depended upon its acceptance by the public. But, while the public might take it for a while, the public would not take it indefinitely. In an inarticulate, irrational, and emotional way, the American people still adhered to the attitudes to which Harold Lasswell had given intellectualized expression in his garrison-state essays. The traditional responses refused to die. If the troops sided with the Administration, the public sided with the generals. Indeed, as Walter Millis pointed out, the real problem of morale was not at the front but at home. The dissidence of the generals became the focus and crystallizing point of public discontent. The accumulated public irritation and frustration was a political fact which the opposition party could not ignore. Eisenhower might well have won without the Korean War. But even his appeal as a personality was largely tied in with the feeling that he would "do something" about foreign policy. Insofar as there was a dominant issue in the election, it was certainly Korea.[19] The Van Fleet letter, the promise to visit Korea, the assertion that Asians should fight Asians, the front-page publicity for casualty lists and pictures of the dead and wounded — all reminded the American people of the unpleasant realities in East Asia and stimulated them to cast their vote for the hope that these might be brought to a quick halt.

THE JOINT CHIEFS IN THE FIRST TWO YEARS
OF THE EISENHOWER ADMINISTRATION

UNITY. Certainly one of the most fundamental changes which the Eisenhower Administration made in the governmental pattern of its predecessor was to reunite foreign and domestic policy according to a common outlook. In a sense, this was what the American people had voted for in 1952. The new unity was reflected most obviously in the leadership of the government. The Republican Administration was, literally, a team. Its principal executives were recruited from the ranks of business, particularly manufacturing, or from those who shared the business philosophy. "We're here in the saddle," said the Secretary of the Interior quite truthfully, "as an Administration representing business and industry." The proportion of business executives in top positions in the government was just about double that of the Truman Administration.[20] It was unfair to refer to the cabinet as composed of eight millionaires and a plumber, but the element of truth in this wisecrack was emphasized by the early and controversial departure of the plumber. In general, cabinet officials displayed not only an amazing homogeneity of outlook but also an extraordinary continuity and stability in office.

Unlike the Truman Administration, the same type of men ran both the domestic agencies and the foreign-defense units of the government. The proportion of businessmen in the Defense Department was about as high as the proportion in the Commerce Department. At the end of the Administration's first year in office, seventeen out of twenty-four officials of secretarial rank in the Department of Defense were business or corporation executives.[21] The sharp cleavage of background and outlook characteristic of the Truman Administration had disappeared. Forrestal did not talk the language of Hannegan or Chapman. But Wilson had no difficulty communicating with Summerfield or McKay: they had all been connected with the same industrial complex. The Administration, moreover, was all of the same party. The State and Defense Departments, which under Truman had been part Democrat and part Republican, became thoroughly Republican under Eisenhower.

The unity of the Eisenhower Administration reflected a fairly profound development in politics and public opinion. Traditionally American liberalism was split between a Whig branch, reflecting the interests of business and the economically better-off groups of society, and the popular democratic branch of reform liberalism with its roots in the farmers, small business, and labor. While there was little fundamental ideological conflict between these two segments, there were differences of economic interest. In periods of economic distress the party of reform or popular liberalism was usually able to outvote its rival. Since 1932 this had been the means whereby the Democrats had maintained themselves in office. The Republicans, consequently, had to surmount the prevailing tendency to think in terms of a conflict between the interests of business and the interests of the people. The Eisenhower Administration achieved an identification of interest between business liberalism and popular liberalism by shifting the locus of controversy from domestic policy to foreign policy. In this area popular attitudes reinforced business interests. Business, instead of being the opponent of the popular will, became its champion. The split between the business and popular viewpoints on domestic affairs had made the Democratic Party the majority party so long as economic issues were preëminent. The unity of the business and popular viewpoints on foreign-defense policy gave the Republicans the majority when those problems came to the fore.

DEFENSE LIBERALISM. The traditional proclivities of American liberalism manifested themselves in the Eisenhower Administration's defense policies in a variety of ways. The foreign policy of the Administration was to be guided by "openness, simplicity, and righteousness." [22] The liberal tendency to absolutize and dichotomize war and peace was reflected in the Administration's hostility toward persistent limited involvements. The Korean War was brought to a close, and the "massive retaliation" policy was enunciated with the hope of averting further conflicts of this nature. In the spring of 1954 the Administration did consider intervention in Indochina but the opposition of Congress and the British caused it to abandon this proposal. Liberal optimism was reflected in the Administration's evaluation of the strength of the Russian foe. Secretary Wilson and Deputy Secretary Kyes early indicated their disbelief of pessimistic service estimates and consistently maintained that American military forces were the best in the world, and that the United States had a long lead over the Russians in weapons technology. The Administration also tended to define the goals of American policy in more sweeping and universalistic terms than did its predecessor. The goal of the "liberation" of Eastern Europe was emphasized in the 1952 campaign, and even after coming into office, the Administration continued to stress the desirability of a "more dynamically anti-communist" policy. The leaders of the Defense Department tended to adhere to the liberal belief that domestic and economic solutions were applicable to the problems of military security. The same techniques, policies, and organization which produced success in business could also produce success in government. The traditional liberal hostility to military institutions and military force manifested itself in the Administration's efforts to find substitutes for large military forces as a means to national security. In the Administration's first year it was argued that a strong economy was our first line of defense and military forces should not be maintained which might threaten financial stability or national solvency. In the second year of the Administration the technological substitute was emphasized: American possession of a variety of nuclear and thermonuclear weapons would justify a reduction in conventional military forces. In the Administration's third year stress was placed upon the creation of a substantial reserve of citizen-soldiers as the alternative to a large standing army. Throughout this period the Administration gave high priority to a balanced budget and reduced taxes and, consequently, reduced military expenditures. It was here, of course, that in practical terms the business liberalism of the Administration most closely coincided with the popular desires of the people.

The Eisenhower Administration expected the Joint Chiefs of Staff to share in this liberal philosophy. This meant that the qualifications of a desirable JCS member for the Eisenhower Administration differed considerably from those of one for the previous administration. The Truman Administration needed military leaders with the political prestige to carry the Administration's policies. The Eisenhower Administration wanted agreement not advocacy from its military Chiefs. They were, in Secretary Wilson's words, to be members of the team — not spokesmen for it. The initial appointments to the JCS in the spring of 1953 reflected this desire to secure men who would share the "new look" of the Administration rather than ones who would have political weight with Congress and the public. This same tendency was carried even further two years later with the selection of Rear Admiral Burke as Chief of Naval Operations. The Truman Administration probably could never have afforded politically to dip so low into the flag officer ranks. The appointment of the Chiefs for no specified term and the stated intention to review all appointments after two years indicated that the Administration was more interested in securing agreement than in enhancing the status of its military leaders. The Rockefeller Committee which drew up the reorganization plan for the Pentagon in the spring of 1953 emphasized the desirability of a unified civilian-military thinking. It was impossible, the Committee said, "to make a sufficiently clear distinction between military affairs, on the one hand, and on the other hand civilian affairs (such as political, economic, and industrial affairs) to serve as a practicable basis for dividing responsibility between military and civilian officers, or for establishing two parallel lines of command." [23] The report also urged the Secretary of Defense to participate in meetings of the Joint Chiefs. Whereas the Truman Chiefs had argued that they spoke purely "from the military viewpoint," a directive from Secretary Wilson in the summer of 1954 ordered the Chiefs in discharging their statutory responsibilities to "avail themselves of the most competent and considered thinking that can be obtained representing every pertinent point of view, including military, scientific, industrial and economic." [24] The President reportedly declared that he wanted only unanimous decisions from the Joint Chiefs. Subsequently, when he found himself dissenting from the Administration viewpoint, General Ridgway charged that he had been subjected to "incessant pressure" to persuade him to "conform to a preconceived politico-military 'party line.'" When the general refused to adjust his thinking, it was made clear to him that he was not to let his "nonconcurrence publicly be known." [25]

Despite these various efforts by the Administration to insure a harmonious viewpoint, it took a while for the new Joint Chiefs to adjust their thinking to the new philosophy. Upon taking office in the summer of 1953 they were directed to formulate a "new look" military strategy taking into consideration both military factors and the new Administration's fiscal policy. Despite this injunction they came up in the fall with virtually the same force level proposals as their Truman predecessors. The National Security

Council, however, rejected these recommendations and directed the military to produce a strategic plan which would cost less money.[26] This in itself, of course, did not transgress civil-military responsibilities, nor would the Joint Chiefs have abandoned a military role if they had simply complied with the directive and produced the best recommendations possible within the NSC budgetary limit. But the evidence suggests that some members of the Joint Chiefs went beyond this. They did not just accept the limits set by the political authorities; they also incorporated into their own thinking the assumptions which were uppermost in the minds of the political leaders. This was particularly true of the chairman of the JCS, Admiral Radford. To a lesser degree it was also true of Admiral Carney and General Twining. It was not true of General Ridgway who essayed a strictly professional role adhering to his independent military judgment yet accepting the subordination of this judgment to that of the President and his civilian advisers. Rejecting Bradley's warning of the previous summer that military men should not make economic and political judgments, Radford argued that the Joint Chiefs should begin with estimates of the total national income and then

. . . make an assumption as to the amount that might be allotted for defense . . .

Without any reservation, I subscribe to the theory that as military men, in trying to work out plans for the long pull . . . we must take economic factors into consideration . . .

From figures that we obtained on prospective national income over the long pull, we eliminated the more or less fixed expenses, and within the remaining estimated amount, we did feel . . . that we came up with a military program which was adequate . . .[27]

Subsequently, Admiral Radford indicated his complete support for the reduced budget of the "New Look," a position which he took again the following year when the second stage of the Administration's military reductions were before Congress. The Eisenhower Joint Chiefs also tended to adopt as a part of their thinking the assumptions advanced by Secretary Dulles as to the desirability of a more active anticommunist policy. In the spring of 1954, Admiral Radford urged intervention in the Indochinese War by carrier air strikes at the enemy forces attacking Dienbienphu.[28]

In the fall of 1954 the Joint Chiefs (Ridgway dissenting) recommended that the United States intervene by bombing the Chinese mainland if necessary in order to defend the Nationalist held offshore islands (Quemoy) against Communist attack. Still later, after touring the Far East, Admiral Radford was apparently able to secure a partial and somewhat beclouded endorsement by the Administration of his position. At about the same time he indicated that he would support a blockade of the Chinese coast if this were necessary to secure the release of Americans held by the Communists.[29]

The full extent to which Admiral Radford's outlook deviated from the military ethic was revealed in the document on *Militant Liberty* which he sponsored.[30] Prepared in the admiral's office, this eighteen-page pamphlet attempted to state for the guidance of the Armed Forces "the principles upon which our nation was founded." Defining the conflict between the Western and Soviet blocs in purely ideological terms, *Militant Liberty* drew a neat dichotomy between the two: the strength of Communism was the *"Annihilated* Conscience of the Individual"; the strength of the Free World was the *"Sensitive* Conscience of the Individual." The nations of the world, it was argued, can be rated on a scale of from plus-one hundred to minus-one hundred, in terms of the extent to which they balance rights and responsibilities in six areas of human activity. Coming from any place outside of the Government of the United States, the pamphlet would be put down as the naïve, amusing, and harmless work of an eccentric. Issuing from the Pentagon, however, it was a warning symptom of the derangement of American civil-military relations: at one and the same time a measure of the civilian abdication and a devastating example of what can happen when generals and admirals follow fusionist advice to abandon their military knitting and venture into political philosophy.

IMPLEMENTATION. The political strength of the Eisenhower Administration, the popularity of its civilian leaders, and the popularity of its policies made it unnecessary for the Joint Chiefs to become involved in the public advocacy of policy on anything like the scale of their predecessors. Whereas the Truman Administration had encouraged its military leaders to speak out on policy questions, the Eisenhower Administration preferred silence. It rebuffed military chiefs such as Admiral Carney when they did speak out of turn and instituted elaborate clearance procedures for statements and articles issuing from the military. The Administration felt little need or desire for the military leaders to plead for Administration policies before the public. During his last two years as Chairman of the JCS during the Truman Administration (January 1951–January 1953), General Bradley made fifty-seven public appearances before Congress, civilian groups, and over radio and television in which he discussed important issues of military policy. In contrast, Admiral Radford, in his first two years as JCS Chairman (August 1953–August 1955), made only thirty-nine such statements.* General Bradley delivered the classic exposition of the Truman military policy in his "Gibraltar" speech and frequently made broad statements on foreign policy. The classic formulation of the military policy of the Eisenhower Administration, on the other hand, was not made by a general nor even by the Secretary of Defense, but rather by Secretary Dulles in his "massive retaliation" speech. The rejoinder to Democratic attacks upon this policy was also made by the Secretary at a press conference and in an article in *Foreign Affairs* and by Vice President Nixon in a national radio address. The only significant contribution of the Joint Chiefs to the debate were the qualifying remarks made by Admiral Radford in a speech on March 9, 1954 and at a military budget hearing before the Senate Appropriations Committee two days after the Vice President's talk. The Indochinese crisis followed a similar pattern. Although Admiral Radford was a prime mover in the development of policy, he played only a minor role in its public announcement. The lead was taken initially by the President in his statements on March 24 and April 7 and by Secretary Dulles in his New York speech of March 29. The Vice President again played a key role with his famous "off the record" talk to the newspaper editors on April 16. When intervention was finally rejected, it was Dulles who signaled the change in the Administration's intentions. Radford's one significant public statement came in a speech on April 15 which, however, only repeated what the President and

* These include: formal, public congressional hearings: Bradley, 18–Radford, 16; addresses before nonmilitary groups: Bradley, 26–Radford, 23; additional radio and TV appearances: Bradley, 13–Radford, none. Compiled from public documents and information supplied by General Bradley and Admiral Radford.

the Secretary of State had already said, and which was quickly forgotten with the Vice President's more extreme pronouncement the following day.

The Administration's failure to utilize the military leaders for purposes of advocacy reflected its lack of need for political support from this source. Bradley was a strong ally for Truman, but what need did Eisenhower have for Radford? The Administration also in many respects paid a more respectful attention to the views of Congress on defense policy matters such as Indochina and Formosa, and consequently was less in need of means of persuading Congress to validate its own viewpoint. At times the Eisenhower Chiefs made speeches on policy and argued for Administration programs before Congressional committees. But these roles were considerably less important for them than for their predecessors.

CONCLUSION

The patterns of civil-military relations in the two administrations reflected differing efforts to ease the tension between military professionalism and liberal politics. So long as basic American attitudes toward war and the military continue in their traditional mold, the Joint Chiefs will be pushed toward either an advocatory political role, a substantive political role, or some combination of the two. Since it is unlikely that the military themselves will possess again the prestige and popularity which they did immediately after World War II, it is unlikely that any subsequent administration will be able to utilize their political support to the extent that the Truman Administration did. But if the party in power does attempt to follow a conservative and unpopular line, whatever aid the military can contribute will certainly be invoked in merchandising that policy to the public. If a more popular policy is followed, on the other hand, the Joint Chiefs will be expected to adhere to the prevailing views. Inevitably, the Chiefs must be either representatives of public opinion or pleaders before it.

15

The Separation of Powers and
Cold War Defense

THE IMPACT OF THE SEPARATION OF POWERS

The continued high level of defense activities required by the Cold War intensified the impact of the separation of powers on civil-military relations in three ways. First, it enhanced the role of Congress with respect to both military policy and military administration. Second, it shifted the focus of congressional-military relations from the supply units of the military departments to the professional heads of the services and thereby heightened the tension between the separation of powers and military professionalism. Third, it tended to produce a pluralistic or balanced national military strategy.

THE SEPARATION OF POWERS VERSUS THE SEPARATION OF FUNCTIONS

THE CHANGE IN CONGRESSIONAL INTEREST. The increased importance of military affairs during the Cold War necessarily and legitimately resulted in increased congressional involvement in military policy and military administration. Prior to 1940 Congress had little concern with military policy as such. It viewed the activities of the War and Navy Departments from a relatively limited, narrow perspective. Congressional interest focused upon the location of Army posts and Navy yards, military construction, military procurement, and, in general, upon where and to whom military expenditures were made rather than for what they were made. Sectional, economic, and local interests were the motivating factors in congressional concern with military matters. Debates on military appropriations were lightly attended and discussion frequently ran far afield on topics quite unrelated to military spending.[1] Congressional consideration of major issues of military policy was limited to occasional bills on Army organization such as the National Defense Acts of 1916 and 1920 and to major authorizations of naval construction such as those of 1916, 1934, and 1938. Apart from these instances, however, Congress gave little attention to military policy for the simple reason that military policy was not politically significant enough to warrant its attention.

In the ten years following World War II, however, Congress was almost constantly occupied with major substantive issues of military policy: selective service, universal military training, the size of the active forces, the composition of the reserve forces, the organization of the defense establishment, the conditions of service for officers and enlisted men. Each year, in addition, the annual appropriations for the armed services raised the most significant issues of military policy, and the annual authorizations for military and naval construction and for military assistance necessitated important decisions. The transformation of military affairs into an area of vital public concern made it impossible to maintain the constitutional division of function which assigned to the President the authority of the English king to command and administer the military forces and gave to Congress the authority of the English Parliament to determine their existence, size, and composition.

THE DUPLICATION OF FUNCTIONS. One of the peculiarities of American national government is the conflict between the constitutional separation of powers and the constitutional separation of functions. The Framers made Congress and the President independent of each other, drawing authority from separate clauses of the Constitution and acquiring power and influence from separate constituencies through different systems of election. These separate sources of power have been further enhanced by the "differential access of interest groups" to Congress and the President: some interests are better able to achieve their ends by working through the President, others by working through Congress. The independence of Congress and President from each other and from any other higher institutional authority means that both share in the ultimate power to govern. Inevitably, the result is continuous rivalry and friction. The Constitution, however, also provides for a separation of functions. In the broadest terms, Congress has the legislative function and the President the executive function, although the Constitution does assign some executive duties to Congress and some legislative duties to the President. In actual practice, however, the constitutional separation of powers undermines the constitutional separation of functions. The constant rivalry between Congress and President leads each to invade the constitutional realm of the other in any major substantive area of governmental activity. In pursuing their ends, neither the President nor congressional leaders recognize theoretical, legal distinctions between legislative and executive functions. Congress investigates, calls administrative officials to account, doles out funds in limited quantities and for specific purposes, and in many ways penetrates far deeper into the administrative process than does the President. The Chief Executive, on the other hand, formulates major policies, initiates the legislative program for each session, implements sweeping grants of authority through executive orders and regulations, and in reality determines the over-all direction of government policy. Under the separation of powers, Congress and the President must both administer and legislate. That is the iron law of institutional survival. The power to govern cannot be restricted or divided. If each branch is to share in it, each branch must exercise it at every opportunity. The separation of powers thus leads inevitably to the duplication of functions.

The collapse of the separation of functions before the separation of powers is normally lamented by reactionaries who attack the President for usurping the policy-making functions of Congress and by academics who criticize Congress for busying itself with administrative detail. In reality, however, the widespread distribution of power rather than the efficient allocation of function is the central value of the American constitutional pantheon. Divided power results in continuous overlapping and conflicting jurisdictions between the national government and the states, among the three branches of the national government, among executive bureaus and agencies, and between rival congressional committees. Many people do the work of others, and the legal profession and the courts acquire exceptional importance because of the constant need to adjudicate rival powers and claims. Other results of the dispersion of power, however, are the need to secure the agreement of virtually all interested parties (Calhoun's concurrent majority) before taking action, the democratic multiplication of the avenues of access to government, and the mutual restraint which all groups and governmental bodies exercise on each other and which prevents the arbitrary and dictatorial use of power. In moving in on each other's functional preserves, Congress and the President exemplify the basic genius of American government.

THE POLICY AND ADMINISTRATIVE ROLES OF CONGRESSIONAL COMMITTEES. Congress discharges its responsibilities for policy and administration through its committees, a majority of which become involved in one way or another with military affairs.[2] Its principal instrumentalities with respect to military policy and military administration in the postwar decade were, however, six in number.* The House and Senate Armed Services Committees were preëminent, combining extensive interests in both policy and administration. The House military appropriations subcommittees used the budgetary process for the detailed probing of military administration. The Senate military appropriations subcommittee attempted a more general consideration of military policy. The House Government Operations Committee went deeply into military administration. The Senate Foreign Relations Committee dealt with the important issues of military policy raised by treaties and the annual mutual assistance acts.

Virtually all bills dealing directly with the military establishment, except military appropriations and reorganization plans, were considered by the House Armed Services Committee. In the Eightieth through the Eighty-second Congresses it held extensive

* This estimate of the role of congressional committees with respect to military affairs is based on their operations from 1947 through 1954. The Senate Government Operations Committee, with the exception of a well-publicized series of hearings on the Army in 1953 and 1954, only rarely probed military matters, and its infrequent incursions into this field were generally offshoots of investigations whose primary foci were elsewhere, for example, subversion or influence in government procurement. The House Committee on Foreign Affairs considered the annual military assistance bill, but otherwise did not go deeply into military matters. The Joint Committee on Atomic Energy, of course, dealt regularly with issues in which the Defense Department had a direct interest.

hearings upon measures dealing with officer promotion policy, universal military training, selective service, Army organization, the uniform code of military justice, the National Security Act Amendments of 1949, military pay scales, Air Force organization, and the armed forces reserve bill. In addition, its investigation of "Unification and Strategy" in 1949 occasioned the most thorough probing of postwar national military policy prior to the MacArthur hearings. Its chairmen and members maintained a constant interest in the actions of the appropriations committees with respect to the size and composition of the armed forces. The House Committee also went deeply into essentially administrative matters. No aspect of the military establishment was held to be outside its legitimate area of concern. The investigations of the Committee probed into conditions at various military posts and stations, the administration of the military medical services, Air Force safety procedures and air hitchhikers, procurement methods, the operation of ordnance facilities. The extent of the Committee's administrative involvement was reflected in the requirement that each military department secure the approval of the House and Senate Armed Services Committees before it acquired or disposed of any real estate valued at more than $25,000. The House Naval Affairs Committee first achieved this power with respect to the Navy Department in 1944. At the beginning of the Eighty-first Congress in 1949, Carl Vinson, the new Democratic chairman of the Armed Services Committee and former chairman of the House Naval Affairs Committee, announced the appointment of a special subcommittee to exercise the Committee's responsibilities with respect to Navy real estate transactions. In a colloquy which strikingly illustrated the tendency of the constitutional separation of functions to become a nullity, he then went on to say:

THE CHAIRMAN. Now, in that connection, while this subject is up, I think it highly important that we have our staff prepare a bill covering the Army and Air Force with reference to all acquisitions and disposals of land and that we should have the same jurisdiction over those two Departments as well as over the Navy Department . . .

MR. KILDAY. May I suggest, Mr. Chairman, that we put that in some other legislation to avoid the possibility of veto?

THE CHAIRMAN. Well, that might be a good idea. But it is sufficient to stand on its own merits. It is clearly within the authority of Congress to have a voice in disposals.

Now, there may be some doubt as to the constitutionality of acquisitions, but there is not any question as to disposals . . . Now, of course, the weakness of our position is that it is not Congress but it is the committee. That might raise a question. But we will cross that bridge when we get to it. So, Mr. Smart, fix up a bill and we will have that to consider . . .

Now, we will designate Mr. Brown, of the professional staff, to carry on this work [on Navy transactions] as he did under Mr. Bates. I want to compliment you on your work and I hope your records are all up to date. I have not checked on it but I am trusting it is all right, so that we will all know what is going on . . .

Well, I think it is a fine control. I want this committee to have something to do with running the departments instead of the departments just telling the committee what they are going to do.

The next matter is the appointment of the special committee to handle the disposal of special properties by the Department of the Navy.

You see, gentlemen, a great many of these things relate specifically to the Navy because when we were guiding the destinies of the Navy we felt that the committee should have a hand in a great many things.

I feel that same way with reference to all the armed services.[3]

Despite Mr. Kilday's warnings, Chairman Vinson attempted to secure his authority in a separate piece of legislation. The President vetoed it. Mr. Vinson then wrote these provisions into the Military and Naval Construction Act of 1951, which, perforce, Mr. Truman had no choice but to sign. The Committee has not infrequently used this power to veto military real estate transactions or to force changes in the terms of the contract.

The Senate Armed Services Committee normally devoted a larger proportion of its effort to major pieces of legislation than did its House counterpart. Unlike the latter, it participated in the consideration of military assistance legislation with the foreign affairs committees, and it maintained close ties with the Senate military appropriations subcommittee. In 1951 it joined with the Foreign Relations Committee in the two major investigations of national military policy concerning the relief of General MacArthur and the assignment of additional American forces to Europe. Investigations were normally carried out by special subcommittees. Most significant in the period under discussion was the Preparedness Subcommittee under the leadership of Senator Lyndon Johnson which during the Korean War investigated a wide variety of subjects in military policy and administration including military tables of organization, the rate of build-up of the Air Forces, the shortage of tungsten, the administration of the Munitions Board, the construction of the North African air bases, the operation of military induction centers, the Army's procurement of paint, and the comparative firepower of American and Russian divisions. In the Eighty-third Congress two special preparedness subcommittees carried out investigations of the shortage of ammunition in Korea and the procurement of aircraft. The Senate Committee also shared with the House Armed Services Committee responsibility for authorizing the detailed public works expenditures and for approving military real estate transactions. At the beginning of the Eighty-third Congress, the Committee called a halt to the spending of fifty to sixty million dollars on overseas air base construction until a study could be made of the military construction program. The Senate Committee had the additional important power of acting upon all promotions in the armed services and the appointment of the Chiefs of Staff and top-level civilian officials of the Department of Defense. Occasionally the Committee refused to approve the promotion of officers who had been publicly criticized for misperformance of duty. On the other hand, the Committee was also able to secure the promotion of officers who apparently had been neglected or discriminated against by the executive branch.*

The National Security Act of 1947 and the reorganization of the Defense Department in 1953 were both considered in the House by its Committee on Government Operations (formerly the Committee on Expenditures in the Executive Departments). Aside from these major issues of organizational policy, the military in-

* In 1953 the Committee successfully threatened to hold up promotions in the Navy unless provision was made for the advancement of the Navy's atomic submarine expert, Captain Hyman Rickover, to flag rank. In 1955 the Committee attempted to limit the discretion of the President in making job assignments of high-level officers by demanding that the promotions of individuals to be lieutenant generals and full generals should only be for specific posts. The executive, on the other hand, maintained that promotions should be made without consideration of future assignment. The Committee's position was in effect a return to the preprofessional system in which rank was dependent upon office instead of being a prerequisite to office. See *Army Navy Air Force Journal,* XCII (Mar. 19, 1955), 848, (May 7, 1955), 1053, 1064.

terest of the Government Operations Committee was almost entirely in administration, management, supply, and procurement. Its Subcommittee on Government Operations in 1951 and 1952, under the chairmanship of Porter Hardy, carried out extensive inquiries into irregularities in Army procurement and the techniques and procedures of military construction. The Intergovernmental Relations Subcommittee, under Representative Herbert C. Bonner, during the same period investigated military property disposal and military supply management. Other subcommittees went into the military aspects of the federal catalog program and the publicity operations of the War Department with respect to universal military training. In 1953 and 1954 the Riehlman Military Operations Subcommittee continued the interest of its Democratic predecessors in procurement, supply management, and surplus property disposal. In addition it carried out an extensive probe of the organization and administration of military research and development. The operations of the subcommittees frequently involved them in most detailed questions of administration and management in the armed services.[4]

THE MILITARY APPROPRIATIONS PROCESS. The military budget is the single most important annual contact between the military and Congress. It affords Congress the opportunity to consider and lay down the broad lines of military policy and to review in exhaustive detail military procedure and administration. A distinguishing aspect of the military budget process in Congress is the relative freedom possessed by the military appropriations subcommittees in dealing with the budget. In most areas of governmental activity, the fundamental policies and programs are set forth in substantive legislation previously considered by the subject-matter legislative committees and approved by the Congress. The Appropriations Committees operate within these boundaries in determining each year how much money is to be spent in implementing the substantive legislation. With respect to military affairs, however, the pattern is considerably different. The role of substantive legislation in furnishing a guide to the Appropriations Committees is less important than in most other fields. The basic legislation authorizing the personnel and organization strength of the armed forces usually only sets a ceiling which is seldom approached in actuality. The same authorizing legislation may serve as the basis for a budget of thirty billion dollars or for one of sixty billion dollars. In 1950, after the outbreak of the Korean War, moreover, the strength authorizations of the armed services were first suspended and then set at such a high level — five million — as to have no practical effect. Consequently, full responsibility for making the congressional decisions on the size of the military establishment and the relative importance of the various types of force devolved upon the appropriations process. The only major aspects of the military program for which there were detailed authorizations were military pay scales, military assistance to foreign countries, and military public works. Thus, in effect, the Armed Services Committees were excluded from the most important yearly decisions on military policy. Efforts to bridge this gap were made in the Senate by overlapping membership between the Appropriations and Armed Services Committees. The House Armed Services Committee, on the other hand, attempted to influence military appropriations through a variety of means. In 1949, for instance, the Committee passed a resolution urging the expansion of the Air Force to seventy groups, the staff of the Committee prepared a comprehensive military budget which the chairman presented to the Appropriations Committee, and the chairman himself played a key role in securing congressional approval of increased Air Force appropriations and in endeavoring to increase naval air funds. In 1955 the House Armed Services Committee introduced and considered legislation authorizing an extensive naval shipbuilding program while the Appropriations Committee was considering funds for this purpose. The Armed Services Committee hearings gave the Navy an opportunity to make a public case for its program, and particularly for the construction of an additional Forrestal-class carrier, at a time when the leadership of the Appropriations Committee was reported to be opposed to further carrier construction. In general, however, the Appropriations Committees have an unusual degree of latitude in determining military appropriations.

The absence of detailed substantive legislation implies that the military appropriations subcommittees should give careful and extensive attention to broad policy issues. The Appropriations Committees have, however, been subject to vigorous and informed criticism for giving too little attention to military policy issues and for concentrating instead upon matters of administrative detail. The implication of this criticism is that Congress in dealing with the military budget should not get involved in the details of military command and administration, and that it does not give adequate attention to major issues of public policy.[5] The critics, however, are wrong on both counts. The separation of powers demands that Congress become involved in administrative detail in the budget process as in other areas. In practice, moreover, Congress also gives considered and effective attention to the major issues of military policy involved in the budget. Through a division of labor in the military budget process, the House military appropriations subcommittee makes a detailed review of administrative efficiency, waste, and duplication, and the Senate military appropriations subcommittee focuses upon the major issues of military policy. While the implicit rivalry of the two houses tends to lead each into both policy and administration, this division of function between them is nonetheless a reality in practice.

The difference in function of the military appropriations process in the two houses is reflected in differences in organization and procedure. The House appropriations subcommittee normally goes over the military budget first, giving it much longer consideration than it receives in the Senate. As a result, the House is able to analyze proposed and previous expenditures in great detail. Since the House usually does not finish with the military appropriations bill until late spring and since it is desirable to complete action upon it before the end of the fiscal year on June 30, the Senate committee is frequently pressed for time. Hence, it is compelled to focus upon the major issues. Also, the fact that its action follows that of the House gives the Senate an appellate function. The services usually accept the House cuts in less important items and only ask the Senate to restore those which they consider most crucial. The House appropriations subcommittee, moreover, is usually broken down into subsubcommittees on each service while the Senate hearings take place before a single military appropriations subcommittee or before the full Appropriations Committee itself. The hundreds of officials who testify before the House committees are mostly medium level civilian administrators and military officers expert in the fiscal and administrative details of their programs. Testimony before the Senate Committee, on the other hand, is usually monopolized by the Secretaries and the military chiefs, who are concerned with policy rather than administration. In addition, the House hearings are normally secret, although the record is subsequently published, while the Senate hearings since 1947 have usually been public. The former procedure, of course, is more applicable to the probing of administrative detail, while the latter is more appropriate for the broad discussion of public policy. Finally, while the military appropriations subcommittee of the House has relatively few contacts with the House Armed Services Committee, close ties exist between the military appropriations subcommittee of the Senate and the Armed Services Committee in the Senate. In 1953, for instance, four of the fifteen members of the military appropriations subcommittee were also members of the Armed Services Committee. In addition, three other members of the Armed Services Committee participated in appropriation hearings as ex officio representatives of that Committee. This custom, standard practice in the Senate, also tends to make the legislative committee more conscious of the fiscal implications of its actions.

An excellent example of the roles of the two houses in affecting military policy and administration through the budget process was furnished by the Defense Department Appropriations Bill for Fiscal 1953. For three months, from January 10 to April 3, 1952, the bill was before the House military appropriations subcommittee. The subcommittee was divided into four subsubcommittees on the Army, Navy, Air Force, and Military Public Works. Hearings before the full subcommittee lasted twenty-six days: six days for general policy issues concerning the Defense Department as a whole; twelve days devoted to the policy issues of the individual military departments; eight days for the detailed review of proposed appropriations for the Office of the Secretary of Defense. The item by item consideration and justification of the appropriation requests for the military services took twenty-three days before the Navy subsubcommittee, twenty days before the Air Force subsubcommittee, and twenty-two days before the Army subsub-

committee. Twenty-three civilians and 93 officers appeared on behalf of the Navy, 43 civilians and 132 officers for the Army, and
30 civilians and 102 officers for the Air Force. Virtually none of
the testimony of these witnesses dealt with problems of service-
wide policy and interest, and virtually all of it concerned specific
items of minor importance. The subcommittee eventually made
cuts totaling $4,230,000,000 in seventy-eight different items from
the recommended appropriations of $50,921,000,000. The de-
bate on the floor of the House the second week in April brought
to the fore three general policy issues which had not previously
been subject to considered discussion: (1) the size of Air Force
appropriations involving the issue of whether to achieve a 143
wing Air Force in mid-1955, 1956, or later; (2) the size of naval
construction funds involving the issue of building another Forrestal-class carrier; and (3) a proposed limitation of Defense Department expenditures (not appropriations) for fiscal 1953 to
$46 billion. On all three issues the House voted in favor of
economy. But the significance of its action was not in the careful
consideration of these issues — they did not receive that either in
committee or on the floor — but rather that the three were separated out from the mass of other minor issues and details as the
three problems which involved major and controversial considerations of public policy. Fifteen of the twenty days of hearings
before the Senate military appropriations subcommittee between
April 10 and June 21 were devoted almost exclusively to these
and other major policy issues. Most of the testimony came from
secretaries, assistant secretaries, and military chiefs. The nature of
the Soviet threat, the impact of the military budget on the national
economy, the relative desirability of different types of military
force, the strategic role of carrier air power, manpower policy and
procurement, the significance of alternative readiness dates in the
military build-up — all received extensive, intelligent, and thoughtful discussion. The Committee voted to reverse two of the snap
decisions made by the House, recommending elimination of the
expenditures limitation and approval of the Forrestal-class carrier. In two days of Senate debate, June 28 and 30, discussion
again centered upon the major policy issues. The Senate approved
the Committee recommendations in two cases, but also voted in

favor of a 143 wing Air Force by the middle of 1955, restoring $600,000,000 to Air Force procurement funds. The decisions of the Senate reversing the House on all three major issues of policy were accepted by the conference committee and written into law.

It is difficult to see how this budget process could be improved upon. Appropriations details were considered first by a number of small committees working upon different parts of the budget. Their actions were then brought together and approved by the House. Out of this process developed major issues which were then explored thoroughly by the Senate committee and voted upon by the Senate. In general, the Senate tended to be successful in getting the House to accept its decisions on these issues. Throughout recent years the discussion of military policy before the Senate military appropriations subcommittee has been informed, intelligent, and focused upon the most important current issues. The green volumes of Senate hearings are, in fact, one of the best sources for the general nature of American military policy. It was in this forum, for instance, that the implications of the 1953 and 1954 cuts by the Eisenhower Administration in the Air Force and Army were most thoroughly explored. Indeed, so far as one can tell from the information available, it would appear that the 1953 Air Force cuts received somewhat more careful consideration in the Senate committee than they received in the executive branch itself.

THE SEPARATION OF POWERS VERSUS MILITARY PROFESSIONALISM

THE PREWAR PATTERN OF MILITARY-CONGRESSIONAL RELATIONS. Throughout most of American history, the inherent conflict between the separation of powers and objective civilian control has been more latent than overt: the separation of powers exercised a delaying, restraining influence upon the development of military professionalism. The Cold War, however, with its requirement of continued high level defense activity, markedly increased the tension existing between military professionalism and the separation of powers. The increased importance of military policy made the pattern of congressional-military relations which prevailed after 1947 distinctly different from that which existed prior to 1940. The earlier relations were primarily between Congress and the more civilian, supply, and logistic elements in the armed services. The technical services of the Army — the Corps of Engineers, the Quartermaster Corps, the Ordnance Department, the Signal Corps — and the bureaus in the Navy — Yards and Docks, Ordnance, Supplies and Accounts, Construction and Repair, Steam Engineering — had the most intensive and sustained contacts with Congress. The contact of the professional chiefs of the military forces with Congress tended, on the other hand, to be distant and sporadic. This pattern was to be expected, so long as Congress was more interested in the disbursing side of the military establishment than in its fighting side. In dealing with Congress, the chiefs of the technical services and bureaus functioned in part as expert technical advisers and to an even greater extent simply as the representatives of specific organizational interests within the military departments. They did not act in a professional military role. Indeed, they might just as well have been the representatives of civilian agencies. No real elements of civil-military relations were involved in these contacts. The bureaus and services in many cases built up close relations with particular congressional blocs and congressional committees based upon simple mutuality of economic interest. The extreme case, of course, was the complicated pattern of relationships existing among the Army Corps of Engineers, the rivers and harbors lobby, and congressmen from southern and midwestern states. The connections of the Engineers with Congress were fundamentally similar to the congressional relations of other executive bureaus in the Agriculture and Interior Departments which likewise had closely associated client-groups.[6]

The relative lack of importance of military policy issues and the relative disinterest of Congress in such issues also permitted the professional military chiefs in dealing with Congress to act primarily as spokesmen for the executive branch. So long as Congress did not give considered attention to military policy matters, it did not require professional military advice. Consequently, the military chiefs in dealing with Congress, particularly with respect to the military budget, did not present their own independent professional estimates of military needs but instead loyally supported the recommendations of the President. This behavior in part reflected the injunction of the Budget and Accounting Act of 1921 that "No estimate or request for an appropriation and no request for an increase in an item of such estimate or request . . . shall be submitted to Congress or any committee thereof by any officer or employee of any department or establishment, unless at the request of either House of Congress." [7] So long as Congress was not interested in arriving at its own conclusions on military policy and drawing out of the officers their independent views on defense spending, all that the military could do was to support the President. Looking back to the early twenties, General Marshall once commented that

> Speaking very intimately, I saw General Pershing [Chief of Staff of the Army] in the position where his views didn't count at all. He never could get them up for consideration. And yet he was a man of great prestige in this country. But the cuts, and cuts and cuts came despite what he felt. The main reason for this was that he had no opportunity to give public expression without being in the position of disloyalty. Of course, he never would have done that.[8]

Military officers universally felt bound by the President's decisions: "In the Budget we are presenting," said General MacArthur in 1935, "we are merely the agent of the President." [9] Earlier, the Army Chief of Finance had explicitly informed Congress that the President's policy was the controlling factor which prevented the War Department from presenting its needs directly to Congress: "I think when the Budget has once been approved by the President and transmitted to Congress, it is his budget estimate and no officer or official of the War Department would have any right to come up here and attempt to get a single dollar more than is contained in that estimate." [10] This was standard military thinking and practice prior to 1940. The only significant exceptions occurred with respect to the naval construction acts. The greater importance of the Navy to national security led to direct dealings between Congress and its professional leaders, and the General Board of the Navy did not hesitate to make its views known even when they lacked presidential approval. Even with respect to the Navy, however, communication was limited. The issue only really arose in connection with the occasional acts of great importance, and prior to 1913, the views of the General Board were not even made public. The astonishing aspect of this entire pattern of relations was the extent to which Congress acquiesced in the subordination of the military professionals to the President and accepted the denial to it of direct professional advice. This could only happen because military policy was in general not particularly important and Congress was in general not particularly interested. Where it was important as in the Navy bills and the National Defense Acts of 1916 and 1920, Congress did insist upon hearing directly from the professional chiefs. But these were exceptions to the prevailing pattern.

CONGRESSIONAL ACCESS OF THE MILITARY CHIEFS. The continuing importance of military policy after 1945 shifted the principal locus of congressional-military relations from the technical services and bureaus to the professional military chiefs. The full implications of the separation of powers could no longer be avoided; the relations between Congress and the military became a problem in civil-military relations. If Congress was to play its part in determining national military policy, it required the same independent professional advice which the President received. Previously congressmen had only occasionally asserted their right to the direct views of the military chiefs. After World War II they regularly insisted in earnest that the military leaders be free to present their views directly to congressional committees. With respect to the military budget in particular it was argued that Congress could only discharge its constitutional responsibilities if it was able to compare the purely "military" recommendations of the Joint Chiefs with the President's budget "compounded of a number of extramilitary considerations . . ." * The legal mile-

---

* Carl Vinson went on to argue in this speech that:

"The responsibility of Congress is greater than merely to accept or reduce the totals proposed by the Bureau of the Budget . . .

"Where do we look mainly in this country for the best judgment on what is needed for an adequate national defense? The ultimate responsibility for the executive branch rests, of course, with the President. But his is not the expert military view. It can never be so, nor does our system so intend. Our top source for military judgment is the Joint Chiefs of Staff who, under the law, are charged among other things with the Nation's strategic and logistic planning. It is these men, who have risen to the top in the Nation's armed forces after a generation of experience and effort in military life, to whom we must look, and to whom

stone marking the shift from the prewar pattern was the provision in the National Security Act of 1949 permitting a member of the Joint Chiefs of Staff to present to Congress "on his own initiative, after first informing the Secretary of Defense, any recommendation relating to the Department of Defense that he may deem proper." [11] This was the first statute in American history authorizing a professional military chief to take his views directly to Congress. While it did not make the Chiefs of Staff the principal military advisers to Congress as it made them with respect to the President, the National Security Council, and the Secretary of Defense, it did nonetheless free them from the legal restrictions of the 1921 Budget and Accounting Act. This legal authorization, however, could become inoperative without the political means of protecting the military chiefs against pressure or retaliation from the executive branch. After the dismissal in 1949 of Admiral Denfeld, Chief of Naval Operations, following his participation in the B-36 hearings, the House Armed Services Committee warned that any further "intimidation" of this nature would lead it to "ask the Congress to exercise its constitutional power of redress." [12] This "constitutional power," however, is one which it is easier for Congress to assert than to exercise. Few effective devices are available to it to protect military officers against executive action.

This vulnerability of the chiefs places a tremendous burden upon them as to whether to speak up or to remain silent. What is the proper course of professional behavior when called before a congressional committee and invited to criticize the President's recommendations? How strong should be the doubts and disagreements of a chief with the President's policy before he takes the

the President must look, for the most authoritative advice on our national-defense requirements.

"This being so, I have taken the President's military budget, which is compounded of a number of extra-military considerations, and contrasted it with the lowest budget recommended by the Joint Chiefs of Staff, which is exclusively military in nature. By that process, I believe the Congress can arrive more soundly at our national-defense needs than if the President's budget alone is taken as the criterion."

Vinson's examination of the two budgets led him to recommend appropriations of $16,364,000,000 compared with the JCS figure of $17,439,000,000 and the President's estimate of $14,765,000,000. *Cong. Record,* XCV (Mar. 30, 1949), 3540.

initiative in criticizing it before Congress? The annual psychic
crisis of the Chiefs of Staff before the congressional appropriations committees is a new but apparently enduring phenomenon
in American government. If the military chief accepts and defends
the President's policies, he is subordinating his own professional
judgment, denying to Congress the advice to which it is constitutionally entitled, and becoming the political defender of an
administration policy. If the military chief expresses his professional opinions to Congress, he is publicly criticizing his Commander in Chief and furnishing useful ammunition to his political
enemies. There is no easy way out of this dilemma. Military leaders
in the postwar period varied in their behavior from more or less
active campaigning against presidential policies (the admirals with
respect to unification and the B-36 controversy) to the defense of
presidential policies which ran counter to their professional judgment (General Bradley with respect to the Fiscal 1951 budget).
A middle course, however, appears to be the most professionally
desirable one. Complete silence before Congress or rigid adherence to the presidential line is no longer the proper behavior. The
military chief has the professional duty to speak frankly to both
President and Congress. As Admiral Radford stated in contrast
to the military opinion of the 1920's:

. . . we cannot function under our form of Government unless the
Congress of the United States is able to get full and frank and truthful
answers from any witnesses who appear before their committees. I
feel that military men appearing before committees of Congress, if asked
for their own opinion, should give it as truthfully and frankly as they
can.[13]

General Ridgway's behavior under Senate questioning in 1954
and 1955 reflected an effort to find the proper path. In both cases,
the general emphasized his acceptance of higher level executive
decisions fixing the size of the Army which obviously did not accord with his own judgment. In 1954 he gave his own views in
executive session; in 1955 he presented in public his military
opinion on the desirable strength of his service.[14]

The maintenance of this pattern of behavior requires the mutual restraint and conscious cooperation of military man, legisla-

tor, and executive. Military professionalism and objective civilian control become impossible if the administration punishes officers for presenting their professional opinions to Congress, if congressmen insist upon using the soldiers to embarrass the administration, or if the soldiers stray beyond their field of expertise into those of politics and diplomacy.*

THE SEPARATION OF POWERS VERSUS STRATEGIC MONISM

INTERBRANCH RIVALRY AND NATIONAL STRATEGY. While it is almost constitutionally impossible for the United States to have a highly effective system of civilian control, it is also constitutionally impossible for it to suffer from a condition which civilian control and military professionalism normally serve to prevent. This condition is prolonged adherence to a national military policy of strategic monism, that is, primary reliance upon a single strategic concept, weapons system, or military service as the means of achieving military security. The opposite, strategic pluralism, requires a wide variety of forces and weapons to meet a diversity of potential security threats. Strategic monism is incompatible with a high level of military professionalism because it presupposes an ability to predict and control the action of possible enemies, a willingness to pursue a more activistic and, possibly, more aggressive foreign policy, a reluctance to "play it safe" by covering all bets, and, usually, an acceptance of a lower level of total military expenditures.[15] A system of civil-military relations which maximizes civilian control and military professionalism normally tends to produce decisions favoring a pluralistic strategy. In the United States, however, a pluralistic tendency is achieved not through a high level of professionalism but through the operation of the separation of powers.

The broad and diverse composition of Congress includes supporters of virtually every military concept, military program, and

* The Jenner subcommittee investigating the conduct of the Korean War, for instance, criticized the efforts of the Truman Administration to control the military and urged that steps be taken "to eliminate political interference in the conduct of hostilities and negotiations of a military armistice." It also solicited the views of the retired Korean War commanders on American participation in the United Nations and the severance of diplomatic relations with the Soviet Union. Internal Security Subcommittee, Committee on the Judiciary, *The Korean War and Related Matters*, 84th Cong., 1st Sess. (1955).

military service. When the executive appears to emphasize one military interest to the detriment of others, the aggrieved interests can normally find sympathetic backing in Congress, strong enough at times to alter executive policy. The congressional coalition which forms to help the military interests rejected by the executive usually consists of three elements with quite different motives. The hard core of support comes from those congressmen who are simply interested in the protection of the one particular program or service. They are reinforced, however, by a second group who support stronger military forces in general and who oppose executive cuts in any defense program. While probably the weakest element in most congressional coalitions of this nature, this group alone in the coalition is motivated by a conscious desire for a pluralistic strategy. In the House this group centered about the Armed Services Committee and most particularly its chairman, Representative Vinson. The report of the Committee in the B-36 controversy, for instance, explicitly endorsed strategic pluralism. In the Senate, the "strong defense" bloc was more nebulous, with Stuart Symington at the end of the postwar decade emerging as its most articulate member. The supporters of particular military programs and those of all military programs would not normally carry great weight in Congress or prevail against the executive if they were not able to enlist the assistance of a third, more diffuse, but larger congressional group, consisting of those who oppose presidential policies either for partisan reasons or from the desire to enhance the position of Congress in the separation of powers. The aggrieved military interest can frequently rally to its support all the inherent jealousy and antagonism which Congress has for executive leadership. While the separation of powers tends to produce an identity of function between Congress and President, it also tends to produce a divergence of policy. The rivalry of the two bodies requires each to distinguish itself from the other by advancing its own contributions to national policy. At times, one branch adopts a policy differing from that of the other branch not because it has any strong opinions on the issue, but simply because it feels that it must assert itself as at least a coequal in running the government. Continued acquiescence by one branch in the policies advocated by the other, even if they were desirable policies, would eventually lead to the subordination of the approving branch to the initiating branch.

Unusual unanimity among executive branch agencies frequently leads Congress to react with suspicion and hostility. In the unification controversy in 1947, for example, the House Committee on Government Operations was in part motivated to open hearings and search out opposition to unification because of the apparently united front of the Army and Navy in support of the interservice agreements of the previous winter.[16] A few years later Carl Vinson persuaded the House of Representatives to pass the Marine Corps Bill of 1952 by stressing the virtually unanimous opposition to it by executive military leaders:

> I want to make clear [he argued] that this is in all respects a congressional measure. It is not sponsored by the Department of Defense. Our Defense leaders are, in fact, strongly opposed to the enactment of this bill. The Deputy Secretary of Defense sent correspondence to the committee in opposition to the bill and the Joint Chiefs of Staff testified against it. They also testified against the bill in the Senate, but the Senate approved the principles of the bill unanimously despite that opposition. The House Committee, with the same testimony before it, has favorably reported the bill to the House with only one dissenting vote.
>
> So there can be no doubt but that this bill, as much as any measure ever to come before the House, is by and of the Congress and not a bill drawn up in the Pentagon and passed up here for the Congress to enact.[17]

Under the peculiar dialectic of the separation of powers, in other words, too much executive support for a bill may lead to its defeat and too much executive opposition may lead to its passage.

Congressional military policy in the postwar decade apparently lacked any logic or consistency. All the military services and most of the significant military programs were at one time or another the recipients of congressional protection and support. Those services or groups which were weak in the executive branch appealed to Congress for support — they identified civilian control with congressional control — while the services and groups strong in the executive branch decried congressional intrusion into military affairs. In 1944–1947 when the President favored the Army views on unification, Congress supported the Navy. In 1948 and

1949, when the President opposed the expansion of the Air Force, Congress twice voted additional funds for this purpose. In 1947 and 1948 when the executive limited National Guard funds, Congress similarly increased them over the presidential requests. In 1946–1948 when there were reports of executive hostility to the Marine Corps, Congress protected the Corps by defining explicitly its functions in the National Security Act and demanding from civilian executive officials assurances of their respect for the integrity and existence of the Marines. Subsequently, when the executive branch almost unanimously opposed the Marine Corps Bill of 1952, Congress passed it anyway. In 1953, when the Eisenhower Administration cut back Air Force appropriations, a strong although unsuccessful effort was made in Congress to restore them. In 1954, when the Administration cut back Army funds, the pattern was repeated. In 1955, when the Administration wanted to reduce Marine Corps funds, Congress this time refused to go along and voted the extra money. In 1956, due to antipathy toward Secretary Wilson as well as from fear of the Soviets, Congress approved additional funds for the Air Force despite the Administration's opposition.

The fact is Congress does not have fixed and definite views on national strategy. Congress, as a whole, is not basically pro-Army, pro-Navy, pro-Air Force, or even pro-Marine Corps. It is simply pro-Congress. Its sympathies and policies change with the needs of the times and against the desires of the executive. The one consistent result of Congress' actions is to produce a strong trend toward strategic pluralism: the multiplication of programs and activities and a tendency to equalize the division of resources among competing military claims. Congress is frequently criticized for its susceptibility to narrow pressures and interests, its vulnerability to lobbies, its lack of responsibility and discipline, and its inability to develop an integrated approach to policy. In military affairs, however, this dispersion and openness of Congress tend to produce a policy coinciding closely with that demanded by the professional military ethic. Whatever its merits with respect to tariff legislation, tax policy, and agricultural subsidies, the strength of particularism and parochialism in Congress works to enhance the military security of the United States.

ORGANIZATIONAL PLURALISM. The principal means by which Congress tended to produce a pluralistic strategy were through investigations which furnished an opportunity to aggrieved military interests to express their views, statutory prescription of the organization of the defense establishment, statutory assignment of functions to the various military units, and, most significantly, control of the military budget. Congress' opposition to the executive led it to oppose the centralization of authority in the executive branch and to support military units attempting to defend their independence and autonomy. In the unification controversy of 1944–1947, Congress consistently supported a more dispersed form of organization than advocated by the President. The initial presidential plan, transmitted to Congress in December 1945, proposed a single department of the armed forces with a single chief of staff. Congress compelled this proposal to be dropped. A second presidential plan worked out in June 1946 and concurred in by the Secretaries of War and of the Navy also established a single executive department to house all three services. Again opposition stopped it in Congress. Finally, in the fall and winter of 1946–1947, the two services agreed to a third compromise plan which Congress eventually approved in the summer of 1947. Throughout the proceedings, the naval opponents of unification stressed the extent to which centralized executive authority would diminish congressional influence, and Congress insisted upon a loose organization both to protect the Navy and Marines against possible Army domination and to secure congressional participation in the exercise of civilian control. In considering the National Security Act Amendments of 1949, Congress at first hesitated to create a Chairman for the Joint Chiefs of Staff and eventually agreed to the establishment of such an office only when it was surrounded by strict safeguards and had its powers narrowly defined. President Eisenhower's reorganization of the Defense Department in 1953 which proposed to increase the authority of the JCS Chairman was disapproved by the House Committee on Government Operations, and approved in the House itself by a vote of 108 to 234. The strength and fervor of the plan's opponents indicated that Congress had gone just about as far as it would go for the time in acquiescing in the centralization of authority in the defense

Separation of Powers

establishment. In its postwar consideration of the organization of the individual services, Congress likewise favored decentralization and dispersion of authority.[18] Congress also strengthened the tendency toward pluralism by preferring explicit and closely defined legal grants to broad and vague powers. In the 1947 unification act, for instance, it attempted to balance what it believed to be executive hostility to the Navy and Marine Corps by defining the functions and duties of those services in much more concrete terms than those of the Army and Air Force.

Congressional support of dispersion existed irrespective of whether there were significant units within the military establishment favoring it also. In the unification debate of 1944–1947, the interests of Congress coincided with the interests of the Navy. In 1953, substantial congressional elements opposed Eisenhower's reorganization plan despite the absence of open opposition from within the military establishment itself. Congress' constant concern with the dangers of the "Prussian General Staff System" reflected not so much a fear of enhanced military power as a fear of enhanced executive power.

BUDGETARY PLURALISM: ADMINISTRATIVE REDUCTIONS AND POLICY INCREASES. Highly conscious of its role as custodian of the purse, Congress virtually always feels compelled, except during a war crisis, to make some changes in the President's military budget. Normally congressional alteration occurs in one of two forms. If Congress in general agrees with presidential military policy, and if no aggrieved interests plead strongly before it, Congress then approaches the budget with economic policy rather than military policy uppermost in its mind. Its policy goal is to reduce the military budget as much as possible without challenging fundamentally the military policy embodied in the budget. Consequently, it tends to make a broad, general, but small reduction in the proposed estimates. Congress here is acting in the general interests of economy and efficiency. It does not tend to make substantial cuts in any particular program but instead distributes its cuts throughout the budget in the hope that each program will be able to absorb its share without serious impairment. In the 1953 budget, for instance, the House Committee total reduction of 8 per cent in military appropriations was distributed among

423

seventy-eight different items. Frequently Congress will simply cut the executive requests back to the next lower round figure. Or the demand will be made for an across the board percentage reduction in all items or for the elimination of a round sum such as one billion dollars from the total military budget. Congress at times may dictate a reduction in military spending but leave it to the executive to determine where the cuts should be made. In making these reductions Congress asserts itself against the President not in the realm of military policy but in the realm of military administration. It is accepting the basic assumptions of the President's military planning and is challenging the military to produce the same programs with less money.

The second method by which Congress may play an independent role in the budget process is to advance a military policy and national strategy different from that of the President. Its normal way of expressing this more fundamental challenge to presidential recommendations is to support an increase in the funds allocated to one particular service or program. While congressional reductions in military appropriations are generally broad, unspecific, and small, congressional increases are usually specific, concentrated, and substantial. In the one case Congress is acting in behalf of the general interests of economy and efficiency, and in the other it is acting in behalf of the specific interests of some particular military program or service. Prior to 1940, because of its lack of interest in military policy as such, Congress seldom made significant program increases. Its typical method of asserting its role in the budget process was to reduce executive recommendations. Since World War II, however, the increased involvement of Congress in the substance of military policy has enhanced its willingness to increase specific elements in the President's budget.* While

* Congress may well, of course, make administrative reductions and policy increases simultaneously. In the Fiscal 1950 Air Force budget the House Committee eliminated $51,000,000 from civilian personnel, subsistence, clothing, equipage, and transportation, and added $851,000,000 to aircraft funds to maintain a fifty-eight-group Air Force. As Huzar points out, the reductions "reflected continued Congressional dissatisfaction with administration in the National Military Establishment" while the increase "expressed Congressional dissatisfaction with the Administration's strategic program." Elias Huzar, *The Purse and the Sword: Control of the Army by Congress through Military Appropriations, 1933–1950* (Ithaca, N.Y., 1950), p. 187.

most increases involve minor issues of policy, at times major programs and fundamental policies are at stake. The most significant instance of this type of congressional action was Congress' increasing the authorizations for the Air Force in the 1948 supplemental budget and in the fiscal year 1950 regular appropriation. As both the President and congressional leaders agreed, a "major question of policy" was at issue in this conflict. On other occasions, mentioned above, Congress increased National Guard and Marine Corps funds, and groups within Congress made strong efforts to restore funds to other aggrieved services. In all these instances, Congress or congressional elements voiced their dissent from presidential military policy by supporting limited specific increases in the military budget.

The relatively few instances in which Congress overrode the Administration and increased the funds for a particular service or program in part reflect the extent to which Congress and President have similar views on defense policy. To some degree, however, it also reflects the extent to which the President takes into consideration likely congressional reaction to budget recommendations. The executive undoubtedly attempts to protect itself against congressional administrative reductions by asking more than it actually needs to carry out its program. Similarly, with respect to congressional policy increases, the executive tends to follow Carl J. Friedrich's law of anticipated reactions and to refrain from making drastic cuts in any one service or program which might invite congressional attack. Executive approval in 1951, for instance, of the increase in the Air Force goal from 95 to 143 wings was dictated in part by the likelihood that Congress would appropriate the funds for the increase anyway. Similarly, early in 1956 the Eisenhower Administration requested additional funds for B-52 procurement in an apparent though unsuccessful attempt to forestall even larger congressional increases. Thus, while upon the surface Congress almost always makes a net reduction in presidential military estimates, its more subtle and pervading influence is toward a multiplication of military programs and a higher level of military spending.

The extent to which Congress' actions on the budget further a pluralistic strategy depends, of course, on the extent to which

Congress can force the executive to accept and to implement its increases in the military forces. If Congress were unable to compel adherence to its demands for increased spending, no restraints, prior or otherwise, would exist upon executive concentration upon one specific arm or service. In the absence of such authority, Congress might be able to criticize the executive and arouse public opinion, but it would be unable to apply the ultimate sanction. Consequently, the constitutional issue as to whether Congress can compel the executive to spend money which it appropriates assumes considerable significance. The issue arose most dramatically with respect to the actions of the executive impounding research and development funds in 1946, the extra money for the fifty-eight group Air Force in 1949, and the increase in Marine Corps appropriations in 1955. Few people, and certainly no one in Congress, would challenge the power of the President to refrain from spending money if he found that programs could be implemented with less funds than previously thought necessary. Congress is all in favor of administrative savings and reductions. But it draws a sharp distinction between these and executive refusal to carry out a congressional policy decision. As Representative Mahon remarked, apropos of the impounding of Air Force funds:

> I do not think it would be proper for the will of Congress on matters of policy to be circumvented. I would not object, as I know other Members would not object, to any reasonable economies in Government. But economy is one thing, and the abandonment of a policy and program of the Congress another thing.[19]

Congressional opinion has generally agreed with Mahon. The House Appropriations Committee condemned President Truman's impounding of Air Force funds as the unconstitutional usurping of a function of Congress. The House Armed Services Committee termed the action a flagrant denial of the wishes of Congress and recommended legislation requiring the executive to consult with the Appropriations Committees before withholding funds. Secretary Johnson, on the other hand, defended the President's action on the grounds of his inherent powers as Chief Executive and Commander in Chief.[20]

The merits of this argument are definitely with Congress. If the President has the power to sign an appropriations statute into law and then nullify a major policy embodied in that statute by refusing to spend a substantial portion of the funds appropriated, he has in effect an item veto. More than that, he has an absolute veto exercised without danger of being overridden by a two-thirds vote of Congress. Neither the Commander in Chief clause nor any other clause in the Constitution gives him an item veto or an absolute veto. Congress not the President has the final authority to determine the size and composition of the armed forces. The powers of Congress to "raise and support armies" and to "provide and maintain a navy" are positive powers not limited to establishing a ceiling on the services. The constitutional authority of Congress to provide funds for the military and other executive departments necessarily implies the constitutional power to compel the funds to be expended.

The power of Congress to enforce increased expenditures is intimately related with the legal right and duty of the military chiefs to present their professional opinions directly to Congress. Inevitably with respect to the budget, the chiefs wish more funds than the executive is willing to approve. But their right to appeal to Congress becomes a nullity unless Congress also possesses the right to act upon their appeal. These two authorities are inseparably connected, and together they are essential to the operation of the separation of powers. The right of the chiefs to speak frankly to Congress has been established in law and has been more or less accepted in practice. The authority of Congress to require military expenditures likewise should be explicitly sanctioned and acquiesced in by legislature and executive.

16

Departmental Structure of Civil-
Military Relations

Departmental organization of civil-military relations must provide for the performance of three distinct functions. The *professional military function* includes representing the nation's military requirements, advising on the military implications of proposed courses of action and of the military needs necessary to carry out adopted policies, and directing the military forces in the implementation of national policy. The *administrative-fiscal function* includes representing the interests of economy and efficiency, advising on fiscal, budgetary, and management matters, and administering "civilian" activities such as supply, procurement, construction, nonmilitary personnel, and the budget. The *policy-strategy function* includes balancing the professional military and administrative-fiscal viewpoints, formulating the departmental recommendations on force levels and the military budget, and defending departmental views before outside groups. In a vertical system of departmental organization the civilian secretary and the military chief share responsibility for all three functions. In a coordinate organizational pattern, the civilian secretary has the administrative-fiscal function, the military chief the professional military function, and both share in the policy-strategy function. A balanced system of departmental civil-military relations maximizes objective civilian control and military professionalism through a greater degree of specialization. Each of the three functions is performed by a distinct unit within the department: the secretary is responsible for policy strategy, the military chief for the professional military function, and a separate set of officials, civilian or military, for the administrative-fiscal affairs.

The principal issue of civil-military relations in the executive branch after World War II involved the distribution of these three functions at the central service level, that is, at a level above the individual military services (Army, Navy, Air Force) but below the highest political authority in the government (President, National Security Council).* The problem arose because the United States came out of World War II with an organized military unit at this level, the Joint Chiefs of Staff, which, in addition to performing professional military functions, discharged policy-strategy and administrative-fiscal functions. The absence of any significant civilian institution at this level left no effective restraints on the Joint Chiefs. They were, as Admiral Leahy remarked, "under no civilian control whatever." Consequently, the fundamental need was to "militarize" the Joint Chiefs, to divest them of their non-military functions and to develop appropriate organs to discharge the administrative-fiscal and policy-strategy responsibilities. In a sense, the JCS existed in 1945 as the one completed room of a mansion begun in 1941. Although designed for a limited purpose, this room for four years had met the needs normally served by an entire house. In the postwar years it became necessary to build the

* At the military service level, the Navy continued to maintain its balanced system of organization. The Army initially returned to the vertical general staff system, but the impact of the Cold War and particularly of the Korean War subsequently forced it to begin the high level segregation of the professional military and administrative-fiscal functions. The need, in the words of the Secretary of the Army, to "distinguish between activity which is primarily military . . . and activity which, although it is in support of military activity, partakes more of the industrial or commercial" characteristics led to the creation of a Deputy Chief of Staff for Logistics with authority over all seven technical services. The Air Force, less involved in immediate Cold War military operations and more concerned with planning for total war, was organized along more strictly vertical lines. See Navy Organization Act of 1948, 62 Stat. 66; Robert H. Connery, *The Navy and Industrial Mobilization in World War II* (Princeton, 1951), chs. 19, 20; Dept. of the Navy, Office of the Management Engineer, *The United States Navy: A Description of its Functional Organization* (Washington, 1952); *Report* of the Committee on Organization of the Department of the Navy, April 16, 1954 (Washington, 1954); *Organization of the Army*, Report of the Advisory Committee on Army Organization, December 18, 1953; *Army Navy Air Force Journal*, XCI (June 26, 1954), 1298, (July 3, 1954), 1335; Air Force Organization Act of 1951, 65 Stat. 326; H. Rept. 9, 82d Cong., 1st Sess. (1951); S. Rept. 426, 82d Cong., 1st Sess. (1951).

rest of the mansion about the Joint Chiefs and to transfer to these additions much of the furniture and fixtures which had become solidly established in the JCS.

The development of a balanced system of organization was complicated by three factors. First, the simple existence of the Joint Chiefs with their existing powers and functions had a determining influence upon the nature of the American defense establishment. The organization planners did not start with a *tabula rasa* upon which to draw an ideal system. They began with the established fact of the Joint Chiefs. Throughout all the defense organization debates of 1944 through 1947, the continued existence of the Joint Chiefs was the one point never disputed at any time by Army, Navy, Air Force, civilian administrators, or Congress. Born to power in wartime and antedating all other central defense institutions by six years, the Joint Chiefs experienced great difficulty in adjusting to a purely professional role. Reared in an environment in which the performance of political functions by military institutions was accepted practice, civilian offices were diffident about asserting political leadership.

A second difficulty sprang from the widespread acceptance of the fusionist approach to civil-military relations in the postwar years. Starting from the liberal preference for subjective civilian control, this theory rejected as inherently undesirable and impossible the segregation of military and political responsibilities. It furnished an intellectual rationale for opposing a balanced structure and for continuing the existing merger of functions in the Joint Chiefs.

Thirdly, the issue of civil-military relations at the central defense level was inextricably intertwined with the issue of the relative powers of the central defense organization and the military services. Two military departments could exist without supervision. Three military departments required a fourth agency to coordinate them. The powers of this fourth agency vis-à-vis the other three was not a problem of civil-military relations. It was a problem of administrative federalism, of centralization versus decentralization, and the unification debate had both its Alexander Hamiltons and its Luther Martins. The federalism problem, however, was directly related to the civil-military relations problem. Any change in the balance of power between the central organization and the military services would affect the civil-military balance within the central organization. Conversely, any alteration of the civil-military alignment within the central organization would affect the distribution of power beween the central office and the services. The 1949 amendments to the National Security Act, for example, were designed primarily to centralize control in the Department of Defense. One means to this end was to strengthen the budgetary authority of the Secretary of Defense. This action, however, tended to establish in the Comptroller's Office a significant counterweight to the Joint Chiefs of Staff. The 1953 reorganization, on the other hand, was conceived primarily in terms of a redistribution of authority and functions within the central organization. Yet, despite disclaimers to the contrary, it had the incidental effect of still further reducing the influence of the military departments. The general trend with respect to federalism was from a loose organization to a unified organization. The separation of powers and functions within the central organization thus tended to assume greater significance than the distribution of power between the central organization and the federal units.*

Despite the obstacles, the central organization in the postwar decade tended to evolve toward a balanced pattern of civil-military relations. The Joint Chiefs retreated from their wartime heights; the office of the Comptroller emerged as the focus of administrative-fiscal functions; Secretaries of Defense essayed the policy-strategist role. Nonetheless, the formal organization still fell short of a fully balanced pattern. The fundamental defect was the weakness of the

* The appropriate role for the Secretaries of the Army, Navy, and Air Force presents a major problem. Theoretically, they should be policy-strategists at a lower level than the Secretary of Defense. In actual practice, they have difficulty functioning in this capacity because they have no place in the central defense organization, while their military chiefs do have such a role through the JCS. The obvious solutions are either to divorce the Joint Chiefs from the services (suggested by Forrestal and Lovett) or to provide some means for the secretaries to participate in the central organization. Efforts to achieve the latter through the Joint Secretaries have not been particularly successful: the grounds for unity and the specificity of function which existed for the military chiefs were absent from the civilian side. The most satisfactory role for the service secretaries is probably to represent the principle of decentralization by serving as spokesmen for the military and civilian needs of their services.

office of the Secretary.* Both the Joint Chiefs and the Comptroller continued to tread upon ground which the Secretary should have occupied if he were to discharge his responsibilities in the realm of policy and strategy. The Joint Chiefs were part military and part political; the Comptroller was part fiscal and part political; the Secretary was part political and part vacuum.

THE JOINT CHIEFS OF STAFF: LEGAL FORM AND POLITICAL REALITY

For eight years after the passage of the National Security Act of 1947 a curious gap existed between the role of the Joint Chiefs as defined by statute and the role of the Joint Chiefs in practice. By law, the Joint Chiefs were to perform only the professional military function. In actual fact, they participated in a variety of political and administrative roles. The primary reasons for this failure of behavorial patterns to conform to statutory prescriptions derived from American opinion toward military affairs, the operation of the separation of powers, and the failure of the lawmakers to prescribe the organizational forms necessary to realize their intent.

Most of the service proposals for unification in 1944–1947 envisioned legal perpetuation of the wartime status and roles of the Joint Chiefs. This made all the more remarkable the fact that the National Security Act of 1947 did not codify the World War II pattern, but instead prescribed for the Joint Chiefs a strictly military role. This surprising result was less the outcome of conscious thought than it was a product of the clash of views between the Army and Navy over the powers which should be assigned to the central defense organization. Broadly speaking, the Army wanted to concentrate power in the military component of the central organization. The Navy wanted the central organization to have as little power as possible, and, for this reason, countered the Army proposal for a rigid military integration with a plan for the loose coordination of all the departments and agencies concerned with

---

* Legally, the Office of the Comptroller, the Joint Chiefs, the assistant secretaries of defense, and certain other units are all within the Office of the Secretary of Defense (OSD). Since the significant issues, however, concern the relations among the components of the OSD, when I speak of the Secretary of Defense or the office of the Secretary I mean only the individual and his immediate staff.

national security. The clash between these two approaches produced a compromise in which the central defense organization was made stronger than the Navy wanted it. Within that central organization, however, the civilian component (the secretary) was given more authority than the Army wanted it to have.

Congress spelled out the purely military character of the Joint Chiefs in four ways.[1] First, the composition of the JCS was purely military. Congress in 1947, and again in 1949, rejected suggestions that the Secretary of Defense be a member of the Joint Chiefs or that the chairman be a civilian. In practice, the Secretary of Defense at times attended JCS meetings. Civilian participation, however, was appropriate only to the extent that the Joint Chiefs performed civilian functions.* Second, the National Security Act assigned purely military responsibilities to the Joint Chiefs. They were the "principal military advisers" to the principal organs of the executive branch.† The more specific duties assigned them in the act and in the implementing Functions Paper were also strictly military. Thirdly, the Act placed the Joint Chiefs within the defense establishment with respect to which the Secretary of Defense is the principal adviser to the President. To be sure, the Chiefs were unique among the agencies of that establishment in that they were under the "authority and direction" of the President as well as the Secretary, and were advisers to the President and the NSC as well as to the Secretary. The Act avoided, however, a fully developed coordinate system. It was presumed that although the Joint Chiefs would participate in many different dramas with Congress, the President, the National Security Council, and the Secretary of Defense, they would play the same military role in each drama. In

---

* In Great Britain the Prime Minister was until 1946 ex officio chairman of the Chiefs of Staff Committee. Since then the Minister of Defense may, if he so desires, act as chairman. The system worked best, however, when the civilians stayed away from the Chiefs of Staff meetings. Churchill declared that it was his practice to leave the Chiefs "alone to do their own work, subject to my general supervision, suggestion and guidance." He presided at only 44 of 462 meetings of the Chiefs in 1940 and 1941. Maurice Hankey, *Government Control in War* (Cambridge, 1945), pp. 55–56; *H.C. Debates* (5th Series), CCCLXXVIII (Feb. 24, 1942), 41–42; *Central Organisation for Defence,* Cmd. 6923, pp. 6, 9 (1946).

† It could be argued that the adjective "military" might describe either the persons of the advisers or the nature of their advice. Common usage has accepted the latter interpretation. Other provisions of the Act require the Chiefs to be military men, and the canons of statutory interpretation require that Congress never be considered guilty of redundancy if it can be avoided.

many ways, this was an unrealistic assumption. But it was also an unavoidable one, for the constitutional relationships of the President and Congress to the military chiefs could not be ignored.

Finally, the National Security Act and other legislation divested the Joint Chiefs of many nonmilitary functions which they performed during the war. A common phenomenon of civil-military relations is the initial assignment to the military services of new activities related to defense. As these activities expand, however, their nonmilitary applications and implications become more significant; they gradually lose their predominantly military character; and they are eventually transferred from the services to an appropriate civilian agency. The early postwar years saw this process at work with respect to six major functions. (1) The responsibility for advising the President on over-all *national security policy* which had been performed by the Joint Chiefs during the war was assigned to the National Security Council composed of top civilian officials. The creation of this agency was more important than any other organizational development in restricting the Joint Chiefs to military activities.[2] (2) Central coordination of *military research and development* was removed from the Joint Chiefs in 1946 by Secretaries Forrestal and Patterson. The National Security Act assigned this function to a board directly under the Secretary of Defense; in 1953 the board was abolished and the functions given to an assistant secretary of defense. (3) During the war the military services created "full political and economic intelligence staffs," and the Joint Intelligence Committee of the JCS was the principal *coordinator of the national intelligence* of the services, the OSS, the State Department, and the Foreign Economic Administration. In 1946 and 1947 executive action and the National Security Act established an independent Central Intelligence Agency directly under the NSC which assumed responsibility for the coordinating function.[3] (4) *Atomic energy* had been handled during the war by the Army's Manhattan District Project. Following considerable controversy over the merits of civilian versus military control, the McMahon Act of 1946 assigned primary responsibility for atomic programs to a civilian commission. (5) Eventually, either by the transfer of authority to another agency, as in the case of Germany, or the disappearance of the function, the Joint Chiefs lost their immediate postwar responsibilities for the *government of occupied areas*. (6) Prior to World War II an agency closely associated with the military chiefs, the Joint Army and Navy Munitions Board, was responsible for *planning national economic mobilization*. After the war, however, the military realized, in Admiral Sherman's words that "Politically, any plans of national scope prepared by the Army and Navy Munitions Board are bound to be still-born." [4] The National Security Act assigned the planning of economic mobilization to a unit in the Executive Office of the President and limited the Munitions Board to the supervision and coordination of military procurement and the purely military aspects of industrial mobilization.

The extent and forms of JCS deviation in practice from its assigned military role have been analyzed previously. While descending from their wartime peaks of power and glory, the Joint Chiefs still remained conspicuously above the timber line separating the sequestered shades of professionalism from the bare and open rocks of politics. Throughout the postwar decade informed observers of the defense establishment commented on the extent to which JCS political power exceeded that appropriate for a purely military organ. In wandering afield from military planning, the Chiefs also tended to get bogged down in minor administrative matters.* The performance by the Joint Chiefs of their primary military functions suffered seriously from the time and energy devoted to these extraneous issues, the absence of effective objective civilian control adversely affecting the achievement of military security.[5] The extent to which JCS practice was divorced from its statutory role was manifested in one peculiar characteristic of JCS behavior: the repeated assertions by the Chiefs or their Chairman that they spoke purely from the "military viewpoint." The ritualistic incantation of this phrase was the deference which they paid to the theory of the National Security Act. The extent to which that phrase in the mouths of the Chiefs was followed by political advice on nonmilitary subjects was an index of the difference between structural form and political reality.

* It was reported that during the last two years of the Truman Administration the Joint Chiefs made 600 decisions relating to strategic planning; 500 on purely administrative matters; and 500 on issues combining administrative and military considerations. *New York Times,* Feb. 8, 1953, p. E5.

The most important reasons for the failure of the Joint Chiefs to conform to their statutory role lay deep in the currents of American politics and public opinion. One organizational factor which supplemented these other forces, however, was the position of the Chairman of the JCS. The Chairmanship was created in 1949 upon the recommendation of Forrestal to aid the Chiefs in rising above service loyalties and in reaching agreement on major military policies. His creation was urged because it would aid unification, and it was opposed because it would aid unification too much. Consequently, Congress carefully circumscribed his powers. The principal impact of the Chairmanship, however, was not on unification but on civil-military relations. In the absence of total war, military policy occupied a relatively small proportion of the President's time, and consequently he did not regularly consult with the Joint Chiefs as a body. Instead, the Chairman emerged as the link between the Chiefs and the White House. Although by statute the Joint Chiefs collectively were the military advisers to the President and the NSC, it was the Chairman who regularly briefed the President on military matters and represented the Chiefs at NSC meetings.* In acting as an intermediary, however, the Chairman went beyond a military role: he represented the political views of the Administration to the Joint Chiefs as well as the military views to the government. In addition, the first two occupants of the Chairmanship — General Bradley and Admiral Radford — were men of exceptional stature, intelligence, and vigor. They tended to become symbols of the military policy of the administrations they served: Bradley representing containment, land warfare, and Europe; Radford identified with a more dynamic approach, sea-air power, and Asia. In six short years they made the office of Chairman one of the most significant posts in the national government. They were true samurai, military statesmen rather than military experts, assuming many roles which more properly belonged to the Secretary of Defense. At times the reluctance of the Secretary to take the initiative in policy matters resulted in a tendency toward a co-

---

* During his four years as Chairman, General Bradley made 272 visits to the White House and attended 68 NSC meetings. In the first year of the Eisenhower Administration, the Chairman briefed the President weekly on the military situation. *New York Times,* Aug. 14, 1953, p. 2; Charles J. V. Murphy, "Eisenhower's White House," *Fortune,* XLVIII (July 1953), 176.

ordinate organization with the Secretary handling administration and the Chairman handling policy. Only the strengthening of the Secretary so that he could become the dominant figure representing administration policy would permit the Chairman to serve as the spokesman for the more permanent professional military viewpoint.

THE COMPTROLLER: SUPEREGO OF THE DEPARTMENT OF DEFENSE

The principal antagonist of the Joint Chiefs within the central defense organization was the Comptroller. Like the JCS, however, his office afforded an excellent illustration of the deceptive quality of formal legal structure. On the organization charts the Comptroller was lost among the crowd of nine assistant secretaries of defense. In the actual operation of the Department, however, he was a political force rivaled only by the military leaders themselves. He became the preëminent representative of the civilian demands for economy and efficiency in the military establishment. Just as the power of the Joint Chiefs extended beyond the purely military, the power of the Comptroller extended beyond the bounds of strictly administrative and fiscal matters. His influence rested on four pillars: theoretical, legal, functional, and personal.

The theoretical foundation of the power of the Comptroller was the identification of civilian control with budget control. The Comptroller's office was thoroughly civilian in both psychology and personnel. At the end of 1953, for instance, it included only 6 military personnel among a total staff of 160 people, a ratio of military to civilian personnel far lower than that of any other major unit in the Department. The Comptroller's staff and the Budget Bureau officials who cooperated with it looked upon the fiscal-administrative function as the principal means by which the Secretary could control his Department. In the words of Ferdinand Eberstadt: "The budget is one of the most effective, if not the strongest, implement of civilian control over the Military Establishment." [6] This outlook was carried to the point where cuts in the military budget were justified simply on the grounds that they were necessary to remind the military of the supremacy of civilian authority.[7] The identification of civilian control with budget control enhanced the authority of the Comptroller, but it weakened the authority of the Secretary. For it oriented the Secretary away from policy and toward a function which was inherently at a lower level than where he should operate. It downgraded him from umpire to participant. Furthermore, as Secretary Lovett pointed out, in any crisis, the budget, as an instrument of civilian control, would dissolve in his hands. Effective and responsible civilian control must be policy control not budgetary control.

The identification of civilian control with fiscal control received legal embodiment in Title IV of the National Security Act Amendments of 1949. Prior to this, one of the three assistants to the Secretary of Defense advised him on budgetary and fiscal matters. The authority of the central organization in this area was, however, somewhat hazy, and the Hoover Commission Task Force recommended a thoroughgoing overhaul of Pentagon budget procedures and a strengthening of the central budget office. Title IV established the Assistant Secretary of Defense (Comptroller) as the adviser and assistant to the Secretary in the performance of his budgetary and fiscal functions. The Comptroller was to supervise and direct the preparation of the budget estimates of the Defense Department and generally to supervise the fiscal and accounting aspects of the Department. These provisions, which were not included in either Forrestal's recommendations or the presidential message on defense organization, reflected the joining of the administrative management approach of the Hoover Commission with the existing concern with fiscal devices on the part of the Secretary's budgetary adviser. They were in part responsible for the subsequent exclusion of the Joint Chiefs from the budget process except for the formulation of the initial statement of force levels.[8]

The position of the Defense Department Comptroller after the passage of Title IV was unusual among federal agencies. The only other executive department to have a comptroller at the departmental level was the Post Office. Normally in the national government the principal representation of the interests of economy with respect to an agency's program comes from outside the agency itself, from the Treasury, the Budget Bureau, and the Appropriations Committees. But to an extent unique among federal agencies, the Department of Defense internalized the representation and implementation of the economy viewpoint. The primary reason for this was simply the size of the Department. It was, in effect, a defense government within a government, larger in personnel and funds than all the rest of the national government combined. It was difficult if not impossible for any agency outside this defense government to exercise effective control over its farflung operations. It would be a pigmy on the back of an elephant. The agency principally responsible for representing the economy viewpoint, the Bureau of the Budget, did not have in its Military Division the staff, the knowledge, or the influence necessary to master the defense establishment. Consequently, there was a unique fusing of the activities of the Budget Bureau with those of the Comptroller, the staffs of the two agencies cooperating together closely. For the fiscal years 1952 through 1955, the Budget Bureau and the Comptroller conducted a joint review of budget estimates, a practice not generally duplicated elsewhere in the federal government.[9] Thus, the Comptroller's office developed as the Freudian superego of the Department: an internal mechanism of restraint and control reflecting external demands and interests. It was the "garrison in the conquered city," giving powerful representation to an essentially unmilitary and alien element within the Department.

A final factor enhancing the power of the Comptroller was the continuity in office of Wilfred J. McNeil. McNeil had been the Fiscal Director of the Navy under Forrestal. In 1947 he became the budgetary and fiscal assistant to Forrestal as Secretary of Defense. In 1949 he became Comptroller, a position he still held in 1955. He was unique among the higher leaders of the Defense Department in that he performed the same job for all of the first five Secretaries of Defense. It is not surprising that he was labeled the "virtually indispensable man" of the Pentagon.[10] The Comptroller's office possessed knowledge and experience in a way which even the military could not rival and which was quite beyond the grasp of transient political appointees. Thus, McNeil was able to maintain his position as the principal balance to the JCS, despite occasional challenges from other civilian units, such as the General Counsel's office, the Joint Secretaries, and General McNarney's Defense Management Committee.[11]

The combination of these theoretical, legal, functional, and personal factors put the Comptroller's office deep into matters of strategy and policy. Here, as with the military, there was a contrast between ritualistic form and substantive reality. Just as the Chiefs argued that their advice was solely "from the military viewpoint," McNeil and his associates claimed that their recommendations dealt only with "fiscal management." In actuality, the Comptroller's office played a key role in determining the nature of America's military policy. For the fiscal years from 1950 through 1954, the Comptroller carried an important share of the responsibility for eliminating $62 billion from total service budget requests of $273 billion.[12] A reduction of 5 per cent in military estimates might be the result of acute fiscal management; a reduction of 22 per cent necessarily implied basic decisions on strategy. In formulating the budget for Fiscal 1954, McNeil played a major role in removing $5 billion from the Air Force request for $16.7 billion, thus bringing about a shift in Air Force goals from 143 wings in 1955 to 120 wings in 1956. So long as the Secretary of Defense was unable to arrive at an independent balancing of military and fiscal demands, the basic decisions on military policy were inevitably the result of the political battle of the Comptroller versus the Chiefs.

THE ROLE OF THE SECRETARY

The most important duty of the Secretary is to make the annual force-level recommendation to the President. This includes advice as to: (1) the strength of forces: how many divisions, ships, wings; (2) the level of forces: percentage strengths of divisions, etc.; (3) readiness dates of forces; and (4) deployment of forces. The translation of this advice into dollar terms furnishes the basis of the military budget recommendations. The decision on force levels and the budget is, of course, made by the President and ratified by Congress through appropriations. But the recommendation has to come from someone who devotes time and study to the problem. This official can be no one else but the Secretary of Defense. Normally the President would be expected to accept his recommendations. If there were continued serious disagreement between the two, the President would have to get another Secretary.

The responsibility for the force-level recommendation is one which the Secretary cannot avoid. It is the basic element of military policy. If he attempts to escape this duty, he is only delegating it to someone else and tacitly approving his conclusions. Consequently, the real issue is not whether the Secretary will discharge this responsibility, but rather how he will discharge it. There are three broad ways in which he may act. He may simply endorse the views of his military advisers and pay little heed to the demands of economy and efficiency. In this event, he is acting as a military spokesman. He may listen to the fiscal experts, and adopt their recommendations without reference to strategic implications. Here he functions as a business manager. He may attempt to integrate military and economic considerations into an overall defense policy. In this case, he acts as a policy strategist.

The National Security Act is sufficiently broad and ambiguous to permit him to function in any or all of these capacities. In practice, each Secretary has embodied some elements of each role. Nonetheless, the roles are essentially conflicting. Each requires somewhat different legal authority, staff assistance, and outlook and ability on the part of the Secretary. More important, each implies a fundamentally different pattern of civil-military relations. No one role for the Secretary and no one pattern of civil-military relations has yet emerged as dominant. During war, the military spokesman conception appears to prevail. In peace, the practice has been to oscillate between the other two. In the end, accumulated practice rather than statutory enactment will determine the place of the Secretary in the national scheme of civil-military relations.

MILITARY SPOKESMAN. The requirement that the Secretary be a civilian, the permeation of the government with liberal values, the widespread acceptance of those values by the military themselves, all combined to make the military-spokesman concept of the office the least prevalent one. The Secretary has been more the delegate of the American people to the military than the delegate of the military to the American people. If no professional military organ existed, the Secretary might legitimately attempt to act as military spokesman, as, for instance, the Navy secretary did during the nineteenth century. But, with the Joint Chiefs in existence, the Secretary, if he essayed that role, could only endorse what they said, which would be useless, or offer conflicting advice, which would be confusing. There is, of course, a sense in which the Secretary must function, in the phrase of *The Economist,* as the "Defender of Defense." [13] But the interest which the Secretary defends before the legislature and the people should be broader than mere military interest.

No American Secretary of Defense has ever functioned purely as a military spokesman. As Secretary of War and Secretary of the Navy, Stimson and Knox tended to play this role in World War II. Since 1947, however, the closest approximation was perhaps achieved by Secretary Marshall from September 1950 to September 1951. This was due both to personality and circumstance. As a professional officer, Marshall's attitudes were similar to those of the Joint Chiefs. As an Army man, he leaned toward the vertical system of civil-military relations under which the Army had operated since 1903. His service also coincided with the Korean rearmament when the needs of the military necessarily had high priority. The United States, after going through the famine period of its normal cycle, was swinging back toward the other extreme. Marshall's inclination toward the military spokesman role was indicated by the essentially passive concept he had of his duties. He did not attempt to be a positive, creative initiator of, and contributor to, policy and the resolution of policy conflicts. Nor did he organize his office for this role. The supplementary budget estimates formulated under his direction in the fall of 1951 reflected the preëminence of the military requirements determined by the Joint Chiefs as the "principal item" of concern. The requests of the Chiefs were not, in Marshall's view, to be balanced off against the needs of economy and other claims. Failure to meet the minimum requirements of the Chiefs would seriously endanger the security of the nation and of its military forces.[14]

BUSINESS MANAGER. The business-manager Secretary devotes his energies primarily to the civil activities of the Department: administration, organization, logistics, supply, fiscal management, construction, procurement, and personnel. He also conceives of himself as primarily the representative of the civilian interest in economy. He sides with the Comptroller against the Joint Chiefs. The two Secretaries whose performance in office most closely approximated the business-manager role were Louis Johnson and Charles E. Wilson. Their tendencies in this direction were one aspect of their general embodiment and reflection of liberal values and forces. Both stressed the importance of a strong economy to the nation's defense. Johnson justified economies in the name of unification and unification in the name of economies. Wilson argued for "more defense for less money." Both leaned primarily upon their fiscal advisers and organized their offices so as to de-emphasize staff aids which might enable them to function as independent policy strategists. Johnson ended the policy secretariat which Forrestal had strived to develop under John Ohly and instead created a Defense Management Committee because of the necessity for "a continuing program to reduce Department of Defense expenditures." [15] Similarly, Wilson did not follow the recommendations of his predecessor for a combined civil-military policy staff. He believed that government should be organized on the same principles as business, and he added six additional functional assistant secretary "vice presidents" to the Office of the Secretary of Defense.[16]

The tendency of the business-manager Secretary to concentrate primarily on the civil side of his job to the exclusion of strategy was perhaps best exemplified in Wilson's first year in Washington. Wilson summed up his concept of his role with: "Leave the military stuff up to the military, production up to us." Secretary Lovett had defined his duty as "the establishment of policies under the guidance of the President." Wilson, on the other hand, it was reported, thought his function was "to manage military policy rather than to make it." As one Washington correspondent summed up Wilson after a few months: "He is no strategist, has no intention of trying to be. That is the military job. What he must do is supervise the organization of buying, manpower, construction and operation, in the field and in the Pentagon for efficiency and to eliminate waste and duplication." This emphasis was not unnatural, since, as one of his subordinates in the Defense Department put it, his chief qualifications for the job were his "managerial genius, his ability to choose men, and his unique skill at production." [17]

Both Johnson and Wilson in determining the size of the military budget and military force levels relied primarily upon the internal advice and assistance of the Comptroller and the external support and pressure of the Budget Bureau and Treasury. Military advice played a minor role in their decisions. Thus, in the early fall of

1949, on the recommendation of the Management Committee and without asking the services as to its implications for their programs, Johnson ordered a reduction of $929 million in service expenditures for Fiscal 1950.[18] The formulation of Wilson's first defense budget began with the Secretary's pledge that his Department would reduce its share of the national budget deficit. The first decision was on the size of the cut in the earlier Truman-Lovett estimates. Then, after the budget had been fixed, the calculations were made as to the military forces that could be supported by the reduced estimates. It was not clear until the end of the budget-making process what the impact of the cuts would be on force levels and national strategy. The budget was primarily the work of Deputy Secretary Roger Kyes and Comptroller McNeil. While obviously the Joint Chiefs were aware that reductions were under way, it was apparently not until the last moment that they knew of the actual amounts to be allocated to each service. Although they protested these decisions, it was by then too late. In General Vandenberg's words, "the Chiefs, as the Joint Chiefs of Staff, have not been participants in the makeup of this budget." Ironically, the Secretary of the Air Force also declared that he had not participated in the decision on the cut because that "is not the province" of a civilian secretary: "I think that is a military decision and one that must be made by those who are competent to make that decision." [19] While Wilson like Talbott could avoid considering strategy, he could not avoid the effects that his actions, in identifying himself with McNeil, would have on strategy. Inevitably, the reduction in the goals of the Air Force build-up from 143 wings in 1955 to 120 wings in 1956 had significant implications for American military policy.

POLICY STRATEGIST. Two Secretaries of Defense, James Forrestal and Robert A. Lovett, conceived of themselves primarily as policy strategists. Both accepted the responsibility of balancing military requirements and economic demands. Both played an active and creative mediating role in the formulation of force levels and budget estimates. Both were hampered and frustrated by the lack of sufficient legal authority and, even more, by the lack of adequate staff assistance. Both urged the creation of staff organs which would enable the Secretary to discharge his functions in a responsible and effective manner. The contrast between their methods of operation and those of Marshall on the one hand, and Johnson and Wilson on the other, may be illustrated by their roles in the formulation of the 1950 and 1953 military budgets.

Forrestal and the 1950 Budget. From the start, Forrestal was faced with a presidential ceiling of $15 billion on the military budget. The President had established this on the advice of the Budget Bureau apparently without consulting either the JCS or the NSC. The uncoordinated original estimates of the three military services, on the other hand, totaled $30 billion.[20] The task of the Secretary was to find the optimum balance of security and economy between these two extremes. When it appeared unlikely that the Joint Chiefs would be able to arrive at an allocation of the presidential figure among the services, Forrestal first considered appointing a special board of high-ranking officers to advise him directly on this problem. Subsequently, however, he instead directed the Chiefs to appoint a Budget Advisory Committee (the McNarney Board) to review service requests and attempt to bring them to some acceptable level. He also tried unsuccessfully to get guidance from the NSC as to the foreign-policy assumptions which should underlie the budget. Forrestal constantly emphasized the relation between strategy and money. The McNarney Board, for instance, reduced the service requests to $23.6 billion, which, it was said, would put the United States in a reasonable degree of readiness in the event of war. A budget of $15 billion, on the other hand, Forrestal eventually drew from the JCS, would only permit the United States to mount a strategic bombing offensive from Britain. Forrestal presented these alternatives to the President, but the latter appeared definite on the $15 billion ceiling. Nonetheless, Forrestal obtained tacit permission to go ahead along two lines: the $15 billion budget and another "intermediate" budget which would permit not only the air offensive from Britain, but which would also enable the United States to maintain control of the Mediterranean. The JCS estimated that this second strategy would require $16.9 billion. The alternatives in terms of dollars and policy were thus clear. When submitted to the President a few weeks before the budget was due to be presented to Congress, Truman again reaffirmed his decision in favor of the $15 billion, British air offensive choice. In one last effort, Forrestal then proposed that the President grant the military an additional $770 million so that they could add a half dozen more bomber groups. If the United States was to limit its capabilities to a strategic air offensive, he wanted to have sufficient air strength to insure success. The President still maintained a deaf ear, however, and in the end the Budget Bureau even reduced the budget somewhat below the $15 billion ceiling.

The 1950 military budget was thus a case where a firm presidential ceiling was set and maintained. This did not, however, prevent Forrestal from functioning as a creative policy strategist. Both sides of the coin were constantly before him. An increase in the budget had to be justified in terms of its "functional" strategic gains. A decrease in the budget had to be weighed in terms of its effect on American capabilities in the event of war. Every dollar had a strategic implication and justification.

Lovett and the 1953 Budget. The formulation of the 1953 military budget was in many respects quite different from that of 1950, yet Secretary Lovett played essentially the same role then that Secretary Forrestal had played previously. The starting point for 1953 was not a Budget Bureau ceiling, but rather the force-level estimate of the Joint Chiefs, in which the key element was the recommendation that the Air Force goal be increased from 95 wings to 143 wings in 1954. These force levels were approved by the NSC in October 1951. The initial uncoordinated requests of the military services based on these forces totaled $71 billion in new obligational authority. Faced with this imposing figure, Secretary Lovett and the NSC directed the military services to prepare an alternative "point of departure" budget based on new appropriations of $45 billion. As in 1951, preparation of both budgets went on simultaneously. In the end, Lovett recommended a budget of $55 billion to the President based upon the achievement of the recommended force levels in 1953 and 1954. Over the protests of Lovett and the Joint Chiefs, the President reduced this to $52 billion, which delayed the date of achieving the 143-wing Air Force from 1954 to 1955. Here, too, the Secretary played a creative, mediating role balancing extra expenditures against calculated risks. On the one hand, in Lovett's words, the budget did "not give us, within the time that the military leaders feel desirable, the strengths which they feel necessary." On the other hand, neither did the Comptroller-Budget Bureau viewpoint completely prevail.[21]

Both Forrestal and Lovett were frustrated by the lack of an adequate staff equipped to develop over-all policies. Both recognized this deficiency and attempted to remedy it. Forrestal appointed his first statutory special assistant, John Ohly, as head of an office of the Secretariat. Ohly advised the Secretary on the co-ordination of plans and programs, served as executive secretary of the War Council and other policy committees, and collected and analyzed the facts and opinions relevant to important decisions. He also was the Defense Department liaison with the State Department and the NSC. In title and substance this office was inspired by the English Cabinet Secretariat and was to provide the same sort of services for Forrestal which that office does for the Prime Minister.[22] In addition to this civilian policy staff, Forrestal attempted to develop an independent source of military advice, relying primarily on Major General Alfred M. Gruenther, Director of the Joint Staff. Forrestal viewed Gruenther as his "principal military adviser" and utilized him as his intermediary in dealing with the Joint Chiefs. Gruenther was in constant attendance at all important meetings, accompanied the Secretary on his travels, and placed at his disposal "real ability" in "achieving resolution of differences." [23] At various times, Forrestal also attempted to develop other sources of military judgment which would furnish him with an independent check on the conclusions of the Joint Chiefs.* He was, indeed, engaged in an almost constant search for unbiased military advice. But, in the end, he usually fell back on Gruenther.

Lovett's experience led him to conclude that the Secretary of Defense should be furnished with a "combined military-civilian staff" responsible to him alone. This staff would aid him in resolving disputes among the services, distributing shortages among them,

---

* Forrestal at times turned to *ad hoc* military groups such as the Advisory Committee on the 1950 budget and the Spaatz-Towers committee. He also consulted frequently with General Eisenhower after the latter went on inactive service and brought him back to Washington at the beginning of 1949 to serve as temporary chairman of the JCS. In the spring of 1948, the Army had blocked his efforts to get General Bradley made his principal military adviser. Forrestal's use of General Gruenther in this capacity made difficult Gruenther's relations with Admiral Leahy, presiding officer of the JCS.

and helping him formulate policies on the budget, procurement, logistics, manpower, personnel, and intelligence. In the absence of such a staff, the Secretary was forced to turn many administrative and policy matters unrelated to their principal functions over to the Joint Chiefs, and to rely upon them exclusively for military facts and "experienced military judgment." Only if the Secretary had a civil-military policy staff would it be possible to confine the Chiefs to their proper concern with war plans.[24]

THE NEEDS OF THE OFFICE

A balanced system of civil-military relations in the Department of Defense requires that the Secretary function as a policy strategist. The principal obstacles to the achievement of a balanced system are political forces outside the realm of structure and organization. Nonetheless, administrative means exist which would enhance the ability of the Secretary to act as a policy strategist even within the prevailing political framework. The three prerequisites are: (1) adequate legal authority for the Secretary; (2) adequate staff assistance in the Secretary's office; and (3) the appointment as Secretary of individuals equipped to perform a policy-making role.

LEGAL AUTHORITY. The National Security Act of 1947 gave the Secretary of Defense inadequate control over the National Military Establishment. The 1949 amendments to the Act extended his authority in four ways. The military services were reduced from the status of executive departments to that of military departments within a single Department of Defense presided over by the Secretary. The limiting word "general" was removed from the 1947 provisions granting the Secretary "general direction, authority, and control" over the military establishment. The Secretary was designated as the "principal assistant to the President in all matters relating to the Department of Defense." The "Tenth Amendment" clause in the 1947 act giving the services all authority not specifically granted to the Secretary of Defense was eliminated.

Events after 1949 demonstrated that a further clarification of the Secretary's authority was desirable, particularly with respect to the Joint Chiefs of Staff. Some "legal beavers," Secretary Lovett complained, argued that the provision which placed the Joint Chiefs under the "authority and direction of the President and the

Secretary of Defense" meant that the JCS was not "directly under" the Secretary. Lovett suggested that the complete authority of the Secretary over the Chiefs and the military departments be spelled out in additional legislation. In 1953, the Rockefeller Committee on Defense Organization agreed with Lovett as to the proper scope of the Secretary's control, but declared that existing law gave him this power, and that challenges to it were based on an erroneous interpretation of the National Security Act. A legal opinion by the Committee's counsel defined the scope of the Secretary's authority in sweeping and forceful terms. It held that the clause making the Secretary the "principal assistant" to the President in Defense Department affairs made him Deputy Commander in Chief and "the highest military officer of the Department." No grounds existed for claiming that the Joint Chiefs were outside his authority, and the statutory provision making them the principal military advisers to the President should be interpreted in this light.[25] So long as the legal opinion of the Rockefeller Committee was accepted as the authoritative definition of the powers of the Secretary, he possessed all the power needed to perform his proper role. The issue would only finally be settled, however, if Congress confirmed by statute the interpretation of the powers of the Secretary advanced by the Committee.

STAFF ASSISTANCE. The greatest single deficiency in the organization of the Department of Defense was the absence of the proper staff assistance for the Secretary. Legal authority was meaningless without the organizational means to exercise it. "The creation of the staff facilities," Forrestal said in 1949, "is paramount even to the increase of power." [26] The Secretary was surrounded by antagonists. In front were the State Department and the NSC, presumably pointing out the path of national policy; behind him, the Treasury and the Budget Bureau, always acting as a drag; on either side, the Joint Chiefs and the Comptroller, pushing him off the road in one direction or another. The Secretary, however, was institutionally naked and defenseless. It was not surprising that his functions were encroached upon by other agencies or that he himself found it necessary to identify his interests and role with that of some other agency. He had no support with which to maintain an independent stand.

One argument raised against the need for more staff assistance for the Secretary was the already great size of the Office of the Secretary of Defense. The OSD was intended, it was said, to be a small policy-oriented unit but it had expanded to gigantic proportions with a staff of over two thousand. What use could the Secretary possibly have for any more staff assistance? He was surfeited with staff. The reply to this, of course, was that the important issue was not how much staff the Secretary had, but rather what kind of staff he had, and to what extent the staff was actually his. A staff is only a real aid to an executive when its outlook is his outlook and its interest is his interest. No one of the Secretary's principal staff organs had a scope or an interest as broad as that of the Secretary. The Joint Chiefs gave him military advice; the Comptroller gave him budgetary advice and represented the needs of economy; his other eight assistant secretaries all had limited functional responsibilities and interests; the service secretaries defended their own service needs. The Secretary's office as formally defined was not really his office. It contained agencies and officials representing forces independent of him and whom it was his job to balance and control. The Secretary had assistance to help him in accomplishing everything except the discharge of the one responsibility which was his and his alone: the formulation and enforcement of over-all defense policy. What was needed was the institutionalization of the secretarial viewpoint: a small, competent, corporate body to aid the Secretary in developing the interests and advice surrounding him into a comprehensive military program.

This absence of staff agencies with a secretarial perspective made the Secretary unable to play an independent role and to formulate his own viewpoint. Instead of rising above the subordinate interests within his department, the Secretary was forced to lower himself and identify his interest with that of one of his subordinate agencies. The lack of an effective secretarial office was the institutional reflection of the feast or famine approach to American military policy. In the quiet years of peace, the economy viewpoint held sway, and the Secretary became its instrument. In the years of war, military demands were unquestioned, and the Secretary became a military advocate. If the nation was to have a continuing and consistent military policy along the Aristotelian path between these extremes, however, it needed an organ to represent and embody that interest at the level of the Secretary of Defense. This organ would be an institutional gyroscope designed to keep military policy on an even keel. When political pressures were directed toward a slash in military spending, it would remind political leaders of the needs of security. When the reverse was true, and the military were riding high, it would serve as a counterbalance in the other direction. So long as the nation remained in a state of half-peace and half-war, such an agency was essential. The National Security Act met some of the institutional needs of the Cold War in establishing the NSC and legalizing the Joint Chiefs. But it left a yawning gap at the level of the Secretary of Defense. As the Hoover Commission Task Force pointed out in 1948, the Secretary of Defense "lacked the clarity of authority, the staff assistance, the organizational instrumentalities, and the sheer time" necessary to remain on top of his job. Four years later the same defects still persisted.[27] The need for over-all policy assistance for the Secretary was recognized by virtually all those who had given thoughtful attention to the problem. The weakness of the staff serving the American Secretary was also highlighted by the comparison with that which served his counterpart in Great Britain. There the Minister of Defense was aided by about fifty military officers and high level civil servants headed by a Chief Staff Officer and a Permanent Secretary.* Almost every

* The Chief Staff Officer was the principal military assistant to the Minister and his link with the Chiefs of Staff Committee. The post was at various times filled by a lieutenant general, an Air Marshal, and a retired major general. The staff included twelve to twenty officers. On the civil side, the Permanent Secretary was aided by a deputy secretary, two under secretaries, and seven assistant secretaries. This staff enabled the Minister to play an independent and constructive role in the formulation of defense policy and the defense budget.

In the United States, Admiral Sherman, one of the drafters of the National Security Act, thought the Secretary should have a staff of fifteen to twenty-five military and civilian "$10,000 a year men." *Hearings* before Senate Committee on Armed Services on S. 758, 80th Cong., 1st Sess., p. 155 (1947). Lovett and Vannevar Bush urged a mixed civil-military staff. Generals Bradley and Collins and the 1949 Hoover Commission Task Force stressed the Secretary's need for military advisers. *New York Times,* Jan. 10, 1953, p. 4, Apr. 21, 1953, p. 20; Commission on Organization, *Task Force Report on National Security Organization* (Appendix G, 1949), pp. 12–14, 56–57. Former Air Force Secretary Thomas Finletter suggested a permanent under secretary of defense. *Power and Policy* (New York, 1954), pp. 281–283. The 1955 Hoover Commission proposed the

other executive department in the American government had an
over-all policy staff to assist its secretary. The Hoover Commission
Task Force on Departmental Management recognized this in 1948
and recommended that all departments heads "should have the
necessary machinery for the systematic review of department-wide
policies and programs." [28] The need for this was obviously much
greater in the Department of Defense with its tripartite structure
and its far-flung operations than it was in many of the smaller
domestic departments.

The purpose of a defense policy staff would be to assist the
Secretary of Defense in integrating the conflicting interests of
economy and security and the conflicting interests of the three
services into a comprehensive military program. It would serve
no useful function if it did not rise above all other interests in
the Department and serve only the Secretary. With its assistance
he could establish for the Joint Chiefs the maximum level of defense expenditures permissible from the viewpoint of the national
economy and then insist that they produce the best military plan
within this economic limitation. The Secretary could also establish for the Comptroller the minimum military forces essential for
the nation's security and then insist that he produce a budget
which would provide in the most economic fashion possible for
those military forces. In this manner the Joint Chiefs would be
removed from economics and politics, and the Comptroller would
no longer determine key issues of strategy. Economics and strategy
would be tied together in the hands of the Secretary with the
policy staff as his agent. To fulfill this function the staff would
have to be small, consisting perhaps of no more than a score of
officials. Its membership might be drawn from three sources.
High-level civil servants would contribute experience and continuity. The most promising graduates of the war colleges of field
and general officer rank would bring military expertise and, assuming a three-year detail, a certain element of continuity. Civilian experts and consultants from outside the government would
furnish a fresh approach, specialized knowledge, and would be

creation in the OSD of "a civilian position invested with sufficient stature and
authority to insure the establishment and maintenance of effective planning and
review of military requirements." Commission on Organization, *Business Organization of the Department of Defense* (June 1955), p. 19.

a link between the staff and business, science, and the universities. The head of the staff would be a civilian, possessing the confidence of the Secretary, but so far as possible a permanent official divorced from politics. The ranking military officer on the staff, a major general or lieutenant general or his equivalent, would be the deputy director. He would be the link between the staff and the Joint Chiefs and would normally attend meetings of the latter.

THE CALIBER OF THE MAN. The final essential to the proper functioning of the Department of Defense is the appointment as Secretary of individuals qualified for the office. In a Cold War the Secretary of Defense is by any standard one of the two or three most important men in the government. As the head of a defense government within a government, he has responsibilities significantly different from and greater than those of other departmental chiefs. His office, however, is still young as government offices go. Its powers and prerogatives have not been defined and frozen into a fixed pattern. It is still primarily the man who shapes the office rather than the office which shapes the man. Personality and tradition are more important than statutes. The Secretary of State acquired a primacy among cabinet officers, not because of his legal power or the importance of his functions. For a hundred years, from 1815 to 1917, these were relatively minor. The stature of the office was determined by the stature of its secretaries: Jefferson, Madison, John Quincy Adams, Clay, Webster, Calhoun, Seward, Hay, Root, Hughes, Stimson, Hull. The Defense Secretaryship deserves men of no less caliber.

What are the desirable characteristics of a Secretary of Defense? First, he should be a man of experience, possessing some familiarity with the problems with which he will be dealing. This is probably best achieved by service in one of the subordinate secretaryships within the Department. Marshall's prior experience as Army Chief of Staff, 1939–1945, and Secretary of State, 1947–1949, although not of this sort was no less valuable. On the other hand, Forrestal had been Under Secretary of the Navy in World War II and Secretary of the Navy from 1944 to 1947. Lovett had been Assistant Secretary of War for Air during World War II, Under Secretary of State in 1947 and 1948, and Deputy Secretary of Defense for a year before moving up to the top position. Louis

Johnson had been Assistant Secretary of War from 1937 to 1940. An awareness of the complexity of defense issues, the relations among the services, the problems of phasing, procurement, intelligence, and an appreciation of the multiplicity of interests and functions can only be achieved through this type of prior service.

Second, the Secretary should be a man of respect, commanding the admiration of informed public opinion. He must be publicly recognized as a man of stature, integrity, responsibility, and respectability. His ability and honesty must inspire confidence if not consensus. He must, in short, have some of the makings of a statesman. This is essential for the public image of the office. The American people will permit many individuals to be Attorney General or Postmaster General whom they would never permit to be Secretary of State. We demand statesmen in the latter case; we accept, if we do not prefer, machine politicians, special-interest representatives, or personal cronies in the other. The public image of the Secretary of Defense should be similar to that of the Secretary of State.

Third, he should be a man of dedication, acting and thinking purely in terms of the needs of the office. He must concentrate on those alone and be free of external influences, interests, and ambitions. Forrestal at one point indicated that the Secretary of Defense should be nonpolitical in the partisan sense. Whether he has been a partisan figure at the time of his appointment to office really matters little except insofar as it may affect the respect in which he is held. But it is still possible for men to be partisan leaders and to command bipartisan respect. What is essential, however, is that he cease to act and think as a partisan when he takes office. The Secretaryship of Defense was the end of their public career for its first four incumbents. With Forrestal this was a matter of necessity; with Johnson a matter of circumstance; and with Marshall and Lovett a matter of choice. Nonetheless, the precedent has been established. The office of Secretary of Defense should be the end point not a stepping stone in a public career. Only if this tradition is maintained will it be possible for the Secretary to dedicate himself to his job with the singleminded concern which is essential for success.

Finally, the Secretary must be a man of policy. His greatest needs are breadth, wisdom, insight, and, above all, judgment. He is neither operator, administrator, nor commander. But he is policy maker. He must accept this arduous role with good cheer, and neither try to escape its duties nor abdicate its responsibilities. He does not need the dynamic drive, the organizing flair, the energetic ruthlessness of the forceful manager whether civilian or military. He does need the capacity to analyze, to discriminate, to evaluate, and to reconcile conflicting claims and interests. He should have his own ideas on policy, and he needs initiative. But he also requires patience and humility. Men who combine these characteristics are rare, but experience indicates that America is not without them.

17

Toward a New Equilibrium

THE REQUISITE FOR SECURITY

The tension between the demands of military security and the values of American liberalism can, in the long run, be relieved only by the weakening of the security threat or the weakening of liberalism. During the decade after World War II the immediate dangers to American security varied in intensity. At times, the United States moved close to total war, became involved in limited war, or lagged dangerously behind in the armaments race. At other times, the threats seemed to recede, the Soviets and their allies acquiesced in peaceful coexistence and apparently surrendered, at least temporarily, their ambitions to extend their sway. The United States oscillated between the December spirit of the Yalu and the July spirit of Geneva. Whatever the fluctuations in the international temperature, however, American involvement as a major participant in world politics remained an undeniable fact, and the Cold War rivalry between the United States and the Soviet states appeared a relatively permanent aspect of the international scene. Under these circumstances, the United States necessarily had to maintain military forces on a level far higher than that to which it was accustomed prior to 1940. Military considerations remained important in American foreign policy. Military men and institutions continued to wield significant influence and authority. These imperatives rendered impossible the restoration of the old balance of civil-military relations which had prevailed until World War II. On the other hand, the furtherance of national security required the maximizing of civilian control and military professionalism. The achievement of these ends was hampered by institutional and ideological obstacles. The institutional hindrances, however, were relatively secondary. The constitutional separation of powers was the only really significant institution complicating the achievement of civilian control and military professionalism. Aside from that, professional military institutions could be fitted without undue difficulty into the American political, economic, and social structure. Civilian institutions were preëminently liberal in character, but no necessary conflict existed between them and professional military institutions, so long as each was kept within its proper sphere. The real problem was the ideological one, the American attitude of mind which sought to impose liberal solutions in military affairs as well as in civil life. This tendency constituted the gravest domestic threat to American military security. So long as the Cold War continued, that security would depend upon the ability of the United States to evolve an intellectual climate more favorable to the existence of military professionalism and the achievement of objective civilian control.

CHANGES IN THE IDEOLOGICAL ENVIRONMENT

While liberalism continued to dominate the American approach to civil-military relations in the postwar decade, some evidence also existed of the beginnings of a fundamental change which might herald the emergence of a new, more sympathetically conservative environment for military institutions. These beginnings by no means constituted a major revolution in the American intellectual climate. But, if continued and enlarged upon, they would facilitate the establishment of a new equilibrium in civil-military relations compatible with the security demands of the Cold War. This undercurrent, after all, was not to be unexpected. The revolution in the American security position since the 1930's could hardly fail to leave some imprint on the varied patterns of American thought.

The New Conservatism. The "new conservatives" were in some respects less conservative than they claimed to be. The views expressed in much of their writing came closer to a more sophisticated version of business liberalism than to a true conservatism. Nonetheless, the appearance of a reasonably articulate group of American intellectuals and writers eager to assume the title of "conservative" and to expound the virtues of Burke and Calhoun was in itself a noteworthy event in American intellectual history. Some of the publicists appeared to be rather self-consciously conservative, thereby giving the movement many of the characteristics of a passing intellectual fad. Other thinkers and authors, however, such as Reinhold Niebuhr, T. S. Eliot, and Eric Voegelin, were, without embracing the conservative label, expressing fundamentally conservative values. No one, furthermore, could question Eliot's popular literary preëminence in the postwar decade, and Niebuhr seemed to have some chance of being looked back upon by subsequent generations as the most significant American social thinker of the mid-century. The currents of the new conservatism, moreover, if they did not cut deep into the liberal waters, at least spread wide across the cultural surface. In education a mounting reaction developed against John Dewey's progressivism. In religion, neo-orthodoxy, sparked by Niebuhr, represented the most vigorous element in American Protestantism; and significant conservative currents existed in Catholicism and Judaism. The revival of popular interest in religion was itself possibly a sign of changing times. In the social sciences, economists and political scientists abandoned the mood of the 1930's and early 1940's which had been highly critical of American political and economic institutions. New virtues were discovered in the old facts of American capitalism and the American Constitution. Writers such as Boorstin and Hartz analyzed the inherently conservative tone of American institutions and the fundamentally liberal character of American thought. Positing the need for an absolute moral code, Walter Lippmann expressed grave doubts as to the ability of unguided popular democracy to conduct public affairs. All these disparate developments hardly made up a coherent intellectual movement. Nonetheless, they were signs of a reëxamination of American society and American values from a more conservative viewpoint. Their significance for civil-military relations was that in due course they might result in the widespread acceptance by Americans of values more like those of the military ethic. Present in virtually all the strands of the new conservatism were a stress on the limitations of man, an acceptance of institutions as they were, a critique of utopianism and "solutionism," and a new respect for history and society as against progress and the individual. While having, perhaps, little immediate relevance to the achievement of objective civilian control and military professionalism, the broad currents of the new conservatism offered the greatest hope that these goals might be more fully realizable in the future.[1]

Academic Realism. The postwar decade saw a startling change in the prevailing academic approach to international relations. In the 1930's, the emphasis had been almost entirely upon the questions of form and structure studied in courses in international law and international organization. The basic value premise was usually the desirability of world organization. By the late 1940's, however, American writers were vying with each other in denouncing the moralism, legalism, utopianism, Wilsonism, and sentimentalism of the American diplomatic past. The State Department Policy Planning group, particularly George Kennan, played some part in the new appreciation of power politics, but the preëminent figure was Hans J. Morgenthau, whose books on international relations achieved an unrivaled acceptance during this period. "The statesman," Morgenthau warned, in contrast to earlier American viewpoints, "must think in terms of the national interest conceived as a power among powers." In this new realism, American civilian thought essentially accepted the interpretation of international politics preached by American military writers since the 1870's.[2] Another aspect of the academic change was the increasing attention given in colleges and universities to the problems of national security. Courses were established in foreign policy, military history, and defense policy, and institutes blossomed to further research in these areas. Most of the earlier American writing on military affairs had focused primarily upon the danger the security programs presented to other social values such as civil rights and free enterprise. Much of the immediate postwar writing continued in this vein. By 1955, however, concern for the achievement of security itself was the more frequent motivation apparent behind the scholarly studies of military affairs.

The Waning of Fusionism. By the end of the postwar decade some doubts were being expressed as to the advantages of encouraging political thinking by professional military officers and the assumption of political responsibilities by professional military institutions. It became obvious that the Joint Chiefs of Staff could not participate in the "good" politics of policy without also becoming enmeshed in the "bad" politics of partisanship. The need for some secure fount of impartial professional judgment became more widely accepted.[3] If military considerations are vital to national policy, and if the generals and admirals do not represent the military viewpoint, who will? Considerable uneasiness was aroused by the role of the Chiefs in the MacArthur controversy and the subsequent Republican attacks on the Truman Chiefs and Democratic attacks on the Eisenhower Chiefs. As Walter Lippmann warned at the time, a schism between the generals of the Republican Party and the generals of the Democratic Party would be "an almost intolerable thing" in the Republic. The conflict between the Senate Permanent Investigations Subcommittee under the chairmanship of Joseph R. McCarthy and the Department of the Army dramatically demonstrated some of the more blatant results of the prostitution of military organization to political goals. It was one of the few instances in American history where the organs of opinion rallied to the defense of military institutions against the attacks of a civilian politician with a sizable popular following. The coalition of interests and viewpoints on the Army side extended from the extreme left which had previously been so bitterly critical of the "military mind" to rightist groups as far over as *The Chicago Tribune.* If they accomplished nothing else, the Army-McCarthy hearings made many reform liberals aware for the first time of the fundamental distinction between traditional conservatism and nihilistic reaction.

Restoring Military Integrity. The early postwar drive to civilianize the military services which had been symbolized by the Doolittle Board lost some of its momentum during the Korean War years. In its place appeared a fairly widespread concern in civilian as well as military circles for the declining prestige of the military career and the shaky morale of the officer corps. The Womble Committee report in 1953 and the persistent warnings of Hanson Baldwin and others called public attention to the plight of the military, the press generally reacting favorably to the military pleas, and even Congress manifesting a sympathetic interest. While this shift in intellectual environment did not reverse the tendencies in the opposite direction, it did enable a number of measures to be taken in 1953–1955 toward restoring the integrity of the officer corps and the attractiveness of the military career. Congress improved retirement benefits, liberalized promotion opportunities, and increased military pay. Within the services, more emphasis was placed upon developing combat leaders instead of technical specialists. The Uniform Code of Military Justice was widely criticized, and proposals were submitted to restore the authority of commanding officers to punish minor infractions without court martial. While measures such as these did not immediately stop military deterioration, they were, nonetheless, signs of a widespread apprehension as to the ultimate affects of any further encroachment upon the integrity and status of the officer corps.[4]

The Literary Image of the Officer. Changes in the fictional portrayal of any social type usually reflect and help shape more general changes in public attitudes. Perhaps one of the more significant developments toward the end of the postwar decade was the appearance of a more appreciative interpretation of the military in popular fiction. This represented a distinct change from the main tradition of American literature on military subjects which had carried over into the early postwar years. The first outstanding postwar "war" novel, Norman Mailer's *The Naked and the Dead* published in 1948, presented the traditional liberal stereotype of the Regular Army officer: Major General Cummings is a fascist at heart, expounding a philosophy derived from Nietzsche and Spengler of power for its own sake and of fear as the basis of authority which would have well become Dostoievski's Grand Inquisitor. Cummings' foil, and the book's principal hero, is Lieutenant Robert Hearn, a Harvard-educated intellectual liberal, who, however, agrees with the major general that the power morality is the wave of the future. Hearn thus reflects the liberal pessimism of Lasswell's garrison-state theory, a pessimism evidently shared by Mailer who titles his flashback of Hearn's early life "The Addled Womb" while that of Cummings is described as "A Peculiarly American Statement." *The Naked and the Dead* falls squarely within the great American tradition of antiwar, antimilitary literature.

Three years after the publication of Mailer's novel, however, definite signs of change were evident. The second great war novel, James Jones's *From Here to Eternity,* appears also to have a simple liberal theme: the individual versus the organization. There is, however, more to Jones's book than this. Running throughout it is a sense of identification with the Army and the military way of life which begins with its dedication to "The United States Army" and its prefacing quote from Kipling: "I've eaten your bread and salt . . ." The Army and its values are necessary to the individual. The hero, Private Robert E. Lee Prewitt, an ideal military type (symbolized in his name), finds a home in the Army, but comes to a tragic end because, like all human institutions, the Army falls short of its ideal. Prewitt is destroyed in the gap between the Army Militant and the Army Spiritual. In contrast to Mailer, Jones's ideals are military ideals; his heroes, Prewitt and Sergeant Warden, are true soldiers; the villain, Captain Holmes, falls short of the soldierly code. Like Mailer, Jones focuses on the psychological implications of the conflict of freedom and authority. But while Hearn's rebellion against Cummings is fundamentally petty, meaningless, and negative, affirming nothing except ego-irritation, Prewitt's rebellion against Holmes is the affirmation of the true spirit of the Army, an appeal to the military conscience of the Army, from which it has departed in practice. Infused throughout *From Here to Eternity* is a sensitivity to the beauty, appeal, and meaning of the military life, its rewards and richness.

The third outstanding war novel was Herman Wouk's *The Caine Mutiny,* which sold two million copies after its publication in 1951 and also appeared in highly successful screen and stage versions. Throughout most of the book, Wouk deceives his readers as to the moral of his tale. Captain Queeg, the Regular Navy officer, combines the vices of Cummings and Holmes into a distinctly psychotic personality. His opponents are Keefer, the liberal intellectual, and Maryk, the simple fisherman representing the Rousseauian natural goodness of the common man. Only after the court martial in which Maryk is acquitted for relieving Queeg of his command does the author suddenly reverse direction and bluntly reveal his true point in black and white terms. Queeg was right. Maryk was wrong. Keefer, who prompted Maryk to the mutiny, is the real villain. And the real hero is none of the individual figures, but the United States Navy itself. The junior officers of the *Caine* should have served in silence under Queeg because he was part of the system, and the disruption of the system does more harm than the suffering of individual injustice. The court martial repudiated Queeg because Queeg, like Holmes, had failed to measure up to the military ideal. While the citizen officers of the *Caine* were freely pursuing their own delights in peacetime civil life, however, Queeg and the Regular Navy were mounting guard over the nation's security. Whatever Queeg's faults, the regular officers are a superior breed: "you can't be good in the Army or Navy unless you're goddam good," drunkenly argues Greenwald, Maryk's attorney, "though maybe not up on Proust 'n' *Finnegan's Wake* and all." In the few years separating *The Caine Mutiny* from *The Naked and the Dead* the regular officer and the liberal intellectual had neatly exchanged roles.

CONSERVATISM AND SECURITY

The problem of civilian control and military professionalism has existed on both sides of the Iron Curtain. American and Soviet patterns of civil-military relations have been similar in many respects. In both countries the dominance of a single antimilitary ideology has put obstacles in the way of military professionalism. In both countries, also, the professional officer corps when it did emerge became a force for caution, sanity, and realism. The stronger the military voice, the less the likelihood of conflict. The probability of continued peaceful adjustment between the two nations depends to a large extent on the degree to which communism in the Soviet Union and liberalism in the United States are supplanted by a conservative outlook, divorced from universalistic pretensions, and simply content to preserve and secure what it has. In the Soviet Union, as well as in the United States, this event is not beyond the realms of possibility.

The emergence of a conservative environment in the United

States would reduce the danger of progressive deterioration in American officership. The leadership produced by the American officer corps has so far been extraordinary. Only a small handful of the hundreds of general and flag officers have proved incapable in battle, and the top commanders in all three twentieth-century wars have been men of exceptional ability. This success, however, was to a large extent the product of the old pattern of civil-military relations. Since 1940 the American people have been coasting on the quality of the past. Unless a new balance is created, the continued disruption of American civil-military relations cannot help but impair the caliber of military professionalism in the future. A political officer corps, rent with faction, subordinated to ulterior ends, lacking prestige but sensitive to the appeals of popularity, would endanger the security of the state. A strong, integrated, highly professional officer corps, on the other hand, immune to politics and respected for its military character, would be a steadying balance wheel in the conduct of policy. During the twenty years prior to 1939 the political leaders of Europe brushed aside the warnings of the professional diplomats who were working cautiously and quietly to protect their nations from disaster. Even greater calamity would follow if in the twenty years after World War II the voice of the professional soldier went similarly unheeded. In a liberal society the power of the military is the greatest threat to their professionalism. Yet, so long as American military security is threatened, that power is not likely to diminish significantly. The requisite for military security is a shift in basic American values from liberalism to conservatism. Only an environment which is sympathetically conservative will permit American military leaders to combine the political power which society thrusts upon them with the military professionalism without which society cannot endure.

THE WORTH OF THE MILITARY IDEAL

Just south of the United States Military Academy at West Point is the village of Highland Falls. Main Street of Highland Falls is familiar to everyone: the First National Bank with venetian blinds, real estate and insurance offices, yellow homes with frilly victorian porticos, barber shops, and wooden churches —

the tiresome monotony and the incredible variety and discordancy of small-town commercialism. The buildings form no part of a whole: they are simply a motley, disconnected collection of frames coincidentally adjoining each other, lacking common unity or purpose. On the military reservation the other side of South Gate, however, exists a different world. There is ordered serenity. The parts do not exist on their own, but accept their subordination to the whole. Beauty and utility are merged in gray stone. Neat lawns surround compact, trim homes, each identified by the name and rank of its occupant. The buildings stand in fixed relation to each other, part of an over-all plan, their character and station symbolizing their contributions, stone and brick for the senior officers, wood for the lower ranks. The post is suffused with the rhythm and harmony which comes when collective will supplants individual whim. West Point is a community of structured purpose, one in which the behavior of men is governed by a code, the product of generations. There is little room for presumption and individualism. The unity of the community incites no man to be more than he is. In order is found peace; in discipline, fulfillment; in community, security. The spirit of Highland Falls is embodied in Main Street. The spirit of West Point is in the great, gray, Gothic Chapel, starting from the hill and dominating The Plain, calling to mind Henry Adams' remarks at Mont St. Michel on the unity of the military and the religious spirits. But the unity of the Chapel is even greater. There join together the four great pillars of society: Army, Government, College, and Church. Religion subordinates man to God for divine purposes; the military life subordinates man to duty for society's purposes. In its severity, regularity, discipline, the military society shares the characteristics of the religious order. Modern man may well find his monastery in the Army.

West Point embodies the military ideal at its best; Highland Falls the American spirit at its most commonplace. West Point is a gray island in a many colored sea, a bit of Sparta in the midst of Babylon. Yet is it possible to deny that the military values — loyalty, duty, restraint, dedication — are the ones America most needs today? That the disciplined order of West Point has more to offer than the garish individualism of Main Street? Historically, the virtues of West Point have been America's vices, and the vices of the military, America's virtues. Yet today America can learn more from West Point than West Point from America. Upon the soldiers, the defenders of order, rests a heavy responsibility. The greatest service they can render is to remain true to themselves, to serve with silence and courage in the military way. If they abjure the military spirit, they destroy themselves first and their nation ultimately. If the civilians permit the soldiers to adhere to the military standard, the nations themselves may eventually find redemption and security in making that standard their own.

NOTES

INDEX

Notes

Chapter 1 — Officership as a Profession

1. This author has discovered only one volume in English which analyzes officership as a profession: Michael Lewis, *England's Sea Officers: The Story of the Naval Profession* (London, 1939). More typical is the standard history of the professions in Great Britain which omits mention of the military "because the service which soldiers are trained to render is one which it is hoped they will never be called upon to perform." A. M. Carr-Saunders and P. A. Wilson, *The Professions* (Oxford, 1933), p. 3. Sociological studies, following Max Weber, have usually analyzed the military as a bureaucratic structure. See H. H. Gerth and C. Wright Mills (eds.), *From Max Weber* (New York, 1946), pp. 221–223; C. D. Spindler, "The Military — A Systematic Analysis," *Social Forces*, XXVII (October 1948), 83–88; C. H. Page, "Bureaucracy's Other Face," *Social Forces*, XXV (October 1946), 88–94; H. Brotz and E. K. Wilson, "Characteristics of Military Society," *Amer. Jour. of Sociology*, LI (March 1946), 371–375. While bureaucracy is characteristic of the officer corps, it is, however, a secondary not an essential characteristic. Other writers have followed the liberal tendency to identify the military with the enemies of liberalism and have stressed the feudal-aristocratic elements in militarism. See Alfred Vagts, *A History of Militarism* (New York, 1937), and Arnold Rose, "The Social Structure of the Army," *Amer. Jour. of Sociology*, LI (March 1946), 361–364. For definitions of professionalism, see Carr-Saunders and Wilson, *The Professions*, pp. 284–285, 298, 303, 365, 372; A. M. Carr-Saunders, *Professions: Their Organization and Place in Society* (Oxford, 1928), p. 5; Talcott Parsons, "A Sociologist Looks at the Legal Profession," *Essays in Sociological Theory* (Glencoe, Ill., rev. ed., 1954), p. 372, and *The Social System* (Glencoe, Ill., 1951), p. 454; Abraham Flexner, "Is Social Work a Profession?" *Proceedings*, National Conference of Charities and Correction (1915), pp. 578–581; Carl F. Taeusch, *Professional and Business Ethics* (New York, 1926), pp. 13–18; Roy Lewis and Angus Maude, *Professional People* (London, 1952), pp. 55–56, 64–69, 210; Roscoe Pound, *The Lawyer from Antiquity to Modern Times* (St. Paul, 1953), pp. 4–10; R. H. Tawney, *The Acquisitive Society* (New York, 1920), p. 92; Graham Wallas, *Our Social Heritage* (New Haven, 1921), pp. 122–157; M. L. Cogan, "The Problem of Defining a Profession," *Annals* of the American Academy, CCXCVII (January 1955), 105–111. Professional education is discussed in T. Parsons, "Remarks on Education and the Professions," *Intntl. Jour. of*

Ethics, XLVII (April 1937), 366–367, and Robert M. Hutchins, *The Higher Learning in America* (New Haven, 1936), pp. 51–57. The ups and downs of the legal profession in the United States may be traced in terms of the liberal education requirement. See Pound, *Lawyer from Antiquity to Modern Times,* p. 229; M. Louise Rutherford, *The Influence of the American Bar Association on Public Opinion and Legislation* (Philadelphia, 1937), pp. 46ff. On professional ethics, see Taeusch, *Professional and Business Ethics;* Benson Y. Landis, *Professional Codes* (New York, 1927); R. D. Kohn, "The Significance of the Professional Ideal: Professional Ethics and the Public Interest," *Annals* of the American Academy, CI (May 1922), 1–5; R. M. MacIver, "The Social Significance of Professional Ethics," *ibid.,* pp. 6–7; Oliver Garceau, *The Political Life of the American Medical Association* (Cambridge, 1941), pp. 5–11; James H. Means, *Doctors, People, and Government* (Boston, 1953), pp. 36–40; George Sharswood, *An Essay on Professional Ethics* (Philadelphia, 5th ed., 1907, first published 1854); Samuel Warren, *The Moral, Social, and Professional Duties of Attornies and Solicitors* (Edinburgh and London, 1848); Henry S. Drinker, *Legal Ethics* (New York, 1953); "Ethical Standards and Professional Conduct," *Annals* of the Amer. Academy, CCXCVII (January 1955), 37–45. For the origins of occupational values in general, see E. C. Hughes, "Personality Types and the Division of Labor," *Amer. Jour. of Sociology,* XXXIII (March 1928), 762.

Chapter 2 — The Rise of the Military Profession in Western Society

1. See John U. Nef, *War and Human Progress* (Cambridge, Mass., 1950), pp. 93ff.; Robert G. Albion, *Introduction to Military History* (New York, 1929), pp. 98ff.; John W. Fortescue, *A History of the British Army* (London, 13 vols., 1899–1930), IV, 212–213, V, 223–225; Walter L. Dorn, *Competition for Empire, 1740–1763* (New York, 1940), pp. 82–83; Albert Duruy, *L'Armée Royale en 1789* (Paris, 1888), pp. 26–34; Curt Jany, *Geschichte der Königlich Preussischen Armee* (Berlin, 4 vols., 1928–1933), I, 679–699, III, 60–64, 435–449; Herbert Rosinski, *The German Army* (London, 1939), pp. 17–19.

2. On entry into the French Army, see Duruy, *L'Armée Royale,* pp. 81, 87ff.; Louis Tuetey, *Les Officiers sous L'Ancien Régime: Nobles et Routuriers* (Paris, 1908), *passim;* Spenser Wilkinson, *The French Army Before Napoleon* (Oxford, 1915), pp. 86ff., 92–93, 101; R. Quarré de Verneuil, *L'Armée en France depuis Charles VII jusqu'à la Révolution* (Paris, 1880), p. 261; Edgard Boutaric, *Institutions Militaires de la France* (Paris, 1863), pp. 413–451. For the rationale behind using the army as a means of subsidizing the nobility, see Henry Guerlac, "Science and War in the Old Regime" (Ph.D. Thesis, Harvard Univ., 1941), pp. 251–254. The regular French naval officer corps was, like the Army, a monopoly of the

The Rise of the Military Profession

aristocracy. Dorn, *Competition for Empire*, pp. 117–118. On entry into the Prussian Army, see Karl Demeter, *Das Deutsche Heer und seine Offiziere* (Berlin, 1935), pp. 6–8, 11–13; Jany, *Preussischen Armee*, I, 724–728, II, 219–222, III, 34–37, 420; Felix Priebatsch, *Geschichte des Preussischen Offizierkorps* (Breslau, 1919), p. 13; Rosinski, *German Army*, pp. 30–35; Hans Speier, "Militarism in the Eighteenth Century," *Social Research*, III (August 1936), 309–316. On the purchase system, see Charles M. Clode, *The Military Forces of the Crown* (London, 2 vols., 1869), I, Appendix XVII; Clifford Walton, *History of the British Standing Army, 1660–1700* (London, 1894), pp. 447–456; Fortescue, *British Army*, II, 29–30, IV, 213; Robert Biddulph, *Lord Cardwell at the War Office* (London, 1904), pp. 80–87; C. W. C. Oman, *Wellington's Army, 1809–1814* (New York, 1912), pp. 198–201. For the British Navy, see Michael Lewis, *England's Sea Officers: The Story of the Naval Profession* (London, 1939), pp. 81ff.

3. For French advancement policies, there is C. A. Thomas, *Les Transformations de L'Armée Française* (Paris, 2 vols., 1887), I, 409–410, 415–416; Duruy, *L'Armée Royale*, pp. 73–76, 83–87, 99–102; Léon Mention, *L'Armée de L'Ancien Régime de Louis XIV à la Révolution* (Paris, 1900), pp. 136–141; Wilkinson, *French Army*, pp. 87–88, 93; Albert Babeau, *La Vie Militaire sous L'Ancien Régime* (Paris, 2 vols., 1890), II, ch. ix; Louis Hartmann, *Les Officiers de L'Armée Royale et de la Révolution* (Paris, 1910), pp. 5–22. For comment by one of France's most distinguished eighteenth-century soldiers on the effects of French personnel policies, see Maurice de Saxe, *Reveries on the Art of War* (Harrisburg, 1944), p. 28. On the Prussian system, see Jany, *Preussischen Armee*, I, 541–543, 722–724, 740, II, 223–225; Priebatsch, *Preussischen Offizierkorps*, pp. 7–9; Gerhard Ritter, *Staatskunst und Kriegshandwerk* (Munich, 1954), I, 211; Robert Ergang, *The Potsdam Führer* (New York, 1941), pp. 78–80.

4. A. Stenzel, *The British Navy* (London, 1898), p. 114; Lewis, *England's Sea Officers*, pp. 85–86; Clode, *Military Forces*, I, 192–194, II, 93–94, 336–339; J. S. Omond, *Parliament and the Army, 1642–1904* (Cambridge, 1933), pp. 45–49; Fortescue, *British Army*, IV, 296–298; Alfred Vagts, *A History of Militarism* (New York, 1937), pp. 49, 67–68.

5. *Les Officiers*, pp. 37–38. On the French schools, see Mention, *L'Armée de L'Ancien Régime*, pp. 78–84; Babeau, *La Vie Militaire*, II, 1–78; Jules Clère, *Histoire de L'École de la Flèche* (La Flèche, 1853), *passim;* Guerlac, "Science and War in the Old Regime," chs. 9, 12, pp. 228, 246ff. For Prussian education, see Jany, *Preussischen Armee*, I, 727–728, III, 38–41, 423–426; Priebatsch, *Preussischen Offizierkorps*, pp. 10–22; Henry Barnard, *Military Schools and Courses of Instruction in the Science and Art of War* (Philadelphia, 1862), pp. 284–288; William O. Shanahan, *Prussian Military Reforms: 1786–1813* (New York, 1945), pp. 29, 133–134. On English schools, see Clode, *Military Forces*, I, 457–461; Lewis, *England's Sea Officers*, pp. 87–88; F. G. Guggisberg, *'The Shop': The Story of the Royal Military Academy* (London, 1900), *passim.*

6. J. D. Hittle, *The Military Staff* (Harrisburg, Pa., 1949), pp. 75–85; Jany, *Preussischen Armee*, III, 157–158; Ritter, *Staatskunst und Kriegs-handwerk*, I, 207–209; D. D. Irvine, "The Origins of Capital Staffs," *Jour. of Modern History*, X (June 1938), 166–170.

7. Gordon A. Craig; *The Politics of the Prussian Army, 1640–1945* (Oxford, 1955), pp. 24–26; Priebatsch, *Preussischen Offizierkorps*, pp. 10–11, 15–17; Demeter, *Deutsche Heer*, pp. 9–13, 80; Rosinski, *German Army*, pp. 37, 40; Shanahan, *Prussian Military Reforms*, pp. 95–96; Duruy, *L'Armée Royale*, pp. 211–212; Mention, *L'Armée de L'Ancien Régime*, pp. 141–144; Louis Ducros, *French Society in the Eighteenth Century* (London, 1926), pp. 299–300; Fortescue, *British Army*, I, 573–574, II, 26, VII, 424–426, IX, 86–88, 96, X, 204–206.

8. Military historians have perhaps tended to give eighteenth-century military thought more credit than it deserves. See B. H. Liddell Hart, *The Ghost of Napoleon* (New Haven, 1934), ch. 1; Max Jähns, *Geschichte der Kriegswissenschaften* (Munich and Leipzig, 3 vols., 1889–1891), III, 1769–1770; Henri Mordacq, *La Stratégie: Historique Évolution* (Paris, 3rd ed., 1921), pp. 19–29. Henry Lloyd's *The History of the Late War in Germany* (London, 2 vols. 1781) was a military best seller and was read carefully by Napoleon. See Liddell Hart, *ibid.*, p. 190; Jähns, *ibid.*, pp. 2102–2114; and, for the influence of Lloyd on Clausewitz, Hans Rothfels, *Carl von Clausewitz; Politik und Krieg* (Berlin, 1920), pp. 40–41. Guibert's *Essai General de Tactique* appeared in Paris in 1770 and was translated into English in 1781. For Guibert's influence, see R. R. Palmer, "Frederick the Great, Guibert, Bülow: From Dynastic to National War," in Edward Mead Earle (ed.), *Makers of Modern Strategy* (Princeton, 1952), pp. 62–68; Liddell Hart, *ibid.*, pp. 69–100; Wilkinson, *French Army*, pp. 54–84. On the "classicism" of eighteenth-century thinking, see Liddell Hart, *ibid.*, pp. 15–18, 187; Jähns, *ibid.* III, 1774, 1823–1837. The writings of Pusegur, Guischardt, Mesnil-Durand, Maizeroy, and Zanthier are excellent examples of the classical preoccupation. In general the term "strategy" throughout the eighteenth century was still associated with stratagem. See J. J. Graham, *Elementary History of the Art of War* (London, 1858), pp. 201–202. Flavius Vegetius Renatus, *The Military Institutions of the Romans* (Harrisburg, Pa., 1944), was, according to T. R. Phillips, the "most influential military treatise in the western world from Roman times to the 19th Century."

9. *Reveries*, p. 17.

10. Lloyd, *History*, II, i, vi–x, xxx–xxxi, 69–97.

11. Lloyd, *History*, II, vii, xxi; Saxe, *Reveries*, pp. 119–120; J. A. H. Guibert, *A General Essay on Tactics* (London, 2 vols, 1781), I, xxvi, xlvi–xlvii, lvii, II, 184–185. Compare Vagts, *History of Militarism*, pp. 81ff., who argues that the genius theory was fundamentally progressive.

12. "Reglement über die Besetzung der Stellen der Portepee-Fähnriche, und über die Wahl zum Officier bei der Infanterie, Kavallerie und Artillerie, 6 August 1808," published in Prussian General Staff, *Die Reorganisation*

der Preussischen Armee nach dem Tilsiter Frieden (Berlin, 1857), vol. II, Sec. 3, pp. 366–369. See, generally, Jany, *Preussischen Armee*, III, 426–428, IV, 14–17; Max Lehmann, *Scharnhorst* (Leipzig, 2 vols., 1886), II, ch. 1; Shanahan, *Prussian Military Reforms, passim;* Guy Stanton Ford, *Stein and the Era of Reform in Prussia, 1807–1815* (Princeton, 1922), *passim,* but esp. ch. 8; J. R. Seeley, *Life and Times of Stein* (Boston, 2 vols., 1879), I, 397–423; Hans Delbrück, *Gneisenau* (Berlin, 2 vols., 1882), I, 117–145; Ritter, *Staatskunst und Kriegshandwerk,* I, 97–101; Craig, *Prussian Army,* pp. 37–75.

13. On Germany, see Ritter, *Staatkunst und Kriegshandwerk,* I, 100–101; Lehmann, *Scharnhorst,* II, 62–63; Vagts, *History of Militarism,* pp. 139–145; Demeter, *Deutsche Heer,* pp. 12–14. The best source on France is Raoul Girardet, *La Société Militaire dans la France Contemporaine (1815–1939)* (Paris, 1953), ch. 1.

14. *Democracy in America* (Cambridge, 2 vols., 1863), II, 334–335. In Germany, the struggle between bourgeoisie and aristocrats not only facilitated the emergence of the military profession but also produced an enormous monographic literature on the roles of the two classes in the officer corps.

15. Thomas, *Transformations,* I, 420–422; Girardet, *Société Militaire,* pp. 125–133; Jean Lucas-Dubreton, *The Restoration and the July Monarchy* (New York, 1929), pp. 54–55; Eyre Crowe, *History of the Reigns of Louis XVIII and Charles X* (London, 2 vols., 1854), I, 392ff., II, 37–40; J. Monteilhet, *Les Institutions Militaires de la France (1814–1924)* (Paris, 1926), pp. 9–12; E. Guillon, *Les Complots Militaires sous la Restauration* (Paris, 1895), *passim.*

16. Shanahan, *Prussian Military Reforms,* pp. 75–82, 150ff.; G. S. Ford, "Boyen's Military Law," *Amer. Hist. Rev.,* XX (April 1915), 528–538; Max Jähns, *Das Franzosische Heer von der Grossen Revolution bis zur Gegenwart* (Leipzig, 1873), pp. 291–293, 317–319, 380–383; Thomas James Thackery, *The Military Organization and Administration of France* (London, 2 vols., 1857), I, 61–63; Biddulph, *Lord Cardwell,* p. 211; Omond, *Parliament and the Army,* pp. 118–119; Fortescue, *British Army,* XIII, 560.

17. See Hoffman Nickerson, *The Armed Horde, 1793–1939* (New York, 1940), *passim,* and Vagts, *History of Militarism,* pp. 221–241.

18. General von Holleben, quoted in Great Britain, Military Education Commission, *Account of the Systems of Military Education in France, Prussia, Austria, Bavaria, and the United States* (London, 1870), p. 198. See also: Jany, *Preussischen Armee,* IV, 168–172; Demeter, *Deutsche Heer,* pp. 73–86, 95, 260–265.

19. See Barnard, *Military Schools,* pp. 11–132, 225–240; C. J. East, *The Armed Strength of France* (London, 1877), pp. 74ff.; C. de Montzey, *Institutions d'Education Militaire* (Paris, 1886), *passim;* James R. Soley, *Report on Foreign Systems of Naval Education* (Washington, 1880), ch. 14. On the social composition of the French services, see Girardet, *Société*

Militaire, pp. 50, 61–63, 79–84, 185ff.; Theodore Ropp, "The Development of a Modern Navy: French Naval Policy, 1871–1909" (Ph.D. Thesis, Harvard Univ., 1937), pp. 95–97.

20. On army entry, see Fortescue, *British Army,* IV, 927, XIII, 558ff.; Clode, *Military Forces,* II, 91–92. On navy entry and education, see Lewis, *England's Sea Officers,* pp. 87–111 and "Report of the Committee on the Education of Naval Executive Officers," *Accounts and Papers* (Cmd. 4885, 1886), pp. xxv, xxviii.

21. Theodore Schwan, *Report on the Organization of the German Army* (War Dept., Adjutant General's Office, Mil. Information Div., No. 2, Washington, 1894), pp. 17–18; D. D. Irvine, "The French and Prussian Staff Systems before 1870," *Jour. of the Amer. Mil. Hist. Foundation,* II (1938), 195–196; Christian W. Gässler, *Offizier und Offizierkorps der Alten Armee in Deutschland* (Wertheim a.M., 1930), pp. 24–25, 38.

22. Thomas, *Transformations,* I, 422–423; East, *Armed Strength of France,* pp. 157, 172–183, 200; Thackery, *Military Organization,* I, 73–87, 100–111; Louis Trochu, *L'Armée Française en 1867* (Paris, 1867), pp. 108–111; Ropp, "French Naval Policy," pp. 87–94; J. L. de Lanesson, *La Marine Française au Printemps de 1890* (Paris, 1890), pp. 273–296.

23. Biddulph, *Lord Cardwell,* pp. 114–117 and 73–77; Fortescue, *British Army,* IV, 871–880, XIII, 20–21, 557–558; Omond, *Parliament and the Army,* pp. 66–67, 120–121; Clode, *Military Forces,* II, 92, 161, 347–348, 352–353, 739.

24. Vagts, *History of Militarism,* p. 242.

25. Great Britain, *Military Education,* pp. 333–334. See also Barnard, *Military Schools,* pp. 331–336, 395–399; Spenser Wilkinson, *The Brain of an Army* (London, new ed., 1913), pp. 147–191.

26. Quoted in Hittle, *Military Staff,* p. 107.

27. D. D. Irvine, "The French Discovery of Clausewitz and Napoleon," *Jour. of the Amer. Mil. Institute,* IV (1940), 149–153; East, *Armed Strength of France,* pp. 79–80; L. Jablonski, *L'Armée Française à travers Les Ages* (Paris, 5 vols., 1894), V, 319ff.

28. Soley, *Foreign Systems of Naval Education,* pp. 49ff.; A. F. Mockler-Ferryman, *Annals of Sandhurst* (London, 1900), pp. 86–87.

29. Quoted in John W. Wheeler-Bennett, *The Nemesis of Power: The German Army in Politics, 1918–1945* (London, 1953), p. 97. On the General Staff, see also Walter Görlitz, *History of the German General Staff* (London, 1953), pp. 15–23, 57–58, 66–69; Rudolf Schmidt-Bückeburg, *Das Militärkabinett der Preussischen Könige und Deutschen Kaiser* (Berlin, 1933), pp. 10–14, 57–96; Paul Bronsart von Schellendorff, *The Duties of the General Staff* (London, 3rd ed., 1893), pp. 15–22.

30. See Col. E. B. Hamley, *The Operations of War* (Edinburgh, 3rd ed., 1872), pp. ix–x; Wilkinson, *Brain of an Army,* pp. 102–107. Moltke's statement of the theory is quoted in F. E. Whitton, *Moltke* (London, 1921), pp. 74–75.

The Rise of the Military Profession

31. See Irvine, *Jour. Amer. Mil. Hist. Found.*, II, 198–203; Hittle, *Military Staff*, pp. 89–107; Schellendorff, *Duties of the General Staff*, pp. 80–83; Jablonski, *L'Armée Française*, V, 317ff.

32. Hittle, *Military Staff*, pp. 127–145; John K. Dunlop, *The Development of the British Army, 1899–1914* (London, 1938), pp. 23, 198–213; Schellendorff, *Duties of the General Staff*, pp. 97–108.

33. Viscount Wolseley, "The Standing Army of Great Britain," *Harper's*, LXXX (February 1890), 346–347.

34. Irvine, *Jour. of the Amer. Mil. Institute*, IV, 146–148; Girardet, *Société Militaire*, pp. 94–95. For the contrast between French and German war planning, see Helmuth von Moltke, *The Franco-German War of 1870–71* (London, 2 vols., 1891), I, 3–10.

35. Lascelles Wraxall, *The Armies of the Great Powers* (London, 1859), pp. 99–100.

36. *Military Education*, p. 168.

37. Emory Upton, *The Armies of Europe and Asia* (New York, 1878), pp. 319–320.

38. For typical adulatory comments on Clausewitz, see Stewart L. Murray, *The Reality of War: A Companion to Clausewitz* (London, 1914), ch. ii; D. K. Palit, *The Essentials of Military Knowledge* (Aldershot, 1950), p. 78; Rosinski, *German Army*, pp. 121–122. For a brief critical analysis, see Hans Rothfels, "Clausewitz," in Earle (ed.), *Makers of Modern Strategy*, pp. 93–113. Lloyd, Guibert, Behrenhorst, and Bülow were the most important immediate precursors. For Lloyd and Guibert, see above, pp. 29–30. On Behrenhorst, see Jähns, *Kriegswissenschaften*, III, 2121–2128; Ernst Hagemann, *Die Deutsche Lehre vom Kriege: Von Behrenhorst zu Clausewitz* (Berlin, 1940), pp. 6–20; Vagts, *History of Militarism*, pp. 92–95. Bülow's *Der Geist des Neuren Kriegssystems* (1799, English trans., *The Spirit of Modern Warfare*, London, 1806) has been rightly criticized for its eighteenth-century strategic ideas, yet it nonetheless reflects a highly systematic approach to the study of war. See Palmer, in Earle (ed.), *Makers of Modern Strategy*, pp. 68–74; von Caemmerer, *The Development of Strategical Science During the Nineteenth Century* (London, 1905), pp. 1–10. Clausewitz's most important contemporary was the Swiss Henri Jomini whose *Precis de L'Art de la Guerre* (Paris, 2 vols., 1838) was second only to *On War* in its influence on subsequent military thinking. All quotations from *On War* in this chapter and elsewhere in this book are from the translation by O. J. Matthijs Jolles, Modern Library edition, copyrighted and published by Random House, New York, 1943, and are used by permission of the publishers. See particularly pp. 34–39, 16–21, 45, 128ff., 568–571, 594ff.

39. *Ghost of Napoleon*, pp. 120–122. See also his *The British Way in Warfare* (London, 1932), ch. 1, and for a similar interpretation, A. Lauterbach, "Roots and Implications of the German Idea of Military Society," *Military Affairs*, V (Spring 1941), pp. 3ff. Erich Ludendorff, a true glorifier

of violence as an end in itself, however, was a more perceptive reader of *On War* and recognized the basic difference between Clausewitz and himself. See *The Nation at War* (London, 1936), pp. 11–24. In his more recent *Strategy* (New York, 1954), pp. 352–357, Liddell Hart tempers somewhat his earlier strictures of Clausewitz.

Chapter 3 — The Military Mind

1. For discussion of the military mind, see Walter Bagehot, *Physics and Politics* (New York, 1948), p. 83; Alfred Vagts, *A History of Militarism* (New York, 1937), pp. 11–21; Herbert Richmond, "The Service Mind," *Nineteenth Century and After,* CXIII (June 1933), 90–97; R. P. Patterson, "The Military Mind," *Infantry Journal,* LXI (July 1947), 13; W. R. Kintner, "Sound Thinking in the Army," *ibid.,* LXIII (October 1948), 17–22; "The U.S. Military Mind," *Fortune,* XLV (February 1952), 91ff.; A. M. Schlesinger, Jr., "Generals in Politics," *Reporter,* VI (April 1, 1952), 33–36; Drew Middleton, "The Enigma Called 'The Military Mind,' " *New York Times Magazine,* Apr. 18, 1948, pp. 13ff.; J. P. Marquand, "Inquiry Into the Military Mind," *ibid.,* Mar. 30, 1952, pp. 9ff.; L. B. Blair, "Dogs and Sailors Keep Off," U.S. Naval Institute *Proceedings,* LXXVI (October 1950), 1095–1103; Burton M. Sapin, Richard C. Snyder, and H. W. Bruck, *An Appropriate Role for the Military in American Foreign Policy-making: A Research Note* (Foreign Policy Analysis Series No. 4, Organizational Behavior Section, Princeton Univ., July 1954), pp. 24–33, 42–51. W. R. Schilling's contrasts between civilian and naval thinking in World War I may also be extended into general patterns. "Civil-Naval Politics in World War I," *World Politics,* VII (July 1955), 578–579. For pungent attacks on the quality of the military mind, see David Lloyd George, *War Memoirs* (Boston, 6 vols., 1933–37), VI, 338–344; J. F. Dobie, "Samples of the Army Mind," *Harper's,* CXCIII (December 1946), 529–536; and *contra,* J. J. McCloy, "In Defense of the Army Mind," *ibid.,* CXCIV (April 1947), 341–344. On the military personality, see Hanson Baldwin in Lester Markel (ed.), *Public Opinion and Foreign Policy* (New York, 1949), pp. 118–120; W. T. Colyer, "The Military Mind," *Independent,* LXXXIX (Jan. 1, 1917), 22; Field Marshal Earl Wavell, *The Good Soldier* (London, 1948), pp. 27–28; Field Marshal Viscount Montgomery, *Military Leadership* (London, 1946), pp. 15–16; Cdr. H. E. Smith, "What is the Military Mind?" U.S. Naval Institute *Proceedings,* LXXIX (May 1953), pp. 509ff.; *The Officer's Guide* (Harrisburg, Pa., 19th ed., 1952), p. 270. For *a priori* definitions of the substance of the military mind, see W. O. Douglas, "Should We Fear the Military?" *Look,* XVI (Mar. 11, 1952), 34; Albert Salomon, "The Spirit of the Soldier and Nazi Militarism," *Social Research,* IX (February 1942), 95; Quincy Wright, "The Military and Foreign Policy," in

The Military Mind

Jerome Kerwin (ed.), *Civil-Military Relationships in American Life* (Chicago, 1948), pp. 116–120; Louis Smith, *American Democracy and Military Power* (Chicago, 1951), pp. 111–113. For literary portrayals, see Tolstoy, *War and Peace;* Stendhal, *Lucien Leuwen;* and Proust, *The Guermantes Way.* Among contemporary fiction, there is Norman Mailer, *The Naked and the Dead;* James Gould Cozzens, *Guard of Honor;* James Jones, *From Here to Eternity;* and, most especially, John P. Marquand, *Melville Goodwin, USA.*

    2. Friedrich von Bernhardi (Gen, Ger), *On War of To-Day* (London, 1912), p. vi. On the universality of conflict, see Sir Reginald Bacon (Adm, GB) and Francis E. McMurtrie, *Modern Naval Strategy* (London, 1940), pp. 15–16; W. D. Bird (Gen, GB), *The Direction of War: A Study of Strategy* (Cambridge, 1920), p. 1; Hermann Foertsch (Col, Ger), *The Art of Modern Warfare* (New York, 1940), p. 3; Stewart L. Murray (Maj, GB), *The Peace of the Anglo-Saxons* (London, 1905), p. 9.

    3. J. F. C. Fuller (Gen, GB), *The Foundations of the Science of War* (London, 1926), pp. 34–35; Ardant du Picq (Col, Fr), *Battle Studies: Ancient and Modern Battle* (New York, 1921), pp. 48–51, 96–97, 111, 118; U.S. Dept. of Defense, *The Armed Forces Officer* (Washington, 1950), p. 131.

    4. *On War* (New York, 1943), pp. 32–33, 53–55; Foertsch, *Modern Warfare,* p. 24; U.S. Dept. of Defense, *Armed Forces Officer,* p. 131; Ardant du Picq, *Battle Studies,* pp. 39–40; U.S. Dept. of War, *Field Service Regulations: Operations* (FM 100–5, June 15, 1944), p. 27.

    5. Colmar von der Goltz (Lt Col, Ger), *The Nation in Arms* (London, 1887), p. 37.

    6. Charles de Gaulle, (Gen, Fr), *The Army of the Future* (Philadelphia, 1941), pp. 115–116; Clausewitz, *On War,* pp. 128–131; Auguste Frederic Marmont (Marshal, Fr), *The Spirit of Military Institutions* (Philadelphia, 1862), pp. 243–256, 271.

    7. B. H. Liddell Hart (Capt, GB), *The Strategy of Indirect Approach* (London, 1941), ch. 1; von Moltke, quoted in Spenser Wilkinson, *The Brain of an Army* (London, rev. ed., 1913), pp. 164–165; Sir H. W. Richmond (Adm, GB), *National Policy and Naval Strength and Other Essays* (London, 1928), pp. 255–293; A. T. Mahan (Adm, US), "Subordination in Historical Treatment," *Naval Administration and Warfare* (Boston, 1918), pp. 245–272.

    8. Field Marshal Viscount Montgomery, quoted in *Combat Forces Journal,* IV (July 1954), 14.

    9. J. F. C. Fuller, *Armament and History* (New York, 1945), pp. 11–14, 20–21.

    10. The classic formulation of course is Clausewitz, *On War,* pp. 594–601. See also Jomini, *Summary of the Art of War* (New York, 1854), p. 25; Bernhardi, *On War of To-Day,* II, 182–202; Foertsch, *Modern Warfare,* pp. 6–8; B. H. Liddell Hart, *Paris or the Future of War* (London, 1925),

p. 91; von der Goltz, *Nation in Arms,* p. 117. On the limitation of war, see Fuller, *Armament and History,* pp. 35ff., 343ff., and Vagts, *A History of Militarism,* pp. 397, 410.

11. Liddell Hart, *Paris,* p. 8; Lopez Valencia (Gen, Sp), quoted in *Military Review,* XXIX (January 1950), 83; J. J. Graham (Lt Col, GB), *Elementary History of the Progress of the Art of War* (London, 1858), p. 1; J. F. C. Fuller, *The Reformation of War* (London, 1923), p. 7; von der Goltz, *Nation in Arms,* p. 386.

12. Murray, *Peace of the Anglo-Saxons,* p. 13; Bacon and McMurtrie, *Naval Strategy,* p. 30; Moltke quoted in Vagts, *History of Militarism,* p. 427; von der Goltz, *Conduct of War,* p. 2; Liddell Hart, *Paris,* pp. 7ff.; Cecil Battine (Maj, GB), "What is Militarism?" *Fortnightly,* CXI (March 1919), 378–379.

13. See U.S. Army, *Field Service Regulations: Operations* (FM 100–5, June 15, 1944), p. 36.

14. Sir Richard Gale (Gen, GB), "The Impact of Political Factors on Military Judgment," *Journal* of the Royal United Service Institution, XCIX (February 1954), 37.

15. See von Seeckt (Gen, Ger), *The Future of the German Empire* (New York, 1930), pp. 151–153.

16. See Bird, *Direction of War,* p. 8; Walter H. James (Lt Col, GB), *Modern Strategy* (Edinburgh, 1907), p. 10. For the attitudes of the military and others on preventive war, see Alfred Vagts, *Defense and Diplomacy: The Soldier and the Conduct of Foreign Relations* (New York, 1956), ch. 8.

17. Quoted respectively in Vagts, *History of Militarism,* p. 13, and Carlos G. Calkins (Lt, US), "How May the Sphere of Usefulness of Naval Officers Be Extended in Time of Peace with Advantage to the Country and the Naval Service?" U.S. Naval Institute *Proceedings,* IX (1883), 178. See also De Tocqueville's comments, *Democracy in America* (Cambridge, 2 vols. 1863), II, 333–335.

18. See Ashton, *Nineteenth Century and After,* CXXXVI, 633–634; Vagts, *History of Militarism,* p. 15; Ardant du Picq, *Battle Studies,* pp. 14, 224; V. Derrécagaix (Col, Fr), *Modern War* (Washington, 3 vols., 1888), I, 81.

19. Moltke, quoted in Wilkinson, *Brain of an Army,* p. 165. Prior to the nineteenth century the word "strategy" was generally employed in the sense of stratagem. Since then it has been used to identify the permanent core of military science. See Admiral Castex (Fr), *Théories Stratégiques* (Paris, 5 vols., 1929–1935), I, 3–27; A. R. Maxwell (Gen, US), "This Word 'Strategy'" *Air Univ. Quarterly Review,* VII (Spring 1954), 66–74. For the principles of war, see Cyril Falls (Capt, GB), *Ordeal by Battle* (London, 1943), ch. 5; Bernhardi, *On War of To-Day,* I, 30–43; Alfred Higgins Burne (Lt Col, GB), *The Art of War on Land* (London, 1944); C. R. Brown (Adm, US), "The Principles of War," U.S. Naval Institute *Proceedings,* LXXV (June 1949), 621–633; Marshal Foch, *Precepts and*

Judgments (London, 1919), pp. 215–218; Sir F. Maurice (Gen, GB), *British Strategy* (London, 1929), ch. 2; and for a critical discussion, Bernard Brodie, "Strategy as a Science," *World Politics*, I (July 1944), 466–488.

20. Gale, *Jour. Royal United Service Inst.*, XCIX, 37.

21. Von Moltke, quoted in Liddell Hart, *Strategy of Indirect Approach*, p. 185; pp. 184–189 of this volume contain an excellent brief statement of the responsibilities of the military commander in relation to the statesman.

22. A. T. Mahan, "The Military Rule of Obedience," *Retrospect and Prospect* (Boston, 1902), p. 283; Derrécagaix, *Modern War*, I, 78. For an excellent statement by a civilian, see T. V. Smith, "Ethics for Soldiers of Freedom," *Ethics*, LX (April 1950), 157–168.

23. See B. H. Liddell Hart, *The Ghost of Napoleon* (New Haven, 1934), pp. 171–177; Richmond, *National Policy and Naval Strength*, pp. 217–230.

Chapter 4 — Power, Professionalism, and Ideology

1. For other theoretical analyses of civil-military relations, see Alexis de Tocqueville, *Democracy in America*, vol. II, bk. 3, chs. 22–26; Gaetano Mosca, *The Ruling Class* (New York, 1939), ch. 9; Karl Mannheim, *Freedom, Power, and Democratic Planning* (New York, 1950), pp. 127–131; Stanislaw Andrzejewski, *Military Organization and Society* (London, 1954); Morris Janowitz, "The Professional Soldier and Political Power: A Theoretical Orientation and Selected Hypotheses" (Bureau of Government, Institute of Public Administration, Univ. of Michigan, 1953; mimeo.); Burton Sapin, Richard C. Snyder, and H. W. Bruck, *An Appropriate Role for the Military in American Foreign Policy-making: A Research Note* (Foreign Policy Analysis Series No. 4, Organizational Behavior Section, Princeton Univ., 1954).

Friedrich's general distinction between objective functional responsibility and subjective political responsibility in the public service is relevant to the distinctions here made between the varieties of civilian control. Carl J. Friedrich, *et al.*, *Problems of the American Public Service* (New York, 1935), pp. 36–37.

2. The analysis of the concept of "power" goes back, of course, to Machiavelli and Aristotle. Some of the more helpful recent discussions are: Harold D. Lasswell, *Politics: Who Gets What, When, How* (New York, 1936), and *Power and Personality* (New York, 1948); Charles E. Merriam, *Political Power* (New York, 1934), and *Systematic Politics* (Chicago, 1945); Bertrand Russell, *Power: A New Social Analysis* (New York, 1938); Gaetano Mosca, *The Ruling Class* (New York, 1939); Carl J. Friedrich, *Constitutional Government and Democracy* (Boston, 1950); Robert M. MacIver, *The Web of Government* (New York, 1947); Bertrand de Jouvenel, *On Power* (New York, 1949); Karl Mannheim, *Freedom, Power, and Democratic Planning* (New York, 1950); Harold D. Lasswell and Abraham

Notes to Chapter 4

Kaplan, *Power and Society* (New Haven, 1950); H. Goldhamer and E. A. Shils, "Types of Power and Status," *Amer. Jour. of Sociology*, XLV (1939), 171–182; Reinhard Bendix, "Bureaucracy and the Problem of Power," *Public Administration Review*, V (1945), 194–209; H. A. Simon, "Notes on the Observation and Measurement of Political Power," *Journal of Politics*, XV (November 1953), 500–516; Robert Bierstedt, "An Analysis of Social Power," *American Sociological Review*, XV (December 1950), 730–738; F. L. Neumann, "Approaches to the Study of Political Power," *Pol. Science Quarterly*, LXV (June 1950), 161–180.

3. Classic statements of the Liberal position will be found in the writings of Locke, the French Enlightenment thinkers, Bentham, Adam Smith, John Stuart Mill, Kant, T. H. Green, and Croce. For analysis of the historical components of liberalism, see Harold J. Laski, *The Rise of Liberalism* (New York, 1936), Guido de Ruggiero, *The History of European Liberalism* (London, 1927), and A. D. Lindsay, *The Modern Democratic State* (New York, vol. I, 1947). The best sources for fascist ideology are Hitler's *Mein Kampf*, Mussolini's *The Doctrine of Fascism*, and Alfred Rosenberg, *Der Mythus des 20. Jahrhunderts*. For analysis of fascist ideas, see W. Y. Elliott, *The Pragmatic Revolt in Politics* (New York, 1928); Hermann Rauschning, *The Revolution of Nihilism* (New York, 1939); Franz L. Neumann, *Behemoth* (New York, 2d ed., 1944); William Ebenstein, *The Nazi State* (New York, 1943). I have attempted to place this analysis of fascist ideas at a sufficiently abstract level so as to include both Italian and German fascism, although there are of course many specific differences between the two. The most useful writings for the political theory of Marxism are Karl Marx and Friedrich Engels, *The Communist Manifesto*, and V. I. Lenin, *The State and Revolution* and *Imperialism*. Emile Burns, *Handbook of Marxism* (New York, 1935) is a useful compendium. An excellent brief critical analysis is R. N. Carew Hunt, *The Theory and Practice of Communism* (New York, 1951). The classic statement of conservatism is, of course, by Edmund Burke, particularly in *Reflections on the French Revolution* and *Appeal from the New to the Old Whigs*. For analysis of conservatism as an ideology, see Karl Mannheim, "Conservative Thought," *Essays on Sociology and Social Psychology* (New York, ed. by Paul Kecskemeti, 1953).

Chapter 5 — Germany and Japan

1. Quoted in Paul von Hindenburg, *Out of My Life* (London, 1920), p. 220; Friedrich von Bernhardi, *On War of To-Day* (London, 2 vols., 1912), II, 182–183; Hajo Holborn, "Moltke and Schlieffen: The Prussian-German School," in Edward Mead Earle (ed.), *Makers of Modern Strategy* (Princeton, 1952), pp. 175–176. Compare Gerhard Ritter, *Staatskunst und*

Germany and Japan

Kriegshandwerk (Munich, 1954), I, 246–261; Gordon A. Craig, *The Politics of the Prussian Army, 1640–1945* (Oxford, 1955), pp. 195–196, 216.

2. Quoted in John W. Wheeler-Bennett, *The Nemesis of Power: The German Army in Politics, 1918–1945* (London, 1953), p. 86, n. 3. See also *Essays, Speeches, and Memoirs of Count Helmuth von Moltke* (London, 2 vols., 1893), II, 50; Helmuth von Moltke, *The Franco-German War of 1870–1871* (London, 1891), p. 1. Moltke did say in a much quoted letter that "Eternal peace is a dream and not even a beautiful dream," but this was immediately followed by a lamenting of the horrible sufferings which inevitable war occasioned.

3. Quoted in Alfred Vagts, "Land and Sea Power in the Second German Reich," *Jour. of the Amer. Mil. Institute, III* (Winter 1939), 213.

4. Herbert Rosinski, *The German Army* (London, 1939), pp. 107–108; Walter Görlitz, *The German General Staff: Its History and Structure, 1657–1945* (London, 1953), p. 139; Christian W. Gässler, *Offizier und Offizierkorps der Alten Armee in Deutschland* (Wertheim a.M., 1930), Appendix 4.

5. Rosinski, *German Army,* pp. 96–98; Görlitz, *General Staff,* p. 95; Friedrich Meinecke, *The German Catastrophe* (Cambridge, 1950), p. 12.

6. Quoted in G. P. Gooch, *Germany* (New York, 1925), p. 96. On the fundamental shift in German values, see also Meinecke, *German Catastrophe,* pp. 1–24; Koppel S. Pinson, *Modern Germany: Its History and Civilization* (New York, 1954), pp. 251–273, 291–312; Hans Kohn (ed.), *German History: Some New German Views* (Boston, 1954), *passim;* John H. Hallowell, *The Decline of Liberalism as an Ideology in Germany* (Berkeley, 1943), *passim.*

7. *German Army,* pp. 100–104.

8. See John W. Wheeler-Bennett, *Wooden Titan: Hindenburg in Twenty Years of German History, 1914–1934* (New York, 1936), pp. 137–140; Albrecht Mendelssohn-Bartholdy, *The War and German Society* (New Haven, 1937), pp. 106–117; and R. H. Lutz (ed.), *The Causes of the German Collapse in 1918* (Stanford University, 1934), pp. 22–24, 199–201, for the failure of German civilian leadership.

9. *The Nation at War* (Eng. trans of *Der Totale Krieg,* London, 1936), pp. 23–24, 175, 180.

10. Quoted in Telford Taylor, *Sword and Swastika: Generals and Nazis in the Third Reich* (New York, 1952), p. 16.

11. Seeckt, *Thoughts of a Soldier* (London, 1930), pp. 5–6.

12. Quoted in Wheeler-Bennett, *Nemesis of Power,* p. 116.

13. Seeckt, *Thoughts of a Soldier,* pp. 77–80.

14. Wheeler-Bennett, *Nemesis of Power,* pp. 108–110.

15. Görlitz, *General Staff,* p. 302; Hermann Foertsch, *The Art of Modern Warfare* (New York, 1940).

16. Görlitz, *General Staff*, p. 294. On the general contrast between military and Nazi values, see Hermann Rauschning, *The Revolution of Nihilism* (New York, 1939), pp. 123–176.

17. General Dittmar, quoted in B. H. Liddell Hart, *The Other Side of the Hill* (London, rev. ed., 1951), p. 59.

18. On the November meeting, the Czech crisis, Beck's opposition, and the Halder plot, see Office of U.S. Chief of Counsel for Prosecution of Axis Criminality, *Nazi Conspiracy and Aggression* (Washington, 8 vols. and 2 supplements, 1946), I, 377–387; Görlitz, *General Staff*, pp. 324–339; Wheeler-Bennett, *Nemesis of Power*, pp. 395–424; Hans Rothfels, *The German Opposition to Hitler* (Hinsdale, Ill., 1948), pp. 58–63.

19. Quoted in Fabian von Schlabrendorff, *They Almost Killed Hitler* (New York, 1947), pp. 34–35.

20. See, generally, Chester Wilmot, *The Struggle for Europe* (New York, 1952), pp. 89–90, 162, 188, 332; Hans Speidel, *Invasion: 1944* (Chicago, 1950), pp. 27–30; E. A. Shils and Morris Janowitz, "Cohesion and Disintegration of the Wehrmacht in World War II," *Public Opinion Quarterly*, XII (Summer 1948), 303–308; N. W. Caldwell, "Political Commissars in the Luftwaffe," *Jour. of Politics*, IX (February 1947), 57–79; H. A. Sheen, "The Disintegration of the German Intelligence Services," *Military Review*, XXIX (June 1949), 38–41.

21. General Dittmar, quoted in Liddell Hart, *The Other Side of the Hill*, p. 59.

22. See Schlabrendorff, *They Almost Killed Hitler*, pp. 39–40; Görlitz, *General Staff*, pp. 329–330; Gen. Günther Blumentritt, *Von Rundstedt: The Soldier and the Man* (London, 1952), pp. 34, 39–40; Rauschning, *Revolution of Nihilism*, pp. 151–152, 169–170.

23. Quoted in Wheeler-Bennett, *Nemesis of Power*, p. 381. See also Hans Bernd Gisevius, *To the Bitter End* (Boston, 1947), pp. 223–267; Taylor, *Sword and Swastika*, pp. 337–343.

24. Hans Speier, "German Rearmament and the Old Military Elite," *World Politics*, VI (January 1954), 150, n. 4; H. A. DeWeerd, "The German Officer Corps versus Hitler," *Military Affairs*, XIII (Winter 1949), 200–207; Kurt Assmann, "Hitler and the German Officer Corps," U.S. Naval Institute *Proceedings*, LXXXII (May 1956), 520.

25. Ulrich von Hassell, *The Von Hassell Diaries, 1938–1944* (New York, 1947), p. 6; Speidel, *Invasion: 1944*, p. 16. Compare Blumentritt, *Von Rundstedt*, p. 25.

26. *New York Times*, Nov. 10, 1952, p. 7; Gordon A. Craig, "NATO and the New German Army," in William W. Kaufmann (ed.), *Military Policy and National Security* (Princeton, 1956), pp. 203–204, 209.

27. D. C. Holtom, *Modern Japan and Shinto Nationalism* (Chicago, rev. ed., 1947), pp. 7ff. See also Uichi Iwasaki, *The Working Forces in Japanese Politics* (New York, 1921), pp. 12–13; E. E. N. Causton, *Militarism and Foreign Policy in Japan* (London, 1936), ch. 1; Ruth Benedict,

The Chrysanthemum and the Sword: Patterns of Japanese Culture (Boston, 1946), pp. 43–75; J. F. Steiner, "Basic Traits of Japanese Character," *Proceedings,* Institute of World Affairs, V (1944–45), 44; Inazo Nitobe, *Bushido: The Soul of Japan* (New York, 10th ed., 1905), *passim.*

28. J. C. Balet, *Military Japan: The Japanese Army and Navy in 1910* (Yokohama, 1910), p. 3; John M. Maki, *Japanese Militarism: Its Cause and Cure* (New York, 1945), p. 182.

29. Alfred Vagts, *A History of Militarism* (New York, 1937), p. 319.

30. Robert Leurquin, "The Japanese Punitive Expedition in China," *The Army Quarterly* (April 1938), quoted in Paul W. Thompson, *et al., The Jap Army* (Army Orientation Course, Series I, No. I, 1942), pp. 23–24. See also Hillis Lory, *Japan's Military Masters* (New York, 1943), pp. 94–95.

31. Nitobe, *Bushido,* p. 188.

32. Quoted in Lory, *Japan's Military Masters,* p. 37.

33. Quoted in Benedict, *Chrysanthemum and the Sword,* pp. 22–23.

34. M. D. Kennedy, *Some Aspects of Japan and her Defence Forces* (London, 1928), p. 164, and *The Military Side of Japanese Life* (London, 1924), pp. 311–312, 355; Alexander Kiralfy, "Japanese Naval Strategy," in Earle (ed.), *Makers of Modern Strategy,* pp. 457–462.

35. Lory, *Japan's Military Masters,* pp. 81, 41–47, 79–95; Balet, *Military Japan,* p. 7; Kennedy, *Japan and her Defence Forces,* p. 153; Causton, *Militarism and Foreign Policy,* p. 83; Benedict, *Chrysanthemum and the Sword,* pp. 38ff.

36. War Ministry Pamphlet, 1934, quoted in Kenneth W. Colegrove, *Militarism in Japan* (Boston, 1936), pp. 52–53.

37. General Mazaki, quoted in Hugh Byas, *Government by Assassination* (New York, 1942), p. 150.

38. Quoted in K. W. Colegrove, "The Japanese Cabinet," *Amer. Pol. Sci. Rev.,* XXX (October 1936), 916–917. See also Chitoshi Yanaga, "The Military and the Government in Japan," *ibid.,* XXXV (June 1941), 529–530; Causton, *Militarism and Foreign Policy,* ch. 2; Lory, *Japan's Military Masters,* pp. 239–245.

39. Quoted in Lory, *Japan's Military Masters,* pp. 139–140.

40. *Ibid.,* pp. 116, 122, 126–128; M. F. Gibbons, Jr., "The Japanese Needed Unification," *Military Review,* XXIX (August 1949), 20–27.

41. Quoted in Lory, *Japan's Military Masters,* p. 114.

42. Lt. Gen. Tamon, quoted in O. Tanin and E. Yohan, *Militarism and Fascism in Japan* (London, 1934), p. 186. See also Tatsuji Takeuchi, *War and Diplomacy in the Japanese Empire* (Garden City, N.Y., 1935), pp. 349–357.

43. Quoted in Tanin and Yohan, *Militarism and Fascism,* p. 187.

44. Kennedy, *Military Side,* pp. 108–109.

Notes to Chapter 6

Chapter 6 — The Ideological Constant

1. *Journals of the Continental Congress 1774–1789*, XXVII (June 2, 1784), 518, 524; Memorandum of General Tasker H. Bliss in Frederick Palmer, *Newton D. Baker: America at War* (New York, 2 vols., 1931), I, 40–41.

2. The implications of the prevalence of liberalism in the United States have been brilliantly probed by Louis Hartz, *The Liberal Tradition in America* (New York, 1955). See also Daniel J. Boorstin, *The Genius of American Politics* (Chicago, 1953), and Clinton Rossiter, *Conservatism in America* (New York, 1955).

3. Quoted in Harold Stearns, *Liberalism in America* (New York, 1919), p. 80.

4. See Merle Curti, *Peace or War: The American Struggle, 1636–1936* (New York, 1936), and Arthur A. Ekirch, Jr., *The Civilian and the Military* (New York, 1956).

5. Carl J. Friedrich, *et al.*, *Problems of the American Public Service* (New York, 1935), p. 12.

6. Quoted in Dorothy Burne Goebel and Julius Goebel, Jr., *Generals in the White House* (Garden City, N.Y., 1945), p. 147.

7. *Public Papers* (New York, 6 vols., ed. by Ray Stannard Baker and William E. Dodd, 1925–1927), V, 83, 86.

8. On military heroes in American politics, see: Goebel and Goebel, *Generals in the White House;* Albert Somit, "The Military Hero as Presidential Candidate," *Public Opinion Quarterly,* XII (Summer 1948), 192–200; L. B. Wheildon, "Military Leaders and the Presidency," *Editorial Research Reports* (Dec. 5, 1947), pp. 869–883; Frank Weitenkampf, "Generals in Politics," *American Scholar,* XIII (Summer 1944), 375–378; Sidney Hyman, *The American President* (New York, 1954), pp. 210–217; P. F. Boller, Jr., "Professional Soldiers in the White House," *Southwest Review,* XXXVII (Autumn 1952), 269–279.

9. *The Hero in America* (New York, 1941), p. 12.

10. Quoted in Hyman, *American President*, p. 211.

Chapter 7 — The Structural Constant

1. William Blackstone, *Commentaries on the Laws of England* (Oxford, 3rd ed., 4 vols., 1768), I, 407, 413–414.

2. For the discussion of this clause, see Max Farrand (ed.), *The Records of the Federal Convention of 1787* (New Haven, 4 vols., 1911–1937), I, 380, II, 286–290; Jonathan Elliot (ed.), *The Debates in the Several Conventions* (Washington, 4 vols., 1836), III 372–373. For the few instances in which the clause has been invoked in practice, see *Hind's Prece-*

The Structural Constant

dents of the House of Representatives (Washington, 1907), ch. XVI, and *Cannon's Precedents* (Washington, 1935), ch. 16.

3. Farrand, *Records,* II, 326, 329–330, 563, 640, III, 207; Elliot, *Debates,* I, 326, 328, 335, II, 77–80, 136–137, III, 381, 660, IV, 244; Charles Warren, *The Making of the Constitution* (Cambridge, 1947), pp. 474, 483; James Madison, No. 41, *The Federalist* (Modern Library ed.), pp. 262–263.

4. Farrand, *Records,* I, 465, II, 385; No. 8, *The Federalist,* pp. 42–43; Elliot, *Debates,* II, 520–521, III, 169, 378, 410–411. Patrick Henry commented with respect to the nationalist claim: "This argument destroys itself. It demands a power, and denies the probability of its exercise."

5. Farrand, *Records,* II, 136, 168, 182, 330, 385, II, 332; Elliot, *Debates,* III, 382, IV, 422–424.

6. See Emory Upton, *The Military Policy of the United States* (Washington, 1912), pp. 100–103; F. B. Wiener, "The Militia Clause of the Constitution," *Harvard Law Review,* LIV (December 1940), 192–193; Leonard D. White, *The Jeffersonians* (New York, 1951), pp. 540–541. Compare Washington's revolutionary difficulties. James B. Scott, *The Militia* (S. Doc. 695, 64th Cong., 2d Sess., 1917), pp. 25–26.

7. F. P. Todd, "Our National Guard: An Introduction to Its History," *Military Affairs,* V (Summer, Fall 1941), 73–86, 152–170, at pp. 162–163. Aside from these brief articles and a few law review pieces, little scholarly work has been done on the National Guard and the National Guard Association. There is a gold mine here for an enterprising student of American political history.

8. *Official Proceedings of the Natl. Guard Assoc., 66th Annual Convention, 1944,* pp. 28–29, 44; *1948,* pp. 111, 242–244, 254–255; *1949,* pp. 202–210. For the Gray Board recommendations, see Committee on Civilian Components, *Reserve Forces for National Security* (Washington, 1948), pp. 9–24.

9. *Statement of Policy Adopted by the Natl. Guard Assn. and the Adjutants General Assn. in Joint Convention,* Baltimore, May 4, 1944, pp. 1, 4; *Proceedings, NGA Convention, 1944,* p. 100; *1945,* pp. 65–66; *1946,* pp. 114–115; *1948,* p. 65; Public Administration Clearing House, *Public Administration Organizations, 1954* (Chicago, 1954), pp. 102, 119.

10. *Proceedings, NGA Convention, 1943,* pp. 89, 93–96; *1945,* pp. 50–55.

11. *Proceedings, NGA Convention, 1945,* p. 47; *1946,* p. 43; *1948,* pp. 34, 66, 80–81; *1950,* pp. 264–265; *1953,* pp. 288–290.

12. *Proceedings, NGA Convention, 1943,* pp. 56, 67, 88; *1944,* pp. 44, 53, 55, 58, 65, 69, 73, 74; *1945,* p. 56; *1946,* pp. 28–32; *1948,* pp. 47–49, 57, 91–92; *1953,* p. 28; *Time,* LXIII (Mar. 1, 1954), 18.

13. *Proceedings, NGA Convention, 1948,* pp. 33–34; *1950,* p. 245.

14. For discussion of royal and parliamentary authority, see Blackstone, *Commentaries,* I, 257–258, 262, 412–413; J. S. Omond, *Parliament and*

the Army, *1642–1904* (Cambridge, 1933), pp. 7–8; John W. Fortescue, *A History of the British Army* (London, 13 vols., 1899–1930), II, 568. The Framers at first adopted *in toto* the language of the basic English statute, 13 Car. II, c. 6 (1661), but then realized that they could not make the President, like the king, commander in chief of the militia in peace as well as war. See Farrand, *Records,* I, 139–140, II, 185, 426–427; No. 69, *The Federalist,* p. 448. For the continuing debate as to whether the war power was properly legislative or executive, see Farrand, *Records,* I, 64–66; Alexander Hamilton, *Works* (New York, 12 vols., ed. by H. C. Lodge, 1904), IV, 145–146; James Madison, *Writings* (New York, 9 vols., 1900–1910), VI, 145; Clarence A. Berdahl, *War Powers of the Executive in the United States* (Urbana, Ill., 1921), p. 79. Compare W. W. Crosskey, *Politics and the Constitution* (Chicago, 2 vols., 1953), I, 422–428.

15. Fleming v. Page, 9 How. 603, 615, 618 (1850). The powers of the British king as general of the kingdom extended to many nonmilitary areas. Blackstone, *Commentaries,* I, 262ff. For the views of the Framers on the Commander in Chief power, see Farrand, *Records,* I, 244, 292, II, 145, 319, 426–427, III, 624; Elliot, *Debates,* IV, 114; *The Federalist,* pp. 448, 482.

16. For the boundaries between presidential and congressional military powers, see Edward S. Corwin, *The President: Office and Powers* (New York, 1948), ch. vi; Ex Parte Milligan, 4 Wall. 2 (1866); Berdahl, *War Powers, passim;* Howard White, *Executive Influence in Determining Military Policy in the United States* (Urbana, Ill., 1924), ch. iii; and R. G. Albion's interesting, if unconvincing, views, "The Naval Affairs Committee, 1816–1947," U.S. Naval Institute *Proceedings,* LXXVIII (November 1952), 1929.

17. Quoted in T. H. Williams, "The Committee on the Conduct of the War: An Experiment in Civilian Control," *Jour. Amer. Mil. Institute,* III (Fall 1939), 141.

18. Lloyd M. Short, *The Development of National Administrative Organization in the United States* (Baltimore, 1923), p. 119; Berdahl, *War Powers,* pp. 111–114; Upton, *Military Policy,* pp. 250–251; Pendleton Herring, *The Impact of War* (New York, 1941), pp. 141–142; Arthur A. Maass, *Muddy Waters: The Army Engineers and the Nation's Rivers* (Cambridge, Mass., 1951), *passim;* White, *Executive Influence,* pp. 237–238, 263; Otto L. Nelson, Jr., *National Security and the General Staff* (Washington, 1946), pp. 130–166; John Dickinson, *The Building of an Army* (New York, 1922), p. 320; Bradley A. Fiske, *From Midshipman to Rear Admiral* (New York, 1919), pp. 563–571.

19. Donald W. Mitchell, *History of the Modern American Navy from 1883 through Pearl Harbor* (New York, 1946), pp. 62–63.

20. Farrand, *Records,* I, 244, III, 217–218, 624, IV, 53; Elliot, *Debates,* II, 408, 412, 522–523, III, 59–60, 496–498; Leonard D. White, *The Jef-*

fersonians, p. 220, and *The Jacksonians* (New York, 1954), pp. 51–57; Herring, *Impact of War,* pp. 146–147.

21. The theoretical rationale of the balanced pattern was developed in A. T. Mahan, "The Principles of Naval Administration," *Naval Administration and Warfare* (Boston, 1908), pp. 3–48, and Spenser Wilkinson, Preface to the 2d edition of *The Brain of an Army* (London, 1913). Mahan's essay and Wilkinson's preface are brilliant analyses of executive military organization and are basic to an understanding of the subject.

22. Secretary of Defense, *Semiannual Report, July 1 to December 31, 1954,* p. 58; *New York Times,* January 13, 1956, p. 6; *New York Herald Tribune,* November 22, 1953, p. 1, November 20, 1955, Sec. 2, p. 3.

Chapter 8 — The Roots of the American Military Tradition before the Civil War

1. *The Writings of Thomas Jefferson* (New York, 10 vols., ed. by Paul L. Ford, 1892–1899), X, 239; William A. Ganoe, *The History of the United States Army* (New York, 1932), p. 95.

2. Secretary of War to Congress, Jan. 13, 1800, *American State Papers: Military Affairs,* I, 133–135 (hereafter cited as ASP:MA). This communication by McHenry and a subsequent one of Jan. 31, 1800 (ASP:MA, I, 142) were based on Hamilton's letter to him of Nov. 23, 1799, Alexander Hamilton, *Works* (New York, 12 vols., ed. by H. C. Lodge, 1904), VII, 179ff. For further expression of Hamilton's views, see his *Works,* IV, 457, 464, VII, 11, and *The Federalist* (Modern Library ed.), pp. 42, 62–69, 206–207. Washington's words in his Farewell Address were suggested by Hamilton. See Edward Mead Earle, "Adam Smith, Alexander Hamilton, Friedrich List: The Economic Foundations of Military Power," in Earle (ed.), *Makers of Modern Strategy* (Princeton, 1952), pp. 128–138. For Washington's views, see P. F. Boller, Jr., "Washington and Civilian Supremacy," *Southwest Review,* XXXIX (Winter 1954), 10–12; William R. Tansill, *The Concept of Civil Supremacy in the United States* (Library of Congress, Legislative Reference Service, Public Affairs Bulletin No. 94, 1951), pp. 3–5.

3. *The Writings of Thomas Jefferson* (Washington, 20 vols., Thomas Jefferson Memorial Association ed., 1905), IV, 218, XIII, 261. For further expression of Jeffersonian military policy, see *ibid.,* II, 242, X, 365, XIV, 261; *The Works of Thomas Jefferson* (New York, 12 vols., ed. by Paul L. Ford, 1905), V, 386, 426–428, IX, 18, X, 190–191, 206ff., 222–223, XI, 68–69, 426, 436–437.

4. Samuel Tillman, "The Academic History of the Military Academy, 1802–1902," *The Centennial of the United States Military Academy at West Point, New York, 1802–1902* (Washington, 1904), p. 276; H. Wager

Halleck, *Elements of Military Art and Science* (New York, 1846), p. 134; Sidney Forman, *West Point* (New York, 1950), pp. 43–44, 51–58; R. Ernest Dupuy, *Men of West Point* (New York, 1951), p. 13. French texts used in the early days of the Academy included Gay de Vernon, *Treatise on the Science of War and Fortification* (New York, 2 vols., 1817); Louis de Tousard, *American Artillerist's Companion* (Philadelphia, 3 vols., 1809); H. Lallemand, *A Treatise on Artillery* (New York, 1820).

5. Hamilton to McHenry, Nov. 23, 1799, *Works,* VII, 179ff.; ASP:MA, I, 133ff.

6. Jacob D. Cox, *Military Reminiscences of the Civil War* (New York, 2 vols., 1900), I, 172, 177–179; Forman, *West Point,* pp. 23, 74ff., 82, 87–89; W. V. Judson, "The Services of Graduates," *Centennial,* pp. 833–835; Tillman, *ibid.,* pp. 282–283, 374; Eben Swift, "Services of Graduates of West Point in Indian Wars," *ibid.,* p. 527; W. S. Chaplin, "The Services of Graduates in Civil Life, 1802–1902," *ibid.,* pp. 876–877; William Baumer, Jr., *Not All Warriors* (New York, 1941), p. xi, and *West Point: Moulder of Men* (New York, 1942), pp. 241–242; R. Ernest Dupuy, *Where They Have Trod* (New York, 1940), pp. 368–371, 399–402, and Appendix A; Report of Committee on the General Condition of the Military Academy, June 20, 1826, ASP:MA, III, 375; Report of the Board of Visitors to the Military Academy, 1830, ASP:MA, IV, 603; Ann. Report of the Secy. of War, 1828, ASP:MA, IV, 2ff.

7. Exec. Doc. No. 2, 27th Cong., 2d Sess., p. 364 (1841); *Amer. State Papers: Naval Affairs* (hereafter cited as ASP:NA), I, 320, II, 44, III, 350; James R. Soley, *Historical Sketch of the United States Naval Academy* (Washington, 1876), pp. 7–61; W. D. Puleston, *Annapolis: Gangway to the Quarterdeck* (New York, 1942), pp. 11–47.

8. Art. 63, Articles of War, Act of Apr. 10, 1806, 2 Stat. 367; Act of Mar. 3, 1813, 2 Stat. 819; Leonard D. White, *The Jeffersonians* (New York, 1951), pp. 236–240.

9. "Report of the secretary of the navy, of a plan for reorganization of the navy department," *Niles' National Register,* Jan. 25, 1840, pp. 343–345. On nineteenth-century naval organization, see S. B. Luce, "Naval Administration," U.S. Naval Institute *Proceedings* (hereafter cited as USNIP), XIV (1888), 574–575, 582–583; "Naval Administration, II," USNIP, XXVIII (1902), 841–844; "The Board of Naval Commissioners," USNIP, XXXVII (December 1911), 1123–1124; C. O. Paullin, "Naval Administration Under the Naval Commissioners, 1815–1842," USNIP, XXXIII (1907), 598–599, 606–611, and "A Half Century of Naval Administration in America, 1861–1911," USNIP, XXXVIII (December 1912), 1315ff.; Act of Feb. 7, 1815, 3 Stat. 202; Act of Aug. 31, 1842, 5 Stat. 579; Rept. of the Secy. of the Navy, Dec. 4, 1841, S. Doc. 1, 27th Cong., 2d Sess., p. 378 (1841); Rolf Haugen, "The Setting of Internal Administrative Communication in the United States Naval Establishments, 1775–1920" (Ph.D. Thesis, Harvard Univ., 1953), p. 133.

The Roots of the Military Tradition

10. Emory Upton, *The Military Policy of the United States* (Washington, 1912), p. 225; James D. Richardson (ed.), *Messages and Papers of the Presidents, 1789–1910* (New York, 11 vols., 1908), II, 438; Joseph L. Blau (ed.), *Social Theories of Jacksonian Democracy* (New York, 1947), p. 64.

11. Rept., Com. on Mil. Affs., H. of Reprs., May 17, 1834, ASP:MA, V, 347; Rept. of Select Committee on the United States Military Academy, Mar. 1, 1837, ASP:MA, VII, 14. For the decline of the legal profession and the diplomatic service under the Jacksonian impact, see Roscoe Pound, *The Lawyer from Antiquity to Modern Times* (St. Paul, Minn., 1953), pp. 226–228, 232–233; J. Rives Childs, *The American Foreign Service* (New York, 1948), p. 4.

12. ASP:MA, IV, 285, 683, V, 307, 347, VI, 988, VII, 1ff., 89; Forman, *West Point*, pp. 49–51.

13. Act of Mar. 1, 1843, 5 Stat. 604; Act of Mar. 3, 1845, 5 Stat. 794; Act of Aug. 31, 1852, 10 Stat. 102; *Congressional Globe*, XI (May 13, 1842), 499–500, XII (Feb. 7, 1843), 224–225, XXIV (Aug. 30, 1852), 2442–2444; ASP:MA, III, 616; H.Doc. 167, 20th Cong., 1st Sess., pp. 3–4 (1828).

14. Paullin, USNIP, XXXIII, 632; Halleck, *Military Art and Science*, pp. 404–405; Swift, *Centennial*, pp. 528ff.; Upton, *Military Policy*, pp. 212–213; Truman Seymour, *Military Education: A Vindication of West Point and the Regular Army* (1861), p. 6; J. F. C., "Hints on Manning the Navy, Etc.," *Naval Magazine*, I (March 1836), 185.

15. Halleck, *Military Art and Science*, p. 398; James Fenimore Cooper, *History of the Navy of the United States of America* (London, 2 vols., 1839), I, xxix.

16. *Army and Navy Chronicle*, II (Jan. 7, 1836), 13 (Feb. 18, 1836), 108–109, (Mar. 2, 1836), 139–140, (May 19, 1836), 315–316.

17. ASP:MA, II, 450.

18. H. Rept. 46, 23rd Cong., 2d Sess., p. 4. See also Secy. Spenser's similar views in 1842, S. Rept. 555, 45th Cong., 3rd Sess., pp. 408–409 (1878).

19. Art. XXXIX, Par. 1, Army Regulations, Dec. 31, 1836. For subsequent appearances of this clause, see Par. 48, Art. X, in the 1841 and 1847 Regulations, Pars. 186, 187, 813, *Regulations for the Army of the United States* (Washington, 1889). On the evolution of this provision, see G. Norman Lieber, *Remarks on the Army Regulations* (Washington, 1898), pp. 63–73.

20. S. Rept. 555, 45th Cong., 3rd Sess., p. 120 (1878). For post-Civil War efforts to introduce a vertical organization, see *ibid.*, pp. 7–8, 121; William H. Carter, *The American Army* (Indianapolis, 1915), pp. 185–186; Report of the Commission Appointed by the President to Investigate the Conduct of the War Dept. in the War with Spain, S. Doc. 221, 56th Cong., 1st Sess., pp. 115–116 (1900).

21. Colonel H. L. Scott, *Military Dictionary* (New York 1864), pp.

17, 233, 548–549; Upton, *Military Policy,* p. 129; S. Rept. 555, 45th Cong., 3rd Sess., pp. 398–399. On the bureaus, see Carter, *American Army,* pp. 188 ff., and General S. V. Benet, "Historical Statement of the Rise and Progress of the Ordnance Department," 1876, quoted in L. D. Ingersoll, *A History of the War Department of the United States* (Washington, 1879), p. 317.

22. S. Rept. 555, 45th Cong., 3rd Sess., pp. 410–411; Leonard D. White, *The Jacksonians* (New York, 1954), pp. 194–196; Upton, *Military Policy,* p. 365; John McA. Schofield, *Forty-Six Years in the Army* (New York, 1897), ch. 22, pp. 468–475, 536–538; John McAuley Palmer, *Washington, Lincoln, Wilson: Three War Statesmen* (Garden City, N.Y., 1930), pp. 157–158; William H. Carter, *Creation of the American General Staff* (S. Doc. 119, 68th Cong., 2d Sess., 1924), p. 19, and *American Army,* pp. 185–192; Otto L. Nelson, Jr., *National Security and the General Staff* (Washington, 1946), pp. 25–28; Rachel Sherman Thorndike (ed.), *The Sherman Letters* (New York, 1894), pp. 331–332, 339, 346; Elihu Root, *Five Years of the War Department* (Washington, 1900), p. 330; J. D. Hittle, *The Military Staff* (Harrisburg, Pa., 1949), p. 166.

23. See Rollin G. Osterweis, *Romanticism and Nationalism in the Old South* (New Haven, 1949), pp. 90–94; W. J. Cash, *The Mind of the South* (New York, 1941), pp. 43–44. For a comprehensive description of the Southern military tradition, see John Hope Franklin, *The Militant South, 1800–1860* (Cambridge, Mass., 1956), esp. pp. 138–170 on Southern military education. Unfortunately, this book was published too late to be used in the writing of this section.

24. Seymour, *Military Education,* pp. 3ff.; Alfred T. Mahan, *From Sail to Steam* (New York, 1907), p. 151.

25. United States Military Academy, Department of Economics, Government, and History, *Military Policy of the United States, 1775–1944* (West Point, 1945), pp. 15–16; Upton, *Military Policy,* pp. 238–241; Oliver L. Spaulding, *The United States Army in War and Peace* (New York, 1937), pp. 243–244; E. R. Humphreys, *Education of Officers: Preparatory and Professional* (Boston, 1862), p. 10; Seymour, *Military Education,* pp. 5–6; Ellsworth Eliot, Jr., *West Point in the Confederacy* (New York, 1941), *passim.* For the significance of the Union government's acceptance of Southern resignations, see Joseph E. Johnston, *Narrative of Military Operations* (New York, 1874), p. 11.

26. John A. Logan, *The Volunteer Soldier of America* (Chicago, 1887), pp. 243–246, 431–435; Mahan, *Sail to Steam,* pp. 85–87; Lloyd Lewis, *Sherman: Fighting Prophet* (New York, 1932), pp. 54–55; William A. Gordon, *A Compilation of Registers of the Army of the United States from 1815 to 1837* (Washington, 1837), pp. 575ff.; *Congressional Globe,* XI (May 13, 1842), 498–500; Puleston, *Annapolis,* pp. 8–9, 14–19, 27–29, 68–69; A. Howard Meneely, *The War Department, 1861* (New York, 1928), pp. 26–28; Paullin, USNIP, XXXIII, 1437–1438; P. Melvin, "Stephen Russell

Mallory, Southern Naval Statesman," *Jour. of Southern History*, X (May 1944), 137–160.

27. On Calhoun's administrative reforms, see Ingersoll, *War Department*, pp. 79–107, and White, *The Jeffersonians*, pp. 233–250. For his views on military policy, see ASP:MA, I, 780–781, 799, 834–835, II, 75–76, 188–191, 699.

28. Paullin, USNIP, XXXIII, 637, 1473ff.; "U.S. Naval Lyceum," *Naval Magazine*, I (January 1836), 21–28.

29. Benjamin Blake Minor, *The Southern Literary Messenger, 1834–1864* (New York, 1905), pp. 84–85, 90, 119; Frank L. Mott, *A History of American Magazines, 1741–1850* (New York, 1930), p. 643. On pre-Civil War military periodicals generally, see Max L. Marshall, "A Survey of Military Periodicals" (M.A. Thesis, Univ. of Missouri, 1953), pp. 10–17.

30. See his "Scraps from the Lucky Bag," *Southern Literary Messenger*, VI (April 1840), 235–237, (May 1840), 312–317, (Dec. 1840), 793–795, VII (Jan. 1841), 5, 24.

31. Mahan, *Sail to Steam*, pp. ix–xiv, 89, 151. The most relevant portions of Dennis Mahan's writings are *Advanced Guard, Out Post, and Detachment Service of Troops* (New York, new ed., 1863), pp. 7, 19–20, 26–28, 33, 169, 266; *Notes on the Composition of Armies and Strategy* (West Point, Lithographed), pp. 2–3, 5, 11; *A Treatise on Field Fortifications* (New York, 1856), pp. vi–vii. On Mahan, generally, see Dupuy, *Where They Have Trod*, pp. 272–274, and *Men of West Point*, ch. 2.

32. *Military Art and Science*, pp. 11–13, 15–21, 29, 142, 381–382, 398–407; Report on the Means of National Defense, S. Doc. 85, 28th Cong., 2d Sess., pp. 2, 7 (1845).

Chapter 9 — The Creation of the American Military Profession

1. For business pacifist expressions, see Spencer, *The Principles of Sociology* (New York, 3 vols., 1888), I, 473–491, 568–667; Fiske, *Outlines of Cosmic Philosophy* (Boston, 2 vols., 11th ed., 1890), II, 240ff.; Sumner, *War and Other Essays* (New Haven, ed. by A. G. Keller, 1913), pp. 28–29, 33, 35, 39–40, 323, 348; Sumner and A. G. Keller, *The Science of Society* (New Haven, 4 vols., 1927), I, 407–410; Carnegie, *Autobiography* (Garden City, N.Y., 1933), pp. 271ff., 321; *The Gospel of Wealth and Other Timely Essays* (Garden City, N.Y., 1933), pp. 140, 159, 166–167; *Miscellaneous Writings* (Garden City, N.Y., 2 vols., ed. by B. J. Hendrick, 1933), II, 221, 237, 254–255, 260–267, 275, 284; *New Republic*, I (Jan. 9, 1915), 9–10. Compare Brooks Adams, *The Law of Civilization and Decay* (London, 1895), esp. pp. vii–viii. On Sumner and Carnegie, generally, see Robert G. McCloskey, *American Conservatism in the Age of Enterprise* (Cambridge, Mass., 1951), chs. 2, 3, 6. Spencer's popularity

in the United States is described in Richard Hofstadter, *Social Darwinism in American Thought, 1860–1915* (Philadelphia, 1945), pp. 18–22. For the activities of Carnegie and his pacifist predecessors among American businessmen, see Merle Curti, *Peace or War: The American Struggle, 1636–1936* (New York, 1936), pp. 37, 43–44, 59, 78–79, 127, 164–165, 200–206, 212. For the role of the economics-politics contrast in liberal thought generally, see Hans J. Morgenthau, *Scientific Man vs. Power Politics* (Chicago, 1946), pp. 75–81.

2. As late as 1908, regulars could not vote in Kansas, Missouri, Oregon, and Texas. Frederic S. Stimson, *The Law of the Federal and State Constitutions of the United States* (Boston, 1908), p. 222.

3. T. Bentley Mott, *Twenty Years as a Military Attaché* (New York, 1937), p. 338; B. A. Fiske, "American Naval Policy," U.S. Naval Institute *Proceedings* (hereafter cited as USNIP), XXXI (1905), 69–72; William Carter, "Army as a Career," *North American,* CLXXXIII (Nov. 2, 1906), 873; Liggett Hunter, S. Doc. 621, 62d Cong., 2d Sess., pp. 22–26 (1912); Sidney Forman, *West Point* (New York, 1950), pp. 216–217. On the effects of business pacifism on technological development, see Harold and Margaret Sprout, *The Rise of American Naval Power, 1776–1918* (Princeton, 1946), pp. 167–171; William A. Ganoe, *The History of the United States Army* (New York, 1932), pp. 348–349; C. Joseph Bernardo and Eugene H. Bacon, *American Military Policy* (Harrisburg, Pa., 1955), pp. 234–261.

4. See Lloyd Lewis, *Sherman: Fighting Prophet* (New York, 1932), pp. 411, 531, 635–637. For Sherman's views, see *Ann. Rept. of the Commanding General, 1880,* I, 6, *1883,* pp. 44–45; Rachel Sherman Thorndike (ed.), *The Sherman Letters* (New York, 1894), pp. 340–342; W. T. Sherman, *Memoirs* (New York, 2 vols., 1875), II, 385–386, 406; M. A. DeWolfe Howe (ed.), *Home Letters of General Sherman* (New York, 1909), p. 387.

5. B. A. Fiske, "Stephen B. Luce: An Appreciation," USNIP, XLIII (September 1917), 1935–1939. For a summary of Luce's ideas, see J. D. Hayes, "The Writings of Stephen B. Luce," *Military Affairs,* XIX (Winter 1955), 187–196. On Upton, see Peter S. Michie, *The Life and Letters of Emory Upton* (New York, 1885), pp. 454–457; W. H. Carter, "The Evolution of Army Reforms," *United Service,* III (May 1903, 3rd Series), 1190ff.; R. C. Brown, "General Emory Upton — The Army's Mahan," *Military Affairs,* XVII (Fall 1953), 125–131.

6. Letter of Sherman to Sheridan, Nov. 22, 1881, Ira L. Reeves, *Military Education in the United States* (Burlington, Vt., 1914), p. 205; *Ann. Repts. of the Commanding General, 1880,* I, 6, *1883,* pp. 44–45.

7. *The Armies of Europe and Asia* (New York, 1878), pp. 51–54, 319–320, 324, 354–358, 360–362.

8. Upton, *The Military Policy of the United States* (Washington, 1912), p. 258; Sherman, *Memoirs,* II, 388; Arthur L. Wagner, *The Cam-*

paign of Königgratz (Fort Leavenworth, 1889), pp. 9, 11, 15, 23; Major Theodore Schwan, *Report on the Organization of the German Army* (War Dept., Adj. Gen'l.'s Office, Mil. Inf. Div., No. 2, 1894); Captain T. A. Bingham, "The Prussian Great General Staff," *Journal of the Military Service Institution* (hereafter cited as JMSI), XIII (July 1892), 669; Mott, *Twenty Years as a Military Attaché*, p. 336; Captain F. E. Chadwick, "Explanation of Course at the Naval War College," USNIP, XXVII (1901), 332; A. T. Mahan, *Naval Strategy* (London, 1912), pp. 297–301; A. T. Mahan, "The Practical Character of the Naval War College," USNIP, XIX (1893), 163; W. E. Puleston, *Mahan* (New Haven, 1939), pp. 75–80, 295–298; J. H. Russell, "A Fragment of Naval War College History," USNIP, LVIII (August 1932), 1164–1165.

9. Albert Gleaves, *Life and Letters of Rear Admiral Stephen B. Luce* (New York, 1925), p. 101.

10. See Luce's letter to William Conant Church, 1882, quoted by Rear Admiral John D. Hayes, *Military Affairs*, XVIII (Fall 1954), 166; Gleaves, *Luce*, pp. 168–171; Puleston, *Mahan*, p. 69; R. Ernest Dupuy, *Men of West Point* (New York, 1951), pp. 116–118.

11. Quoted in Samuel E. Tillman, "The Academic History of the Military Academy, 1802–1902," *The Centennial of the United States Military Academy at West Point, 1802–1902* (Washington, 1904), pp. 289–290.

12. For military discussion and criticism of the Academy curricula see JMSI, XIV (1893), 1019–1026, XVI (1895), 1–24, XX (1897), 23; *Inf. Jour.*, I (Oct. 1, 1904), 7; USNIP, XXXVII (1911), 447–451, XXXVIII (1912), 187–194, 1397–1403, XXXIX (1913), 138; *United Serv.*, VIII (1883), 173. Also: W. D. Puleston, *Annapolis* (New York, 1942), pp. 108, 114; Mott, *Twenty Years as a Military Attaché*, pp. 41–42; Charles W. Larned, "The Genius of West Point," *Centennial*, pp. 467, 479; U.S. Military Academy, Board of Visitors, *Report*, 1889, p. 40.

13. Major Eben Swift, *Remarks*, Introductory to the Course in Military Art at the Infantry and Cavalry School, Fort Leavenworth, Kansas (September 1904), pp. 1–3. On Leavenworth, see also Report of the Secy. of War, H. Ex. Doc. 1, 42d Cong., 3rd Sess., p. 79 (1871); Report of the Cmdg. Genl., 1878, p. 8; Ganoe, *United States Army*, pp. 363, 422–423; Reeves, *Military Education*, pp. 213–233; Major Eben Swift, "An American Pioneer in the Cause of Military Education," JMSI, XLIV (January–February 1909), 67–72. On naval postgraduate education, see Gleaves, *Luce*, pp. 330–336; Puleston, *Annapolis*, pp. 119–120; Ralph Earle, *Life at the U.S. Naval Academy* (New York, 1917), p. 259; Belknap, USNIP, XXXIX. 135–153; Paullin, USNIP, XL, 681–682; Ernest J. King and Walter Whitehill, *A Naval Record* (New York, 1952), pp. 146–149.

14. For Luce's views, see USNIP, IX (1883), 635, XII (1886), 528, XXXVI (1910), 560ff. For other aspects of War College history, see USNIP, IX (1883), 155ff., XXXVII (1911), 353–377, LIII (1927), 937–947, LVIII (1932), 1157–1163.

15. Reeves, *Military Education,* p. 198. Typical military views are in JMSI, XIV (1893), 452ff., XX (1897), 1–54, 453–499. For Root's attitudes, see *Five Years of the War Department* (Washington, 1904), pp. 62–65, 335–336, and *The Military and Colonial Policy of the United States* (Cambridge, Mass., 1916), pp. 121–129. In general, see *The Army War College: A Brief Narrative, 1901–1953* (Carlisle Barracks), pp. 1–3.

16. JMSI, XVI, 19, XX, 1–54; "Memorandum for a General Order — Subject: Instruction of Officers," November 27, 1901, Root, *Five Years of the War Department,* pp. 414–418; "Report and Recommendations of a Board Appointed by the Bureau of Naviation Regarding the Instruction and Training of Line Officers," USNIP, XLVI (August 1920), 1265–1292.

17. On the Naval Institute, see "Sixty Years of the Naval Institute," USNIP, LIX (October 1933), 1417–1432, and on the Military Service Institution, Colonel J. B. Fry, "Origin and Progress of the Military Service Institution of the United States," JMSI, I (1879), 20–32. For the military publications and associations generally, see Max L. Marshall, "A Survey of Military Periodicals" (M.A. Thesis, Univ. of Missouri, 1951), pp. 18ff.; "The Journal's First Half Century," *Combat Forces Journal,* V (October 1954), 17–20; U.S. Dept. of the Army, *The Army Almanac* (Washington, 1950), pp. 883–908. For other aspects of the emerging military scholarship, see Paullin, USNIP, XXXIX (September 1913), 1252, (December 1913), 1499; Lt. G. R. Catts, "Post Professional Libraries for Officers," JMSI, XLIV (January–February 1909), 84–89.

18. On the Navy, see Act of Aug. 5, 1882, 22 Stat. 284; Act of Mar. 3, 1901, 31 Stat. 1129; Ann. Rept. of the Secy. of the Navy, 1882, H. Ex. Doc. 1, 47th Cong., 2d Sess., p. 8; Puleston, *Annapolis,* p. 223. For the Army: Acts of June 11, 1878, 20 Stat. 111; June 18, 1878, 20 Stat. 150; July 30, 1892, 27 Stat. 336; Mar. 2, 1899, 30 Stat. 979; Larned, *Centennial,* pp. 494–496; Herman Beukema, *The United States Military Academy and Its Foreign Contemporaries* (West Point, 1944), pp. 33–34; Peyton C. March, *The Nation at War* (Garden City, N.Y., 1932), pp. 53–56; *Inf. Jour.,* XV (February 1919), 681–682; Richard C. Brown, "Social Attitudes of American Generals, 1898–1940" (Ph.D. Thesis, Univ. of Wisconsin, 1951), pp. 17–19.

19. On naval conditions, see Secy. Chandler, *Ann. Rept. of the Secy. of the Navy, 1882,* pp. 9, 41–42, *1883,* p. 14, *1884,* p. 41. For professional naval opinion pro and con selection, see USNIP, XXII (1896), 85–86, XXVII (1901), 25–26, XXXI (1905), 401–454, XXXII (1906), 20ff., 801–806, XXXIV (1908), 1129–1140. The relevant statutes are: Acts of July 16, 1862, 12 Stat. 584; Apr. 21, 1864, 13 Stat. 53; Mar. 3, 1899, 30 Stat. 1004; Aug. 29, 1916, 39 Stat. 578–579. On the Army, see Root, *Five Years of the War Department,* pp. 61–65; JMSI, XIV (1893), 954–955, XXXVII (1905), 1–7, 289–294, XL (1907), 167–183, LI (1912), 1–12; *Inf. Jour.,* XI (1914), 128–131; *United Serv.,* I (1902, 3rd Series), 373–

389; William H. Carter, *The American Army* (Indianapolis, 1915), pp. 225–230; Act of Oct. 1, 1890, 26 Stat. 562.

20. Acts of Feb. 28, 1855, 10 Stat. 616; Aug. 3, 1861, 12 Stat. 289. For the Navy: Acts of Dec. 12, 1861, 12 Stat. 329; July 16, 1862, 12 Stat. 587; July 28, 1866, 14 Stat. 345; July 15, 1870, 16 Stat. 333; March 3, 1873, 17 Stat. 547, 556; March 3, 1899, 30 Stat. 1004. For the Army: Acts of July 17, 1862, 12 Stat. 596; July 15, 1870, 16 Stat. 317, 320; June 30, 1882, 22 Stat. 118; Emory Upton, "Facts in Favor of Compulsory Retirement," *United Service*, II (March 1880), 269–288, III (December 1880), 649–666, IV (January 1881), 19–32.

21. Acts of July 15, 1870, 16 Stat. 319; Feb. 27, 1877, 19 Stat. 243; July 31, 1894, 28 Stat. 205; *Regulations for the Government of the United States Navy, 1876,* Ch. vi, Art. 33, *1896,* Pars. 219, 236, *1900,* Par. 232; *Regulations for the Army of the United States, 1895,* Art. I, Par. 5. For subsequent problems caused by this legislation, see *New York Times,* Oct. 22, 1951, p. 10; *Hearings* before House Committee on the Armed Services on H. R. 5946, 84th Cong., 1st Sess. (1955).

22. Act of Feb. 2, 1901, 31 Stat. 755; Root, *Five Years of the War Department,* pp. 64, 139; Carter, *American Army,* p. 235; USNIP, XXIV (1898), 4–6, XXVIII (1902), 231–242, XXXI (1905), 823–944, XL (1914), 676.

23. *Ann. Rept. of the Secy. of the Navy, Nov. 30, 1885,* pp. xxxviii–xl.

24. The most important expressions of the views of the naval traditionalists are those of Luce, USNIP, XIV (1888), 561–588, XVIII (1902), 839–849, XXIX (1903), 809–821, and Mahan, "The Principles of Naval Administration," *Naval Administration and Warfare* (Boston, 1908), pp. 1–48, and Certain Needs of the Navy, S. Doc. 740, 60th Cong., 2d Sess. (1909). See also USNIP, XI (1885), 55ff., XII (1886), 362–363, XIV (1888), 726ff., XX (1894), 498ff., XXVII (1901), 3–10, XXXI (1905), 318ff., XXXIX (1913), 443–444, 965–974. For early support of the vertical system, see Paullin, USNIP, XXXIX, 756–757, 1261–1262; *Ann. Rept. of the Secy. of the Navy, 1886,* pp. 66–67. The best expression of the insurgent view is H. C. Taylor, "Memorandum on a General Staff for the U.S. Navy," USNIP, XXVI (1900), 441–448. But, see also USNIP, XXVII (1901), 307–308, XXVIII (1902), 254–255, XXIX (1903), 805–807, XXXIII (1907), 574–576; Bradley A. Fiske, *From Midshipman to Rear Admiral* (New York, 1919), pp. 558–559; Elting E. Morison, *Admiral Sims and the Modern American Navy* (Boston, 1942), pp. 114–115.

25. Act of Mar. 3, 1915, 38 Stat. 929; Act of August 29, 1916, 39 Stat. 558; U.S. Navy Dept., *Naval Administration: Selected Documents on Navy Department Organization, 1915–1940,* p. I–3; Paullin, USNIP, XXXIX, 737, XL, 118; J. A. Mudd, "The Reorganization of the Naval Establishment," USNIP, XXXV (1909), 37–44; *Ann. Rept. of the Secy. of the Navy, 1885,* pp. xxxix–xl.

26. See Root, *Five Years of the War Department*, pp. 297–298, 485; William H. Carter, *Creation of the American General Staff* (S. Doc. 119, 68th Cong., 1st Sess., 1924), pp. 2, 8, 20–23, and *American Army*, pp. 197, 204.

27. *United Serv.*, IX (1883), 663, I (1902, 3rd Series), 604–631; *Inf. Jour.*, IX (1912), 117–137, 255–261; USNIP, III (1877), 5ff., IX (1883), 155–194, 661, XII (1886), 527–546, XIV (1888), 632–633, XXII (1896), 2–3, XXIV (1898), 269, XXVII (1901), 27, 255, XXIX (1903), 538–539, 801, XXXI (1905), 76ff., XXXIII (1907), 485–487; Colonel J. B. Wheeler, *The Elements of the Art and Science of War* (New York, 1893), pp. 7–8, 317–319; Captain James S. Pettit, *Elements of Military Science* (New Haven, rev. ed., 1895), p. 150; Lt. Col. G. J. Fiebeger, *Elements of Strategy* (1906), pp. 73, 105; Captain Arthur L. Wagner, *Organization and Tactics* (New York, 1895), p. 2; Captain A. T. Mahan, *Naval Strategy* (London, 1912), pp. 2–5, 113–115.

28. *Inf. Jour.*, IX (1912), 296–297; *United Serv.*, IX, 663, III (1903, 3rd Series), 694–697; USNIP, XII (1886), 535, XXX (1904), 343, XXXI (1905), 323, XXXIII (1907), 127–130, 476, 527, 559; JMSI, X (1889), 624, XLII (1908), 26, 30, XLIX (1911), 2–4; General Hugh L. Scott, *Some Memories of a Soldier* (New York, 1928), p. 145; Mott, *Twenty Years as a Military Attaché*, pp. 340–341; Mahan, *Naval Strategy*, pp. 121, 135–136, 149, 191.

29. JMSI, XVI (1895), 211–250, XXI (1897), 226–228, 544–587, XXII (1898), 269, XXXVIII (1904), 329, XLII (1908), 22–23, XLVI (1910), 225–256; USNIP, XI (1885), 5, XII (1886), 530–543, XIII (1887), 178–180, XIV (1888), 4, XXIV (1898), 8–10, XXVII (1901), 5, 7, 16, XXIX (1903), 323, XXX (1904), 615–618; H. M. Chittenden, *War or Peace: A Present Duty and A Future Hope* (Chicago, 1911), p. 238; Rear Adm. Bradley A. Fiske, *The Navy as a Fighting Machine* (New York, 1916), pp. 13–16, 19–21, and *Midshipman to Rear Admiral*, p. 538; Richard Stockton, Jr., *Peace Insurance* (Chicago, 1915), pp. 41–42, 75, 77; Wagner, *Organization and Tactics*, Introduction; Capt. Harrison S. Kerrick, *Military and Naval America* (Garden City, N.Y., 1917), p. 382; Colonel James Mercur, *Elements of the Art of War* (New York, 3rd ed., 1894), pp. 11–15; Mahan, *Naval Administration and Warfare*, pp. 245–272; Wheeler, *Elements of the Art and Science of War*, p. v.

30. JMSI, XII (1891), 225–231, XVII (1895), 255, XXI (1897), 277–279, XXXVIII (1906), 38, XL (1907), 199–203; USNIP, V (1879), 126, IX (1883), 175–176, XIV (1888), 3–7, XXIV (1898), 8–9; *United Serv.*, V (1881), 620–630, VII (1905, 3rd Series), 654–660; Wheeler, *Elements of the Art and Science of War*, p. 58; Mercur, *Elements of the Art of War*, p. 273; Scott, *Memories of a Soldier*, pp. 469–471, 545; Mahan, *Naval Strategy*, p. 21; U.S. War Dept., General Staff, *Report on the Organization of the Land Forces of the United States* (Washington, 1912), p. 12; Truman Seymour, *Military Education* (New York, 1864), p. 4.

31. JMSI, XVII (1895), 239, XXI (1897), 276, XL (1906), 203; USNIP, XXIV (1898), 11, XXVII (1901), 257, XXXI (1905), 79, XXXII (1906), 127–130, XXXIII (1907), 32–33, XXXVIII (1912), 567; *Inf. Jour.*, X (1913), 473–485; Army War College, *Statement of a Proper Military Policy for the United States* (Supplementary War Dept. Doc. No. 526, September 1915), pp. 6–10; Mercur, *Elements of the Art of War*, pp. 11–15; Bradley A. Fiske, *The Art of Fighting* (New York, 1920), p. 365; Pettit, *Elements of Military Science*, p. 151; Captain J. M. Caleff, *Notes on Military Science and the Art of War* (Washington, 1898), pp. 61–62; Mahan, *Naval Administration and Warfare*, pp. 137–138. For military recommendations for a national defense council, see USNIP, XXXVIII (1912), 563–593, XXXIX (1913), 479–482, 1709–1710, XL (1914), 3–15, 636–638; Genl. Staff, *Organization of the Land Forces*, pp. 63–64; Fiske, *Midshipman to Rear Admiral*, pp. 537–538; A. T. Mahan, *Armaments and Arbitration* (New York, 1912), pp. 57–77; Nelson, *National Security and the General Staff*, p. 237.

32. USNIP, V (1879), 160, XI (1885), 4, XVI (1890), 201, 368, XXIV (1898), 41, XXVIII (1902), 266–267, 840, XXX (1904), 476–479, 493–494, 620–621, XL (1914), 1301; JMSI, XIV (1893), 238, XXI (1897), 239–240, XLII (1903), 336, XLIV (1909), 385, XLVI (1910), 193–194, 213–214; *Inf. Jour.*, IX (1912), 151–160, X (1914), 777; *United Serv.*, IX (1883), 658–666; Wagner, *Organization and Tactics*, p. v; Fiske, *Navy as a Fighting Machine*, pp. 5–6, 21–29, and ch. 4, and *Midshipman to Rear Admiral*, pp. 555–560; Chittenden, *War or Peace*, pp. 201ff., 230–231; Stockton, *Peace Insurance*, chs. 3, 4; Scott, *Memories of a Soldier*, p. 218; A. T. Mahan, *Some Neglected Aspects of War* (Boston, 1907), pp. 45–52, and *The Interest of America in Sea Power* (Boston, 1898), p. 193; Lt. Col. A. L. Wagner and Cdr. J. D. J. Kelley, *The United States Army and Navy* (Akron, 1899), pp. 100–103, Kerrick, *Military and Naval America*, ch. 46. The White quotation is from Allen Westcott (ed.), *Mahan on Naval Warfare* (Boston, 1941), p. xix. For other analysis of military views on this subject, see Morison, *Admiral Sims and the Modern American Navy*, ch. 23; Brown, "Social Attitudes," pp. 266–268, 272–273; Puleston, *Mahan*, ch. 20. For a rare military adherence to the bellicose version of Social Darwinism, see *United Serv.*, IV (1903, 3rd Series) 390–398.

33. Major R. L. Bullard, JMSI, XXVI (January–February 1905), 104–114. See also JMSI, XXIX (1906), 331, XXXVI (1910), 268, XXXVIII (1906), 1–38, 327, 363, XXXIX (1907), 329–340, XL (1907), 384, XLII (1908), 1–12, 18, 340, XLIV (1909), 378, 384, XLVI (1910), 214–215; USNIP, V (1879), 162, VI (1880), 382–383, XIV (1888), 625–626, XX (1894), 796ff., XXVII (1901), 16, XXIX (1903), 323, XXXIX (1913), 516–536, 546, XL (1914), 1073–1074; *Inf. Jour.*, IX (1912), 300–303; A. T. Mahan, *From Sail to Steam* (New York, 1907), p. 7; Carter, *American Army*, p. 26; Army War College, *Proper Military Policy*, p. 9; Homer

Lea, *The Valor of Ignorance* (New York, 1909), pp. 19–20, 24–28, 58–71; General M. B. Stewart, "Soldiering — What Is There in It?" *Harper's Weekly,* LIII (Dec. 11, 1909), 16, "Shame of the Uniform" *ibid.,* LVII (May 24, 1913), 12–13; Colonel C. W. Larned, "Modern Education from a Military Viewpoint," *North American Review,* CLXXXVII (April 1908), 506; Mott, *Twenty Years as a Military Attaché,* pp. 30–31.

Chapter 10 — The Failure of the Neo-Hamiltonian Compromise

1. The literature on Neo-Hamiltonian personalities and ideas is voluminous, but only a small portion deals with their approach to military affairs. For a concise analysis of Theodore Roosevelt's philosophy of international relations, see Robert E. Osgood, *Ideals and Self-Interest in America's Foreign Relations* (Chicago, 1953), pp. 88–91, and, for the Neo-Hamiltonian approach generally, pp. 58–70. Gordon C. O'Gara, *Theodore Roosevelt and the Rise of the Modern Navy* (Princeton, 1943), explores the impact of the Colonel on that service. For Root's views, see *Five Years of the War Department* (Washington, 1904) and *The Military and Colonial Policy of the United States* (Cambridge, Mass., 1916), Richard W. Leopold, *Elihu Root and the Conservative Tradition* (Boston, 1954), *passim,* and Philip C. Jessup, *Elihu Root* (New York, 2 vols., 1938), I, 215–264. Brooks Adams' ideas are discussed in Thornton Anderson, *Brooks Adams, Constructive Conservative* (Ithaca, N.Y., 1951). Croly's philosophy is set forth in *The Promise of American Life* (New York, 1909). For the opinions of Croly, Lippmann, and their associates on the *New Republic,* see *New Republic,* I (Dec. 12, 1914), 6–7, (Jan. 8, 1915), 9–10, II (Mar. 20, 1915), 166–167.

2. A. T. Mahan, *From Sail to Steam* (New York, 1907), pp. xiv, 274. Mahan expressed his religious philosophy in *The Harvest Within: Thoughts on the Life of the Christian* (Boston, 1909). On this aspect of his life, see also W. D. Puleston, *Mahan* (New Haven, 1939), pp. 15–17, 24, 37, 44, 63, 72–73; C. C. Taylor, *The Life of Admiral Mahan* (London, 1920), p. ix.

3. Mahan, *Naval Strategy* (London, 1912), pp. 20–21, 107–108, *The Interest of America in Sea Power* (Boston, 1897), pp. 104, 121–122, 223, *Armaments and Arbitration* (New York, 1912), pp. 15–35, 70–77, 100–120, *Naval Administration and Warfare* (Boston, 1908), pp. 1–86, 175–242, *Retrospect and Prospect* (Boston, 1902), pp. 17, 20–21, 39–53, *Lessons of the War with Spain and Other Articles* (Boston, 1899), pp. 207–240; William E. Livezey, *Mahan on Sea Power* (Norman, Okla., 1947), pp. 175–187, 263–270, 292–293.

4. Mahan, *From Sail to Steam,* p. 313; Mahan to Samuel Ashe, Nov. 24, 1893, quoted in Livezey, *Mahan,* pp. 12–13; Puleston, *Mahan,* p. 148.

5. Livezey, *Mahan,* pp. 89–90, 254.

6. *Ibid.,* pp. 272–273.

The Neo-Hamiltonian Compromise

7. Mahan, *Retrospect and Prospect*, p. 24, *From Sail to Steam*, pp. 7, 276, *Armaments and Arbitration*, pp. 121–154, 211–212; Puleston, *Mahan*, pp. 206, 274–275, 292, 323; Osgood, *Ideals and Self-Interest*, pp. 39–40.

8. For Wood's adherence to the military ethic, see his *Our Military History* (Chicago, 1916), pp. 28, 31–54, 84–85, and *The Military Obligation of Citizenship* (Princeton, 1915), pp. 40–41, 62. For his activities in Army reform, see Hermann Hagedorn, *Leonard Wood* (New York, 2 vols., 1931), II, 109, 125–128; Eric F. Wood, *Leonard Wood: Conservator of Americanism* (New York, 1920), pp. 268–270. Hagedorn's book is the best source on Wood but it is blind to even his most obvious shortcomings. A critical biography of this fascinating man is definitely needed.

9. H. L. Stimson to W. G. Harding, Jan. 9, 1921, quoted in Hagedorn, *Wood*, II, 101.

10. See Wood, *Military History*, pp. 169, 177ff., 188–190, 194–195, 206, and *Military Obligation of Citizenship*, pp. 69–76.

11. *Inf. Jour.*, XXV (1924), 520; *Ann. Rept. of the Secy. of War, 1920*, pp. 8–9.

12. *Inf. Jour.*, XVI (1920), 623–29, 827–831, XXX (1927), 253; *Ann. Rept. of the Secy. of War, 1924*, pp. 12–13, 27, *1928*, pp. 14–16.

13. AR 600–10, Change 1, Dec. 31, 1927, Secs. 6a–6d; *Inf. Jour.*, XXI (1922), 454–455, XXIV (1924), 36–39, XXV (1925), 41–43, 520, XXVI (1925), 618, 651–656.

14. *Ann. Rept. of the Superintendent of the United States Military Academy, 1920*, p. 4; *Inf. Jour.*, XXVIII (1926), 276–283, 324, XXIX (1926), 391–395.

15. *Ann. Rept. of the Secy. of the Navy, 1921*, pp. 6–7, *1923*, pp. 16–22; U.S. Office of Naval Intelligence, *The United States Navy in Peacetime: The Navy in Its Relation to the Industrial, Scientific, Economic, and Political Development of the Nation* (Washington, 1931); *Ann. Rept. of the Secy. of War, 1925*, p. 3; *Inf. Jour.*, XXV (1924), 521, XXVI (1925), 288–289, XXX (1927), 2–7.

16. *Ann. Rept. of the Secy. of War, 1920*, pp. 16–17, *1926*, pp. 22–24; *Inf. Jour.*, XV (1918), 325–333, XVI (1920), 725–729, (1919–20), 70–71, 593, 725–729, XVIII (1921), 217–218, 325–328, XIX (1921), 7–11.

17. *Inf. Jour.*, XVIII (1921), 31–33, XXII (1923), 271–286, XXIV (1924), 25ff., XXXIII (1928), 229–230. The most influential anti-ROTC brochure was Winthrop D. Lane, *Military Training in Schools and Colleges of the United States* (New York, 2d ed., 1926). For an excellent analysis of the opposition to "militarism in education," see Arthur A. Ekirch, Jr., *The Civilian and the Military* (New York, 1956), ch. 14.

18. *Inf. Jour.*, XXVIII (1926), 485–489, XXI (1922), 214–216, XXVII (1925), 62–66, 242–249, 432–436, XXVIII (1926), 196, XXXI (1927), 493, 611–615, XXXIV (1929), 618ff.; U.S. Naval Institute *Proceedings*, LVII (1931), 604; *Ann. Rept. of the Secy. of War, 1923, passim, 1930*, pp. 94–98; Sidney Forman, *West Point* (New York, 1950), pp. 192–

193; Harold and Margaret Sprout, *Toward a New Order of Sea Power* (Princeton, 1946), esp. pp. 104–121.

Chapter 11 — The Constancy of Interwar Civil-Military Relations

1. *Liberalism in America* (New York, 1919), pp. viii, 17, 200–202. This remarkable volume sets the tone for reform thought between Wilson and the New Deal. For Stearns's influence, see John Chamberlain, *Farewell to Reform* (New York, 1932), pp. 301–305, and Eric F. Goldman, *Rendezvous with Destiny* (New York, 1952), pp. 276–281.

2. *U.S. Foreign Policy: Shield of the Republic* (Boston, 1943), p. xi.

3. Stuart Chase, "The Tragedy of Waste," *New Republic,* XLIII (Aug. 12, 1925), 312–316; Lewis Mumford, *Technics and Civilization* (New York, 1934), p. 93.

4. Margery Bedinger, "The Goose Step at West Point," *New Republic,* LXIV (Sept. 24, 1930), 146; F. B. Johnson, "Discipline," *ibid.,* XIX (July 2, 1919), 280–283; T. M. Pease, "Does the Military Caste System Work in War?" *ibid.,* XX (Aug. 6, 1919), 27–28; "The Military Idea of Manliness," *Independent,* LIII (April 18, 1901), 874–875.

5. Maxim's book, *Defenseless America* (New York, 1915), was almost a caricature of the reformer's critique, the machine gun manufacturer arguing at one point, that "The quick-firing gun is the greatest life-saving instrument ever invented."

6. Simeon Strunsky, "Armaments and Caste," *Annals* of the American Academy, LXVI (July 1916), 237–246; C. E. Jefferson, "Military Preparedness a Peril to Democracy," *ibid.,* pp. 232–233; Stearns, *Liberalism in America,* pp. 84–85; H. C. Engelbrecht, *Merchants of Death* (New York, 1934), pp. 113–114, 143–144; H. F. Ward, "Free Speech for the Army," *New Republic,* LI (July 13, 1927), 194–196.

7. F. H. Giddings, "The Democracy of Universal Military Service," *Annals* of the American Academy, LXVI (July 1916), 175; Josephus Daniels, *The Wilson Era: Years of Peace — 1910–1917* (Chapel Hill, N.C., 1944), pp. 253–278, 386–403.

8. *Ann. Rept. of the Secy. of the Navy, 1932,* p. 190; U.S. Naval Institute *Proceedings* (hereafter cited as USNIP), LI (1925), 274–279, LVI (1930), 123–131, LVII (1931), 1364–1366, LVIII (1932), 1110–1115, LIX (1933), 1438–1441; *Inf. Jour.,* XXXIX (1932), 355–357, XLIV (1937), 254; Sidney Forman, *West Point* (New York, 1950), p. 200; William H. Baumer, Jr., *West Point: Moulder of Men* (New York, 1942), pp. 108–109.

9. On Navy promotion, see Acts of June 10, 1926, 44 Stat. 717; June 22, 1926, 44 Stat. 761; Mar. 3, 1931, 46 Stat. 1482; June 23, 1938, 52 Stat. 944; *Ann. Rept. of the Secy. of the Navy, 1926,* pp. 138–39, *1930,* pp. 177–178; and USNIP files for 1935 and 1936 where promotion received

constant attention, esp. Admiral W. S. Sims, "Service Opinion upon Promotion and Selection," USNIP, LXI (June 1935), 791–806. On the Army, see Acts of June 4, 1920, 41 Stat. 771–774, and July 31, 1934, 49 Stat. 505; *Ann. Rept. of the Secy. of War, 1922*, p. 20, *1924*, pp. 33–34, *1932*, p. 73; *Ann. Rept. of the Chief of Staff, 1927*, p. 53, *1930*, p. 141, *1931*, p. 41, *1932*, pp. 64–66, 69–70, *1933*, p. 35, *1938*, p. 36; *Inf. Jour.*, XVI (1920), 591, XLII (1935), 119–125, XLIV (1937), 532–535.

10. Henry L. Stimson and McGeorge Bundy, *On Active Service in Peace and War* (New York, 1947), p. 33; General Peyton C. March, *The Nation at War* (New York, 1932), p. 373; Charles G. Washburn, *The Life of John W. Weeks* (Boston, 1928), p. 288; Pendleton Herring, *The Impact of War* (New York, 1941), ch. 4.

11. On these battles, see Stimson and Bundy, *On Active Service*, p. 36; Otto L. Nelson, Jr., *National Security and the General Staff* (Washington, 1946), pp. 132–166, 187–210, 247–253; Maj. Gen. Robert L. Bullard, *Personalities and Reminiscences of the War* (Garden City, N.Y., 1925), p. 26; Maj. Gen. James G. Harbord, *The American Army in France, 1917–1919* (Boston, 1936), pp. 22–23, 110–111; March, *The Nation at War*, pp. 49–50, 371; General John J. Pershing, *My Experiences in the World War* (New York, 1931), pp. 185–192.

12. William H. Carter, *The American Army* (Indianapolis, 1915), p. 200; Nelson, *National Security and the General Staff*, p. 65.

13. Herring, *Impact of War*, p. 82; Frederick Palmer, *Newton D. Baker: America at War* (New York, 2 vols., 1931), I, 11.

14. On the breakdown of the War Department in World War I, see Nelson, *National Security and the General Staff*, pp. 220ff.; Bullard, *Personalities and Reminiscences*, pp. 21–23; Paul Y. Hammond, "The Secretaryships of War and the Navy: A Study of Civilian Control of the Military" (Ph.D. Thesis, Harvard Univ., 1953), pp. 114–132.

15. See *Hearings* before House Committee on Military Affairs on H. R. 8287, 66th Cong., 1st Sess., pp. 1803–1804 (1919); Nelson, *National Security and the General Staff*, pp. 282–287, 301–307; John Dickinson, *The Building of an Army* (New York, 1922), pp. 307–322; Mark S. Watson, *Chief of Staff: Prewar Plans and Preparations* (Washington, 1950), pp. 60–64, 75–76; John D. Millett, *The Organization and Role of the Army Service Forces* (Washington, 1954), pp. 14–18.

16. On the World War II reorganization, see Millett, *Army Service Forces*, ch. 2, pp. 173–181, 429, 480, 514–516; Ray S. Cline, *Washington Command Post: The Operations Division* (Washington, 1951), pp. 70, 91–93, 99, 270–274, 352–361; Nelson, *National Security and the General Staff*, pp. 328–334, 373–382; Stimson and Bundy, *On Active Service*, pp. 449–452.

17. See U.S. Navy Dept., *Naval Administration: Selected Documents on Navy Department Organization, 1915–1940, passim;* R. E. Coontz, *From the Mississippi to the Sea* (Philadelphia, 1930), p. 400; Ernest J. King and Walter Whitehill, *Fleet Admiral King: A Naval Record* (New York, 1952),

pp. 261ff., 471–478; Hammond, "Secretaryships of War and the Navy," pp. 223–246, 293–305. For naval support for the vertical system, see USNIP, XLII (1916), 1137–1170, 1451–1452, LI (1925), 521–561, LXVI (1940), 52–57. On the evolution of the office of CNO prior to World War II, see the articles by H. P. Beers, *Military Affairs*, X–XI (1946–47).

18. U.S. Navy Dept., *Naval Administration*, pp. VI–202–203, VI–224; *Ann. Rept. of the Secy. of the Navy, 1920*, pp. 199–210, 348, 380.

19. *Ann. Rept. of the Secy. of the Navy, 1920*, p. 207.

20. Stimson and Bundy, *On Active Service*, p. 506. For further comments on the insularity and parochialism of the Navy from one who should know, Franklin D. Roosevelt, see Marriner S. Eccles, *Beckoning Frontiers* (New York, 1951), pp. 335–336.

21. *Ann. Rept. of the Superintendent of the U.S. Military Academy, 1921*, p. 245; *Inf. Jour.*, XV (1918), 159–160, XXXI (1927), 304–305, 633, XXXII (1928), 78, 323–324; USNIP, XLVII (1921), 877–882, LII (1926), 1–14, LVII (1931), 1157–1162, LXI (1935), 475, 1074, LXIV (1938), 1601–1606, LXVII (1941), 1437.

22. See *Inf. Jour.*, XXXIX (1926), 30–34, XLI (1934), 117–119; USNIP, XLVI (1920), 1609–1618, LII (1926), 484–491, LIV (1928), 257–264, LIX (1933), 1747–1758, LXII (1936), 473–486, LXIII (1937), 1724–1731, LXVII (1941), 621–622; Command and General Staff School, *Military Intelligence* (1937), pp. 7–10.

23. W. T. R. Fox, "Interwar International Relations Research: The American Experience," *World Politics*, II (October 1949), 67–79.

24. USNIP, LIX (1933), 1747–1758, LX (1934), 774–783, 961–972; *Inf. Jour.*, XVIII (1921), 384, XXXVIII (1930), 186.

25. For the classic Clausewitz approach of the United States military generally, see USNIP, LX (1934), 1377ff., LXV (1939), 945–948, LXVI (1940), 650; Oliver P. Robinson, *The Fundamentals of Military Science* (Washington, 1928), *passim*, but esp. pp. viii–ix. For the military demand for a defense council, see: *Inf. Jour.*, XIV (1918), 861–862, XXXV (1929), 476–479; USNIP, LX (1934), 465–467, 779, LXI (1935), 842–844, LXV (1939), 1395, LXVII (1941), 619ff.; Robinson, *Military Strategy*, pp. 14, 56–58. For the fate of the various military proposals, see W. R. Schilling, "Civil-Naval Politics in World War I," *World Politics*, VII (July 1955), 572–575; E. R. May, "The Development of Political-Military Consultation in the United States," *Political Science Quarterly*, LXX (June 1955), 167–172; Lawrence J. Legere, Jr., "Unification of the Armed Forces" (Ph.D. Thesis, Harvard Univ., 1951), pp. 75–77.

26. Command and General Staff School, *Principles of Strategy*, pp. 19–20; USNIP, XLVI (1920), 1615–1616.

27. See Captain Hoffman Nickerson, "U.S. Military Writing Today," *Inf. Jour.*, XLIX (November 1941), 34–35.

28. *Inf. Jour.*, XXXI (1927), 4–6, XLIII (1936), 237–238, XLV

(1938), 504ff., XLVII (1940), 12–17, 322, 536–538, XLVI (1939), 22ff., XLVII (1940), 12–17, 172–175, 322, 536–538.

29. USNIP, LVII (1931), 1158, LXIV (1938), 1602ff.; *Inf. Jour.*, XLV (1938), 504ff., XLVI (1939), 312–313.

30. Compare *Inf. Jour.*, XVIII (1921), 396–397, XIX (1921), 331–332, XXI (1922), 219, XXII (1923), 378–379 with *Inf. Jour.*, XXXIII (1928), 335, XLVI (1939), 309, 313, XLVII (1940), 536–537 and USNIP, LXI (1935), 1478, 1497.

31. Major J. H. Burns, *Inf. Jour.*, XLVII (September–October 1940), 419–423.

Chapter 12 — World War II: The Alchemy of Power

1. Henry L. Stimson and McGeorge Bundy, *On Active Service in Peace and War* (New York, 1947), pp. 389, 409; Cordell Hull, *Memoirs* (New York, 2 vols., 1948), II, 1109; *Cong. Record*, LXXXIX (June 19, 1943), 6155–6156, quoted in Elias Huzar, *The Purse and the Sword* (Ithaca, N.Y., 1950), p. 160.

2. *Federal Register*, IV (July 7, 1939), 2786; E. O. 8984, Dec. 18, 1941; E. O. 9096, Mar. 12, 1942; E. O. 9028, Feb. 28, 1942. See also Ernest J. King and Walter Whitehill, *Fleet Admiral King: A Naval Record* (New York, 1952), pp. 349–359.

3. Hull, *Memoirs*, II, 1111; William D. Leahy, *I Was There* (New York, 1950), pp. 3–4, 98–101; Ray S. Cline, *Washington Command Post: The Operations Division* (Washington, 1951), p. 44; Maurice Matloff and Edwin M. Snell, *Strategic Planning for Coalition Warfare, 1941–1942* (Washington, 1953), pp. 51–52; Robert E. Sherwood, *Roosevelt and Hopkins* (New York, 1948), pp. 11, 100–101.

4. Stimson and Bundy, *On Active Service*, pp. 414–415. On Knox, see Paul Y. Hammond, "The Secretaryships of War and the Navy: A Study of Civilian Control of the Military" (Ph.D. Thesis, Harvard Univ., 1953), pp. 306–311.

5. Lucius Clay, *Decision in Germany* (Garden City, N.Y., 1950), pp. 3–6; Sherwood, *Roosevelt and Hopkins*, pp. 269–270, 661–662, 757; Hull, *Memoirs*, II, 1109–1110; John J. McCloy, *The Challenge to American Foreign Policy* (Cambridge, 1953), pp. 36–37; H. Bradford Westerfield, *Foreign Policy and Party Politics: Pearl Harbor to Korea* (New Haven, 1955), pp. 139–145, 184–186.

6. Sherwood, *Roosevelt and Hopkins*, pp. 446, 615, 948; Leahy, *I Was There*, p. 213; King and Whitehill, *Fleet Admiral King*, pp. 525–526.

7. Colonel H. D. Kehm, "Comparison Between British and American Joint Planning," quoted in Cline, *Washington Command Post*, pp. 104–106, 314; Otto L. Nelson, Jr., *National Security and the General Staff* (Washington, 1946), p. 399.

8. See Cline's brilliant analysis of the changing character of the Army planning staffs and the mixed feelings of the military at this development, *Washington Command Post,* pp. 189, 327–332.

9. George A. Lincoln, W. S. Stone, and T. H. Harvey, *Economics of National Security* (New York, 1950), pp. 420–421; Huzar, *Purse and the Sword,* pp. 55–56, 58, 162.

10. S. Rept. 10, 78th Cong., 1st Sess., Part 9, p. 1 (1943), quoted in Louis Smith, *American Democracy and Military Power* (Chicago, 1951), p. 216; Harry A. Toulmin, Jr., *Diary of Democracy: The Senate War Investigating Committee* (New York, 1947), *passim.*

11. Stimson and Bundy, *On Active Service,* pp. 414–415, 453; Sherwood, *Roosevelt and Hopkins,* pp. 405, 739, 756–757; Hull, *Memoirs,* II, 922–923, 1110.

12. See, for example, Wallace Carroll, *Persuade or Perish* (Boston, 1948), p. 74; Robert Payne, *The Marshall Story* (New York, 1951), p. 230; Chester Wilmot, *The Struggle for Europe* (New York, 1952), pp. 714–716.

13. *Roosevelt and Hopkins,* p. 446; *I Was There,* p. 95.

14. King and Whitehill, *Fleet Admiral King,* pp. 525–526; Sherwood, *Roosevelt and Hopkins,* p. 615; Matloff and Snell, *Strategic Planning,* pp. 282–306.

15. See Dwight D. Eisenhower, *Crusade in Europe* (New York, 1952), p. 19.

16. See Mark S. Watson, *Chief of Staff: Prewar Plans and Preparations* (Washington, 1950), pp. 23–56, 110–119, 388–389, 406–407; Matloff and Snell, *Strategic Planning,* pp. 12–16, 51–52; William L. Langer and S. Everett Gleason, *The Undeclared War, 1940–1941* (New York, 1953), pp. 35, 41–43, 649–651, 844–847, 894–901.

17. Quoted in Matloff and Snell, *Strategic Planning,* pp. 28–31, and Watson, *Chief of Staff,* pp. 370–373.

18. Sherwood, *Roosevelt and Hopkins,* pp. 410ff.; Langer and Gleason, *Undeclared War,* pp. 739–740; Watson, *Chief of Staff,* pp. 352–357.

19. *On Active Service,* pp. 472, 565–566; Cline, *Washington Command Post,* p. 313.

20. On these decisions, see Hull, *Memoirs,* II, 1165ff.; Sumner Welles, *Seven Decisions That Shaped History* (New York, 1950), ch. 5; Matloff and Snell, *Strategic Planning,* pp. 30, 380; Leahy, *I Was There,* p. 145; Sherwood, *Roosevelt and Hopkins,* pp. 695–696; Watson, *Chief of Staff,* pp. 124–125.

21. Notes on Conference in Office of the Chief of Staff, Cline, *Washington Command Post,* p. 44.

22. Sherwood, *Roosevelt and Hopkins,* p. 164.

23. Quoted, *ibid.,* p. 948.

24. Payne, *Marshall Story,* p. 230; Cline, *Washington Command Post,* p. 313.

25. Sherwood, *Roosevelt and Hopkins,* p. 748; Hull, *Memoirs,* II, 1470, 1705–1706.

26. *I Was There,* pp. 284–285; Welles, *Seven Decisions,* p. 134.

27. See, for example, "It Will Take Something More," *Inf. Jour.,* LII (February 1943), 6–7; Lt. Cdr. E. M. Eller, "How Shall We Win," U.S. Naval Institute *Proceedings* (hereafter cited as USNIP), LXVIII (April 1942), 465–472; Cdr. Harley Cope, "When Peace Comes," USNIP, LXIX (February 1943), 165–168; C. A. Weil, "An American Way of Peace or War," USNIP, LXIX (May 1943), 674–694; Cdr. H. H. Smith-Hutton, "Post-War Problems and the Navy," USNIP, LXIX (June 1943), 785–793; Lt. Col. H. N. Kenyon, USMC, "Executing the National Policy," USNIP, LXIX (August 1943), 1045–1051; 1st Lt. R. Sunderland, "The Soldier's Relation to Foreign Policy," USNIP, LXIX (September 1943), 1170–1175; Cdr. Isaiah Olch, "National and Naval Policy," USNIP, LXIX (July 1943), 925–932.

28. *Great Mistakes of the War* (New York, 1949), pp. 44–45.

29. Memo to the Chief of Staff, July 23, 1940, Cline, *Washington Command Post,* pp. 43–44, 105–106, 314ff.

30. *Hearings* before Senate Committee on Military Affairs on S. 84, 79th Cong., 1st Sess., p. 521 (1945); *I Was There,* p. 239 (italics are the admiral's).

31. King and Whitehill, *Fleet Admiral King,* pp. 631–632; E. O. 9635, Sept. 29, 1945; Naval Organization Act of 1948, 62 Stat. 66 (Mar. 5, 1948).

32. *Hearings* before House Select Committee on Postwar Military Policy on a Single Department of the Armed Forces, 78th Cong., 2d Sess., pp. 34–38 (1944).

33. *Hearings* before Senate Military Affairs Committee on S. 84, pp. 157, 411ff.

34. *Ibid.,* pp. 589ff.; *Report* by Ferdinand Eberstadt to Secretary of the Navy Forrestal on Unification, Senate Committee on Naval Affairs, 79th Cong., 1st Sess. (1945); Walter Millis (ed.), *The Forrestal Diaries* (New York, 1951), p. 19.

35. The Hopkins-Nelson-WPB viewpoint may be found in Donald M. Nelson, *Arsenal of Democracy* (New York, 1946), Bruce Catton, *The War Lords of Washington* (New York, 1948), and the Bureau of the Budget history, *The United States at War* (Washington, n.d.). For the Patterson-Somervell-Army approach, see John D. Millett, *The Organization and Role of the Army Service Forces* (Washington, 1954), and Stimson and Bundy, *Active Service,* ch. 19. The Baruch-Eberstadt-Forrestal interpretations are reflected in Eliot Janeway, *The Struggle for Survival* (New Haven, 1951) and Robert H. Connery, *The Navy and Industrial Mobilization in World War II* (Princeton, 1951). The picture as it seemed from the angle of James Byrnes and OWMR is given in H. M. Somers, *Presidential Agency: OWMR* (Cambridge, Mass., 1950). The Somers vol-

ume and the official history of the War Production Board, Civilian Production Administration, *Industrial Mobilization for War*, vol. I, *Program and Administration* (Washington, 1947) probably achieve the best combination of comprehensiveness and objectivity.

36. Industrial Mobilization Plan, Revision of 1939. S. Doc. 134, 76th Cong., 2nd Sess. (1939).

37. See Connery, *Navy and Industrial Mobilization*, ch. 8; Millett, *Army Service Forces*, pp. 201–212, 291–293.

38. Executive Order 9024, Jan. 16, 1942, *Federal Register*, VII (Jan. 17, 1942), 330.

39. Civilian Production Administration, *Industrial Mobilization for War*, I, 971. See also, for a brief summary, Somers, *Presidential Agency*, pp. 28–31.

40. See Somers, *Presidential Agency*, pp. 125–137.

41. The mismanagement of German War production is convincingly described in the United States Strategic Bombing Survey, *The Effects of Strategic Bombing on the German War Economy* (Washington, 1945), and Wilmot, *Struggle for Europe*, chs. 3, 4, 7.

Chapter 13 — Civil-Military Relations in the Postwar Decade

1. "Sino-Japanese Crisis: The Garrison State versus the Civilian State," *China Quarterly*, II (Fall 1937), 643–649; "The Garrison State and Specialists on Violence," *Amer. Jour of Sociology*, XLVI (January 1941), 455–468, reprinted in *The Analysis of Political Behavior* (New York, 1947); "The Interrelations of World Organization and Society," *Yale Law Journal*, LV (August 1946), 889–909; "The Prospects of Cooperation in a Bipolar World," *Univ. of Chicago Law Rev.*, XV (Summer 1948), 877–901; " 'Inevitable' War: A Problem in the Control of Long-Range Expectations," *World Politics*, II (October 1949), 1–39; "The Threat Inherent in the Garrison-Police State," in *National Security and Individual Freedom* (New York), 1950, pp. 23–49; "The Universal Peril: Perpetual Crisis and the Garrison-Prison State," in Lyman Bryson, Louis Finkelstein, and R. M. MacIver (eds.), *Perspectives on a Troubled Decade: Science, Philosophy, and Religion, 1939–1949* (New York, 1950), pp. 323–328; "Does the Garrison State Threaten Civil Rights?" *Annals* of the American Academy, CCLXXV (May 1951), 111–116; "The Threat to Privacy," in Robert M. MacIver, (ed.), *Conflict of Loyalties* (New York, 1952), pp. 121–140; "The World Revolutionary Situation," in Carl J. Friedrich (ed.), *Totalitarianism* (Cambridge, Mass., 1954), pp. 360–380.

2. See, for example, Townsend Hoopes, "Civilian-Military Balance," *Yale Review*, XLIII (Winter 1954), 221–222; *Report* of the Rockefeller Committee on Department of Defense Organization, April 11, 1953, pp.

3–4; H. Struve Hensel, "Changes Inside the Pentagon," *Harvard Business Review,* XXXII (January–February 1954), 102–103.

3. *National Security and Individual Freedom,* pp. 186–187.

4. *Sword and Swastika* (New York, 1952), pp. 368–370. One of the most acute critical analyses by an American of the responsibility of the German generals is G. A. Craig, "Army and National Socialism 1933–1945: The Responsibility of the Generals," *World Politics,* II (April 1950), 426–438.

5. Speech to the Massachusetts legislature, July 25, 1951, *New York Times,* July 26, 1951, p. 12.

6. Lawrence J. Legere, Jr., "Unification of the Armed Forces" (Ph.D. Thesis, Harvard Univ., 1951), p. 406. Quoted by permission of the author. See also Crommelin's statement, *New York Times,* Nov. 9, 1949, p. 33.

7. Compare General Ridgway's comments in *Soldier: The Memoirs of Matthew B. Ridgway* (New York, 1956), pp. 239–240. On this problem generally, see William Yandell Elliott and associates, *United States Foreign Policy: Its Organization and Control* (New York, 1952), pp. 168–172, and G. C. Reinhardt and W. R. Kintner, "The Need for a National Staff," U.S. Naval Inst. *Proceedings,* LXXVII (July 1952), 721–727.

8. Richard C. Snyder and H. Hubert Wilson, *The Roots of Political Behavior* (New York, 1949), p. 557.

9. For civilian criticism, see Hanson Baldwin, "The Military Move In," *Harper's,* CXCV (December 1947), 481–489; J. F. Dobie, "Samples of the Army Mind," *ibid.,* CXCIII (December 1946), 529–536; L. B. Wheildon, "Militarization," *Editorial Research Reports* (May 12, 1948), pp. 301–310; William R. Tansill, *The Concept of Civil Supremacy over the Military in the United States* (Library of Congress, Legislative Reference Service, Public Affairs Bulletin No. 94, Washington, 1951), pp. 38–59; *Cong. Record* (Daily ed.), CI (May 17, 1955), 5518 (July 14, 1955), 9069–9071 (Aug. 1, 1955), 11024–11026, CII (Mar. 20, 1956), 4595–4597 (Mar. 21, 1956), 4691–4706. For the military defense, see *Inf. Jour.,* LX (April 1947), 71, CXII (January 1948), 76–77; J. W. Stryker, "Are the Military Moving In?", U.S. Naval Inst. *Proceedings,* LXXV (March 1949), 295–301; L. B. Blair, "Dogs and Sailors Keep Off," *ibid.,* LXXVI (October 1950), 1102.

10. The activities of former officers are reported weekly in the "Retired Service Notes" in the *Army Navy Air Force Journal.* For lists of some of the more notable business appointments, see "The Military Businessmen," *Fortune,* XLVI (September 1952), 128ff.; *Cong. Record,* CI (July 14, 1955, daily ed.), 9070–9071; *U.S. News and World Report,* XL (Apr. 27, 1956), 55–56.

11. Walter H. McLaughlin, Jr., "Business Attitudes Towards Defense Policy During the Cold War" (Honors Thesis, Harvard Univ., 1955), pp. 36–59; U.S. Dept. of the Army, *The Army Almanac* (Washington, 1950), pp. 883–908.

12. "The Macs and the Ikes: America's Two Military Traditions," *American Mercury*, LXXV (October 1952), 32–39.

13. For aspects of the MacArthur versus Marshall and Eisenhower feud, see Clark Lee and Richard Henschel, *Douglas MacArthur* (New York, 1952), pp. 98–102, 115–131; Richard H. Rovere and Arthur Schlesinger, Jr., *The General and the President* (New York, 1951), pp. 70–71; Robert E. Sherwood, *Roosevelt and Hopkins* (New York, 1948), p. 759, and "The Feud between Ike and Mac," *Look*, XVI (July 1, 1952), 17ff.; Marquis Childs, "Soldiers and 1952 Politics," *Washington Post*, July 8, 1952, p. 12; Frazier Hunt, *The Untold Story of Douglas MacArthur* (New York, 1954), *passim;* Robert Payne, *The Marshall Story* (New York, 1951), pp. 108–110; James K. Eyre, Jr., *The Roosevelt-MacArthur Conflict* (Chambersburg, Pa., 1950), *passim.*

14. "The Necessity for Military Forces," *Inf. Jour.*, XXX (March 1927), 330; Speech to the Rainbow Division, July 14, 1935, in Frank C. Waldrop (ed.), *MacArthur on War* (New York, 1942), pp. 31ff.

15. Address, Los Angeles, Jan. 26, 1955, *U.S. News and World Report*, XXXVIII (Feb. 4, 1955), 86–88; Douglas MacArthur, *Revitalizing a Nation* (Chicago, John M. Pratt, ed., 1952), p. 16.

16. *New York Times*, July 26, 1951, p. 12; *Hearings* before the Senate Committee on the Armed Services and the Committee on Foreign Relations on the Military Situation in the Far East, 82d Cong., 1st Sess., pp. 39–40, 44–45, 114–115 (1951).

17. *New York Times*, May 24, 1953, p. 34, July 2, 1953, p. 1.

18. Quoted by Stewart Alsop, *New York Herald Tribune*, Apr. 24, 1955, Sec. 2, p. 1.

Chapter 14 — *The Political Roles of the Joint Chiefs*

1. Walter Millis (ed.), *The Forrestal Diaries* (New York, 1951), pp. 13, 203; *New York Times*, Dec. 9, 1952, p. 26.

2. Millis, *Forrestal Diaries*, p. 341; Edgar A. Mowrer, *The Nightmare of American Foreign Policy* (New York, 1948), pp. 249–250; *State Department Bulletin*, XVIII (May 16, 1948), 623–625.

3. Millis, *Forrestal Diaries*, p. 529.

4. See Harry S. Truman, *Memoirs: Vol. I, Year of Decision* (Garden City, N.Y., 1955), pp. 70–72, 79–82, 411–412, 550–552, 555–560.

5. See John C. Campbell (ed.), *The United States in World Affairs, 1947–1948* (New York, 1948), pp. 8–9, n. 4; Mowrer, *Nightmare of American Foreign Policy*, pp. 211–212.

6. See George Kennan, *Realities of American Foreign Policy* (Princeton, 1954), as well as his earlier *American Diplomacy, 1900–1950* (Chicago, 1951); Louis Halle, *Civilization and Foreign Policy* (New York,

1955); Charles B. Marshall, *The Limits of Foreign Policy* (New York, 1954).

7. "A Soldier's Farewell," *Saturday Evening Post*, CCXXVI (Aug. 22, 1953), 63–64.

8. Millis, *Forrestal Diaries*, pp. 195, 312, 315–316; *Hearings* before Senate Armed Services and Foreign Relations Committees on Military Situation in the Far East, 82d Cong., 1st Sess., pp. 2572–2576 (1951); A. L. Warner, "How the Korea Decision was Made," *Harper's*, CCII (June 1951), 99–106.

9. Probably the classic expression on civilian control was by General Vandenberg, *Hearings* before Senate Committee on Appropriations on Department of Defense Appropriation Bill for 1951, 81st Cong., 2d Sess., p. 226 (1950).

10. Gabriel A. Almond, *The American People and Foreign Policy* (New York, 1950), pp. 122–126.

11. For a trenchant criticism of the Kennan philosophy, see Joseph and Stewart Alsop, "That Washington Security Curtain," *Saturday Evening Post*, CCXXVII (Feb. 19, 1955), 128.

12. For further analysis of the relations among budgetary policy, foreign policy, and strategy, see this author's "Radicalism and Conservatism in National Defense Policy," *Journal of International Affairs*, VIII (1954), 206–222.

13. For text of the speech, see *U.S. News and World Report*, XXXII (March 28, 1952), 84–86, and for Baldwin's comments, *New York Times*, April 2, 1952, p. 20. See also Burton M. Sapin and Richard C. Snyder, *The Role of the Military in American Foreign Policy* (Garden City, N.Y., 1954), pp. 46–49.

14. *New York Times*, April 27, 1951, p. 4; Dulles, *War or Peace* (New York, 1950), pp. 233–238.

15. George Barrett, "That's the Way the Ball Bounces," *New York Times Magazine*, Nov. 23, 1952, p. 14; Peter Braestrup, "Korea: The New Professional," in Yale Daily News, *Seventy-Five — A Study of a Generation in Transition* (New Haven, 1953), p. 81; Bill Mauldin, *Bill Mauldin in Korea* (New York, 1952), pp. 10–11; John Groth, *Studio: Asia* (Cleveland, 1952).

16. *Hearings* before Senate Committees on Foreign Relations and Armed Services on Military Situation in the Far East, pp. 380–381.

17. *New York Herald Tribune*, Jan. 20, 1953, p. 1.

18. *The Korean War and Related Matters*, Report of the Internal Security Subcommittee, Senate Committee on the Judiciary, 84th Cong., 1st Sess., p. 2 (1955); Mark W. Clark, *From the Danube to the Yalu* (New York, 1954), p. 81; Matthew B. Ridgway, *Soldier: The Memoirs of Matthew B. Ridgway* (New York, 1956), pp. 219–220.

19. See Angus Campbell, Gerald Gurin, and Warren E. Miller, *The*

Voter Decides (Evanston, Ill., 1954), ch. 4, esp. pp. 65–67; Samuel Lubell, *Revolt of the Moderates* (New York, 1956), pp. 39–45.

20. See John McDonald, "The Businessman in Government," *Fortune,* L (July 1954), 68–70.

21. Charles J. V. Murphy, "Strategy Overtakes Mr. Wilson," *Fortune,* XLIX (January 1954), 80.

22. Merlo J. Pusey, *Eisenhower the President* (New York, 1956), p. 129.

23. *Report* of the Rockefeller Committee on Department of Defense Organization, p. 3 (1953). For further elaboration of the philosophy behind this, see H. Struve Hensel, "Changes Inside the Pentagon," *Harvard Business Review,* XXXII (January–February 1954), 102–103; Paul L. Davies, "A Business Look at the Army," *Military Review,* XXXIV (December 1954), 41–42.

24. "Method of Operation of the Joint Chiefs of Staff and Their Relationships with Other Staff Agencies of the Office of the Secretary of Defense," Department of Defense Directive No. 5158.1, July 26, 1954.

25. M. B. Ridgway, "My Battles in War and Peace," *Saturday Evening Post,* CCXXVIII (Jan. 21, 1956), 46.

26. "Defense and Strategy," *Fortune,* XLVIII (September 1953), 75, (December 1953), 77–78; *New York Times,* Oct. 14, 1953, p. 18, Oct. 15, 1953, p. 21.

27. *Hearings* before Senate Committee on Appropriations on Department of Defense Appropriation Bill for 1955, 83rd Cong., 2d Sess., p. 83 (1954); *New York Times,* Dec. 15, 1953, p. 31, Jan. 22, 1954, p. 12, Apr. 5, 1955, p. 1; *New York Herald Tribune,* Mar. 17, 1954, p. 1; *Army Navy Air Force Journal,* XCII (Jan. 29, 1955), 630. Compare Ridgway's views, *Soldier,* pp. 271–272.

28. See Marquis Childs in the *Washington Post,* June 15, 16, 1954; Chalmers Roberts, "The Day We Didn't Go To War," *The Reporter,* XI (Sept. 14, 1954), 31–35.

29. See Stewart Alsop, *New York Herald Tribune,* Jan. 26, 1955; Chalmers Roberts, "The Battle on 'The Rim of Hell': President vs. War Hawks," *The Reporter,* XI (Dec. 16, 1954), 11–14. For analysis of Radford's earlier views, see Arthur Krock, *New York Times,* May 14, 1953, p. 28. For Admiral Carney's opinion, see his speech before the National Security Industrial Association, May 27, 1954, *New York Times,* May 28, 1954, p. 2. Any conclusive judgment as to the role played by military and civilians in the defense policy decisions of the Eisenhower Administration must, of course, wait upon the availability of more extensive and better documented evidence.

30. *Militant Liberty: A Program of Evaluation and Assessment of Freedom* (Washington, 1955). See also W. H. Hale, "Militant Liberty and the Pentagon," *The Reporter,* XIV (Feb. 9, 1956), 30–34.

Separation of Powers

Chapter 15 — The Separation of Powers and Cold War Defense

1. Pendleton Herring, *The Impact of War* (New York, 1941), pp. 115–117; Elias Huzar, *The Purse and the Sword: Control of the Army by Congress through Military Appropriations, 1933–1950* (Ithaca, N.Y., 1950), pp. 46–52, 133–156; Lawrence H. Chamberlain, *The President, Congress, and Legislation* (New York, 1946), ch. 5.

2. See Carey Brewer, "An Analysis of Defense Legislation and Congressional Committee Jurisdiction," Report prepared for the Senate Committee on Expenditures in the Executive Departments, 82d Cong., 1st Sess., August 24, 1951; Francis Shackelford, "The Separation of Powers in Time of Crisis," in Harvard Law School, *Government Under Law* (Cambridge, Mass., 1955), pp. 174–180.

3. Organization of the Armed Services Committee, 81st Cong., 1st Sess., pp. 9–10 (1949); Title IV, Act of Sept. 28, 1951, 65 Stat. 365–366; Act of Apr. 4, 1944, 58 Stat. 189. For a good summary of the Committee's investigatory activities in the Eighty-second Congress, see *Report on Investigations by Armed Services Committee,* H. Rept. 2489, 82d Cong., 2d Sess. (1952).

4. See, for example, H. Rept. 307, 82d Cong., 1st Sess. (1951); H. Rept. 857, 83rd Cong., 1st Sess. (1953); and Francis Shackelford's comments, Harvard Law School, *Government Under Law,* pp. 166–167.

5. See Huzar, *The Purse and the Sword,* pp. 398–407; Arthur Smithies, *The Budgetary Process in the United States* (New York, 1955), pp. 139–142, 163–164, 183ff.; Edward L. Katzenbach, Jr., "How Congress Strains at Gnats, Then Swallows Military Budgets," *The Reporter,* XI (July 20, 1954), 31–35.

6. See Arthur A. Maass, *Muddy Waters: The Army Engineers and The Nation's Rivers* (Cambridge, Mass., 1951).

7. Sec. 206, Act of June 10, 1921, 42 Stat. 21.

8. *Hearings* before House Committee on the Armed Services on Unification and Strategy, 81st Cong., 1st Sess., p. 604 (1949).

9. *Hearings* before House Committee on Appropriations on War Appropriation Bill (Military Activities) for 1936, 74th Cong., 1st Sess., p. 18 (1935), quoted in Huzar, *Purse and the Sword,* p. 147.

10. Quoted in Mark S. Watson, *Chief of Staff: Prewar Plans and Preparations* (Washington, 1950), pp. 21–22; Huzar, *Purse and the Sword,* p. 128.

11. Sec. 202(c)(6), National Security Act, Act of Aug. 10, 1949, 63 Stat. 578.

12. Committee on Armed Services, House of Representatives, *Unification and Strategy,* H. Doc. 600, 81st Cong., 2d Sess., pp. 10–12, 45, 53 (1950).

Notes to Chapter 15

13. *Hearings* before Senate Armed Services Committee on JCS Nominations, 83rd Cong., 1st Sess., pp. 15–16 (1953).

14. *Hearings* before Senate Committee on Appropriations on Dept. of Defense Appropriation Bill for 1955, 83rd Cong., 2d Sess., pp. 43–44 (1954); *Hearings* before Senate Committee on Appropriations on Dept. of Defense Appropriation Bill for 1956, 84th Cong., 1st Sess., pp. 211–212, 215–219 (1955). For an acute analysis of this problem, see E. L. Katzenbach, Jr., "Should Our Military Leaders Speak Up?" *New York Times Magazine,* April 15, 1956, pp. 17ff.

15. See this author's "Radicalism and Conservatism in National Defense Policy," *Journal of International Affairs,* VIII (1954), 206–222.

16. See Lawrence J. Legere, Jr., "Unification of the Armed Forces" (Ph.D. Thesis, Harvard Univ., 1951), p. 344.

17. *Cong. Record,* XCVIII (May 16, 1952), 5347.

18. *Hearings* before Senate Committee on Armed Services on S. 758, 80th Cong., 1st Sess., pp. 100, 113, 209, 211 (1947); *Hearings* before House Committee on Armed Services on Army Organization Bill, 81st Cong., 2d Sess., pp. 6013, 6023, 6036, 6046ff., 6125, 6128, 6202, 6208, 6235 (1950).

19. *Cong. Record,* XCV (Oct. 18, 1949), 14922.

20. H. Rept. 1797, 81st Cong., 2d Sess., pp. 309–311 (1950); H. Doc. 600, 81st Cong., 2d Sess., pp. 49–50 (1950); *Hearings* before House Armed Services Committee on Unification and Strategy, pp. 97–99, 300–301; *Hearings* before House Committee on Appropriations on Department of Defense Appropriations for 1951, 81st Cong., 2d Sess., pp. 50–62 (1950); J. D. Williams, *The Impounding of Funds by the Bureau of the Budget* (University, Ala., ICP Case Series: No. 28, 1955).

Chapter 16 — Departmental Structure of Civil-Military Relations

1. Public Law 253, 80th Cong., 61 Stat. 495 (July 26, 1947), amended by Public Law 216, 81st Cong., 63 Stat. 578 (Aug. 10, 1949), Public Law 416, 82d Cong., 66 Stat. 283 (July 22, 1952). Reorganization Plan No. 6 of 1953 tended to modify the previous theory in some respects.

2. On the origins and background of the NSC, see *Hearings* before Senate Committee on Military Affairs on S. 84, 79th Cong., 1st Sess., p. 588 (1945); *Report* by Ferdinand Eberstadt to Secretary of the Navy Forrestal on Unification, Senate Committee on Naval Affairs, 79th Cong., 1st Sess.; Walter Millis (ed.), *The Forrestal Diaries* (New York, 1951), pp. 19, 61–63, 315–316; E. R. May, "The Development of Political-Military Consultation in the United States," *Political Science Quarterly,* LXX (June 1955), 161–180. On the comparable British institution, see Maurice Hankey, *Government Control in War* (Cambridge, 1945), pp. 22–31, and *Diplo-*

macy by Conference (New York, 1946), pp. 83–104; Franklyn A. Johnson, "Defense by Committee: The Origin and Early Development of the British Committee of Imperial Defense, 1885–1916" (Ph.D. Thesis, Harvard Univ., 1952). On the operations of the NSC, see: J. and S. Alsop, "How Our Foreign Policy Is Made," *Saturday Evening Post*, CCXXI (Apr. 30, 1949), 30ff.; S. W. Souers, "Policy Formation for National Security," *Amer. Pol. Sci. Rev.*, XLIII (June 1949), 534–543; H. P. Kirkpatrick, "The National Security Council," *American Perspective*, VII (February 1949), 443–450; The Brookings Institution, *The Administration of Foreign Affairs and Overseas Operations* (Report to the Budget Bureau, June, 1951), *passim;* John Fischer, *Master Plan USA* (New York, 1951), ch. 2; W. Y. Elliott *et al., United States Foreign Policy* (New York, 1952), pp. 83–96; J. S. Lay, Jr., "National Security Council's Role in the U.S. Security and Peace Program," *World Affairs*, CXV (Summer 1952), 37–39; Cabell Phillips, "The Super-Cabinet for our Security," *New York Times Magazine,* Apr. 4, 1954, pp. 14ff.; G. A. Wyeth, Jr., "The National Security Council," *Jour. of International Affairs,* VIII (1954), 185–195; Anthony Leviero, " 'Untouchable, Unreachable, and Unquotable,' " *New York Times Magazine,* Jan. 30, 1955, pp. 12ff.; Dillon Anderson, "The President and National Security," *Atlantic Monthly, CXCVII* (January 1956), 42–46; Robert Cutler, "The Development of the National Security Council," *Foreign Affairs,* XXXIV (April 1956), 441–458. For other reports on the evolution of the NSC, see the *New York Times:* Apr. 22, 1949, p. 14; Apr. 2, 1951, p. 1; Mar. 12, 1953, p. 22; Mar. 24, 1953, p. 24; May 4, 1953, p. 9; Sept. 4, 1953, p. 1; Mar. 18, 1955, p. 24.

3. *Hearings* before Senate Committee on Armed Services on S. 758, 80th Cong., 1st Sess., pp. 491ff. (1947); Sherman Kent, *Strategic Intelligence* (Princeton, 1949), p. 79; Public Law 110, 81st Cong., 63 Stat. 208 (June 20, 1949).

4. *Hearings* before Senate Committee on Armed Services on S. 758, pp. 215 -216.

5. See, for example, Commission on Organization, *The National Security Organization* (Report to Congress, February 1949), p. 11; Hanson Baldwin, *New York Times,* Aug. 15, 1951, p. 10, and April 23, 1953, p. 16; Robert A. Lovett, Letter to the President, Nov. 18, 1952, pp. 5–6; Vannevar Bush, Address at the Mayo Clinic, Rochester, Minn., Sept. 26, 1952, p. 8; L. E. Denfeld, "Why I Was Fired," *Collier's,* CXXV (Mar. 25, 1950), 47.

6. *Hearings* before Senate Committee on Armed Services on National Security Act Amendments, 81st Cong., 1st Sess., p. 209 (1949).

7. Frederick C. Mosher, *Program Budgeting: Theory and Practice with Particular Reference to the U.S. Department of the Army* (Public Administration Service, 1954), pp. 184, 216–217.

8. See *Hearings* before Senate Committee on Armed Services on Na-

tional Security Act Amendments, p. 195; S. Rept. 366, 81st Cong., 1st Sess. (1949); Secy. of Defense, *First Report, 1948*, pp. 3–4, 40–42; Mosher, *Program Budgeting*, pp. 31–42, 46, 220.

9. Mosher, *Program Budgeting*, pp. 180–185, 192; Francis Shackelford, "The Separation of Powers in Time of Crisis," in Harvard Law School, *Government Under Law* (Cambridge, Mass., 1955), p. 146.

10. *New York Times*, Nov. 6, 1952, p. 15; Charlotte Knight, "Mystery Man of the Pentagon," *Collier's*, CXXXIII (Jan. 22, 1954), 30ff.

11. See *Unification and Strategy*, Report by House Committee on Armed Services, H. Doc. 600, 81st Cong., 2d Sess., pp. 52–53 (1949), for an example of congressional support of the Comptroller against the Management Committee.

12. Knight, *Collier's*, CXXXIII (Jan. 22, 1954), 32–34.

13. CLXXII (Aug. 28, 1954), 639–640.

14. *Hearings* before House Committee on Appropriations on Second Supplemental Appropriation Bill for 1951, 81st Cong., 2d Sess., pp. 17, 20, 53–54, 62–63 (1950); *Hearings* before Senate Committee on Appropriations on Second Supplemental Appropriation Bill for 1951, 81st Cong., 2d Sess., p. 88 (1950); Secy. of Defense, *Semiannual Report, Jan. 1–June 30, 1951*, p. 70.

15. *Hearings* before House Committee on Armed Services on Unification and Strategy, 81st Cong., 1st Sess., p. 624 (1949).

16. Charles E. Wilson, Address, Secretaries' Conference, Quantico, Va., July 23, 1953, p. 14; P. R. Leach, *Boston Daily Globe*, Apr. 17, 1953, p. 18.

17. J. and S. Alsop, *New York Herald Tribune*, Jan. 26, 1953, p. 17; Lovett, Letter to the President, p. 5; Walter Millis, *New York Herald Tribune*, Nov. 24, 1952, p. 14; P. R. Leach, *Boston Daily Globe*, Apr. 17, 1953, p. 18; Fred Seaton, quoted in D. Norton-Taylor, "The Wilson Pentagon," *Fortune*, L (December 1954), 96; "Defense and Strategy," *Fortune*, XLVII (June 1953), 89.

18. *Hearings* before House Committee on Armed Services on Unification and Strategy, pp. 305–306, 357–358, 608–609, 624.

19. *Hearings* before Senate Committee on Appropriations on Department of Defense Appropriation Bill for 1954, 83rd Cong., 1st Sess., pp. 36, 38–39, 216, 230–231, 340–342, 355, 561–562 (1953); *New York Times*, Mar. 21, 1953, p. 1.

20. Commission on Organization, *Task Force Report on National Security Organization* (Appendix G, 1949), p. 38; Millis, *Forrestal Diaries*, p. 435. Except where otherwise indicated the sources for this description of the formulation of the 1950 budget are Millis, *Forrestal Diaries*, ch. 13 and pp. 435, 450, 500–506, 510, 535, 537, and *Hearings* before House Committee on Appropriations on Department of Defense Appropriation Bill for 1950, 81st Cong., 1st Sess., pp. 12, 16, 205ff. (1949).

21. *Hearings* before House Committee on Appropriations on Department of Defense Appropriation Bill for 1953, 82d Cong., 2d Sess., pp. 1, 57, 87–90, 97, 110–111, 142–145 (1952); *Hearings* before Senate Committee on Appropriations on Department of Defense Appropriation Bill for 1953, 82d Cong., 2d Sess., pp. 1, 5, 145–151 (1952).

22. Secretary of Defense, *First Report, 1948,* pp. 30–31; *Semiannual Report July 1–December 31, 1949,* p. 31. For Forrestal's views on the necessity of a permanent cadre of trained civilian personnel upon whom successive secretaries may rely on coming into office, see James Forrestal, "Managing the Public's Business," in Joseph E. McLean, *The Public Service and University Education* (Princeton, 1949), pp. 236–237.

23. Millis, *Forrestal Diaries,* pp. 314, 317, 335, 352, 404, 415, 434, 497, 500, 502, 519ff.; *New York Times,* Feb. 12, 1949, p. 1.

24. Lovett, Letter to the President, pp. 2–8.

25. Lovett, Letter to the President, pp. 3–4; *Report* of the Rockefeller Committee on Department of Defense Organization (1953) p. 2, Appendix A.

26. *Hearings* before Senate Committee on Armed Services on National Security Act Amendments, p. 20.

27. Commission on Organization, *Task Force Report on National Security Organization,* pp. 37–38; Vannevar Bush, "What's Wrong at the Pentagon," *Collier's,* CXXX (Dec. 27, 1952), 32.

28. Commission on Organization, *Task Force Report on Departmental Management* (Appendix E, Jan. 1949), pp. 16, 51–54.

Chapter 17 — Toward a New Equilibrium

1. The best concise summary and classification of American conservatism, past and present, is Clinton Rossiter's *Conservatism in America* (New York, 1955). Among the better expressions of the more conscious conservatism are Peter Viereck, *Conservatism Revisited* (New York, 1949), Francis G. Wilson, *The Case for Conservatism* (Seattle, 1951), Russell Kirk, *The Conservative Mind* (Chicago, 1953), and Gordon Harrison, *Road to the Right* (New York, 1954). Profound statements of a fundamentally conservative viewpoint will be found in the writings of Reinhold Niebuhr, particularly his magistral *The Nature and Destiny of Man* (New York, one vol. ed., 1948), the poems, plays, and essays of T. S. Eliot among which *The Idea of a Christian Society* (New York, 1940) is the most explicit, and Eric Voegelin's *The New Science of Politics* (Chicago, 1952). Niebuhr's *Christian Realism and Political Problems* (New York, 1953) applies neoorthodoxy to current issues. Among Catholic political analyses are Ross J. S. Hoffman, *The Spirit of Politics and the Future of Freedom* (Milwaukee, 1951), Martin Hillenbrand, *Power and Morals* (New York, 1949),

Notes to Chapter 17

and Thomas P. Neill, *The Rise and Decline of Liberalism* (Milwaukee, 1953). Will Herberg's *Judaism and Modern Man* (New York, 1951) and the volumes of *Commentary* eloquently express conservative elements in the Jewish tradition. Gordon K. Chalmers' *The Republic and the Person* (Chicago, 1952) ranks high among the many critiques of Dewey's educational philosophy. Thoughtful defenses of American political institutions will be found in Arthur N. Holcombe, *Our More Perfect Union* (Cambridge, Mass., 1950), Ernest S. Griffith, *Congress: Its Contemporary Role* (New York, 1951), and the essays of Don K. Price. Hans J. Morgenthau, *Scientific Man vs. Power Politics* (Chicago, 1946), and John H. Hallowell, *The Decline of Liberalism as an Ideology* (Berkeley, 1943) and *Main Currents in Modern Political Thought* (New York, 1950) are analyses of political theory by conservative political scientists. Representative of what one critic has described as "the economics of self-congratulation" are John K. Galbraith, *American Capitalism: The Concept of Countervailing Power* (Boston, 1952), A. A. Berle, *The Twentieth Century Capitalist Revolution* (New York, 1954), and David Lilienthal, *Big Business: A New Era* (New York, 1953). Penetrating analyses of the American political tradition reflecting the new stress on the uniqueness of the American experience and the dichotomy between American ideas and institutions include Reinhold Niebuhr, *The Irony of American History* (New York, 1952), Louis Hartz, *The Liberal Tradition in America* (New York, 1955), and Daniel J. Boorstin, *The Genius of American Politics* (Chicago, 1953). Lippmann's views are expressed in *The Public Philosophy* (Boston, 1955). Some recognition of the coherence of the new conservatism as an intellectual movement is afforded by the reaction against it expressed in that stimulating periodical, *Dissent*. For further references to the literature of American conservatism, see the comprehensive bibliography in Rossiter's book.

2. Morgenthau's views are expressed in *Politics Among Nations* (New York, 1948), *In Defense of the National Interest* (New York, 1951), and "Another 'Great Debate': The National Interest of the United States," *American Political Science Review*, XLVI (December 1952), 961–988. For opposing views, see Frank Tannenbaum, "The Balance of Power versus the Coordinate State," *Political Science Quarterly*, LXVII (June 1952), 173–197, and T. I. Cook and Malcolm Moos, "The American Idea of International Interest," *Amer. Pol. Sci. Review*, XLVII (March 1953), 28–44.

3. See, for example, Hanson Baldwin, "Military in Politics," *New York Times*, Apr. 1, 1952, p. 22, Apr. 2, 1952, p. 20; Senator Mike Mansfield, "The Role of the Military in American Foreign Policy," *Cong. Record*, CI (Feb. 21, 1955, daily ed.), A-1091–A-1093.

4. Hanson Baldwin, "What's Wrong With the Regulars?" *Saturday Evening Post*, CCXXVI (Oct. 31, 1953), 19ff., "The Problem of Army Morale," *New York Times Magazine*, Dec. 5, 1954, pp. 9ff., and his regular column in the *Times;* Department of Defense, Press Release, Dec. 3, 1953,

A New Equilibrium

"Final Report — Ad Hoc Committee on the Future of Military Service as a Career that will Attract and Retain Capable Career Personnel" (Womble Committee Report); *New York Times,* Apr. 19, 1954, p. 22; H. W. Blakeley, "Esprit de What? Our Army and Morale," *The Reporter,* XI (Sept. 23, 1954), 35–37; D. J. Carrison, "Our Vanishing Military Profession," *American Mercury,* LXXVII (November 1953), 77–81.

INDEX

Acheson, Dean, 377–378, 385, 387
Adams, Brooks, 224, 270, 272
Adams, Henry, 270, 465
Adams, John, 194
Adams, John Quincy, 147, 453
Adjutants General Association, 174
Administrative budgetary reductions, 423–424
Administrative-fiscal function, Department of Defense, 428, 437–440
Adolphus, Gustavus, 21, 26
Advancement, purchase, birth, and politics, 23–24; professional standard for in Prussia, 45; France, 45–46; England, 46–48; Army and Navy (U.S.), 206–207, 297, 406
Ageton, Rear Admiral Arthur A., 360 fn.
Ainsworth, Adjutant General Fred, 298
Air Force, congressional interest in expansion, 408, 411–412, 425, 426; cutback controversy, 421; vertical system of organization, 429 fn., 440, 444–446
Air Force Association, 366
Air Force Organization Act of 1951, 429 fn.
Air National Guard, 191
Aircraft Industries Association, 366
Alger, Russell Alexander, 210
Amalgamation, Jacksonian principle of, 204
American militarism, roots of, 193–194
American Military Enlightenment, 217–221
American Ordnance Association, 366
American society, image in the military mind, 266; military influence in, 354–373
Angell, Norman, 258; The Great Illusion, 279
Annapolis. See United States Naval Academy
Annapolis Postgraduate School, 295 fn.
Anticommunist policy, 394, 396–397
Appropriations. See Military appropriations

Araki, General (Japan), 127, 129, 132, 134
Arbitration, view of the military, 264
Archer, Gleason L., The History of Radio to 1926, 363 fn.
Aristocracy, in conflict with democracy, 33–34; identified with military control, 81–82
Aristocratic institutions, in eighteenth-century military affairs, 20–28
Aristocrats, in Prussian officer corps, 39–40, 103; in France, 42; in England, 43
Armed Forces Chemical Association, 365
Armed Forces Communications Association, 365
Armstrong, John, 208
Army (U.S.), staff organization, 200; seniority system, 206–207; a lateral entry into officer corps, 206–207; coordinate organization, 208–211; prevalence of Southerners, 213; years of isolation and rejection, 226–229; reform movement, 230–236; organizational problem, 247; subordination to civil power, 261; promotion system, 297; presidential favoring of, 420; vertical system, 429 fn.; views on unification, 432–433; one of four great pillars of society, 465. See also Defense, Department of; Military; Officer Corps; Professionalism and War Department
Army and Navy Chronicle, 207, 219
Army Appropriation Act of 1867, 182
Army Industrial College, 295 fn.
Army-McCarthy hearings, 460
Army Navy Munitions Board, 338, 339
Army Service Forces, 339
Army Services of Supply, 339
Army War College, 237
Arsenal, The (S.C.), 219
Articles of Confederation, 168
Artillery officers, training of, 25
Artillery School (Fort Monroe, Va.), 217, 236
Atlantic Charter, 331, 334

Index

Index

and reforming tendencies of, 270; *New Republic* and *The Promise of American Life,* 272

Crommelin, Captain Henry, 353

Cromwell, Oliver, 21, 26

Crosby, Ernest, 292

Crowell, Benedict, 299 fn., 300

Crowinshield, Benjamin, 201

Czechoslovakia, 115

Daniels, Josephus, 157, 250–251, 263, 294, 303

Dartmouth (England) training ship at, 44

Davis, General George B., 264

Davis, Jefferson, 210

Defense, Department of, relations with business, 362, 364, 365; reorganizations, 375, 406, 422–423; unity with Eisenhower administration, 392; liberalism in, 393–397; organizational problems of postwar decade, 428–432; Joint Chiefs of Staff role, 432–437; Comptroller the superego of, 437–440; General Counsel's office, 439; role of the Secretary, 440–448; needs of the OSD, 448–455

Defense conservatism, under Truman, 378–382

Defense industry, growth and identification with the military attitude, 364–366

Defense liberalism under Eisenhower, 393–397

Defense Management Committee, 439, 443, 444

Defense policy, effect of separation of powers on, 400–427. *See also* Military security

Democracy, conflict with aristocracy, 33–34; civilian control identified with, 82; and militarism, 260–261

Democratic ideals, factor in growth of professionalism, 33–34

Democratic Party, essentially domestic interests of, 382–383; attack on Joint Chiefs of Staff, 460

Denfeld, Admiral Louis E., 416

Dewey, Admiral George, 161, 183

Dewey, John, 311, 458

Dick Act (1903, 1908), 171, 176

Dienbienphu, 396

Doolittle Board, civilianizing of military service, 460

Douglas, Lewis W., 378

Draper, William H., 377

Dulles, Allen, 377

Dulles, John Foster, 378; on Joint Chiefs of Staff role in politics, 386; more active anti-communist policy, 396; spokesman on defense matters, 398; article in *Foreign Affairs,* 398

Durbin, E. F. M., 148

Earle, Edward Mead, *Makers of Modern Strategy,* 128 fn.

Eberstadt, Ferdinand, 337; chairman of ANMB, 339; on WPB, 340, 341; quoted on military budget control, 437

Ebert, Friedrich, 109, 112

École d'Application d'État Major, 49

École Militaire, 24–25

École Militaire Supérieure, 49

École Polytechnique, 42, 43, 49, 197

Economic liberalism, a source of business pacifism, 223

Economic mobilization, civil-military relations in, 337–342; and JCS, 435

Economist, on Minister of Defense, 441–442

Education, nobles and technicians, 24–25; requirements for entry into officer corps in Prussia, 39–41; in France, 42–43; in England, 44, 43 fn.; advanced in Prussia, 48–49; in France, 49; in England, 49–50; engineering school at West Point, 198–199; military's attitude toward, 311. *See also* United States Military Academy, United States Naval Academy

Eisenhower, Dwight David, 161, 162, 323; prestige and civilian activity, 367–373; in Truman administration, 377, 378; effect of Korean War on election of, 391; and Congress, 422–423; consulted by Forrestal, 447 fn.

Eisenhower Administration, military officers in, 358, 360; JCS in, 375, 391–399; Air Force cuts under, 412; attempts to forestall congressional budgetary increases, 425

Eliot, T. S., 458

Endicott, William C., 210

Engineers, Corps of, 182, 198, 247–248, 413

Engineers, training of, 25

England, eighteenth-century aristocra-

formers, 234–235, 251, 257; U.S. military governorship in, 355–356. *See also* Prussia

Gerry, Elbridge, 144

Gessler, Otto, 110, 112

Gleason, S. Everett, 331

Gneisenau, Count August von, 31

Godkin, E. L., 258

Goltz, Count August von der, 105, 235 fn.

Göring, Hermann, 118

Grant, Ulysses S., 182, 367

Gray Board, Report of, 172, 173

Great Britain, advanced education, 49–50; distribution of military powers, 164; influence on pattern of American constitution, 164, 177–178; civil-military relations, 187; military organization, 210, 433 fn.; system of conducting war compared with America's, 328–329; Minister of Defense compared with Secretary of Defense, 451, 451 fn. *See also* England

Greenwich (England) naval college at, 50

Gregory, Major General Edmund B., 360 fn.

Grey, Charles, Second Earl, 47

Gröner, Wilhelm, 103, 112, 113

Gruenther, General Alfred M., 356, 447

G-2 (Military Intelligence), staff study by, 335

Guderian, Heinz, 119

Guibert, Comte Jacques de, 28, 29, 30

Haeften, Count von, 107

Hague Conferences, 264

Halder, Franz, 115–116

Hall, Captain R. A., 68 fn.

Halleck, General H. Wager, 197, 234; *Elements of Military Art and Science*, 221

Halsey, Admiral William F., 362

Hamaguchi, Premier Yuko, 138

Hamilton, Alexander, 148, 178, 198, 430; abortive professionalism of, 194, 195

Hancock, General Winfield Scott, 158 fn., 159, 160, 162

Hannegan, Robert E., 376

Harbord, General James G., 298, 363 fn.

Hardy, Porter, 407

Harriman, W. Averill, 377

Harrison, W. H., 158 fn.

Hart, Liddell, 57, 64

Hartz, Louis, 458

Hay, John M., 453

Hayashi, General Senjuro, 132

Heroes, in liberal politics, 157–160; prestige, 367–373

Hertling, Count von, 107

Heye, Colonel General Wilhelm, 112

Highland Falls (N.Y.), 464–465

Hilldring, Major General John H., 360 fn.

Himmler, Heinrich, 117–118

Hindenburg, Paul von, 106, 112

Hines, Brigadier General Frank T., 360 fn.

Hirota, Koki, 132

Hitler, Adolf, 77, 113–116, 117

Hitlerism, guilt of generals in, 353–354

Hoffman, Paul, 377, 378, 385

Holcomb, Major General Thomas, 360 fn.

Holt, Colonel Lucius, 296

Hooker, General Joseph, 181

Hoover, Herbert, 93 fn., 386

Hoover Commission Task Force, 451, 452

Hopkins, Harry, 319, 323, 330

House Armed Services Committee, 403–407, 408, 410, 416, 419, 426

House Committee on Foreign Affairs, 403 fn.

House Government Operations Committee, 403–407, 420, 422

House military appropriations subcommittees, 403, 407–412, 423, 426

House Naval Affairs Committee, increased power of, 404

Hughes, Charles Evans, 453

Huidekoper, Frederick Louis, *The Military Unpreparedness of the United States*, 280 fn.

Hull, Cordell, Secretary of State, 317, 321, 322, 326, 333, 453

Hundred Years War, 21

Huzar, Elias, *The Purse and the Sword*, 424 fn.

Hydrogen bomb, 383

Index

Ickes, Harold L., 330, 380
Ideologies, and military ethic, 94–96
Ikes and Macs, 367–373
India, source of ideas of professional reformers, 235
Indians, 211
Individualism, attacks on, 258, 267
Indochina, 393, 396, 398
Industrial Mobilization Plan, 338
Industrialism, and militarism, 224–226
Infantry Journal, 268, 283, 288 fn., 311
Infantry School *Quarterly*, 294 fn.
Ingles, Major General Harry C., 366 fn.
Institutional policy, 1
Intelligence coordination and JCS, 434
Interbranch rivalry, 418–421
Internal security policy, 1
International military commands, 355, 356–357
International politics, 305–307
Interwar civil-military relations, 289–312 *passim*
Inukai, Premier Ki, 138
Investigations, 422
Isherwood, Benjamin, 232
Ismay, Hastings, 356
Isolationalism, 271
Item veto, 427

Jackson, Andrew, 158 fn., 208, 270, 368
Jacksonian democracy, 193
Jacksonians, attitude on military affairs, 156, 193, 203–204; hostility toward West Point, 204–205; hostility to the military, 224; attitude on war, 225
Japan, pattern of civil-military relations, 98–99; national ideology, 124–125; the Japanese military mind, 125–130; military authority in dual government, 130–134; National Mobilization Law, 134; clan support of the military, 134–135; navy, 135; popular support, 137; military's terroristic methods, 137–138; destruction of officer corps, 138; future civil-military relations, 138–139; as a garrison state, 348; U.S. military governorship, 355–356
Jefferson Thomas, 196–198, 270, 453
Jeffersonians, views on military, 156,

224; contributions to military tradition, 193; attitude on war, 225
Jenner subcommittee on conduct of the Korean War, 390, 418 fn.
Jessup, Brigadier General T. S., 213
Jodl, Alfred, 117, 119
Johnson, Louis, as Secretary of Defense, 378, 442–444, 453–454; opposed to defense spending, 384; on impounding of Air Force funds, 426
Johnson, Lyndon, Preparedness Subcommittee, 406
Johnston, R. M., *Arms and the Race*, 280 fn.
Joint Army-Navy Munitions Board, 317, 318–319, 330–331, 338, 339, 435; balance of power policy, 379
Joint Chiefs of Staff, 318–324, 336; World War II policies, 333–334; problems of administrative coordination with State Department, 351–352; political role in Truman administration, 374–387; in Korean War, 387–391; in Eisenhower administration, 391–399; congressional access of, 415–418; Chairman of, 422, 436–437; postwar function of, 429–432; legal form and political reality, 432–437; and Comptroller, 439–440, 444; and Secretary of Defense, 440–448, 449, 452–453; current attitude toward, 460
Joint Committee on Atomic Energy, 403 fn.
Joint Intelligence Committee of JCS, 434
Jomini, Baron Henri, 197, 255, 277
Jones, James, *From Here to Eternity*, 462
Jones, Colonel Roger, 213
Jones, William, 200
Joy, Admiral Turner, 390
Judaism, 458
Junker aristocracy, 103

Kato, Admiral Tomosaburo, 136
Keitel, Wilhelm, 117, 119
Kennan, George, 377; "Sources of Soviet Conduct," 381; appreciation of power politics, 383–384, 459
Kentucky Military Institute, 219
Kilday, Paul J., 404–405
King, Admiral Ernest J., 302, 319, 336

Index

Index

writings, 220; contribution to American military professionalism, 220–221

Mahon, George H., on impounding of Air Force funds, 426

Mailer, Norman, *The Naked and the Dead*, 461–462

Manhattan District Project (Army), 434

March, General Peyton C., 282 fn.; Chief of Staff, 299

Marine Corps Bill of *1952*, 420

Marine Corps controversy, 420, 421, 425, 426

Marshall, General George C., 319, 325, 363 fn.; political appointments in Truman Cabinet, 359, 360–361; in anti-MacArthur group, 368–369, 389; importance to Truman foreign and defense policies, 377–380; returns to professional military ethic, 381; on Korean War, 387; on Pershing's loyalty, 414; military spokesman role when Secretary of Defense, 442; high caliber, 453, 454

Marxism, 92–93

Mason, George, 165, 177–178

Massenbach, Colonel Christian von, 50

Maury, Matthew Fontaine, 218, 219, 232; views on naval organization, 219–220

Maxim, Hudson, 293

Mercenary system, 20–22

Mexican punitive expedition of *1916*, 389

Meyer, George von L., 303

Michaelis, Georg, 107

Michels, Robert, *Political Parties*, 95

Miles, General Nelson A., 210

Militant Liberty, sponsored by Admiral Radford, 397

Militarism, Jeffersonian contribution toward, 193; Southern sources of, 211–213; and religious moralism, 223; and industrialism, 224, 226; and democratic government, 260–261; pragmatic usages of, 290–294. *See also* Professionalism

Military, definition of, 433 fn.

Military, The, and the state, 70–78, 80–89; conservatism, 154, 257–258; participation in politics, 180–184, 367–373; business pacifist's attitude

toward, 226; professionalization of, 230–237; relations with society, 282–289; role within the government, 307–309; and civilian ethics, 309–310; and Congress, 324–325, 412–418; adjustment to wartime power and postwar plans, 326–337; rapprochement with business, 361–367; departmental structure of, 428–455 *passim*

Military and Naval Construction Act of *1951*, 405

Military and Naval Magazine, 219

Military Appropriations process, 407–412

Military budget, congressional pluralism in, 423–427

Military chiefs, congressional access of, 415–418

Military conservatism, problem of postwar tension with liberalism, 345–346

Military dictatorship, Germany, 106–109

Military Enlightenment, 234

Military ideal, 464–466

Military integrity, 460–461

Military literature, 28–30

Military Magazine, 219

Military mind, 59–61, 254–268

Military obedience, and professional competence, 74–76

Military officer, 7, 11–18; the Framers' concept of, 165–166; in civil governmental positions, 355–361

Military organization, executive and legislative positions on, 181–183

Military power, basis of, 317, 318

Military professionalism, developed by Prussia, 30–32; in modern Germany, 99–101; clash with Nazi approach, 114–116; and business reform hostility, 289–290; versus separation of powers, 412–418. *See also* Professional Military Ethic

Military research and development, 434

Military Review, 294 fn., 394 fn.

Military schools, 24–25. *See also individual schools by name*

Military science, 71; recognition of, 218

Military security, postwar problem, 345–346; enhanced by Congress,

Index

Policy strategy, function of Department of Defense, 428, 440–455 *passim*

Political ideologies, and professional military ethic, 89–94

Political influence, of high commands, 24; of officer corps, 86–89

Political-military fusion, 350–354

Political roles, substantive and advocatory, 374–375; of Joint Chiefs of Staff, 374–399

Politics, and military science, 70–72; military participation in, 207–208, 210, 259–260; tradition of neutrality, 231–232

Polk, James K., 183, 185

Pompadour, Madame de, 24

Popularism, roots in Jacksonians, 193; in American military tradition, 203–210

Portsmouth, Royal Naval College at, 44

Power, definition, 86; forms of, 86–89

Power politics, new interest in, 459

Powers, separation of, 400–427 *passim*

Pratt, Admiral W. V., 301

Preparedness, military attitude on, 264–265

Preparedness Subcommittee, 405–406

President, and Joint Chiefs of Staff, 318–319, 416–417; versus Congress, 400–427 *passim;* and Department of Defense, 429, 433, 436, 440, 445–446; and Secretary of Defense, 448, 449

Proctor, Redfield, 183

Production Requirements Plan, 339

Profession, concept of, 7–10

Professional competence, versus military obedience, 74–76

Professional military ethic, formulation of, 55–58, 61–62, 254; with respect to basic values and perspectives, 62–64; with respect to military policy and state, 64–78; realistic and conservative, 79; compared with political ideologies, 89–94; compatibility with political ideology, 94–96; dominance in German military mind, 100; Seeckt's formulation of, 111; and the Japanese military mind, 126–127, 129; American attitude toward, 153–154; elements in Neo-Hamil-

tonism of, 270; interwar, 303–309; abandonment by military, 355

Professional military function, of Defense Department, 428, 429–437

Professional organizations, 10

Professionalism, of modern officer, 7, 8–10, 19, 30–39; and universal service, 37–39; Upton's summary of, 54; development affected by separation of powers, 177–184; Southern contribution to military tradition, 193, 211–214; Hamilton's views on, 194–195; Calhoun's efforts to cause, 214–217; and Military Enlightenment, 217–221; the creative core, 230–237; compared with other countries, 233; during interwar period, 289–290. *See also* Military, The

Promotion, system revised, 297

Promotion, congressional power over, 406

Property requirement, in military service, 23, 24

Prussia, 21; eighteenth-century aristocratic institutions in the military, 22–28; advancement, 23, 45; education, 24, 48–49; staff system, 25, 26, 50–51; ineptness of officer corps, 27; development of military professionalism, 30–34, 36–42, 53–54, 99; universal service, 37–38. *See also* Germany

Prytanée Militaire, 43

Public Advertiser, 219

Purchase system, in British and French armies, 23; abolished in England, 43, 47

Quartermaster Association, 365

Quartermaster Corps, 413

Quartermaster General, in early staffs, 26

Quemoy, 397

Radford, Admiral Arthur W., as Chairman of JCS, 396–399, 436; on congressional access, 417

Radio Corporation of America, 363 fn., 366 fn.

Rainbow war plans, 317

Randolph, Edmund, 166

Reform liberalism, 289, 290–291

Reich, armies under, 118. *See also* Germany *and* Prussia

Reichstag, 102, 110

Index

Index

VINTAGE POLITICAL SCIENCE
AND SOCIAL CRITICISM

A free catalogue of VINTAGE BOOKS *will be sent at your request. Write to* Vintage Books, 457 Madison Avenue, New York, New York 10022.

VINTAGE HISTORY—AMERICAN

A free catalogue of VINTAGE BOOKS *will be sent at your request. Write to* Vintage Books, 457 Madison Avenue, New York, New York 10022.

VINTAGE HISTORY—WORLD